Lecture Notes in Computer Science 5805

Commenced Publication in 1973
Founding and Former Series Editors:
Gerhard Goos, Juris Hartmanis, and Jan van Leeuwen

T0189926

Idit Keidar (Ed.)

Distributed Computing

23rd International Symposium, DISC 2009
Elche, Spain, September 23-25, 2009
Proceedings

 Springer

Volume Editor

Idit Keidar
Technion – Israel Institute of Technology
Department of Electrical Engineering
Haifa, 32000 Israel
E-mail: idish@ee.technion.ac.il

Library of Congress Control Number: 2009934036

CR Subject Classification (1998): C.1.4, C.2.1, C.2.4, D.1.3, D.4.3, D.4.7, E.1, H.2.4, H.3.4

LNCS Sublibrary: SL 1 – Theoretical Computer Science and General Issues

ISSN   0302-9743
ISBN-10   3-642-04354-2 Springer Berlin Heidelberg New York
ISBN-13   978-3-642-04354-3 Springer Berlin Heidelberg New York

springer.com

© Springer-Verlag Berlin Heidelberg 2009
Printed in Germany

Typesetting: Camera-ready by author, data conversion by Scientific Publishing Services, Chennai, India
Printed on acid-free paper   SPIN: 12756209   06/3180   5 4 3 2 1 0

Preface

This volume contains 33 15-page-long regular papers and 15 2-page-long brief announcements selected for the 23rd International Symposium on Distributed Computing (DISC 2009), held during September 23-25, 2009, in Elche, Spain. This volume also includes the citation of the 2009 Edsger W. Dijkstra Prize in Distributed Computing, which was awarded at DISC this year, as well as abstracts of talks delivered in a mini symposium honoring the 60th birthdays of Michel Raynal and Shmuel Zaks.

There were 121 submissions to DISC this year, of which 116 were considered for regular presentations, and the rest for brief announcements only. Every submitted paper was read and evaluated by Program Committee members assisted by external reviewers. The final decisions regarding acceptance or rejection of each paper were made during the phone-based Program Committee meeting held during June 2009. Some papers that were not selected for regular presentation were invited to be presented as brief announcements.

The Program Committee nominated five best papers as candidates for awards. The award nominees were presented in a special session at DISC 2009, and appear first in this volume. The winners of the Best Paper Award and Best Student Paper Award were chosen among these five nominees, and announced at the conference.

Although all submissions were carefully read and evaluated, the papers were not formally refereed. It is expected that many of these papers will appear in a more complete and polished form in refereed scientific journals. Revised and expanded versions of a few best selected papers will be considered for publication in a special issue of the journal *Distributed Computing* dedicated to DISC 2009.

Brief announcements present ongoing work or recent results whose full description is not yet ready; it is expected that full papers containing those results will soon appear in other conferences or journals.

Five workshops were co-located with DISC this year: "What Theory for Transactional Memory?" organized by Rachid Guerraoui (EPFL) and Vincent Gramoli (EPFL and University of Neuchâtel); "BFTW3: Why? When? Where? (Workshop on Theory and Practice of Byzantine Fault Tolerance)" organized by Petr Kuznetsov (TU Berlin/Deutsche Telekom Laboratories) and Rodrigo Rodrigues (Max Planck Institute for Software Systems MPI-SWS); "Workshop on Reliability and Security in Wireless Networks" organized by Seth Gilbert (EPFL) and Dariusz Kowalski (University of Liverpool); "Workshop on Game Theoretic Aspects of Distributed Computing" organized by Chryssis Georgiou (University of Cyprus) and Paul Spirakis (CTI and University of Patras); and "Workshop on Theoretical Aspects of Dynamic Distributed Systems (TADDS)" organized by Roberto Baldoni (University of Rome La Sapienza) and Alexander A. Shvartsman (University of Connecticut and MIT).

On behalf of the Program Committee, I would like to thank the workshop organizers, as well as all authors who submitted papers to the conference. I would also like to thank the numerous additional reviewers who provided valuable input to the selection process. I am also grateful to Vicent Cholvi Juan and Antonio Fernández Anta, who played a key role in the success of the conference in their capacity as the Local Arrangements Chairs.

The following institutions are gratefully acknowledged for providing financial support, materials, and human resources to DISC 2009: Ministerio de Ciencia e Innovación, Spain; Microsoft Research; Grupo de Sistemas y Comunicaciones (GSyC), European Association for Theoretical Computer Science (EATCS); Instituto Tecnológico de Informática (ITI), Universidad Politécnica de Valencia (UPV); Universidad del País Vasco/Euskal Herriko Unibertsitatea (UPV/EHU); IMDEA Networks; Asociación de Técnicos de Informática (ATI); Tumsme D'Elx; Cultura D'Elx Universitat Jaume I (UJI); Universidad Rey Juan Carlos (URJC); Yahoo!

July 2009   Idit Keidar

Organization

DISC is an international symposium on the theory, design, analysis, implementation and application of distributed systems and networks. DISC is organized in cooperation with the European Association for Theoretical Computer Science (EATCS). The symposium was established in 1985 as a biannual International Workshop on Distributed Algorithms on Graphs (WDAG). The scope was soon extended to cover all aspects of distributed algorithms as WDAG came to stand for International Workshop on Distributed AlGorithms, and in 1989 it became an annual symposium. To reflect the expansion of its area of interest, the name was changed to DISC (International Symposium on DIStributed Computing) in 1998. The name change also reflects the opening of the symposium to all aspects of distributed computing. The aim of DISC is to reflect the exciting and rapid developments in this field.

Program Committee Chair

Idit Keidar   Technion, Haifa, Israel

Organization Committee Co-chairs

Vicent Cholvi Juan   Universitat Jaume I, Spain
Antonio Fernández Anta   Universidad Rey Juan Carlos, Spain

Steering Committee Chair

Rachid Guerraoui   EPFL, Switzerland

Program Committee

Ittai Abraham   Microsoft Research SVC, USA
Yehuda Afek   Tel-Aviv University, Israel
Marcos K. Aguilera   Microsoft Research SVC, USA
James Aspnes   Yale, USA
Christian Cachin   IBM Zurich Research Laboratory, Switzerland
Gregory V. Chockler   IBM Haifa Research Laboratory, Israel
Carole Delporte-Gallet   University of Paris Diderot, France
Pascal Felber   University of Neuchâtel, Switzerland
Seth Gilbert   EPFL, Switzerland
Danny Hendler   Ben-Gurion University, Israel
Ricardo Jiménez-Peris   Universidad Politécnica de Madrid, Spain
Idit Keidar (Chair)   Technion, Israel

Zvi Lotker	Ben-Gurion University, Israel
Thomas Moscibroda	Microsoft Research, USA
David Peleg	Weizmann Institute, Israel
Eric Ruppert	York University, Canada
Elad M. Schiller	Chalmers University and Gothenburg University, Sweden
Mark R. Tuttle	Intel, USA
Robbert van Renesse	Cornell University, USA
Jay J. Wylie	HP Labs, USA
Lidong Zhou	Microsoft Research Asia, China

Organizing Committee

Sergio Arévalo Viñuales	Universidad Rey Juan Carlos, Spain
Vicent Cholvi Juan (Co-chair)	Universitat Jaume I, Spain
Juan Echagüe	Universitat Jaume I, Spain
Antonio Fernández Anta (Co-chair)	Universidad Rey Juan Carlos, Spain
Vicente Galiano Ibarra	Universidad Miguel Hernández, Spain
Chryssis Georgiou (Publicity)	University of Cyprus, Cyprus
Pedro de las Heras Quirós	Universidad Rey Juan Carlos, Spain
Ernesto Jiménez Merino	Universidad Politécnica de Madrid, Spain
Flavio Junqueira	Yahoo! Research, Spain
Mikel Larrea Alava	The University of the Basque Country, Spain
Miguel A. Mosteiro	Rutgers and Universidad Rey Juan Carlos, Spain
Francesc Muñoz-Escoí	Polytechnic University of Valencia, Spain
Luis Rodero-Merino	Telefónica Investigación y Desarrollo, Spain

Steering Committee

Antonio Fernández Anta	Universidad Rey Juan Carlos, Spain
Chryssis Georgiou	University of Cyprus, Cyprus
Rachid Guerraoui (Chair)	EPFL, Switzerland
Idit Keidar	Technion, Haifa, Israel
Andrzej Pelc	University of Quebec, Canada
Nicola Santoro	Carleton University, Canada
Gadi Taubenfeld	IDC, Israel

External Reviewers

Dan Alistarh	Dariusz Kowalski
Nir Amira	Peter Kropf
Liat Atsmon	Fabian Kuhn
Hagit Attiya	Shay Kutten
Chen Avin	Petr Kuznetsov
Leonid Barenboim	Ron Lavi
Amit Berman	Julia Lawall
Yitzhak Birk	Pierre Leone
Olivier Bournez	Walther Maldonado
Franck van Breugel	Patrick Marlier
Keren Censor	Fabien Mathieu
Hana Chockler	Moti Medina
Michael Clarkson	Alessia Milani
Michele Colajanni	Adam Morrison
Lenore Cowen	Michael Neely
Ajoy Datta	Calvin Newport
Stéphane Devismes	Israel Nir
Ronald de Wolf	Gopal Pandurangan
Partha Dutta	Boaz Patt-Shamir
Michael Elkin	Dmitri Perelman
Faith Ellen	Seth Pettie
Yuval Emek	Dror Rawitz
Amir Epstein	Oded Regev
Shimi Ezra	Torvald Riegel
Rui Fan	Thomas Sauerwald
Hugues Fauconnier	Stefan Schmid
Jeremy Fineman	Yee Jiun Song
Cyril Gavoille	Mike Spreitzer
Vincent Gramoli	Gadi Taubenfeld
Rachid Guerraoui	Andreas Tielmann
Maxim Gurevich	Vinod Vaikuntanathan
Nicolas Hanusse	Ymir Vigfusson
Derin Harmanci	Martin Wahlén
Ted Herman	Jennifer Welch
Chi Ho	Josef Widder
Michel Hurfin	Udi Wieder
Erez Kantor	Junfeng Yang
Jonathan Katz	Haifeng Yu
Gabriel Kliot	Uri Zwick

Table of Contents

Transactional Memory (Session 1A)

Shared Memory (Session 1B)

Distributed and Local Graph Algorithms (Session 1C)

Modeling Issues (Session 1D)

Game Theory (Session 2A)

Consensus and Byzantine Agreement (Session 3C)

Radio Networks (Session 3D)

The 2009 Edsger W. Dijkstra Prize in Distributed Computing

The Edsger W. Dijkstra Prize in Distributed Computing is awarded for an outstanding paper on the principles of distributed computing, whose significance and impact on the theory and/or practice of distributed computing has been evident for at least a decade.

The Dijkstra Award Committee has selected Joseph Halpern and Yoram Moses as the recipients of this year's Edsger W. Dijkstra Prize in Distributed Computing. The prize is given to them for their outstanding paper: "Knowledge and Common Knowledge in a Distributed Environment" published in Proceedings of the Third Annual *ACM Symposium on Principles of Distributed Computing (PODC'84)* pp. 50–61, 1984, and in *Journal of the ACM (JACM)*, 37:3.

The "Knowledge and Common Knowledge in a Distributed Environment" paper presented by Halpern and Moses in PODC 1984 provided an effective new way of reasoning about distributed systems, which has proven incredibly influential in ensuing years; its influence continues to be felt today. This influence extends far beyond the distributed systems community, and can be seen in current work in AI, security, and game theory. This demonstrates how research in distributed computing is relevant to and applicable in a variety of settings involving multi-agent interaction.

The paper provided a novel rigorous and elegant framework supporting the intuition that the most fundamental characteristic of distributed algorithms is the fact that they must cope with uncertainty (i.e., lack of knowledge). When reasoning informally about distributed protocols, researchers naturally think (and speak) in terms of agents "knowing" certain facts about the global system state. The key insight of Halpern and Moses was that this informal notion of knowledge could be given a rigorous mathematical formulation. The resulting new "knowledge framework" shed useful, new light on old results and enabled the discovery of new ones.

The paper is seminal in many respects. First, the paper introduced a model of knowledge, which is now essentially standard in the distributed systems, formal methods, and multi-agent systems communities. The second key aspect of the paper is perhaps its most famous and possibly most cited result: common knowledge cannot be achieved in systems where the receipt of messages is not guaranteed. This result, and the role of common knowledge in the associated "coordinated attack problem", are now part of the computing folklore; they are known and cited by many, many researchers, including many who no doubt have never read the original paper, and are not even part of the distributed systems community. Although common knowledge had been introduced before, this paper for the first time identified its role in distributed systems, and particularly coordination problems. Third, the "hierarchies" of knowledge identified in the paper have been very influential. The different levels of knowledge (distributed/implicit

I. Keidar (Ed.): DISC 2009, LNCS 5805, pp. 1–2, 2009.

knowledge, through to common knowledge) and their relationships have subsequently been extended, challenged, championed, and refined by many others.

For a long while, this paper provided the foundation for many negative and impossibility results, showing that certain tasks cannot be performed in a distributed environment, such as the impossibility of gaining common knowledge where none was initially present. However, subsequent developments have shown that the terminology and notation of the logic of knowledge introduced in this seminal paper can also be used in a positive way to derive new distributed algorithms and re-derive existing ones. Thus, the framework developed in this paper can serve as a high-level language for the natural and intuitive development of new distributed algorithms. With the recent renewed interest in synthesis of code from logical specifications we can expect that this foundation will find new and exciting applications.

In the context of security, since at least the late 1970s, it has been recognized that matters of belief and knowledge are central to the design and to the understanding of systems for security-critical tasks. However, the reasoning used in this context was informal and, although fruitful, also error-prone. Clearly, more rigorous ways of analyzing belief and knowledge are of great value in this context. Later research on security protocols relied on more precise definitions and on more systematic procedures for protocol design and analysis, which were influenced by the work of Halpern and Moses.

In an explicit attempt to address the common knowledge paradox raised by the nominated paper, the notion of internal knowledge consistency was later considered, not only by the distributed computing community, but also by Nobel laureates in the economics community.

More generally, this paper sparked a considerable effort in the study of logics of knowledge involving multi-agent settings (most earlier work in philosophy dealt with the knowledge of a single agent in isolation). Indeed, the excitement and activity generated by this work had a central role in bringing about the biennial TARK conference (Theoretical Aspects of Reasoning about Knowledge, recently renamed Theoretical Aspects of Rationality and Knowledge), with its community consisting of theoretical computer scientists, AI researchers, economists and philosophers.

Award Committee 2009:

Lorenzo Alvisi, Chair	UT Austin
Rachid Guerraoui	EPFL
Prasad Jayanti	Dartmouth
Idit Keidar	Technion
Shay Kutten	Technion
Jennifer Welch	Texas A&M

Computing, Observing, Controlling, Checkpointing: Symbiosis Is Even Better Than Agreement!

Jean-Michel Hélary

Retired from IRISA, University of Rennes 1, France

This talk is a tribute to Michel Raynal, and more precisely to the nice work I had the great pleasure to share with him during twenty years of close collaboration (1985-2004).

Why this title *"Symbiosis is better than Agreement"*? Despite the famous FLP (1985) impossibility result, Michel and I often succeeded to reach agreement. Perhaps none of us was faulty? Perhaps our context was not as asynchronous as it could appear? Well, I don't believe so! The deep reason lies rather in the symbiosis that prevailed between Michel (a tree) and me (a mushroom). This symbiosis not only allowed us to reach agreement, but, more interestingly, to obtain important and fundamental results in several fields of distributed computing. From "old" problems or paradigms – e.g. Network traversal, Detection of stable properties, Election of a leader, Mutual exclusion, Distributed evaluation – to advances in new ones – e.g., related to fault tolerance such as Checkpointing –, we have always strived to bring out design principles and to obtain generic solutions.

During these allocated 30' talk, I will try to overcome another impossibility: make an exhaustive presentation of those about 25 journal and 30 conference papers, appeared in such high quality titles such as Acta Informatica, Distributed Computing, IEEE TPDS, IEEE TSE, Information and Computation, IPL, JCSS, JPDC, and other journals, and such prestigious conferences such as FTCS/DSN, ICDCS, OPODIS, PODC, SIROCCO, SRDS, WDAG/DISC, etc.

Let me just recall two examples of what I consider as very significant results: - The first one is the concept of *Non Simultaneous Delayed Evaluation* (NSDE) [1]. In an asynchronous distributed context, the detection of a property generally rests upon consistent detection of a predicate. This may be very difficult since it impossible to observe at same time all components of a distributed program, and this impossibility is the core of the difficulties encountered in the control of distributed programs. The NSDE concept formalizes this difficulty. Moreover, an operational solution is proposed. It generalizes to the distributed context the usual iteration derivation techniques known in the sequential context, namely the expression of a result as the conjunction of an invariant and a stop condition. It is based on the new notion of *guarded waves*, expressing how the repeated traversal of the network, necessary to collect values, is submitted to the satisfaction of an invariant.

I. Keidar (Ed.): DISC 2009, LNCS 5805, pp. 3–4, 2009.

4   J.-M. Hélary

- The second one is the concept of *Interval Consistency* [2]. In some situations, consecutive events of a sequential process can be merged into a single interval. When a set of sequential processes constitute a distributed computation, the classical Lamport's precedence relation on events is naturally generalized to a precedence relation on intervals (I-precedence). The IC concept answers the following question: *Is the interval-based abstraction associated with a distributed computation consistent?*. To answer this question, a consistency criterion named interval consistency (IC) is introduced. Intuitively, this criterion states that an interval-based abstraction of a distributed computation is consistent if its I-precedence relation does not contradict the sequentiality of each process. More formally, IC is defined as a property of a precedence graph. Interestingly, the IC criterion can be operationally characterized in terms of timestamps (whose values belong to a lattice). This characterization is used to design a versatile protocol that, given intervals defined by a daemon whose behavior is unpredictable, breaks them (in a nontrivial manner) in order to produce an abstraction satisfying the IC criterion. Applications to communication-induced checkpointing are suggested.

Clearly, all these nice results are also due to the collaboration with other talented companions, namely Roberto Baldoni, Jerzy Brzezinski, Achour Mostefaoui, for the closest of them. In fact, one of the Michel's quality, as a group leader, has always been to be able to detect new and promising brilliant fellows, and to give them the opportunity of an excellent walk in scientific life[1]. Would it be only for this, I will stay grateful to Michel for having trusted me and having allowed me to enjoy a rich and thrilling professional life.

Another notable Michel's quality is his terrific sense of pedagogy. This is testified by his numerous text books – and I am very proud to have contributed to one of the most famous of them[2], by his constant implication in his teaching activities at the University, and by the clearness of his papers. I'm sure that many brilliant scientific vocations rose out while attending his beautiful lessons or reading his nice papers. What comes out from his inestimable teaching seems to me fully summarized in the following aphorism (adapted from Mark Rothko):

Each algorithm should be a revelation, the unexpected and unprecedented resolution of an eternally familiar necessity.

References

1. Helary, J.M., Raynal, M.: Towards the construction of Distributed Detection Programs, with an application to distributed termination. Dist. Comp. 7(3), 137–147 (1994)
2. Helary, J.M., Mostefaoui, A., Raynal, M.: Interval Consistency of Asynchronous Distributed Computations. Journal of Computer and System Sciences (JCSS) 64(2), 329–349 (2002)

---

[1] See, more recently, these outstanding young researchers such as Mathieu Roy, Corentin Travers, Frederic Tronel, to cite just a few.
[2] *Synchronization and control of Distributed Systems and Programs* (J.Wiley, 1990).

What Agreement Problems Owe Michel

Achour Mostefaoui

Ifsic/Inria, Université de Rennes, 35042 Rennes, France
achour@irisa.fr

Agreement problems are at the heart of the design of dependable and reliable distributed services. Distributed systems that run such services may experience unpredictable processing and communication delays, and some of their components can fail in various ways. It has been proved that in such settings, the consensus problem, the most popular and fundamental of the agreement problems has no deterministic solution.

Therefore, researchers started investigating ways of circumventing the impossibility result. Two main directions were explored: relaxing the requirements of the consensus problem, and strengthening the assumptions on the system. At least two ways of relaxing the consensus requirements have been investigated: randomization (termination is achieved only with high probability) and approximate agreement. Also, at least two ways of strengthening the assumptions on the system have been considered: adding synchrony assumptions to the system and abstracting the details of how a processor suspects a failure has occurred, without referring to particular synchrony assumptions by the mean of the *Unreliable Failure Detectors* that provides processes with a list of processes suspected to have crashed.

Michel Raynal has contributed to both directions and also to the combination of the two. He has co-authored more than a hundred papers on the topic. Moreover, he has with his co-authors initiated and investigated a new direction: the *condition-based* approach. The *condition-based* approach consists in looking at certain combinations of input values of a given distributed problem. It is often the case in practice that some combinations of the input values of processes occur more frequently than others.

After the specification of necessary and sufficient conditions that allow to solve some problems, a hierarchy of classes of conditions has been exhibited that allow to solve an agreement problem more and more efficiently when the condition is more constraining. Then, a first connection has been made with synchronous systems as the weakest condition that allows to solve consensus in the asynchronous model is the exact condition that allows to solve the same problem in a synchronous system but in the most efficient way revealing a continuum between synchronous and asynchronous systems. Moreover, a connection has been made between the Interactive Consistency agreement problem and error-correcting codes. Indeed, any error-correcting code can be used to parametrize a generic agreement protocol to solve the interactive consistency problem.

The talk will present the different facets of the contribution of Michel Raynal to the understanding of agreement problems (decidability, efficiency, algorithmic mechanisms, etc.).

I. Keidar (Ed.): DISC 2009, LNCS 5805, p. 5, 2009.

Shmuel Zaks - The Early Years:
A Combinatorialist in Distributed Computing

Nicola Santoro

School of Computer Science, Carleton University, Ottawa, K1S 5B6, Canada

Abstract. Celebrating Shmuels Zaks' 60th birthday and his remarkable career, the focus of this talk is on his early contributions to Distributed Computing. In particular, in this talk I examine how this young combinatorialist/graph theorist, upon discovering the beauty and fun of distributed algorithms, was so captured by the area that he never left it. In these early explorations, his research contributions have been many, some very important (e.g. lower bound for election in complete graphs) and some very beautiful (e.g. guessing games in synchronous networks). In this talk, a few of these research results are described and commented, and some of his other contributions to the Distributed Computing community during those years are highlighted.

I. Keidar (Ed.): DISC 2009, LNCS 5805, p. 6, 2009.

Shmuel Zaks - The Mathematician, Computer Scientist and Personality

Mordechai Shalom

TelHai Academic College, Upper Galilee, 12210, Israel
cmshalom@telhai.ac.il

Abstract. Shmuel Zaks received his BSc (cum laude) and MSc degrees in Mathematics from the Technion, Haifa, Israel, in 1971 and 1972, respectively, and his PhD degree in Computer Science from the University of Illinois at Urbana-Champaign in 1979. He is a full professor at the Department of Computer Science at the Technion, where he has been since 1979. He is an author over 100 journal and conference papers, which span his research interests, including Distributed Computing, ATM networks, Optical Networks,Graph and Combinatorial Algorithms, and Discrete Mathematics.

I had the honor to be supervised by Shmuel Zaks (and jointly of Shlomo Moran) during my MSc studies in years 1982-1985. At that period the main research interest of Shmuel was Distributed Algorithms, and my MSc thesis was on this subject. His numerous contributions to this field are subject of another talk.

In the first half of the 1990's his major contributions was in the field of ATM networks. In part of this talk I will describe a beautiful result from [CGZ96].

He has numerous contributions in Optical Networks. I had the opportunity to collaborate with him in part of these works, which are mostly approximation algorithms to NP-hard optimization problems. In my talk will describe one of these results ([FMSZ08]).

Shmuel is a father of 4 children and grandfather of 4 grandchildren. It is impossible to talk about him without mentioning that he is an exceptional family man and enjoys helping people at every possible occasion and in every possible way.

References

[CGZ96] Cidon, I., Gerstel, O., Zaks, S.: The layout of virtual paths in atm networks. IEEE/ACM Trans. Netw. 4(6), 873–884 (1996)

[FMSZ08] Flammini, M., Moscardelli, L., Shalom, M., Zaks, S.: Approximating the traffic grooming problem. Journal of Discrete Algorithms 6(3), 472–479 (2008)

I. Keidar (Ed.): DISC 2009, LNCS 5805, p. 7, 2009.
© Springer-Verlag Berlin Heidelberg 2009

The Disagreement Power of an Adversary

Carole Delporte-Gallet[1], Hugues Fauconnier[1],
Rachid Guerraoui[2], and Andreas Tielmann[1]

[1] LIAFA, Université Paris Diderot
Paris, France
[2] Distributed Programming Laboratory, EPFL
Lausanne, Switzerland

Abstract. At the heart of distributed computing lies the fundamental result that the level of agreement that can be obtained in an asynchronous shared memory model where t processes can crash is exactly $t + 1$. In other words, an adversary that can crash any subset of size at most t can prevent the processes from agreeing on t values. But what about the remaining $(2^{2^n} - n)$ adversaries that might crash certain combination of processes and not others?

This paper presents a precise way to characterize such adversaries by introducing the notion of *disagreement power*: the biggest integer k for which the adversary can prevent processes from agreeing on k values. We show how to compute the disagreement power of an adversary and how this notion enables to derive n *equivalence* classes of adversaries.

1 Introduction

The theory of distributed computing is largely related to determining what can be computed against a specific adversary. Most results so far have been devoted to *one* specific form of adversaries: those that can control any subset of size t of the processes, i.e., the *t-failures* adversary. In particular, a seminal result in distributed computing says that the level of agreement that can be obtained deterministically in a shared memory model where t processes can crash is exactly $t + 1$ [1,2,3]. In other words, an adversary that can crash any subset of size at most t can prevent the processes from agreeing on t values. In the case of consensus for instance ($t = 1$), this translates into FLP [4].

In a sense, these results are very incomplete. Indeed, the *t*-failures assumption covers only the n "uniform" adversaries in a system of size n. What about the other $(2^{2^n} - n)$ adversaries that can crash certain subsets of processes of a certain size but not others of the same size? In particular, given any adversary $\mathcal{A}$, for what k does $\mathcal{A}$ prevent k-set agreement [5]? This paper addresses this question and derives from the answer equivalence classes between adversaries. More specifically, we characterize the power of an adversary $\mathcal{A}$ by the biggest k for which k-set agreement cannot be solved with $\mathcal{A}$, which we call here the *disagreement power* of $\mathcal{A}$. We show how to compute the disagreement power of

I. Keidar (Ed.): DISC 2009, LNCS 5805, pp. 8–21, 2009.

an adversary and we show that adversaries within the same class solve the same set of (colorless[1]) tasks.

Beyond intellectual curiosity, studying "non-uniform" adversaries might even be practically motivated by modern multicore architectures where the failures of processes in the same core might all be correlated [8,9,10].

Determining the disagreement power of certain adversaries is trivial. For others, it is not. Consider, in a system of 3 processes, $\{1, 2, 3\}$, an adversary $\mathcal{A}$ that can fail either no process, both processes 2 and 3, or process 1 i.e. $\mathcal{A} = \{\emptyset, 23^2, 1\}$. It is easy to show that $\mathcal{A}$ can prevent consensus but not 2-set agreement. In this sense, adversary $\mathcal{A}$ has the same disagreement power as the 1-failure adversary, i.e., 1. Consider now a more involved scenario: a system of 4 processes and another adversary $\mathcal{A}'$ that can fail any element of $\{\emptyset, 4, 23, 14, 12, 134, 124, 123\}$. What is the disagreement power of $\mathcal{A}'$? We prove in this paper that it is also 1.

We give a general characterization of adversaries that enables one to automatically compute their disagreement power. Namely, we introduce a *structure predicate* on adversaries, parameterized by an integer k, and which, intuitively, checks for any set of faulty processes of size less or equal k, whether there is some adequate superset in the adversary. We prove that any adversary that satisfies the predicate has disagreement power k. We first show (sufficient condition) that if k-set agreement can be solved with some adversary that satisfies the predicate for some k, then k-set agreement can be solved with the k-failures adversary which in turn is known to be impossible [1,2,3]. Hence, an adversary that satisfies the predicate has disagreement power at least k. We do this through a new simulation between adversaries, which we call the *conservative back-off simulation*, and which we believe is interesting in its own right. The idea underlying our simulation is the following: a process backs-off and skips its simulation step if the process thinks that it is faulty in some set where the simulated algorithm is known to work. Conversely (necessary condition), we show how to solve k-set agreement with any adversary $\mathcal{A}$ that does not satisfy the predicate for some k. We do this by showing how to implement failure detector k-anti-Ω [11], known in turn to implement k-set agreement. (Each query to k-anti-Ω returns $n - k$ process ids; the specification ensures that there is a correct process whose id is eventually never output.)

We then use our characterization to split the set of all adversaries into n disjoint *equivalence* classes, one for every level of disagreement: we show that for any two adversaries with the same disagreement power, exactly the same set of (colorless) tasks can be solved. The key to our proof of the equivalence is that for every adversary with disagreement power k, it is possible to simulate a wait-free system of $k + 1$ processes which in turn can simulate every other k-failure adversary [6,12]. This is technically achieved by implementing $(k+1)$-anti-Ω for the adversary and translating it to a vector of $k + 1$ Ω failure detectors [13] of

---

[1] Intuitively, in a colorless task [6,7] any process can adopt any input or output value of any other process without violating the task specification.

[2] When appropriate, we will use e.g. 23 as shorthand for the set $\{2, 3\}$.

which at least one is a "real" Ω (i.e. it outputs eventually everywhere the same correct process). Then, each of the $k + 1$ simulated processes can be associated with one of the Ω's and a consensus-object can be built to agree on the simulated steps of such a process.

Since we can compute automatically the disagreement power of an adversary (using our structural predicate), we can thus automatically derive results for an adversary from known results from another adversary with the same disagreement power.

Indirectly, our partitioning contributes to the idea that a very small subset of results and ad-hoc proofs in distributed computing should suffice to derive all others. In particular, if indeed needed to reason about $(n-1)$-set agreement for the "wait-free" adversary, topology is not needed for all the other ones. Results concerning other k-failures ("uniform") adversaries can be deduced by [6,12], whereas results for all other ("non-uniform") $(2^{2^n} - n)$ adversaries can be deduced from our characterization.

The remainder of the paper is structured as follows. We first define our model in Section 2. We then introduce our notion of disagreement power and our structural predicate in Section 3. We present our conservative back-off simulation and use it in Section 4 to show that any adversary that satisfies the predicate for k can be reduced to the k-failure adversary (thus the predicate is sufficient for the simulation). We show in Section 5 how to implement k-set agreement with any adversary that does not satisfy the predicate (therefore, the predicate is necessary). We then show that adversaries with the same disagreement power are actually in the same equivalence class in Section 6 and conclude the paper with some general remarks in Section 7.

2   Model and Definitions

We assume systems of deterministic processes that communicate asynchronously using read-write atomic registers. We recall below the necessary elements to describe our model and introduce the notion of an adversary.

Processes and registers. Our system consists of a set $\Pi = \{p_1, p_2, ..., p_n\}$ of n processes sharing atomic registers. Processes might crash. Processes that crash are called faulty and a process that never crashes is said to be correct.

Adversaries and runs. Intuitively, an *adversary* can choose which set of processes will crash. More precisely, we represent an adversary as a set of sets of processes (we call these sets *faulty-sets*) and the adversary can choose one of these faulty-sets. Here, we consider only adversaries $\mathcal{A}$ for which there is always at least one correct process, i.e. $\Pi \notin \mathcal{A}$.

A run of an algorithm A is an infinite sequence of steps of the processes. Given an adversary $\mathcal{A}$, associated with every run is a set of processes $a \in \mathcal{A}$ that will crash. This set is chosen by the adversary and the processes in a may crash at any time. The set of processes that make an infinity of steps in some run associated with a is then exactly $\Pi \setminus a$.

The classical n process k-failure adversary, denoted $\mathcal{B}_k^n$ is the adversary for which at most k $(0 \leq k \leq n-1)$ processes may crash: $\mathcal{B}_k^n = \{b \subseteq \Pi \mid |b| \leq k \wedge |\Pi| = n\}$. Where the number of processes is clear from the context, we will omit the n (i.e. $\mathcal{B}_k = \mathcal{B}_k^n$).

Tasks. Generally, we say that algorithm A solves a task T in adversary $\mathcal{A}$ if every run of A with associated $a \in \mathcal{A}$ satisfies the specification of T (we say also A implements T for adversary $\mathcal{A}$). More specifically, a task is a tuple $(\mathcal{I}, \mathcal{O}, \Delta)$, where $\mathcal{I}$ is a set of vectors of input values and $\mathcal{O}$ is a set of vectors of output values such that the value of every process p_i corresponds to the i-th entry of a vector. Δ is a total relation from $\mathcal{I}$ to $\mathcal{O}$. Then, a task is solved if for input vector $I \in \mathcal{I}$, an output vector $O \in \mathcal{O}$ is computed such that $O \in \Delta(I)$.

In the following, we restrict ourselves to specific colorless tasks [6,7]. Let $val(V)$ be the set of values in some vector V. A *colorless* task is such that if $O \in \Delta(I)$, then for every I' with $val(I') \subseteq val(I)$: $I' \in \mathcal{I}$ and $\Delta(I') \subseteq \Delta(I)$. Furthermore, for every O' with $val(O') \subseteq val(O)$: $O' \in \mathcal{O}$ and $O' \in \Delta(I)$. As a result, the specification of a colorless task is independent of the number of processes. In this sense, such a task specifies a *family of tasks*, one for every possible number of processes.

k-Set agreement. The canonical example of a colorless task is *k-set agreement*. Let S be any set of values with $|S| \geq k+1$. In k-set agreement, $\mathcal{I}$ and $\mathcal{O}$ are the sets of all vectors of values from S such that for all $O \in \mathcal{O}$, $|val(O)| \leq k$ and for every $I \in \mathcal{I}$: $O \in \Delta(I)$ iff $val(O) \subseteq val(I)$.

Consensus is 1-set agreement. k-set agreement can be solved in $\mathcal{B}_l$ iff $0 \leq l \leq k-1$ [1,2,3].

In one of our proofs, we will use a distributed oracle called k-anti-Ω [11]: each query to k-anti-Ω returns $n-k$ process ids, with the guarantee that there is a correct process whose id is returned only a finite number of times. If $k = 1$, k-anti-Ω is equivalent to the eventual leader Ω failure detector, the weakest failure detector for consensus [13,14]. If $k = n-1$, k-anti-Ω is anti-Ω, the weakest failure detector to solve $(n-1)$-set agreement [11].

3   Disagreement Power

We define the *disagreement power* of an adversary $\mathcal{A}$ to be the maximal k for which it is impossible to implement k-set agreement in $\mathcal{A}$. More precisely:

Definition 1. *An adversary $\mathcal{A}$ has disagreement power k, denoted $dis(\mathcal{A})$, if (1) it is impossible to implement k-set agreement in $\mathcal{A}$, and (2) it is possible to implement $(k+1)$-set agreement in $\mathcal{A}$.*

If an adversary cannot prevent agreement for any k, then we say that its disagreement power is 0. As established in [1,2,3], it is possible to implement $(k+1)$-set agreement in $\mathcal{B}_k$ but it is impossible to implement k-set agreement in $\mathcal{B}_k$. Hence, the disagreement power of $\mathcal{B}_k$ is k.

Proposition 1. $dis(\mathcal{B}_k) = k$

To compare the power of two adversaries, we define what it means for an adversary to be *stronger* than another adversary:

Definition 2. *An adversary $\mathcal{A}$ is stronger than an adversary $\mathcal{B}$ (denoted $\mathcal{A} \succcurlyeq \mathcal{B}$) if every colorless task that can be solved in $\mathcal{A}$ can be solved in $\mathcal{B}$.*

We also compare our adversaries with a (structural) *domination* property without considering the tasks that they can solve. The interesting point, as we will show later, is that this property captures exactly the power of an adversary. For our domination property, we implicitly assume that both adversaries are built upon the same set of processes Π.

Definition 3. *Let $\mathcal{A}$ and $\mathcal{B}$ be any two adversaries. We say that a faulty-set $a \in \mathcal{A}$ dominates a faulty-set $b \in \mathcal{B}$ in $\mathcal{A}$ and $\mathcal{B}$ (denoted $D(a, \mathcal{A}, b, \mathcal{B})$), if*

$$(a \supseteq b) \quad and \quad (\forall b' \in \mathcal{B}, b' \supsetneq b, \exists a' \in \mathcal{A}, a' \supseteq a : D(a', \mathcal{A}, b', \mathcal{B}))$$

In the base case, when there is no strict superset of b in $\mathcal{B}$, then this translates to $a \supseteq b$. Where $\mathcal{A}$ and $\mathcal{B}$ are clear from the context, we will simply write $D(a, b)$. With a slight abuse of the D-symbol, we extend the notion of domination to adversaries:

Definition 4. *We say that an adversary $\mathcal{A}$ dominates an adversary $\mathcal{B}$ (denoted $D(\mathcal{A}, \mathcal{B})$) if and only if the following property is satisfied:*

$$\forall b \in \mathcal{B}, \exists a \in \mathcal{A} : D(a, \mathcal{A}, b, \mathcal{B}).$$

This property is intricate. One may think that if for all $b_0 \subset b_1 \ldots \subset b_x$ in $\mathcal{B}$ there exist $a_0 \subseteq a_1 \ldots \subseteq a_x$ in $\mathcal{A}$ such that $b_i \subseteq a_i$ for all i then $D(\mathcal{A}, \mathcal{B})$. But this is not the case. Consider the following example:

Example 1. Assume $n = 3$ and consider two adversaries (we use $ij \ldots$ as a shorthand for the set $\{p_i, p_j, \ldots\}$):

$$\mathcal{A} = \{\emptyset, 2, 12, 13, 23\}$$
$$\mathcal{B}_2 = \{\emptyset, 1, 2, 3, 12, 13, 23\}$$

In this example for all $b_0 \subset b1 \subset b2$ there exist $a_0 \subseteq a1 \subseteq a2$. But $\neg D(\mathcal{A}, \mathcal{B}_2)$, because for all $a \in \mathcal{A}$, $\neg D(a, 3)$.

Example 2. Consider now a slightly different example with $n = 4$ and the following adversaries :

$$\mathcal{A} = \{\emptyset, 12, 34, 123, 124, 134, 234\}$$
$$\mathcal{B}_2 = \{\emptyset, 1, 2, 3, 4, 12, 13, 14, 23, 24, 34\}$$

In this example, $D(\mathcal{A}, \mathcal{B}_2)$, i.e. for every $b \in \mathcal{B}_2$ there exists an $a \in \mathcal{A}$ such that $D(a, b)$ (e.g. $D(\emptyset, \emptyset)$, $D(12, 2)$ and $D(124, 24)$).

Interestingly, concerning adversary $\mathcal{B}_k$, our definitions induce the following property:

Theorem 1. *Consider any k with $1 \leq k \leq n-1$ and any element $b \in \mathcal{B}_k$. Then $\neg D(\mathcal{B}_k \setminus \{b\}, \mathcal{B}_k)$.*

Proof. We show that for all $a \in \mathcal{B}_k \setminus \{b\}$, $\neg D(a, b)$. If $|b| = k$, then this is immediately clear, because there cannot be any superset of b in $\mathcal{B}_k \setminus \{b\}$. Otherwise, if $|b| < k$ then assume that $a \in \mathcal{B}_k$ is any set such that $D(a, b)$. Hence, there is some set $b' \supsetneq b$ with $|b'| = k$ such that the number of processes not in a is maximal in b'. Assume there exists some $a' \supseteq a$ and $a' \supseteq b'$. Then $|a'| \geq |a \cup b'| > k$, because $|b'| = k$ and there is at least one element in $a \setminus b'$. Thus $a' \notin \mathcal{B}_k$ and we have a contradiction.

4   The Conservative Back-Off Simulation (Sufficient Condition)

In this section we show that if, for adversaries $\mathcal{A}$ and $\mathcal{B}$, we have $D(\mathcal{A}, \mathcal{B})$, then $\mathcal{A}$ is stronger than $\mathcal{B}$. Given that k-set agreement cannot be implemented in $\mathcal{B}_k$, we get a sufficient condition for the impossiblity of implementing k-set agreement, namely if $D(\mathcal{A}, \mathcal{B}_k)$, then k-set agreeement cannot be implemented in $\mathcal{A}$.

Assume $D(\mathcal{A}, \mathcal{B})$ for some adversaries $\mathcal{A}$ and $\mathcal{B}$ over the same set of processes Π. Let Alg be any algorithm which solves a colorless task T in $\mathcal{A}$. Then, the *conservative back-off simulation* in Algorithm 1 solves T with Alg in $\mathcal{B}$.

The goal of the simulation is to identify, in every possible run with a set of faulty processes $b^* \in \mathcal{B}$, a set of processes $a^* \in \mathcal{A}$ with $b^* \subseteq a^*$ (i.e. more failures in a^* than in b^*). Hence, the processes outside a^* can use the given algorithm which is known to terminate for every $a^* \in \mathcal{A}$. The processes in a^* that are not in b^* can then just back-off and omit to take simulation steps, since the others are enough to ensure termination. Thus, termination is achieved by simply letting some correct processes take only finitely many steps, i.e. to simulate their crashes.

To determine a^*, we first narrow down the possibilities in b^* in the run. This is achieved by simply using step-counters. The current estimations are stored in *possibly-faulty*. Then, starting from the smallest set $b \in$ *possibly-faulty*, every process tries to stepwise approximate a^*.

In these steps, our property $D(\mathcal{A}, \mathcal{B})$ is needed. For every $b \in$ *possibly-faulty*, starting from the smallest, some $a \in \mathcal{A}$ with $D(a, b)$ that is a superset of all other elements in *faulty* is deterministically chosen and added to *faulty*. Since $D(a, b)$, and every next $b' \in$ *possibly-faulty* is a superset of b, it is guaranteed that in the following there will always be an $a' \in \mathcal{A}$ that is a superset of a and $D(a', b')$. This sequence of a's is stored in *faulty*. Since the subsets of b^* in *possibly-faulty* are stable (i.e. they are eventually always in *possibly-faulty*), even if the supersets of b^* change infinitely often, the a added in the step in b^* is such that $b^* \subseteq a$. Then, the a^* we are trying to seek is just the smallest set in *faulty* where $b^* \subseteq a^*$. Although we do not know which one of the elements of *faulty* it is, it is safe for a process to take a step if it does not belong to some $a \in$ *faulty* and has reason to believe that all other processes that are not in a are alive. This is simply achieved by determining which processes took steps since the last own simulation step using the variable *lastsimsteps*. A process not in a^* will not block here forever, because all non-faulty processes increase their step-counters infinitely often.

If some process decides, it writes its decision value into a special register. If some other process observes that another process has decided, it adopts its decision value and decides also.

Consider the adversaries from Example 2: $\mathcal{A} = \{\emptyset, 12, 34, 123, 124, 134, 234\}$, $\mathcal{B}_2$ and $n = 4$. If the actual faulty-set is 3, then eventually *possibly-faulty* can only be: $\{\emptyset, 3, 23\}$, $\{\emptyset, 3, 13\}$ or $\{\emptyset, 3, 34\}$, because process 3 takes the least number of steps. By construction, *faulty* will be $\{\emptyset, 34, 234\}$, $\{\emptyset, 34, 134\}$ or $\{\emptyset, 34, 234\}$ respectively. For the three processes p_1, p_2 and p_4 that take infinitely many steps, eventually *alive* $\subseteq$ 124. If one of these processes takes only finitely many simulation steps, then *alive* = 124 at this process. In this case, for p_1 and p_2 there is always the set 34 in *faulty* such that *alive* $\cup$ 34 $= \Pi$ and p_1 respectively p_2 are not in 34. But this is not the case for p_4. Thus, p_4 takes only finitely many steps and only processes p_1 and p_2 take infinitely many steps. Therefore, the simulated algorithm is executed as if the faulty set is 34.

Algorithm 1. The conservative back-off simulation for process p_i and $D(\mathcal{A}, \mathcal{B})$.

```
1   Stepc_i := 0;                                        /* a SWMR register */
2   lastsimsteps_i := [0, ..., 0];         /* the state at the last simulated step */

3   while true do
4   |   if some other process has decided then adopt its decision value and decide;
5   |   let p_{i_1}, ..., p_{i_n} be the processes ordered by increasing Stepc (ties broken
    |       deterministically);
6   |   possibly-faulty_i := {∅, {p_{i_1}}, {p_{i_1}, p_{i_2}}, ..., {p_{i_1}, ..., p_{i_{n-1}}}} ∩ B;
7   |   faulty_i := ∅;
8   |   foreach b ∈ possibly-faulty_i, ordered by inclusion do
9   |   |   add some a ∈ A to faulty_i s.t. D(a, b) and ∀a' ∈ faulty_i, a ⊇ a' (choose
    |   |       deterministically);
10  |   alive_i := {p_j | Stepc_j > lastsimsteps_i[j]};
11  |   if ∃a ∈ faulty_i, alive_i ∪ a = Π and p_i ∉ a then
12  |   |   execute a step of Alg;
13  |   |   if decided then write decision value into special register;
14  |   |   lastsimsteps_i := [Stepc_1, ..., Stepc_n];
15  |   Stepc_i := Stepc_i + 1;
```

Theorem 2. *If $D(\mathcal{A}, \mathcal{B})$, then $\mathcal{A} \succcurlyeq \mathcal{B}$.*

Proof. We show that Algorithm 1 decides for any algorithm Alg and any colorless task T in all runs of $\mathcal{B}$. For this, it is sufficient if the simulation of Alg decides, *because T is a colorless task and every other process can decide on the decision value of any other decided process.*

Let $b^* \in \mathcal{B}$ be the actual set of faulty processes in some run. Then, eventually always $b^* \in$ possibly-faulty and all $b \in$ possibly-faulty with $b \subseteq b^*$ are the same at all processes, because all the step counters at processes in sets $b \subseteq b^*$ change only finitely often and the step counters of some of the processes in all other sets increase infinitely often.

In the "for"-loop, for every $b \in$ possibly-faulty, some $a \in \mathcal{A}$ with $D(a,b)$ is chosen such that $\forall a' \in$ faulty$_i$, $a \supseteq a'$. It is here where we need $D(\mathcal{A},\mathcal{B})$. If b is the smallest set in possibly-faulty, we simply have to choose some set a where $D(a,b)$. In all following steps, the recursiveness of the domination predicate is needed. Let a' be the set that has been added to faulty in the previous step in $b' \in$ possibly-faulty. Thus $D(a',b')$ and we need in fact some $a \supseteq a'$ with $D(a,b)$ where $b \supsetneq b'$. And this follows immediately from $D(a',b')$.

Let $a^* \in \mathcal{A}$ be the smallest set with $a^* \supseteq b^*$ that is eventually always added to faulty$_i$. Such a set has to exist (e.g. the one that is added in the step where $b = b^*$). Then, eventually, and at all correct processes, for all sets $a \in$ faulty$_i$ where $a \cup$ alive$_i = \Pi$, a is a superset of a^*, because for all strict subsets a' of a^* there is at least one process $p \notin a'$ that makes only finitely many steps. Since eventually only processes that are not in such an a take steps, processes in a^* simulate only finitely many steps of Alg.

Assume some process p_j that is not in a^* simulates only finitely many steps of Alg. Since $a^* \supseteq b^*$, all these processes take infinitely many steps. Therefore, eventually, alive$_j \supseteq \Pi \setminus a^*$. But then, alive$_j \cup a^* = \Pi$. A contradiction to the fact that p_j simulates only finitely many steps of Alg. Therefore, exactly the processes not in a^* simulate infinitely many steps. Since $a^* \in \mathcal{A}$, Alg has to terminate.

From this Theorem follows, that if $D(\mathcal{A},\mathcal{B}_k)$, then k-set agreement cannot be implemented in $\mathcal{A}$, since it is impossible in $\mathcal{B}_k$ [1,2,3].

Corollary 1. *If $D(\mathcal{A},\mathcal{B}_k)$, then k-set agreement cannot be implemented in $\mathcal{A}$.*

5 k-Set Agreement Protocol (Necessary Condition)

In this section, we show that if for adversaries $\mathcal{A}$ and $\mathcal{B}_k$ we have $\neg D(\mathcal{A},\mathcal{B}_k)$, then k-set agreement can be implemented in $\mathcal{A}$. By the contrapositive, we get a necessary condition for the impossibility of implementing k-set agreement, namely if k-set agreement cannot be implemented in $\mathcal{A}$, then $D(\mathcal{A},\mathcal{B}_k)$

We compare an adversary $\mathcal{A}$ with the k-failure adversary which contains all sets of size less or equal k. We show that if $\neg D(\mathcal{A},\mathcal{B}_k)$, then it is possible to implement k-set agreement for $\mathcal{A}$. For this, it is sufficient to show how to implement k-anti-Ω, since this is sufficient to implement k-set agreement in adversary $\mathcal{A}$ [11]. Basically, k-anti-Ω outputs, whenever queried, at least $n - k$ processes, s.t. at least one correct process is output only finitely often. Algorithm 2 implements k-anti-Ω.

The key to the implementation is to find a set b^* such that b^* contains at least one non-faulty process, i.e. if the actual set of faulty processes is a^*, then $b^* \not\subseteq a^*$. It is sufficient though, that we eventually always find supersets of b^* of size at most k. The output for k-anti-Ω is then just the complement of these sets.

As in the previous section, we first try to narrow down the possibilities for the actual faulty set a^*. This is again achieved by using step-counters. The current estimations are stored in *possibly-faulty*. Then, we take the smallest set $b_{init} \in \mathcal{B}_k$ that is not dominated by any $a \in \mathcal{A}$ (since $\neg D(\mathcal{A}, \mathcal{B}_k)$, there has to exist at least one). Although this set is not dominated by any a, it may contain no correct process (in particular, b_{init} may be the empty set). However, if so, then by the recursive nature of the domination property, there has to exist a strict superset of b_{init} which is not dominated by any $a \in \mathcal{A}$ with $a \supseteq b_{init}$ (if $b_{init} = \emptyset$, then this applies to all $a \in \mathcal{A}$). By an iterated use of this property, for every possible $a \in$ *possibly-faulty*, the inner "while"-loop ends. Thus, for all $a \in$ *possibly-faulty*: $a \not\supseteq est$ for the corresponding est after the loop. Since a^* is eventually always in *possibly-faulty*, we eventually always choose the same $b^* \not\subseteq a^*$ in the step for a^*. Although the supersets of a^* in *possibly-faulty* may differ in each round, our estimate will eventually always contain b^*, because some prefix in *possibly-faulty* is stable.

Consider Example 1 with $n = 3$ and $k = 2$: $\mathcal{A} = \{\emptyset, 2, 12, 13, 23\}$ and $\mathcal{B}_2$ and recall that $\neg D(\mathcal{A}, \mathcal{B}_2)$. Then, for example $b_{init} = 3$ and thus est is initially set to 3.

Assume first that the actual faulty-set is 1. Eventually *possibly-faulty* will be $\{\emptyset, 12\}$ or $\{\emptyset, 13\}$. In any case, if $a = \emptyset$ is considered, then est remains 3. If $a = 12$ is considered, then est remains 3 and thus the failure detector output does not contain 3.

Assume now that all the processes are correct i.e. the faulty-set is $\emptyset$. We have to avoid, in this case, that the output alternates between 1, 2 and 3. Eventually *possibly-faulty* will be $\{\emptyset, 1, 12\}$, $\{\emptyset, 1, 13\}$, $\{\emptyset, 2, 12\}$, $\{\emptyset, 2, 23\}$, $\{\emptyset, 3, 13\}$ or $\{\emptyset, 3, 23\}$. In any case, if $a = \emptyset$ is considered, then est remains 3. After that, est can be augmented, but 3 will eventually never be in the ouput of k-anti-Ω. Therefore, eventually there is a correct process (3) that is not in the output of k-anti-Ω.

Theorem 3. *For all $\mathcal{A}$, if $\neg D(\mathcal{A}, \mathcal{B}_k)$, then it is possible to implement k-anti-Ω in $\mathcal{A}$.*

Proof. If $\neg D(\mathcal{A}, \mathcal{B}_k)$, then:

$$\exists b \in \mathcal{B}_k, \forall a \in \mathcal{A}, \neg D(a, b).$$

Thus, this b can be chosen as b_{init}. If a does not dominate b for $\mathcal{A}$ and $\mathcal{B}_k$, then

$$(a \not\supseteq b) \quad \vee \quad (\exists b' \in \mathcal{B}_k, b' \supsetneq b, \forall a' \in \mathcal{A}, a' \supseteq a, \neg D(a', b')). \tag{1}$$

Let $a^* \in \mathcal{A}$ be the actual set of faulty processes in some run. Then, eventually, *possibly-faulty* contains a^* and all $a \in$ *possibly-faulty*, $a \subseteq a^*$ are the same at all processes, because all the step counters at these processes change only finitely

---

Algorithm 2. Implementation of k-anti-Ω

---

1 $Stepc_i := 0;$ /* a SWMR register */
2 $b_{init} :=$ some set in $\mathcal{B}_k$ s.t. for all $a \in \mathcal{A}, \neg D(a, b_{init});$

3 **while** *true* **do**
4   let $p_{i_1}, \ldots, p_{i_n}$ be the processes ordered by increasing $Stepc$ (ties broken deterministically);
5   *possibly-faulty*$_i := \{\emptyset, \{p_{i_1}\}, \{p_{i_1}, p_{i_2}\}, \ldots, \{p_{i_1}, \ldots, p_{i_{n-1}}\}\} \cap \mathcal{A};$
6      $est_i := b_{init};$
7   **foreach** $a \in$ *possibly-faulty*$_i$, *ordered by inclusion* **do**
8   **while** $a \supseteq est_i$ **do**
9          $est_i :=$ determin. choose some $b \in \mathcal{B}_k, b \supsetneq est_i$ s.t. $\forall a' \in \mathcal{A}, a' \supseteq a:$
           $\neg D(a', b);$
10   **if** $|est_i| < k$ **then** add some processes to est_i until $|est_i| = k$
11     $Stepc_i := Stepc_i + 1;$
12   output $\Pi \setminus est_i;$

---

often and the step counters of some of the processes in all supersets increase infinitely often.

Since $\neg D(\mathcal{A}, \mathcal{B}_k)$, there exists some good b_{init}. For every $a \in$ *possibly-faulty* in every step in the "for"-loop, $\neg D(a, est)$, because otherwise it would not have been chosen as b_{init} or in the inner "while"-loop. Thus, either $a \not\supseteq est$ and the inner "while"-loop immediately terminates, or it follows from (1), that there exists some some $b \in \mathcal{B}_k, b \supsetneq est_i$ s.t. $\forall a' \in \mathcal{A}, a' \supseteq a: \neg D(a', b)$, i.e. the loop continues. Since in every step of the inner "while"-loop, est grows and $est \in \mathcal{B}_k$, the loop ends after at most k steps.

Let $b^* \supseteq b_{init}$ be the maximal set such that b^* is eventually always a subset of est_i at the end of the "for"-loop. Since the prefix of the subsets of a^* is stable in *possibly-faulty*, $a^* \supseteq b^*$, because this is the terminating condition of the inner "while"-loop. Therefore, $a^* \not\supseteq b^*$ and there exists a process $p \in b^*$ which is not in a^* and the properties of k-anti-Ω are fulfilled.

Then, we get:

Corollary 2. *If k-set agreement cannot be implemented in $\mathcal{A}$, then $D(\mathcal{A}, \mathcal{B}_k)$.*

If we gather together Theorem 2 and Theorem 3, we obtain a necessary and sufficient condition in terms of structured predicate under which an adversary can solve the k-set agreement.

Theorem 4. *k-set agreement can be implemented in $\mathcal{A}$ if and only if $\neg D(\mathcal{A}, \mathcal{B}_k)$*

We can now directly derive the disagreement power of an adversary by our structural predicate:

Theorem 5. *$dis(\mathcal{A}) = k$ if and only if (1) $D(\mathcal{A}, \mathcal{B}_k)$, and (2) $\neg D(\mathcal{A}, \mathcal{B}_{k+1})$*

6   Equivalence Classes

In this section we show that if two adversaries have the same disagreeement power then they solve exactly the same set of colorless tasks: $dis(\mathcal{A}) = dis(\mathcal{B})$ if and only if $\mathcal{A} \succcurlyeq \mathcal{B}$ and $\mathcal{B} \succcurlyeq \mathcal{A}$.

Before showing that all adversaries with the same disagreement power solve the same set of (colorless) tasks, we show that the ability of an adversary to prevent agreement is independent of the number of processes (as long as $n \geq k+1$). After that, we show that for any two adversaries $\mathcal{A}$ and $\mathcal{B}$ with the same disagreement power k, $\mathcal{A} \succcurlyeq \mathcal{B}$.

6.1   Robustness against the Number of Processes

Before we state our results, we recall a theorem from [6] that, in our notation, states the following:

Theorem 6. *(BG [6]). For all n, for all k with $n > k$: $\mathcal{B}_k^n \succcurlyeq \mathcal{B}_k^{k+1}$.*

Theorem 7. *For every adversary $\mathcal{A}^n$ built upon a set of n processes, for every $k < n$: if k-set agreement for $k + 1 \leq n$ processes can be implemented in $\mathcal{A}^n$, then k-set agreement can be implemented in $\mathcal{A}^n$.*

Proof. Assume k-set agreement can be implemented for $k + 1$ processes in adversary $\mathcal{A}^n$. Assume for contradiction that $D(\mathcal{A}^n, \mathcal{B}_k^n)$. Then, with Theorem 2, k-set agreement for $k+1$ processes can be implemented in $\mathcal{B}_k^n$ and with Theorem 6 it follows that k-set agreement can be implemented in $\mathcal{B}_k^{k+1}$. A contradiction to [1,2,3]. Thus, $\neg D(\mathcal{A}^n, \mathcal{B}_k^n)$ which means by Theorem 3 that k-set agreement can be implemented in $\mathcal{A}^n$.

Thus, the ability of an adversary to prevent an agreement of k values is independent from the number of processes, i.e. if it cannot prevent agreement for $k + 1$ processes, then it cannot prevent agreement for any $n > k$ processes. In this sense, the disagreement power is robust against the number of processes.

6.2   Simulating k Processes with k-anti-Ω

In the following, we will show how to use k-anti-Ω to simulate a set of k processes, such that at least one of the simulated processes takes infinitely many steps (this simulation, although seemingly simple, may be of independent interest). With the simulation, we can show that every colorless task that can be solved in $\mathcal{B}_{k-1}^k$ can be solved with any adversary $\mathcal{A}$ where k-anti-Ω is implementable. We use here the fact that it is possible to extract an array of k Ω-failure detectors $\Omega_1, \ldots, \Omega_k$ from k-anti-Ω with the property that at least one of them is a "real" Ω (i.e. it eventually outputs everywhere always the same correct process) [11]. Thus we can build k consensus objects [14], one for every Ω and we have the property, that at least one consensus terminates infinitely often. Note that for the consensuses associated with a bogus Ω (i.e. one that outputs infinitely often faulty processes or does not stabilize on one process), in [14], the agreement and validity properties of consensus are never violated.

We denote with consensus$_{j,r}$ the r-th invocation of the consensus object associated with Ω_j. Furthermore, we associate with every $1 \leq j \leq k$ a "virtual" process q_j and all processes use the consensus$_{j,r}$-objects to agree on the simulated steps of q_j.

Without loss of generality, we assume that the algorithm that implements the task in $\mathcal{B}_{k-1}^k$ uses only one single-writer multiple-reader (SWMR) register per process. Three types of steps need to be considered:

— a *write(v)*-step in which a process writes v to its associated SWMR register,
— a *read(p_j)*-step in which a process reads the SWMR register associated to process p_j
— and an internal step which does not involve any registers

These assumptions do not restrict the set of solvable tasks [15].

The simulation works as follows: at the beginning, all processes propose their initial values to all k consensuses in parallel. Since the algorithm is deterministic, the internal steps of q_j can just be executed. To simulate the write-steps of q_j, every simulator p_i writes the value to be written together with the number of the currently simulated step to its own register $R[i,j]$. To simulate a read step of q_j, a process scans all other processes registers associated with q_j and returns the "freshest" value (i.e. the value associated with the maximal step-number). Then, it proposes this value to the consensus corresponding to q_j and returns the result for the read-operation. In this way, it is ensured that all simulators will return exactly the same values for every q_j and all will simulate exactly the same steps. If some virtual process q_j has decided, the simulator just adopts that value and halts.

Theorem 8. *For every adversary $\mathcal{A}^n$ build upon a set of n processes, for every $k < n,$: if $\neg D(\mathcal{A}^n, \mathcal{B}_k^n)$, then $\mathcal{B}_{k-1}^k \succcurlyeq \mathcal{A}^n$.*

Proof. We assume an algorithm that solves a colorless task in $\mathcal{B}_{k-1}^k$ and use Theorem 3 to extract k-anti-Ω from $\mathcal{A}^n$ and thus create consensus$_{j,r}$-objects for every j and k. Since there is some j such that Ω_j contains eventually always a correct process, all correct processes simulate infinitely many steps of q_j.

Furthermore, since the execution of the simulated algorithm depends only on the values read (i.e. the algorithm is deterministic), for all j, all processes execute exactly the same steps for virtual process q_j. By the definition of colorless tasks, it is allowed that any process picks up any other processes input and output value and particularly, it is allowed that several processes have the same input or output values. It remains to show that every run of the virtual processes is indeed a run of the simulated algorithm in $\mathcal{B}_{k-1}^k$, i.e. it is indistinguishable from a real run. For this, we need to show that the sequence of the simulated operations on the registers is linearizable. But this follows from the fact that the sequence of the real registers is linearizable and every simulated operation corresponds to some operation of the real run.

Algorithm 3. Simulation of $\mathcal{B}_{k-1}^k$ for process p_i

---

1 **for** $1 \leq j \leq k$ **do** $R[i,j] := (\perp, 0)$;
2 $init_i :=$ initial value;

3 **foreach** $1 \leq j \leq k$ *in parallel* **do**
4 $\quad$ $init_j := \text{consensus}_{j,0}(init_i)$;
5 $\quad$ $r_j := 1$;
6 $\quad$ **while** q_j *has not decided* **do** start simulating steps of q_j with initial value $init_j$
7 $\quad\quad$ **if** *next step of q_j is a write(v)-step* **then**
8 $\quad\quad$ $\quad$ $R[i,j] := (v, r_j)$;
9 $\quad\quad$ **else if** *next step of q_j is a read(p_x)-step* **then**
10 $\quad\quad$ $\quad$ select v s.t. r is max. $\forall (v,r)$ where $\exists y : R[y,x] = (v,r)$;
11 $\quad\quad$ $\quad$ return $\text{consensus}_{j,r_j}(v)$ for the read;
12 $\quad\quad$ **else**
13 $\quad\quad$ $\quad$ take internal step of q_j;
14 $\quad\quad$ $r_j := r_j + 1$;
15 $\quad$ decide on q_j's decision value; halt;

Thus, every simulated run will eventually terminate at at least one virtual process and every simulator decides.

If we put all other theorems together, we get the following result:

Theorem 9. *For any two adversaries $\mathcal{A}$ and $\mathcal{B}$: $dis(\mathcal{A}) = dis(\mathcal{B})$ if and only if $\mathcal{A} \succcurlyeq \mathcal{B}$ and $\mathcal{B} \succcurlyeq \mathcal{A}$*

Proof. Since $\mathcal{A}$ has disagreement power k, it is impossible to implement k-set agreement in $\mathcal{A}$. Thus $D(\mathcal{A}, \mathcal{B}_k)$ (Theorem 3) and therefore $\mathcal{A} \succcurlyeq \mathcal{B}_k$ (Theorem 2). Furthermore, since $\mathcal{B}$ has also disagreement power k, it is possible to implement $(k+1)$-set agreement in $\mathcal{B}$. Therefore, since it is impossible to implement $(k+1)$-set agreement in $\mathcal{B}_{k+1}$ [8,9,10]: $\neg D(\mathcal{B}, \mathcal{B}_{k+1})$ (Theorem 2). Thus, with Theorem 8, $\mathcal{B}_k^{k+1} \succcurlyeq \mathcal{B}$. With Theorem 6 (BG), $\mathcal{B}_k \succcurlyeq \mathcal{B}$. If we put all these results together, $\mathcal{A} \succcurlyeq \mathcal{B}$. We obtain $\mathcal{B} \succcurlyeq \mathcal{A}$ in the same way.

7 Concluding Remarks

This paper presents a novel way to precisely characterize *adversaries*: the notion of *disagreement power*, i.e., the biggest integer k for which an adversary can prevent processes from agreeing on k values. This notion partitions the set of all adversaries into n distinct *equivalence* classes, one for every disagreement power. Any two adversaries with the same disagreement power solve exactly the same set of (colorless) tasks (Section 6). We believe that our result could be extended to colored tasks but this is subject to future work.

At the heart of our partitioning lies our simulation between adversaries (Section 4). Interestingly, the simulation works also if we assume the existence of stronger objects than registers or even non-deterministic object types. Furthermore, the simulation (as well as our implementation of k-set agreement with a given adversary in Section 5) remains correct even if the adversary is known only eventually, i.e., not necessarily from the beginning.

References

1. Herlihy, M., Shavit, N.: The topological structure of asynchronous computability. J. ACM 46(6), 858–923 (1999)
2. Borowsky, E., Gafni, E.: Generalized flp impossibility result for t-resilient asynchronous computations. In: STOC, pp. 91–100 (1993)
3. Saks, M.E., Zaharoglou, F.: Wait-free k-set agreement is impossible: The topology of public knowledge. SIAM J. Comput. 29(5), 1449–1483 (2000)
4. Fischer, M.J., Lynch, N.A., Paterson, M.S.: Impossibility of distributed consensus with one faulty process. J. ACM 32(2), 374–382 (1985)
5. Chaudhuri, S.: Agreement is harder than consensus: set consensus problems in totally asynchronous systems. In: PODC, pp. 311–324 (1990)
6. Borowsky, E., Gafni, E., Lynch, N.A., Rajsbaum, S.: The BG distributed simulation algorithm. Distributed Computing 14(3), 127–146 (2001)
7. Herlihy, M., Rajsbaum, S.: The decidability of distributed decision tasks (extended abstract). In: STOC, pp. 589–598 (1997)
8. Junqueira, F.P., Marzullo, K.: Designing algorithms for dependent process failures. In: Future Directions in Distributed Computing, pp. 24–28 (2003)
9. Fitzi, M., Maurer, U.M.: Efficient byzantine agreement secure against general adversaries. In: DISC, pp. 134–148 (1998)
10. Ashwinkumar, B.V., Patra, A., Choudhary, A., Srinathan, K., Rangan, C.P.: On tradeoff between network connectivity, phase complexity and communication complexity of reliable communication tolerating mixed adversary. In: PODC, pp. 115–124 (2008)
11. Zielinski, P.: Anti-Omega: the weakest failure detector for set agreement. In: PODC, pp. 55–64 (2008)
12. Chandra, T.D., Hadzilacos, V., Jayanti, P., Toueg, S.: Generalized irreducibility of consensus and the equivalence of t-resilient and wait-free implementations of consensus. SIAM J. Comput. 34(2), 333–357 (2004)
13. Chandra, T.D., Hadzilacos, V., Toueg, S.: The weakest failure detector for solving consensus. In: PODC, pp. 147–158 (1992)
14. Lo, W.K., Hadzilacos, V.: Using failure detectors to solve consensus in asynchronous shared-memory systems (extended abstract). In: WDAG, pp. 280–295 (1994)
15. Vitanyi, P.M.B., Awerbuch, B.: Atomic shared register access by asynchronous hardware. In: SFCS, Washington, DC, USA, pp. 233–243. IEEE Computer Society Press, Los Alamitos (1986)

New Bounds for the Controller Problem

(Extended Abstract)

Yuval Emek[1,*] and Amos Korman[2,**]

[1] Tel Aviv University, Tel Aviv, 69978 Israel
[2] CNRS and University Paris Diderot, France

Abstract. The (M, W)-*controller*, originally studied by Afek, Awer-buch, Plotkin, and Saks, is a basic distributed tool that provides an abstraction for managing the consumption of a global resource in a distributed dynamic network. The input to the controller arrives online in the form of *requests* presented at arbitrary nodes. A request presented at node u corresponds to the "desire" of some entity to consume one unit of the global resource at u and the controller should handle this request within finite time by either *granting* it with a *permit* or *denying* it. Initially, M permits (corresponding to M units of the global resource) are stored at a designated *root* node. Throughout the execution permits can be transported from place to place along the network's links so that they can be granted to requests presented at various nodes; when a permit is granted to some request, it is eliminated from the network. The fundamental rule of an (M, W)-controller is that a request should not be denied unless it is certain that at least $M - W$ permits are eventually granted. The most efficient (M, W)-controller known to date has message complexity $O(N \log^2 N \log \frac{M}{W+1})$, where N is the number of nodes that ever existed in the network (the dynamic network may undergo node insertions and deletions).

In this paper we establish two new lower bounds on the message complexity of the controller problem. We first prove a simple lower bound stating that any (M, W)-controller must send $\Omega(N \log \frac{M}{W+1})$ messages. Second, for the important case when W is proportional to M (this is the common case in most applications), we use a surprising reduction from the (centralized) *monotonic labeling problem* to show that any (M, W)-controller must send $\Omega(N \log N)$ messages. In fact, under a long lasting conjecture regarding the complexity of the monotonic labeling problem, this lower bound is improved to a tight $\Omega(N \log^2 N)$. The proof of this lower bound requires that $N = O(M)$ which turns out to be some-what inevitable due to a new construction of an $(M, M/2)$-controller with message complexity $O(N \log^2 M)$.

* Supported in part by the Israel Science Foundation, grant 664/05.
** Supported in part by the ANR project ALADDIN, by the INRIA project GANG, and by COST Action 295 DYNAMO.

I. Keidar (Ed.): DISC 2009, LNCS 5805, pp. 22–34, 2009.

1 Introduction

1.1 Background

A centralized online algorithm typically makes decisions based on past information, lacking any knowledge of what the future holds. In a distributed setting the input is spread over distant nodes in a network, hence introducing an additional kind of uncertainty, where nodes should make decisions based on local information without knowing what already happened in remote parts of the network. This paper addresses a basic problem which is affected by both kinds of uncertainties: controlling the consumption of a global resource. (For other problems that deal with both kinds of uncertainties, see, e.g., [5,20].)

Consider for example the case in which some finite amount of money (the global resource) resides somewhere in the network (in one node, or in several), and occasionally different nodes wish to withdraw a certain amount of money. A withdrawal request made by node u is either *granted*, in which case the requested amount of money is transferred to u (a portion of the global resource is consumed), or *rejected*. We are interested in a *distributed bank* protocol that handles these withdrawal requests while guaranteeing that a request is not rejected if there is still enough money available in the network.

Controllers (originally studied in [1] and later in [17]) provide an abstraction for such a distributed bank protocol and more generally, for global resource consumption management. Considered as one of the elementary and fundamental tools in distributed computing (cf. [2]), controllers serve as a key ingredient in the state of the art solutions for various problems such as majority commitment in a network where some of the nodes failed before the algorithm started [3,6,13,21], routing (and other informative labeling problems) in dynamic trees [15,16,18,19], and dynamic name assignment [1,16,17].

The (M, W)-Controller Problem. We consider a distributed network operating in an asynchronous environment. Initially, a set of *permits* resides at some designated node called the *root*. A subset of permits may be delivered from node u to any of its neighbors v by sending a single message from u to v (this message essentially encodes the number of permits that are being delivered). Therefore throughout the execution the permits are distributed among the nodes of the network and different nodes may hold different numbers of permits. The input to the controller arrives online in the form of *requests* presented at arbitrary nodes. When a request is presented at node u, the controller must respond within finite time in one of the following two manners: (1) it may *grant* the request by delivering a permit to u in which case the permit is eliminated from the network (corresponding to consuming one unit of the global resource at node u); or (2) it may *reject* the request.

In an (M, W)-*controller*, the number of permits that initially reside at the root is M, indicating that at most M requests can be granted. On the other hand, the (M, W)-controller may reject a request only if it is certain that at most W permits eventually remain in the network. In other words, if an (M, W)-controller rejects a request, then it is guaranteed that at least $M - W$ requests were already granted (or will be granted within finite time).

It is assumed in [1,17] that a spanning tree T rooted at some node r is maintained in the network and that the controller relies on the links of T for communication. The global resource whose consumption is managed by the controller may be of various types. However, since the concept of an (M, W)-controller finds many applications in dynamic networks, a special attention has been given to the case where a request presented at node u represents the desire to perform a topology change at the vicinity of u. Such a request is referred to as a *topological request*. Specifically, the topology changes considered in this context are: (i) inserting a new child of u as a leaf in T; (ii) inserting a new child of u as an internal node in T by subdividing a link that connects u to one of its children; and (iii) deleting a child v of u and turning the children of v into children of u (the root r is never deleted). In all three cases the actual topology change is assumed to occur once the topological request is granted a permit[1].

The number of nodes that ever existed in the network (including the deleted ones) is denoted by N. Note that N cannot exceed the initial network size by more than M since the insertion of every new node should be granted a permit by the controller (in fact, the combined number of node insertions and deletions is at most M).

The efficiency of an (M, W)-controller is measured by means of its *message complexity*, namely, the total number of messages sent during the execution. This is usually expressed as a function of M, W, and N. Consider for example the following naive implementation for an (M, W)-controller. Upon receiving a request at node u, the naive controller sends a message to the root r asking for a permit. The root returns a permit in response to each of the first $M - W$ arriving messages; afterwards, it broadcasts some "out of permits" message to all nodes, so that subsequent requests are rejected with no further consideration. Exchanging messages between u and r in an N-node network may require $\Omega(N)$ messages, hence the message complexity of this naive (M, W)-controller can be as large as $\Omega(N(M - W))$ even if the requests are spaced in time so that each request is granted before the next request is presented (which is typically far from being the case in an asynchronous network).

The Monotonic Labeling Problem. Vital to our techniques is the *monotonic labeling problem*. In this (centralized) problem n distinct elements from some dense totally ordered set S (e.g., the real numbers) are introduced, one at a time. Upon introduction, each element $x \in S$ should be assigned with a *label* $\lambda(x)$ taken from some discrete totally ordered set L of adequate ($|L| \geq n$), yet limited, cardinality (e.g., the integers $1, \ldots, |L|$). The order of the labels must agree with

---

[1] The protocols responsible for executing the actual topology change may be interesting by their own right, however, for simplicity, previous works ignored the details of these protocols by assuming that the requesting entity is taking care of performing the topology change. For further details regarding the dynamic model and its applications see [17].

the order of the elements, that is, for every two elements $x, y \in S$, if $x < y$, then $\lambda(x) < \lambda(y)$. Therefore from time to time some previously introduced elements must be *relabeled* to "make room" for new elements. The objective function of an algorithm for the monotonic labeling problem is to minimize the total number of labeling operations (including relabeling previously introduced elements). This is typically measured as a function of n and with respect to the cardinality of the label set L (clearly, the problem becomes easier as $|L|$ grows).

1.2   Related Work

The most relevant works to this paper, are the works of [1] and [17]. In [1], Afek et al. construct the first (M, W)-controller which admits message complexity $O(N \log^2 N \log \frac{M}{W+1})$. It is based on the following principle. The M permits, which initially reside at the root, are disseminated and moved by the controller in order to grant arriving requests. At any time, the remaining permits are stored at specific bins which are organized according to an underlying structure called the *bin hierarchy*. This bin hierarchy is employed in order to preserve some "sparseness" properties of the distribution of the remaining permits which are essential for the analysis. In terms of topology changes, the controller of Afek et al. only supports the insertion of leaves.

Korman and Kutten [17] introduce an (M, W)-controller with a similar message complexity[2] which supports all three types of topology changes (i.e., the insertion of leaves, the insertion of internal nodes, and the deletion of nodes). The improvement is achieved by relaxing the hierarchy of bins and constructing it on the fly, in a more local fashion.

Both the (M, W)-controller of [1] and that of [17] are implemented by first constructing an $(M, M/2)$-controller with message complexity $O(N \log^2 N)$, and then invoking it in $O(\log \frac{M}{W+1})$ iterations. Observe that the iterative argument does not hold if W is large so that $\log \frac{M}{W+1} = o(1)$. Indeed, it is implicitly assumed in [1,17] that $W \le M(1 - \Omega(1))$. The controller of [17] encodes each message using $O(\log N)$ bits, while the (more restricted) controller of [1] encodes each message using $O(\log \log N)$ bits.

On the negative side, it is easy to see that an $\Omega(N)$ term in the message complexity of any (M, W)-controller is inevitable. (In the case of an N-node path, for example, merely delivering a permit from the root to a request presented at the other end requires N messages.) However, no non-trivial lower bounds were previously known.

The monotonic labeling problem is essentially introduced in [14] and studied further in [9,23,22,11,4,12,7,10], mainly in the context of maintaining an ordered

---

[2] The message complexity of the protocol of [17] is actually sometimes slightly better than $O(N \log^2 N \log \frac{M}{W+1})$. The total number of messages sent by that protocol is $O(N_0 \log^2 N_0 \log \frac{M}{W+1}) + O(\sum_i \log^2 N_i \log \frac{M}{W+1})$, where N_0 is the initial number of nodes in the network and N_i denotes the number of nodes after the ith topology change occurs. The parameter N can be thought of as N_0 plus the number of node insertions. Note, that if $M < N_0$ then the message complexity of both the controller of [17] and the controller of [1] is $O(N \log^2 N \log \frac{M}{W+1})$.

data structure. With label sets of cardinality n, $n(1+\epsilon)$, and $n^{1+\epsilon}$, where ϵ is any positive constant, the known upper bounds for the number of labeling operations are $O(n \log^3 n)$ [4], $O(n \log^2 n)$ [14,23,7], and $O(n \log n)$ [9,22,11]. An $\Omega(n \log n)$ lower bound for the number of labeling operations with label sets of cardinality polynomial in n is established in [10], thus showing that the upper bound of [9,22,11] is tight. Based on a lower bound established in [12] for the special class of *smooth* algorithms, the authors of [12,10] conjecture that any monotonic labeling algorithm with $O(n)$ labels requires $\Omega(n \log^2 n)$ labeling operations, hence the upper bound of [14,23,7] is also tight.

1.3   Our Contribution

In this paper we establish new bounds on the message complexity of the controller problem. As a warm up, we first prove a simple lower bound stating that any (M, W)-controller must send $\Omega(N \log \frac{M}{W+1})$ messages. Although this lower bound is meaningful for small values of W, it is not very informative when W is proportional to M, which is the typical case in many applications of the controller problem.[3]

Subsequently, we turn our attention to the case where W is proportional to M and prove that for every constant $\epsilon > 0$, an $(M, M(1 - \epsilon))$-controller on a dynamically growing path of initial size M must admit message complexity $\Omega(M \log M) = \Omega(N \log N)$. This lower bound is obtained due to a surprising reduction from the (centralized) monotonic labeling problem to the (distributed) controller problem. Through this reduction, the $\Omega(n \log n)$ lower bound on the number of labeling operations that must be performed by any monotonic labeling algorithm with a label set of cardinality polynomial in n translates to the desired $\Omega(N \log N)$ lower bound on the message complexity of a controller. In fact, the reduction holds for monotonic labeling algorithms with label sets of cardinality $O(n)$, and therefore as it turns out, under the conjecture of [12,10], we obtain a tight $\Omega(N \log^2 N)$ lower bound on the message complexity of any $(M, M(1-\epsilon))$-controller.

Both our lower bounds hold even when the message size is unbounded. Furthermore, they do not rely on concurrency considerations, and therefore remain valid even if the system is synchronous and the requests are "spaced in time" so that the next request is presented only after the controller finished handling all previous ones.

As previously mentioned, the proof of the $\Omega(N \log N)$ lower bound (and also of the conjectured tight $\Omega(N \log^2 N)$ lower bound) relies on a network of initial size M which, in particular, implies that $N = \Theta(M)$. It turns out that this is no coincidence: such a lower bound cannot hold if M is much smaller than N. We prove it by constructing a novel $(M, M/2)$-controller with message complexity $O(N \log^2 M)$. Apart from demonstrating the inherent limitation of our

---

[3] In particular, the case $W = M/2$ is the one used to derive the state of the art solutions for the routing problem (and other labeling problems) on dynamic trees [15,16,18,19] as well as for the dynamic name assignment problem [1,17].

lower bound proof technique, the new controller is interesting as it can be generalized (c.f. Section 5 in [1]) to an (M, W)-controller with message complexity $O(N \log^2 M \log \frac{M}{W+1})$, thus exhibiting an asymptotic improvement to the state of the art in the case that M is sub-polynomial in N. Moreover, the structure of our new controller is completely different than the previously known controllers and bears an independent algorithmic interest.

2 Lower Bounds

2.1 The $\Omega(N \log \frac{M}{W+1})$ Lower Bound

We begin the technical part with a simple lower bound that provides a good demonstration of the definition of a controller. Let P be an N-node (static) path and let π be any (M, W)-controller that supports non-topological requests on P. We prove that there exists a scenario Γ that forces π to send $\Omega(N \log \frac{M}{W+1})$ messages. Note that if $\log \frac{M}{W+1} = O(1)$, then the required lower bound is dominated by the trivial $\Omega(N)$ lower bound. We may therefore assume that $\log \frac{M}{W+1} = \omega(1)$. Moreover, we assume for simplicity that both $M + 1$ and $W + 1$ are powers of 2. (The proof can be easily modified to handle an arbitrary choice of parameters.)

Let u and v be the two end nodes of P. The desired request sequence Γ admits the following two features. First, each request in Γ is presented after all actions of π in response to the previous request are completed. Second, each request is presented at either u or v. The sequence Γ is divided to $\lambda = \log \frac{M+1}{W+1} - 1$ subsequences denoted $\Gamma = \gamma_1 \cdot \gamma_2 \cdots \gamma_\lambda$. For every $1 \le i \le \lambda$, the ith subsequence γ_i consists of $(M + 1)/2^i$ requests which are presented (all of them) either at u or at v. The proof relies on designing the request subsequences γ_i so that in response to each one of them, π must send $\Omega(N)$ messages.

We construct the request subsequences γ_i, by induction on i. Let γ_0 denote the empty subsequence. Given $1 \le i \le \lambda$, assume that the prefix $\Gamma_{i-1} = \gamma_0 \cdot \gamma_1 \cdots \gamma_{i-1}$ is already determined and construct the subsequence γ_i as follows.

Let $\gamma(u)$ (respectively, $\gamma(v)$) denote a sequence of $(M + 1)/2^i$ requests presented at u (resp., at v). Consider the subsequences

$$\Gamma(u) = \Gamma_{i-1} \cdot \gamma(u) \quad \text{and} \quad \Gamma(v) = \Gamma_{i-1} \cdot \gamma(v) .$$

Observe, that both $\Gamma(u)$ and $\Gamma(v)$ contain

$$(M + 1)(1 - 1/2^{i-1}) + (M + 1)/2^i = (M + 1)(1 - 1/2^i) < M - W$$

requests (the last inequality follows from the fact that $i < \log \frac{M+1}{W+1}$). Therefore π cannot deny any request in response to either $\Gamma(u)$ or $\Gamma(v)$.

Now, consider the request sequence

$$\Gamma(u, v) = \Gamma_{i-1} \cdot \gamma(u) \cdot \gamma(v) .$$

As $\Gamma(u, v)$ contains

$$(M + 1)(1 - 1/2^{i-1}) + 2(M + 1)/2^i = M + 1$$

requests, at least one of them should be denied by π. This means that π somehow "distinguishes" $\Gamma(u,v)$ from both $\Gamma(u)$ and $\Gamma(v)$. More formally, after handling the prefix Γ_{i-1}, either $\Omega(N)$ messages are sent in response to $\gamma(u)$ or $\Omega(N)$ messages are sent in response to $\gamma(v)$ (or both). If the former is true, then we fix $\gamma_i = \gamma(u)$; otherwise, we fix $\gamma_i = \gamma(v)$.

To summarize, our construction of the request sequence $\Gamma = \gamma_1 \cdots \gamma_\lambda$ guarantees that π sends $\Omega(N)$ messages for each $1 \leq i \leq \lambda$. This sums up to $\Omega(N \log \frac{M}{W+1})$ in total.

2.2 The $\Omega(N \log N)$ Lower Bound

We now turn to prove the main result of the paper, namely, that for every constant $\epsilon > 0$, an $(M, M(1-\epsilon))$-controller on a dynamically growing path of initial size M must send $\Omega(M \log M) = \Omega(N \log N)$ messages (recall that N is proportional to M when the initial size of the network is M).

Our method is based on reducing the monotonic labeling problem to the controller problem. Specifically, we show that an $(n, n(1-\epsilon))$-controller that supports node insertion requests on a path of initial size n with message complexity $f(n)$ implies an algorithm for the monotonic labeling of n elements with label set of cardinality $2n$ that performs $O(f(n))$ labeling operations. It is known that such a monotonic labeling algorithm does not exist unless $f(n) = \Omega(n \log n)$ [10] and it is conjectured that $f(n)$ must be $\Omega(n \log^2 n)$ [12,10]. This implies the following theorem.

Theorem 1. *The existence of an $(n, n(1-\epsilon))$-controller with message complexity $f(n)$ for a path of initial size n implies $f(n) = \Omega(n \log n)$ ($f(n) = \Omega(n \log^2 n)$ under the conjecture of [12,10]).*

To prove Theorem 1, consider some instance of the monotonic labeling problem on n elements with label set $\{1, \ldots, 2n\}$. Let $x_1, \ldots, x_n$ denote the n elements in order of introduction. We label the first $\lceil 1/\epsilon \rceil$ elements $(x_1, \ldots, x_{\lceil 1/\epsilon \rceil})$ arbitrarily (since ϵ is constant, this incurs $O(1)$ labeling operations) and deal with the remaining elements in iterations. Let n_i denote the number of elements which were already introduced (and labeled) at the beginning of iteration i ($n_1 = \lceil 1/\epsilon \rceil$), so that the elements introduced during this iteration are $x_{n_i+1}, \ldots, x_{n_{i+1}}$. We label these $n_{i+1} - n_i$ elements in accordance with the execution of an $(n_i, n_i(1-\epsilon))$-controller invoked on a path P. This is done as follows.

At all times, the size of P equals the number of elements that were already introduced. In particular, at the beginning of iteration i we have $|P| = n_i$. Consider the path $P = (u_1, \ldots, u_k)$ after the elements $x_1, \ldots, x_k$ were introduced for some $n_i \leq k \leq n_{i+1}$. The nodes of P are mapped from left to right to the elements $x_1, \ldots, x_k$ according to their rank, that is, u_j is mapped to the jth smallest element in $x_1, \ldots, x_k$. Let $x(u_j)$ denote the element to which node u_j is mapped. Note that $x(u_j) < x(u_{j+1})$ for every $1 \leq j < k$.

The labels $\lambda(\cdot)$ assigned to $x_1, \ldots, x_k$ are determined by the permit distribution along the path $P = (u_1, \ldots, u_k)$. For every $1 \leq j \leq k$, the element $x(u_j)$

is assigned with the label $\lambda(x(u_j)) = j + p_j$, where p_j denotes the number of permits stored in the subpath $(u_1, \ldots, u_{j-1})$. Note that this is a valid labeling scheme since it guarantees that

(i) $\lambda(x(u_j)) < \lambda(x(u_{j+1}))$; and
(ii) all labels are taken from the set $\{1, \ldots, 2n_i\} \subseteq \{1, \ldots, 2n\}$.

(To verify that (ii) holds, observe that the sum of $|P|$ and the number of permits stored in P is $2n_i$ throughout the iteration.)

Upon introduction of the next element x_{k+1}, we present a node insertion request to P in a position that corresponds to the rank of x_{k+1} in $x_1, \ldots, x_{k+1}$. If this request is granted, then a new node is inserted into P and x_{k+1} is labeled in accordance with the aforementioned scheme (which may cause some relabeling of previously introduced elements). Otherwise (the request is rejected), iteration i is halted, $n_{i+1} \leftarrow k$, and iteration $i+1$ starts by invoking an $(n_{i+1}, n_{i+1}(1-\epsilon))$-controller on a path of initial size n_{i+1}, where the first request corresponds to the insertion of a node mapped to x_{k+1} (this was rejected in iteration i). Note that the invocation of the new $(n_{i+1}, n_{i+1}(1 - \epsilon))$-controller may change the labels of elements $x_1, \ldots, x_{n_{i+1}}$ due to changes in the permit distribution along the path P.

Let l be the index of the last iteration (in which element x_n was labeled). For every $1 \leq i < l$, we know that the $(n_i, n_i(1 - \epsilon))$-controller that operates in iteration i does not reject any request before at least ϵn_i requests were granted (and that many new nodes were inserted into P), thus $n_{i+1} \geq n_i(1 + \epsilon)$. Since $n_1 = \lceil 1/\epsilon \rceil$ and $n_l < n$, we conclude that $l = O(\log n)$.

This is a valid monotonic labeling algorithm: each element is labeled upon introduction and the order of the labels always agrees with the order of the elements. It remains to bound the number of labeling operations performed by our monotonic labeling algorithm. In attempt to do so, we distinguish between two types of labeling operations: (1) those that occur during the execution of one of the controllers; and (2) those that occur when one iteration halts and a new iteration begins (recall that when a new iteration begins the labels of the elements that were already introduced may change). At most n_i labeling operations occur when iteration i begins, hence the total number of labeling operations of type (2) is bounded from above by $\sum_{i=1}^{l} n_i = O(n)$.

We now turn to analyze the number of labeling operations of type (1). Suppose that for every $1 \leq i \leq l$, we have an $(n_i, n_i(1 - \epsilon))$-controller that supports node insertion requests on a path of initial size n_i with average message complexity at most $f(n_i)$, where $f : \mathbb{Z}_{>0} \to \mathbb{Z}_{>0}$ is a non-decreasing function. This means that at most $2n_i f(n_i)$ messages were sent in iteration i, which sums up to at most $\sum_{i=1}^{l} 2n_i f(n_i) = O(nf(n))$ messages all together.

The key argument in our analysis is that each type (1) labeling operation accounts for at least one message sent by the controllers, and hence the total number of type (1) labeling operations is $O(nf(n))$. To justify this argument, consider the path $P = (u_1, \ldots, u_k)$ at some stage of iteration i and observe that the element $x(u_j)$ is assigned with a new label only when the sum S of the number of nodes to the left of u_j and the number of permits stored in these nodes changes. Note that the number of nodes to the left of u_j may increase due to the insertion of a new node in the subpath (u_1, u_{j-1}), but this comes together with the elimination of one permit stored at one of the nodes $\{u_1, \ldots, u_{j-1}\}$. Therefore the sum S changes only when some permits were shifted from $\{u_1, \ldots, u_{j-1}\}$ to $\{u_j, \ldots, u_k\}$ or vice versa which requires the exchange of a message along the path link (u_{j-1}, u_j). It follows that our monotonic labeling algorithm performs $O(nf(n))$ labeling operations in total, thus establishing Theorem 1.

3   An (M, W)-Controller

In this section we consider a dynamic rooted tree T of initial size N_0 and construct an $(M, M/2)$-controller for T with message complexity $O(N_0 \log^2 M)$ assuming that $M < N_0$. This is done in two stages. First, we reduce the $(M, M/2)$-controller problem from arbitrary trees to simple paths by a novel technique[4] presented in Section 3.1. Therefore the remaining challenge is to construct an $(M, M/2)$-controller with message complexity $O(N_0 \log^2 M)$ for simple paths of initial size $N_0 > M$; this is done in Section 3.2.

3.1   A Reduction from Trees to Paths

In this section we design a transformation from the $(M, M/2)$-controller problem on a tree T to the $(M, M/2)$-controller problem on a path P. A scenario of requests on T is translated under this transformation to an induced scenario of requests on P. An $(M, M/2)$-controller protocol on P handles this (path) scenario and its actions are simulated by the nodes of T. A natural attempt to do so is to map every node in T to a unique node in P (a bijection) so that each tree node simulates the actions taken by its corresponding path node. The efficiency of this method depends on the stretch induced by the mapping: delivering a message from node u to an adjacent node v in P is simulated by delivering a message from u' to v' in T, where u' and v' are the preimages of u and v, respectively. Therefore if u' and v' are far apart in T, then many messages should be sent in T in order to simulate a single message in P and the reduction fails.

Although it is always possible to design a (bijective) mapping that guarantees a constant stretch for every pair of adjacent path nodes, the methods known to us that do so are not very simple to describe (we are unaware of previous works that studied this issue). More importantly, we do not know how to adapt these methods to the dynamic distributed setting. Instead of relying on such a bijection, we shall map every node in T to *several* nodes in P. For simplicity of presentation, we shall first describe the desired transformation assuming that all requests are non-topological. In this case, the topology of the tree remains fixed throughout the execution and in particular, the number of nodes N remains unchanged.

---

[4] A similar technique was used in [16], where a preliminary version of the current paper is credited.

At any given time during the execution, the N-vertex rooted tree T is associated with a $2N$-node path P rooted at its leftmost node. This is done by associating each tree node with a pair of path nodes, as follows. Recall that a DFS tour (starting at the root) associates every node u in T with two *timestamps* $1 \leq d[u] < f[u] \leq 2N$, where $d[u]$ records the time step when u was first visited and $f[u]$ records the time step when the examination of u was over (see [8]). (In particular, the root r satisfies $d[r] = 1$ and $f[r] = 2N$ and if u is a leaf, then $d[u] = f[u] - 1$.) Enumerate the $2N$ nodes in P from left to right by the integers $1, \ldots, 2N$ and let each vertex u in T be associated with the nodes $d[u]$ and $f[u]$. Note that each path node x is associated with a single tree node $\mathrm{pre}(x)$, referred to as the *preimage* of x.

A scenario of requests in T is translated to a scenario of requests in P as follows: a request presented at some tree node v is translated to a request presented at the path node $d[v]$. This defines an induced request scenario on P for every request scenario on T. An $(M, M/2)$-controller for P is invoked on this induced request scenario. The actions taken by the path nodes are simulated by their preimages in T. Specifically, if some path node x wishes to send a message to one of its neighbors y in P, then this message is sent from $\mathrm{pre}(x)$ to $\mathrm{pre}(y)$ in T. The permits of the tree controller are subjected to the path controller so that if x delivers some subset of permits to y, then $\mathrm{pre}(x)$ delivers that subset of permits to $\mathrm{pre}(y)$. (Initially, the M permits are stored in the root of the path whose preimage is the root of the tree.) Recall that a request was presented at the path node $d[v]$ under the induced scenario only when a request was presented at the tree node v under the original scenario. If this request is granted a permit (respectively, rejected) by the path controller, then the corresponding request is granted a permit (resp., rejected) by the tree controller. The above simulation clearly implements an $(M, M/2)$-controller on T.

We argue that the distance in T between the preimages $\mathrm{pre}(x)$ and $\mathrm{pre}(y)$ of any two path neighbors x and y is at most 2. Indeed, as demonstrated by Table 1, $\mathrm{pre}(x)$ and $\mathrm{pre}(y)$ are either siblings in T or a child and a parent. Note that in order to simulate the actions of the path controller a tree node u does not have to know the exact DFS timestamps of its associated path nodes

Table 1. The DFS timestamps of the left and right neighbors of some path node

path node	left neighbor	right neighbor
$d[u]$	$f[v]$, where v is the left sibling of u, if u has a left sibling in T; $d[v]$, where v is the parent of u, if u does not have a left sibling in T;	$d[v]$, where v is the leftmost child of u, if u has a child in T; $f[u]$ if u does not have a child in T;
$f[u]$	$f[v]$, where v is the rightmost child of u, if u has a child in T; $d[u]$ if u does not have a child in T;	$d[v]$, where v is the right sibling of u, if u has a right sibling in T; $f[v]$, where v is the parent of u, if u does not have a right sibling in T;

$d[u]$ and $f[u]$, but rather the structure of its local neighborhood in T, that is, whether it admits any children, whether it admits a left sibling, and whether it admits a right sibling. The bound on the message complexity of the resulting $(M, M/2)$-controller on the tree T follows.

The case of topological requests follows from a similar approach, but requires some additional technicalities which are omitted from this extended abstract. This completes the proof of the following theorem.

Theorem 2. *An $(M, M/2)$-controller on a tree can be implemented by an $(M, M/2)$-controller on a path with asymptotically the same message complexity.*

3.2   An $(M, M/2)$-Controller for a Path — Overview

In this section we design an $(M, M/2)$-controller that operates on a path P of initial size N_0. We follow the convention that P is rooted at its leftmost node so that the sole child of a path node is its right neighbor. The controller supports topological requests which means that the path may undergo node insertions and deletions, but since we assume that $M < N_0$, the size of P is $O(N_0)$ at all times. Our controller operates in an asynchronous environment under the *FIFO channel* assumption, that is, if node u sends message m_1 at time t_1 and message m_2 at time $t_2 > t_1$, both to the same neighbor v, then m_1 is received at v before m_2 (this assumption can be easily lifted by using standard acknowledging techniques). Due to lack of space, we provide here an overview of the construction and omit the full detail from this extended abstract.

A central component of our controller is an implicit complete binary tree T which is simulated by the nodes of P (see also [7]). The height h of T is proportional to $\log M$. Each vertex x in T is associated with a subpath P_x of P so that every level of T induces a pairwise disjoint partition of P. Moreover, if x is a child of y in T, then P_x is a subpath of P_y. The behavior of each vertex x in T is simulated by some node in P_x.

In a preprocess stage the controller spreads the M permits evenly among the leaves of T. Subsequently, a path node u handles a newcoming request by sending a message to the leaf ℓ such that $u \in P_\ell$ and asking for a permit. While waiting for the permit, u is *locked* which means that it does not handle subsequent requests. A request presented at the locked node u is stored in a queue denoted by $\mathcal{Q}(u)$; when u gets *unlocked*, the request stored at the head of $\mathcal{Q}(u)$ is dequeued and its handling procedure starts. The protocol guarantees that ℓ responds to u's message (by either granting the request with a permit or denying it) within finite time, thus a request cannot remain in the queue indefinitely.

A tree vertex x (that may be a leaf) learns that some nodes in P_x are waiting for permits via an invocation of Procedure Update at x. Procedure Update first makes sure that all nodes in P_x are locked. Afterwards it counts how many permits remained in the leaves of the subtree T_x and how many requests in P_x wait for a permit. If the difference is larger than some threshold ρ_i that depends on the level $0 \le i \le h$ of x in T, then Procedure Update grants permits to the awaiting requests, spreads (evenly) the remaining permits among the leaves of $\mathcal{T}_x$, and unlocks all nodes in P_x. Otherwise, x invokes Procedure Update at its parent in $\mathcal{T}$. The threshold ρ_i is designed so that if the root z finds out that the difference of the number of permits in the leaves of $\mathcal{T}_z = \mathcal{T}$ to the number of permit-awaiting requests in $P_z = P$ is smaller than its threshold ρ_h, then more than $M/2$ permits must have been granted and all subsequent requests are rejected.

It is crucial for the analysis of the message complexity that every leaf in $\mathcal{T}$ is assigned with $O(N_0/2^h)$ path nodes. For this purpose, Procedure Update is slightly more complicated than what we described in the previous paragraph. Since some of the requests that currently wait for permits at P_x may be topological, granting them may change the size of P_ℓ for some leaves ℓ in $\mathcal{T}_x$, hence the procedure has to ensure that the size of P_x does not become too large after the current requests will be granted. Indeed, if $|P_x|$ is soon to exceed some threshold σ_i that (just like the threshold ρ_i) depends on the level i of x in $\mathcal{T}$, then the execution of Procedure Update at x is halted and the procedure is reinvoked at the parent of x in $\mathcal{T}$. Otherwise, the nodes in P_x are reassigned to leaves in $\mathcal{T}_x$ in a manner that keeps $|P_\ell|$ sufficiently small for all leaves ℓ in $\mathcal{T}_x$. The threshold σ_i is designed so that $\sigma_h = 3N_0/2$, thus if $|P|$ exceeds the threshold σ_h, then at least $N_0/2 > M/2$ node insertion requests must have been granted.

References

1. Afek, Y., Awerbuch, B., Plotkin, S.A., Saks, M.: Local management of a global resource in a communication network. J. ACM 43, 1–19 (1996)
2. Afek, Y., Ricklin, M.: Sparser: a paradigm for running distributed algorithms. J. Algorithms 14(2), 316–328 (1993)
3. Afek, Y., Saks, M.E.: Detecting global termination conditions in the face of uncertainty. In: Proc. 7th ACM Symp. on Principles of Distributed Computing (PODC), pp. 109–124 (1987)
4. Andersson, A., Lai, T.W.: Fast updating of well-balanced trees. In: Proc. 2nd Scandinavian Workshop on Algorithm Theory (SWAT), pp. 111–121 (1990)
5. Awerbuch, B., Kutten, S., Peleg, D.: Competitive distributed job scheduling (Extended Abstract). In: Proc. 24th ACM Symp. on Theory of Computing (STOC), pp. 571–580 (1992)
6. Bar-Yehuda, R., Kutten, S.: Fault tolerant distributed majority commitment. J. Algorithms 9(4), 568–582 (1988)
7. Bender, M.A., Cole, R., Demaine, E.D., Farach-Colton, M., Zito, J.: Two simplified algorithms for maintaining order in a list. In: Proc. 10th Ann. European Symp. on Algorithms (ESA), pp. 152–164 (2002)
8. Cormen, T.H., Leiserson, C.E., Rivest, R.L., Stein, C.: Introduction to Algorithms, 2nd edn. The MIT Press, Cambridge (2001)
9. Dietz, P.F.: Maintaining Order in a Linked List. In: Proc. 14th ACM Symp. on Theory of Computing (STOC), pp. 122–127 (1982)
10. Dietz, P.F., Seiferas, J.I., Zhang, J.: A tight lower bound for online monotonic list labeling. SIAM J. Discrete Math. 18(3), 626–637 (2004)
11. Dietz, P.F., Sleator, D.D.: Two algorithms for maintaining order in a list. In: Proc. 19th ACM Symp. on Theory of Computing (STOC), pp. 365–372 (1987)

12. Dietz, P.F., Zhang, J.: Lower bounds for monotonic list labeling. In: Proc. 2nd Scandinavian Workshop on Algorithm Theory (SWAT), pp. 173–180 (1990)
13. Fischer, M.J., Lynch, N.A., Paterson, M.: Impossibility of distributed consensus with one faulty process. J. ACM 32(2), 374–382 (1985)
14. Itai, A., Konheim, A., Rodeh, M.: A sparse table implementation of priority queues. In: Proc. 8th Colloq. on Automata, Languages and Programming (ICALP), pp. 417–431 (1981)
15. Korman, A.: General compact labeling schemes for dynamic trees. J. Distributed Computing 20(3), 179–193 (2007)
16. Korman, A.: Improved compact routing schemes for dynamic trees. In: Proc. 27th ACM Symp. on Principles of Distributed Computing (PODC), pp. 185–194 (2008)
17. Korman, A., Kutten, S.: Controller and estimator for dynamic networks. In: Proc. 26th ACM SIGACT-SIGOPS Symp. on Principles of Distributed Computing (PODC), pp. 175–184 (2007)
18. Korman, A., Peleg, D., Rodeh, Y.: Labeling schemes for dynamic tree networks. Theory Comput. Syst. 37(1), 49–75 (2004)
19. Korman, A., Peleg, D.: Labeling schemes for weighted dynamic trees. J. Information and Computation 205(12), 1721–1740 (2007)
20. Lund, C., Reingold, N., Westbrook, J., Yan, D.C.K.: Competitive on-line algorithms for distributed data management. SIAM J. Comput. 28(3), 1086–1111 (1999)
21. Kutten, S.: Optimal fault-tolerant distributed construction of a spanning forest. Inf. Process. Lett. 27(6), 299–307 (1988)
22. Tsakalidis, A.K.: Maintaining order in a generalized linked list. Acta Inform. 21, 101–112 (1984)
23. Willard, D.: Maintaining dense sequential files in a dynamic environment. In: Proc. 14th ACM Symp. on Theory of Computing (STOC), pp. 114–121 (1982)

On Set Consensus Numbers

Eli Gafni[1] and Petr Kuznetsov[2]

[1] Computer Science Department, University of California, Los Angeles, USA
eli@ucla.edu
[2] TU Berlin/Deutsche Telekom Laboratories, Berlin, Germany
pkuznets@acm.org

Abstract. We propose a complete characterization of a large class of distributed tasks, with respect to a weakened solvability notion called *weak termination*. A task is weak-termination solvable if there is an algorithm by which at least one process outputs.

The proposed categorization of tasks is based on the weakest failure detectors needed to solve them. We show that every task T in the considered class is equivalent (in the failure detector sense) to some form of set agreement, and thus its solvability with weak termination is completely characterized by its *set consensus number*: the maximal integer k such that T can be (weak-termination) solved using read-write registers and k-set agreement objects.

The characterization goes through showing that $\neg\Omega_k$, recently shown to be the weakest failure detector for the task of k-set agreement, is necessary to solve *any* task that is k-resilient impossible.

1 Introduction

One of the central challenges in distributed computing is characterizing the conditions under which a given problem is solvable. In this paper we consider a large class of problems, called *tasks*, in a distributed system of n asynchronous processes, subject to the *crash* failures, communicating via reading and writing in the shared memory. Informally, the correctness of a task solution depends only on the inputs the processes receive in the beginning of the computation and the outputs they produce at the end of it. A conventional liveness property of a task solution is *wait-freedom*: every *correct* process, i.e., a process that never crashes, must eventually *decide* (return a value).

An example of a distributed task is k-set agreement [1], in which each process starts with an input in $\{0, \ldots, k\}$ and the set of outputs must be a subset of inputs of size at most k. There is no wait-free solution for $k + 1$-process k-set agreement [2,3,4]. More generally, for all $n \geq k + 1$, there is no algorithm that solves n-process k-set agreement (or simply (n, k)-set agreement) tolerating k faulty processes [4,5]. In other words, the lack of synchrony and the presence of failures make k-resilient (n, k)-set agreement impossible. To circumvent the impossibility, assuming that we still want to tolerate failures, we need to introduce some synchrony into the system. But how much synchrony is enough?

I. Keidar (Ed.): DISC 2009, LNCS 5805, pp. 35–47, 2009.
© Springer-Verlag Berlin Heidelberg 2009

Synchrony assumptions can be described using *failure detectors* [6,7], distributed oracles that provide processes with some (possibly inaccurate and incomplete) hints about failures. The exact amount of synchrony needed to circumvent an asynchronous impossibility is captured through the notion of the *weakest failure detector* [7]: $\mathcal{D}$ is the weakest failure detector for solving a problem $\mathcal{M}$ if $\mathcal{D}$ is both (1) *sufficient* to solve $\mathcal{M}$, i.e., there exists an algorithm that solves $\mathcal{M}$ using $\mathcal{D}$, and (2) *necessary* to solve $\mathcal{M}$, i.e., any failure detector that is sufficient to solve $\mathcal{M}$ provides at least as much information about failures as $\mathcal{D}$ does. Every distributed computing problem has a weakest failure detector [8].

It has been recently shown [9,10] that, for all $0 < k < n$, the weakest failure detector for solving k-set agreement is $\neg\Omega_k$, regardless of the assumptions on when and where failures might occur. $\neg\Omega_k$ outputs, when queried, a set of $n - k$ processes so that some correct process is output only finitely many times.

In this paper, we show that, for all $0 < k < n$, $\neg\Omega_k$ is necessary to solve *any* n-process task that cannot be *weak-termination* solved k-resiliently, i.e., tolerating k faulty processes. Weak termination means here that to solve a task we only require *one* process to output. We also show that $\neg\Omega_k$ is sufficient to solve any task that can be weak-termination solved *actively* $k - 1$-resiliently, i.e., tolerating k failures among the processes that *participate* (invoke the task).

Thus, our results provide a complete categorization of tasks which do not distinguish between k-resilience and active k resilience, i.e., tasks for which k-resilient solvability implies *active* k-resilient solvability), for all k. We call these tasks *participation-oblivious*, and observe that many popular tasks, including set agreement, are participation-oblivious.

We derive therefore that the weak-termination solvability of a participation-oblivious task $\mathcal{T}$ is completely characterized by its *set consensus number*: the integer k such that $\mathcal{T}$ and k-set agreement are, in the failure detector sense, equivalent. Formally, set consensus number of $\mathcal{T}$ is the lowest k such that $\mathcal{T}$ cannot be (weak-termination) solved k-resiliently. As a result, we derive a complete characterization of participation-oblivious tasks into n equivalence classes (set consensus hierarchy), each class $k = 1, \ldots, n$ consists of tasks that are equivalent to k-set agreement. In particular, class 1 in the hierarchy consists of "universal" tasks (e.g., consensus) that can be used to solve any task, and class n consists of "trivial" tasks that can be solved wait-free.

The sufficiency part of our result builds upon the recently established equivalence of k-set agreement, k-*concurrency*, and active k-resilience [11]: the set of tasks that are solvable k-concurrently (when at most k processes are active at a time) coincides with both the set of tasks that can be wait-free solved using k-set agreement objects and read-write registers and the set of tasks that are solvable actively $(k - 1)$-resiliently. This allows us to conclude that any task that can be solved actively k-resiliently can also be solved using $\neg\Omega_k$.

The rest of the paper is organized as follows. Section 2 describes our system model. Sections 3 proves that $\neg\Omega_k$ is necessary to solve any k-resilient unsolvable task, and presents the implications of this result: a characterization criterion for participation-oblivious distributed tasks. Section 4 overviews the related work and Section 5 concludes the paper by discussing limitations of our results and interesting open questions.

2   Model

We consider a system of n processes $\Pi = \{p_1, \ldots, p_n\}$. Processes communicate reading and writing in the shared memory and can query the failure detector. Processes are subject to *crash* failures. More details on the model can be found in [7,9].

2.1   Failure Patterns and Failure Detectors

A *failure pattern* F is a function from the time range $\mathbb{T} = \{0\} \cup \mathbb{N}$ to 2^{Π}, where $F(t)$ denotes the set of processes that have crashed by time t. Once a process crashes, it does not recover, i.e., $\forall t : F(t) \subseteq F(t+1)$. We define $faulty(F) = \cup_{t \in \mathbb{T}} F(t)$, the set of faulty processes in F. Respectively, $correct(F) = \Pi - faulty(F)$. A process $p \in F(t)$ is said to be *crashed* at time t. An *environment* is a set of failure patterns. By default, we assume that at least one process is correct in every failure pattern.

A *failure detector history H with range $\mathcal{R}$* is a function from $\Pi \times \mathbb{T}$ to $\mathcal{R}$. $H(p_i, t)$ is interpreted as the value output by the failure detector module of process p_i at time t. A *failure detector $\mathcal{D}$ with range $\mathcal{R_D}$* is a function that maps each failure pattern to a (non-empty) set of failure detector histories with range $\mathcal{R_D}$. $\mathcal{D}(F)$ denotes the set of possible failure detector histories permitted by $\mathcal{D}$ for failure pattern F. We do not restrict possible ranges of failure detectors.

The failure detector $\neg\Omega_k$ [12] outputs, at each process and each time, a set of $n - k$ processes. $\neg\Omega_k$ guarantees that there is a time after which some correct is never output. By definition, $\neg\Omega_{n-1}$ is equivalent to anti-Ω [13]. Also, $\neg\Omega_1$ is equivalent to Ω [7].

2.2   Algorithms

We define an *algorithm $\mathcal{A}$ using a failure detector $\mathcal{D}$* as a collection of deterministic automata, one automaton $\mathcal{A}_i$ for each process p_i. In each step of $\mathcal{A}$, process p_i can first invoke an atomic operation on a shared object (in our case - register) receive a response or query its module of $\mathcal{D}$ and receive a value, and then perform a state transition according to its automaton and the received value.

If the state transitions of the algorithm automata do not depend on the failure detector values, we say that the algorithm $\mathcal{A}$ is *asynchronous*.

2.3   Runs

A *state* of $\mathcal{A}$ defines the state of each process and each object in the system. An *initial state I* of $\mathcal{A}$ specifies an initial state for every automaton $\mathcal{A}_i$ and every shared object.

A *run of algorithm* $\mathcal{A}$ *using a failure detector* $\mathcal{D}$ in an environment $\mathcal{E}$ is a tuple $R = \langle F, H, I, S, T \rangle$ where $F \in \mathcal{E}$ is a failure pattern, $H \in \mathcal{D}(F)$ is a failure detector history, I is an initial state of $\mathcal{A}$, S is an infinite *schedule*, i.e., the sequence of process ids, and T is a non-decreasing sequence of values in $\mathbb{T}$ such that $\forall \ell$: $S[k] \notin F(T[k])$.

Let $inf(R)$ denote the set of processes that appear infinitely often in its schedule S. We say that a run $R = \langle F, H, I, S, T \rangle$ is *fair* if $correct(F) = inf(R)$, and *k-resilient* if $|inf(R)| \geq n - k$. A *partial run* of an algorithm $\mathcal{A}$ is a finite prefix of a run of $\mathcal{A}$. Note that for an asynchronous algorithms, runs that share I and S are indistinguishable.

2.4 Distributed Tasks

A *task* is defined through a set $\mathcal{I}$ of input n-vectors (one output value for each process), a set $\mathcal{O}$ of output n-vectors (one input value for each process) and a total relation Δ that associates each input vector with a set of possible output vectors. In the *n-process k-set agreement* task (we simply write (n, k)-set agreement), each process takes a value in $\{0, \ldots, k\}$ as an input, and the set of non-$\perp$ output values is a subset of the input values of size at most k.

In this paper, we only consider tasks that have finite sets of inputs $\mathcal{I}$.

2.5 Weak Termination

In this paper, we focus on the *weak termination* condition: a run is considered terminated based on a finite prefix of it.

More precisely, we say that an algorithm $\mathcal{A}$ *solves a task* $\mathcal{T} = (\mathcal{I}, \mathcal{O}, \Delta)$ (with weak termination) in an environment $\mathcal{E}$ using a failure detector $\mathcal{D}$, if in every *fair* run $\langle F, H, I, S, T \rangle$ of $\mathcal{A}$, where I is the input vector in $\mathcal{I}$ and $F \in \mathcal{E}$, *at least one* process eventually *decides*, i.e., reaches a special state with an irrevocable non-$\perp$ output value, and the vector O gathering the values output in that run satisfies $(I, O) \in \Delta$. Weak termination condition is sufficient to solve (n, k)-set agreement: any process that reaches an output writes the output value in the shared memory and every process that finds the value adopts it as the output. A state of an algorithm in which some process decides is called *deciding*.

2.6 Resilience and Active Resilience

A task is can be solved *k-resiliently* if there is an *asynchronous* (i.e., without using a failure detector) algorithm that solves the task in an environment in which any k processes may fail. A task can be solved *actively k-resiliently* if an asynchronous algorithm solves the task in every run in which not more than k processes that took at least one step fail.

Obviously, if a task is solvable actively k-resiliently, then its is also solvable k-resiliently. It is shown in [4] that k-set agreement is impossible to solve k-resiliently, and thus also actively k-resiliently.

We say that a task $\mathcal{T}$ is *participation-oblivious* if for all $0 < k < n$, k-resilient solvability of $\mathcal{T}$ implies active k-resilient solvability of $\mathcal{T}$.

2.7 Comparing Failure Detectors

We say that an algorithm $\mathcal{A}$ using $\mathcal{D}'$ *extracts the output of $\mathcal{D}$ in an environment $\mathcal{E}$*, if $\mathcal{A}$ implements a distributed variable $\mathcal{D}$-*output* such that for every run of $\mathcal{A}$ with failure pattern $F \in \mathcal{E}$, there exists $H \in \mathcal{D}(F)$ such that for all $p_i \in \Pi$ and $t \in \mathbb{T}$, $\mathcal{D}$-$output_i(t) = H(p_i, t)$, i.e., the value of $\mathcal{D}$-*output* at p_i at time t is $H(p_i, t)$. We call $\mathcal{A}$ a *reduction* algorithm.

If, for failure detectors $\mathcal{D}$ and $\mathcal{D}'$, there is a reduction algorithm that extracts the output of $\mathcal{D}$ using $\mathcal{D}'$ in $\mathcal{E}$, then we say that $\mathcal{D}$ *is weaker than* $\mathcal{D}'$ in $\mathcal{E}$.

$\mathcal{D}$ is the *weakest failure detector* to solve a task $\mathcal{M}$ in $\mathcal{E}$ if (i) there is an algorithm that solves $\mathcal{M}$ using $\mathcal{D}$ in $\mathcal{E}$ and (ii) $\mathcal{D}$ is weaker than any failure detector that can be used to solve $\mathcal{M}$ in $\mathcal{E}$. Every task can be shown to have a weakest failure detector [8]. In any environment, $\neg \Omega_k$ is the weakest failure detector to solve (n, k)-set agreement [9].

2.8 The BG-Simulation Technique

Borowsky and Gafni proposed a simulation technique (called *BG-simulation*) by which $k + 1$ processes $q_1, \ldots, q_{k+1}$, called *simulators*, can wait-free simulate a k-resilient execution of any asynchronous n-process protocol [4,5]. Each simulator tries to promote steps of all simulated processes in the breadth-first-manner, one by one, by running an agreement protocol for each step. The agreement protocol is guaranteed to terminate if every simulator that started the protocol is correct. BG-simulation makes sure that a simulator can block the agreement protocol for at most one simulated code at a time, and thus, as long as at least one simulator is live, at most k simulated processes can be faulty (appear only finitely often) in the simulated execution.

The original BG-simulation technique has been extended in order to reduce the question of k-resilient solvability of an n-process task $\mathcal{T}$ defined for processes $p_1, \ldots, p_n$, to *wait-free* solvability of a $k+1$-process task $\mathcal{T}'$ defined for simulators $q_1, \ldots, q_{k+1}$ [14]. Task $\mathcal{T}'$ is defined as follows. Every simulator q_i receives, as an input in task $\mathcal{T}'$, an input value of p_i in task $\mathcal{T}$ and $n - k - 1$ inputs of processes p_j such that $j > i$. All inputs must belong to an input vector I of $\mathcal{T}$. Respectively, an output of q_i in $\mathcal{T}'$ consists of an output value for p_i in $\mathcal{T}$ as well as $n - k - 1$ outputs of processes p_j such that $j > i$. All outputs must belong to the same output vector O such that (I, O) satisfies the task specification of $\mathcal{T}$. Task $\mathcal{T}$ is solvable k-resiliently if and only if $\mathcal{T}'$ is solvable wait-free [14]. Unlike [4,5] where simulators did not care about which codes make progress, as long as there at least $n - k$ of them, the simulation technique of [14] associates each simulator q_i with a distinct process p_i, and q_i is required to move the code of p_i forward until p_i (and at least $n - k - 1$ codes of processes with ids higher than i) outputs a value for task $\mathcal{T}$. But since we consider the weak termination condition, to solve $\mathcal{T}'$, it is sufficient to make sure that at least one simulator observes that some simulated process has decided.

In BG-simulation [4,5], every (infinite) *schedule* (sequence of ids of simulators $q_1, \ldots, q_{k+1}$) σ implies a unique (k-resilient) schedule for the simulated processes

$p_1, \ldots, p_n$, denoted $BG(\sigma)$. Moreover, if σ is *fault-free* (every simulator appears infinitely often in σ), then so is $BG(\sigma)$. If a simulated process p_i is blocked in a finite schedule σ by some simulator q_j (q_j started the agreement protocol for a step of p_i but has not terminated it), then any q_j-free extension σ' of σ produces an execution in which p_i is faulty, and all appearances of p_i in $BG(\sigma')$ take place in $BG(\sigma)$, a prefix of it.

3   The Main Result

In this section we show that, for any environment $\mathcal{E}$, if a failure detector $\mathcal{D}$ solves a k-resiliently impossible task $\mathcal{T}$ in $\mathcal{E}$, then $\mathcal{D}$ is stronger than $\neg \Omega_k$ in $\mathcal{E}$.

3.1   Overview

Let $\mathcal{A}$ be the algorithm that solves $\mathcal{T}$ in $\mathcal{E}$ using $\mathcal{D}$. We devise a *reduction algorithm* that uses $\mathcal{A}$ and $\mathcal{D}$ to derive, in each run, the output of $\neg\Omega_k$, regardless of the environment, i.e., of the assumptions on when and where failures are supposed to take place. The reduction algorithm consists of two components that are running in parallel: the *communication component* and the *computation component*.

In the communication component, the run of the reduction algorithm induces a *directed acyclic graph* (DAG) that contains a sample of the failure detector history of this run and captures some causal relations between the values returned by $\mathcal{D}$ to different processes at different times [7]. A vertex $[p_j, d, m]$ of the DAG corresponds to the value d returned to process p_j when it queried its module of $\mathcal{D}$ for the m-th time. The DAG contains an edge $([p_j, d, m], [p_\ell, d', m'])$ when the m-th query performed by p_j and returned value d *causally precedes* the m'-th query performed by p_ℓ and returned value d'.

To maintain its version of the DAG, every process periodically queries its module of $\mathcal{D}$, creates a new vertex in the graph and adds an edge from every other vertex to the newly created vertex (Figure 1). Also, the process periodically writes its version of the graph in the shared memory, scans the memory and updates its version with the vertices added by other processes. As a result, the ever-growing DAGs maintained at the correct processes tend to the same infinite DAG $\bar{G}$ every vertex of which originates a path that contains infinitely many vertices of each correct process. More details on the DAG maintenance can be found in [7].

In the computation component, every process uses the ever-growing DAG for simulating locally a number of runs of the whole system and extracting the output of $\neg\Omega_k$ from the simulated runs. We use the observation that every constructed $\mathcal{D}$-based DAG G induces an *asynchronous* algorithm $\mathcal{A}^G$ that is almost like $\mathcal{A}$, except that, instead of $\mathcal{D}$, $\mathcal{A}^G$ uses G to *simulate* (finite and possibly unfair) ever-growing runs of $\mathcal{A}$ [13]. We strengthen this observation slightly and consider algorithm $\mathcal{A}^{G,\beta}$, where β is a mapping from the set of vertices of G to $\mathbb{N}$. (We call β a *delay* map.) To simulate the next step of $\mathcal{A}$ at a process p_j, $\mathcal{A}^{G,\beta}$ locates the first vertex $[p_j, d, m]$ in G that causally succeeds

Shared variables: for all $p_i \in \Pi$: V_i, initially $\perp$

```
1    k_i := 0
2    while true do
3        for all p_j ≠ p_i do  G_j := V_j; G_i := G_i ∪ G_j
4        d_i := query failure detector D
5        k_i := k_i + 1
6        add [p_i, d_i, k_i] and edges from all other vertices of G_i to [p_i, d_i, k_i], to G_i
7        V_i := G_i
```

Fig. 1. Communication component of the reduction algorithm (building a DAG): the code for each process p_i

all simulated steps that are currently observed. Then p_i takes $\beta([p_j, d, m])$ local steps, and if the next step p_j takes in $\mathcal{A}$ is a failure detector query, then the simulated step is assumed to return d. These local steps are have no effect on the simulated run of $\mathcal{A}$, and we use the delay map β to reconcile the evolutions of DAGs G_i constructed at different processes p_i.

The asynchronous algorithm $\mathcal{A}^{G,\beta}$ is *safe*: the runs produced in the simulated runs of $\mathcal{A}$ comply with the specification of task $\mathcal{T}$. Also, if every correct (in the current failure pattern F) process appears in a simulated run of $\mathcal{A}^{\bar{G},\beta}$, where $\bar{G}$ is the limit infinite DAG in this run, infinitely often (we call such a run *fair*), then the run must be *deciding*, i.e., every correct process must decide in it [9].

The computation component uses BG-simulation [4,5] to simulate, for each subDAG G and a delay map β, a number of runs of $\mathcal{A}^{G,\beta}$ on $k+1$ *simulators* $q_1, \ldots, q_{k+1}$. Each simulator q_i accepts as an input $n - k$ input values of task $\mathcal{T}$ for p_i and $n - k - 1$ processes of ids higher than i. It is required that all these inputs are consistent with some input vector of $\mathcal{T}$. In the beginning of the simulation, each simulator registers its input value in the shared memory. To simulate a step of a process p_i, a simulator q_j first checks if p_i has an input value, i.e., if any simulator registered an input containing a value for p_i. If no value is found, then q_j tries to simulate a "nop" step that makes no effect on the shared memory, otherwise it simulated a step of $\mathcal{A}^{G,\beta}$. In accordance with our weak termination condition, the run is considered *deciding* if at least one simulates process p_i returns an output of $\mathcal{T}$ at some simulator q_j.

The fact that the $(k+1)$-process task $\mathcal{T}'$ is not wait-free solvable [14] (see also Section 2.8) implies that the described BG-simulation must produce at least one infinite non-deciding run that, in turn, corresponds to an infinite k-resilient non-deciding run of some $\mathcal{A}^{\bar{G},\beta}$. To emulate $\neg\Omega_k$, it is thus sufficient to output the set of $n - k$ processes that appear the latest in the *first* such run (appropriately defined). Since every fair run of $\mathcal{A}^{\bar{G},\beta}$ is deciding [9], at least one correct process will eventually never be output in that run. Thus, the output of $\neg\Omega_k$ is extracted.

Of course, we still need to make sure that all correct processes eventually agree on simulating the same ever-growing non-deciding run. We address this issue using the *corridor-based* ordering of the simulated executions introduced in [9], some details are given below.

3.2 Preliminaries

Let G and G' be two finite DAGs, β and β' be two delay maps defined on G and G', respecpctively. We say that G' and β' extend G and β if $G \subseteq G'$, and for every vertex v in $G' - G$, $\beta'(v)$ is more than the length of the longest path in G. Note that for each input vector I and schedule σ, the run of $\mathcal{A}$ produced by $\mathcal{A}^{G',\beta'}$ with I and σ extends the run produced by $\mathcal{A}^{G,\beta}$. We are going to use the following result:

Theorem 1. *[9] Let $\bar{G}$ be the limit DAG produced in a fair run of the algorithm in Figure 1, with failure pattern F. Let G be any finite subDAG of $\bar{G}$, β be any delay map on G, and R' be any run of $\mathcal{A}^{G,\beta}$ with an input vector I and schedule σ. Then the sequence of steps simulated in R' belongs to a (partial) run of $\mathcal{A}$, $R_{\mathcal{A}}$, with I and F. If $correct(F) \subseteq inf(R')$, then there exists a subDAG G' of $\bar{G}$ and a delay map β' extending G and β, such that the run of $\mathcal{A}^{G',\beta'}$ with I and σ is deciding.*

Below we recall the notions of the corridor-based ordering [9].

Let $<$ be any deterministic order on subsets of $\mathcal{Q} = \{q_1, \ldots, q_{k+1}\}$, that is consistent with $\subseteq$: for all distinct $Q, Q' \in 2^{\mathcal{Q}}$, $Q \subseteq Q' \Rightarrow Q < Q'$. A *corridor* is a sequence $Q_1, Q_2, \ldots$ of non-empty subsets of $\mathcal{Q}$ such that $\forall \ell : Q_{\ell+1} \subseteq Q_\ell$. Since the elements of an infinite corridor eventually stabilize on the same non-empty subset Q_ℓ, each infinite corridor allows for a finite representation $Q_1, Q_2, \ldots, Q_{\ell-1}, (Q_\ell)^*$. Corridors C and C' of the same length are compared lexicographically, consistently with $<$ (slightly abusing notation we write $C < C'$).

We say that a (finite or infinite) schedule $\sigma = q_{i_1}, q_{i_2}, \ldots$ belongs to a (finite or infinite, resp.) corridor $C = Q_1, Q_2, \ldots$ (of the same length), and we write $\sigma \in C$, if $\forall \ell, q_{i_\ell} \in Q_\ell$. Similarly, we say that a corridor $C = Q_1, Q_2, \ldots$ belongs to a corridor $C' = Q'_1, Q'_2, \ldots$, and we write $C \subseteq C'$, if $\forall \ell, Q_\ell \subseteq Q'_\ell$.

The *narrowest corridor* of σ, denoted $crd(\sigma)$, is the smallest corridor σ belongs to. For an infinite schedule σ, let Q be the non-empty set that $crd(\sigma)$ eventually stabilizes on. It is then immediate that $live(\sigma) = Q$.

Schedules of the same length are compared lexicographically, consistently with some deterministic order on $\mathcal{Q}$. This implies a lexicographic order on tuples (I, C, σ) such that C and σ have the same length, and $\sigma \in C$.

In the following, let G be any finite subDAG of $\bar{G}$ and β be any delay map on G. We say that a (finite or infinite) schedule σ is *deciding with G, β and I*, if the run of $\mathcal{A}^{G,\beta}$ with schedule σ and I produces a deciding run of $\mathcal{A}$. We also use the following result:

Theorem 2. *[9] There exists a tuple $(\tilde{I}, \tilde{C}, \tilde{\sigma})$, where $\tilde{\sigma}$ is infinite and $\tilde{C} = crd(\tilde{\sigma})$, such that (i) $\forall G, \beta$, there exists $(I, C, \sigma) < (\tilde{I}, \tilde{C}, \tilde{\sigma})$ such that σ is not deciding with G, β and I, and (ii) for all $(I, C, \sigma) < (\tilde{I}, \tilde{C}, \tilde{\sigma})$, there exist G and β such that for all $(I', C', \sigma') \leq (I, C, \sigma)$, σ' is deciding with G, β and I'.*

In other words, $(\tilde{I}, \tilde{C}, \tilde{\sigma})$ is the smallest tuple such that, for every finite DAG G, $(\tilde{I}, \tilde{C}, \tilde{\sigma})$ is higher than the *highest* deciding tuple over all subDAGs of G and

8   **repeat forever**
9   **for all** G, subgraphs of G_i, and all β on G **do**
10   **for all** I, input vectors of T' **do**
11   BG simulate (on $q_1, \ldots, q_{k+1}$) all possible runs of $\mathcal{A}^{G,\beta}$ with I
12   let (I', C', σ') be the smallest tuple that is higher
                than the highest deciding tuple over all G and β
13        $\neg\Omega_k\text{-}output := n - k$ processes that appear the latest in $BG(\sigma')$

Fig. 2. Computational component of the reduction algorithm: code for each process p_i

all delay maps β. Intuitively, the existence of such $(\tilde{I}, \tilde{C}, \tilde{\sigma})$ follows from the fact that task T' on $q_1, \ldots, q_{k+1}$ is not wait-free solvable [14].

3.3   Main Result

Our reduction algorithm is described in Figures 1 and 2. In the communication component (Figure 1), processes simply take a sample of their failure detector outputs, exchange this information, and maintain ever-growing DAGs that capture temporal relations between values output by the failure detector at different processes.

In the computation component (Figure 2), a process p_i takes every subgraph G of its DAG G_i and every delay nap β on G to simulate $k+1$ processes $q_1, \ldots, q_{k+1}$ that, in turn, run the BG-simulation algorithm to simulate k-resilient runs of $\mathcal{A}^{G,\beta}$ on n processes $p'_1, \ldots, p'_n$. (To avoid confusion, for all $1 \le j \le n$, p'_j denotes here the process that represents p_j in the local simulation.) The simulation goes through all possible input vectors I of the $(k+1)$-process task T' corresponding to T [14]. [1] Simulating a schedule σ of $q_1, \ldots, q_{k+1}$ applied to an input vector terminates when the simulated run of $\mathcal{A}^{G,\beta}$ with schedule $BG(\sigma)$ and input vector I decides or reaches a vertex of G_i that has no causal successors. The levels of simulation that takes place at every process p_i are summarized below:

$$p_i$$
simulates runs of Extended BG-simulation on
$$q_1, \ldots, q_{k+1}$$
simulate runs of $\mathcal{A}^{G,\beta}$ on
$$p'_1, p'_2, \ldots, p'_{n-1}, p'_n$$
simulate runs of $\mathcal{A}$

Then p_i chooses (I', C', σ'), the smallest tuple that is higher than the *highest* deciding tuple over all G and β (by Theorem 2 it exists). The current output of $\neg\Omega_k$ is evaluated as the set of $n - k$ processes that appear the latest in $BG(\sigma')$ (here each p'_j is replaced with p_j).

Theorem 3. *Let $\mathcal{E}$ be any environment and T be any weak-termination k-resilient impossible task. Let $\mathcal{D}$ be a failure detector that solves T in $\mathcal{E}$. Then $\mathcal{D}$ is stronger than $\neg\Omega_k$ in $\mathcal{E}$.*

---

[1] Here we use the assumption that the set of inputs of T is finite.

Proof sketch. Consider a run of the reduction algorithm with failure pattern F. Let G_i be the DAG maintained at a correct process p_i and G' be a subgraph of G_i. For each G, a subDAG of G and every delay map β, p_i periodically simulates all possible finite schedules of BG-simulation of $\mathcal{A}^{G,\beta}$ using all possible input vectors of $\mathcal{T}'$. For uniformity, we consider schedules of the same length, sufficiently long to cover all possible runs of $\mathcal{A}$ that can be simulated using G. Here we use the assumption that there are only finitely many input vectors of $\mathcal{T}$.

Let $(\tilde{I}, \tilde{C}, \tilde{\sigma})$ be the infinite tuple satisfying properties (i) and (ii) of Theorem 2. We observe that there is a time after which for every (I', C', σ') evaluated by p_i in line 12, $I' = \tilde{I}$, C' extends longer and longer prefixes of $\tilde{C}$, and σ' extends longer and longer prefixes of $\tilde{\sigma}$. This is because for each (I, C, σ), a prefix of $(\tilde{I}, \tilde{C}, \tilde{\sigma})$, there is a time after which p_i considers every $(I'', C'', \sigma'') < (I, C, \sigma)$ "deciding": there exist G and β such that for every infinite extension of (I'', C'', σ'') that is smaller than $(\tilde{I}, \tilde{C}, \tilde{\sigma})$, the run of $\mathcal{A}^{G,\beta}$ with I'' and σ'' is deciding. Thus, eventually, the output of $\neg\Omega_k$ maintained in line 13 consists of $n - k$ processes that is a subset of $live(BG(\tilde{\sigma}))$.

Now we observe that $live(BG(\bar{\sigma}))$ cannot include all correct (in F) processes. Otherwise, by Theorem 1, for some subDAG G and some β, and for all $(I, C, \sigma) \leq (\tilde{I}, \tilde{C}, \tilde{\sigma})$, $\mathcal{A}^{G,\beta}$ produces a deciding run with I and σ — a contradiction with the definition of $(\tilde{I}, \tilde{C}, \tilde{\sigma})$.

Finally, the output produced in line 13 consists of $n - k$ processes, and, eventually, at least one correct process is never output — the output of $\neg\Omega_k$ is extracted. □

3.4 Set Consensus Number: Categorizing Distributed Tasks

It has been recently shown that, for all $0 < k < n$, every actively $(k-1)$-resiliently solvable task can be solved wait-free if, in addition to read-write registers, we are allowed to use k-set agreement task as a shared object [11]. By a simple substitution, we derive that $\neg\Omega_k$ solves any actively $(k - 1)$-resiliently solvable task in any environment. On the other hand, our Theorem 3 implies that every task $\mathcal{T}$ that is not k-resilient solvable requires $\neg\Omega_k$, in any environment. Thus:

Corollary 1. *Let $0 < k < n$. Let task $\mathcal{T}$ be actively $(k-1)$-resilient solvable but not k-resilient solvable. Then the weakest failure detector to solve $\mathcal{T}$ is $\neg\Omega_k$.*

Corollary 1 implies that the (weak-termination) solvability of any participation-oblivious task $\mathcal{T}$ in any environment is precisely captured by its *set consensus number*: the maximal k such that $\mathcal{T}$ can be solved wait-free using read-write registers and k-set agreement objects. If $\mathcal{T}$'s set consensus number is k, then the weakest failure detector for solving $\mathcal{T}$ is $\neg\Omega_k$.

4 Related Work

The notion of the weakest failure detector was introduced by Chandra et al [7] who showed that Ω, the failure detector that eventually outputs the same correct process id at every correct process, is the weakest failure detector to solve consensus (1-set agreement) in the message-passing model. An extension of this result to the read-write shared memory model appears in [15,16,9].

Zieliński [12,13] introduced anti-Ω ($\neg\Omega_{n-1}$ in our notation) and proved that it is the weakest failure detector to solve wait-free $(n-1)$-set agreement in every environment. The result has been recently generalized to the case of $\neg\Omega_k$ and k-set agreement in [9]. [2] The reduction algorithm of [9] used both the fact that ensuring weak termination for k-set agreement implies that every correct process decides, and the "symmetry" of inputs: every process participating in a k-set agreement run can give up its input value in favor of any input value it sees without affecting the correctness of decision. In this paper we generalize the result to any task that is not k-resiliently solvable with weak termination and eliminated the input-symmetry requirement. Our reduction algorithm employed the BG-simulation technique [4,5], and used the equivalence result in [14]. The DAG-based simulation framework is done following the general strategy proposed in [7], and generalizes our recent result [9]. Unlike [7], the computation component of our algorithm bases solely on the fact that the given task is k-resilient impossible. Our task characterization is based on the equivalence of k-concurrency, k-set agreement, and active k-resilience established in [11].

5   In Place of Conclusion

Viewed collectively, our result imply that n-process participation-oblivious distributed tasks can be categorized into n equivalence classes, $1, \ldots, n$. For each $k = 1, \ldots, n$, the weakest failure detector for solving any task in class k is $\neg\Omega_k$. Class 1 consists of *universal* task: whenever a universal task is solvable, any other task is solvable [18]. Class n consists of *trivial* tasks that can be solved asynchronously. More generally, a task $\mathcal{T}$ in class k is equivalent to k-set agreement: any failure detector that solves $\mathcal{T}$ can solve k-set agreement, and vice versa. The classes are totally ordered in decreasing strength: any failure detector that solves a task $\mathcal{T}$ in class k solves any task in classes $k' \geq k$.

For our reduction algorithm, we make, however, certain restrictions on tasks. First, we assume that a task has a finite set of inputs. We use the assumption when we establish that inability to locate a non-deciding run implies that k-set agreement is solvable k-resiliently which goes through exploring all possible runs for $k+1$ BG simulators starting from all possible input vectors. Most of the tasks we can think of either satisfy this requirement or can be shown equivalent to such a task (cf. the equivalence between $k+1$-valued and multi-valued k-set agreement).

Another restriction, which looks more serious, is that we reason about solvability assuming the weak termination condition, instead of conventional "strong" termination ("every correct process eventually decides"). Intuitively, we need the weak-termination assumption for our reduction algorithm because the set of correct processes is not known in advance, so we may never be able to conclude

---

[2] Two papers [10,17] concurrently derived similar results ([17] for the case of k-resilient environments).

that every correct process decided in the simulated run. We therefore consider deciding any run in which at least one simulated process decides.

But circumventing a weak-termination k-resilient impossibility potentially requires stronger failure detector than the conventional one, which makes our result weaker: we can imagine k-resilient impossible tasks that *can* be solved k-resiliently with weak termination. Consider, for instance, a task $T^{k+1,k}$ which requires each subset of $k+1$ processes to solve $(k+1, k)$-set agreement ($T^{2,1}$, the consensus variant of this task, is considered in [19]). It turns out that this task is weak-termination solvable k-resiliently. In fact, there is an algorithm which makes at least $n - k - 1$ processes decide in every k-resilient run: every process tries to solve, one by one, k-set agreement for each set of $k+1$ processes it belongs to using a k-resilient variant of BG-agreement [4,5]. Since at most k processes fail, at most one of these $(k + 1, k)$-set agreements can block forever, and thus, at least $n - k - 1$ processes that are not involved in the blocked agreement will be able to terminate. However, it is impossible to make sure that at least $n - k$ processes produce outputs in every k-resilient run: otherwise, we could derive a k-resilient k-set agreement algorithm, contradicting [2,3,4].

We can therefore consider a task $T_{n-k}^{k+1,1}$, similar to $T^{k+1,k}$, in which every process starts with a set of $n - k$ input values and produces a set of at least $n - k$ output values, so that all inputs (resp., outputs) belong to the same input (resp., output) vector of $T^{k+1,k}$ such that the input-output realtion of $T^{k+1,k}$ is preserved. It is immediate that the task is not solvable k-resiliently *with weak termination*, and thus, by our Theorem 3, requires $\neg\Omega_k$ to be solved.

The missing link now is to establish that every failure detector that circumvents k-resilient impossibility for a task T, also circumvents the weak-termination impossibility for T_{n-k}. We cannot however expect this claim to hold for all tasks: there are k-resilient impossible "asymmetric" tasks, specification of which do not withstand permutations of process ids, that do not require $\neg\Omega_k$ to be solved. But we conjecture that for symmetric tasks, like $T^{k+1,k}$, the claim is indeed true. This, once proved, gives a natural generalization of the fundamental equivalence result [19] that solving consensus among any pair of processes requires exactly the same amount of synchrony as solving consensus among all processes (Ω). So we have here an intersting open question which can be seen as a generalization of the "extended BG" equivalence [14] to the world of failure detectors.

References

1. Chaudhuri, S.: Agreement is harder than consensus: Set consensus problems in totally asynchronous systems. In: PODC, pp. 311–324 (1990)
2. Herlihy, M., Shavit, N.: The asynchronous computability theorem for t-resilient tasks. In: STOC, pp. 111–120 (1993)
3. Saks, M., Zaharoglou, F.: Wait-free k-set agreement is impossible: The topology of public knowledge. In: STOC, pp. 101–110. ACM Press, New York (1993)
4. Borowsky, E., Gafni, E.: Generalized FLP impossibility result for t-resilient asynchronous computations. In: STOC, pp. 91–100. ACM Press, New York (1993)

5. Borowsky, E., Gafni, E., Lynch, N.A., Rajsbaum, S.: The BG distributed simulation algorithm. Distributed Computing 14(3), 127–146 (2001)
6. Chandra, T.D., Toueg, S.: Unreliable failure detectors for reliable distributed systems. Journal of the ACM 43(2), 225–267 (1996)
7. Chandra, T.D., Hadzilacos, V., Toueg, S.: The weakest failure detector for solving consensus. Journal of the ACM 43(4), 685–722 (1996)
8. Jayanti, P., Toueg, S.: Every problem has a weakest failure detector. In: PODC, pp. 75–84 (2008)
9. Gafni, E., Kuznetsov, P.: The weakest failure detector for solving k-set agreement. In: PODC (2009),
   http://www.net.t-labs.tu-berlin.de/~petr/pubs/wfd-kset.pdf
10. Delporte-Gallet, C., Fauconnier, H., Guerraoui, R., Tielmann, A.: The disagreement power of an adversary (brief announcement). In: PODC (2009)
11. Gafni, E., Guerraoui, R.: Simulating few by many: Limited concurrency=set consensus. Unpublished manuscript (2009),
    http://www.cs.ucla.edu/~eli/eli/kconc.pdf
12. Zieliński, P.: Automatic classification of eventual failure detectors. In: Pelc, A. (ed.) DISC 2007. LNCS, vol. 4731, pp. 465–479. Springer, Heidelberg (2007)
13. Zieliński, P.: Anti-omega: the weakest failure detector for set agreement. In: PODC (2008)
14. Gafni, E.: The extended BG-Simulation. In: STOC (2009),
    http://www.cs.ucla.edu/~eli/eli/230-gafni1.pdf
15. Lo, W.K., Hadzilacos, V.: Using failure detectors to solve consensus in asynchronous shared memory systems. In: Tel, G., Vitányi, P.M.B. (eds.) WDAG 1994. LNCS, vol. 857, pp. 280–295. Springer, Heidelberg (1994)
16. Guerraoui, R., Kuznetsov, P.: Failure detectors as type boosters. Distributed Computing 20(5), 343–358 (2008)
17. Anta, A.F., Rajsbaum, S., Travers, C.: Weakest failure detectors via an egg-laying simulation (brief announcement). In: PODC (2009)
18. Herlihy, M.: Wait-free synchronization. ACM Transactions on Programming Languages and Systems 13, 123–149 (1991)
19. Delporte-Gallet, C., Fauconnier, H., Guerraoui, R.: (Almost) all objects are universal in message passing systems. In: Fraigniaud, P. (ed.) DISC 2005. LNCS, vol. 3724, pp. 184–198. Springer, Heidelberg (2005)

The Abstract MAC Layer*

Fabian Kuhn, Nancy Lynch, and Calvin Newport

MIT CSAIL, Cambridge, MA
{fkuhn,lynch,cnewport}@csail.mit.edu

Abstract. A diversity of possible communication assumptions complicates the study of algorithms and lower bounds for radio networks. We
address this problem by defining an Abstract MAC Layer. This service
provides reliable local broadcast communication, with timing guarantees stated in terms of a collection of abstract *delay functions* applied
to the relevant contention. Algorithm designers can analyze their algorithms in terms of these functions, independently of specific channel
behavior. Concrete implementations of the Abstract MAC Layer over
basic radio network models generate concrete definitions for these delay
functions, automatically adapting bounds proven for the abstract service to bounds for the specific radio network under consideration. To
illustrate this approach, we use the Abstract MAC Layer to study the
new problem of *Multi-Message Broadcast*, a generalization of standard
single-message broadcast, in which any number of messages arrive at
any processes at any times. We present and analyze two algorithms for
Multi-Message Broadcast in static networks: a simple greedy algorithm
and one that uses regional leaders. We then indicate how these results
can be extended to mobile networks.

1 Introduction

The study of bounds for mobile ad hoc networks is complicated by the numerous possible communication assumptions: Do devices operate in slots or asynchronously? Do simultaneous transmissions cause collisions? Can collisions be
detected? Is message reception determined by geographical distances? Or is it
determined by a more complex criteria, such as signal-to-noise ratio? And so on.
This situation causes problems. Results for one set of communication assumptions might prove invalid for a slightly different set. In addition, these low-level
assumptions require algorithm designers to grapple with low-level problems such
as contention management, again and again, making it difficult to highlight interesting high-level algorithmic issues. This paper proposes a possible solution
to these concerns. (A technical report with more details is also available [19].)

---

* This work has been support in part by Cisco-Lehman CUNY A New MAC-Layer
  Paradigm for Mobile Ad-Hoc Networks, AFOSR Award Number FA9550-08-1-0159,
  NSF Award Number CCF-0726514, and NSF Award Number CNS-0715397.

I. Keidar (Ed.): DISC 2009, LNCS 5805, pp. 48–62, 2009.

The Abstract MAC Layer. We introduce an *abstract MAC layer* service for mobile ad hoc networks (MANETs). We intend this service to be implemented over real MANETs, with very high probability. At the same time, we intend it to be simple enough to serve as a good basis for theoretical work on high-level algorithms in this setting. The use of this service allows algorithm designers to avoid tackling issues as contention management and collision detection. They can instead summarize their effects with abstract delay bounds.

The abstract MAC layer service delivers transmitted messages reliably within its local neighborhood, and provides feedback to the sender of a message in the form of an acknowledgement that the message has been successfully delivered to all nearby receivers. The service does not provide the sender with any feedback about particular recipients of the message. The service provides guaranteed upper bounds on the worst-case amount of time for a message to be delivered to all its recipients, and on the total amount of time until the sender receives its acknowledgement. It also may provide a (presumably smaller) bound on the amount of time for a receiver to receive *some message* among those currently being transmitted by neighboring senders. These time guarantees are expressed using *delay functions* applied to the current amount of contention among senders that are in the neighborhoods of the receivers and the sender.

To implement our abstract MAC layer over a physical network one could use popular contention-management mechanisms such as carrier sensing, backoff, receiver-side collision detection with NACKs, or perhaps even network coding methods, such as the ZigZag Decoding approach of Gollakota and Katabi [11]. Our MAC layer encapsulates the details of these mechanisms within the service implementation, presenting the algorithm designer with a simple abstract model that involves just message delivery guarantees and time bounds.[1] We believe that this MAC layer service provides a simple yet realistic basis for theoretical work on high-level algorithms and lower bounds for MANETs.

Multi-Message Broadcast and Regional Leader Election. In this paper, we validate our formalism by studying two problems: *Multi-Message Broadcast (MMB)* and *Regional Leader Election (RLE)*. The MMB problem is a generalization of single-message broadcast; c.f., [1,2,3,4,6,5,7,8,16,14,15,17,18]. In the MMB problem, an arbitrary number of messages originate at arbitrary processes in the network, at arbitrary times; the problem is to deliver all messages to all processes. We present and analyze two MMB algorithms in static networks, and indicate how the second of these can be extended to mobile networks.

Our first MMB algorithm is a simple greedy algorithm, inspired by the strategy of the single-message broadcast algorithm of Bar-Yehuda et al. [3]. We analyze this algorithm using the abstract MAC layer delay functions. We obtain an upper bound on the time for delivery of each message that depends in an

---

[1] Note that MAC layer implementations are usually probabilistic, both because assumptions about the physical layer are usually regarded as probabilistic, and because many MAC layer implementations involve random choices. Thus, these implementations implement our MAC layer with very high probability, not absolute certainty.

interesting way on the *progress bound*—the small bound on the time for a receiver to receive *some* message. Specifically, the bound for MMB to broadcast a given message m, is of the form $O\left((D + k)F_{prog} + (k - 1)F_{ack}\right)$, where D is the network diameter, k is a bound on the number of messages whose broadcast overlaps m, and F_{ack} and F_{prog} are upper bounds on the acknowledgement and progress delay functions, respectively. Note that a dependency on a progress bound was implicit in the analysis of the single-message broadcast algorithm in [3]. Our use of the abstract MAC layer allows us to make this dependency explicit.

Our second MMB algorithm achieves better time complexity by exploiting geographical information; in particular, it uses a solution to the RLE problem as a sub-protocol. In the RLE problem, the geographical area in which the network resides is partitioned statically into regions; the problem is to elect and maintain a leader in each occupied region. Regional leaders could be used to form a backbone network that could, in turn, be used to solve many kinds of communication and coordination problems. We give an RLE algorithm whose complexity is approximately bF_{prog}, where b is the number of bits required to represent process ids.

Using the RLE algorithm, our second MMB algorithm works as follows: After establishing regional leaders, the MMB algorithm runs a version of the basic greedy MMB algorithm, but using just the leaders. In order to transfer messages that arrive at non-leader processes to leaders, all the processes run a *collect* sub-protocol in parallel with the main broadcast algorithm. The complexity of the resulting MMB algorithm reduces to $O\left(D + k + bF_{prog} + F_{ack}\right)$, a significant improvement over MMB without the use of leaders.

Finally, to extend our second MMB algorithm to the mobile case, we provide a preliminary theorem that says that the MMB problem is solved given certain restrictions on mobility and message arrival rates.

Contributions. The contributions of this paper are: (a) the definition of the abstract MAC layer, and the suggestions for using it as an abstract layer for writing mobile network algorithms, and; (b) new algorithms for Multi-Message Broadcast and Regional Leader Election, and their analysis using the abstract MAC Layer.

2   Model

We model a Mobile Ad Hoc Network (MANET) using the Timed I/O Automata (TIOA) formalism. Our model captures n user processes, which we label with $\{1, ..., n\}$, in a mobile wireless network with only local broadcast communication.

2.1   System Components

Our system model consists of three component automata, the *network automaton*, the *abstract MAC layer automaton*, and the *user automaton*, connected as

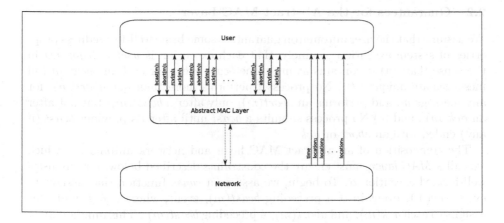

Fig. 1. The MANET system

shown in Figure 1. The *network automaton* models the relevant properties of the physical world: time, mobile node locations, and physical network behavior. It provides a physical layer interface for low-level communication on the radio channel. It outputs the time and mobile node locations; we assume here that this information is accurate. The network automaton comes equipped with a pair of functions f_G and $f_{G'}$ that map from states to directed graphs whose vertices V are the mobile nodes. The graph $G = (V, E) = f_G(s)$ is the *communication graph* in state s, indicating the processes that are within communication range in s. The graph $G' = (V, E') = f_{G'}(s)$ is the *interference graph* in state s, indicating the processes within interference range. We consider communication separately from interference because in many practical radio network models the interference range exceeds the reliable communication range.[2]

The *abstract MAC layer automaton* mediates the communication of messages between the user processes and the network. Each user process i interacts with the MAC layer automaton via MAC layer inputs $bcast(m)_i$ and $abort(m)_i$ and MAC layer outputs $rcv(m)_i$ and $ack(m)_i$, where m is a message from some message alphabet. (The *abort* is used in cases where the sender is satisfied that "enough" neighbors have already received the message, and so is willing to terminate efforts by the MAC layer to continuing broadcasting.) The abstract MAC layer automaton connects to the network through the physical layer interface. Finally, the *user automaton* models n user processes, numbered $1, \ldots, n$. Each process i connects to the MAC layer through the $(bcast, abort, rcv, ack)$ interface described above, and might also receive the network's location and time outputs.

---

[2] To capture some physical layer models, notably a Signal to Interference-plus-Noise Ratio model, we might need to extend our definition of G' to allow weights on the edges; that is, capture not just who might interfere but also how much interference they contribute. We do not make this extension here but leave it as interesting future work.

2.2   Guarantees for the Abstract MAC Layer

We assume that the user automaton guarantees some basic well-formedness properties of system executions, namely, that each execution is *user-well-formed* in the sense that: (a) it contains at most one *bcast* event for each message m (all messages are unique); (b) No process i performs more than one $abort(m)_i$ for any message m, and performs an $abort(m)_i$ only after a $bcast(m)_i$ but not after an $ack(m)_i$; and (c) No process submits a *bcast* until after its previous *bcast* (if any) ended with an *abort* or *ack*.

The composition of an abstract MAC layer and network automaton, which we call a *MAC layer*, must ensure the constraints described below, for any user-well-formed execution α. To begin, we assume a *cause* function that assigns to every $rcv(m)_j$ event in α a preceding $bcast(m)_i$ event, where $i \neq j$, and that assigns to each $ack(m)_i$ and $abort(m)_i$ a preceding $bcast(m)_i$. This function must satisfy:

1. **Receive correctness:** Suppose that $bcast(m)_i$ event π causes $rcv(m)_j$ event π' in α. Then: (a) *Proximity:* At some point between events π and π', $(i, j) \in E'$ (notice, we use the edge set from the interference graph, E', instead of the edge set from the communication graph, E, because the former captures edges where communication *might* occur, while the latter captures edges where communication *is guaranteed* to occur); (b) *No duplicate receives:* No other $rcv(m)_j$ event caused by π precedes π'; and (c) *No receives after acknowledgements:* No $ack(m)_i$ event caused by π precedes π';
2. **Acknowledgment correctness:** Suppose that $bcast(m)_i$ event π causes $ack(m)_i$ event π' in α. Then: (a) *Guaranteed communication:* If for every point between events π and π', $(i, j) \in E$ (the edge set of the communication graph), then a $rcv(m)_j$ event caused by π precedes π'; (b) *No duplicate acknowledgements:* No other $ack(m)_i$ event caused by π precedes π'; and (c) *No acknowledgements after aborts:* No $abort(m)_i$ caused by π precedes π';
3. **Termination:** Every $bcast(m)_i$ causes either an $ack(m)_i$ or an $abort(m)_i$.

We also impose upper bounds on the time from a $bcast(m)_i$ event to its corresponding $ack(m)_i$ and $rcv(m)_j$ events. These bounds are expressed in terms of the contention involving i and j during the broadcast interval. Let f_{rcv}, f_{ack}, and f_{prog} be monotonically non-decreasing functions from natural numbers to nonnegative reals. We use these to bound the delay for a specific message to be delivered, for an acknowledgement to be received, and for *some* message among many to be received, all with respect to a given amount of contention. For many MAC layer implementations, f_{prog} is smaller than f_{ack}, because the time to deliver some message is smaller than the time to deliver a specific message. Let ϵ_a be a small constant, used to bound the amount of time beyond an *abort* when the message could still be received somewhere.

We define a "message instance" to be a matched pair of $bcast_i$ and ack_i, or $bcast_i$ and $abort_i$ events. Let α be an execution, α' a closed execution fragment within α and j a process. Then $contend(\alpha, \alpha', j)$ is the set of message instances in α that intersect with fragment α', and such that $(i, j) \in E'$ at some point in this intersection, where i is the sender from the instance in question. These are the message instances that might reach j during α'. Similarly, $connect(\alpha, \alpha', j) \subseteq contend(\alpha, \alpha', j)$ is the set of message instances such that α' is entirely contained between the corresponding $bcast_i$ and ack_i events and $(i, j) \in E$ for the duration of α', where i is the sender. These are the messages instances that must reach j if α' is long enough. For an execution α and events π and π', $\alpha[\pi, \pi']$ denotes the execution fragment within α that spans from π to π'.

We can now formalize our time bounds with the *receive, acknowledgment,* and *progress* properties. These bound the time for a specific message to be received, a specific message to be acknowledged at the sender, and some message from among many to be received, respectively.

5. **Receive:** Suppose that a $bcast(m)_i$ event π causes a $rcv(m)_j$ event π' in α. Then the time between π and π' is at most $f_{rcv}(c)$, where c is the number of distinct senders of message instances in $contend(\alpha, \alpha[\pi, \pi'], j)$. Thus, the bound for j's receipt of m grows with the number of *nearby* processes (incoming neighbors, according to G') that have message instances intersecting with the instance in question. Also, if π causes an $abort(m)_i$ event π'', then π' occurs at most ϵ_a time after π''.

6. **Acknowledgement:** Suppose that a $bcast(m)_i$ event π causes an $ack(m)_i$ event π' in α. Let $ackcon$ be the set containing i and every process j such that there exists a $rcv(m)_j$ with cause π. Then the time between π and π' is at most $f_{ack}(c)$, where c is the number of distinct senders of message instances in $\bigcup_{j \in ackcon} contend(\alpha, \alpha[\pi, \pi'], j)$. This bound is similar to the receive bound, except that we now consider the contention at the sender and at all receivers. This is intended to allow enough time for the receivers to somehow communicate their receipt of the message back to the sender.

7. **Progress:** For every closed fragment α' within α, for every process j, and for every integer $c \geq 1$, it is not the case that *all* three of the following conditions hold:

   (a) The total time described by α' is strictly greater than $f_{prog}(c)$; (b) The number of distinct senders of message instances in $contend(\alpha, \alpha', j)$ is at most c, and $connect(\alpha, \alpha', j)$ is non-empty; and (c) No $rcv(m)_j$ event from a message instance in $contend(\alpha, \alpha', j)$ occurs by the end of α'.

   Thus, the time bound for j to receive *some* message (when at least one message is being sent by an incoming neighbor in G), grows with the total number of processes that are in interference range.

Fixed Bounds on Message Delivery. In some results, we will use constant upper bounds F_{rcv}, F_{ack}, and F_{prog} on f_{rcv}, f_{ack}, and f_{prog}, respectively, all defined with respect to a particular execution α. These upper bounds take the maximum values of the functions over all graphs that occur in α and all possible amounts of contention, as defined by the node degrees that occur in those graphs. In the design of algorithms, we sometimes use F_{rcv}^+, F_{ack}^+, F_{prog}^+, which are defined with respect to all *executions* of a given network automaton.

2.3   Implementing an Abstract MAC Layer

It is beyond the scope of this paper to offer a detailed implementation of an abstract MAC layer automaton. Here we discuss, only informally, some basic ideas for implementations with the aim of providing some intuition regarding the type of concrete definitions our delay functions might adopt in practice. We consider the simple case where G and G' are the same for all network states (that is, the network is static) and undirected, and $G = G'$. (See [12] for an example of how a scheme could be adapted to tolerate mobility and transient faults.) We assume a physical network that corresponds to the slotted radio broadcast model of [2,3,10,20,22,13]. This model assumes that communication occurs in synchronized slots, and that a message from a sender i is correctly received by a neighbor j in a time slot s if and only if i is the only neighbor of j broadcasting during s. The model includes no collision detection—a collision cannot be distinguished from silence.

In this setting, a simple *Decay* strategy [2,3] can be used to implement the abstract MAC layer. In this approach, time is divided into synchronized epochs of $\Theta(\log \Delta)$ time slots, where Δ is the maximum degree in G. A process with a message to broadcast starts broadcasting at the beginning of the next epoch. During an epoch, a sending process decreases its probability of broadcasting exponentially, from 1 to $1/\Delta$. It is guaranteed that every process with at least one neighbor sending a message during an epoch receives at least one message, with constant probability. Thus, the progress delay function f_{prog} is $O(\log \Delta)$ (with high probability). The receive and acknowledgement delay functions, f_{rcv} and f_{ack}, are both $O(\Delta \log \Delta)$.

2.4   Multiple Abstract MAC Layer Automata

To simplify the analysis of multiple user protocols running on the same physical network, it is sometimes useful to include several independent abstract MAC automata in the same system. In this scheme, each protocol connects with its own MAC automaton, all of which connect with the same network automaton. Each MAC automaton satisfies the specifications given above, with respect to the common network. This approach allows an algorithm designer to prove properties of the behavior of the individual protocols and assert that they still hold when the protocols are combined, thus evading issues of contention among the protocols. Note that there are practical realizations of multiple MAC automata. For example, most radio-equipped computing devices have access to many communication frequencies. If a device has several transmitters, it can execute several simultaneous MAC protocols on independent frequencies. If the device has a single transceiver and/or access to only a single frequency, it can use a Time-Division Multiplexing scheme to partition use of the frequency among the logical MAC layers.

3   Multi-Message Broadcast

The Multi-Message Broadcast (MMB) problem assumes that the environment submits messages to the user processes at arbitrary times during an execution. The goal is to propagate every such message to *all* of the users in the network. In this section we assume a *static* network, that is all states generate the same G and G' graphs. Furthermore, we assume $G = G'$ and the graphs are undirected. We use the notation $D(G)$ to refer to the diameter of graph G.

An *MMB protocol* for a message alphabet $\mathcal{M}$ is a user automaton whose external interface includes an $arrive(m)_i$ input and $deliver(m)_i$ output for each user process i and message m. We say that an execution of an MMB protocol is *MMB-well-formed* if it contains at most one $arrive(m)_i$ event for each m. (Each broadcast message is unique). An MMB protocol *solves the MMB problem* if, for every MMB-well-formed execution: (a) For every $arrive(m)_i$ and every process j, there is a $deliver(m)_j$; and (b) For every m and j, there is at most one $deliver(m)_j$, and it comes after some $arrive(m)_i$.

Our first MMB algorithm is a simple greedy algorithm, inspired by the single-message broadcast algorithm of Bar-Yehuda et al. [2,3].

The Basic Multi-Message Broadcast (BMMB) Protocol
Every process i maintains a FIFO queue named *bcastq* and a set named *rcvd*. Both are initially empty. If process i is not currently broadcasting a message (i.e., not waiting for an *ack* from the MAC layer) and *bcastq* is not empty, it broadcasts the message at the head of the queue. If i receives an $arrive(m)_i$ event it immediately performs a $deliver(m)_i$ output and adds m to the back of *bcastq*. It also adds m to *rcvd*. If i receives a broadcast message m from the MAC layer it first checks *rcvd*. If $m \in rcvd$ it discards it. Else, i immediately performs a $deliver(m)_i$ event, and adds m to the back of *bcastq* and to the *rcvd* set.

Theorem 1. *The BMMB protocol solves the MMB problem.*

The proof is presented in the full version of this paper [19]. We continue with a collection of definitions used by our complexity proof. In the following, let α be some MMB-well-formed execution of the BMMB protocol composed with a MAC layer.

The get Event. We define a $get(m)_i$ event with respect to α, for some arbitrary message m and process i, to be one in which process i first learns about message m. Specifically, $get(m)_i$ is the first $arrive(m)_i$ event if message m arrives at process i, otherwise, $get(m)_i$ is the first $rcv(m)_i$ event.

The clear Event. Let $m \in \mathcal{M}$ be a message for which an $arrive(m)_i$ event occurs in α. We define $clear(m)$ to describe the final $ack(m)_j$ event in α for any process j.[3]

---

[3] Notice, by the definition of BMMB if an $arrive(m)_i$ occurs then i eventually broadcasts m, so $ack(m)_i$ occurs. Furthermore, by the definition of BMMB, there can be at most one $ack(m)_j$ event for every process j. Therefore, $clear(m)$ is well-defined.

The Set $K(m)$. Let $m \in \mathcal{M}$ be a message such that $arrive(m)_i$ occurs in α for some i. We define $K(m) = \{m' \in \mathcal{M} :$ an $arrive(m')$ event precedes the last $deliver(m)$ event and the $clear(m')$ event follows the $arrive(m)_i$ event$\}$. That is, $K(m)$ is the set of messages whose processing overlaps the interval between the the $arrive(m)_i$ event and the last $deliver(m)$ event.

The obvious complexity bound would guarantee the delivery of a given message m in $O(D(G)kF_{ack})$ time, for $k = |K(m)|$, as there can be no more than k messages ahead of m at each hop, and each message is guaranteed to be sent, received, and acknowledged within F_{ack} time. The complexity theorem below does better. By separating kF_{ack} from the diameter, $D(G)$, instead multiplying by the smaller progress bound, F_{prog}. This captures an implicit pipelining effect that says *some* message always makes progress in F_{prog} time.

Theorem 2. *Let k be a positive integer and α be an MMB-well-formed execution of the BMMB protocol composed with a MAC layer. Assume that an $arrive(m)_i$ event occurs in α. If $|K(m)| \leq k$ then the time between the $arrive(m)_i$ and the last $deliver(m)_j$ is at most:*

$$(D(G) + 2k - 2)F_{prog} + (k - 1)F_{ack}.$$

Theorem 2 is a direct consequence of the following lemma.

Lemma 1. *Let α be an MMB-well-formed execution of the BMMB protocol composed with a MAC layer. Assume that at time t_0, $arrive(m)_{i_0}$ occurs in α for some message $m \in \mathcal{M}$ and some process i_0. Let j be a process at distance $d = d_G(i_0, j)$ from the process i_0. Further, let $\mathcal{M}' \subseteq \mathcal{M}$ be the set of messages m' for which $arrive(m)_{i_0}$ precedes $clear(m')$. For integers $\ell \geq 1$, we define*

$$t_{d,\ell} := t_0 + (d + 2\ell - 2) \cdot F_{prog} + (\ell - 1) \cdot F_{ack}.$$

For all integers $\ell \geq 1$, at least one of the following two statements is true:

(1) The $get(m)_j$ event occurs by time $t_{d,\ell}$ and $ack(m)_j$ occurs by time $t_{d,\ell} + F_{ack}$.
(2) There exists a set $\mathcal{M}'' \subseteq \mathcal{M}'$, $|\mathcal{M}''| = \ell$, such that, for every $m' \in \mathcal{M}''$, $get(m')_j$ occurs by time $t_{d,\ell}$, and $ack(m')_j$ occurs by time $t_{d,\ell} + F_{ack}$.

Proofs of Lemma 1 and Theorem 2 are presented in the full version of the paper [19].

4   Regionalized Networks

Our general model specifies that the network automaton reports node locations, but does not constrain the geography of these locations or their relationship to G and G'. Here we define such constraints; we use these to study the leader election and optimized MMB protocols in Sections 5 and 6, respectively.

Fix L, a set of *locations* (e.g., points in the plane), R, a set of *regions ids*, and *reg*, a *region mapping* that maps locations to region ids. Let $N_R \subseteq N'_R$ be two symmetric neighbor relations among regions in R. We call the graph $G_{region} =$

(R, N_R) a *region communication graph* and the graph $G'_{region} = (R, N'_R)$ a *region interference graph*. We assume that G_{region} is connected and that the maximum node degree in G'_{region} is constant.

We define a physical network $\mathcal{N}$ to be *regionalized* (with respect to L, R, reg, N_R, and N'_R) provided that the following hold. $\mathcal{N}$ uses locations in L; in any particular state of $\mathcal{N}$, let $loc(i)$ denote the location of node i as encoded by $\mathcal{N}$. Then at any point in any execution of $\mathcal{N}$: (a) If $reg(loc(i)) = reg(loc(j))$ or $(reg(loc(i)), reg(loc(j))) \in N_R$, then $(i, j) \in E$; and (b) If $(i, j) \in E'$, then either $reg(loc(i)) = reg(loc(j))$ or $(reg(loc(i)), reg(loc(j))) \in N'_R$. That is, if two nodes are in the same region or neighboring regions in the region communication graph G_{region}, then they must be connected in G, and if two nodes are connected in G' then they are in the same or neighboring regions in the region interference graph G'_{region}. Thus, G_{region} describes which regions must be in communication range while G'_{region} describes which regions might be in interference range.

Fixing a Regionalized Network. For Sections 5 and 6 we fix a static network $\mathcal{N}$ that is regionalized with respect to some parameters L, R, reg, N_R, and N'_R. As in Section 3 we assume that $G = G'$ and the graphs are undirected. We also assume that the network occupies every region in every execution. When we refer to MAC layers in these sections, we implicitly mean MAC layers that include $\mathcal{N}$. When we refer to any region r, we implicitly assume that $r \in R$.

5   Leader Election

The BMMB protocol does not take advantage of location information. In Section 6 we describe a new MMB algorithm, the *Regional Multi-Message Broadcast algorithm*, which leverages this information to achieve a better complexity bound. The Regional MMB algorithm uses a backbone of leaders—one per region of the regionalized network—that are each elected using a local leader election protocol. This leader backbone forms a connected dominating set (CDS), as studied, for example, in [23,21,20,24,9]. Our algorithm, however, is simpler than those in prior work, because we use location information and the abstract MAC layer masks contention.

An *Regional Leader Election (RLE) protocol* is a user automaton that has a $leader(r)_i$ and $notleader(r)_i$ output for every process i and every region r. Such a protocol *solves the RLE problem for region r by time t* if in every execution, by time t, exactly one process i in region r outputs $leader(r)_i$, and every other process j in region r outputs $notleader(r)_j$.

We begin by describing the Fast Regional Leader Election (FRLE) protocol whose complexity depends only on F^+_{prog} (which we typically assume to be much smaller than F^+_{ack}), and the size of the id space. In the following, let b be the number of bits needed to describe the id space, and let ϵ_b be a fixed small constant. We use this latter value in both leader election protocols to add a small *buffer* after the time required to receive a message.[4]

---

[4] This is required by a technicality of the TIOA definition that allows multiple events to occur at the same time.

The r-Fast Regional Leader Election (FRLE) Protocol
In the r-FRLE protocol for some region r, each process i in r behaves as follows. Let $\epsilon'_a = \epsilon_a + \epsilon_b$. Divide the time interval from 0 to $b(F^+_{prog} + \epsilon'_a)$ into b phases each of length $F_{prog} + \epsilon'_a$. We associate phase p with bit p of the id space. At the beginning of phase 1, process i broadcasts the phase number and its id if it has a 1 bit in location 1 of its id. Otherwise it does not broadcast. After F^+_{prog} time has elapsed in the phase, if i broadcast and has not yet received an *ack*, it submits an *abort*. At the end of the phase (i.e., ϵ'_a time after the potential *abort*), i processes its received messages. If i did not broadcast in this phase yet received at least one message, it outputs $notleader(r)_i$ and terminates the protocol. Otherwise, it continues with the next phase, which proceeds the same as before with respect to bit position 2. This continues until i terminates with a $notleader(r)_i$ output or finishes the last phase without terminating. In the latter case, i submits a $leader(r)_i$ output.

Theorem 3. *For any region r, the r-FRLE protocol solves the RLE problem for region r by time $b(F^+_{prog} + \epsilon_a + \epsilon_b)$.*

FRLE works correctly because it is impossible for all processes that are non-terminated at the beginning of a phase to submit $notleader(r)$ outputs at the end of the phase. Moreover, two or more processes cannot survive all b phases to become leaders, because their ids differ in at least one bit position. The formal correctness proof is presented in the full version of the paper [19].

We continue by describing the Complete Regional Leader Election (CRLE) Protocol, which elects a leader in *every* region. It uses FRLE within each region and a Time-Division Multiplexing (TDM) strategy to avoid interference among the FRLE instances. As before, let b be the bits needed to describe the id space. This protocol uses a *minimal-sized region TDMA schedule* T defined with respect to the region interference graph for the regionalized network.[5] (Notice, by the definition of regionalized, $|T| = O(1)$.)

The Complete Regional Leader Election (CRLE) Protocol
In the CRLE protocol each process i behaves as follows. We dedicate $b(F^+_{prog} + \epsilon'_a)$ time to each set in T. Process i does nothing until the start of the time dedicated to the single set in T that contains i. Process i runs the $reg(loc(i))$-FRLE protocol during the time interval dedicated to this set. It first adds, however, a fixed offset to the time input used by FRLE to transform the time at the beginning of the interval to evaluate to 0, as expected by FRLE.

Theorem 4. *The CRLE protocol solves RLE problem for every region by time $\Theta\left(b \cdot (F^+_{prog} + \epsilon_a)\right)$*

The proof is presented in the full version [19].

---

[5] That is, T describes minimally-sized sequence of sets of region ids such that: (a) every region id shows up in exactly one set; (b) no set contains two region ids that are neighbors in the region interference graph.

6   Regional Multi-Message Broadcast

The *Regional MMB (RMMB)* protocol runs a version of the basic greedy MMB algorithm over a connected backbone of leaders elected by the CRLE protocol. To transfer messages that arrive at non-leader processes to leaders, the processes run a *Collect* protocol in parallel with the main broadcast algorithm. The complexity of RMMB is just $O\left(D + k + bF_{prog} + F_{ack}\right)$, a significant improvement over Basic MMB. The improvement arises because RMMB confines the propagation of messages to the low-degree backbone of leaders elected by CRLE.

The Regional Multi-Message Broadcast (RMMB) Protocol
The protocol uses three independent MAC automata (see Section 2.4), which we call the *Collect*, *Leader*, and *Broadcast* MAC automata. We use the *Leader MAC* to elect regional leaders using CRLE, the *Broadcast MAC* to run BMMB on the leader backbone once CRLE terminates, and the *Collect MAC* to transfer messages that arrive at non-leaders to the regional leaders. The Collect protocol runs concurrently with the CRLE and BMMB protocols. Before CRLE completes, all processes running Collect queue messages in case they are elected leader. Each process i in region r maintains a *broadcast* queue and an *arrive* queue, both initially empty. It also maintains a *leader* flag, initially *false*, and two sets, *delivered* and *rcvd*, both initially empty.

Leader Election: Starting at time 0, process i executes the CRLE leader election protocol, using the *Leader* MAC. At the end of the protocol, process i sets its *leader* flag to *true* if and only if it performed a $leader(r)_i$ output.

Collect: When an $arrive(m)_i$ or $rcv((m,r))_i$ event occurs, process i adds the message (m or (m,r)) to its *arrive* queue. When i's *arrive* queue is non-empty it does the following. If the element at the head of the queue is a single message m', process i removes m' from the *arrive* queue, outputs $deliver(m')_i$, adds m' to the *delivered* set and to the *broadcast* queue, and *propagates* m'. Then it moves on to the next element in the *arrive* queue. The propagate step depends on the value of the *leader* flag: If *leader* = *true*, then propagate is a *noop*. If *leader* = *false* then i broadcasts (m',r) using the Collect MAC, and then waits for the corresponding $ack((m',r))_i$. If the element at the head of the *arrive* queue is (m',r), then i removes (m',r) from the queue, outputs $deliver(m')_i$, adds m' to the *delivered* set and to the *broadcast* queue. (It does not propagate in this case.)

Broadcast: Process i waits for the fixed amount of time required for the CRLE protocol to complete. If i has *leader* = *true* at this point, then it executes the BMMB protocol using the Broadcast MAC, using the *broadcast* queue maintained by the Collect protocol, and using its *delivered* set *in addition* to the list *rcvd* used by BMMB to determine when to pass along a message. If i is not a leader, then for each m received from the Broadcast MAC, if m is not in the delivered set then it outputs $deliver(m)_i$ and adds m to the *delivered* set.

The proofs to the following theorems are presented in the full version of the paper [19].

Theorem 5. *The RMMB protocol solves the MMB problem.*

For the time complexity, the key observation is that RMMB executes on a backbone of leaders. So the contention on the broadcast MAC automaton is at most the maximum degree of G'_{region}, which is constant, reducing the F_{ack} and F_{prog} to constants. For the following theorem, we assume that the rate of *arrive* events at each process is $O(1/F_{ack})$, preventing any process from having more than a constant number of messages in its *arrive* queue at once. Let $K(m)$ and $D(G)$ be defined the same as in Section 3.

Theorem 6. *Let k be a positive integer and α be an MMB-well-formed execution of the RMMB protocol composed with three MAC automata and a network. Assume that an $arrive(m)_i$ event occurs in α. If $|K(m)| \leq k$ then the length of the interval between $arrive(m)_i$ and the last $deliver(m)_j$ is:*

$$O\left(max\{b(F^+_{prog} + \epsilon_a), F_{ack}\} + D(G) + k\right).$$

7   Adapting RMMB for Mobile Networks

In the full version of this paper [19] we describe mobile RMMB—a modification of RMMB for a mobile setting. In addition to the protocol description, we prove a preliminary theorem that establishes bounds on RMMB's message delivery, under certain mobility constraints. We reproduce the theorem below to provide intuition regarding the type of results that can be proved in a mobile setting. (The full details of the protocol, and the proof of theorem, are in [19].)

In the statement below, we assume each process maintains a *region exit bound* state variable. This variable contains a time value that is no later than the time when the process will next exit its current region. We assume that while a process remains within a region, this value does not change. We say a network is T-*stable*, for some nonnegative real T, if and only if every process calculates an exit bound at least T past the current time upon entering a new region, and for all regions and for all times there exists at least one process with an exit bound at least T past the current time. Finally, we use t_{CF} to describe the running time of CRLE and D to describe the maximum diameter of G in the mobile network.

We obtain the following theorem:

Theorem 7. *Let k be a positive integer, F^{max}_{ack} and t^{max}_{CF} be nonnegative reals, and $T = (D + 1)2kF^{max}_{ack} + kF^{max}_{ack}$. If we restrict the rate of arrive events such that no more than k such events happen in any interval of length T, and consider only regionalized $(2kF^{max}_{ack} + max\{kF^{max}_{ack}, t^{max}_{CF}\})$-stable networks with $F_{ack} \leq F^{max}_{ack}$, and $t_{CF} \leq t^{max}_{CF}$, then the mobile RMMB protocol, executed with $kF^{max}_{ack} + t^{max}_{CF}$ passed as the parameter to the mobile leader election sub-protocol, solves the MMB problem.*

8   Conclusion

We presented the abstract MAC layer for MANETs. This service is intended to be implemented over real MANETs, with high probability. It abstracts the complexities of programming for this environment—including contention management and collision behavior—allowing the algorithm designer to focus on the issues unique to the problem being solved.

This approach generates many interesting open questions. For example, exploring how we can use the layer to implement basic primitives such as neighbor discovery and unicast communication, or complex protocols such as spanning trees and dominating sets. Extensions to the MMB problem, such as calculating throughput bounds and the cost of sender acks, are also important. Another direction is to improve the abstract MAC layer formalism itself. We might generalize the G and G' model to capture the effects of signal to interference-plus-noise ratios (SINR), or perhaps replace the deterministic delay functions with probability distributions over the different possible delays. This latter change would support more advanced analysis of the system's probabilistic behavior. Finally, it will prove useful to analyze specific MAC layer strategies for specific radio network models, providing concrete definitions for the delay functions.

Acknowledgements

We thank those who contributed comments and suggestions towards this project. In particular, we acknowledge Jennifer Welch and Seth Gilbert for their careful readings and helpful suggestions, and thank Rotem Oshman and Majid Khabbazian for their helpful discussions and comments.

References

1. Alon, N., Bar-Noy, A., Linial, N., Peleg, D.: On the complexity of radio communication. In: Proceedings of the ACM Symposium on Theory of Computing (1989)
2. Bar-Yehuda, R., Goldreich, O., Itai, A.: Efficient emulation of single-hop radio network with collision detection on multi-hop radio network with no collision detection. Distributed Computing 5, 67–71 (1991)
3. Bar-Yehuda, R., Goldreich, O., Itai, A.: On the time-complexity of broadcast in multi-hop radio networks: An exponential gap between determinism and randomization. Journal of Computer and System Sciences 45(1), 104–126 (1992)
4. Chlamtac, I., Kutten, S.: On broadcasting in radio networks - problem analysis and protocol design. IEEE Transactions on Communications 33(12), 1240–1246 (1985)
5. Chlebus, B.S., Gasieniec, L., Gibbons, A., Pelc, A., Rytter, W.: Deterministic broadcasting in unknown radio networks. In: Proceedings of the ACM-SIAM Symposium on Discrete Algorithms (2000)
6. Chlebus, B.S., Gasieniec, L., Gibbons, A., Pelc, A., Rytter, W.: Deterministic broadcasting in ad hoc radio networks. Distributed Computing 15(1), 27–38 (2002)
7. Clementi, A., Monti, A., Silvestri, R.: Round robin is optimal for fault-tolerant broadcasting on wireless networks. Journal of Parallel and Distributed Computing 64(1), 89–96 (2004)
8. Czumaj, A., Rytter, W.: Broadcasting algorithms in radio networks with unknown topology. In: Proceedings of the Symposium on Foundations of Computer Science (2003)

9. Das, B., Bharghavan, V.: Routing in ad-hoc networks using minimum connected dominating sets. In: Proceedings of the IEEE International Conference on Communications (1997)
10. Gasieniec, L., Pelc, A., Peleg, D.: The wakeup problem in synchronous broadcast systems. SIAM Journal of Discrete Mathematics 14(2), 207–222 (2001)
11. Gollakota, S., Katabi, D.: Zigzag decoding: Combating hidden terminals in wireless networks. In: Proceedings of the ACM SIGCOMM Conference (2008)
12. Hernman, T., Tixeuil, S.: A distributed TDMA slot assignment algorithm for wireless sensor networks. In: Proceedings of the International Workshop on Algorithmic Aspects of Wireless Sensor Networks (2004)
13. Jurdzinski, T., Stachowiak, G.: Probabilistic algorithms for the wakeup problem in single-hop radio networks. In: Proceedings of the Symposium on Algorithms and Computation (2002)
14. Kowalski, D., Pelc, A.: Broadcasting in undirected ad hoc radio networks. In: Proceedings of the International Symposium on Principles of Distributed Computing (2003)
15. Kowalski, D., Pelc, A.: Time of radio broadcasting: Adaptiveness vs. obliviousness and randomization vs. determinism. In: Proceedings of the Colloquium on Structural Information and Communication Complexity (2003)
16. Kowalski, D., Pelc, A.: Time of deterministic broadcasting in radio networks with local knowledge. SIAM Journal on Computing 33(4), 870–891 (2004)
17. Kowalski, D.R., Pelc, A.: Deterministic broadcasting time in radio networks of unknown topology. In: Proceedings of the Symposium on Foundations of Computer Science (2002)
18. Kranakis, E., Krizanc, D., Pelc, A.: Fault-tolerant broadcasting in radio networks. In: Proceedings of the Annual European Symposium on Algorithms (1998)
19. Kuhn, F., Lynch, N., Newport, C.: The abstract MAC layer. Technical Report, MIT-CSAIL-TR-2009-021 (2009), http://hdl.handle.net/1721.1/45515
20. Kuhn, F., Moscibroda, T., Wattenhofer, R.: Initializing newly deployed ad hoc and sensor networks. In: Proceedings of the International Conference on Mobile Computing and Networking (2004)
21. Kuhn, F., Moscibroda, T., Wattenhofer, R.: Fault-tolerant clustering in ad hoc and sensor networks. In: Proceedings of the IEEE International Conference on Distributed Computing Systems (2006)
22. Moscibroda, T., Wattenhofer, R.: Maximal independent sets in radio networks. In: Proceedings of the International Symposium on Principles of Distributed Computing (2005)
23. Scheideler, C., Richa, A., Santi, P.: An o(log n) dominating set protocol for wireless ad-hoc networks under the physical interference model. In: Proceedings of the International Symposium on Mobile Ad Hoc Networking and Computing (2008)
24. Wan, P.-J., Alzoubi, K., Frieder, O.: Distributed construction of connected dominating set in wireless ad hoc networks. Mobile Networks and Applications 9(2), 141–149 (2004)

Randomization Can Be a Healer: Consensus with Dynamic Omission Failures*

Henrique Moniz, Nuno Ferreira Neves, Miguel Correia, and Paulo Veríssimo

University of Lisboa, Faculdade de Ciências, LASIGE

Abstract. Wireless ad-hoc networks are being increasingly used in diverse contexts, ranging from casual meetings to disaster recovery operations. A promising approach is to model these networks as distributed systems prone to dynamic communication failures. This captures transitory disconnections in communication due to phenomena like interference and collisions, and permits an efficient use of the wireless broadcasting medium. This model, however, is bound by the impossibility result of Santoro and Widmayer, which states that, even with strong synchrony assumptions, there is no deterministic solution to any non-trivial form of agreement if $n - 1$ or more messages can be lost per communication round in a system with n processes. In this paper we propose a novel way to circumvent this impossibility result by employing randomization. We present a consensus protocol that ensures safety in the presence of an unrestricted number of omission faults, and guarantees progress in rounds where such faults are bounded by $f \leq \lceil \frac{n}{2} \rceil (n - k) + k - 2$, where k is the number of processes required to decide, eventually assuring termination with probability 1.

1 Introduction

Wireless ad-hoc networks are being increasingly used in diverse contexts, ranging from casual meetings to disaster recovery operations. The ability of distributed processes to execute coordinated activities despite failures is important to distributed systems, including those based in wireless ad-hoc networks. Such coordination requires agreement among the processes, a problem that has taken many incarnations in the literature: consensus, Byzantine generals, and interactive consistency are just a few examples [12,17,23]. The prevalent aspect of these formulations is that at some point in their execution the processes involved have to agree on a common item of information.

In the traditional models for distributed systems, faults are static and component-bound, i.e., a fault is associated to a particular component that is forever considered faulty. The faulty component can be a process or a communication link (e.g., [23,24]). These models are referred to as *component failure models*. For systems based on these models to operate correctly, a certain number of components must not exhibit failures during their entire operation time.

* This work was partially supported by the FCT through the Multiannual and the CMU-Portugal Programs.

I. Keidar (Ed.): DISC 2009, LNCS 5805, pp. 63–77, 2009.
© Springer-Verlag Berlin Heidelberg 2009

This approach, however, is not well adapted to wireless ad-hoc networks. First, in these environments, faults have a more dynamic and transient nature. The nodes are usually subject to momentary disconnection due to node mobility and other environmental phenomena such as electromagnetic interference, fading, collisions, etc. These events may result in message loss or corruption, but should not be sufficient to permanently assume a process or link as faulty, specially because they can possibly affect many processes during the lifetime of the system. Due to the emergence of wireless networks, there is an increasing need for models that accurately capture the reality of these environments.

Second, the openness of wireless ad-hoc networks provides a natural broadcasting medium, where the cost of transmitting a message to multiple processes can be just the same of transmitting it to a single process, as long as they are within communication range. To take advantage of this feature, it becomes necessary to depart from the common modeling assumption of reliable point-to-point channels, usually employed by the component failure models. Developing a system based on this assumption forces the implementation of end-to-end message delivery mechanisms (similar to TCP), which significantly increase the medium access contention, impairing the overall performance. The unreliability inherent to radio communications has to be dealt with in some other way. Models that assume unreliable communication links are more adjusted to wireless networking. Tolerance to message loss becomes integrated within the semantics of the algorithms, instead of being abstracted by typically inefficient implementations.

More adapted to the wireless ad-hoc environments is the *communication failure model* [28,27]. This model differs from the component failure models in the sense that it focuses on the effects of faults rather than their source. On message-passing systems, any failure, regardless of its nature, will ultimately manifest itself as transmission faults. For example, a process crash will manifest into a series of transmission omission faults with the crashed process as sender, and a process that is attacked and falls under the control of a maliciously adversary may manifest into a series of transmission corruption faults where the contents of the messages are modified relative to the original protocol. Such an approach implicitly allows every component of the system to eventually fail. The only restriction is placed on the number of faults that simultaneously manifest in the system.

Research in this model, however, has been limited mainly due to two fundamental reasons. When the model was introduced by Santoro and Widmayer in 1989, a stringent impossibility result came along with it [28]. This result applies to the k-*agreement* problem among n processes, in which k out of n processes must agree on a binary value $v \in \{0, 1\}$. The Santoro-Widmayer impossibility result applies to non-trivial agreement, i.e., for $k > \lceil n/2 \rceil$. It states that there is no finite time deterministic algorithm that allows n processes to reach k-*agreement* if more than $n - 2$ transmission failures occur in a communication step. This is a very discouraging result since the crashing of a single process necessarily results in $n - 1$ transmission failures, rendering this form of agreement impossible. Moreover, this result is produced under strong time assumptions where both the processes' relative processing times and communication delays are bound by known constants (i.e., a synchronous system).

The second reason has probably to do with some lack of practical interest of this model prior to the emergence of wireless ad-hoc communication. For distributed systems based on wired networks, it was safe and convenient to assume end-to-end reliable delivery mechanisms, since the implementation of such mechanisms did not represent a significant performance overhead. Interestingly, these models are also bound by an impossibility result: the FLP result [13]. It states that consensus is impossible to solve deterministically in asynchronous systems (i.e., where there are no assumptions about the processes' relative processing times and communication delays) if just a single process can fail.

Thus, on one hand we have asynchronous systems, bound by the FLP impossibility result, where agreement is impossible even if communication is reliable. On the other hand, we have systems that are synchronous but the communication is unreliable so they are bound by the Santoro-Widmayer impossibility result, also making agreement impossible. While several solutions have been proposed over the years to circumvent the FLP result (e.g., partial synchrony models [10], failure detection [7], wormholes [21]), the result of Santoro and Widmayer, for the reasons stated above, has not received comparable attention. Nevertheless, getting past the current upper bound of $n-2$ transmission failures is paramount to the embracing of the communication failure model for emergent networking environments.

This paper proposes a protocol that circumvents the Santoro-Widmayer impossibility result in both a practical and efficient way. We achieve this by employing *randomization*, which has never been applied before in the context of the communication failure model. The Santoro-Widmayer impossibility result rules out deterministic solutions to agreement in this model. Randomization takes a probabilistic approach to the problem, and has been used in the past to solve consensus in FLP-bound systems (starting with [3,25]). It overcomes previous limitations by supplying processes with access to random information (e.g., a coin flip) and combining this with a refinement of the problem statement where a decision is ensured with a probability of 1.

The paper describes a randomized binary *k-consensus* algorithm that tolerates omission faults. The algorithm allows at least k processes to decide on a common binary value in a system with n processes such that $k > \frac{n}{2}$. The safety properties of consensus (i.e., validity and agreement) are ensured even with an unrestricted number of faults, while the liveness property (i.e., termination) is ensured if the number of faults per round does not exceed $\lceil \frac{n}{2} \rceil (n-k) + k - 2$. This algorithm is adequate for wireless ad-hoc networks because it allows one to take advantage of the broadcasting medium in an efficient way and, at the same time, ensures safety under severe communication problems that lead to many message losses. The termination is achieved with probability 1 when communication becomes stable, i.e., when the threshold above is satisfied. Furthermore, the algorithm is efficient in the sense that it is *fast-learning* [16], i.e., it terminates in 2 communication steps under favorable conditions (i.e., with no message losses, benign patterns of message losses, and/or all processes having the same initial value).

The remainder of the paper is organized as follows: Section 2 discusses the related work. Section 3 formalizes the *k-consensus* problem, and the next section presents the system model. Section 5 describes the algorithm, and the correctness proofs are provided in the following section. Section 7 discusses some performance aspects of the algorithm, and finally, Section 8 concludes the paper.

2   Related Work

The problem of reaching agreement with unreliable communication links goes back as far as 1975 when Akkoyunlu et al. pointed out that an agreement between two processes connected by unreliable communication paths leads to an infinite exchange of messages [2]. In 1978 Gray identified essentially the same problem by formulating the *generals paradox* [14]. He showed that there is no fixed length protocol that allows agreement between two processes connected through an unreliable communication link. This problem is often referred to as the *coordinated attack problem* from the formalization of Lynch [18]. Varghese and Lynch later proposed a randomized solution to the coordinated attack problem where the protocol runs for a fixed number of rounds and agreement is reached with a probability proportional to the number of rounds [30].

The previous result was generalized to an arbitrary number of processes by Santoro and Widmayer [28,27]. Their contribution provides an important impossibility result. It states that there is no fixed-time solution to the problem of *k-agreement* (i.e., $k > \lceil \frac{n}{2} \rceil$ processes decide the same value 0 or 1) in a system with n processes if more than $n - 2$ links are allowed to lose messages. Their problem statement represents a weaker form of agreement than ours. The definition of *k-agreement* allows processes to decide different values as long as k decide the same value, while in our definition (i.e., *k-consensus*) no process is allowed to decide a different value.

The work of Chockler et al. presents algorithms that solve consensus in systems where nodes fail only by crashing and messages can be lost due to collisions [9]. Their solution assumes that processes have access to a collision detector that determines when message collisions occur, which allows nodes to take recovery measures when messages are lost. Message omissions other than those due to collisions, however, are not covered by their model. By contrast, our model assumes message omissions regardless of their nature.

Two other works also solve consensus under dynamic communication failures. The work of Biely et al. does so by addressing the problem in the context of the *heard-of model* of Charron-Bost and Schiper [4,8]. This model permits a fine-grained specification of the fault patterns allowed in the system, thus being able to distinguish the cases where the fault pattern exceeds the lower bound of Santoro and Widmayer but is not harmful to the system as a whole (e.g., $n - 1$ faults are harmful to the system if they originate at the same process, but may not be if they originate each one at a different process). The work of

Schmid et al. presents an analogous contribution in the sense that it restricts the number of faults that each process may experience such that the harmful fault patterns are avoided [29]. None of these two contributions, however, deal with the problematic essence of the Santoro-Widmayer impossibility result, which is the failure of every transmission from a single process rendering consensus impossible. This implies that consensus remains unsolvable if, for instance, in a wireless ad-hoc network, a single node falls out of range of every other node for an unknown period of time.

Crash-recovery models based on failure detection mechanisms can also be applied to wireless environments because of their ability to capture the disconnection and eventual reconnection of processes [11,15,22,1]. The granularity of these models, however, was not intended to capture connectivity scenarios likely to arise in wireless environments. For example, consensus cannot be solved in scenarios where every *good* process (i.e., one that is not crashed) has some faulty link to another good process. Such configuration violates the eventual weak accuracy property required by failure detectors.

3   The k-Consensus Problem

The *k-consensus* problem considers a set of n processes where each process p_i proposes a binary value $v_i \in \{0, 1\}$, and at least $k > \frac{n}{2}$ of them have to decide on a common value proposed by one of the processes. The remaining $n - k$ processes do not necessarily have to decide, but if they do, they are not allowed to decide on a different value. Our problem formulation is designed to accommodate a randomized solution and is formally defined by the properties:

Validity. If all processes propose the same value v, then any process that decides, decides v.

Agreement. No two processes decide differently.

Termination. At least k processes eventually decide with probability 1.

4   System Model

The system is composed by a fixed set of n processes $\Pi = \{p_0, p_1, ..., p_{n-1}\}$. The timing model is assumed to be synchronous. This implies that (1) there is a known upper bound on time required by a process to execute a step, (2) there is a known upper bound on message transmission delays, and (3) every process has a local clock with a known bounded rate of drift with respect to real-time.

The communication between processes proceeds in synchronous rounds. At each round, every process $p_i \in \Pi$ executes the following actions: (1) transmits a message m to every process $p_j \in \Pi$, including itself, by invoking broadcast(m), (2) receives the messages broadcast in the current round by invoking receive(), and (3) performs a local computation based on its current state and the set of messages received so far. We should note that the assumption of a broadcast operation generating n transmissions arises from the necessity of modeling the possibility of non-uniform message delivery by the processes. In practice, this operation can still be implemented efficiently by transmitting a single message.

Processes are modeled so as not to exhibit faulty behavior, i.e., they correctly follow the protocol until termination. The notion of a faulty process is instead captured by the assumption of faulty message transmissions. For example, a crashed process can be expressed by the loss of every message transmitted by it. The model considers omission transmission failures. A transmission between two processes p_i and p_j is subject to an omission failure if the message sent by p_i is not received by p_j.

In rounds where omission faults are bounded by $f \leq \lceil \frac{n}{2} \rceil (n-k) + k - 2$ out of the n^2 transmissions that occur (where k is the number of processes required to decide), the protocol necessarily makes some progress that eventually leads to a decision. Therefore, if enough of these rounds occur, then the protocol ensures termination with probability 1. Nevertheless, to simplify the correctness proofs we will assume that there is some unknown time after which at most f faulty transmissions occur at each round. The number of faults per round prior to this is unrestricted and can for instance match the total number of transmissions n^2.

Finally, every process $p_i \in \Pi$ has access to a local random bit generator that returns unbiased bits observable only by p_i, and access to a function $\#_x(V)$ that returns the number of occurrences of an element x in a vector V.

5 The Algorithm

This section presents a k-consensus algorithm (Algorithm 1). The algorithm is tolerant to omission faults and relies on each process p_i having access to a *local coin*[1] mechanism that returns random bits observable only by p_i (e.g., [3,5]). Safety (i.e., the *validity* and *agreement* properties of consensus) is ensured by the algorithm regardless of the number of omission faults that occur per round, while liveness (i.e., the *termination* property) is ensured if, after some arbitrary number of rounds, the number of omission faults per round does not exceed the threshold $f \leq \lceil \frac{n}{2} \rceil (n-k) + k - 2$.

The internal state of a process p_i is comprised by three variables: (1) the *phase* $\phi_i \geq 1$, (2) the *proposal value* $v_i \in \{0,1\}$, and finally, (3) the *decision status* $status_i \in \{decided, undecided\}$. Each process starts its execution with $\phi_i = 1$, $status_i = undecided$, while v_i is set to the initial proposal value indicated by the input register $proposal_i$.

A round of the algorithm is executed as follows. Upon every clock tick (line 5), each process p_i broadcasts a message of the form $\langle \phi_i, v_i, status_i \rangle$ containing the variables that comprise its internal state, and receives the messages broadcast by all processes (lines 6-7). Some of the messages that a process is supposed to receive may be lost. Any *new* messages that a process p_i receives at every round are accumulated in a vector V_i (line 8). A message $\langle \phi, v, status \rangle$ transmitted by a process p_j is considered new if it does not exist in V_i any message with phase value ϕ from p_j. This implies that it is impossible to accumulate in vector V_i

---

[1] As opposed to a *shared coin* that returns bits observable by all processes (e.g., [25,6]).

Algorithm 1. k-consensus algorithm

Input: Initial binary proposal value $proposal_i \in \{0, 1\}$
Output: Binary decision value $decision_i \in \{0, 1\}$

1 $\phi_i \leftarrow 1$;
2 $v_i \leftarrow proposal_i$;
3 $status_i \leftarrow undecided$;
4 $V_i \leftarrow \emptyset$;

5 **for each** *clock tick* **do**
6 $\quad$ broadcast($\langle \phi_i, v_i, status_i \rangle$);
7 $\quad$ receive();
8 $\quad$ $V_i \leftarrow V_i \bigcup \{$new messages received in the current round$\}$;

9 $\quad$ **while** $\exists_{\langle \phi, v, status \rangle \in V_i} : \phi > \phi_i$ **do**
10 $\quad\quad$ $\phi_i \leftarrow \phi$;
11 $\quad\quad$ $v_i \leftarrow v$;
12 $\quad\quad$ $status_i \leftarrow status$;
13 $\quad$ **end**

14 $\quad$ **if** $\#_{\langle \phi_i, *, * \rangle}(V_i) > \frac{n}{2}$ **then**
15 $\quad\quad$ **if** $\phi_i \bmod 2 = 1$ **then**   /* odd phase */
16 $\quad\quad\quad$ **if** $\exists_{v \in \{0,1\}} : \#_{\langle \phi_i, v, * \rangle}(V_i) > \frac{n}{2}$ **then**
17 $\quad\quad\quad\quad$ $v_i \leftarrow v$;
18 $\quad\quad\quad$ **else**
19 $\quad\quad\quad\quad$ $v_i \leftarrow \perp$;
20 $\quad\quad\quad$ **end**
21 $\quad\quad$ **else**   /* $\phi_i \bmod 2 = 0$: even phase */
22 $\quad\quad\quad$ **if** $\exists_{v \in \{0,1\}} : \#_{\langle \phi_i, v, * \rangle}(V_i) > \frac{n}{2}$ **then**
23 $\quad\quad\quad\quad$ $status_i \leftarrow decided$;
24 $\quad\quad\quad$ **end**
25 $\quad\quad\quad$ **if** $\exists_{v \in \{0,1\}} : \#_{\langle \phi_i, v, * \rangle}(V_i) \geq 1$ **then**
26 $\quad\quad\quad\quad$ $v_i \leftarrow v$;
27 $\quad\quad\quad$ **else**
28 $\quad\quad\quad\quad$ $v_i \leftarrow coin_i()$;
29 $\quad\quad\quad$ **end**
30 $\quad\quad$ **end**
31 $\quad\quad$ $\phi_i \leftarrow \phi_i + 1$;
32 $\quad$ **end**

33 $\quad$ **if** $status_i = decided$ **then**
34 $\quad\quad$ $decision_i \leftarrow v_i$;
35 $\quad$ **end**
36 **end**

---

more than one message with the same phase value ϕ from any single process. Based on its current internal state and the messages accumulated so far in vector V_i, each process p_i performs a state transition (i.e., modifies ϕ, v or $status$).

Before explaining how a process performs a state transition, it is important to note the distinction between round and phase. The term *round* pertains to a periodic execution of the protocol activated by a synchronous event, a clock tick in this case. The term *phase* pertains to a monotonic variable ϕ_i that is part of the internal state of a process p_i, and whose value increases as p_i accumulates messages of a certain form in vector V_i. How exactly ϕ_i is updated is explained below. For now, it is beneficial to retain that for any given round, any two processes p_i and p_j can have different phase values $\phi_i \neq \phi_j$.

A process p_i performs a state transition when one of two conditions occur:

1. The vector V_i holds one message from some process p_j whose phase ϕ_j is *higher* than the phase ϕ_i of p_i.
2. The vector V_i holds more than $\frac{n}{2}$ messages whose phase is *equal* to the phase ϕ_i of p_i.

The first case is straightforward (lines 9-13). When the condition is met (line 9), the process p_i updates its state to match exactly the state of the received message (lines 10-12).

The second case is more complex (lines 14-32). The way a process p_i updates its state depends on whether the current number of its phase ϕ_i is odd (i.e., $\phi_i \bmod 2 = 1$) or even (i.e., $\phi_i \bmod 2 = 0$). The odd phase essentially guarantees that if two processes set their proposal to a value 1 or 0, they do it for the same value. The even phase is where a process decides if it learns that a majority of processes have the same proposal value.

If $\phi_i \bmod 2 = 1$ (lines 15-20), then the proposal value v_i is updated in the following way: if there are more than $\frac{n}{2}$ messages of the form $\langle \phi_i, v, * \rangle$ in V_i with the same value v, then v_i is set to v (lines 16-17), otherwise it is set to a special value $\bot \notin \{0, 1\}$ indicating a lack of preference (lines 18-19).

If $\phi_i \bmod 2 = 0$ (lines 21-30), then the process sets $status_i$ to *decided* if there are more than $\frac{n}{2}$ messages of the form $\langle \phi_i, v, * \rangle$ in V_i with the same value $v \neq \bot$ (lines 22-24). The proposal value v_i is updated to v if there is at least one message of the form $\langle \phi_i, v, * \rangle$ in V_i with a value $v \neq \bot$, otherwise v_i is set to the value of function `coin()`, which returns a random number 0 or 1, each with a probability $\frac{1}{2}$ (lines 25-29). Regardless of whether the phase ϕ_i is odd or even, its value is always incremented by one unit at line 31.

At the end of each round, a process p_i checks if $status_i$ has been set to *decided*. If so, it decides by setting the output variable $decision_i$ to the current proposal value v_i (lines 33-35). Any further accesses to this variable do not alter its value. Hence, they have no impact on the correctness of the algorithm.

In the presented algorithm, processes do not voluntarily stop sending messages. The fact that the system stabilization time is unknown combined with the assumed fault model means that processes have no way of knowing when other processes have decided. This limitation can be easily overcome by having the processes execute for an additional round after deciding, where the broadcast operation is performed through a reliable (and possibly asynchronous) channel. Raynal and Roy showed that it is possible to implement reliable and asynchronous communication on top of an unreliable and synchronous model, and vice-versa [26]. One can assume the presence of a reliable channel that is judiciously used in such situations.

6   Correctness Proof

In this section we prove the correctness of the algorithm. Up to Theorem 2 we prove *validity* and *agreement* properties, which are made on the assumption that the system might be subject to an unbounded number of faults per round. From Lemma 4 and on, we address the *termination* property and assume the number of faults per round is $f \leq \lceil \frac{n}{2} \rceil (n - k) + k - 2$.

Lemma 1. *If every process p_i with phase value $\phi_i = \phi$ has the same proposal value $v_i = v$, then every process p_j that sets $\phi_j = \phi + 1$ also sets $v_j = v$.*

Proof. The lemma is going to be proved by induction on the number of processes that reach phase $\phi + 1$. *Basis:* Without loss of generality, let p_1 be the first process that sets $\phi_1 = \phi + 1$. In this case, process p_1 must have received more than $\frac{n}{2}$ messages of the form $\langle \phi, *, * \rangle$ (Line 14). Since every process p_i with $\phi_i = \phi$ has the same value $v_i = v$, every broadcast message of the form $\langle \phi, *, * \rangle$ carries the same proposal value v (Line 6). This implies that the more than $\frac{n}{2}$ messages received by process p_1 have the form $\langle \phi, *, * \rangle$ with the same value v. Therefore, p_1 must set its proposal value to v (either on Line 17 or 26). *Inductive step:* Assume that every process p_u with $1 \leq u \leq j-1$ has $\phi_u = \phi + 1$ and $v_u = v$, and now we want to demonstrate that when p_j sets $\phi_j = \phi + 1$ it will also set $v_j = v$. In order for process p_j to set $\phi_j = \phi + 1$ it must have in vector V_j (1) more than $\frac{n}{2}$ messages of the form $\langle \phi, *, * \rangle$ (Line 14) or (2) at least a message of the form $\langle \phi + 1, *, * \rangle$ (Line 9). Condition (1) corresponds to the basis case, and therefore it has already been shown that p_j sets $v_j = v$. Condition (2) also results in the same outcome, since by hypothesis message $\langle \phi+1, *, * \rangle$ must have been transmitted by one of the p_u processes, and therefore p_j also sets $\phi_j = \phi+1$ and $v_j = v$ (Lines 10-11).   □

Lemma 2. *Let ϕ be some odd phase (i.e., $\phi \bmod 2 = 1$). If every process with phase value ϕ has the same proposal value v, then every process that sets its phase to any value $\phi' > \phi + 1$ decides v.*

Proof. Since every process with odd phase value ϕ has the same proposal value v, by Lemma 1, every process that reaches even phase $\phi + 1$ also has proposal value v (either on Lines 10-11 or Lines 17 and 31). Let p_i be the first process to set phase value $\phi_i = \phi + 2$. Since there is no other process p_j with phase value $\phi_j > \phi + 1$, the only way for p_i to go from phase $\phi + 1$ to $\phi + 2$ is to receive more than $\frac{n}{2}$ messages of the form $\langle \phi + 1, *, * \rangle$ (Line 14). Since $\phi + 1$ is even and all these messages carry the same proposal value v, this implies that p_i sets $status_i = decided$, $v_i = v$ and $\phi_i = \phi + 2$ (Lines 23, 26, 31). Consequently, process p_i can now decide v (Line 34).

  The next process that sets its phase value to $\phi + 2$ also decides v because it either accumulates more than $\frac{n}{2}$ messages with phase value $\phi + 1$ and same proposal value v (Lines 23, 26, 31 and 34), or receives a message from p_i of the form $\langle \phi + 2, v, decided \rangle$ (Lines 10-12 and 34). This reasoning can be applied recursively to any other process that sets its phase value to $\phi + 2$. It follows that any process that sets its phase value to $\phi' \geq \phi + 2$ must either had been at phase $\phi + 2$, and hence decided, or it must have received some message from a process that went through phase $\phi + 2$, and thus also deciding. Therefore, every process that sets its phase to any value $\phi' > \phi + 1$ decides v. □

Theorem 1. *If all processes propose the same value v, then every process that decides, decides v.*

Proof. If every process has the same initial proposal value v, then they all start in odd phase 1 and set proposal value to v (Lines 1-2). Therefore, by Lemma 1, every process p_j that sets phase $\phi_j = 2$ also has proposal value $v_j = v$. Moreover, by Lemma 2, every process p_i that sets its phase to $\phi_i > 2$, decides v. □

Lemma 3. *In some even phase ϕ, there are no two process p_i and p_j that receive messages of the form $\langle \phi, 0, * \rangle$ and $\langle \phi, 1, * \rangle$, respectively.*

Proof. Suppose otherwise. Then p_i and p_j are two processes with phase value ϕ that, respectively, receive a message $\langle \phi, 0, * \rangle$ from p_u and a message $\langle \phi, 1, * \rangle$ from p_w. This implies that process p_u sets $v_u = 0$ either because on odd phase $\phi - 1$ it accumulated more than $\frac{n}{2}$ messages of the form $\langle \phi - 1, 0, * \rangle$ (Lines 16-17, 31), or because it received a message $\langle \phi, 0, * \rangle$ (Lines 10-11) from a process that had accumulated that majority of $\langle \phi - 1, 0, * \rangle$ messages. Using a similar reasoning, in order for process p_w to set $v_w = 1$, some process must have received on odd phase $\phi - 1$ more than $\frac{n}{2}$ messages of the form $\langle \phi - 1, 1, * \rangle$. But this is a contradiction because only one of the proposal values 0 and 1 can be in a majority of the messages broadcast for any particular phase number. □

Theorem 2. *No two processes decide differently.*

Proof. Let p_i be the first process to decide, and do so when phase $\phi_i = \phi$ (Line 34). Without loss of generality, let the decision value be 1. Then, vector V_i must contain more than $\frac{n}{2}$ messages of the form $\langle \phi - 1, 1, undecided \rangle$, and $\phi - 1$ must be even (to allow the execution of Lines 23, 26, and 31). By Lemma 3, no other process p_j can receive a message of the form $\langle \phi - 1, 0, * \rangle$. Therefore, every other process p_j with phase $\phi_j = \phi$ has proposal value $v_j = 1$ either because it accumulates more than $\frac{n}{2}$ messages with at least one being of the form $\langle \phi - 1, 1, * \rangle$ (Line 26), or because it receives a message $\langle \phi, 1, * \rangle$ (Line 11) transmitted by process p_i (or another process that sets its proposal value to 1). Additionally, since all processes with phase ϕ have proposal value 1, then by Lemmas 1 and 2, every process that decides in phase $\phi' > \phi$ will do it for value 1. □

The remainder of the proof serves to prove the *termination* property of consensus (Theorem 3) and is made on the assumption that the message scheduling falls under the control of an adversary that can cause no more than f faults per round for $f \leq \lceil \frac{n}{2} \rceil (n - k) + k - 2$.

Lemma 4. *If some process p_i has some phase value $\phi_i > 1$, then there is a set of processes S such that $\forall_{p_j \in S} : \phi_j \geq \phi_i - 1$ and $|S| > \frac{n}{2}$.*

Proof. Given a phase number $\phi > 1$, then there must be some process p_i that is the first to set its phase to $\phi_i = \phi$. In order to do this, p_i must have more than $\frac{n}{2}$ messages of the form $\langle \phi - 1, *, * \rangle$ in vector V_i (Line 14). It follows that there are more than $\frac{n}{2}$ processes that were at some point in time in phase $\phi - 1$.   □

Lemma 5. *If some process p_i has phase value $\phi_i = \phi$, then eventually there is a set of processes S such that $\forall_{p_j \in S} : \phi_j \geq \phi - 1$ and $|S| \geq k$.*

Proof. Suppose otherwise. By Lemma 4, if some process p_i has $\phi_i = \phi > 1$, then there is a set of processes S such that $\forall_{p_j \in S} : \phi_j \geq \phi - 1$ and $|S| > \frac{n}{2}$. Let $R^+ = S$ where $\frac{n}{2} < |R^+| < k$, and R^- be the set of remaining processes, i.e., $\forall_{p_u \in R^-} : \phi_u < \phi - 1$ where $n - k < |R^-| < \frac{n}{2}$.

By assumption, the adversary can create at most $f = f_1 + f_2$ message omissions per round, where $f_1 = \lceil \frac{n}{2} \rceil (n - k)$ and $f_2 = k - 2$. In order to prevent processes in R^- from reaching $\phi_u \geq \phi - 1$, the adversary must omit every message from processes of R^+ to R^- (due to Lines 9-13). This implies the elimination of more than $\frac{n}{2}$ messages in more than $n - k$ processes because $|R^+| > \frac{n}{2}$ and $|R^-| > n - k$. It is clear that after consuming f_1 faults, there are at most $n - k$ processes in R^- that do not receive any message from R^+.

Since by definition $|R^-| - (n - k) = k - |R^+| > 0$, there must be $k - |R^+|$ processes in R^- that could still receive messages from every process in R^+. Let R_*^- denote the set of processes in this situation. To prevent every process p_u in R_*^- from reaching $\phi_u \geq \phi - 1$, the adversary must create $|R^+||R_*^-|$ omissions, where $|R^+| + |R_*^-| = k$. However, the adversary only has $f_2 = k - 2 = |R^+| + |R_*^-| - 2$ faults available. This creates a contradiction because $|R^+||R_*^-| > |R^+| + |R_*^-| - 2$, for all $|R^+| \geq 1$ and $|R_*^-| \geq 1$. This implies that some process in $|R^-|$ always increases its phase value when $\frac{n}{2} < |R^+| < k$.   □

Lemma 6. *Let R^+ be the set of processes such that $\forall_{p_i \in R^+} : \phi_i \geq \phi$, with $|R^+| = k + \alpha$ and $0 \leq \alpha \leq n - k$. Let α or more processes in R^+ have phase ϕ and the remaining processes of R^+ have phase $\phi + 1$. Let R^- be the set of process such that $\forall_{p_j \in R^-} : \phi_j < \phi$, with $|R^-| = n - k - \alpha$. Whenever a round has such configuration, some process increases its phase value.*

Proof. Suppose otherwise. Then, under the Lemma conditions, there must be a message schedule where at some round no process increases its phase value.

In order to prevent every process in R^- from increasing its phase value, the adversary must omit every message from R^+ to R^- (due to Lines 9-13). This requires that $|R^+||R^-|$ faults must be spent. Since $|R^+||R^-| = (k + \alpha)(n - k - \alpha)$ and the total number of omissions per round is $f = \lceil \frac{n}{2} \rceil (n - k) + k - 2$, then the adversary is left with no more than $f - |R^+||R^-| \leq (\alpha + \lceil \frac{n}{2} \rceil + k - n)\alpha + k - 2$ faults.

In order to block each of the α processes in R^+ with phase ϕ, the adversary must omit all messages from processes in R^+ with phase $\phi + 1$ (Line 9) and it must prevent the reception of more than $\frac{n}{2}$ messages of the form $\langle \phi, *, * \rangle$ also from processes in R^+ (Line 14). This implies that each of the α processes with phase ϕ can receive the $n - k - \alpha$ messages from processes in R^- and at most

$\lfloor \frac{n}{2} \rfloor$ messages from processes in R^+. Therefore, the adversary must create at least $\left[n - (\lfloor \frac{n}{2} \rfloor + n - k - \alpha) \right] \alpha$ faults to stop the progression of the α processes. Since $\left[n - (\lfloor \frac{n}{2} \rfloor + n - k - \alpha) \right] \alpha = (\alpha + \lceil \frac{n}{2} \rceil + k - n)\alpha$, the adversary is left with no more than $k - 2$ faults.

For the remaining k processes in R^+, there are two possible cases:

1. First consider the two extreme situations, where all k processes either have phase value ϕ or $\phi + 1$. Since the adversary only has $k - 2$ faults left, some process has to receive more than $\frac{n}{2}$ messages with the same phase ϕ or $\phi + 1$. Therefore, some process increases its phase value (Line 14).
2. Second consider that some of the k processes have phase value $\phi + 1$ and the others have phase value ϕ. Let H be the set of processes with $\phi + 1$ and L the set of processes with ϕ, such that $|H| + |L| = k$. To block the processes in L, the adversary has to omit $|H|\|L|$ messages (due to Line 9). Since the adversary only has $k - 2 = |H| + |L| - 2$ faults left, it cannot prevent some process from increasing its phase because $|H|\|L| > |H| + |L| - 2$ for all $|H| \geq 1$ and $|L| \geq 1$.   □

Lemma 7. *Let $\phi_{init} = 1$ be the initial phase value for all processes. Some process p_i eventually sets $\phi_i > \phi_{init}$.*

Proof. If every process has the same phase value ϕ_{init}, then according to the conditions of Lemma 6, this is equivalent of having every process in set R^+ with phase ϕ_{init}, such that $|R^+| = n$. Therefore, by Lemma 6, some process has to increase its phase value and set $\phi_i > \phi_{init}$.   □

Lemma 8. *If some process has phase value ϕ, then eventually some process must have phase value $\phi + 1$.*

Proof. If some process has phase value ϕ, then by Lemma 5, eventually there is a set R^+ of k or more processes such that $\forall_{p_i \in R^+} : \phi_i \geq \phi - 1$. This implies that the system must reach a configuration where there are two sets of processes R^+ and R^- according to the conditions of Lemma 6. When this happens, by the same Lemma, some process will increase its phase. This process can be in one of three possible cases: (1) a process of R^-; (2) a process with phase number $\phi - 1$ of R^+; or (3) a process with phase number ϕ of R^+. The system configuration resulting from cases (1) and (2) falls under the conditions of Lemma 6, and therefore more processes will continue to increase their phase. Consequently, in the most extreme scenario, the system will evolve to a configuration where all process are in phase number ϕ, and case (3) will necessarily have to occur, and some process p_i will set its phase number to $\phi_i = \phi + 1$.   □

Theorem 3. *At least k processes eventually decide with probability 1.*

Proof. The proof is organized in two parts. First, we show that as messages are received, processes make progress on the protocol execution and continue to increase their phase number. Second, we demonstrate that due to this progression, eventually the system will reach to a configuration where at least k processes decide with probability 1.

First part: By Lemma 7, some process p_i eventually increases its phase number from the initial phase number, i.e., $\phi_i = \phi > \phi_{init}$. Then, by Lemma 8, some process will eventually set its phase number to $\phi + 1$. Moreover, by Lemma 5, k or more processes set their phase value to at least ϕ. Since these Lemmas can be applied repeatedly, this ensures that at least a set of k processes continue to increase their phase numbers.

Second part: By Lemma 3, no two processes with the same even phase value ϕ can receive messages $\langle \phi, 0, * \rangle$ and $\langle \phi, 1, * \rangle$. Therefore, any process p_i that enters the **if** condition of Line 14, and sets $\phi_i = \phi + 1$ (Line 31), must set its proposal value v_i either to a common value v (Line 26) or to a random value 1 or 0 (Lines 28). Let S be the processes that eventually reach phase value $\phi + 1$, with $|S| \geq k$ due to the above discussion. Then, at least k processes in S will set their proposal values to the same v with probability $p = 2^{-k}$. Therefore, the probability that k processes do not set the same proposal value v is $(1 - p)$.

As the protocol progresses, and the phase number of processes increases, the probability of not existing a phase where k processes propose the same value v is $\lim_{\phi \to \infty} (1 - p)^{\phi} = 0$. Thus, eventually there will be a phase ϕ_t where k processes have the same proposal value v with probability 1. According to Lemma 2, every process that sets its phase value to $\phi > \phi_t$ decides v. Consequently, at least k processes decide. □

7 Performance

The algorithm guarantees the termination property of consensus in a probabilistic fashion. Since the execution of the algorithm may need to extend for any number of rounds and any process may reach an arbitrarily high phase, eventually there will be a phase where all processes flip the same coin value v and decide (Theorem 3). The number of expected rounds for this to happen is $O(2^n)$ after the system stabilizes in at most f faults per round. Note that this is the most extreme possible scenario. In fact, the presence of an adversary that enforces a worst-case scheduling is very unlikely to happen in practice [19,20]. A simple inspection of the protocol suffices to observe that the algorithm is fast-learning, i.e., it decides within two communication rounds in runs with no faults or with certain fault patterns. This is true even if processes have different initial proposal values. As long as the fault distribution is benign enough, k processes will see the majority of one value during the first phase, propose the same value for the second phase and decide.

8 Conclusions

Despite its usefulness to represent wireless ad-hoc communication environments, research on the communication failure model has been limited. This is related to an associated impossibility result, which states that no agreement is possible in a synchronous system if at every communication round more than $n - 2$ messages can be lost [28,27]. This paper presents a k-*consensus* algorithm tolerant to transmission omission faults, the first to circumvent the Santoro-Widmayer impossibility result using randomization. In a system with n processes, our algorithm makes consensus possible among $k > \frac{n}{2}$ processes. It maintains safety despite an unrestricted number of faults and ensures liveness if the number of omission faults does not exceed $\lceil \frac{n}{2} \rceil (n - k) + k - 2$. Furthermore, the algorithm can be fast learning in the sense that it terminates in two communication steps under favorable conditions.

References

1. Aguilera, M., Chen, W., Toueg, S.: Failure detection and consensus in the crash-recovery model. Distributed Computing 13(2), 99–125 (2000)
2. Akkoyunlu, E.A., Ekanadham, K., Huber, R.V.: Some constraints and tradeoffs in the design of network communications. In: Proceedings of the 5th ACM Symposium on Operating Systems Principles, pp. 67–74 (1975)
3. Ben-Or, M.: Another advantage of free choice: Completely asynchronous agreement protocols. In: Proceedings of the 2nd ACM Symposium on Principles of Distributed Computing, pp. 27–30 (1983)
4. Biely, M., Widder, J., Charron-Bost, B., Gaillard, A., Hutle, M., Schiper, A.: Tolerating corrupted communication. In: Proceedings of the 26th ACM Symposium on Principles of Distributed Computing, pp. 244–253 (2007)
5. Bracha, G.: An asynchronous $\lfloor (n - 1)/3 \rfloor$-resilient consensus protocol. In: Proceedings of the 3rd ACM Symposium on Principles of Distributed Computing, pp. 154–162 (1984)
6. Cachin, C., Kursawe, K., Shoup, V.: Random oracles in Constantinople: Practical asynchronous Byzantine agreement using cryptography. Journal of Cryptology 18(3), 219–246 (2005)
7. Chandra, T., Toueg, S.: Unreliable failure detectors for reliable distributed systems. Journal of the ACM 43(2), 225–267 (1996)
8. Charron-Bost, B., Schiper, A.: The heard-of model: Computing in distributed systems with benign failures. Technical Report LSR-REPORT-2007-001, EPFL (2007)
9. Chockler, G., Demirbas, M., Gilbert, S., Lynch, N., Newport, C., Nolte, T.: Consensus and collision detectors in radio networks. Distributed Computing 21(1), 55–84 (2008)
10. Dolev, D., Dwork, C., Stockmeyer, L.: On the minimal synchronism needed for distributed consensus. Journal of the ACM 34(1), 77–97 (1987)
11. Dolev, D., Friedman, R., Keidar, I., Malkhi, D.: Failure detectors in omission failure environments. In: Proceedings of the 16th ACM Symposium on Principles of Distributed Computing, pp. 286–295 (1997)
12. Fischer, M.J.: The consensus problem in unreliable distributed systems (A brief survey). In: Karpinski, M. (ed.) FCT 1983. LNCS, vol. 158, pp. 127–140. Springer, Heidelberg (1983)
13. Fischer, M.J., Lynch, N.A., Paterson, M.S.: Impossibility of distributed consensus with one faulty process. Journal of the ACM 32(2), 374–382 (1985)

14. Gray, J.: Notes on data base operating systems. In: Bayer, R., Graham, R.M., Seegmüller, G. (eds.) Operating Systems. LNCS, vol. 60. Springer, Heidelberg (1978)
15. Hurfin, M., Mostefaoui, A., Raynal, M.: Consensus in asynchronous systems where processes can crash and recover. In: Proceedings of the the 17th IEEE Symposium on Reliable Distributed Systems, pp. 280–286 (1998)
16. Lamport, L.: Lower bounds for asynchronous consensus. Distributed Computing 19(2), 104–125 (2006)
17. Lamport, L., Shostak, R., Pease, M.: The Byzantine generals problem. ACM Transactions on Programming Languages and Systems 4(3), 382–401 (1982)
18. Lynch, N.A.: Distributed Algorithms. Morgan Kaufmann, San Francisco (1997)
19. Moniz, H., Neves, N.F., Correia, M., Veríssimo, P.: Experimental comparison of local and shared coin randomized consensus protocols. In: Proceedings of the 25th IEEE Symposium on Reliable Distributed Systems, pp. 235–244 (2006)
20. Moniz, H., Neves, N.F., Correia, M., Veríssimo, P.: RITAS: Services for randomized intrusion tolerance. In: IEEE Transactions on Dependable and Secure Computing (to appear, 2009)
21. Neves, N.F., Correia, M., Veríssimo, P.: Solving vector consensus with a wormhole. IEEE Transactions on Parallel and Distributed Systems 16(12), 1120–1131 (2005)
22. Oliveira, R., Guerraoui, R., Schiper, A.: Consensus in the crash-recover model. Technical Report 97-239, EPFL (1997)
23. Pease, M., Shostak, R., Lamport, L.: Reaching agreement in the presence of faults. Journal of the ACM 27(2), 228–234 (1980)
24. Perry, K.J., Toueg, S.: Distributed agreement in the presence of processor and communication faults. IEEE Transactions on Software Engineering 12(3), 477–482 (1986)
25. Rabin, M.O.: Randomized Byzantine generals. In: Proceedings of the 24th Annual IEEE Symposium on Foundations of Computer Science, pp. 403–409 (1983)
26. Raynal, M., Roy, M.: A note on a simple equivalence between round-based synchronous and asynchronous models. In: Proceedings of the 11th IEEE Pacific Rim International Symposium on Dependable Computing, pp. 387–392 (2005)
27. Santoro, N., Widmayer, P.: Agreement in synchronous networks with ubiquitous faults. Theoretical Computer Science 384(2-3), 232–249 (2007)
28. Santoro, N., Widmayer, P.: Time is not a healer. In: Proceedings of the 6th Symposium on Theoretical Aspects of Computer Science, pp. 304–313 (1989)
29. Schmid, U., Weiss, B., Keidar, I.: Impossibility results and lower bounds for consensus under link failures. SIAM Journal on Computing 38(5), 1912–1951 (2009)
30. Varghese, G., Lynch, N.A.: A tradeoff between safety and liveness for randomized coordinated attack. Information and Computation 128(1), 57–71 (1996)

Interrupting Snapshots and the Java™ Size() Method

Yehuda Afek[1], Nir Shavit[1,2], and Moran Tzafrir[1]

[1] Tel-Aviv University, Tel-Aviv, Israel
[2] Sun Microsystems, Burlington, MA

Abstract. The Java™ developers kit requires a `size()` operation for all objects. Unfortunately, the best known solution, available in the Java concurrency package, has a blocking concurrent implementation that does not scale. This paper presents a highly scalable wait-free implementation of a concurrent `size()` operation based on a new lock-free *interrupting snapshots* algorithm for the classical atomic snapshot problem. This is perhaps the first example of the potential benefit from using atomic snapshots in real industrial code (the concurrency package is currently deployed on over 10 million desktops).

The key idea behind the new algorithm is to allow snapshot scans to interrupt each other until they agree on a shared linearization point with respect to updates, rather than trying, as was done in the past, to have them coordinate the collecting of a shared global view. As we show, the new algorithm scales well, significantly outperforming existing implementations.

Keywords: atomic, consistent state, fault-tolerance, snapshot, global state.

1 Introduction

The Java developers kit requires a `size()` operation, counting the number of elements in the data structure, to be made available for all objects. Accordingly, the Java concurrency package (currently deployed on over 10 million desktops), includes a concurrent implementation of the `size()` operation. Unfortunately, this implementation has two problems: (a) it is *blocking*, so non-blocking structures such as the ConcurrentSkipListMap, unfortunately have a blocking `size()` operation during which other operations on the structure are delayed, and (b) if all modifying operations update the size, the implementation simply does not scale. To allow scalability one must update infrequently and accordingly relax the specification so that `size()` is only *an approximation* of the actual data structure size.

This paper overcomes the above limitations, presenting a wait-free, linearizable, and highly scalable implementation of the Java `size()` operation that can be added seamlessly to any concurrent data structure. Our solution is based on a new *interrupting snapshots* algorithm for the classical atomic snapshots problem [1,2].

I. Keidar (Ed.): DISC 2009, LNCS 5805, pp. 78–92, 2009.
© Springer-Verlag Berlin Heidelberg 2009

1.1 Atomic Snapshots

To implement a scalable size counter, the frequent operations that update size must have a very low overhead, and the burden of the implementation should be placed on the relatively infrequent calls to size (). One solution that immediately pops to mind is to use localized individual counters, one for each of the n threads, to track changes to the structure. One can then use an atomic snapshot operation [1,2] to collect an instantaneous coherent view of all the individual counters.

An atomic snapshot object has two operations, an update() that writes to its given location and a scan() that collects a view of all locations. Unfortunately, a straightforward application of the above approach will not work.

The approach taken by the Java concurrency package is to attempt a scan() using a double collect in the style of [1], that is, make several passes over all counters, hoping to detect no intervening update() between some pair of them. However, since such intervening updates are quite likely, the scan() in the Java concurrency package defaults to locking all counters in order to guarantee a valid snapshot. This results in rather poor non-scalable performance.

The classical wait-free read-write register-based snapshot algorithms such as [1,2,3] also do not provide a solution since they have an $O(n)$ and higher update complexity even when contention is low (see [4] for a survey).

The only practical non-blocking algorithm with an $O(1)$ common case update complexity is the coordinated collect algorithm of Riany et. al [4]. However, it requires $O(n)$ costly read-modify-write operations (such as compare-and-swap (CAS)) to shared locations to coordinate the collection of a shared snapshot view. To implement a scalable size() operation, we must therefore devise a new type of snapshot algorithm, one that uses a small number of CAS operations to collect the snapshot view.

1.2 Interrupting Snapshots in a Nutshell

Our quest for an algorithm begins with an implementation of a new lock-free snapshot algorithm. As a basis, we start out with the single scanner algorithm of Riany et. al [4] which is in turn based on the single scanner algorithm of [5]. This single scanner algorithm uses an array of $2n$ entries, a recent and a previous entry per thread, and a *scan sequence number* incremented by the single scanner at the start of every scan (the structure is depicted in part (a) of Fig. 1). The recent and previous values are tagged with a scan sequence number. Updaters start by reading the scan counter and then update the recent field as long as the field's sequence number is the same as the counter value they read. Upon detecting a newer scan counter value, the updater performs a "copy on write", it copies the recent field to the previous field before writing the new value into recent. To collect a snapshot, the single scanner, increments the scan counter. It then traverses the array, collecting, for every location, the recent value if the sequence number is less than the scan's sequence number, and the previous value if the recent sequence number is equal to the scan's number (because there is a single scanner it cannot be greater). The collection of values forms a snapshot

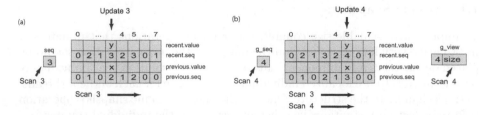

Fig. 1. Sample executions of the algorithm. Part (a) describes an execution of the single scanner algorithm. A scan increments the global sequence number g_seq to 3, then while it collects its view an updater with value y reads this new global sequence number. It must therefor copy its old value x from recent to previous and update its recent field to y with sequence 3. When the scan reads this recent field it will see that its seq is 3, so it started after the scan, and will therefore use the previous value x. In part (b) we see a wait-free algorithm with the seq number now shared among scans. A scan of seq 3 is concurrent with a scan with seq 4, and an updater thread reads 4, updates its recent field to a new value y with sequence 4. When the scan with seq 3 reads this recent field it will see that its seq 4 is greater than 3 and will be forced to retry the scan. Even if it misses this update and completes collecting values, it will be forced to retry when it finally checks that the global sequence number has remained 3. It will perform the retry with a value of 4, unless when it checks the g_view field it finds that the scan with 4 has updated the view, in which case it adopts and returns this new view.

because the counter increment is a linearization point for the scan: any update that starts after this point will not be collected as we will always collect the latest previous value.

To make this algorithm support multiple scanners, one cannot simply have all scanners increment a shared sequence counter using a CAS operation because different scanners can collect old and new values forming inconsistent views. Riany et. al [4] solved the problem by having threads coordinate the collection of a single shared snapshot view, a process which unfortunately entails using n CAS operations even in the uncontended case.

The key to our new *interrupting snapshots* algorithm is to avoid collecting a shared view. As we noted, we start by describing a lock-free implementation, and then turn it into a wait-free one. Instead of collecting a shared view, our algorithm allows scanners to interrupt each other, forcing a retry of the scan. We add a new shared g_view field that contains the sequence number of the last successful scanner. Each scanner begins by incrementing the shared scan counter g_seq using a CAS (this is done per scan, not per update). It next collects its own snapshot view, checking to see that there are no updated fields with a sequence number greater than its own. If there are such sequence numbers, then clearly a later scan has started concurrently (See the example in part (a) of Fig. 1). If a scan does complete the collection of values, it checks to see that the shared g_seq counter still contains its own sequence number, and if this number has changed, it again was interrupted. Our idea then is to have the interrupted scan retry collecting its snapshot again. However, this time it *does not* increment the shared g_seq counter. Instead, it uses the sequence number of the scan that interrupted it. This way, if no scan succeeds, then eventually all scans agree on the same sequence number and no longer interrupt each other. The final step in our algorithm is that each scan that successfully collected a view tries to be the next successful scan by increasing the g_view field to its sequence number. If it detects that the g_view field already has a higher value, then it has failed and restarts from the beginning, incrementing the g_seq etc.

How does this help us in collecting a lock-free scan? Well, as we prove, every time a scanner is interrupted it must be because it has seen a sequence number of a later scan, and it adopts this scan's number. After at most $n - 1$ threads have all started a scan, if none of them succeed they will all eventually agree on the highest sequence number. They will all collect a view and one of them will succeed in CASing g_view to the new sequence number and complete the scan. Thus, the only way in which new sequence numbers can be continuously generated and prevent a scanner from completing is if at least one scan successfully completed and increased the g_view field, implying that scans are lock-free.

We can now extend the lock-free interrupting snapshot to implement a wait-free size() implementation in a straightforward fashion. As in Fig. 1, we add to g_view a field that contains the snapshot view (in our case an integer representing the collected size) of the last successfully completed scan, and as before, it also contains its sequence number. Successful scans CAS both their sequence number and the view they collected into this location. If a thread is interrupted while performing its lock-free interrupting scan, it checks to see if the g_view field has a sequence greater than its own, that is, it contains a size value collected by some interrupting scan that has started after it did. If it finds one then it can safely return that size. Otherwise, it continues in the lock-free collection attempt. The algorithm is wait-free because either a scanner is eventually not interrupted and completes a scan, or it must be that there are other successful scans continuously interrupting it, implying that it can return the size collected by one of them. Notice that we expect size method calls, and therefore scans, to be relatively infrequent, so overflow should not be a practical concern.

Our new wait-free size() algorithm thus has a "take the view of some thread that interrupted you" flavor of former algorithms such as [1], but unlike these algorithms, the interruptions are between scans, not between scans and updates, which is the key to the new algorithm's efficiency.

1.3 Benefits of the New Algorithm

As we prove, unlike existing solutions, our new size algorithm is wait-free, linearizable, and has an update() operation that in the uncontended case requires only a couple of loads and one store and a scan() operation that requires $O(n)$ loads and two CAS operations. We show that it can be added to any data structure to provide a linearizable size() implementation.

We also note that the wait-free size() implementation we presented can be extended to allow a general scalable wait-free snapshot implementation with a view larger than a single word (in the case of size() we use the fact that the view is contained in a single word to transform the lock-free snapshot scan() to a wait-free size().[1]

In the performance section we compare our new wait-free size() implementation to the one offered by the Java concurrency package as well as one implemented using the practical snapshot algorithm of Riany et. al. [4]. Our benchmarking was performed on two state-of-the-art multiprocessor machines: an Azul Vega2 (7200 series) distributed shared memory with up to 768 processors and a Sun Maramba 128-way multicore machine. As can be seen, our algorithm shows impressive scalability while the other algorithms simply do not scale.

In summary, the strong progress and coherence properties combined with high scalability of the new algorithm lead us to suggest that it is a good candidate for replacing the current size operation in the Java concurrency package. It is perhaps satisfying that a theoretically motivated data structure, the atomic snapshot object, introduced in the late 80s [1,2], can finally find real-world applicability.

2   The Algorithm

Our computation model and specification of atomic snapshots follows [1,4], with the small exception of replacing load-linked/store conditional operations (LLSC) by compare-and-swap (CAS) operations.

Following [1] an atomic snapshot object provides two methods, update() and scan(), with the usual semantics.

Section 1.2 provided a high level view of our new algorithm. Here we provide a more detailed walk through the pseudo-code. As we did earlier, we start by describing our lock-free *interrupting snapshots* algorithm, and then modify it into a wait-free size method. The main difference between a size() method and an atomic snapshot is that to store a full snapshot we need an array of values, while for size, one integer word is enough.

The pseudo-code of the lock-free snapshot algorithm is provided in Fig. 2. Each updater maintains two values, recent and previous, each with an associated sequence number which is the value the updater observed in the global-counter just before updating this value. The two values together are stored in a **struct** called Data (Line 2). The data of thread i is in g_mem[i]. To keep track of which value belongs to which snapshot, we maintain a global g_seq counter, which each scanner atomically fetches and increments when it starts the scan, and each updater reads before writing a new value. Each scan is identified by the sequence number it obtained in this atomic fetch and increment at the beginning of the scan. The scanner obtains a snapshot by reading from the updater's locations in Lines 20 to 33. The point in time where the scanner increments g_seq is a "line in the sand": all updates starting after this point are ignored, and those before it can be part of the snapshot.

---

[1] The most straightforward practical way to do this is to have a scanner allocate a structure in which its view is collected and use the CASable shared location to store a reference to this structure.

```
1    struct    view  { view [1],  view [2],  ... ,  view[n]  };
2    struct    Data { int _value,  _seq;  }; //a pair <value; seq_number>
3    struct    Thread {
4              Data _recent;
5              Data _previous; };
6    int       g_seq;          //global snapshot sequence(counter)
7    Thread*   g_mem;          //array of Thread struct, with an entry for each thread
8    int       g_view_seq; //holds the latest global view seq#
9
10   method wait_free_update(i, new_value)
11     if(g_seq != g_mem[i]._recent._seq) { g_mem[i]._previous := g_mem[i]._recent; }
12     g_mem[i]._recent := {new_value, g_seq};
13
14   method lock_free_scan()
15       start_view_seq := g_view_seq;
16       scan_seq :=AtomicFetchAndInc(g_seq);
17   do
18          n_scan := view[1,...n];
19          scan_ok := true;
20          for (i := 0;  i < N; ++i) {
21              recent := g_mem[i]._recent;
22              previous := g_mem[i]._previous;
23              if (recent._seq < scan_seq) {
24                  n_scan[i] := recent._value;
25              } else if (previous._seq < scan_seq) {
26                  n_scan[i] := previous._value;
27              } else {
28                  scan_ok := false;
29                  start_view_seq := g_view_seq;
30                  scan_seq := g_seq;
31                  break;
32              }
33          } //end for
34          if (scan_ok) {
35              if (CAS (g_view_seq, start_view_seq, scan_seq))
36                  return n_scan;
37              start_view_seq := g_view_seq;
38              scan_seq := g_seq;
39          }
40          if (scan_seq ≤ start_view_seq)
41              scan_seq := AtomicFetchAndInc(g_seq);
42   while (true);
```

Fig. 2. The lock-free *interrupting snapshots* algorithm

Consider a read from the j-th location. If thread j's recent sequence number is smaller than the scanner's sequence number, then clearly the value that thread j had in its recent field (associated with the read sequence number) was its valid value at the time that the scanner performed its increment of g_seq. The scanner thus adds this value into the snapshot view (Line 24). If thread j's recent number was equal the scanner's sequence number, then the scanner adds j's previous value into the snapshot view. If however, thread j's recent sequence number is greater than the scan's sequence number, then the scanner has been interrupted by a later scanning thread. In this case the scanner starts a new attempt to collect a snapshot, this time adopting the higher number of the interrupting scanner (Line 38). The CAS in Line 35 ensures the linearization of the scan method, by checking that no scan operation completed during its associated interval. To see why the algorithm is lock-free, notice that if no scanner succeeds, the scanners continue to execute forever, and the highest sequence number scanner must eventually succeed or a new scanner must have joined in. But the number of scanners is bounded so the algorithm is lock-free.

A scanner that succeeds cannot just return the scan it obtained, because it may not be linearized with other successful and concurrent scans. To this end we add a global view location g_view_seq storing the sequence number of the most recent scan that successfully collected a view. In effect we guarantee that at any point of time there is (in retrospect) only one scan that is going to succeed. A scan will complete and return if it can successfully CAS its sequence number into the g_view_seq (Line 35) replacing the global view sequence number it has seen just before starting its most recent scan attempt. This is also the motivation of the CAS: to ensure linearizability by maintaining the invariant that at any point in time, there is in effect only one uninterrupted scan that is going to succeed.

The wait-free update() for thread i is described in Fig. 3. A thread i starts in Line 8 by checking if there might be a concurrent scan() method that requires the current recent value (e.g the current g_seq is larger than recent's sequence number). If such a scan() potentially exists, we copy thread i's recent value to its previous one (Line 8). Then, in Line 9, thread i updates its associated location to the new_value tagged with the current g_seq value.

The wait-free size () is described in Fig. 3. It is a modification of the lock-free code presented above. The key to turning the above lock-free snapshot algorithm into a wait-free size () algorithm, is that either a scanner succeeds in the lock-free scan attempt, or it is interrupted by another scan with a higher sequence number. Since such repeated failures can only happen if some thread continuously succeeds, then if each interrupted scanner checks the g_view, it will eventually observe a value with a larger sequence number than its own in g_view. It can safely adopt the size stored in this view, because the execution interval of the scan of the interrupting thread started after its own.

In more detail, a thread i starts in Line 13 by assigning to start_view the global-view g_view. It then atomically increments the global g_view._seq, and assigns the new sequence to scan_seq. It keeps in first_seq the initial scan_seq, used to detect when the scan() started. The for-loop in Line 19 starts the snapshot, and in each iteration the scanning thread tries to get some thread i's value with sequence $<$ scan_seq. In Line 23 it adds thread i's recent._value to the sum, since recent._value was updated before this scan(). In Line 25, the scanning thread sums thread i's previous._value, since recent._value was updated before this

```
1   struct    Data { int _value, _seq ; }; //a pair <value; seq_number>
2   struct    Thread { Data _recent; Data _previous; };
3   int       g_seq;   //global snapshot sequence(counter)
4   Thread*   g_mem; //array of Thread struct, with an entry for each thread
5   Data      g_view; //holds the latest size result with its associated seq#
6
7   method wait_free_update(i, new_value) //threads count locally the new value.
8       if(g_seq != g_mem[i]._recent._seq) { g_mem[i]._previous := g_mem[i]._recent;}
9       g_mem[i]._recent := { new_value, g_seq};
10
11  method wait_free_size()
12      smart backoff;
13      start_view := g_view;
14      scan_seq   := AtomicFetchAndInc(g_seq);
15      first_seq  := scan_seq;
16      do
17          size := 0;
18          scan_ok := true;
19          for (i := 0; i < N; ++i) {
20              recent := g_mem[i]._recent;
21              previous := g_mem[i]._previous;
22              if (recent._seq < scan_seq) {
23                  size += recent._value;
24              } else if (previous._seq < scan_seq) {
25                  size += previous._value;
26              } else { scan_ok := false;
27                       start_view := g_view;
28                       scan_seq := g_seq;
29                       break; }
30          } //end for
31          if ( first_seq ≤ (g_view._seq)) {
32              return (g_view._value); }
33          if (scan_ok) {
34              if (CAS (g_view, start_view, [scan_seq, size ]))
35                  return size;
36              start_view := g_view;
37              scan_seq := g_seq;
38          }
39      while (true);
```

Fig. 3. The wait-free size () algorithm

scan(). When the scanner exits the for-loop, either the snapshot succeed or it failed (e.g.scan_ok is true or false). Regardless of the outcome, in Line 31, the scanner checks if the global g_view has higher sequence than first_seq . If it does, the scanner returns the size field of the global g_view. If the snapshot succeed (Line 34), the thread tries to substitute its *new-view* with g_view using a CAS. If it succeeds, it can return size , but if it failed to commit its *new-view*, the scan() attempt fails, and it starts over.

2.1 Using the Size Object

To use our wait-free size() object with any linearizable object that has modifying methods, one adds the update() method as the last operation in the modifying method.

For example the JDK's *ConcurrentHashMap*, there is a local counter per segment of the table, where segment access is lock protected. The JDK's size() makes two attempts at a successful "double collect" in the style of [1] . If it does not succeed, it locks all segments and counts the size.

To use our wait-free size() solution, we simply add the new size object to the JDK's ConcurrentHashMap, and initialize its number of threads to the number of threads in the system (i.e., the concurrency level in the JDK). Then we replace the JDK's size() method with a call to wait_free_size (). The add() remove() methods for a given segment call the wait_free_update () and no other changed were required as each thread maintains locally the total number of keys in the table that it inserted.

3 Performance Evaluation

To test our new approach, we implemented the size() method of the of the original JDK's *ConcurrentHashMap* using four different algorithms. The first is *JDK*, the original JDK ConcurrentHashMap with the blocking size(). The second, *NWF*, is our new wait-free implementation of size(). The third, *NLF*, is our implementation of size() based on the lock-free snapshot. The fourth, *RST*, is an implementation of size using the *coordinated collect* snapshot algorithm of [4].

We tested the *ConcurrentHashMap* implementations on two architectures. The first was a 128-way Sun UltraSPARC® T2 Plus multicore machine running Solaris™ 10. It has two eight-core 1.2GHz processors and up to 256GB of memory. The second is an Azul Vega2® Java-machine, the 7200 series contains up to 768 processing cores on 16 processor chips with 768GB of memory. We did not test the algorithms on Intel or AMD systems because we only had access to machines with limited (8-way) concurrency. On such machines we can report that we found little scalability differences between the algorithms.

Evaluations were performed with micro-benchmarks similar to those used by [4]. The add() (add a key) and remove() (remove a key) perform update()s and the scan() method is the equivalent of size() (get the number of keys). The contain() typical to hash tables has no effect on the size(). In our benchmarks we measured throughput: the number of successful methods completed per millisecond. Each point in the graphs, is an average of 5 samples. We used only 1 million keys to eliminate overheads related to hash table resizing.

3.1 Benchmark I: Mixed Methods Per Thread

In this benchmark we assigned to each thread a predefined mixture of method calls, where the relative fraction of calls is equal for all threads.

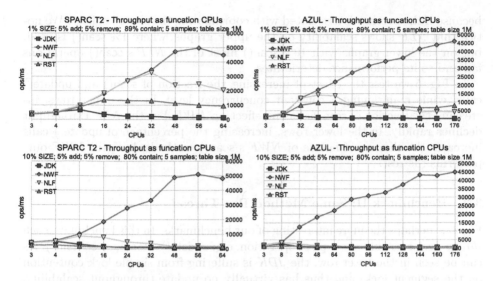

Fig. 4. Benchmark I: (i) in the upper row throughput as a function of concurrency with 1% Scans and (ii) in the lower row with 10% Scans

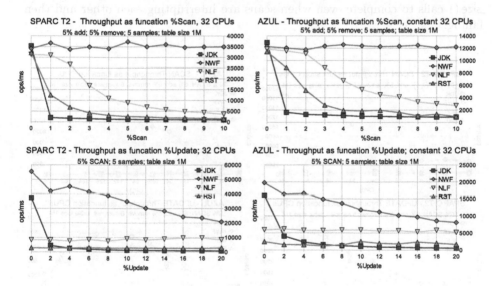

Fig. 5. Benchmark I: (i) in the upper row throughput of a mix of operations, as function of the % of Scans and (ii) in the lower row as function of % of Updates

In Fig. 4, one can see that on both machines the algorithms show similar behavior. Our *NWF* implementation scales nicely on both architectures. On the other hand, the *JDK* and *RST* schemes do not scale at all because *JDK* essentially ends up locking the structure repeatedly, and *RST* gives similar behavior because if the overheads associated with coordinating the shared collect. We notice that *NLF* shows scalability on the upper graphs, where 1% scan() is used, but on the lower graphs with 10% scan() most of the *NLF*'s scan() operations fail and so its performance deteriorates.

In Fig. 5 we test the effect of increasing the fraction of scan() and update() calls, while maintaining a constant concurrency level. In the upper rows, increasing the fraction of scan()s has no effect on *NWF*, but the *NLF* throughput declines rapidly. In the lower rows, increasing the percentage of update() calls increases the chances of failure of *NWF*'s scan() methods, but still *NWF* outperforms the rest.

3.2   Benchmark II: Same Method Per Thread

Fig. 6 is perhaps the more interesting of our benchmarks. In this benchmark each *thread* performs only one type of operation, e.g. update(), scan(), or contain(). As can be seen in the lower row, the *JDK* is suffering from simple lock contention on the segment locks and thus has virtually no update throughput scalability. All the other algorithms have nice update throughput scalability. However, the successful updates are hurting the scan throughput. The only algorithm that scales is *NWF* because it adopts the view of interrupting scans which allows size() calls to complete even when scans are interrupting each other and then failing.

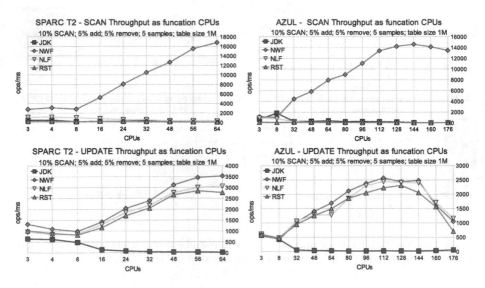

Fig. 6. Benchmark II: (i) in the upper row scan throughput as function of concurrency and (ii) in the lower row update throughput as function of concurrency

4   Correctness Proof

We provide a correctness proof for the wait-free version of the Interrupting Snapshots algorithm. We prove that the update() and scan() methods are wait-free and linearizable [6,7].

4.1   Model

Interrupting snapshots is an atomic snapshot object [1,2]. We use a shared-memory model similar to [4], allowing atomic reads and writes from memory together with CAS operations, together with method invocations and responses. Without loss of generality one can assume that all machine level operations in a given execution history can be totally ordered, and that method calls are sequences of such machine operations starting with an invocation and ending with a response.

4.2   Sequential Specification

The sequential specification of an Interrupting Snapshot object provides two kinds of methods for each thread i, $(0 \leq i \leq N - 1)$:

- A $update_i(d)$, invocation whose response is $ACK_i()$, where d is the input data of thread i.
- A $scan_i()$, an invocation whose response is $RETURN_i(V)$, where V is an N-element vector called a view.

A sequence of scan() and update() method calls is a valid execution of an interrupting snapshot if and only if, for each V returned by a given scan() method call, for all i, $V[i]$ equals d, the input parameter of the latest preceding $update_i(d)$ method call. If there is no preceding $update_i()$ method call, then $V[i]$ is the initial value.

4.3   Proof of Wait-Free Progress

Lemma 1. *The wait_free_update method completes within a bounded number of machine operations.*

Proof. From Figure 3 we can deduce that the execution ends after a constant number of instructions, regardless of any other scan() or update() method call.   □

Because g_seq is updated only in Line 14, it follows that

Lemma 2. *The g_seq's value is strictly increasing.*

Looking at Lines 23, 25, and 28, we can deduce that scan_seq is updated only to bigger values. It follows that

Lemma 3. *The values in the scan()'s local-variable scan_seq are strictly increasing.*

Lemma 4. *The* g_view's *sequence numbers in an execution are strictly increasing.*

Proof. Since scan_seq is strictly increasing, we know that first_seq $\leq$ scan_seq, and from Line 31, we deduce that the g_view sequence is updated only to larger values Line 34. □

Lemma 5. *The* wait_free_scan *method completes within a bounded number of machine instructions.*

Proof. Assume by way of contradiction that the method does not end after $N-1$ iterations of the for-loop. This implies that N times either the **else** in Line 26 was reached, or the **if** in Line 34 failed. Both imply that g_view changed, so by Lemma 4 we know that g_view 's sequence increased by at least one. But since there are only N threads, the difference between first_seq and g_view's sequence number is bounded by $N - 1$, so the **if** in Line 34 should have succeeded, a contradiction. □

The immediate conclusion from Lemma 1 and Lemma 5 is that

Theorem 1. *Both the* update() *and* scan() *method calls are wait-free.*

4.4 Linearizability Proof

An atomic snapshot object has the property that a scan() method call, which reads all the thread's data from g_mem, can be linearized (i.e. thought of as occurring at a single point within its execution interval).

Definition 1. *A successful-scan is a* scan() *method call that created new view (*g_view*), e.g. successfully executed the CAS in Line 34.*

We uniquely identify successful scan() method calls in a given execution using $scan_i^j$ to denote the j-th scan which happens to be executed by thread i.

Definition 2. g_view$_i^j$ *is the new view* V *with sequence number* g_view_seq$_i^j$ *that is returned by a successful* scan$_i^j$.

Theorem 2. *The interrupting snapshot object with its* update() *and* scan() *methods is linearizable to a sequential snapshot object.*

Proof. Let us linearize an update$_i(d)$ method call by a thread i at Line 9, which is the point of updating g_mem[i].recent to the new value d tagged with g_seq.

Let us also linearize a successful scan$_i^j$ at the point T_i^j in which g_seq is incremented using an AtomicFetchAndInc (Line 14) to g_view_seq$_i^j$. Notice that the AtomicFetchAndInc could have been executed by another thread. Let us linearize the unsuccessful scan$_i^j$ at the linearization point of the successful scan() whose view it returned. Let I_i^j be the execution interval of a scan$_i^j$ method call.

For a successful-scan we need to prove two things: (i) that T_i^j is in I_i^j, and that (ii) for all k, the value of g_view$_i^j[k]$ is the input d of the latest preceding update$_k(d)$ method call before T_i^j according to the updates linearization points.

Proof of (i): If scan$_i^j$ by thread i itself incremented g_seq to g_view_seq$_i^j$ in Line 14, then clearly T_i^j is in I_i^j. Otherwise, scan$_i^j$ assigned g_view_seq$_i^j$ (g_seq) to scan_seq) in Line 28 or 37. But, since the initial value of scan_seq is g_seq (Line 14), and since by Lemma 3 g_seq are strictly increasing, we know that T_i^j is in I_i^j.

Proof of (ii): Assume by way of contradiction the existence of a successful-scan, scan$_i^j$, that returned g_view$_i^j$ and for at least one index k, had g_view$_i^j[k]$ not equal the input of the latest preceding linearized update$_k(d)$ method call. There are two cases:

- g_view$_i^j[k]$ is equal to the input d of update$_k(d)$ that wrote to g_mem$[k]$ (Line 9) after T_i^j. This means that the seq number value the update$_k(d)$ wrote is greater than the value used by scan$_i^j$ because the scan uses g_view_seq$_i^j$, the g_seq before the AtomicFetchAndInc. In this case, the value of recent. _seq (Line 22) or previous. _seq (Line 24) must be greater than g_view_seq$_i^j$ (scan_seq). But then the values would not have been collected.

- g_view$_i^j[k]$ is equal to the input d of an update$_k(d)$ method call that is linearized *before* the latest preceding update$_k()$ before T_i^j. But this could not have happened because the scanning thread sets its g_view. _seq before it reads any location g_mem$[k]$. This value cannot be read from the recent field in g_mem$[k]$ because the latest linearized update was written to recent and recent is an atomic register. It could thus only be that it read the problematic value (that was earlier than the latest preceding update$_k()$ before T_i^j) from the previous field. However, for any update of g_mem$[k]$, previous is read and returned only if the sequence number of recent is greater than g_view. _seq (Line 9). We know that for any k, the value of the latest value written to the recent field must have been copied to the previous (Line 8) before a new value was written to recent (Line 9). Thus, the value of the latest preceding update$_k()$ before T_i^j must have been copied to previous before a value of an update$_k()$ with a sequence greater than g_view. _seq was written to recent. Since scan$_i^j$ first reads and tests recent, and only then reads previous (Line 22), and since both are atomic registers, it cannot be that a value earlier than the latest linearized update$_k()$ before T_i^j was read. A contradiction.

For an unsuccessful-scan scan$_i^j$ we need only show that the last sequence of reads of g_mem[k] by the successful scan, the ones whose view it returned, is completely within its execution interval. To see why this is true, notice that the scan$_i^j$ returns in Line 31 the view of another successful-scan whose sequence number is greater than or equal to the one the scan$_i^j$ started with initially. Thus, this successful scan must have started its sequence of reads of g_mem[k] after the start of scan$_i^j$ and it clearly ended this sequence before the end of scan$_i^j$.   □

Acknowledgments

We thank Dave Dice and Doug Lea for their help during the writing of this paper.

References

1. Afek, Y., Dolev, D., Attiya, H., Gafni, E., Merritt, M., Shavit, N.: Atomic snapshots of shared memory. In: PODC, pp. 1–13 (1990)
2. Anderson, J.H.: Multi-writer composite registers. Distrib. Comput. 7(4), 175–195 (1994)
3. Attiya, H., Rachman, O.: Atomic snapshots in o (n log n) operations. SIAM J. Comput. 27(2), 319–340 (1998)
4. Riany, Y., Shavit, N., Touitou, D.: Towards a practical snapshot algorithm. In: ISTCS, pp. 121–129 (1995)
5. Kirousis, L.M., Spirakis, P.G., Tsigas, P.: Simple atomic snapshots: A linear complexity solution with unbounded time-stamps. In: Dehne, F., Fiala, F., Koczkodaj, W.W. (eds.) ICCI 1991. LNCS, vol. 497, pp. 582–587. Springer, Heidelberg (1991)
6. Herlihy, M.: Wait-free synchronization. ACM Trans. Program. Lang. Syst. 13(1), 124–149 (1991)
7. Herlihy, M.P., Wing, J.M.: Linearizability: a correctness condition for concurrent objects. ACM Transactions on Programming Languages and Systems (TOPLAS) 12(3), 463–492 (1990)

Elastic Transactions*

Pascal Felber[1], Vincent Gramoli[1,2], and Rachid Guerraoui[2]

[1] University of Neuchâtel, Switzerland
[2] EPFL, Switzerland

Abstract. This paper presents *elastic transactions*, a variant of the transactional model. Upon conflict detection, an elastic transaction might drop what it did so far within a separate transaction that immediately commits, and initiate a new transaction which might itself be elastic. Elastic transactions are a complementary alternative to traditional transactions, particularly appealing when implementing search structures. Elastic transactions can be safely composed with normal ones, but significantly improve performance if used instead.

1 Introduction

Background. Transactional memory (TM) is an appealing synchronization paradigm for leveraging modern multicore architectures. The power of the paradigm lies in its abstract nature: no need to know the internals of shared object implementations, it suffices to delimit any critical sequence of shared object accesses using transactional boundaries. Not surprisingly, however, this abstraction sometimes severely hampers parallelism. This is particularly true for search data structures where a transaction do not know a priori where to add an element unless it explores a large part of the data structure. Consider for instance an integer set that supports search, insert, and remove operations. Assume furthermore that the set is implemented with a bucket hash table. A bucket, implemented with a sorted linked list, indicates where an integer should be stored. Consider a situation where one transaction searches for an integer whereas another one seeks to insert an integer after a node that has been read by the first transaction: in a strict sense, there is a read-write conflict, yet this is a false (search-insert) conflict.

We propose *elastic* transactions, a new type of transactions that enables to efficiently implement search data structures and use them with regular transactional applications. As for a regular transaction, the programmer must simply delimit the blocks of code that represent elastic transactions. Nevertheless, during its execution, an elastic transaction can be cut into multiple normal transactions, depending on the conflicts detected. We show that this model is very effective whenever operations parse a large part of the structure while their effective update is localized.

---

* This work was supported in part by the European Velox project (ICT-216852).

I. Keidar (Ed.): DISC 2009, LNCS 5805, pp. 93–107, 2009.

Elastic transactions: a primer. To give an intuition of the idea behind elastic transactions, consider again the integer set abstraction. Each of the insert, remove, and search operations consists of lower-level operations: some reads and possibly some writes. Consider an execution in which two transactions, i and j, try to insert keys 3 and 1 concurrently in the same linked list. Each insert transaction parses the nodes in ascending order up to the node before which they should insert their key. Let $\{2\}$ be the initial state of the integer set and let h, n, t denote respectively the memory locations where the head pointer, the single node (its key and next pointer) and the tail key are stored. Let $\mathcal{H}$ be the following resulting history of operations where transaction j inserts 1 while transaction i is parsing the data structure to insert 3 at its end. (In the following history examples we indicate only operations of non-aborting transactions, thus, commit events have been omitted for simplicity.)

$$\mathcal{H} = r(h)^i, r(n)^i, r(h)^j, r(n)^j, w(h)^j, r(t)^i, w(n)^i.$$

This history is clearly not serializable since there is no sequential history that allows $r(h)^i$ to occur before $w(h)^j$ and also $r(n)^j$ to occur before $w(n)^i$. A traditional transactional model would detect a conflict between transactions i and j, and the transactions could not both commit. Nonetheless, history $\mathcal{H}$ does not violate the high-level linearizability of the integer set: 1 appears to be inserted before 3 in the linked list and both are present at the end of the execution.

To make a transaction elastic, the programmer has simply to label this transaction as being so and use its associated operations to access the shared memory. Assume indeed that transaction i has been labelled as elastic. History $\mathcal{H}$ can now be viewed as a slightly different history, $f(\mathcal{H})$:

$$f(\mathcal{H}) = \boxed{r(h)^i, r(n)^i}^{s_1}, r(h)^j, r(n)^j, w(h)^j, \boxed{r(t)^i, w(n)^i}^{s_2}.$$

The elastic transaction i has been cut in two transactions s_1 and s_2, each being atomic. The cut is only possible because the value returned by the read of t has been the successor of n at some point in time. More precisely, the specific operations inside the elastic transaction ensure that no modifications on n and t have occurred between $r(n)^{s_1}$ and $r(t)^{s_2}$. Otherwise, i would have to abort.

Even though a read value has been freshly modified by another transaction, it might not be necessary to abort and restart from the beginning. Assume that a transaction i searches for a key that is not in the linked list while a transaction j is inserting a node after the kth node. Let $h, n_1, ..., n_\ell, t$ denote respectively the memory locations of the linked list: n_k denotes the memory location of the kth node key and its next pointer. In the following history $\mathcal{H}'$, transaction i reads node n_k and detects that it has freshly been modified by another transaction j.

$$\mathcal{H}' = ..., r(n_k)^j, r(n_{k+1})^j, r(n_{k-1})^i, w(n_k)^j, r(n_k)^i, r(n_{k+1})^i, ...$$

In this example, transaction i does not have to abort and restart from the beginning because it is the first time it accesses n_k and because the preceding node accessed by i has not been overwritten since then. Hence, after making sure that the previously read node n_{k-1} has not been modified, transaction i can resume and commit, as if its read of n_k was part of a new transaction s_k, serialized after j. Hence, we get the following history.

$$f(\mathcal{H}') = ..., r(n_k)^j, r(n_{k+1})^j, r(n_{k-1})^i, w(n_k)^j, \boxed{r(n_k)^i, r(n_{k+1})^i}^{s_k}, ...$$

$\mathcal{E}$-**STM.** We propose $\mathcal{E}$-STM, an implementation of our transactional model that uses timestamps, two-phase-locking, and universal operations. It provides both normal transactions and elastic transactions, allowing the latter ones to be cut to achieve high concurrency, but it retains the abstraction simplicity of transactional memory.

To evaluate the performance and simplicity of our solution, we implement it on four data structure applications: (i) linked list, (ii) skip list, (iii) red-black tree, and (iv) hash table. We compare $\mathcal{E}$-STM with three other synchronization techniques: (i) regular STM transactions, (ii) lock-based, and (iii) lock-free. The regular STM technique relies on TinySTM [1], the fastest STM for microbenchmarks we know of [1, 2]. The lock-based and lock-free implementations are based on the algorithms of Herlihy, Luchangco, Shavit et al. [3, 4], and of Fraser, Harris, and Michael [5, 6, 7], respectively. We also implemented complex operations, move and sum, to illustrate how transactions can be combined.

The results we obtained indicate that $\mathcal{E}$-STM speeds up regular transactions on all workloads and with an average speedup factor of 36%. By lack of space, the detailed experiments are deferred to the companion technical report [8].

Roadmap. In the remainder of this paper, we present our system model (Section 2) and our transactional model (Section 3), and we give an implementation of it, called $\mathcal{E}$-STM (Section 4). Then, we elaborate on the advantages of using $\mathcal{E}$-STM, by illustrating its use in some data structure applications (Section 5). Finally, we present the related work (Section 6) before concluding (Section 7).

2   System Model

Our system comprises transactions and objects similarly to [9]. The states of all objects define the state of the system. A transaction is a sequence of read and write operations that can examine and modify, respectively, the state of the objects. More precisely, it consists of a sequence of events that are an *operation invocation*, an *operation response*, a *commit invocation*, a *commit response*, and an *abort event*.

An operation whose response event occurred is considered as *terminated* while a transaction whose commit response or abort event occurred is considered as *completed*.

The set of transactions is denoted by T and we consider two types of transactions: normal and elastic. We assume that the type of all transactions is initially known. The sets of normal transactions and elastic transactions are denoted by $\mathcal{N}$ and $\mathcal{E}$, respectively. The set of possible objects is denoted by X and the set of possible values is V. An *operation* accessing an object x, belonging to a transaction t, can be of two *types* (read or write), and either takes as an argument or returns a value v. Hence, an operation is denoted by a tuple in $X \times T \times V \times type$.

Histories. We consider only well-formed sequences of events that consist of a set of transactions, each satisfying the following constraints: (i) a transaction must wait until its operation terminates before invoking a new one, (ii) no transaction both commit and abort, and (iii) a transaction cannot invoke an operation after having completed. We refer to these well-formed sequences as *histories*.

A history $\mathcal{H}$ is complete if all its transactions are completed. We define a completing function *complete* that maps any history $\mathcal{H}$ to a set of complete histories by appending an event q to each non-completed transaction t of $\mathcal{H}$ such that:

- q is an abort event if there is no commit request for t in $\mathcal{H}$;
- q is a commit or an abort event if there is a commit request for t in $\mathcal{H}$.

Given a set of transactions T and a history $\mathcal{H}$, we define $\mathcal{H}|T$, the restriction of $\mathcal{H}$ to T, to be the subsequence of $\mathcal{H}$ consisting of all events of any transaction $t \in T$. We refer to the set of transactions that have committed (resp. aborted) in $\mathcal{H}$ as *committed($\mathcal{H}$)* (resp. *aborted($\mathcal{H}$)*). The history of all committed transactions of a given history $\mathcal{H}$ is denoted by *permanent($\mathcal{H}$)* $= \mathcal{H}|committed(\mathcal{H})$. Similarly, for a set of objects X we denote by $\mathcal{H}|X$ the subsequence of $\mathcal{H}$ restricted to X. For the sake of simplicity, to denote $\mathcal{H}|\{x\}$, for $x \in X$ (resp. $\mathcal{H}|\{t\}$, for $t \in T$) we simply write $\mathcal{H}|x$ (resp. $\mathcal{H}|t$).

Let $\rightarrow_{\mathcal{H}}$ be the total order on the events in $\mathcal{H}$. We say that t *precedes* t' in $\mathcal{H}$ (denoted by $t \rightarrow_{\mathcal{H}} t'$) if there are no events $q \in \mathcal{H}|t$ and $q' \in \mathcal{H}|t'$ such that $q' \rightarrow_{\mathcal{H}} q$. Two transactions t and t' are called *concurrent* if none precedes the other, i.e., $t \nrightarrow_{\mathcal{H}} t'$ and $t' \nrightarrow_{\mathcal{H}} t$. A history $\mathcal{H}$ is *sequential* if no two transactions of $\mathcal{H}$ are concurrent.

Operation sequences. For simplicity, we consider a sequence of operations instead of a sequence of events to describe histories and transactions. An operation π is a pair of invocation event and response event such that the invocation and response correspond to the same operation, accessing the same object and being part of the same transaction. A given history $\mathcal{H}$ is thus an operation sequence $S_{\mathcal{H}} = \pi_1, ..., \pi_n$ resulting from $\mathcal{H}$ where commit and operation invocations that do not have a matching response have been omitted. Concurrent operations ordering is determined by the object serial specification described below. We say that two histories $\mathcal{H}$ and $\mathcal{H}'$ are *equivalent* if for any transaction t, $\mathcal{H}|t = \mathcal{H}'|t$.

The serial specification of an object is the set of acceptable sequences of its operations. Each object x is initialized with a default value v_x and accessed either by a write operation, $\pi(x, v)$, that writes a value v or by a read operation, $\pi(x) : v$, that returns a value v. That is, we only focus on read/write objects the serial specification of which requires that a read operation on x returns the last value written on x, or its default value v_x (if the value has not been written before). Without loss of generality, we assume that each written value is unique, hence: let $\pi(x, v)$ and $\pi'(x', v')$ be two write operations, if $v = v'$ then $x = x'$ and $\pi = \pi'$.

We refer to a transaction that never writes an object value in the shared memory as an *invisible* transaction. Observe that an invisible transaction may, however, write some metadata (e.g., lock ownership) in the shared memory. An example is a transaction that acquires some locks before aborting.

3   Elastic Transactions: Definition

An *elastic* transaction is a transaction the size of which may vary depending on conflicts. More precisely, such transaction may cut itself upon conflict detection as if the start of the transaction has moved forward, hence the name elastic. Next, we explain how a cut is achieved.

First, note that a sequence of operations is a totally ordered set, hence, we refer to a history $\mathcal{H}$ as a tuple $\langle S_{\mathcal{H}}, \rightarrow_{\mathcal{H}} \rangle$ where $S_{\mathcal{H}}$ is the corresponding set of operations and $\rightarrow_{\mathcal{H}}$ a total order defined over $S_{\mathcal{H}}$. More generally we refer to any sequence S as a totally ordered set denoted by $\langle S_S, \rightarrow_S \rangle$.

A *sub-history* $\mathcal{H}'$ of history $\mathcal{H} = \langle S_{\mathcal{H}}, \rightarrow_{\mathcal{H}} \rangle$ is a history $\mathcal{H}' = \langle S_{\mathcal{H}'}, \rightarrow_{\mathcal{H}'} \rangle$ such that $S_{\mathcal{H}'} \subseteq S_{\mathcal{H}}$ and $\rightarrow_{\mathcal{H}'} \subseteq \rightarrow_{\mathcal{H}}$. Next, we define the notion of cut and its well-formedness.

Definition 1 (Cut). *A cut of a history $\mathcal{H}$ is a sequence $C = \langle S_C, \rightarrow_C \rangle$ of sub-histories of $\mathcal{H}$ such that:*

1. *each of the cut sub-history contains only consecutive operations of $\mathcal{H}$: for any sub-history $\mathcal{H}' = \pi_1, ..., \pi_n$ in S_C, if there exists $\pi_i \in \mathcal{H}$ such that $\pi_1 \rightarrow_{\mathcal{H}} \pi_i \rightarrow_{\mathcal{H}} \pi_n$, then $\pi_i \in \mathcal{H}'$;*
2. *if one sub-history precedes another in C then the operations of the first precede the operations of the second in $\mathcal{H}$: for any sub-histories $\mathcal{H}_1$ and $\mathcal{H}_2$ in S_C and two operations $\pi_1 \in \mathcal{H}_1$ and $\pi_2 \in \mathcal{H}_2$, if $\mathcal{H}_1 \rightarrow_C \mathcal{H}_2$ then $\pi_1 \rightarrow_{\mathcal{H}} \pi_2$;*
3. *any operation of $\mathcal{H}$ is in exactly one sub-history of the cut: $\bigcup_{\forall \mathcal{H}' \in S_C} S_{\mathcal{H}'} = S_{\mathcal{H}}$ and for any $\mathcal{H}_1, \mathcal{H}_2 \in S_C$, we have $S_{\mathcal{H}_1} \cap S_{\mathcal{H}_2} = \emptyset$.*

For example, there are four cuts of history a, b, c, denoted by $C1 = \{a, b \; ; \; c\}$, $C2 = \{a \; ; \; b, c\}$, $C3 = \{a \; ; \; b \; ; \; c\}$, and $C4 = \{a, b, c\}$, where semi-colons are used to separate consecutive sub-histories of the cut and braces are used for clarity to enclose a cut. In contrast, neither $\{a, c \; ; \; b\}$ nor $\{a \; ; \; a, b, c\}$ are cuts of $\mathcal{H}$. The reason it that the former violates property (1) while the latter violates property (3) of Definition 1.

Definition 2 (Well-formed cut). *A cut C_t of history $\mathcal{H}|t$, where t is a transaction, is well-formed if for any of its sub-histories s_i the following properties are satisfied:*

1. *if s_i contains only one operation, then there is no other $s_j \in S_{C_t}$;*
2. *if $\pi_i \in s_i$ and $\pi_j \in s_j$ are two write operations of t, then $s_i = s_j$;*
3. *if π_i is the first operation of s_i, then either π_i is a read operation or π_i is the first operation of t.*

For example, consider the following history $\mathcal{H}_1|t$ where t is an elastic transaction, and where $r(x)$ and $w(x)$ refer to a read and a write operation on x. (For the following examples, we omit the values returned by the read operations and consider that the object serial specification is satisfied.)

$$\mathcal{H}_1|t = r(u), r(v), w(x), r(y), r(z).$$

There are two well-formed cuts of history $\mathcal{H}_1|t$ that are $C1' = \{r(u), r(v), w(x), r(y), r(z)\}$ and $C2' = \{r(u), r(v), w(x) \; ; \; r(y), r(z)\}$, however, neither $C3' = \{r(u) \; ; \; r(v), w(x) \; ; \; r(y), r(z)\}$ nor $C4' = \{r(u), r(v) \; ; \; w(x), r(y), r(z)\}$ are well-formed. More precisely, the first sub-history of $C3'$ contains only one operation violating property (1) of Definition 2 and the second sub-history of $C4'$ starts with a write operation, that is, property (3) of Definition 2 is violated. In the remainder of this paper, we only consider well-formed cuts.

Next, we define a consistent cut with respect to a history of potentially concurrent transactions. This definition is crucial as it indicates the singularity of elastic transactions. The programmer can label a transaction as elastic if he(she) does not need this transaction to appear as atomic, but still he(she) requires that a set of consecutive operations in this transaction appear as atomic, as formalized below. In a history $\mathcal{H}$, a cut is consistent if there are no writes separating two of its sub-histories each accessing one of the object written by these writes.

Definition 3 (Consistent cut). *A cut C_t of $\mathcal{H}|t$ is consistent with respect to history $\mathcal{H}$ if, for any operation π_i and π_j of any two of its sub-histories s_i and s_j respectively ($s_i \neq s_j$), the two following properties hold:*

- *there is no write operation $\pi'(x)$ from a transaction $t' \neq t$ such that $\pi_i(x) \to_{\mathcal{H}} \pi'(x) \to_{\mathcal{H}} \pi_j(x)$;*
- *there are no two write operations $\pi'(x)$ and $\pi''(y)$ from transactions $t' \neq t$ and $t'' \neq t$ such that $\pi_i(x) \to_{\mathcal{H}} \pi'(x) \to_{\mathcal{H}} \pi_j(y)$ and $\pi_i(x) \to_{\mathcal{H}} \pi''(y) \to_{\mathcal{H}} \pi_j(y)$.*

For example, consider the following history $\mathcal{H}_2$ where e is an elastic transaction and n is a normal transaction, and where $r(x)^t$ and $w(x)^t$ refer to a read and a write operation on x in transaction t.

$$\mathcal{H}_2 = r(x)^e, r(y)^e, w(y)^n, r(z)^e, w(u)^e.$$

Two consistent cuts of $\mathcal{H}_2|e$ with respect to $\mathcal{H}_2$ are possible. One contains two sub-histories $C1 = \{r(x)^e, r(y)^e \; ; \; r(z)^e, w(u)^e\}$ while the other contains one sub-history $C2 = \{r(x)^e, r(y)^e, r(z)^e, w(u)^e\}$. Observe that $C1$ is consistent because there are no two writes from other transactions that occur at objects between the accesses of e to these objects, hence $r(y)^e$ and $r(z)^e$ seem to execute atomically at the time $r(y)^e$ occurs. In contrast, consider history $\mathcal{H}_3$ where e is elastic and n is normal.

$$\mathcal{H}_3 = r(x)^e, r(y)^e, w(y)^n, w(z)^n, r(z)^e, w(u)^e.$$

There is no consistent cut of $\mathcal{H}_3|e$ with respect to $\mathcal{H}_3$ because n writes y and z between the times e reads each of them.

Given a cut $\mathcal{C}_t = s_1^t, ..., s_n^t$ of $\mathcal{H}|t$ for each elastic transaction $t \in \mathcal{H}|\mathcal{E}$, we define a *cutting function* $f_{\mathcal{C}_t}$ that replaces an elastic transaction t by the transactions s_i^t resulting from its cut. More precisely, $f_{\mathcal{C}_t}$ maps a history $\mathcal{H} = \pi_1, ..., \pi_n$ to a history $f_{\mathcal{C}_t}(\mathcal{H}) = \pi_1', ..., \pi_n'$ where if $\pi_i = \langle x, t, v, type \rangle \in s_i^t$ then $\pi_i' = \langle x, s_i^t, v, type \rangle$, otherwise $\pi_i = \pi_i'$, and if $t \in committed(\mathcal{H})$ then $s_i^t \in committed(f_{\mathcal{C}_t}(\mathcal{H}))$, otherwise $s_i^t \in aborted(f_{\mathcal{C}_t}(\mathcal{H}))$. We denote the composition of f for a set of cuts $\mathcal{C} = \{\mathcal{C}_1, ..., \mathcal{C}_m\}$ by $f_{\mathcal{C}} = f_{\mathcal{C}_1} \circ ... \circ f_{\mathcal{C}_m}$.

Next, we define an elastic-opaque transactional system, which combines normal and elastic transactions; this definition relies on Definition 3 of consistent cut, and the definition of opacity [10].

Definition 4 (Elastic-opacity). *A transactional system is* elastic-opaque *if, for any history $\mathcal{H}$ of this system, there exists a consistent cut $\mathcal{C}_t$ for each elastic transaction t of $\mathcal{H}|\mathcal{E}$ with $\mathcal{C} = \{\mathcal{C}_t\}$, such that $f_{\mathcal{C}}(\mathcal{H})$ is opaque.*

As an example, consider the following history $\mathcal{H}_4$ and assume e is elastic while n is normal and both transactions commit:

$$\mathcal{H}_4 = r(x)^e, r(y)^e, r(x)^n, r(y)^n, r(z)^n, w(x)^n, r(t)^e, w(z)^e.$$

This history would clearly not be serializable in a traditional model (with e and n two normal transactions) since there is no sequential histories that allow not only $r(x)^e$ to occur before $w(x)^n$ but also $r(z)^n$ to occur before $w(z)^e$. However, there exists one consistent cut $\mathcal{C}_e$ of $\mathcal{H}_4|e$ with respect to $\mathcal{H}_4$, $\mathcal{C}_e = s_1, s_2$ where $s_1 = r(x)^e, r(y)^e$ and $s_2 = r(t)^e, w(z)^e$ such that, for $\mathcal{C} = \{\mathcal{C}_e\}$, we have:

$$f_{\mathcal{C}}(\mathcal{H}_4) = r(x)^{s_1}, r(y)^{s_1}, r(x)^n, r(y)^n, r(z)^n, w(x)^n, r(t)^{s_2}, w(z)^{s_2}.$$

And $\mathcal{H}_4$ is elastic-opaque as $f_{\mathcal{C}}(\mathcal{H}_4)$ is equivalent to a sequential history: s_1, n, s_2 (and $f_{\mathcal{C}}(\mathcal{H}_4)$ is opaque).

4 Implementation of Elastic Transactions

This section introduces $\mathcal{E}$-STM, a software transactional memory system that implements elastic transactions. The corresponding pseudocode appears in Algorithm 1. $\mathcal{E}$-STM combines two-phase locking, timestamp mechanism, and atomic primitives: compare-and-swap (Lines 79), fetch-and-increment (Line 94), and atomic loads and stores.

Transaction and variable state. A transaction t starts with a begin($type$) indicating whether its type is elastic or normal. Then, it accesses the memory locations using read or write operations. Finally, it completes either by a commit call or by an abort that restarts the same transaction. The try-extend and ver-val-ver are helper functions. A transaction t may keep track of the variable it has accessed since it has lastly started using a r-set to log the reads and a w-set to log

Algorithm 1. $\mathcal{E}$-STM, a transactional memory providing elastic transactions

```
 1: clock ∈ ℕ, initially 0

 2: State of variable x:
 3:    val ∈ V
 4:    tlk a timestamped lock with fields:
 5:       owner ∈ T, the lock owner, initially ⊥
 6:       time ∈ ℕ, a version counter, initally 0
 7:       w-entry ∈ X × V × ℕ, an entry address
 8:          initally ⊥
 9:    // time/w-entry share same location

10: State of transaction t:
11:    type ∈ {elastic, normal}, initially the
12:       ancestor transaction type or ⊥ (if none)
13:    r-set and w-set, sets of entries with fields:
14:       addr ∈ X, an address
15:       val ∈ V, its value
16:       ts ∈ ℕ, its version timestamp
17:    last-r-entry ∈ X × ℕ, an entry,
18:       initally ⊥
19:    lb ∈ ℕ, initially 0 // time lower bound
20:    ub ∈ ℕ, initially 0 // time upper bound

21: begin(tx-type)_t:
22:    ub ← clock
23:    lb ← clock
24:    // if nested inside a normal, be normal
25:    if type ≠ normal then type ← tx-type

26: try-extend()_t:
27:    // make sure read values haven't changed
28:    now ← clock
29:    for all ⟨y, *, ts⟩ ∈ r-set do
30:       ow ← y.tlk.owner
31:       last ← y.tlk.time
32:       if ow ∉ {t, ⊥}∨
33:          (ow = ⊥ ∧ last ≠ ts) then
34:          abort()
35:    ub ← now

36: ver-val-ver(x, evenlocked)_t:
37:    // load a versioned value from memory
38:    repeat:
39:       ℓ₁ ← x.tlk
40:       v ← x.val
41:       ℓ₂ ← x.tlk
42:    until (ℓ₁ = ℓ₂∧
43:       (ℓ₁.owner = ⊥ ∨ evenlocked))
44:    return ⟨ℓ₁, v⟩

45: abort()_t:
46:    for all ⟨x, *, *⟩ ∈ write-set do
47:       x.tlk.owner ← ⊥
48:    begin(type) // restart from the beginning

49: read(x)_t:
50:    // log normal reads for later extensions
51:    if type = normal ∨ w-set ≠ ∅ then
52:       ⟨ℓ_x, v_x⟩ ← ver-val-ver(x, true)
53:       if ℓ_x.owner ∉ {t, ⊥} then ctn_mgt()
54:       else if ℓ_x.owner = t then
55:          v_x ← ℓ_x.w-entry.val
56:       else // ℓ_x.owner = ⊥
57:          if ℓ_x.time > ub then try-extend()
58:          r-set ← r-set ∪ {⟨x, v_x, ℓ_x.time⟩}
59:       // ...or log only the most recent elastic read
60:    if type = elastic ∧ w-set = ∅ then
61:       ⟨ℓ_x, v_x⟩ ← ver-val-ver(x, false)
62:       if ℓ_x.time > ub then
63:          if last-r-entry ≠ ⊥ then
64:             ⟨y, *⟩ ← last-r-entry
65:             ⟨ℓ_y, *⟩ ← ver-val-ver(y, false)
66:             if ℓ_y.time > ub then abort()
67:          ub ← ℓ_x.time
68:       last-r-entry ← ⟨x, ℓ_x.time⟩
69:    return v_x

70: write(x, v)_t:
71:    // lock & postpone the write until commit
72:    repeat:
73:       ℓ ← x.tlk
74:       if ℓ.owner ∉ {⊥, t} then ctn_mgt()
75:       else if ℓ.time > ub then
76:          if type = normal then try-extend()
77:          else abort()
78:       w-entry ← ⟨x, v, ℓ.time⟩
79:       x.tlk ← ⟨t, *, w-entry⟩ // compare&swap
80:    until (x.tlk.owner = t)
81:    lb ← max(lb, ℓ.time)
82:    w-set ← (w-set \ {⟨x, *, *⟩}) ∪ {w-entry}
83:    // make sure last value read is unchanged
84:    if type = elastic ∧ last-r-entry ≠ ⊥ then
85:       (e, time_e) ← last-r-entry
86:       ⟨ℓ_e, *⟩ ← ver-val-ver(e, true)
87:       ow ← ℓ_e.owner
88:       last ← ℓ_e.time
89:       if ow ≠ t ∨ last ≠ time_e then abort()
90:       last-r-entry ← ⊥

91: commit()_t:
92:    // apply writes to memory and release locks
93:    if w-set ≠ ∅ then
94:       ts ← clock++ // fetch&increment
95:       if lb ≠ ts − 1 then try-extend()
96:       for all ⟨x, v, ts⟩ ∈ write-set do
97:          x.val ← v
98:          x.tlk.time ← ts
99:          x.tlk.owner ← ⊥
```

the writes. More precisely, the entries of these sets contain the variable address, *addr*, its value *val*, and its version *ts* (Lines 13–16). If t is elastic, it may only need to keep track of the last read operation, so it uses *last-r-entry* (Lines 17 and 18) to log a single address and its version instead of the entire set *r-set*.

The two last fields of t indicate a lower-bound lb and an upper-bound ub on the logical times at which t can be serialized (Lines 19 and 20).

For the sake of clarity in the pseudocode presentation, we consider that each memory location is protected by a distinct lock. We call it the associated memory location of the lock. More precisely, each shared variable x can be represented by a value (Line 3) *val* and a timestamped lock *tlk*, also called versioned write-lock [11]. A timestamped lock has three fields: (i) the *owner* indicating which transaction has acquired the lock, if any, (ii) the *time* the associated memory location of the lock has the most recently been written, and (iii) *w-entry*, a reference to the corresponding entry in the owner's write set (Lines 4–9). Timestamps are given by a global counter, *clock* (Line 1), that does not hamper scalability [11, 12, 1].

Normal transactions. The algorithm restricted to normal transactions builds upon TinySTM [1] logging all operations. All transactions use two-phase locking when writing to a memory location. While the location is locked by the transaction at the time it executes the write, all updates are buffered into a write-set, *w-set*, until the commit time at which these updates are applied to the memory. When a transaction performs a write$(x, *)$, it acquires the lock of x using a compare-and-swap (Line 79) and holds it until it commits or aborts. When accessing a locked variable, the transaction detects a conflict and calls the contention manager, which typically aborts the current transaction (Lines 53 and 74). Various contention management policies could be used instead to handle conflicts between normal transactions.

When a read request on variable x as part of transaction t is received by $\mathcal{E}$-STM, the value of x is read in a three-step process called ver-val-ver, which consists in loading its timestamped lock $x.tlk$, loading its value $x.val$, and re-loading its lock $x.tlk$. This read-version-value-version is repeated until the two versions read are identical (Line 42) indicating that the value corresponds to that version. Only in some cases needs the value be returned unlocked, hence the use of the boolean *evenlocked*. The transactions of $\mathcal{E}$-STM use the extension mechanism of LSA [12, 1]. Each transaction t maintains an interval of time $[lb, ub]$ indicating the time during which t can be serialized. More precisely, for a given transaction t, lb and ub represent respectively lower and upper bounds on the versions of values accessed by t during its execution. When t reads x, it records the last time x has been modified in its read-set, *r-set*, for future potential check. Later on, if t accesses a variable y that has been recently updated ($y.tlk.time > ub$), t first tries to extend its interval of time by calling try-extend(). Transaction t detects a conflict only if this extension is impossible (Lines 34), meaning that some variables, among the ones t has read, have been updated by another transaction since then.

Elastic transactions. An important difference between normal and elastic transactions is that elastic transactions never use the *r-set* until they read after a write, as there is at most one read operation the transaction has to keep track of: the most recent one. Hence, elastic transactions use the *last-r-entry* field to log the last read operation. In our implementation all reads following a write in an elastic transaction will use the *r-set* like normal transactions (Lines 50–58), however, the implementation could be improved using static analysis to require this only for reads that are both preceded and succeeded by write operations in the same transaction.

Upon reading x (without having written before) an elastic transaction must make sure that the value v_x it reads was present at the time the immediately preceding read occurs. This typically ensures that a thread does not return an inconsistent value v_x after having been pre-empted, for example. If the version v_x of the value is too recent, $\ell_x.time > ub$, then the read operation must recheck the value logged in *last-r-entry* to be sure that the value read has not been overwritten since then (Lines 62–67). This can be viewed as a partial roll-back similar to the one provided by nested models, except that no on-abort definition is necessary and only a single operation would have to be re-executed here. Upon writing x, a similar verification regarding the last value read is made. If the lock corresponding to this address has been acquired, $ow \neq \bot$, or if the version has changed since then, $last \neq time_e$, then the transaction aborts (Line 89). If, however, no other transaction tried to update this address since it has been read, then the write executes as normal (Lines 71–82).

Next, we state the theorem on the correctness of our implementation. The complete proof has been deferred to the companion technical report [8].

Theorem 1. *$\mathcal{E}$-STM is elastic-opaque.*

5   Evaluation

$\mathcal{E}$-STM is simple to program with for two reasons: (i) it indeed provides a high-level abstraction that do not expose synchronization mechanisms to the programmer, and (ii) it enables code composition.

5.1   Abstraction

As with a classical transactional model, the programmer can use $\mathcal{E}$-STM to write a concurrent program almost as if he (she) was writing a sequential program. Like all TMs, $\mathcal{E}$-STM provides the programmer with labels *begin* and *commit* that can delimit the transactions. Hence, all calls to reading and writing the shared memory are redirected to the wrappers read and write of $\mathcal{E}$-STM, but this redirection does not incur efforts from the programmer and can be made automatic: some compilers already detect transaction labels and redirect memory accesses of these transactions automatically even though it is known that over instrumentation of accesses may unnecessarily impact performance.

To illustrate this, consider the sorted linked list implementation of an integer set, where integers (node *keys*) can be searched, removed, and inserted.

Algorithm 2. Linked list implementation built on $\mathcal{E}$-STM (the lock-free harris-ll-find function is given for comparison).

```
 1:  State of process p:                      36:  ll-remove(i)_p:
 2:    node a record with fields:             37:    begin(elastic)
 3:      key, an integer                      38:    ⟨curr, next⟩ ← ll-find(i)
 4:      next, a node                         39:    in ← (next.key = i)
 5:    set a linked-list of nodes with:       40:    if in then
 6:      head at the beginning,               41:      n ← read(next.next)
 7:      tail at the end.                     42:      write(curr.next, n)
 8:    Initially, the set contains head and   43:      free(next)
 9:      tail nodes, and head.key = min       44:    commit()
10:      and tail.key = max.                  45:    return (in)

11:  free(x)_t:                               46:  harris-ll-find(i)_p:
12:    // memory disposal is postponed        47:    loop
13:    write(x, 0)                            48:      t ← set.head
                                              49:      t_next ← read(curr.next)
14:  ll-find(i)_p:                            50:      // 1. find left and right nodes
15:    curr ← set.head                        51:      repeat:
16:    while true do                          52:        if !is_marked(t_next) then
17:      next ← read(curr.next)               53:          curr ← t
18:      if next.key ≥ i then break           54:          curr_next ← t_next
19:      curr ← next                          55:        curr ← unmarked(next)
20:    return ⟨curr, next⟩                    56:        if !t_next then break
                                              57:        t_next ← t.next
21:  ll-insert(i)_p:                          58:      until is_marked(t_next) ∨ (t.key < i)
22:    begin(elastic)                         59:      next = t
23:    ⟨curr, next⟩ ← ll-find(i)              60:      // 2. check nodes are adjacent
24:    in ← (next.key = i)                    61:      if curr_next = next then
25:    if !in then                            62:        if (next.next∧
26:      new-node ← ⟨i, next⟩                 63:           is_marked(next.next) then
27:      write(curr.next, new-node)           64:          goto line 48
28:    commit()                               65:        else return ⟨curr, next⟩
29:    return (!in)                           66:      // 3. remove one or more marked node
                                              67:      if cas(curr.next, curr_next, next) then
30:  ll-search(i)_p:                          68:        if (next.next∧
31:    begin(elastic)                         69:           is_marked(next.next)) then
32:    ⟨curr, next⟩ ← ll-find(i)              70:          goto line 48
33:    in ← (next.key = i)                    71:        else return ⟨curr, next⟩
34:    commit()                               72:    end loop
35:    return (in)
```

Algorithm 2 depicts the entire program that uses $\mathcal{E}$-STM plus a core function of the lock-free Harris [5] implementation, for comparison purpose. It is pretty clear that this harris-ll-find function is more complex than its ll-find counterparts based on $\mathcal{E}$-STM. In fact, harris-ll-find relies on the use of a mark bit to indicate that a node is logically deleted, and must physically delete the nodes that have been logically deleted to ensure that the size of the list does not grow with each operation. Unlike the Harris lock-free function, $\mathcal{E}$-STM-based functions are very simple, as all synchronizations are handled transparently underneath by $\mathcal{E}$-STM. The pseudocode is the same as the non-thread-safe version, except that begin(elastic), and commit have been added at the right places in the code.

5.2 Extensibility

$\mathcal{E}$-STM combines elastic transactions with normal transactions which makes it easily extensible. To illustrate this, we extended the hash table example with operations move and sum. The pseudocode is presented in Algorithm 3.

More specifically, we implemented the insert, search, and remove operations using elastic transactions. Since each bucket of the hash table is implemented with a linked list, we re-used (Lines 12, 18, and 24) the program of the linked list written above. More complex operations like move and sum have been implemented using normal transactions. The elastic transactions nested inside the normal transactions of move (Lines 16 and 22) execute in the normal mode. Although an elastic implementation of move is possible, sum cannot be elastic as it requires an atomic snapshot of all elements of the data structure. This example illustrates the way elastic and normal transactions can be combined.

Observe that, although moving a value from one node to one of its predecessors in the same linked list may lead an elastic search not to see the moved value, the two operations remain correct. Indeed, the search looks for a key associated with a value while the move changes the key of a value v. Hence, if the search looks for the initial key k of v and fails in finding it, then search will be serialized after move, if search looks for the targeted key k' of v and does not find it, then search will be serialized before move. In contrast, a less usual search-value operation looking for the associated value rather than the key of an element would have to be implemented using normal transactions, otherwise, a concurrent move may lead to an inconsistent state. Another issue, pointed out in [13], may arise when one transaction inserts x if y is absent and another inserts y if x is absent. If executed concurrently, these two transactions may lead to an inconsistent state

---

Algorithm 3. Hash table implementation built on $\mathcal{E}$-STM and linked list

```
 1: State of process p:
 2:    node a record with fields:
 3:       key, an integer
 4:       next, a node
 5:    set a mapping from an integer to a
 6:       linkedlist representing a bucket.
 7:    Initially, all buckets of the set are
 8:       empty lists.

 9: ht-search(i)_p:
10:    begin(elastic)
11:    a ← hash(i)
12:    result ← set[a].ll-search(i)
13:    commit()
14:    return result

15: ht-insert(i)_p:
16:    begin(elastic)
17:    a ← hash(i)
18:    result ← set[a].ll-insert(i)
19:    commit()
20:    return result
```

```
21: ht-remove(i)_p:
22:    begin(elastic)
23:    a ← hash(i)
24:    result ← set[a].ll-remove(i)
25:    commit()
26:    return result

27: ht-sum()_p:
28:    begin(normal)
29:    for each bucket in set do
30:       next ← read(bucket.head.next)
31:       while next.next ≠ ⊥ do
32:          sum ← sum + read(next.val)
33:          next ← read(next.next)
34:    commit()
35:    return sum

36: ht-move(i, j)_p:
37:    begin(normal)
38:    ht-remove(i)
39:    ht-insert(j)
40:    commit()
41:    return result
```

where both x and y are present. Again, our model copes with this issue as the programmer can use a normal transaction to encapsulate each conditional insertion. These normal and elastic transactions are safely combined.

Unlike elastic transactions, existing synchronization techniques (e.g., based on locks or compare-and-swap) cannot be easily combined with normal transactions. They furthermore introduce a significant complexity. Using a coarse-grained lock to make the hash table move operation atomic would prevent concurrent accesses to the data structure. In contrast, using fine-grained locks may lead to a deadlock if one process moves from bucket ℓ_1 to bucket ℓ_2 while another moves from ℓ_2 to ℓ_1. With a lock-free approach (e.g., based on an underlying compare-and-swap), one could either modify a copy of the data structure before switching a pointer from one copy to another, or use a multi-word compare-and-swap instruction. Unfortunately, the former solution is costly in memory usage whereas the latter solution requires a rarely supported instruction that is also considered as inefficient. Implementing a lock-free resize operations reveals even more as this requires to replace its internal bucket linked lists by a single linked list imposing to re-implement the whole data structure [14].

5.3   Experiments

Here we compare $\mathcal{E}$-STM and the default version of TinySTM on a 16 core machine. We chose TinySTM as it is the fastest STM on micro-benchmarks we know of [1,2]. We ran the linked list integer set implementation of Algorithm 2 on 16 threads with $\mathcal{E}$-STM and we replaced elastic transaction calls by normal transaction calls to run it with TinySTM. In this experiment, $\mathcal{E}$-STM is almost twice as fast as TinySTM (1.9x faster on average and up to 2.3x faster). For the graphs including other testbed data structures and other synchronization techniques, please refer to the technical report [8].

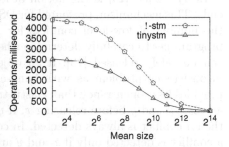

Fig. 1. Performance results when running 5% ll-insert, 5% ll-remove, and 90% ll-search operations as elastic (!-STM) and normal (TinySTM) transactions

6   Discussion and Related Work

One programmer may think of cutting normal transactions himself (herself) instead of using elastic transactions. Nevertheless, hand-crafted cuts must be defined prior to execution which may lead to inconsistencies. As an example, consider that a transaction t searches a linked list. A hand-crafted cut of t between two read operations on x and y may lead to an inconsistent state if another transaction deletes y (by modifying the next pointers of x and y) between those reads: t does not detect that it stops parsing the data structure as soon as it tries to access y. In contrast, elastic transactions avoid this issue by checking dynamically if a transaction can be safely cut and aborting otherwise.

Besides elastic transactions, there have been several attempts to extend the classical transactional model. Open nesting [15] provides sub-transactions that can commit while the outermost transaction is not completed yet. More precisely, open nesting makes sub-transactions visible before the outermost transaction commits. This requires the programmer to define complex roll-backs [16].

Transactional boosting [17] is a methodology for transforming linearizable objects into transactional objects, which builds upon techniques from the database literature. Although transactional boosting enhances concurrency by relaxing constraints imposed by read/write semantics at low-level, it requires the programmer to identify the commutative operations and to define inverse operations for non-commutative ones.

Abstract nesting [18] allows to abort partially in case of low-level conflict. As the authors illustrate, abstract nested transactions can encapsulate independent sub-parts of regular transactions like insert and remove sub-parts of a move transaction. In contrast, abstract nested transactions cannot encapsulate sub-parts of the parsing (as in search/insert/remove) of a data structure. Moreover, abstract nested transactions aim at reducing the roll-back cost due to low-level conflicts, but not at reducing the amount of low-level conflicts.

Early release [19] is the action of forgetting past reads before a transaction ends. This mechanism, presented for DSTM, enhances concurrency by decreasing the number of low-level conflicts for some pointer structures. It requires the programmer to carefully determine when and which objects in every transaction can be safely released [13]: if an object is released too early then the same inconsistency problem as with hand-crafted cuts arises. Finally, early release provides less concurrency than elastic transactions. Consider a transaction t that accesses x and y before releasing x. If y is modified between t accessing x and y then a conflict is always detected. In contrast, if t is an elastic transaction then a conflict is detected only if x and y are consecutively accessed by t and both x and y are modified between those accesses, which is very unlikely in practice.

7   Conclusion

We have proposed a new transactional model that enhances concurrency in a simple fashion. The core idea relies on the combination of traditional transactions with a new type of transactions that are elastic in the sense that their size evolves dynamically depending on conflict detection. We implemented this model in an STM, called $\mathcal{E}$-STM, that only requires to differentiate elastic from traditional transactions, making it simple to program with. Comparisons on data structures have confirmed that elastic transactions are simpler than lock-based and lock-free techniques and faster than regular transactions. It could be interesting to investigate how much performance other applications could gain from using this model. For example, the counter increment on which the rest of the transaction does not depend.

References

1. Felber, P., Fetzer, C., Riegel, T.: Dynamic performance tuning of word-based software transactional memory. In: Proceedings of the 13th ACM SIGPLAN Symposium on Principles and Practice of Parallel Programming, pp. 237–246 (2008)
2. Harmanci, D., Felber, P., Gramoli, V., Fetzer, C.: TMunit: Testing software transactional memories. In: The 4th ACM SIGPLAN Workshop on Transactional Computing (2009)
3. Heller, S., Herlihy, M., Luchangco, V., Moir, M., Scherer III, W.N., Shavit, N.: A lazy concurrent list-based set algorithm. In: Anderson, J.H., Prencipe, G., Wattenhofer, R. (eds.) OPODIS 2005. LNCS, vol. 3974, pp. 3–16. Springer, Heidelberg (2006)
4. Herlihy, M., Lev, Y., Luchangco, V., Shavit, N.: A simple optimistic skiplist algorithm. In: Prencipe, G., Zaks, S. (eds.) SIROCCO 2007. LNCS, vol. 4474, pp. 124–138. Springer, Heidelberg (2007)
5. Harris, T.: A pragmatic implementation of non-blocking linked-lists. In: Welch, J.L. (ed.) DISC 2001. LNCS, vol. 2180, pp. 300–314. Springer, Heidelberg (2001)
6. Michael, M.M.: High performance dynamic lock-free hash tables and list-based sets. In: Proceedings of the 14th Annual ACM Symposium on Parallel Algorithms and Architectures, pp. 73–82. ACM, New York (2002)
7. Fraser, K.: Practical lock freedom. PhD thesis, University of Cambridge (2003)
8. Felber, P., Gramoli, V., Guerraoui, R.: Elastic transactions. Technical Report LPD-REPORT-2009-002, EPFL (2009)
9. Weihl, W.E.: Local atomicity properties: Modular concurrency control for abstract data types. ACM Trans. Program. Lang. Syst. 11(2), 249–283 (1989)
10. Guerraoui, R., Kapałka, M.: On the correctness of transactional memory. In: Proceedings of the 13th ACM SIGPLAN Symposium on Principles and Practice of Parallel Programming, pp. 175–184 (2008)
11. Dice, D., Shalev, O., Shavit, N.: Transactional locking II. In: Dolev, S. (ed.) DISC 2006. LNCS, vol. 4167, pp. 194–208. Springer, Heidelberg (2006)
12. Riegel, T., Felber, P., Fetzer, C.: A lazy snapshot algorithm with eager validation. In: Dolev, S. (ed.) DISC 2006. LNCS, vol. 4167, pp. 284–298. Springer, Heidelberg (2006)
13. Skare, T., Kozyrakis, C.: Early release: Friend or foe? In: Workshop on Transactional Memory Workloads (2006)
14. Shalev, O., Shavit, N.: Split-ordered lists: Lock-free extensible hash tables. J. ACM 53(3), 379–405 (2006)
15. Moss, J.E.B.: Open nested transactions: Semantics and support. In: Workshop on Memory Performance Issues (2006)
16. Ni, Y., Menon, V., Abd-Tabatabai, A.R., Hosking, A.L., Hudson, R.L., Moss, J.E.B., Saha, B., Shpeisman, T.: Open nesting in software transactional memory. In: Proceedings of the 12th ACM SIGPLAN Symposium on Principles and Practice of Parallel Programming, pp. 68–78 (2007)
17. Herlihy, M., Koskinen, E.: Transactional boosting: A methodology for highly-concurrent transactional objects. In: Proceedings of the 12th ACM SIGPLAN Symposium on Principles and Practice of Parallel Programming, pp. 207–216 (2008)
18. Harris, T., Stipić, S.: Abstract nested transactions. In: The 2nd ACM SIGPLAN Workshop on Transactional Computing (2007)
19. Herlihy, M., Luchangco, V., Moir, M., Scherer III, W.N.: Software transactional memory for dynamic-sized data structures. In: Proceedings of the 22nd Annual Symposium on Principles of Distributed Computing, pp. 92–101. ACM, New York (2003)

Brief Announcement: Transactional Scheduling for Read-Dominated Workloads*

Hagit Attiya and Alessia Milani**

Department of Computer Science, Technion, Haifa 32000, Israel
{hagit,alessia}@cs.technion.ac.il

A promising approach to programming concurrent applications is provided by *transactional synchronization*: a *transaction* aggregates a sequence of resource accesses that should be executed atomically by a single thread. A transaction ends either by *committing*, in which case, all of its updates take effect, or by *aborting*, in which case, no update is effective.

The transactional approach to contention management [6,8] guarantees consistency by making sure that whenever there is a conflict, one of the transactions involved is aborted. When aborted, a transaction is later *restarted* from its beginning. Two overlapping transactions T_1 and T_2 conflict, if T_1 reads a resource X and T_2 executes a writing access to X while T_1 is still pending, or T_1 executed a writing access to X and T_2 accesses X while T_1 is still pending. Note that a conflict does not mean that consistency is violated, for example, two overlapping transactions $[read(X), write(Y)]$ and $[write(X), read(Z)]$ can be serialized, despite having a conflict.

A major challenge is guaranteeing *progress* through a *transactional scheduler*, by choosing which transaction to delay or abort and when to restart the aborted transaction, so as to ensure that work eventually gets done, and all transactions commit. This goal can also be stated quantitatively as minimizing the *makespan*—the total time needed to complete a finite set of transactions. Clearly, the makespan depends on the *workload*—the set of transactions and their characteristics, e.g. their arrival times, duration, and, perhaps most importantly, the resources they read or modify.

The *competitive* approach for evaluating the performance of a transactional scheduler A calculates the *ratio* between the makespan provided by A and by an optimal, clairvoyant scheduler, for each workload separately, and then finds the maximal ratio [2,5]. It has been shown that the best competitive ratio achieved by simple transactional schedulers is $\Theta(s)$, where s is the number of resources [2]. However, these prior studies assumed *write-dominated* workloads, in which transactions need exclusive access to resources for most of their duration.

In many situations generated in transactional memory, the workloads are *read-dominated*: most of their duration, transactions do not need exclusive access to resources. This includes *read-only* transactions that only observe data and do not modify it, as well as *mostly-read* transactions, e.g., locating an item by searching a list and then inserting or deleting, or mechanisms that rely on *deferred updates* (in commit time) [3,6,7].

* This research is partially supported by the *Israel Science Foundation* (grant number 953/06).

** On leave from Sapienza, Universitá di Roma; supported in part by a fellowship from the Lady Davis Foundation and by a grant Progetto FIRB Italia- Israele RBIN047MH9.

I. Keidar (Ed.): DISC 2009, LNCS 5805, pp. 108–110, 2009.
© Springer-Verlag Berlin Heidelberg 2009

Contemporary transactional schedulers, like CAR-STM [4], Adaptive Transaction Scheduling [9], and Steal-On-Abort [1], do not perform well under read-dominated workloads. This is because, using somewhat different mechanisms, these schedulers avoid repeated aborts (and hence, wasted work) by *serializing* transactions after a conflict happens. Thus, they all end up serializing more than necessary, in read-dominated workloads. We show that there is a *bimodal* workload, i.e., a workload containing only mostly-write and read-only transactions, for which these schedulers are at best $\Omega(m)$-competitive, where m is the number of cores. This means that, for some workloads, these schedulers utilize at most one core, while an optimal, clairvoyant scheduler exploits the maximal parallelism on all m cores. This can be easily shown to be a tight bound, since at each time, the schedulers do make progress on at least one transaction.

These counter-examples motivate our BIMODAL scheduler, which has a competitive ratio of $O(s)$ on bimodal workloads. BIMODAL alternates between *write epochs*, in which it gives priority to writing transactions, and *read epochs* in which it prioritizes transactions that have issued only reads so far. Taking $\tau_i > 0$ to be the execution time of transaction T_i when it runs uninterrupted to completion, and ω_i to be the total time it requests for exclusive access to resources, we prove:

Theorem 1. *The* BIMODAL *scheduler is* $O(s)$-*competitive for bimodal workloads with equi-length transactions, in which for any writing transaction* T_i, $2\omega_i \geq \tau_i$.

We show that for bimodal traffic, no algorithm can do better than that, extending the lower bound of [2].

BIMODAL also works when the workload is not bimodal, but its behavior deteriorates, and can only be trivially bound to have $O(m)$ competitive makespan when the workload contains mostly-read transactions. We prove that any non-clairvoyant scheduler must suffer a similar degradation, i.e., it is $\Omega(m)$ competitive for some workload (containing mostly-read transactions); this result assumes that the scheduler is *conservative*, i.e., it aborts a transaction whenever a conflict arises.

References

1. Ansari, M., Luján, M., Kotselidis, C., Jarvis, K., Kirkham, C., Watson, I.: Steal-on-Abort: Improving Transactional Memory Performance through Dynamic Transaction Reordering. In: Seznec, A., Emer, J., O'Boyle, M., Martonosi, M., Ungerer, T. (eds.) HiPEAC 2009. LNCS, vol. 5409, pp. 4–18. Springer, Heidelberg (2009)
2. Attiya, H., Epstein, L., Shachnai, H., Tamir, T.: Transactional contention management as a non-clairvoyant scheduling problem. In: PODC 2006, pp. 308–315 (2009)
3. Dice, D., Shalev, O., Shavit, N.N.: Transactional locking II. In: Dolev, S. (ed.) DISC 2006. LNCS, vol. 4167, pp. 194–208. Springer, Heidelberg (2006)
4. Dolev, S., Hendler, D., Suissa, A.: CAR-STM: scheduling-based collision avoidance and resolution for software transactional memory. In: PODC 2008, pp. 125–134 (2008)
5. Guerraoui, R., Herlihy, M., Pochon, B.: Toward a theory of transactional contention managers. In: PODC 2005, pp. 258–264 (2005)

6. Herlihy, M., Luchangco, V., Moir, M., Scherer III, W.N.: Software transactional memory for dynamic-sized data structures. In: PODC 2003, pp. 92–101 (2003)
7. Marathe, V.J., Scherer III, W.N., Scott, M.L.: Adaptive software transactional memory. In: Fraigniaud, P. (ed.) DISC 2005. LNCS, vol. 3724, pp. 354–368. Springer, Heidelberg (2005)
8. Scherer III, W.N., Scott, M.L.: Advanced contention management for dynamic software transactional memory. In: PODC 2005, pp. 240–248 (2005)
9. Yoo, R.M., Lee, H.-H.S.: Adaptive transaction scheduling for transactional memory systems. In: SPAA 2008, pp. 169–178 (2008)

Tight Group Renaming on Groups of Size g Is Equivalent to g-Consensus

Yehuda Afek[1], Eli Gafni[2], and Opher Lieber[1]

[1] The Blavatnik School of Computer Science, Tel-Aviv University, Israel
[2] Computer Science Department, Univ. of California, LA, CA

Abstract. We address two problems, the g-tight group renaming task and what we call, *safe*-consensus task, and show the relations between them. We show that any g-tight group renaming task, the first problem, implements g processes consensus. We show this by introducing an intermediate task, the *safe*-consensus task, the second problem, and showing that g-tight group renaming implements g-safe-consensus and that the latter implements g-consensus. It is known that with g-consensus g-tight group renaming is solvable, making the two problems equivalent.

The *safe*-consensus task, is of independent interest. In it the validity condition of consensus is weakened as follows: if the first processor to invoke the task returns before any other processor invokes, i.e., it runs in solo, then it outputs its input; Otherwise the consensus output can be arbitrary, not even the input of any process. We show the equivalence between safe-(set-)consensus and (set-)consensus.

Keywords: consensus, validity, set-consensus, group renaming, solo run.

1   Introduction

The notion of group solvability was introduced in [9]. The paper in [3] introduced a simpler version of group solvability called tight group solvability and in particular tackled the task of tight group renaming. The tight group renaming task is the renaming problem [2] of groups. Groups have to agree on a slot, and different groups have to agree on different slots. In the g-tight group renaming task there are g processors in each group. In [3] it was shown that g-consensus is sufficient to solve g-tight group renaming. The question whether it is also necessary was left open.

Here we introduce a new task, *safe-consensus*, a weakening of the classic consensus problem, and show the relation between this task, the g-tight group renaming task and the classic g-consensus task. The two basic conditions satisfied by the consensus problem [8] are, *agreement* and *validity*. In the *safe-consensus* task we weaken the *validity* condition of consensus. In the classic consensus problem the output to a participating processor is the input of a participating processor. In a *safe-consensus* task, the validity is weakened to allow the task to return an arbitrary value if initially the number of participating processors is two or more. The agreement property is retained.

I. Keidar (Ed.): DISC 2009, LNCS 5805, pp. 111–126, 2009.
© Springer-Verlag Berlin Heidelberg 2009

Our first result shows that g-tight group renaming implements g processes safe-consensus. Essentially, safe-consensus is an abstraction of tight group renaming. In any deterministic solution to the tight group renaming the output of a solo run is a function of the processor's id and its group id. Since we do not restrict the algorithm there may be two solo runs from the same group that output different values. Thus if two or more processors from the same group come together any new group name may be output, resembling the behavior of a safe-consensus task.

Our next result shows that safe-consensus is in fact as powerful as consensus, which together with the previous result shows its necessity to solve g-tight group renaming.

Following the introduction of *safe-consensus*, we next examine ways to weaken the validity condition of (n, k)-set-consensus. In (n, k)-set-consensus a processor outputs an input of a participating processor, and the cardinality of the output set is no larger than k. Hence the problem becomes non-trivial when initially more than k processors access the task concurrently. Thus the "off-the-cuff" weakening of the validity condition here is, that if more than k processors participate, it can return default non-valid outputs such that the total number of distinct values returned does not exceed k.

We show that this natural weakening is not equivalent to the original problem. Indeed it is strictly weaker than (n, k)-set-consensus. Nevertheless, it is a non-trivial task - it is not read-write wait-free solvable. We then consider strengthening the validity condition of (n, k)-safe-set-consensus to imitate safe-consensus: If a non-valid output is returned to any processors then it must be returned to all. We then show that strong-safe-set-consensus is equivalent to classic set-consensus.

Related Work: In [10], Guerraoui, and Kuznetsov define the weak consensus task. Here processors output 0 or 1 with the validity requirement being only that there exists a run of the task that outputs 0, and there exists a run that outputs 1. They show how weak consensus for n processors can be used to implement n processor consensus with the standard validity condition. Unlike this paper, they rely on the fact that they deal with an *object*, that is a given deterministic implementation of a task. In fact, they need to drive the implementation into particular special state (treating it as a white box). We on the other hand deal just with the specification, i.e., task (as a black box). We do not rely on any particular implementation of the task.

2   Model and Problem Definitions

We follow the standard model of asynchronous shared memory system as in [12,11]. There are n processors in the system $\{1, 2, \ldots, n\}$ that communicate by either atomically reading and writing to the atomic read/write shared memory, or by applying operations to a shared object such as a consensus object.

The g-tight group renaming problem: We follow the definition from [3]: In a tight group renaming task with group size g, n processors with id's from a large domain $\{1, 2, \ldots, N\}$ are partitioned into m groups with id's from a large domain $\{1, 2, \ldots, M\}$, with at most g processors per group. A tight group renaming task renames groups from the domain $1..M$ to $1..l$ for $l << M$, where all processors with the same initial group ID are renamed to the same new group ID, and no two different initial group id's are renamed to the same new group ID.

The n-Safe-consensus problem: In this task n processors with id's $1..n$ each proposes an input value, and outputs a value such that:

– Wait-Free: Each processor finishes executing within a finite number of steps.
– Agreement: All processors output the same output value.
– Weak-Validity: If the output of a processor occurs before the invocation of any other processor then the output is that processor's proposed input value.

Hence, if no processor initially accesses the Safe-consensus task in solo then processors may agree on any value. Notice, a similar task but in which the agreement condition is that each process may return either a fixed default value or the agreement value is read/write implementable.

The (n, k)-Safe-set-consensus problem: In this task n processors with id's $1..n$ each proposes an input value, and outputs a value such that:

– Wait-Free: Each processor finishes executing within a finite number of steps.
– k-Agreement: At most k distinct values are output.
– Weak-Validity: If the first output occurs after no more than k processors have invoked, then all processors output a proposed input value.

The Strong *(n, k)-Safe-set-consensus problem:* In this task n processors with id's $1..n$ each proposes an input value, and outputs a value such that:

– Wait-Free: Each processor finishes executing within a finite number of steps.
– Strong k-Agreement: At most k distinct values are output, and if any output value is not a proposed input value, that output value is the output of all processors which access the task.
– Weak-Validity: If the first output occurs after no more than k processors have invoked, then all processors output a proposed input value.

Task equivalence: We use wait-free constructions to compare two tasks, A and B. We say that *"A can implement B"* if there is a wait-free algorithm C that may use any number of copies of task A and read/write atomic registers to solve task B. If A and B implement each other, the tasks are said to be *equivalent*.

Atomic Snapshots: In several of the algorithms we utilize the ability to perform atomic snapshots of shared memory, as defined in [1].

Correctness proofs for all the algorithms are given in Appendix A.

3 *g*-Tight Group Renaming Implements g-Safe-Consensus

We show that a single g-tight group renaming task can implement g-safe-consensus so long as it supports at least $g + 1$ processor invocations. We then show that any weakening of this requirement is impossible.

Theorem 1. *Any tight group renaming task with group size g supporting n processors s.t., $n > g$ and $M > l$ implements 0/1 safe-consensus for g processors.*

Given an algorithm A which solves tight group renaming we show how to solve safe-consensus for g processors with 0/1 inputs (See code in Algorithm 1). We assume A is of the form $A(processor\text{-}id,group\text{-}id)$, receiving the processor id from $1..N$ and initial group id from $1..M$, and returns the new group ID in range $1..l$, and that A cannot be run more than once with the same processor ID. We also assume that invocation by a single processor in isolation always returns the same result, i.e., the only "non-determinism" is due to concurrency, which is true for any deterministic task.

Lemma 2. *There are two values $k1,k2$, s.t., $k1 \neq k2$ and a solo-run of $A(k1, k1)$ returns the same value as a solo-run of $A(k2, k2)$*

Proof. The pairs $< 1, 1 >$, $< 2, 2 >$,...,$< l + 1, l + 1 >$ are all valid values to call A with, since $M > l$ and $N > l$. Since A returns values in the range $1..l$, there are at least 2 of the above pairs for which $A()$ will return the same value in a solo-run.

Denote this returned value k. Let $k1,k2$ and k be these values for Algorithm A. (Note that these values can be deduced by running $l + 1$ instances of algorithm A, without knowledge of its internal specification, i.e., leaving it as a black-box).

Notice that if more than one processors access the group-renaming concurrently, even if from the same group, then their outputs cannot be deduced (or determined) ahead of time. Their outputs may depend on their interleaving and other parameters such as their ids.

In an attempt to reach consensus we let all g processors run A with group ID $k1$. If $k1$ renamed to k they decide 0, otherwise they decide 1. By definition of tight group renaming $k1$ renames to the same value for all processors, therefore guaranteeing agreement. To achieve the weak-validity requirement of safe-consensus we let all processors first register in memory and take a snapshot. If a processor sees itself alone it runs $A(k1, k1)$, and if it has input 1 it first runs $A(k2, k2)$. This guarantees that if it runs in solo, either $k1$ or $k2$ rename to k according to whether its input is 0 or 1 respectively.

Weak-Renaming: Note that the above construction applies whether the tight group renaming is weak-renaming or strong-renaming (i.e., adaptive).

Notice: The above algorithm can be extended to multivalue safe-consensus with p values, given a g-tight group renaming algorithm which allows at least p groups, s.t. $M > (p - 1)l$, while still using only one instance of algorithm A.

3.1   At Least $g + 1$ Invocations Are Required to Implement Safe-Consensus

In the above construction we showed that tight group renaming with group size g solves binary g-consensus when it may be invoked $g + 1$ times. Taubenfeld

---

Algorithm 1. g processor $0/1$ safe-consensus using a g-tight group renaming box and R/W memory

---

Shared Variables:
    $S[1..g]$: initially NULL
    $temp[1..g]$: g distinct processor ID's which are neither $k1$ nor $k2$
    A(processor-id,group-id) : a g-tight group renaming algorithm instance
procedure consensus(proposal)
1:    S[processor-id] = 'ACTIVE'
2:    SS = atomic snapshot of $S[1..g]$
3:    **if** for all i $\neq$ processor-id SS[i] = NULL
4:        **if** proposal = 1 **then** run A(k2,k2)
5:        value = A(k1,k1)
6:    **else**
7:        value = A(temp[processor-id],k1)
8:    **end if**
9:    **if** value = k **then** decide 0 **else** decide 1
    end consensus

---

then raised the question whether this is a lower bound, i.e., can a tight group renaming task with group size g which supports at most g processor invocations solve g-safe-consensus (and thus g-consensus?)

We prove that a g-tight group renaming task that allows at most g processor invocations cannot solve g-consensus, by showing how to implement such a task using only $(g-1)$-consensus objects and atomic R/W memory.

Theorem 3. *g-tight group renaming that may be invoked by at most g processors can be implemented using only $(g-1)$-consensus objects and atomic R/W memory.*

Proof. In Algorithm 2 we present the code to solve g-tight group renaming for at most g processors in groups of size g. We utilize the fact that $n = g$, which means that if there is some group with more than $g-1$ processors in it, then all g processors are from the same group and they can therefore decide some default value since there are no other groups to collide with.

We associate a $(g-1)$-consensus object with each of the possible M initial group ID's. We also utilize the result from [3] which shows that tight group renaming for groups of size $g-1$ can be implemented using only $(g-1)$-consensus objects and atomic R/W memory. All processors register their ID and group ID in memory and take a snapshot. If there are g processors in the snapshot and all are from the same group the processor simply decides on a default value 0. Otherwise it uses its group's $(g-1)$-consensus object to decide on its output as follows: If all processors in the snapshot are from its group, it proposes the default value 0, otherwise it accesses a $(g-1)$-tight group renaming task (constructed from $(g-1)$-consensus objects and r/w memory) and proposes the value returned from that task (Which returns ID's in range $1..l$ and does not collide with 0). All processors which decide according to their group's $(g-1)$-consensus object decide the same value, and the only time a processor does not access the $(g-1)$-consensus object is if it sees all g processors in memory and they all have the same group ID. In this case it returns 0 and so will all others, since they all propose 0 to the consensus object associated with their group.

Algorithm 2. g-tight group renaming for g processors using $(g-1)$-consensus objects and R/W memory

---

Shared Variables:
  cons[1..M] : M $(g-1)$-consensus objects, one for each group
  S[1..N] : Shared R/W registers, one for each processor, initially NULL
procedure tight-group-renaming(processor-id,group-id)
1:    S[processor-id] := group-id
2:    SS := atomic snapshot of S[1..N]
3:    count-group := $|\{i|SS[i] = \text{group-id}\}|$
4:    count-total := $|\{i|SS[i] \neq NULL\}|$
5:    **if** count-group = count-total = g **then** return 0
6:    **if** count-group = count-total
7:        propose := 0
8:    **else**
9:        propose := $(g-1)$-tight-group-renaming(processor-id,group-id)
10:   **end if**
11:   return cons[group-id] (propose)
  end consensus

---

4   Safe-Consensus Implements Consensus

We now show that n-safe-consensus is equivalent to regular n-consensus for any n, therefore resulting in g-tight group renaming implementing g-consensus for any g, which complements the result from [3] to prove that g-tight group renaming and g-consensus are equivalent.

Theorem 4. *Safe-consensus is equivalent to consensus.*

We implement n processor consensus given enough n processor safe-consensus tasks as black-boxes. Two algorithms are presented, the first one is somewhat simpler but requires $O(2^n)$ copies of the safe-consensus task to solve for n processors. The second algorithm uses a slight improvement and requires only $O(n^2)$ copies of safe-consensus.

4.1   Consensus Using $O(2^n)$ Safe-Consensus Tasks

For n processors we assume inductively we can solve consensus for $n-1$ processors. We implement consensus as follows (The code is given in Algorithm 3): Processors 1..$n-1$ agree on a value P_A recursively using the lower degree version of the task (Line 2) and write the value to shared memory (Line 3). Processors 2..$n-1$ then join processor n to recursively agree on a value using another lower degree version of the task, in which processors $2..n-1$ propose P_A and processor n proposes its own input (Line 6), writing the decision, denoted P_B, to shared memory (Line 7).

They now enter an n-processor safe-consensus task (Line 9), proposing their processor-id, in order to decide between P_A and P_B. If it returns n they decide P_B, otherwise they decide P_A.

Algorithm 3. n-consensus using n-safe-consensus, $(n-1)$-consensus tasks and R/W memory

---

Variables:
      processor-id : ID of the running processor, $1..n$
      P_A, P_B : MWMR registers, initially NULL
procedure consensus(proposal)
1:     **if** processor-id $< n$
2:        proposal := $(n-1)$-$consensus_A(proposal)$
3:        P_A := proposal
4:     **end if**
5:     **if** processor-id > 1
6:        proposal := $(n-1)$-$consensus_B(proposal)$
7:        P_B := proposal
8:     **end if**
9:     winner := n-safe-consensus(processor-id)
10:    **if** winner $= n$
11:       decide P_B
12:    **else**
13:       decide P_A
14:    **end if**
    end consensus

Complexity: $O(2^n)$ as each recursion calls 2 lower degree instances.

4.2 Consensus Using $O(n^2)$ Safe-Consensus Tasks

In Algorithm 4 we implement consensus using only $O(n^2)$ safe-consensus black-boxes. Again, we assume inductively we can solve consensus for $n-1$ processors.

We split the n processors into 2 groups, processors $1..n-1$ on one side, and processor n as a singleton on the other (Denote its input P_B). Processors $1..n-1$ recursively reach consensus among themselves (Line 10), denote this value P_A, and then work together against processor n. The problem here is that with a single safe-consensus task, processors $1..n-1$ can interfere with each other, causing the safe-consensus task to return some arbitrary value, without processor n even being alive. To solve this issue, we use $n-1$ safe-consensus task instances. All n processors run all $n-1$ instances (Lines 4 and 14). Processors $1..n-1$ each start running at a different safe-consensus task. Notice that this guarantees that if processor n is not active, then at least one of the $n-1$ processors will complete a solo-run of a safe-consensus task (The first one to complete running its first instance) and that task will return P_A by definition. On the other hand, if all processors $1..n-1$ are asleep, processor n successfully completes a solo-run of all $n-1$ safe-consensus tasks (Line 4), and they all return P_B. We then have processors $1..n-1$ perform an OR on all their runs, i.e., if at least one of the $n-1$ instances returned P_A they decide on it. Processor n performs an AND, if all instances returned P_B it decides on it. If a processor from $1..n-1$ does not receive P_A from any of the tasks (Line 16), then P_B must be written in memory and it can check if processor n was satisfied (Line 17). If it was not, then they default to deciding P_A. On the other hand if processor n did not receive P_B from all the tasks (Line 6), then P_A must be written in memory and it defaults to P_A (Line 7) as will processors $1..n-1$.

Algorithm 4. n-consensus using $O(n^2)$ safe-consensus tasks and R/W memory

  Variables:
    P_A, P_B : MWMR registers for processors $1..n-1$ and n respectively
    safe-consensus$[1..n-1]$: $n-1$ n-processor or more safe-consensus tasks
    values$[1..n\text{-}1]$: Local registers for each processor
  procedure consensus(proposal)
1:    **if** processor-id $= n$
2:        $P_B :=$ proposal
3:        **for** i := 1 **to** $n-1$
4:            values[i] := safe-consensus[i](proposal)
5:        **end for**
6:        **if** values[i] = proposal for all $i = 1..n-1$ **then** decide P_B
7:        **else** decide P_A
9:    **else**
10:        proposal := $(n-1)$-consensus (proposal)
12:        $P_A :=$ proposal
13:        **for** i := 1 **to** $n-1$
14:            values[i] := safe-consensus$[((i + processor_{id})mod(n-1)) + 1]$(proposal)
15:        **end for**
16:        **if** values[i] = proposal for some $i = 1..n-1$ **then** decide P_A
17:        **elseif** values[i] = P_B for all $i = 1..n-1$ **then** decide P_B
18:        **else** decide P_A
20:    **end if**
  end consensus

Complexity: $n * (n-1)/2$ as it uses $n-1$ safe-consensus tasks and recursively calls one lower degree instance.

Corollary 5. *g-tight group renaming solves g-consensus using* $n*(n-1)/2$ *such black-boxes, and is therefore a g-consensus task for any g.*

5   Safe Set-Consensus

What about (n, k)-set-consensus that may deliver arbitrary values? There are a few possibilities to generalize safe-consensus to a task (n, k)-safe-set-consensus. It may behave as (n, k)-set-consensus so long as no more than k processors initially access the task simultaneously. In case more than k processors initially access it simultaneously, it is allowed to return invalid results (So long as the k-agreement requirement is still satisfied).

5.1   (n,k)-Safe-Set-Consensus

Theorem 6. *Excluding the pair* $(4, 2)$, (n, k)-*set-consensus is implementable from* (n, k)-*safe-set-consensus if f* $n = k + 1$.

For $n > k + 1$, we show we cannot solve (n, k)-set-consensus using (n, k)-safe-set-consensus, except for the case of (4,2). We show how to implement (n, k)-safe-set-consensus using a regular $(k, k - 1)$-set-consensus task for all n (Code in Algorithm 5): Each processor registers in memory and takes an atomic snapshot. If it sees at most k processors (at most k will), it runs the $(k, k-1)$-set-consensus task, posts the result, and decides it. If a processor sees more than k in its snapshot, then if it sees some posted output it decides it, otherwise it defaults to 0. The only time a processor sees more than k in its snapshot but does not see a posted output is if more than k are concurrently executing the task and no processor has returned yet, so deciding an invalid value 0 in this case is allowed.

Since regular $(k, k-1)$-set-consensus can't solve (n, k)-set-consensus for $n/k > k/(k - 1)$ [4], (n, k)-safe-set-consensus can't solve (n, k)-set-consensus for $n > k + 1$, except for the (4,2) case, which is not yet classified.

5.2   Strong (n,k)-Safe-Set-Consensus

Here we strengthen the definition of safe-set-consensus so it can implement regular set-consensus: If an invalid value is returned, *all* processors output that value.

We show that this definition of the task does implement (n, k) set-consensus for all n (See code in Algorithm 6). We use the same idea as in Algorithm 3: We assume inductively we can solve for $(n - 1, k)$. Processors 1..$n - 1$ agree upon k inputs using our $(n - 1, k)$ solution and post the output to a shared vector A[] (Line 3). Processors 2..$n - 1$ each take their results and join another $(n - 1, k)$ set-consensus instance with processor n and post the output to a shared result vector B[] (Line 7). Each processor then runs the (n, k) safe-set-consensus task with its processor ID to decide on up to k winners (Line 9). If the winner is n they go to B[] otherwise they go to A[]. If the 'winner' already wrote a value in its location in the vector, that value is chosen, if not it means the result was

---

Algorithm 5. (n, k) Safe-set-consensus using a $(k, k-1)$ set-consensus task and R/W memory

---

    Shared Variables:
        $S[1..n]$: initialy NULL
        $RES[1..n]$: initialy NULL
    procedure Safe-set-consensus(proposal)
1:      $S[\text{processor-id}]$:= 'ACTIVE'
2:      SS := atomic snapshot of $S[1..n]$
3:      count := $|\{i| SS[i] = \text{'ACTIVE'}\}|$
4:      **if** count $\leq k$
5:          val := $(k, k-1)$-set-cons(proposal)
6:          $RES[\text{processor-id}]$:= val
7:          decide val
8:      **else**
9:          **if** $RES[i]$ = NULL for all $i = 1..n$ decide 0
10:        **else** decide any $RES[i]$ s.t. $RES[i] \neq$ NULL
11:    **end if**
    end Safe-set-consensus

---

invalid and the processors choose any value posted in that array (By the new agreement definition, they all will go to the same array, A[] or B[]).

6 Conclusions

Few questions are left open. We have shown the connection between g-tight group renaming and g processors safe-consensus. That is, if the members of each group must decide on 1 value (new name), then it is equivalent to consensus between the members of the group. The interesting question is then if the members of a group are allowed to decide on two different values, is that equivalent to some form of 2-(safe)-set-consensus? Or in general to try to find a connection between a variant of g-group-renaming which allows up to k new names per group, and the (g, k)-safe-set-consensus problem. Is this variant of group renaming weaker, stronger or equivalent to set-consensus?

For (n, k)-safe-set-consensus we have shown a strong variant of the problem, which is equivalent to (n, k)-set-consensus, and a weaker variant, which is strictly weaker. Is there, or can there be a tighter characterization of safe-set-consensus in between? What is the power of the weaker variant? In the weaker variant of safe-set-consensus, it still remains to show the classification of the $(4, 2)$-safe-set-consensus. Can it solve $(4, 2)$-set-consensus if it is allowed to return 2 invalid values when 3 or 4 processes access it simultaneously? Another question is whether the Weak-Validity considered in this paper is in some sense the weakest validity condition which is still equivalent to the classical consensus definition.

Algorithm 6. (n, k) set-consensus using Strong (n, k) safe-set-consensus and R/W memory

---

Shared Variables:
    A[1..n],B[1..n] : Initially NULL
    $(n - 1, k)$set-consensus-A/B : 2 $(n - 1, k)$ set-consensus tasks
procedure set-consensus(proposal)
1:    **if** processor-id $< n$
2:        proposal := $(n - 1, k)$set-consensus-A(proposal)
3:        A[processor-id] := proposal
4:    **end if**
5:    **if** processor-id > 1
6:        proposal := $(n - 1, k)$set-consensus-B(proposal)
7:        B[processor-id] := proposal
8:    **end if**
9:    winner := safe-set-consensus(processor-id)
10:    **if** winner = n
11:        **if** B[n] $\neq$ NULL decide B[n] else decide any B[i] s.t. B[i] $\neq$ NULL
12:    **else**
13:        **if** winner in 1..n and A[winner] $\neq$ NULL decide A[winner]
14:        **else** decide any A[i] s.t. A[i] $\neq$ NULL
15:    **end if**
    end set-consensus

Acknowledgements. We are in debt to Gadi Taubenfeld for helpful discussions and suggestions.

References

1. Afek, Y., Attiya, H., Dolev, D., Gafni, E., Merritt, M., Shavit, N.: Atomic Snapshots of Shared Memory. Journal of the ACM 40(4), 873–890 (1993)
2. Attiya, H., Bar-Noy, A., Dolev, D., Peleg, D., Reischuk, R.: Renaming in an asynchronous environment. J. ACM 37(3), 524–548 (1990)
3. Afek, Y., Gamzu, I., Levy, I., Merritt, M., Taubenfeld, G.: Group renaming. In: Baker, T.P., Bui, A., Tixeuil, S. (eds.) OPODIS 2008. LNCS, vol. 5401, pp. 58–72. Springer, Heidelberg (2008)
4. Borowsky, E., Gafni, E.: The Implication of the Borowsky-Gafni Simulation on the Set-Consensus Hierarchy. Technical Report 930021, Department of Computer Science, UCLA (1993)
5. Afek, Y., Gafni, E., Rajsbaum, S., Raynal, M., Travers, C.: Simultaneous consensus tasks: A tighter characterization of set-consensus. In: Chaudhuri, S., Das, S.R., Paul, H.S., Tirthapura, S. (eds.) ICDCN 2006. LNCS, vol. 4308, pp. 331–341. Springer, Heidelberg (2006)
6. De Prisco, R., Malkhi, D., Reiter, M.: On k-Set Consensus Problems in Asynchronous Systems. IEEE Transactions on Parallel and Distributed Systems 12(1), 7–21 (2001)
7. Chaudhuri, S.: More Choices Allow More Faults: Set Consensus Problems in Totally Asynchronous Systems. Information and Computation 105, 132–158 (1993)

8. Fischer, M.J., Lynch, N.A., Paterson, M.S.: Impossibility of Distributed Consensus with One Faulty Process. Journal of the ACM 32(2), 374–382 (1985)
9. Gafni, E.: Group-solvability. In: Guerraoui, R. (ed.) DISC 2004. LNCS, vol. 3274, pp. 30–40. Springer, Heidelberg (2004)
10. Guerraoui, R., Kuznetsov, P.: The gap in circumventing the impossibility of consensus. J. Comput. Syst. Sci. 74(5), 823–830 (2008)
11. Herlihy, M.P.: Wait-Free Synchronization. ACM Transactions on Programming Languages and Systems 13(1), 124–149 (1991)
12. Herlihy, M.P., Wing, J.M.: Linearizability: a Correctness Condition for Concurrent Objects. ACM Transactions on Programming Languages and Systems 12(3), 463–492 (1990)

A   Appendix

A.1   Algorithm 1 Proof of Correctness

Wait-Free: Since $A()$ is wait-free and there are no loops.

Agreement: By the code all processors decide according to the value returned by $A()$ when invoking it with group ID $k1$. By the definition of tight group renaming this value is the same for all invocations, and therefore all the processors receive either k and decide 0, or a value different than k and decide 1.

Weak-Validity: Let p be a processor that executes the full algorithm in solo. Processor p therefore sees itself alone in its snapshot. If its input is 1 it first runs $A(k2, k2)$ in solo which by construction returns k. Hence by the definition of tight group renaming the call to $A(k1, k1)$ in Line 5 does not return k since $k1 \neq k2$ and this processor decides 1 in Line 9 and the output is valid. If its input is 0 it does not run $A(k2, k2)$ and its solo-run of $A(k1, k1)$ returns k. It therefore decides 0 in Line 9 and the output is valid in this case as well.

It should also be shown that at most g processors invoke A per initial group ID, and that A is never invoked more than once with the same processor ID: For each "real" processor A is run once with group $k1$ and at most one processor runs it with group $k2$, and it is therefore invoked at most g times with $k1$ and at most one time with $k2$ for a total of at most $g + 1$ invocations.

If no processor sees itself alone then all runs of A are with different processor ID's because all the values in $temp[]$ are different. Since at most one processor can see itself alone, at most one will use values $k1$ and/or $k2$ for processor ID's, which are in any case different from all the values in $temp[]$, and therefore $A()$ is never invoked more than once with a given processor ID.

A.2   Algorithm 2 Proof of Correctness

Suppose all processors return in Line 11. In this case each processor decides the result of its group's consensus task. At most $g - 1$ processors from the same group can reach this line, since at most g can access the task, and if they are all from the same group, the last one to take an atomic snapshot in line 2 will attain: $count - group = count - total = g$ and decide in Line 5. Hence neither the consensus objects nor the $(g-1)$-tight group renaming tasks are ever accessed by more than $g-1$ processors from the same group.

Since the consensus for a certain group always returns the same value, all processors from the same group decide the same value. We need only show that no two groups decide the same value. We claim only one group can see $count - group = count - total$ and propose 0. Since the snapshots are atomic, there cannot be two snapshots in which different group ID's appear alone. Since $(g-1)$-tight-group-renaming(processor-id,group-id) returns a different value for each group by definition, and does not return 0, we have that no two processors from different groups can propose the same value.

We are left with the case that at least one processor does decide in Line 5. This may happen only if all g processors are from the same group and all of them appear in the snapshot. In this case, any processor which sees all g in its snapshot returns 0. All others propose 0 since they all see only their group in Line 6, therefore all proposals are 0 and the consensus in Line 11 must return 0 as well, and all processors return 0.

A.3   Algorithm 3 Proof of Correctness

Wait-Free: By induction and observing the code, since there are no loops.

Agreement: Let v be the value returned at Line 9, which by definition is the same for all processors. Only a single value is written to P_A at Line 3, the value returned by the consensus at line 2, and only a single value is written to P_B at line 7, the result of the consensus at line 6. Therefore we only need to show that if $v = n$, then P_B is not NULL at Line 11, and if $v \neq n$ then P_A is not NULL at line 13.

Suppose a processor finishes executing Line 9, and either P_A or P_B have not yet been written to. If P_B has not yet been written to then this must be processor 1 since processors $2, \ldots, n$ go through line 7. We show that v cannot be n in this case. Since no processor from $2, \ldots, n$ has executed Line 7 then processor 1 runs line 9 in solo and by definition receives 1. Now suppose P_A has not yet been written to and a processor completed line 9. This can only be processor n and processors $1, \ldots, n-1$ have not yet executed Line 3. Therefore processor n runs in solo at Line 9 and by definition receives back n and the decision is therefore P_B.

Validity: We need only to show that the values written to P_A and P_B are valid, i.e., they are proposals of active processors. The result of the consensus at Line 2 is valid, since each processor from $1, \ldots, n-1$ proposes its own input there, therefore P_A is valid. P_B is the result of the consensus at line 6. The proposals there are either P_A, which is valid, or n's input if processor n is alive, thus the result is valid either way.

A.4   Algorithm 4 Proof of Correctness

Wait-Free: By induction: Version n has a constant number of iterations in its loops $(n-1)$, and uses version $n-1$ of our algorithm once.

Lemma 7. *Only a single value is ever written to P_A and a single value to P_B, and any time a processor reads one of these registers in the code, it contains that single value.*

Proof. Processor n only writes once to P_B, at the beginning of its code. Processors $1..n - 1$ each write only once to P_A, first thing after they reach agreement with each other at Line 10, therefore only one value is written to P_A, the value agreed upon at Line 10. Now suppose processor n reads P_A, it therefore reached Line 7. It reaches Line 7 only if not all safe-consensus instances return its proposal. Hence processor n did not run a solo-run in at least one of the tasks. Hence at least one of the other processors from $1..n - 1$ ran at least some part of that safe-consensus task, and it therefore executed its Line 12, therefore P_A contains its value when processor n reads it. Suppose one of the processors from $1..n - 1$ reads P_B. It therefore reached Line 17. It reaches Line 17 only if none of the safe-consensus tasks returned its proposal. Suppose by contradiction that processor n has not executed Line 2 yet. Let p be the first processor from $1..n - 1$ to finish running the first safe-consensus task it ran (At least one has finished, since a processor has reached Line 17). Since processor n has not yet executed line 2, it has not yet executed any part of any of the safe-consensus tasks. Since each of the processors $1..n - 1$ start with a different task instance, processor p must therefore have completed a solo-run of its first instance. Since all processors $1..n - 1$ use the same proposal, and each task guarantees consensus, then all processors $1..n - 1$ will decide at Line 16, in contradiction to the fact that a processor from $1..n - 1$ reached Line 17. Therefore processor n has executed line 2, and its proposal is in P_B whenever any processor reads P_B.

Validity: Since the values written to P_A and P_B are one of the processor's initial proposals (Either processor n's proposal, or the agreed upon proposal of processors $1..n - 1$) and from the fact that the only values decided on in the code are either one of these proposals, or the contents of P_A or P_B, it holds that each processor decides on a valid value.

Agreement: If at least one of the safe-consensus tasks return the agreed upon proposal of processors $1..n - 1$, they all decide that value at Line 16. If processor n had that same proposal, then whether it decides at Line 6 or 7, it will be that value (From the previous lemma we have that it will read that proposal form P_A at line 7). If it did not have the same proposal, it will not decide at Line 6, since at least one of the safe-consensus tasks returned a value which is not its proposal. It therefore decides P_A at Line 7, which is the agreed upon proposal of processors $1..n - 1$, i.e., all processors decide the same value.

If all safe-consensus tasks return the proposal of processor n, then processor n decides that value at Line 6. If processors $1..n - 1$ agreed upon that same proposal, they too all decide that value at line 16 (Since if all tasks returned it, then at least one did as well). If processors $1..n - 1$ had a different agreed upon value, then they will not decide at Line 16, since all tasks returned a different value than their proposal. They therefore read that value at Line 17 (As shown in the previous lemma), see that all the tasks returned it, and decide that value there.

Otherwise, at least one safe-consensus task returned a value different from processor n's proposal, and none of them returned the agreed upon proposal of processors $1..n - 1$. Processor n therefore will not decide at line 6 and will decide P_A at line 7 (Which is updated at this point). Processors $1..n - 1$ will not decide at neither lines 16 nor 17 (Since both those checks will fail), and they too decide P_A, and we reach consensus.

A.5   Algorithm 5 Proof of Correctness

Wait-Free: Since $(k, k - 1)$-set-cons is wait-free so is Algorithm 2 as it has no loops.

k-Agreement: The set of all possible values decided on in the algorithm are the $k - 1$ values returned by the $(k, k - 1)$-set-consensus task and 0, thus at most k values are decided upon, and at most one of them is an invalid value.

Weak-Validity: By the definition of safe-set-consensus, we need to show that if the first processor to output does so after at most $k - 1$ others invoked, then all processors decide on a proposed input value. Suppose the first processor to output does so after no more than $k - 1$ others have invoked. Denote this processor p. Since at most $k - 1$ others have invoked, they all saw at most k processors in their snapshot and accessed the set-consensus object at Line 5 with their proposal. Since this is a standard set-consensus object, it always returns valid values and all these processors therefore decide valid values. Let q be some processor which invoked after p decided and suppose it saw more than k in its snapshot. Since p already decided, it already executed Line 6 and its output is written in memory. Processor q therefore sees a non-NULL value in RES[] and decides it, i.e., no processor decides 0 and all outputs are valid.

A.6   Algorithm 6 Proof of Correctness

Wait-Free: By induction: Since version $n - 1$ is wait-free so is our code as we have no loops.

k-Agreement: We split the proof into two, according to whether the safe-set-consensus at Line 9 returned an invalid value or not. If it did not, then by definition it returned at most k valid values, i.e., at most k processor ID's which proposed themselves at Line 9. Hence if the winner is n, B[n] is not NULL (Since n passed Line 7 in order to propose itself), and if the winner is i in $1..n - 1$ A[i] is not NULL since it must have passed Line 3 in order to propose itself. Thus for each 'winner' at Line 9 exactly one result is decided on at Line 13 or Line 11. Since there are at most k 'winners', and since each A[] and B[] are written only once we have that at most k values are decided on.

Now suppose Line 9 returns an invalid result i. By definition all processors received this result. If the result is n then all processors decide at Line 11 either B[n] or any non-NULL value in B[], while if the result is not n they decide at lines 13 or 14 either A[i] or any non-NULL value in A[]. Since A[] and B[] are each filled respectively with results of separate k-value set-consensus tasks, then at most k values are chosen. It remains only to show that each processor indeed has some value to choose, i.e., if it needs to decide some non-NULL value in A[] or B[], then there exists such a value at that point: Since Line 9 returned an invalid result, then by definition more than k processors invoked before the first processor returned. Hence at least 2 processors invoked. Therefore any decision occurs after at least 2 processors reached Line 9. These processors are either 1 and n, or at least one of them is from $2..n-1$ and in any case at least one of them wrote to A[] and one of them to B[] before reaching Line 9, therefore we will always have a non-NULL value to choose.

Validity: All proposals to the first k-set-consensus task are valid, since they are inputs of active processors. Since this is a regular set-consensus task all its results are valid, and $A[]$ is filled with valid inputs. Since all proposals to the second k-set-consensus are either results of the first one or the input of processor n, it too returns only valid values, therefore $B[]$ is filled with valid values as well. Since all values decided on are non-NULL values from $A[]$ and $B[]$ it holds that all outputs are valid.

The RedBlue Adaptive Universal Constructions*

Panagiota Fatourou[1] and Nikolaos D. Kallimanis[2]

[1] Department of Computer Science, University of Ioannina & FORTH-ICS,
Crete Island, Greece
faturu@ics.forth.gr
[2] Department of Computer Science, University of Ioannina, Greece
nkallima@cs.uoi.gr

Abstract. We present the family of RedBlue algorithms, a collection
of universal wait-free constructions for linearizable shared objects in an
asynchronous shared-memory distributed system with n processes. The
algorithms are adaptive and improve upon previous algorithms in terms
of their time and/or space complexity.

The first of the algorithms achieves better time complexity than all
previously presented algorithms but it is impractical since it uses large
LL/SC registers. This algorithm comprises the keystone for the design of
the other RedBlue algorithms which are of practical interest. The second
algorithm significantly reduces the size of the required registers and it is
therefore practical in many cases. The last two algorithms work efficiently
for large objects improving previous universal constructions for large
objects presented by Anderson and Moir (PODC 1995).

1 Introduction

In a shared memory system processes communicate by accessing shared objects, data structures that can be accessed concurrently by several processes.
We present a collection of wait-free universal constructions that we call RedBlue
algorithms. A universal construction is an algorithm that implements any shared
object in an asynchronous system. A universal construction (or any other algorithm) is *wait-free* [13] if it guarantees that a process completes the operation
it executes in a finite number of its own steps despite the failures or the execution speed of other processes. The algorithms use LL/SC registers; Herlihy has
proved [13] that such algorithms necessarily use strong primitives (with infinite
consensus number) like LL/SC.

In shared memory systems it is often the case that the total number of processes n taking part in a computation is much larger than the actual number of
processes that concurrently access the shared object. For this reason, a flurry of
research [1, 2, 8, 9, 15] has been devoted to the design of *adaptive* algorithms

---

* This work was supported by the European Commission in the context of the SARC
integrated project #27648 (FP6) and by the Research Committee of the University
of Ioannina in the context of the project *"Design and analysis of Distributed shared
data structures"* (project code #80022).

whose time complexity depends on k, the maximum number of processes that concurrently access the shared object. All RedBlue algorithms are adaptive.

The algorithms use two perfect binary trees of $\lceil \log_2 n \rceil + 1$ levels each. The first tree (*red* tree) is employed for the estimation of any encountered contention, while the second tree (*blue* tree) is used for the synchronization with other processes when applying an operation. In each of these trees, a process is assigned a leaf node (and therefore also a path from this leaf to the root node, or vice versa). A process that wants to apply an operation to the simulated object, traverses first its path in the red tree from the root downwards looking for an unoccupied node in this path. Once it manages to occupy such a node, it starts traversing the blue tree upwards from the isomorphic blue node to the occupied red node, transferring information about its operation (as well as about other active operations) towards the tree's root. In this way, each operation traverses at most $O(\min\{k, \log n\})$ nodes in each of the two trees. Once information about the operation reaches the root, the operation is applied to the simulated object.

The first algorithm (F-RedBlue) has time complexity $O(\min\{k, \log n\})$ which is better than any previously presented algorithm but it uses big LL/SC registers; thus it is only of theoretical interest. A lower bound of $\Omega(\log n)$ on the time complexity of universal constructions that use LL/SC registers is presented in [17]. It holds even if an infinite number of unbounded-size registers are employed. Our algorithm is therefore optimal in terms of time complexity.

The second algorithm (S-RedBlue) is a slightly modified version of F-RedBlue that uses smaller registers and it is therefore practical in many cases. S-RedBlue uses $O(n)$ LL/SC registers, one for each of the trees' nodes and $n+1$ single-writer registers per process. Each register of the red tree has size $\lceil \log_2 n \rceil + 1$. Each register of the blue tree stores n bits, one for each process. One of the registers (the register corresponding to the blue root) is big. We implement this register by single-word LL/SC using the technique in [19]. In current systems where registers of 128 bits are available, S-RedBlue works with single-word LL/SC objects for up to 128 processes. In fact, even if $n/128 = c > 1$, where c is any constant, our algorithm can be implemented by single-word LL/SC registers with the same time complexity (increased by a constant factor) using the implementation of multi-word LL/SC from single-word LL/SC [19].

Most of the universal algorithms presented in the past, as well as F-RedBlue and S-RedBlue, copy the entire state of the object each time an update on it should be performed by some process. This is not practical for large objects whose states may require a large amount of storage to maintain. Anderson and Moir [7] presented a lock-free and a wait-free universal construction that are practical for large objects. Their algorithms assume that the object state is represented as a contiguous array which requires B data blocks of size S each for its storage. Each operation can modify at most T blocks and each process can help at most $M \geq 2T$ other processes. We combine some of the techniques introduced in [7] with the techniques employed by the RedBlue algorithms to design two simple wait-free constructions which have the nice properties of the constructions in [7] while achieving better time complexity. More specifically, our algorithms are adaptive. The time complexity of the first algorithm is much better than the wait-free construction presented in [7] but it does not assume an upper bound on the number of processes a process may help as the wait-free construction in [7] does. Our last algorithm (BLS-RedBlue) exhibits all the properties of the wait-free construction in [7] and still achieves better time complexity. In particular, its time complexity is similar to the time complexity of the wait-free algorithm in [7] but with k replacing n. The space complexity of the algorithm is the same as that of the wait-free algorithm in [7]. Our algorithms are much simpler than the constructions presented in [7], and they improve on time complexity upon these algorithms. Table 1 provides the exact time complexities and the space overheads of these algorithms (as well as of other previously published universal constructions discussed below).

Afek, Dauber and Touitou [3] have presented algorithm GroupUpdate which also uses a tree technique to keep track of the list of active processes. They then combine this tree construction with Herlihy's universal algorithm [13, 14] to get a universal construction with time complexity $O(k \log k + W + kD)$, where W is the size (in words) of the simulated object state and D is the time required for performing a sequential operation on it. Our first algorithm retains the basic structure of GroupUpdate but achieves better time complexity ($O(\min\{k, \log n\})$) by employing a faster mechanism to discover the encountered contention and by using large LL/SC registers. Our second algorithm addresses the problem of using large registers still achieving better time complexity than GroupUpdate.

Although the first of the RedBlue algorithms shares a lot of ideas with GroupUpdate, it also exhibits several differences: (1) it employs two complete binary trees each of which has one more level than the single tree employed by GroupUpdate; in each of these trees, each process is assigned its own leaf node which identifies a unique path (from the root to this leaf) in the tree for the process; (2) processes traverse the red tree first in order to occupy a node and this procedure is faster than a corresponding procedure in GroupUpdate. More specifically, GroupUpdate performs a BFS traversal of its employed tree in order for a process to occupy a node of the tree, while each process in any of the RedBlue algorithms always traverses appropriate portions of its unique path. This results in reduced time complexity for some of the RedBlue algorithms.

Afek, Dauber and Touitou [3] present a technique that employs indirection to reduce the size of the registers used by GroupUpdate (each tree register stores a process id and a pointer to a list of ids of currently active processes). A similar technique can be applied to the RedBlue algorithms in case n is too large to have n bits stored in a constant number of LL/SC registers. The resulting algorithms will have just a pointer stored in each of the blue nodes (thus using smaller registers than GroupUpdate which additionally stores a process id in each of its LL/SC registers). However, employing this technique would cause an increase to the step complexity of our algorithms by an $O(k \log n)$ additive term.

Afek, Dauber and Touitou present in [3] a second universal construction (IndividualUpdate) that has time complexity $O(k(W + D))$. IndividualUpdate stores sequence numbers in registers and therefore it requires unbounded size registers

Table 1. Summary of Universal Algorithms

Algorithm	Primitives	Time Complexity	Space Overhead
Herlihy [14]	consensus objects, r/w regs	$O(n)$	$O(n^3 W)$
GroupUpdate, Afek et al. [3]	LL/SC, consensus objects, r/w regs	$O(k \log k + W + kD)$	$O(n^2 W \log n)$
IndividualUpdate, Afek et al. [3]	$LL/VL/SC$	$O(kD \log D)$	$O(nD + W)$
F-RedBlue	LL/SC	$O(\min\{k, \log n\})$	$O(n^2 + W)$
S-RedBlue	$LL/VL/SC$, r/w regs	$O(k + W)$	$O(n^2 + nW)$
Anderson & Moir [6]	$LL/VL/SC$	$O((n/\min\{k, M/T\})(B + MS + nD))$	$O(n^2 + n(B + MS))$
LS-RedBlue	$LL/VL/SC$, r/w regs	$O(B + k(D + TS))$	$O(n^2 + n(B + kTS))$
BLS-RedBlue	$LL/VL/SC$, r/w regs	$O((k/\min\{k, M/T\})(B + MS + k + \min\{k, M/T\}D))$	$O(n^2 + n(B + MS))$

or registers that support the VL operation in addition to LL and SC. The first two RedBlue algorithms achieve better time complexity than IndividualUpdate. Some of our algorithms use single-word registers (however, they also employ $LL/VL/SC$ objects).

Afek, Dauber and Touitou [3] discuss a method similar to that presented in [10] to avoid copying the entire object's state in IndividualUpdate. The resulting algorithm has time complexity $O(kD \log D)$. The work of Anderson and Moir on universal constructions for large objects [7] follows this work. Our last two algorithms improve in terms of time complexity upon the constructions presented in [7]. They achieve this using single-word registers (and the last algorithm with the same space complexity as the wait-free construction in [7]).

Jayanti [18] presented f-arrays, a generalized version of a snapshot object which allows the execution of any aggregation function f on the m elements of an array of m memory cells that can be updated concurrently. As F-RedBlue, f-arrays has time complexity $O(\min\{k, \log n\})$; the algorithm uses a tree structure similar to that employed by GroupUpdate and our algorithm. F-RedBlue is universal, thus achieving wider functionality than f-arrays. Constructions for other restricted classes of objects with polylogarithmic complexity are presented in [11].

Afek et al. [4, 5] and Anderson and Moir [6] have presented universal algorithms for multi-object operations that support access to multiple objects atomically. The main difficulty encountered under this setting is to ensure good parallelism in cases where different operations perform updates in different parts of the object's state. We are currently working on designing appropriate versions of the RedBlue algorithms that can work efficiently for multi-object operations.

2 Model

We consider an asynchronous shared-memory system of n processes which communicate by accessing shared objects. A *read-write register* stores a value from some set and supports two operations: read returns the value of the register leaving its content unchanged, and write(v) writes the value v into the register and returns ack. An *LL/SC register* R stores a value from some set and supports the atomic operations LL and SC; $LL(R)$ returns the current value of R; the execution of $SC(R, v)$ by a process p must be preceded by the execution of an $LL(R)$ by p, and $SC(R, v)$ is successful if and only if no process has performed a successful SC on R since the execution of p's latest LL on R; if $SC(R, v)$ is successful the value of R changes to v and *true* is returned. Otherwise, the value of R does not change and *false* is returned. Some *LL/SC* registers support the operation VL in addition to LL and SC; VL returns *true* if no process has performed a successful SC on R since the execution of p's latest LL on R, and *false* otherwise. A register is *multi-writer* if all processes can change its content; on the contrary, a *single-writer* register can be modified only by one process. A register is *unbounded* if the set of values that can be stored in it is unbounded; otherwise, the register is *bounded*.

A *configuration* consists of a vector of $n + r$ values, where r is the number of registers in the system; the first n attributes of this vector describe the state of the processes, and the last r attributes are the values of the r registers of the system. In the *initial configuration* each process is in an initial state and each register contains an initial value. A process takes a *step* each time it accesses one of the shared registers; a step also involves the execution of any local computation that is required before the process accesses some shared register again (this may cause the state of the process to change). An *execution* is a sequence of steps.

Registers are usually used to simulate more complex objects. A *simulation* of an object O (which supports e.g., l operations) by registers uses the registers to store the data of O and provides l algorithms for each process, to implement each of the l operations supported by the simulated object. The *time complexity of an operation* is the maximum number of steps performed by any process to execute the operation in any execution of the simulation. The *time complexity* of the simulation is defined to be the maximum of the time complexities of its operations. A *universal object* simulates all other objects.

A process is *active* if it has initiated but not yet finished the execution of an operation *op*. When this is true, we also say that *op* is *active*. The portion of an execution that starts with the invocation of an operation *op* and ends with *op*'s response is called the *execution interval* of *op*. The *interval contention* of *op* is the total number of processes that take steps during the execution interval of *op*. The *point contention* of *op* is the maximum number of processes that are active at any configuration during the execution interval of *op*. The interval (point) contention of a simulation is the maximum interval (point) contention of any operation performed in any execution of the simulation. An execution is *serial* if for any two steps executed by the same operation, all steps between them are executed also by the same operation.

We assume that processes may experience *crash failures*, i.e., they may stop running at any point in time. A *wait-free* algorithm [13] guarantees that a process finishes the execution of an operation within a finite number of its own steps independently of the speed of the other processes or the faults they experience. (*Lock-freedom* is a weaker progress property that allows individual processes to starve but guarantees system-wide progress.) We concentrate on *linearizable* implementations [16]. *Linearizability* guarantees that in any execution α of the simulation, each of the executed operations in α appears to take effect at some point, called the *linearization point*, within its execution interval.

3   The F-RedBlue Algorithm

F-RedBlue uses a perfect binary tree (called the *blue tree*) of $\lceil \log n \rceil + 1$ levels, each node of which is an LL/SC register. Each process p owns one of the tree leaves and it is the only process capable of modifying this leaf. For each process p, there is therefore a unique path $pt(p)$ (called *blue path* for p) from the leaf node assigned to p up to the root. The LL/SC register of each node stores an array of n operation types (and their parameters), one for each process p to identify the operation that p is currently executing. The root node stores additionally the state of the simulated object (and for each process, the return value for the last operation (being) applied to the simulated object by the process).

Whenever p wants to apply an operation op to the object, it moves up its path until it reaches the root and ensures that the type $op\_tp(op)$ of op is recorded in all nodes of the path by executing two LL/SC on each node. If any of the LL/SC that p executes on a node succeeds, $op\_tp(op)$ is successfully recorded in it; otherwise, it can be proved that $op\_tp(op)$ is recorded for p in the node by some other process before the execution of the second of the two SC instructions executed by p. In this way, the type of op is propagated towards the root where op is applied to the object.

Process p also records in each node the operations executed by other active processes in an effort to help them finish their executions. Successful SC instructions executed at the root node may cause the application of several operations to the simulated object. In this way, the algorithm guarantees wait-freedom.

Once p ensures that op has been applied, it traverses its path from its leaf up to the root once more to eliminate any evidence of its last operation by overwriting the operation type of it with the special value $\perp$. This allows p to execute more operations on the simulated object; more specifically, a new operation op' executed by p is applied to the simulated object only if its operation type $op\_tp(op')$ reaches the root and finds the value $\perp$ stored for p in it.

This relatively simple algorithm requires $O(\log n)$ steps to execute. In order to make it adaptive, we use one more tree (the *red tree*), isomorphic to the blue tree. Thus, each process p is assigned a leaf node of the red tree which identifies a unique path from the root to this leaf (*red path for p*). The red tree allows processes to obtain information about the encountered contention which is then used to shorten the paths that processes traverse in the blue tree (i.e., the process starts its traversal of its blue path possibly from some internal node of the tree which is at a level that depends on the encountered contention).

Each node of the red tree stores information about one operation, namely the operation that is applied by the process that "occupies" the node. More specifically, each process p first tries to occupy a node of the red tree and then

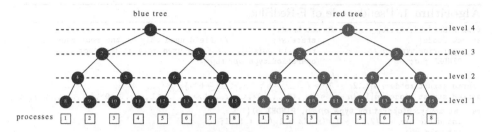

Fig. 1. The blue and the red tree of F-RedBlue for $n = 8$

starts traversing (part of) its blue path. In order to occupy a red node, p traverses its red path downwards starting from the root, until it finds a *clean node* (i.e., a currently unoccupied node with the value $(\perp, -1)$) and manages to occupy it by recording its operation type and its id in it. We prove that each red node is occupied by at most one process at any point in time. An occupied node identifies a process that is currently active, so as long as p reaches occupied nodes, it encounters more contention. We prove that p will eventually reach an unoccupied node and record the appropriate information there. (This, in the worst case, will be its leaf node.) Once p occupies some red node with id z_r, it starts each of the two traversals of its blue path from the node of the blue tree that corresponds to z_r up to the root. By employing the red tree, processes traverse shorter paths in the blue tree. This improves the time complexity of the algorithm to $O(\min\{k, \log n\})$, where k is the interval contention of op.

We continue to provide a technical description of F-RedBlue (Algorithm 1). Since the blue (red) tree is perfect and there is only one such tree with $\lceil \log n \rceil + 1$ levels, we implement it using an array bn (rn) of $2n-1$ elements. The nodes of the tree are numbered so that node z is stored in $bn[z]$ ($rn[z]$, respectively). The root node is numbered with 1, and the left and right children of any node z are nodes $2z$ and $2z + 1$, respectively. The two trees for $n = 8$ are illustrated in Figure 1. Process p, $1 \le p \le n$, is assigned the leaf node numbered $n + p - 1$. We remark that traversing up the path from any node z to the root can be implemented in a straightforward manner: the next node of z in the path is node numbered $\lfloor z/2 \rfloor$. However, the downward traversal of the path requires some more calculations which are accomplished by the lines $5 - 10$ of the pseudocode.

When a process p wants to execute an operation op of type $op\_tp(op)$ it first traverses its red path (lines $1 - 10$). For each node z of this path, it checks if the node is unoccupied (line 3) and if this is so, it applies an SC instruction to it in an effort to occupy it (line 4). If the SC is successful, the traversal of the red path ends (line 4). Otherwise, the next node in the path is calculated (lines $5 - 10$) and one more iteration of the loop is performed.

Once a red node z_r has been occupied, op performs two traversals of (a part of) its blue path starting from the node in the blue tree corresponding ro z_r, up to the root (lines $11 - 15$). This is accomplished by the two calls to **propagate**. Each of these traversals propagates the operation type written into z_r to the

Algorithm 1. Pseudocode of F-RedBlue.

```
type PINDEX {1,...,n};          struct bnode{
struct rnode{                       state st;        // field used only at the root node
    operation_type op_tp;           ret_vals vals[n];  // field used only at the root node
    PINDEX pid;                     operation_type ops_tp[n];
}                               }
shared struct rnode rn[1..2n − 1] = {< ⊥, −1 >, ..., < ⊥, −1 >};
shared struct bnode bn[1..2n − 1]={<⊥,<0,...,0>,<⊥,...,⊥>>, ...,<⊥,<0,...,0>,<⊥,...,⊥>>};
ret_val apply_op(operation_type op_tp, PINDEX p){
    int direction = n/2, z = 1, levels = lg(n) + 1, l;
    ret_vals rv;
```
1. for(l=levels;l ≥ 1;l--){   // traversal of red path
2.   LL(rn[z]);
3.   if(rn[z] == < ⊥, −1 >)
4.   if(SC(rn[z], <op_tp, id>)) break;
5.   if(id ≤ direction){   // find the next node in the path
6.   direction = direction - 2^{l-3};
7.   z = 2 * z;   // move to the left child of z
        }
8.   else{
9.   direction = direction + 2^{l-3};
10.   z = 2 * z + 1;   // move to the right child of z
        }
    }
11. propagate(z, p);   // first traversal of blue path: propagating the operation
12. rv = bn[1].vals[id];
13. LL(rn[z]);
14. SC(rn[z], <⊥, p>);   // the operation occupying rn[z] starts its deletion phase
15. propagate(z, p);   // second traversal of blue path: propagating ⊥
16. LL(rn[z]);
17. SC(rn[z], < ⊥, −1 >);   // re-initialize the occupied red node to ⊥
18. return rv;   // return the appropriate value
}

```
void propagate(int z, PINDEX p){
```
19. while(z!=0){   // traversal of the blue path
20.   for(int i=1 to 2)do{   // two efforts to store appropriate information into each node
21.   LL(bn[z]);
22.   bt=calculate(z, p);
23.   SC(z, bt);
        }
24.   z =⌊z/2⌋;
    }
}

```
struct bnode calculate(int z) {
    struct bnode tmp=< ⊥,< 0,...,0 >,< ⊥,...,⊥ >>, blue=bn[z], lc, rc;
    struct rnode red = rn[z];
```
25. if (2 * z + 1 < 2n) { lc = bn[2 * z]; rc = bn[2 * z + 1]; }   // if z is an internal node
26. if (z == 1) { tmp.ret_val[1..n] = blue.ret_val[1..n]; tmp.st = blue.st; }
27. for q = 1 to n do{
28.   if (red.pid == q) tmp.ops_tp[q] = red.op_pt;   // if process q occupies node red
29.   else if (is_predecessor(z,q,2 * z)) tmp.ops_tp[q]=lc.op_tp[q];
30.   else if (is_predecessor(z,q,2 * z + 1)) tmp.ops_tp[q]=rc.op_tp[q];
31.   if (z == 1 AND tmp.ops_tp[q] ≠ ⊥ AND tmp.ops_tp[q] ≠ blue.ops_tp[q])
32.   apply tmp.ops_tp[q] to tmp.st and store into tmp.ret_vals[q] the return value;
    }
33. return tmp;
}

```
boolean is_predecessor(int z, PINDEX p, int pred){
```
34.   int levels = ⌈log n⌉ + 1, total_nodes = $2^{levels} - 1$, leaf_node = ⌊total_nodes/2⌋ + p;
35.   int pred_height=levels − ⌊lg(2 * z)⌋, real_pred=⌊leaf_node/$2^{pred\_heigth-1}$⌋;
36.   if (pred < 2 * n AND real_pred == pred) return true;
37.   else return false;
}

root node. Notice that p records $\perp$, as its operation type, into z_r (lines $13 - 14$) before it starts its second traversal (we remark that this occurs by performing one more LL/SC since we assume that an LL/SC register supports only read, LL, and SC and not write).

On each node z of the traversed path, propagate performs twice the following: (1) an LL instruction on z (line 21); (2) calculates the appropriate information to write into z by calling function calculate (line 22); (3) an SC to store the result of calculate into z (line 23). Finally, it moves up to the next node of the blue path (line 24). Process p re-initializes its occupied red node by writing in it the value $(\perp, -1)$ (lines $16 - 17$) just before it returns.

Function calculate computes a (potentially new) operation type for each process q (lines $27 - 32$) as described below. If q occupies the isomorphic to z red node (line 28) then q's new operation type is the one which is recorded into the red node. Otherwise, the operation type for q is found in the previous node of z in q's blue path. In case z is the root node and the calculated operation type for q is not already written in z and it is different than $\perp$ (line 31), then the operation of q is a new one and should be applied to the simulated object (line 32). This is simulated by calling function apply.

To prove that F-RedBlue is correct, we first study the execution portion of an operation op that traverses the red tree. Intuitively, we prove that op manages to occupy exactly one red node, and as long as op is executed, no other operation succeeds in occupying this red node. We then study the properties of the execution portion of op that traverses the blue tree. We prove that if op occupies a red node with id z_r, $op\_tp(op)$ will be recorded into all nodes of the path starting from the blue node with id z_r up to the blue root. Therefore, op eventually reaches the root node and it is applied to the object. We also prove that the application of each operation occurs only once and that the calculated response values are correct. Due to lack of space, the formal proof of correctness for F-RedBlue is presented in [12]. Based on the properties of the red tree traversal that we prove, it is easy to argue that F-RedBlue has time complexity $O \min\{k, \log n\}$), where k is the interval contention. A more careful argument proves that this holds even if k is the point contention.

4   Modified Version of F-RedBlue That Uses Small Registers

We present S-RedBlue, a modified version of F-RedBlue that uses small registers. Each red node now stores $\lceil \log n \rceil + 1$ bits. A blue node other than the root stores n bits. The blue root stores n bits, a process id and the state of the object. This LL/SC register is implemented by single-word LL/SC registers using the implementation in [19].

In S-RedBlue, a process p uses a single-writer register to record its current operation (line 1). As in F-RedBlue, the process starts the execution of any of its operations by traversing the red tree. However, to occupy a red node, the process just records its id and sets the bit of the node to *true*.

Algorithm 2. Functions of S-RedBlue that are different from those of F-RedBlue.

```
struct rnode{                          struct bnode{
    boolean op;                            state st; // used only at root
    PINDEX pid;                            PINDEX pid; // used only at root
}                                          boolean ops[n];
                                       }
```

shared struct rnode $rn[1..2n-1]$ = $\{< F, -1 >, ..., < F, -1 >\}$;
shared struct bnode $bn[1..2n-1]$ = $\{< \perp, -1, < F, ..., F >>, ..., < \perp, -1, < F, ..., F >>\}$;
shared ret_val $rvals[1..n][1..n]$ = $\{\{\perp, ..., \perp\}, ..., \{\perp, ..., \perp\}\}$;
shared operation_type $ops[1..n]$ = $\{\perp, ..., \perp\}$;

```
ret_val apply_op(operation_type op_tp,
                 PINDEX p){                 struct bnode calculate(int z, PINDEX p) {
    int direction = n/2, z = 1;                struct bnode blue = bn[z], lc, rc;
    int levels = lg(n) + 1, l;                 struct bnode tmp = < ⊥, -1, < F, ..., F >>;
    ret_vals rv;                               struct rnode red = rn[z];

1.  ops[p] = op_tp;                        15. if (2*z+1 < 2n){lc=bn[2*z]; rc=bn[2*z+1];}
2.  for(l=levels;l ≥ 1;l--){               16. if (z == 1) {tmp.st = blue.st; tmp.pid = p;}
3.      LL(rn[z]);                          17. for(int q = 1 to n do){
4.      if(rn[z] == < F, -1 >)              18.     if (red.pid == q) tmp.ops[q] = red.op;
5.          if(SC(rn[z], <op_tp, id>))      19.     else if (is_predecessor(z,q,2*z))
                break;                      20.         tmp.ops[q] = lc.ops[q];
        //find the next node               21.     else if (is_predecessor(z,q,2*z+1))
6.          lines 5-10 of algorithm 1;     22.         tmp.ops[q] = rc.ops[q];
    }                                       23.     if (z==1 AND tmp.ops[q]==T
7.  propagate(z,p);                                    AND blue.ops[q]==F)
8.  rv = rvals[bn[1].pid][p];              24.         apply ops[q] to tmp.st and store into
9.  LL(rn[z]);                                         rvals[p][q] the return value;
10. SC(rn[z], <F, p>);                     25.     else if(z==1 AND tmp.ops[q]==T)
11. propagate(z,p);                        26.         rvals[p][q] = rvals[b.pid][q];
12. LL(rn[z]);                                 }
13. SC(rn[z], < F, -1 > );                 27. return tmp;
14. return rv;                             }
}
```

Similarly, each process, moving up the path to the root of the blue true, just sets a bit in each node of the path to identify that it is currently executing an operation. Thus, the bit array of the root identifies all processes that are currently active.

To avoid storing the return values in the root node, each process p maintains an array of n single-writer registers, one for each process. When p reaches the root (during the application of one of its operations), it first records the responses for the currently active processes in its appropriate single-writer registers (lines $25 - 26$). Then, it tries to store the new state of the object in the blue root together with its id and the set (bit vector) of active processes. A process finds the response for its current operation in the appropriate single-writer register of the process whose id is recorded in the root node.

The state is updated only at the root node and only when the bit value for a process changes from $false$ (F) to $true$ (T) in the blue root's bit array (line 23). This guarantees that the operation of each process is applied only once to the simulated object. However, all processes reaching the root, record responses for each currently active process p in their single-writer registers, independently of whether they also apply p's operation to the simulated object. This is necessary, since the operation of p may be applied to the object by some process q and later on (and before p reads the root node for finding its response) another process

q' may overwrite the root contents. Process q' will include p in its calculated active set but it will not re-apply p's operation to the object, since it will see that p's bit in the active set of the root node is already set. Still q' should record a response for p in its single-writer registers since p may read q' and not q in $bn[1].pid$ when seeking for its response.

The proof that S-RedBlue is correct closely follows the correctness proof of F-RedBlue. The main difference of the two algorithms is on the way that response values are calculated. If q is the process that applies some operation op, the response for op is originally stored in $rvals[q][p]$ and the id of q is written into the root node. The next process to update the root node will find the id of q in the root node and (as long as op has not yet read its response by executing line 8), it will see that $tmp.ops[p] = T$. Therefore, it will copy the response for op from $rvals[q][p]$ (line 26) to its appropriate single-writer register. So, when p seeks for the response of op it will find the correct answer in the single-writer register of the process recorded at the root node.

S-RedBlue uses $O(n)$ multi-writer LL/SC registers and $O(n^2)$ single-writer read/write registers. One of the multi-writer registers is large and it is implemented using the implementation of a W-word LL/SC object from single-word $LL/VL/SC$ objects presented in [19]. This implementation achieves time complexity $O(W)$ for both LL and SC and has space complexity $O(nW)$. Thus, the number of registers used by S-RedBlue is $O(n^2 + nW)$. In common cases where n bits fit in a constant number of single-word registers, the time complexity of S-RedBlue is $O(k+W)$ since calculate pays $O(k)$ to record k response values in the single-writer registers and $O(W)$ for reading and modifying the root node.

5   Adaptive Universal Constructions for Large Objects

In the universal constructions for large objects presented by Anderson and Moir in [7] the object is treated as if it were stored in a contiguous array. Moreover, the user is supposed to provide sequential implementations of the object's operations which call appropriate read and write procedures (described in [7]) to perform read or write operations in the contiguous array (see [7, Section 4] for more information on what the user code should look like and an example). The universal constructions partition the contiguous array into B blocks of size S each, and during the application of an operation to the object, only the block(s) that should be modified are copied locally (and not the entire object's state). The authors assume that each operation modifies at most T blocks.

S-RedBlue can easily employ the simple technique of the *lock-free* construction in [7] to provide a simple, adaptive, *wait-free* algorithm (called LS-RedBlue) for large objects. As illustrated in Algorithm 3, only routine propagate requires some modifications. Also, data structures similar to those in [7] are needed for storing the array blocks, having processes making "local" copies of them and storing back the changed versions of these blocks. More specifically, array BLK stores the B blocks of the object's state, as well as a set of *copy* blocks used by the processes for performing their updates without any interference by other

Algorithm 3. Pseudocode of LS-RedBlue.

```
type INDEX {1,...,nkT + B};              shared word BLK[1..B + kN * T][1..S];
struct bnode{                            private INDEX copy[1..kT], oldlst[1..kT];
    INDEX BANK[B];                       private pointer ptrs[1..B];
    PINDEX pid;                          private boolean dirty[1..B];
    boolean ops[n];                      private INDEX dcnt, blkidx;
}                                        private word v;

void propagate(int z, PINDEX p){         wordtype read(int addr){
    bnode b;                             15.    v=BLK[ptrs[addrdivS]][addrmodS];
1.    while(z!=0){                       16.    if(VL(BANK)==F)
2.        for(int i = 1 to 2) do {       17.        goto line 27 of calculate (Algorithm 2);
3.            if(z==1){                  18.    else return v;
4.                for(int j = 1 to B) do }
5.                    dirty[j]=F;
6.                dcnt = 0;              void write(int addr, wordtype val){
7.            }                          19.    blkidx=addr div S;
8.            b=LL(bn[z]);               20.    if(dirty[blkidx]==F){;
9.            if (z == 1) ptrs = b.BANK; 21.        memcpy(BLK[copy[dcnt]],
10.           bt=calculate(z,p);                         BLK[ptrs[blkidx]], sizeof(blktype));
11.           if(SC(bn[z], bt) AND z==1) 22.        dirty[blkidx]=T;
12.               for(int l = 1 to dcnt) do  23.        oldlsl[dcnt]=ptrs[blkidx];
13.                   copy[i] = oldlst[i];    24.        ptrs[blkidx]=copy[dcnt];
          }                              25.        dcnt=dcnt + 1;
14.       z = ⌊z/2⌋;                     26.    }
      }                                  27.    BLK[ptrs[blkidx]][addrmodS]=val;
}                                        }
```

processes. Since each operation modifies at most T blocks, a process reaching the blue root, requires at most kT copy blocks in order to make copies of the kT state blocks that it should possibly modify. So, BLK contains $nkT + B$ blocks; initially, the object's state is stored in $BLK[nkT + 1], \ldots, BLK[nkT + B]$ (the blocks storing the state of the object at some point in time are called *active*). The blue root node stores an array named $BANK$ of B indices; the ith entry of this array is the pointer (i.e., the index in BLK) of the ith active block. Each process has a private variable $ptrs$ which uses to make a local copy of the $BANK$ array (line 9).

The application of an active operation to the object is now done by calling (in `calculate`) the appropriate sequential code provided by the user. The codes of the `read` and `write` routines (used by the user code) are also presented in Algorithm 3 (although they are the same as those in [7]). These routines take an index $addr$ in the contiguous array as a parameter. From this index, the block number $blkidx$ that should be accessed is calculated as $blkidx = addr$ div S, and the offset in this block as $addr$ mod S. The actual index in BLK of the $blkidx$-th block can be found through the $BANK$ array. However, the process uses its local copy $ptrs$ of $BANK$ for doing so. Thus, line 15 simply access the appropriate word of BLK. If the execution of the VL instruction of line 16 by some process p does not succeed, the SC instruction of line 11 by p will also not succeed. So, we use the `goto` to terminate the execution of its `calculate`.

The first time that p executes a `write` to the $blkidx$-th block, it copies it to one of its copy blocks (line 21). Array $dirty$ is used to identify whether a block is written for the first time by p. In this case, the appropriate block is copied into the appropriate copy block of p (line 21). Indices to the kT copy blocks of p are stored in p's private array *copy*. The dirty bit for this block is set to *true* (line 22). Counter *dcnt* counts the number of different blocks written by p thus far in the execution of its current operation (line 25). The appropriate entry of *ptrs* changes to identify that the *blkidx*-th block is now one of the copy blocks of p (line 23). The write is performed in the copy block at line 27. A process p uses its copy blocks to make copies of the blocks that it will modify. If later p's SC at line 11 is successful, some of p's copy blocks become active blocks (substituting those that have been modified by p). These old active blocks (that have been substituted) consist the new copy blocks of p which it will use to perform its next operation. This is accomplished with the code of line 12.

LS-RedBlue is wait-free; it has space overhead $\Theta(n^2 + n(B + kTS))$ and time complexity $\Theta(B + k(D + TS))$. The wait-free universal construction presented in [7] assumes that each process has enough copy blocks to perform at most M/T other operations in addition to its own where $M \geq 2T$ is any fixed integer. The algorithm uses a quite complicated helping mechanism with return values written into return blocks which should then be recycled in order to keep the memory requirements low. The construction has time complexity $O((n/min\{n, M/T\})(B + nD + MS))$. LS-RedBlue achieves much better time complexity $(\Theta(B + k(D + TS)))$ and is adaptive. However, it assumes that processes have enough copy blocks to help any number of other active processes.

LS-RedBlue can be slightly modified to disallow processes to help more than M/T other processes. The resulting algorithm (BLS-RedBlue) is much simpler than the wait-free construction of [7] since it does not require the complicated mechanisms of [7] for returning values and verifying the application of an operation. These tasks are performed in BLS-RedBlue in the same way as in S-RedBlue.

The BLS-RedBlue algorithm is presented in Algorithm 4. Propagate executes the same code as in S-RedBlue for all nodes other than the root. The code executed by a process p when it reaches the blue root (lines $27 - 36$) is similar to the one of LS-RedBlue. However, lines $32 - 36$ may have to execute more times in order to ensure that p's operation has been applied to the object. Only when this has occurred, p's propagate returns. To speed up this process, we store one more field, called *help*, in the blue root node. Each process, applying a successful SC on the root node, writes there the index of the last active process it has helped, and next time processes start their helping effort from the next to this process. This has as a result, the body of the while loop (line 31) to execute at most $\min\{k, 2M/T\}$ times. Each time that the loop is executed twice, M/T more active processes are helped. Therefore, after $2k/(\min\{k, M/T\})$ iterations, the operation of p will have been applied to the object.

Each iteration of the loop requires $O(B)$ time to execute lines $27 - 28$, 32, 36 and 34. Each execution of calculate applies at most $\min\{k, M/T\}$ operations. The cost of applying these operations is $O(MS + \min\{k, M/T\}D)$. Finally, the cost of calculating the return values at each execution of calculate is $O(k)$. So, the cost of executing the while loop is $O(k/(\min\{k, M/T\})(B + MS + k + \min\{k, M/T\}D))$. Given that each process requires only $O(\log k)$

Algorithm 4. Algorithm BLS-RedBlue.

```
struct bnode{
    INDEX BANK[B];  // used only at root
    PINDEX pid;     // used only at root
    PINDEX help;    // used only at root
    boolean ops[n];
}

void propagate(int z, int p){
    bnode b;
1.  while(z!=1){
2.      for (int i = 1 to 2) do {
3.          b=LL(bn[z]);
4.          bt=calculate(z, p);
5.          SC(bn[z], bt);
        }
6.      z =⌊z/2⌋;
    }

    // operations to perform at root
7.  b=LL(bn[1]);
8.  while (b.ops[p] == F) {
9.      for (int j=1 to B) do
10.         dirty[j]=F;
11.     dcnt = 0;
12.     b=LL(bn[1]);
13.     ptrs = b.BANK;
14.     bt=calculate(1, p);
15.     if (SC(bn[1], bt))
16.         for (l = 1 to dcnt) do
17.             copy[i] = oldlst[i];
    }
}
```

```
struct bnode calculate(int z, int p) {
    struct bnode tmp =< ⊥,−1,< F,...,F >>,
                      blue = bn[z], lc, rc;
    struct rnode red = rn[z];
    int help=0,q;
17. if (2 ∗ z + 1 < 2n) {
18.     lc=bn[2 ∗ z];
19.     rc=bn[2 ∗ z + 1];
    }

20. if (z==1) {q = blue.help; tmp.pid = p; }
21. else q = 1;
22. for (int i = 1 to n) do{
23.     if (red.pid == q) tmp.ops[q] = red.op;
25.     else if (is_predecessor(z,q,2 ∗ z))
26.         tmp.ops[q] = lc.ops[q];
27.     else if (is_predecessor(z,q,2 ∗ z + 1))
28.         tmp.ops[q] = rc.ops[q];
29.     if (z == 1 AND tmp.ops[q]==T
                  AND blue.ops[q]==F) {
30.         if (help < M/T) {
31.             apply ops[q] and store into
                rvals[p][q] the return value;
32.             help = help + 1;
33.         }
34.         else tmp.ops[q] = F;
35.     }
36.     else if(z == 1 AND tmp.ops[q]==T)
37.         rvals[p][q] = rvals[b.pid][q];
38.     q = (q + 1) MOD n
    }
39. return tmp;
}
```

---

steps to reach the root node, it follows that the time complexity of BLS-RedBlue is $O((k/\min\{k, M/T\})(B+MS+k+\min\{k, M/T\}D))$. Obviously, BLS-RedBlue achieves better time complexity than the wait-free construction of [7] and it is adaptive. This is achieved without any increase to the required space overhead which is $O(n^2 + n(MS + B))$ for both algorithms.

In case a return value has size larger than a single word, i.e., it is at most R words, our algorithms can still work with single-word registers by substituting the array of single-writer registers held by each process with a bidimensional array of nR words. Then, the time complexity of BLS-RedBlue becomes $O((k/\min\{k, M/T\})(B + MS + kR + \min\{k, M/T\}D))$. The wait-free universal construction of [7] has time complexity $O(n/\min\{n, M/T\}(B+nR+nD+MS))$ under this assumption.

If n is very large, a technique like the one used by GroupUpdate [3] can be employed to store a single pointer instead of the bit vector in each blue node. Then, the time complexity of BLS-RedBlue becomes $O(k \log k + (k/\min\{k, M/T\})(B+MS+kR+\min\{k, M/T\}D))$. We expect that $k \log k \in O((k/\min\{k, M/T\})(B+MS + kR + \min\{k, M/T\}D))$ for large objects in most cases.

References

[1] Afek, Y., Attiya, H., Fouren, A., Stupp, G., Touitou, D.: Long-lived renaming made adaptive. In: Proc. of the 18th ACM Symposium on Principles of Distributed Computing, pp. 91–103 (1990)

[2] Afek, Y., Boxer, P., Touitou, D.: Bounds on the shared memory requirements for long-lived & adaptive objects. In: Proc. of the 19th ACM Symposium on Principles of Distributed Computing, pp. 81–89 (2000)

[3] Afek, Y., Dauber, D., Touitou, D.: Wait-free made fast. In: Proc. of the 27th ACM Symposium on Theory of Computing, pp. 538–547 (1995)

[4] Afek, Y., Merritt, M., Taubenfeld, G.: The power of multi-objects. Information and Computation 153, 213–222 (1999)

[5] Afek, Y., Merritt, M., Taubenfeld, G., Touitou, D.: Disentangling multi-object operations. In: Proc. of the 16th ACM Symposium on Principles of Distributed Computing, pp. 262–272 (1997)

[6] Anderson, J.H., Moir, M.: Universal constructions for multi-object operations. In: Proc. of the 14th ACM Symposium on Principles of Distributed Computing, pp. 184–193 (1995)

[7] Anderson, J.H., Moir, M.: Universal constructions for large objects. IEEE Transactions on Parallel and Distributed Systems 10(12), 1317–1332 (1999)

[8] Attiya, H., Fouren, A.: Adaptive and efficient wait-free algorithms for lattice agreement and renaming. SIAM Journal on Computing 31(2), 642–664 (2001)

[9] Attiya, H., Fouren, A.: Algorithms adapting to point contention. Journal of the ACM (JACM) 50, 444–468 (2003)

[10] Barnes, G.: A method for implementing lock-free shared data structures. In: Proc. of the 5th ACM Symposium on Parallel Algorithms and Architectures, pp. 261–270 (1993)

[11] Chandra, T.D., Jayanti, P., Tan, K.: A polylog time wait-free construction for closed objects. In: Proc. of the 17th ACM Symposium on Principles of Distributed Computing, pp. 287–296 (1998)

[12] Fatourou, P., Kallimanis, N.D.: The redblue adaptive universal constructions. Technical Report TR 2009-02, Department of Computer Science, University of Ioannina (February 2009)

[13] Herlihy, M.: Wait-free synchronization. ACM Transactions on Programming Languages and Systems (TOPLAS) 13, 124–149 (1991)

[14] Herlihy, M.: A methodology for implementing highly concurrent data objects. ACM Transactions on Programming Languages and Systems (TOPLAS) 15(5), 745–770 (1993)

[15] Herlihy, M., Luchangco, V., Moir, M.: Space and time adaptive non-blocking algorithms. Electronic Notes in Theoretical Computer Science 78 (2003)

[16] Herlihy, M.P., Wing, J.M.: Linearizability: A correctness condition for concurrent objects. ACM Transactions on Programming Languages and Systems (TOPLAS) 12, 463–492 (1990)

[17] Jayanti, P.: A time complexity lower bound for randomized implementations of some shared objects. In: Proc. of the 17th ACM Symposium on Principles of Distributed Computing, pp. 201–210 (1998)

[18] Jayanti, P.: f-arrays: implementation and applications. In: Proc. of the 21th ACM Symposium on Principles of Distributed Computing, pp. 270–279 (2002)

[19] Jayanti, P., Petrovic, S.: Efficient wait-free implementation of multiword LL/SC variables. In: Proc. of the 25th IEEE International Conference on Distributed Computing Systems, pp. 59–68 (2005)

Help When Needed, But No More: Efficient Read/Write Partial Snapshot

Damien Imbs and Michel Raynal

IRISA, Université de Rennes 1, 35042 Rennes, France
{damien.imbs,raynal}@irisa.fr

Abstract. An atomic snapshot object is an object that can be concurrently accessed by asynchronous processes prone to crash. It is made of m components (base atomic registers) and is defined by two operations: an update operation that allows a process to atomically assign a new value to a component and a snapshot operation that atomically reads and returns the values of all the components. To cope with the net effect of concurrency, asynchrony and failures, the algorithm implementing the update operation has to help concurrent snapshot operations so that they always terminate.

This paper is on *partial snapshot* objects. Such an object provides a snapshot operation that can take any subset of the components as input parameter, and atomically reads and returns the values of this subset of components. The paper has two contributions. The first is the introduction of two properties for partial snapshot object algorithms, called *help-locality* and *freshness*. Help-locality requires that an update operation helps only the concurrent partial snapshot operations that read the component it writes. When an update of a component r helps a partial snapshot, freshness requires that the update provides the partial snapshot with a value of the component r that is at least as recent as the value it writes into that component. (No snapshot algorithm proposed so far satisfies these properties.) The second contribution consists of an update and a partial snapshot algorithms that are wait-free, linearizable and satisfy the previous efficiency properties. Interestingly, the principle that underlies the proposed algorithms is different from the one used so far, namely, it is based on the "write first, and help later" strategy. An improvement of the previous algorithms is also presented. Based on LL/SC atomic registers (instead of read/write registers) this improvement decreases the number of base registers from $O(n^2)$ to $O(n)$. This shows an interesting tradeoff relating the synchronization power of the base operations and the number of base atomic registers when using the "write first, and help later" strategy.

Keywords: Adaptive algorithm, Asynchronous shared memory system, Asynchrony, Atomicity, Efficiency, Concurrency, Linearizability, LL/SC atomic registers, Locality, Partial snapshot, Process crash, Read/Write atomic register, Wait-free algorithm.

1 Introduction

1.1 Context of the Study: Snapshot Objects

Shared memory snapshot objects. Snapshot objects have been introduced in [1,4]. Considering a shared memory system made up of base atomic read/write registers, that can

I. Keidar (Ed.): DISC 2009, LNCS 5805, pp. 142–156, 2009.

be concurrently accessed by asynchronous processes prone to crash, a snapshot object is an object that (1) consists of m components (each component being a base atomic register that can contain an arbitrary value), and (2) provides the processes with two operations, denoted update() and snapshot(). The update() operation allows the invoking process to atomically store a new value in an individual component. Differently, the snapshot() operation returns the values of all the components as if they had been read simultaneously.

From an execution point of view, a snapshot object has to satisfy the safety property called *linearizability*: the update and snapshot operations have to appear as if they had been executed one after the other, each being instantaneously executed at some point of the time line comprised between its start event and its end event [20]. From a liveness point of view, each update or snapshot operation has to terminate if the invoking process does not crash. This liveness property is called *wait-freedom* [17]. It means that an operation issued by a correct process has to terminate whatever the behavior of the other processes (the fact that some processes crash or are very slow cannot prevent an operation from terminating, as long as the issuing process does not crash). Wait-freedom is starvation-freedom despite asynchrony and process failures. In order to implement the wait-freedom property, a process that issues an update() operation can be required to help terminate the processes that have concurrently issued a snapshot() operation (preventing them from looping forever). This helping mechanism is required to ensure that all the snapshot() operations (issued by processes that do not crash) do always terminate [1].

The snapshot abstraction. The snapshot object has proved to be a very useful abstraction for solving many other problems in asynchronous shared memory systems prone to process crashes, such as approximate agreement, randomized consensus, concurrent data structures, etc. A snapshot object hides the "implementation details" that are difficult to cope with in presence of the net effect of concurrency, asynchrony and failures. It is important to notice that, from a computational point of view, a snapshot object is not more powerful than the base atomic read/write objects it is built from. It only provides a higher abstraction level.

Shared memory vs message-passing snapshots. The values returned by a snapshot() operation is a value of the part of the shared memory that is encapsulated in the corresponding snapshot object. It follows from the linearizability property satisfied by a snapshot object that there is a time instant at which the values returned by a snapshot() operation were simultaneously present in the shared memory, this time instant belonging to the time interval associated with that snapshot() operation.

The previous observation is in contrast with the notion of *distributed snapshot* used to capture consistent global states in asynchronous message-passing systems [12] where two distributed snapshots obtained by two processes can be consistent but incomparable in the sense that they cannot be linearized. The set of all the distributed snapshots that can be obtained from a message-passing distributed execution has only a lattice structure (basically, they can be partially ordered but not totally ordered). In that sense, the abstraction level provided by a shared memory snapshot object is a higher abstraction level than the one offered by message-passing distributed snapshots. It hides more asynchrony.

Types of snapshot objects. Two types of snapshot objects have been investigated: single-writer and multi-writer snapshot objects. A single-writer snapshot object has one component per process, and the component associated with a process can be written only by that process. The number of components (m) is then the same as the number of processes (n). The base registers from which a single-writer snapshot object is built are then single-writer/multi-reader atomic registers. Wait-free algorithms implementing single-writer snapshot objects for n processes are described in [1]. Their costs is $O(n^2)$ (when counting the number of shared memory accesses). An algorithm whose cost is $O(n \log(n))$ is described in [10]. An implementation suited to systems with a possibly infinite number of processes (but where finitely many processes can take steps in each finite time interval) is described in [3]. An implementation that is adaptive to total contention (i.e., adaptive to the actual number $k \in [1..n]$ of processes that access the snapshot object during an entire execution [7]) is described in [8]. Its cost is $O(k \log(k))$.

A multi-writer snapshot object is a snapshot object of which each component can be written by any process. So, the base read/write registers on which its implementation relies are multi-writer/multi-reader atomic registers. Wait-free algorithms implementing multi-writer snapshot objects made up of m base components are described in [5,23,25]. The algorithm described in [23] has a linear cost $O(n)$. A short survey of algorithms that implement single-writer and multi-writer snapshot objects is presented in [13].

The notion of partial snapshot. Usually, when a process invokes the snapshot() operation, it is not interested in obtaining the values of all the components, but in the values of a given subset of the components. A *partial snapshot* operation (denoted p_snapshot()) is a generalization of the base snapshot() operation. It takes a sequence $R = < r_1, \cdots, r_x >$ of component indices as input parameter, and returns a sequence $< v_1, \cdots, v_x >$ of values such that the value v_ℓ is the value of the component whose index is r_ℓ (an invocation of p_snapshot() that considers all the components is actually a snapshot() invocation). As before, the invocations of p_snapshot() and update() have to be linearizable, and their implementation has to be wait-free. The notion of partial snapshot object has first been introduced and investigated in [9].

1.2   Content of the Paper and Related Work

Related work. This paper is on efficient wait-free implementations of multi-writer/multi-reader partial snapshot objects in the base read/write shared memory model augmented with underlying *active set* objects [2]. Such an object offers three operations: Join(), Leave() and GetSet(). Basically, Join() adds the invoking process to the active set, while Leave() suppresses it from this set; GetSet() returns the current value of the active set. (There are efficient adaptive read/write implementations of an active set, i.e., implementations whose number of read/write shared memory accesses depends only on the number of processes that invoke Join() and Leave() [2]. So, the base model used in this paper is the read/write atomic register model.)

An algorithm based on read/write atomic registers and an active set object, that implements a partial snapshot object is described in [9] (as far as we know, it is the only such algorithm proposed so far)[1]. That algorithm extends the basic full snap-shot algorithm described in [1]. It is based on the following principle. Each invocation of p_snapshot(R) first makes public the list $R =< r_1, \cdots, r_x >$ of indices of the components it wants to read. Then, it sequentially invokes Join(), an internal embedded_snapshot(R) operation, and finally Leave(). The update operation works as follows. When a process p_i invokes update(r, v, i) (where v is the value it wants to assign to the component whose index is r), it first invokes GetSet() to have a view of all the processes that are concurrently executing a p_snapshot() operation. To guarantee the wait-freedom property (any process that does not crash has to terminate its operations), p_i helps terminate all the concurrent p_snapshot() operations. To that end, it executes an embedded_snapshot() operation whose input includes all the components read by the processes in the active set (whose value has been obtained by the GetSet() invocation). In that way, if p_i does not crash, a concurrent p_snapshot() operation can retrieve the values it is interested in from the values returned by the embedded_snapshot() issued by p_i.

Features of the proposed algorithm. The update and partial snapshot algorithms proposed here have several noteworthy features that make them different from the previous full/partial snapshot algorithms (as far as we know). These features are the "write first, help later" strategy, and the cheap way helping is realized. They result from the additional help-locality and freshness properties the update and snapshot algorithms are required to satisfy.

Freshness. The aim of the *freshness* property is to oblige an update operation that helps a snapshot operation to provide that snapshot with values as recent as possible. More precisely, let up = update(r, v, i) be an update invoked by the process p_i to write the value v in the component r of the partial snapshot object, and psp = p_snapshot(R) be a concurrent snapshot invocation such that psp starts after up (where "starts" means "accesses the shared memory for the first time"). Freshness requires that the value returned for the component r be v or a more recent value (as each component is an atomic register, the notion of "more recent" is well defined)[2]. Stated in another way, freshness requires that the updates be linearized at their first shared memory access.

To obtain that property, the update algorithm proposed in the paper uses the "write first, help later" strategy (differently, the previous algorithms are based on the "help first, then write" strategy).

Help-locality. This property aims at obtaining more efficient update operations by limiting contention. To that end, it reduces the help provided to the partial snapshot operations by the update operations. This property is close to the notion of disjoint-access

---

[1] That paper presents also another algorithm implementing a partial snapshot object, that is based on read/write atomic registers, and more sophisticated registers that support Fetch&Add and Compare&Swap atomic operations. These more sophisticated registers are mainly used to obtain an efficient implementation of the underlying active set object. Here we consider the pure base read/write atomic register model.

[2] As far as we know, none of snapshot algorithms proposed so far satisfies the freshness property. They all provide the snapshot with a component r value that is strictly older than v.

parallelism defined by Israeli and Rappoport [24]. It differs from disjoint-access parallelism by not placing any restriction on the step complexity of operations, and by being more restrictive on the contention that it allows. The goal of the help-locality property is that the underlying shared memory accesses issued by a pair of concurrent operations update$(r, v, -)$ and p_snapshot(R) do not conflict if $r \notin R$.

As for freshness, the help-locality property is not ensured by the algorithms proposed so far to implement the update operation. The snapshot algorithm presented in [1] is very conservative: each update operation is required to compute one helping full snapshot value even when there is no concurrent snapshot. The partial snapshot algorithm described in [9] is a little bit less conservative: an update$(r, -, -)$ operation concurrent with no snapshot operation is not required to help, but an update$(r, -, -)$ operation concurrent with one or more p_snapshot(R_ℓ) operations $(1 \leq \ell \leq z)$ has to help each of them, whatever the sets of entries they access, i.e., even the p_snapshot(R_ℓ) operations that don't access the entry updated by the update$(r, -, -)$ operation.

An additional asynchrony feature. An additional feature of the proposed update algorithm lies in its asynchrony and in the size of the helping snapshot values it computes. Previous (partial or full) snapshot implementations use one base atomic register $REG[r]$ per component r. These registers have to be large. They are made up of several fields, including a field for the last value written, a field storing a snapshot value used to help snapshot operations, and a few other fields containing control data. A snapshot value is made up of one value per component in the case of a full snapshot object, and one value for a subset of the components in the case of a partial snapshot object. Then, each update$(r, v, -)$ operation atomically writes into $REG[r]$ both the new value v and a snapshot value. This means that the implementation of this atomic write can be space and time expensive.

Differently, thanks to the "write first, help later (and individually)" strategy, the proposed update$(r, v, -)$ algorithm separates the write of the value v into $REG[r]$ and the individual writes of helping snapshot values, one for each concurrent p_snapshot(R_ℓ) operation such that $r \in R_\ell$. The fact that an update$(r, v, -)$ operation first writes v, and helps, only later and individually, each concurrent partial snapshot that reads the component r, (1) allows those to obtain a value for the component r that is at least as recent as v, and (2) allows the use of several independent helping atomic registers that are written individually (thereby allowing more efficient atomic write operations). Moreover, the size of these atomic "array-like" registers can be smaller than m^3.

Motivation. As the work described in [9], our aim is to better understand synchronization in presence of failures. From a more practical point of view, a p_snapshot(R) operation can be seen as the reading part of a transaction that needs to obtain mutually consistent and up-to-date values from the base objects specified in R. Such a study can help better understand the underlying foundations of software transactional memories [6,14,15,19,18,21,28].

---

[3] If each partial snapshot by a process p_i is on at most k components, the atomic "array-like" registers used to help p_i need to have only k entries. If $k \ll m$, the writes into such atomic k-size registers can generate less contention that writes into atomic m-size registers.

Roadmap. The paper is composed of 6 sections. Section 2 presents the base asynchronous read/write shared memory prone to process crashes, equipped with an active set object. Section 3 defines the atomic partial snapshot object and the help-locality and freshness properties. Then, Section 4 presents algorithms implementing the update and partial snapshot operations, and proves that they satisfy the previous properties. Section 5 discusses the proposed algorithms and presents a version of them based on LL/SC atomic registers (instead of read/write atomic registers). This improvement, that satisfies the help-locality and freshness properties, is more efficient than the base algorithm from a memory size point of view, namely it requires $O(n)$ LL/SC atomic registers instead of $O(n^2)$ read/write atomic registers. Finally, Section 6 provides a few concluding remarks. (Additional developments are described in [22].)

2   Underlying Shared Memory Model

Asynchronous shared memory model. The system is made up of n processes $p_1, \ldots, p_n$. The identity of p_i is i. These processes communicate through multi-writer/multi-reader atomic registers. Atomic means that each read or write operation on a register appears as if it has been executed sequentially at some point of the time line comprised between its start and end event. The registers are assumed to be reliable (this assumption is without loss of generality -from a computability point of view- as it is possible to build atomic reliable registers on top of crash prone atomic registers [11,16,18,26]).

There is no assumption on the speed of processes: they are asynchronous. Moreover, up to $(n-1)$ processes may crash. Before it crashes (if it ever crashes), a process executes correctly its algorithm. A crash is a premature halt: after it has crashed, a process executes no more step. Given a run, a process that does not crash is *correct* in that run, otherwise it is *faulty* in that run.

Active set object. We assume that the processes can access an *active set* objects. Such an object, first proposed in [2], can be used to solve adaptive synchronization problems (e.g., [29]). As already indicated, its aim is to allow the processes to have a view of which of them are concurrently executing operations. To that end, an active set object provides the processes with three operations, Join(), Leave() and GetSet() (informally described in the Introduction). These operations are not required to be atomic. (So, the definition of an operation cannot assume that the concurrent executions of other operations are both instantaneous and one at a time, they have to explicitly take into account the fact that their execution spans a finite period of time.)

Notation. The shared memory objects are denoted with capital letters, while the local variables are denoted with lower case letters (the subscript i denotes then the corresponding process).

3   Definitions

3.1   Partial Snapshot Object

As already said in the Introduction, a multi-writer/multi-reader partial snapshot object is made up of m components (each being a multi-writer/multi-reader atomic register) that provides the processes with two operations update() and snapshot() such that:

- update(r, v, i) is invoked by p_i to write the value v in the component r ($1 \leq r \leq m$) of the snapshot object. That operation returns the control value ok.
- p_snapshot(R), where R is a sequence $< r_1, \cdots, r_x >$ of component indexes, allows a process to obtain the value of each component in R. It returns a corresponding sequence of values $< v_1, \cdots, v_x >$.

A partial snapshot object is defined by the following properties.

- Termination. Every invocation of update() or p_snapshot() issued by a correct process terminates.
- Consistency. The operations issued by the processes (except possibly the last operation issued by a faulty process[4]) appear as if they have been executed one after the other, each one being executed at some point of the time line between its start event and its end event.

The termination property is wait-freedom [17] (starvation-freedom despite concurrency and process crashes). The consistency property is linearizability [20] (here, it means that a p_snapshot() operation always returns component values that were simultaneously present in the shared memory, and are up-to-date).

3.2 Additional Properties Related to the Implementation

These properties, that have been informally presented in the Introduction, do not concern the definition of the partial snapshot problem, but the way it is solved by the algorithms that implement its operations.

As already indicated, the aim of the help-locality property is reduce shared memory conflicts by preventing an update$(r, -, -)$ to help a concurrent p_snapshot(r) when $r \notin R$. More formally, let L_{op} be the set of (high level) components accessed by operation op (note that L_{op} is a singleton if op is an update$(r, -, -)$ operation). Let M_{op} be the set of base objects (underlying atomic registers and active set objects) accessed by operation op.

Definition 1. *The algorithms implementing the update and partial snapshot operations satisfy the* help-locality *property if, for any pair of concurrent operations $op1$, $op2$ that access a common base object (1) both access a common component, or (2) there exists an operation $op3$ concurrent with $op1$ and $op2$ such that (2.1) both $op1$ and $op3$ access a common component and (2.2) both $op2$ and $op3$ access a common component. More formally, $M_{op1} \cap M_{op2} \neq \emptyset \Rightarrow (L_{op1} \cap L_{op2} \neq \emptyset) \vee (\exists op3 : (L_{op1} \cap L_{op3} \neq \emptyset \wedge L_{op3} \cap L_{op2} \neq \emptyset))$.*

This efficiency-related property follows from the observation that an update$(r, -, -)$ operation and a p_snapshot(R) operation that are concurrent and such that $r \notin R$, are actually independent operations. (This is similar to a read on a register X and a write on a register $Y \neq X$ that are concurrent.) Intuitively, help-locality requires that the implementation does only what is necessary and sufficient.

---

[4] If such an operation does not appear in the sequence, it is as if it has not been invoked.

Definition 2. *The algorithms implementing the update and partial snapshot operations satisfy the* freshness *property if an* update$(r, v, -)$ *operation always happens as if it was executed atomically at the time of its first access to shared memory (i.e., the update is always linearized at its first access to shared memory).*

The aim of this property is to provide the partial snapshot operations with values "as fresh as possible" in the following sense. If update$(r, v, -)$ helps p_snapshot(R) (so we have $r \in R$), then the value returned for r is at least as recent as v. As noticed in the Introduction, (to our knowledge) no pair of update/snapshot algorithms proposed so far satisfies help-locality or freshness.

4   An Efficient Partial Snapshot Construction

This section presents a construction (Figures 1 and 2) of a partial snapshot object that satisfies the help-locality and freshness properties previously defined.

4.1   The Underlying Shared Objects

The algorithms implementing the p_snapshot() and update() operations use the following shared variables.

- An array, denoted $REG[1..m]$, of multi-writer/multi-reader atomic registers. The register $REG[r]$ is associated with the component r of the snapshot object. It is composed of three fields $< value, pid, sn >$, whose meaning is the following. $REG[r].value$ contains the current value of the component r; $REG[r].pid$ and $REG[r].sn$ are control data associated with that value. $REG[r].pid$ contains the id of the process that issued the corresponding update() operation, while $REG[r].sn$ contains its sequence number among all the update() operations issued by that process.
- An array, denoted $AS[1..m]$, of *active set* objects. The object $AS[r]$, associated with the component r of the snapshot object, contains the ids of the processes currently executing a snapshot() operation on r.
- An array, denoted $ANNOUNCE[1..n]$, of single-writer/multi-reader atomic registers. The register $ANNOUNCE[i]$ can be written only by p_i. This occurs when p_i invokes p_snapshot(R): it then stores R in $ANNOUNCE[i]$ (the indexes $r_1, \cdots, r_x$ of the components it wants to read). In that way, if a process p_j has to help p_i to terminate its p_snapshot() operation, it only has to read $ANNOUNCE[i]$ to know the components p_i is interested in.
- An array, denoted $HELPSNAP[1..n, 1..n]$, of single-writer/multi-reader atomic registers. The register $HELPSNAP[i, j]$ can be written only by p_i. When, while executing an update() operation, p_i is required to help p_j terminate its current p_snapshot$(< r_1, \cdots, r_x >)$ operation, it deposits in $HELPSNAP[i, j]$ a sequence of values $< v_1, \cdots, v_x >$ that can be used by p_i as the result of its p_snapshot$(< r_1, \cdots, r_x >)$ operation.

The shared variables are denoted with upper case letters. Differently, the local variables are denoted with lower case letters (those are introduced in the algorithm description).

4.2   The p_snapshot() Operation

The algorithm that implements this operation is described in Figure 1. Similarly to [9], it borrows its underlying principle from [1]. More precisely, it first uses a "sequential double scan" to try to terminate by itself. If it cannot terminate by itself, it looks for a process that could help it terminate (namely, a process that has issued two updates on a component it wants to read).

```
operation p_snapshot(< r_1, · · · , r_x >):    % (code for p_i) %
(01)   ANNOUNCE[i] ←< r_1, · · · , r_x >;
(02)   can_help_me_i ← ∅; for each r ∈ {r_1, · · · , r_x} do AS[r].Join() end for;
(03)   for each r ∈ {r_1, · · · , r_x} do aa[r] ← REG[r] end for;
(04)   while true do % Lin point if return at line 08 %
(05)      for each r ∈ {r_1, · · · , r_x} do bb[r] ← REG[r] end for;
(06)      if (∀r ∈ {r_1, · · · , r_x} : aa[r] = bb[r]) then
(07)         for each r ∈ {r_1, · · · , r_x} do AS[r].Leave() end for;
(08)         return(< bb[r_1].value, · · · , bb[r_x].value >)
(09)      end if;
(10)      for each r ∈ {r_1, · · · , r_x} such that (aa[r] ≠ bb[r]) do
(11)         can_help_me_i ← can_help_me_i ∪ {< w, sn >} where < −, w, sn >= bb[r]
(12)      end for;
(13)      if (∃ < w, sn1 >, < w, sn2 >  ∈ can_help_me_i such that sn1 ≠ sn2) then
(14)         for each r ∈ {r_1, · · · , r_x} do AS[r].Leave() end for;
(15)         return(HELPSNAP[w, i])
(16)      end if;
(17)      aa ← bb
(18)   end while.
```

Fig. 1. An algorithm for the p_snapshot() operation

Startup.   When it invokes p_snapshot(R), a process p_i first announces the components it wants to read (line 01) and invokes $AS[r]$.Join() for each $r \in R$ (line 02). This is in order to allow the processes that concurrently update a component of R to help it.

Sequential double scan.   Then, the process p_i enters a loop (line 04-18). During each execution of the loop body, it uses a pair of scans of the registers $REG[r]$ for the components it is interested in, namely $\{r_1, \ldots, r_x\}$. It is important to notice that these are sequential [1]: the second scan always starts after the previous one has terminated. The values obtained by the first scan are kept in the array aa (line 03 for the first loop, and then line 05 followed by line 17), while the values obtained by the second scan are kept in the array bb (line 05).

Try first to terminate without help.   If, for each $r \in \{r_1, \ldots, r_x\}$, it observes no change in $REG[r]$ (test of line 06), p_i can conclude that at any point of the time line between the end of the first scan and the beginning of the second one, no $REG[r]$, $r \in \{r_1, \ldots, r_x\}$, has been modified. This is called a *successful double scan*. Hence, the values read in bb

were simultaneously present in the snapshot object: they can be returned as the result of the p_snapshot($< r_1, \cdots, r_x >$) invocation (line 08). In that case, before terminating, p_i invokes $AS[r]$.Leave() for each $r \in R$ to announce it does no longer need help (line 07).

Otherwise, try to benefit from the helping mechanism. While until that point, the statements previously described are the same as the ones used in [1,9], the statements that follow are different. This difference is mainly due to the "write first, then help" strategy, and its impact on the way it is exploited by the algorithm.

If the test of line 06 is not satisfied, p_i uses the helping mechanism that (from its side) works as follows. As the test is false, there is at least one component $r \in \{r_1, \cdots, r_x\}$ that has been updated between the two scans. For each such component r, p_i considers the identity of the last write, namely the pair $< w, sn >$ extracted from $bb[r] = < -, w, sn >$ (the last writer of $REG[r]$ is p_w and sn is the increasing sequence number it has associated with the corresponding update); p_i adds this pair to a local set $can\_help\_me_i$ where it stores the processes that could help it (lines 10-12).

Then, p_i checks if it can terminate thanks to the helping mechanism (lines 13-16). The helping termination predicate is as follows: "p_i has observed that there is a process p_w that has issued two different updates (on any pair of components)". From an operational point of view, this is captured by the fact that p_w appears twice in $can\_help\_me_i$ (line 13). As we will see in the proof, the fact that this predicate is true means that p_w has determined a set of values $< v_1, \cdots, v_x >$ (kept in $HELPSNAP[w, i]$) that p_i can use as the result of its p_snapshot($< r_1, \cdots, r_x >$) operation. In that case, p_i invokes $AS[r]$.Leave() for each $r \in R$ to indicate it does no longer need help and returns the content of $HELPSNAP[w, i]$ (lines 14-15).

Finally, if the helping predicate is false, p_i cannot terminate and consequently enters again the loop body (after having shifted the array bb in the array aa, line 17).

4.3   The Update() Operation

The algorithm for the update() operation is described in Figure 2. The invoking process p_i first writes the new value (line 01, where nbw_i is a local sequence number generator), and then (lines 02-31) asynchronously helps the other processes. As indicated in the Introduction, the principles that underlie this mechanism differ from the ones used in previous snapshot/update algorithms. Let update(r, v, i) be an update invocation. The helping mechanism works as follows.

Are there processes to help?   A process p_i first invokes $AS[r]$.GetSet() to learn the set of processes that have concurrently invoked a p_snapshot(R) operation such that $r \in R$ (line 02). It then computes the set to_help_i of the conflicting processes. (Let us notice that a process p_k returned by $AS[r]$.GetSet() may have ended its current snapshot operation and started another one between the executions of lines 02 and 04 by p_i. If p_i helped this other snapshot, it would break the help-locality property. It uses the array $ANNOUNCE$ to exclude such a p_k (lines 03-06).) If there is no conflicting process ($to\_help_i = \emptyset$), p_i does not have to help (help-locality property), and terminates accordingly (line 07).

---

operation update(r, v, i):   % (code for p_i) %
(01) $nbw_i \leftarrow nbw_i + 1$; $REG[r] \leftarrow< v, i, nbw_i >$; % Lin Point %
(02) $readers_i \leftarrow AS[r]$.GetSet(); $to\_help_i \leftarrow \emptyset$;
(03) **for each** $j \in readers_i$ **do**
(04) $announce_i[j] \leftarrow ANNOUNCE[j]$;
(05)   **if** ($r \in announce_i[j]$) **then** $to\_help_i \leftarrow to\_help_i \cup \{j\}$ **end if**
(06) **end for**;
(07) **if** ($to\_help_i = \emptyset$) **then** return(ok) **end if**;
(08) $to\_read_i \leftarrow \left(\bigcup_{j \in to\_help_i} announce_i[j] \right)$ expressed as a sequence $< rr_1, \ldots, rr_y >$;
(09) **for each** $j \in to\_help_i$ **do** $can\_help_i[j] \leftarrow \emptyset$ **end for**;
(10) **for each** $rr \in to\_read_i$ **do** $aa[rr] \leftarrow REG[rr]$ **end for**;
(11) **while** ($to\_help_i \neq \emptyset$) **do**
(12)   **for each** $rr \in to\_read_i$ **do** $bb[rr] \leftarrow REG[rr]$ **end for**;
(13) $still\_to\_help_i \leftarrow \emptyset$;
(14)   **for each** $rr \in to\_read_i$ such that $aa[rr] \neq bb[rr]$ **do**
(15)   **for each** $j \in to\_help_i$ **such that** $rr \in announce_i[j]$ **do**
(16) $still\_to\_help_i \leftarrow still\_to\_help_i \cup \{j\}$;
(17) $can\_help_i[j] \leftarrow can\_help_i[j] \cup \{< w, sn >\}$ **where** $< -, w, sn >= bb[rr]$
(18)   **end for**
(19)   **end for**;
(20)   **for each** $j \in to\_help_i \backslash still\_to\_help_i$ **do**
(21) $HELPSNAP[i, j] \leftarrow < bb[r_1].value, \ldots, bb[r_x].value >$
(22)   **where** $< r_1, \ldots, r_x >= announce_i[j]$
(23)   **end for**;
(24)   **for each** $j \in still\_to\_help_i$ **do**
(25)   **if** ($\exists < w, sn1 >, < w, sn2 > \in can\_help_i[j]$ **such that** $sn1 \neq sn2$) **then**
(26) $HELPSNAP[i, j] \leftarrow HELPSNAP[w, j]$; $still\_to\_help_i \leftarrow still\_to\_help_i \backslash \{j\}$
(27)   **end if**
(28)   **end for**;
(29) $to\_help_i \leftarrow still\_to\_help_i$; $to\_read_i \leftarrow \left(\bigcup_{j \in to\_help_i} announce_i[j] \right)$; $aa \leftarrow bb$
(30) **end while**;
(31) return(ok).

Fig. 2. An algorithm for the update() operation

If $to\_help_i \neq \emptyset$, p_i has to possibly help the processes in to_help_i. To that end, it first computes the set to_read_i of the components it has to read to help these processes (line 08). It also initializes a local array can_help_i to $\emptyset$ (line 09). The entry $can\_help_i[j]$ contains the processes p_w that (to p_i's knowledge) could also help the conflicting process p_j.

How a process helps individually another process. Each process p_j in to_help_i is helped individually by p_i. This is done in the loop (line 11-30), that terminates when the set to_help_i becomes empty.

In each loop iteration, similarly to what is done in the p_snapshot() operation, p_i first executes a double scan (whose values are kept in the local arrays aa and bb) and does the following.

– Part 1: lines 13-19. For each component rr such that $aa[rr] \neq bb[rr]$, let $bb[rr]$ $=< -, w, sn >$, which means that (to p_i's knowledge) p_w is the last process that wrote the component rr (lines 14 and 17). Moreover, this write occurred between the double scan. According to that observation, p_i keeps track of the fact that such a process p_w could help every p_j such that $rr \in announce_i[j]$. This is done by adding the pair $< w, sn >$ to the set $can\_help_i[j]$ (lines 15-17). Additionally, p_i adds j to the set $still\_to\_help_i$ (lines 13 and 16).

– Part 2: lines 20-23. Then, p_i looks for the processes that can be helped directly. Those are the processes p_j such that $j \in to\_help_i \setminus still\_to\_help_i$. The components rr they want to read are such that $aa[rr] = bb[rr]$, which means that the pair (aa, bb) constitutes a successful double scan. Accordingly, p_i writes in $HELPSNAP[i, j]$ a snapshot value that p_j can use if its partial snapshot operation is still pending. This helping snapshot value is $< bb[r_1].value, \ldots, bb[r_x].value >$ where $< r_1, \ldots, r_x >= announce_i[j]$ (line 21).

– Part 3: lines 24-28. For each process p_j that it has not previously helped (line 24), p_i looks if there is a process p_w that can help p_j. The helping termination predicate (line 25) is the same as the one used in the p_snapshot() algorithm (line 13 in Figure 1): there are two writes issued by a process p_w that appear in $can\_help_i[j]$. If the predicate is true, the helping value provided to p_j by p_w is borrowed by p_i to help p_j (line 26).

– Part 4: line 29. Finally, p_i updates to_help_i and to_read_i before entering again the loop. If $to\_help_i = \emptyset$, the loop terminates.

4.4 Proof of the Algorithm

The aim of the following definitions is to help prove that the values returned are "consistent", i.e., they are from the appropriate registers, were simultaneously present in the snapshot object and are recent[5].

Definition 3. *The values $< v_1, \cdots, v_y >$ returned by a p_snapshot($< r_1, \ldots, r_x >$) operation are well defined if $x = y$ and for each ℓ, $1 \leq \ell \leq x$, the value v_ℓ has been read from $REG[r_\ell]$.*

Definition 4. *The values returned by a p_snapshot($< r_1, \ldots, r_x >$) operation are mutually consistent if there is a time at which they were simultaneously present in the snapshot object.*

Definition 5. *The values returned by a p_snapshot($< r_1, \ldots, r_x >$) operation are fresh if, for each ℓ, $1 \leq \ell \leq x$, the value v_ℓ returned for r_ℓ is not older than the last value written into $REG[r_\ell]$ before the partial snapshot invocation[6].*

Due to page limitation, the proof of following theorem can be found in [22].

---

[5] Always returning the initial values would provide well-defined and mutually consistent values, but those would not be fresh and the operations would not be linearizable.

[6] Let us recall that, as each $REG[r_\ell]$ is an atomic register, its read and write operations can be totally ordered in a consistent way. The word "last" is used with respect to this total order.

Theorem 1. *The algorithms described in Figure 1 and Figure 2 satisfy the termination and consistency properties (stated in Section 3.1) that defines a partial snapshot object. Moreover, they satisfy the freshness and help-locality properties.*

5   Using LL/SC Registers Instead of Read/Write Atomic Registers

An array of LL/SC registers. This section shows that using LL/SC registers instead of the atomic read/write registers as underlying base registers reduces the number of base registers from $O(n^2)$ to $O(n)$. More precisely, the array $ANNOUNCE[1..n]$ and the matrix $HELPSNAP[1..n, 1..n]$ both made up of atomic read/write registers can be replaced by a single array $ANNHELP[1..n]$ such that each of its registers is accessed by the pair of LL/SC operations.

The LL/SC pair of operations. An LL/SC register is an atomic register that provides the processes with two operations denoted LL() (Linked Load) and SC() (Store Conditional). Considering an LL/SC register X, X.LL() returns the current value of X. A conditional store X.SC() issued by a process p_i returns *true* (the write succeeded) or *false* (the write failed). Its success depends on the fact that, since the previous X.LL() issued by p_i, other processes have or have not updated X. It succeeds if and only if, since its last reading (whose value has been obtained by X.LL()), X has not been written by another process p_j (whatever the value written by p_j, that value being possibly the same as the current value of X). If X.SC() is successful, p_i knows that X has not been updated since its last reading of X.

The array $ANNHELP[1..n]$. The entry $ANNHELP[i]$ is used both by p_i and by any other process $p_j \neq p_i$ to pass information from one to the other (in both directions). It can contain three types of values, as described below.
  – When it invokes p_snapshot(R), the process p_i sets $ANNHELP[i]$ to $< req, R >$ to announce that it wants to read atomically the components of R.
  – When it returns from p_snapshot(R) without being helped (successful double scan), the process p_i sets $ANNHELP[i]$ to $\perp$ to prevent future help from any other process.
  – When it helps p_i, a process p_j writes into $ANNHELP[i]$ the values corresponding to the components R that p_i wants to read.
So, $< req, R >$, $\perp$ and $< v_1, \ldots, v_x >$ are the three types of values that $ANNHELP[i]$ can contain. Its initial value is $\perp$.

Due to page limitation, the LL/SC-based update() and p_snapshot() operations are described [22].

6   Conclusion

The concept of shared memory snapshot object has first been proposed in [1,4]. The notion of partial snapshot object has then been introduced in [9]. The present paper has first proposed two efficiency properties related to the implementation of partial snapshot objects. It has then addressed the design of a partial snapshot object whose implementation meets these properties. To attain this goal, the proposed implementation takes into account the current concurrency pattern and strives to be as efficient as possible. Its main features are the following[7].

1. The proposed algorithm is the first that (to our knowledge) relies on the "write first, help later and help individually" strategy.
2. An update operation helps a snapshot operation only if needed, and no more. This is formally captured by the help-locality property that states "no help when no conflict".
3. The update algorithms proposed so far issue a single write operation into the shared memory. Differently, the proposed update algorithm separates the write of a new value and the writes of helping snapshot values.
4. The update operation satisfies the following *freshness* property: the value written by an update operation is visible to other processes from the first access to the shared memory by this update.
5. The number of underlying base atomic registers can be reduced from $O(n^2)$ to $O(n)$ when these registers can be accessed by the LL/SC pair of operations instead of the weaker read/write pair of base operations.

More developments can be found in [22].

References

1. Afek, Y., Attiya, H., Dolev, D., Gafni, E., Merritt, M., Shavit, N.: Atomic Snapshots of Shared Memory. Journal of the ACM 40(4), 873–890 (1993)
2. Afek, Y., Stupp, G., Touitou, D.: Long-lived Adaptive Collect with Applications. In: Proc. 40th IEEE Symposium on Foundations of Computer Science Computing (FOCS 1999), pp. 262–272. IEEE Computer Society Press, Los Alamitos (1999)
3. Aguilera, M.K.: A Pleasant Stroll Through the Land of Infintely Many Creatures. ACM Sigact News, Distributed Computing Column 35(2), 36–59 (2004)
4. Anderson, J.: Composite Registers. In: Proc. 9th ACM Symp. on Principles of Distributed Computing (PODC 1990), pp. 15–29 (1990)
5. Anderson, J.: Multi-writer Composite Registers. Distributed Computing 7(4), 175–195 (1994)
6. Attiya, H.: Needed: Foundations for Transactional Memory. ACM SIGACT News 39(1), 59–61 (2008)
7. Attiya, H., Fouren, A.: Algorithms Adapting to Contention Point. Journal of the ACM 50(4), 444–468 (2003)
8. Attiya, H., Fouren, A., Gafni, E.: An Adaptive Collect Algorithm with Applications. Distributed Computing 15, 87–96 (2002)
9. Attiya, H., Guerraoui, R., Ruppert, E.: Partial Snapshot Objects. In: Proc. 20th ACM Symposium on Parallel Architectures and Algorithms (SPAA 2008), pp. 336–343. ACM Press, New York (2008)

---

[7] These features are also the main differences with the partial snapshot algorithm (based on read/write atomic registers) presented in [9], and the algorithms (based on read/write atomic registers) that implement a classical snapshot object (e.g., [1]).

10. Attiya, H., Rachman, O.: Atomic Snapshot in $O(n \log n)$ Operations. SIAM J. of Comp. 27(2), 319–340 (1998)
11. Attiya, H., Welch, J.: Distributed Computing: Fundamentals, Simulations and Advanced Topics, 2nd edn., p. 414. Wiley Interscience, Hoboken (2004)
12. Chandy, K.M., Lamport, L.: Distributed Snapshots: Determining Global States of Distributed Systems. ACM Transactions on Computer Systems 3(1), 63–75 (1985)
13. Ellen, F.: How hard is it to take a snapshot? In: Vojtáš, P., Bieliková, M., Charron-Bost, B., Sýkora, O. (eds.) SOFSEM 2005. LNCS, vol. 3381, pp. 28–37. Springer, Heidelberg (2005)
14. Felber, P., Fetzer, C., Guerraoui, R., Harris, T.: Transactions Are Back–But Are They the Same? ACM SIGACT News 39(1), 47–58 (2008)
15. Guerraoui, R., Kapałka, M.: On the Correctness of Transactional Memory. In: Proc. 13th ACM SIGPLAN Symposium on Principles and Practice of Parallel Programming (PPoPP 2008), pp. 175–184. ACM Press, New York (2008)
16. Guerraoui, R., Raynal, M.: From unreliable objects to reliable objects: The case of atomic registers and consensus. In: Malyshkin, V.E. (ed.) PaCT 2007. LNCS, vol. 4671, pp. 47–61. Springer, Heidelberg (2007)
17. Herlihy, M.P.: Wait-Free Synchronization. ACM Trans. on Progr. Lang. and Systems 13(1), 124–149 (1991)
18. Herlihy, M.P., Shavit, N.: The Art of Mutiprocessor Programming, 508 pages. Morgan Kaufmann Pub., San Francisco (2008)
19. Herlihy, M.P., Luchangco, V.: Distributed Computing and the Multicore Revolution. ACM SIGACT News 39(1), 62–72 (2008)
20. Herlihy, M.P., Wing, J.M.: Linearizability: a Correctness Condition for Concurrent Objects. ACM Transactions on Programming Languages and Systems 12(3), 463–492 (1990)
21. Imbs, D., Raynal, M.: A lock-based STM protocol that satisfies opacity and progressiveness. In: Baker, T.P., Bui, A., Tixeuil, S. (eds.) OPODIS 2008. LNCS, vol. 5401, pp. 226–245. Springer, Heidelberg (2008)
22. Imbs, D., Raynal, M.: Help when needed, but no more: Efficient Read/Write Partial Snapshot. Tech Report # 1907, 24 pages; IRISA, Université de Rennes, France (2008)
23. Inoue, I., Chen, W., Masuzawa, T., Tokura, N.: Linear Time Snapshots Using Multi-writer Multi-reader Registers. In: Tel, G., Vitányi, P.M.B. (eds.) WDAG 1994. LNCS, vol. 857, pp. 130–140. Springer, Heidelberg (1994)
24. Israeli, A., Rappoport, L.: Disjoint-Access-Parallel Implementations of Strong Shared Memory Primitives. In: Proc. 13th ACM Symposium on Principles of Distributed Computing (PODC 1994), pp. 151–160 (1994)
25. Jayanti, P.: An Optimal Multiwriter Snapshot Algorithm. In: Proc. 37th ACM Symposium on Theory of Computing (STOCS 2005), pp. 723–732. ACM Press, New York (2005)
26. Lynch, N.A.: Distributed Algorithms, 872 pages. Morgan Kaufmann Pub., San Francisco (1996)
27. Moir, M.: Practical Implementation of Non-Blocking Synchronization Primitives. In: Proc. 16th ACM Symposium on Principles of Distributed Computing (PODC 1997), pp. 219–228. ACM Press, New York (1997)
28. Shavit, N., Touitou, D.: Software Transactional Memory. Distributed Computing 10(2), 99–116 (1997)
29. Taubenfeld, G.: Synchronization Algorithms and Concurrent Programming, 423 pages. Pearson Prentice-Hall, London (2006)

Contention-Sensitive Data Structures and Algorithms

Gadi Taubenfeld

The Interdisciplinary Center, P.O. Box 167, Herzliya 46150, Israel
tgadi@idc.ac.il
http://www.faculty.idc.ac.il/gadi/

Abstract. A contention-sensitive data structure is a concurrent data structure in which the overhead introduced by locking is eliminated in the common cases, when there is no contention, or when processes with non-interfering operations access it concurrently. When a process invokes an operation on a contention-sensitive data structure, in the absence of contention or interference, the process must be able to complete its operation in a small number of steps and without using locks. Using locks is permitted only when there is interference. We formally define the notion of contention-sensitive data structures, propose four general transformations that facilitate devising such data structures, and illustrate the benefits of the approach by implementing a contention-sensitive consensus algorithm, a contention-sensitive double-ended queue data structure, and a contention-sensitive election algorithm. Finally, we generalize the result to enable to avoid locking also when contention is low.

Keywords: Contention-sensitive, synchronization, locks, shortcut code, disable-free, prevention-free, livelock, starvation, k-obstruction-free, wait-free.

1 Introduction

1.1 Motivation

Concurrent access to a data structure shared among several processes must be synchronized in order to avoid interference between conflicting operations. Mutual exclusion locks are the de facto mechanism for concurrency control on concurrent data structures: a process accesses the data structure only inside a critical section code, within which the process is guaranteed exclusive access. Any sequential data structure can be easily made concurrent using such a locking approach. The popularity of this approach is largely due to the apparently simple programming model of such locks.

When using locks, the *granularity* of synchronization is important. Using a single lock to protect the whole data structure, allowing only one process at a time to access it, is an example of *coarse-grained* synchronization. In contrast, *fine-grained* synchronization enables to lock "small pieces" of a data structure, allowing several processes with non-interfering operations to access it concurrently. Coarse-grained synchronization is easier to program but is less efficient compared to fine-grained synchronization.

Using locks may, in various scenarios, degrade the performance of concurrent applications, as it enforces processes to wait for a lock to be released. Moreover, slow or stopped processes may prevent other processes from ever accessing the data structure.

I. Keidar (Ed.): DISC 2009, LNCS 5805, pp. 157–171, 2009.

Locks can introduce false conflicts, as different processes with non-interfering operations contend for the same lock, only to end up accessing disjoint data.

A promising approach is the design of concurrent data structures and algorithms which avoid locking. The advantages of such algorithms are that they are not subject to priority inversion, they are resilient to failures, and they do not suffer significant performance degradation from scheduling preemption, page faults or cache misses. On the other hand, such algorithms may impose too much overhead upon the implementation and are often complex and memory consuming.

We propose an intermediate approach for the design of concurrent data structures, which incorporates ideas from the work on data structures which avoid locking. While the approach guarantees the correctness and fairness of a concurrent data structure under all possible scenarios, it is especially efficient in the common cases when there is no (or low) contention, or when processes with non-interfering operations access a data structure concurrently.

1.2 Contention-Sensitive Data Structures: The Basic Idea

Contention for accessing a shared object is usually rare in well designed systems. Contention occurs when multiple processes try to acquire a lock at the same time. Hence, a most desired property in a lock implementation is that, in the absence of contention, a process can acquire the lock extremely fast. However, locks were introduced in the first place to resolve conflicts when there is contention, and acquiring a lock *always* introduces some overhead, even in the cases where there is no contention or interference.

We propose an approach which, in common cases, eliminates the overhead involved in acquiring a lock. The idea is simple: assume that, for a given data structure, it is known that in the absence of contention or interference it takes some fixed number of steps, say at most 10 steps, to complete an operation, not counting the steps involved in acquiring and releasing the lock. According to our approach, when a process invokes an operation on a given data structure, it first tries to complete its operation, by executing a short code, called the *shortcut code*, which does not involve locking. Only if it does not manage to complete the operation fast enough, i.e., within 10 steps, it tries to access the data structure via locking. The shortcut code is required to be *wait-free*. That is, its execution by a process takes only a finite number of steps and always terminates, regardless of the behavior of the other processes.

Using an efficient shortcut code, although eliminates the overhead introduced by locking in common cases, introduces a major problem: we can no longer use a sequential data structure as the basic building block, as done when using the traditional locking approach. The reason is simple, many processes may access the same data structure simultaneously by executing the shortcut code. Furthermore, even when a process acquires the lock, it is no longer guaranteed to have exclusive access, as another process may access the same data structure simultaneously by executing the shortcut code.

Thus, a central question which we are facing is: if a sequential data structure can not be used as the basic building block for a general technique for constructing a contention-sensitive data structure, then what is the best data structure to use? Before we proceed to discuss formal definitions and general techniques, which will also help us answering the above question, we demonstrate the idea of using a shortcut code to avoid locking – in the absence of synchronization conflicts – by presenting a contention-sensitive solution to the binary consensus problem using atomic read/write registers and a single lock.

1.3   A Simple Example: Contention-Sensitive Consensus

The *consensus problem* is to design an algorithm in which all correct processes reach a common decision based on their initial opinions. While various decision rules can be considered such as "majority consensus", the problem is interesting even where the decision value is constrained only when all processes are unanimous in their opinions, in which case the decision value must be the common opinion. A consensus algorithm is called *binary* consensus when the number of possible initial opinions is two.

Processes are not required to participate in the algorithm, however, once a process starts participating it is guaranteed that it may fail only while executing the shortcut code. The algorithm uses an array $x[0..1]$ of two atomic bits, and two atomic registers y and *out*. After a process executes a **decide**() statement, it immediately terminates.

CONTENTION-SENSITIVE BINARY CONSENSUS: program for process p_i with input $in_i \in \{0, 1\}$.

shared $x[0..1]$: array of two atomic bits, initially both 0
$\quad\quad\quad$ y, *out* : atomic registers which range over $\{\perp, 0, 1\}$, initially both $\perp$

```
1  x[in_i] := 1                                              // start shortcut code
2  if y =⊥ then y := in_i fi
3  if x[1 − in_i] = 0 then out := in_i; decide(in_i) fi
4  if out ≠⊥ then decide(out) fi                             // end shortcut code
5  |lock| if out = ⊥ then out := y fi |unlock| ; decide(out)     // locking
```

When a process runs alone (either before or after a decision is made), it reaches a decision after accessing the shared memory at most five times. Furthermore, when all the concurrently participating processes have the same preference – i.e., when there is no interference – a decision is also reached within five steps and without locking. Two processes with conflicting preferences, which run at the same time, will not resolve the conflict in the shortcut code if both of them find $y =\perp$. In such a case, some process acquires the lock and sets the value of *out* to be the final decision value. The assignment *out* := y requires two memory references and hence it involves two atomic steps. Memory barriers may be used to prevent reordering [26].

1.4   Summery of Contributions

The full list of our contributions is as follows,

1. We define contention-sensitive data structures by identifying four properties any such data structure must satisfy; and discuss three additional "nice to have" properties. This involves introducing a new notion called a *disable-free* code segment (Section 2).
2. We implement a contention-sensitive double-ended queue. To increase the level of concurrency, *two* locks are used: one for the left-side operations and the other for the right-side operations (Section 3).

3. Three known progress conditions are: (1) livelock-freedom, which guarantees that in the absence of process failures, *some* participating process makes progress; (2) starvation-freedom, which guarantees that in the absence of process failures, *every* participating progress makes progress; (3) obstruction-freedom, which guarantees that a process will be able to complete its pending operations in a finite number of its own steps, if all the other processes "hold still" (i.e., do not take any steps) long enough. That is, obstruction-freedom guarantees progress for any process that eventually executes in isolation long enough. Under contention, obstruction-free data structures may suffer from livelocks. We presents three transformations:
   - Transformation 1, converts any contention-sensitive data structure which satisfies livelock-freedom into a corresponding contention-sensitive data structure which satisfies starvation-freedom. It adds only *one* memory reference to the shortcut code (Section 4.1).
   - Transformation 2, converts any obstruction-free data structure into the corresponding contention-sensitive data structure which satisfies livelock-freedom (Section 4.2).
   - A new progress condition called *prevention-freedom* is presented. Transformation 3, converts any prevention-free data structure into the corresponding contention-sensitive data structure which satisfies livelock-freedom (Section 4.3).
4. We define the notion of a *k-contention-sensitive* data structure in which locks are used only when contention goes above k, and illustrate this notion by implementing a 2-contention-sensitive consensus algorithm. Then, for each $k \geq 1$, we define a progress condition called *k-obstruction-freedom*, and present a transformation that converts any k-obstruction-free data structure into the corresponding k-contention-sensitive data structure which satisfies livelock-freedom (Section 5).
5. We present a contention-sensitive election algorithm, using atomic registers only (Section 6).

1.5 Related Work

Mutual exclusion locks were first introduced by Edsger W. Dijkstra in [6]. Since than, numerous implementations of locks have been proposed [34,40]. Algorithms for several concurrent data structures based on locking have been proposed since at least the 1970's [5,8,20,25]. Speculative lock elision [35], is a hardware technique which allows multiple processes to concurrently execute critical sections protected by the same lock; when misspeculation, due to data conflicts, is detected rollback is used for recovery, and the execution fall back to acquiring the lock and executing non-speculatively.

Implementations of data structures which avoid locking have appeared in many papers [7,11,14,30,38,42]. Several progress conditions have been proposed for data structures which avoid locking. The most extensively studied conditions, in order of decreasing strength, are wait-freedom [15], non-blocking [19], and obstruction-freedom [16]. Wait-freedom guarantees that every process will always be able to complete its pending operations in a finite number of its own steps. Non-blocking guarantees that some process will always be able to complete its pending operations in a finite number of its own steps. All strategies that avoid locks are called lockless [18] or lock-free [29]. (In some papers, lock-free means non-blocking.)

Non-blocking and wait-freedom (although desirable) may impose too much over-head upon the implementation, and are often complex and memory consuming. Re-quiring implementations to satisfy only obstruction-freedom can simplify the design of algorithms, however, since it does not guarantee progress under contention, such algo-rithms may suffer from livelocks. Various contention management techniques have been proposed to improve progress of obstruction-free algorithms under contention while still avoiding locking [12,36]. Other works investigated boosting obstruction-freedom by making timing assumption [4,9,39] and using failure detectors [13].

It is known that even in the presence of only one crash failure, it is not possible to solve consensus using atomic read/write registers only [10,23]. Wait-free consensus algorithms that use read and write operations in the absence of (process) contention, or even in the absence of step contention, and revert to using strong synchronization operations when contention occurs, are presented in [2,24]. A wait-free consensus al-gorithm that in any given execution uses objects with consensus number above k, only when contention goes above k, appeared in [32].

Consistency conditions for concurrent objects are linearizability [19] and sequential consistency [22]. A tutorial on memory consistency models can be found in [1]. Trans-actional memory is a methodology which has gained momentum in recent years as a simple way for writing concurrent programs [17,37,43]. It has implementations that use locks and others that avoid locking, but in both cases the complexity is hidden from the programmer. In [27], a constructive critique of locking and transactional memory: their strengths, weaknesses, and challenges, is presented.

2 Defining Contention-Sensitive Data Structures

We focus on an architecture in which n processes communicate asynchronously via a shared memory. Asynchrony means that there is no assumption on the relative speeds of the processes. Processes may fail by crashing, which means that a failed process stops taking steps forever. Numerous implementations of locks have been proposed to help coordinating the activities of the various processes.

We are not interested in implementing new locks, but rather assume that we can use existing locks. We are not at all interested whether the locks are implemented using atomic registers, semaphores, etc. We do assume that a lock implementation guarantees that: (1) no two processes can acquire the same lock at the same time, (2) if a process is trying to acquire the lock, then in the absence of failures some process, not necessarily the same one, eventually acquires that lock, and (3) the operation of releasing a lock is wait-free. (It is possible to consider also using read-write locks, k-exclusion locks, etc.)

An implementation of a contention-sensitive data structure is divided into *two* con-tinuous sections of code: the *shortcut code* and the *body code*. When a process invokes an operation it first executes the shortcut code, and if it succeeds to complete the oper-ation, it returns. Otherwise, the process tries to complete its operation by executing the body code, where it usually first tries to acquire a lock. If it succeeds to complete the operation, it releases the acquired lock(s) and returns. The problem of implementing a contention-sensitive data structure is to write the *shortcut code* and the *body code* in such a way that the following *four* requirements are satisfied,

- **Fast path:** In the absence of contention or interference, each operation must be completed while executing the shortcut code only.
- **Wait-free shortcut:** The shortcut code must be wait-free – its execution should require only a bounded number of steps and must always terminate. (Completing the shortcut code does not imply completing the operation.)
- **Livelock-freedom:** In the absence of process failures, if a process is executing the shortcut code or the body code, then some process, not necessarily the same one, must eventually complete its operation.
- **Linearizability:** Although operations of concurrent processes may overlap, each operation should appear to take effect instantaneously. In particular, operations that do not overlap should take effect in their "real-time" order.

It is possible to consider replacing linearizability with a weaker consistency requirement, such as sequential consistency [22]. Livelock-freedom may still allow that individual processes may never complete their operations. We will examine also solutions which do not allow such a behavior.

- **Starvation-freedom:** In the absence of process failures, if a process is executing the shortcut code or the body code, then this process, must eventually complete its operation.

Next, we define two additional desirable properties. They are "nice to have", but it is not required that each correct implementation satisfies them. First, we introduce a new notion called *disable-freedom*. A code segment is *disable-free*, if a process that fails while executing that code segment may not prevent other processes from completing their operations.

A disable-free code segment is not necessarily wait-free and vice versa. To illustrate this point, consider the following program for two processes in which a single atomic register, called x, is used. Each process executes the following three lines and terminates: (1) $x := 0$; (2) $x := 1$; (3) **while** $x \neq 1$ **do** skip **od**. Consider the code segment which consists of lines 1 and 2. It is clearly wait-free, but it is not disable-free since a process that fails just before executing line 2 may cause the other process to spin forever (in line 3). On the other hand, the code segment which consists of only line 3 is disable-free but is not wait-free.

- **Disable-free shortcut:** A process that fails (or that is very slow) while executing the shortcut code, may not prevent other processes from accessing the data structure and completing their operations.

We point out that the shortcut code of the consensus algorithm presented in the introduction is disable-free. The second "nice to have" property is,

- **Weak-blocking body:** Let p be a process that has failed while executing the body code, and let q be a process that has started executing the shortcut code after p has failed. Furthermore, assume that the operations of p and q are non-interfering, and that no other process is concurrently participating. Then, the fact that p has failed should not prevent q from completing its operation while executing the shortcut code.

The implementation of the body code can be either coarse-grained, or fine-grained.

3   A Contention-Sensitive Double-Ended Queue Data Structure

In [16], two obstruction-free CAS-based implementations of a double-ended queue are presented; the first is implemented on a linear array, the second on a circular array. In the following, a contention-sensitive double-ended queue data structure implementation, which is based on the implementations from [16], is presented.

The double-ended queue is implemented on an infinite array (denoted Q) and is based on load-link/store-conditional/validate (LL/SC/VL) operations. For a given object o, the operations LL/SC/VL are defined as follows: (1) LL(o) returns o's value. (2) SC(o, v) by process p succeeds if and only if no process has successfully written to o since p's last LL on o. If SC succeeds, it changes o's value to v (or to the value of v, if v is a variable) and returns *true*. Otherwise, o's value remains unchanged and SC returns *false*. (3) VL(o) by process p returns *true* if and only if no process performed a successful SC on o since p's last LL on o. Otherwise, VL returns *false*.

Two locks are used: *llock* (left lock) is used by the left-side operations and *rlock* (right lock) is used by the right-side operations. Two values *lnil* (left null) and *rnil* (right null) that are different from the data values are used, and the following invariant is maintained: For every two integer values $i < j$, $Q[j] = lnil$ implies $Q[i] = lnil$, and $Q[i] = rnil$ implies $Q[j] = rnil$. Two pointers are used: *Lptr* (left pointer) which holds the index of the rightmost *lnil* value, and *Rptr* (right pointer) which holds the index of the leftmost *rnil* value. A *rightpush(value)* (resp. *leftpush(value)*) operation changes the leftmost *rnil* (resp. rightmost *lnil*) value to *value*. A *rightpop* (resp. *leftpop*) operation changes the rightmost (resp. leftmost) data value to *rnil* (resp. *lnil*) and returns that value.

The right-side operations, rightpush and rightpop, are shown in Figure 1. The left-side operations, leftpush and leftpop, are symmetric to the right-side operations, and hence are not presented.

When a process p invokes a right-side operation, p first reads the *Rptr* pointer to find the index of the exact location, say k, it needs to modify in the array Q. Then, it LL($Q[k]$) and also LL $Q[k]$'s adjacent location $Q[k-1]$. In order to prevent interference by another right-side operation, process p first SC to the adjacent location $Q[k-1]$ (without changing that location's value). If this SC succeeds, the process SC to $Q[k]$. As a result of this approach, two concurrent right-side operations can each cause the other to retry. In such a case, p tried to acquire the *rightlock* and, in its critical section, p continually repeats the above sequence of steps trying to complete its operation.

A concurrent left-side and right-side operations can interfere if they try to apply a SC to the same memory location. We observe that in such a case if as a result one of the two type of operations has to retry, then it must be the case that an operation of the other type must be completed.

Since *Rptr* is updated using an atomic write operation, the implementation in Figure 1 does not satisfy the disable-free shortcut and the weak-blocking body properties. These properties can be easily satisfied by letting each process updating *Rptr* (and *Lptr*) using (the more expensive) LL/SC/VL operations, whenever a process finds out that *Rptr* is not updated. For lack of space, all the proofs were omitted.

CONTENTION-SENSITIVE DOUBLE-ENDED QUEUE: program for each one of the n processes

shared $Q[-\infty..\infty]$: infinite array; initially, $Q[i] = lnil$ for all $i < 0$ and $Q[i] = rnil$ for all $i \geq 0$
　　　　$Lptr, Rptr$: integers; initially, $Lptr = -1$ and $Rptr = 0$
local $done, empty$: boolean; $cur, prev$: both range over $\{$all data values, $lnil, rnil\}$
　　　　k: integer

rightpush($value$)   // $value \notin \{lnil, rnil\}$
1   $k := Rptr; prev := \mathrm{LL}(Q[k-1]); cur := \mathrm{LL}(Q[k]);$ // k index of leftmost $rnil$
2   **if** $cur = rnil \wedge prev \neq rnil$ **then**   // $Rptr$ is updated
3   **if** $\mathrm{SC}(Q[k-1], prev)$ **then**   // prevent interfering operations
4   **if** $\mathrm{SC}(Q[k], value)$ **then**   // push new value
5               $Rptr := Rptr + 1;$ **return**("ok") **fi fi fi**   // update $Rptr$
6   $\boxed{\mathrm{lock}(rlock)}$
7   $done := false$ // set local variable
8   **repeat**
9       $k := Rptr; prev := \mathrm{LL}(Q[k-1]); cur := \mathrm{LL}(Q[k])$ // k index of leftmost $rnil$
10   **if** $cur = rnil \wedge prev \neq rnil$ **then**   // $Rptr$ is updated
11   **if** $\mathrm{SC}(Q[k-1], prev)$ **then**   // prevent interfering operations
12   **if** $\mathrm{SC}(Q[k], value)$ **then**   // push new value
13                  $Rptr := Rptr + 1; done := true$ **fi fi fi**   // update $Rptr$
14 **until** ($done$)
15 $\boxed{\mathrm{unlock}(rlock)}$; **return**("ok")   // unlocking section

rightpop()
1   $k := Rptr; prev := \mathrm{LL}(Q[k-1]); cur := \mathrm{LL}(Q[k])$ // k index of leftmost $rnil$
2   **if** $cur = rnil \wedge prev \neq rnil$ **then**   // $Rptr$ is updated
3   **if** $prev = lnil \wedge \mathrm{VL}(Q[k-1])$ **then return**("empty") // adjacent $lnil$ and $rnil$
4   **else if** $\mathrm{SC}(Q[k], rnil)$ **then**   // prevent interfering operations
5   **if** $\mathrm{SC}(Q[k-1], rnil)$ **then**   // pop value
6               $Rptr := Rptr - 1;$ **return**($prev$) **fi fi fi fi**   // update $Rptr$
7   $\boxed{\mathrm{lock}(rlock)}$
8   $done := false; empty := false$ // set local variables
9   **repeat**
10      $k := Rptr; prev := \mathrm{LL}(Q[k-1]); cur := \mathrm{LL}(Q[k])$ // k index of leftmost $rnil$
11   **if** $cur = rnil \wedge prev \neq rnil$ **then**   // $Rptr$ is updated
12   **if** $prev = lnil \wedge \mathrm{VL}(Q[k-1])$ **then** $empty := true$ // adjacent $lnil$ and $rnil$
13   **else if** $\mathrm{SC}(Q[k], rnil)$ **then**   // prevent interfering operations
14   **if** $\mathrm{SC}(Q[k-1], rnil)$ **then**   // pop value
15                  $Rptr := Rptr - 1; done := true$ **fi fi fi fi**   // update $Rptr$
16 **until** ($done \vee empty$)
17 $\boxed{\mathrm{unlock}(rlock)}$; **if** $done$ **then return**($prev$) **else return**("empty") **fi** // unlocking section

Fig. 1. A contention-sensitive double-ended queue data structure. The left-side operations, left-push and leftpop, are symmetric to the right-side operations. The first 5 lines (6 lines, resp.) of the rightpush (rightpop, resp.) operation is the shortcut code. Two locks are used: $llock$ (left lock) is used by the left-side operations and $rlock$ (right lock) is used by the right-side operations.

4   Three Transformations

Recall the question raised in the introduction: If a sequential data structure can not be used as the basic building block for constructing a contention-sensitive data structure, what is the best data structure to use? The following transformations that facilitate devising such data structures provide an answer.

4.1   From Livelock-Freedom to Starvation-Freedom

The transformation converts any contention-sensitive data structure, denoted A, which satisfies livelock-freedom into a corresponding contention-sensitive data structure, denoted B, which satisfies starvation-freedom. It adds only *one* memory reference to the shortcut code. It is an extension of a known transformation, for the mutual exclusion problem, that has appeared in [40] (page 83).

It is assumed that A is implemented using a single lock, and that the *body* of A is divided into three continuous sections of code: *locking*, *main-body*, and *unlocking*. When a process invokes an operation on A it first executes the shortcut code of A, and if it succeeds to complete the operation, it returns. Otherwise, it executes the body code, where it first tries to acquire the single lock by executing the locking code. If it succeeds to acquire the lock, it executes the *main-body*. If it succeeds to complete the operation, it releases the lock.

Using A, we construct B as follows: In addition to the objects used in A, we use an atomic register called *turn* which is big enough to store a process identifier, a boolean array called *flag*, and a boolean bit called *contention*. All the processes can read and write *turn* and the *contention* bit, the processes can read the bit $flag[i]$, but only process i can write $flag[i]$. The processes are numbered 1 through n. The statement "**await** *condition*" is used as an abbreviation for "**while** ¬*condition* **do** *skip*".

Transformation 1: process i's program.
Initially: $flag[i] = false$, *contention* $= false$, the initial value of *turn* is immaterial.

```
1    if contention = true then goto lock fi                    // begin shortcut of B
2    shortcut of A                                              // end shortcut of B

3 lock: flag[i] := true                                         // begin body of B
4    await (turn = i or flag[turn] = false)
5    locking of A

6    contention := true
7    main-body of A
8    contention := false

9    flag[i] := false
10   if flag[turn] = false then turn := (turn mod n) + 1 fi
11   unlocking of A                                             // end body of B
```

Setting the contention bit to true, happens after acquiring the lock which implies that there has been contention and interference. Evaluating the condition $flag[turn] = false$ requires *two* memory references.

4.2 From Obstruction-Freedom to Livelock-Freedom

Next we present a transformation that converts any obstruction-free data structure, de-noted *DS*, into a corresponding contention-sensitive data structure. The idea is to use a lock to choke down parallelism and eventually eliminate interference on an obstruction-free data structure. Let us denote by *first(DS)* the number of steps that a process needs to take in order to complete its operation of *DS* when there is no contention.[1] The trans-formation uses a single lock.

Transformation 2: program for a process which *invokes* operation *op*.

```
1   execute up to first(DS) steps of DS                                      // shortcut
2   if op is completed then return response fi
3   ┌──────┐
    │ lock │                                                                 // body
    └──────┘
4   continue to execute steps of DS until op is completed
5   ┌────────┐
    │ unlock │
    └────────┘
```

First a process tries to complete its operation *op* of *DS* without holding the lock. If there is no contention the process will complete its operation without locking. Otherwise, if after taking *first(DS)* steps, it does not succeed in completing its operation, it tries to acquire the lock. As a result of such an approach, a process that is already holding the lock may experience interference. However, either *some* process will manage to complete its operation without holding the lock, or (since the number of processes is finite) this interference will eventually vanish.

A data structure which is constructed using the above transformation satisfies also the disable-free shortcut property and the weak-blocking body property.

4.3 From Prevention-Freedom to Livelock-Freedom

For a given implementation of a concurrent data structure, DS, assume that each state-ment is uniquely numbered by a natural number. Let S_i denote the set of all the numbers of statements in the code of process p_i (where $i \in \{1, ..., n\}$). For $s \in S_i$, we say that process p_i is at s if the next step of p_i is to execute the statement numbered s. Let G_i be a subset of S_i.

> **Prevention-freedom:** A data structure is *prevention-free* w.r.t. $\{G_1, ..., G_n\}$ if it is guaranteed that each process p_i will be able to complete its pending operations in a finite number of its own steps, if all the other processes simul-taneously "hold still" long enough, where each process $p_j \neq p_i$ "holds still" (i.e., waits) at some $g_j \in G_j$.

Each $g_j \in G_j$ is called a *gate*. Prevention-freedom guarantees that if $n - 1$ processes are suspended or even crash while each one of them is at a gate, the remaining process is not effected and can complete its operation. We assume that when a process does not

---

[1] In simple data structures like a queue or a stack the number of *first(DS)* steps would be a constant. In a data structure like a search tree the number would depend on the size or depth of the tree; this value can be stored in a shared location that each process can read and update.

invoke an operation, it is at a gate. A data structure is obstruction-free if and only if, it is prevention-free w.r.t. $\{S_1, ..., S_n\}$. In an obstruction-free data structure each (number of a) statement is a gate.

Let DS be a data structure that is *prevention-free* w.r.t. some set $\{G_1, ..., G_n\}$. We say that DS is *exit-safe* if, regardless of contention, it is always the case that after a process invokes an operation of DS and takes *first(DS)* steps, either the process completes its operation or the process can always continue taking a small number of additional steps until it reaches a gate. Below we present a transformation which converts any prevention-free exit-safe data structure, denoted DS, into a corresponding contention-sensitive data structure. The transformation uses a single lock.

Transformation 3: First a process tries to complete its operation *op* of DS without holding the lock. If there is no contention the process will complete its operation without locking. Otherwise if the process, after taking *first(DS)* steps, does not succeed in completing its operation it continues taking steps until it reaches a gate, and at that point it "exits" the DS code, and tries to acquire the lock. Once it acquires the lock it "enters" the DS code at the same point where it left it – i.e., through the gate – and continues taking steps trying to complete the operation *op*. If *op* is completed it releases the lock.

A data structure which is constructed using Transformation 3, does not necessarily satisfy the disable-free shortcut property or the weak-blocking body property.

5   Generalizations

A *k-contention-sensitive* data structure is a data structure in which contention resolution (using locks) is used only when contention goes above k. It is defined by modifying the *fast path* requirement as follows: When there is contention of at most k processes, or when there is no interference, each operation must be completed while executing the shortcut code only. We demonstrate this idea, by presenting a 2-contention-sensitive consensus algorithm. The algorithm uses atomic registers and a single swap object.[2]

2-CONTENTION-SENSITIVE CONSENSUS: program for process p_i with input $v_i \in \{0, 1\}$.

shared $x[0..1]$: array of two atomic bits, initially both 0
        y, out : atomic registers which range over $\{\perp, 0, 1\}$, initially both $\perp$
        z : a swap object which ranges over $\{\perp, 0, 1\}$, initially $\perp$
local in_i : a register which ranges over $\{\perp, 0, 1\}$

```
0  in_i := v_i; swap(z, in_i); if in_i = ⊥ then in_i := v_i fi          // start shortcut code
1  x[in_i] := 1
2  if y = ⊥ then y := in_i fi
3  if x[1 − in_i] = 0 then out := in_i; decide(in_i) fi
4  if out ≠ ⊥ then decide(out) fi                                        // end shortcut code
5  lock  if out = ⊥ then out := y fi  unlock ; decide(out)               // locking
```

---

[2] A swap operation takes a shared registers and a local register, and atomically exchange their values. It is known that there is no wait-free consensus algorithm for more than two processes, using atomic registers and atomic swap objects [15].

Processes are not required to participate, however, once a process starts participating it is guaranteed that it may fail only while executing the shortcut code. Once a process decides, it immediately terminates. For a set of processes P, let $|P|$ denotes the size of P. Consider the following generalization of the notion of obstruction-freedom:

> **k-obstruction-freedom:** For any $k \geq 1$, the progress condition k-*obstruction-freedom* guarantees that for every set of processes P where $|P| \leq k$, every process in P will be able to complete its pending operations in a finite number of its own steps, if all the processes not in P do not take steps for long enough.

These progress conditions cover the spectrum between obstruction-freedom and wait-freedom; 1-obstruction-freedom is the same as obstruction-freedom, and in a system of k processes, k-obstruction-freedom is the same as wait-freedom. The following transformation converts any k-obstruction-free data structure, denoted DS, into a corresponding k-contention-sensitive data structure which satisfies livelock-freedom. Let us denote by k-*first*(DS) the number of steps that a process needs to take in order to complete its operation of DS when the contention level is at most k.

> **Transformation 4:** First a process tries to complete its operation op of DS without holding the lock. If the contention level is at most k, the process will complete its operation without locking. Otherwise if the process, after taking k-*first*(DS) steps, does not succeed in completing its operation it "exits" the DS code, and tries to acquire the lock. In this case it is sufficient to use a k-exclusion lock.[3] Once it acquires the lock it "enters" the DS code at the same point where it left it and continues taking steps trying to complete the operation op. If op is completed it releases the lock.

A similar transformation can be designed for the following weaker condition:

> **k-obstacle-freedom:** For any $k \geq 1$, the condition k-*obstacle-freedom* guarantees that for every set of processes P where $|P| \leq k$, **some** process in P with pending operations will be able to complete its operations in a finite number of its own steps, if all the processes not in P do not take steps for long enough.

We notice that, 1-obstacle-freedom is the same as obstruction-freedom, and in a system of k processes, k-obstacle-freedom is the same as non-blocking.

6 A Contention-Sensitive Election Algorithm

The *election problem* is to design an algorithm in which all participating processes choose one process as their leader. More formally, each process that starts participating eventually decides on a value from the set $\{0, 1\}$ and terminates. It is required that exactly one of the participating processes decides 1. The process that decides 1 is the

---

[3] A k-exclusion lock guarantees that: (1) no more than k processes can acquire the lock at the same time, (2) if strictly fewer than k processes fail (are delayed forever) then if a process is trying to acquire the lock, then some process, not necessarily the same one, eventually acquires the lock, and (3) the operation of releasing a lock is wait-free.

elected leader. Processes are not required to participate, however, once a process starts participating it is guaranteed that it will not fail. It is known that in the presence of one crash failure, it is not possible to solve election using atomic registers only [33,41].

The following algorithm solves the election problem for any number of processes, and is related to the splitter constructs from [21,28,31]. A single lock is used. It is assumed that after a process executes a **decide**() statement, it immediately terminates.

CONTENTION-SENSITIVE ELECTION: Process i's program

shared x, z: atomic registers, initially $z = 0$ and the initial value of x is immaterial
          $b, y, done$: atomic bits, initially all 0
local $leader$: local register, the initial value is immaterial

```
1    x := i                                                              // begin shortcut
2    if y = 1 then b := 1; decide(0) fi                                   // I am not the leader
3    y := 1
4    if x = i then z := i; if b = 0 then decide(1) fi fi                  // I am the leader!
                                                                          // end shortcut
5    lock                                                                 // locking
6    if z = i ∧ done = 0 then leader = 1                                  // I am the leader!
7       else await b ≠ 0 ∨ z ≠ 0
8           if z = 0 ∧ done = 0 then leader = 1; done := 1               // I am the leader!
9           else leader = 0                                               // I am not the leader
10          fi
11   fi
12   unlock ; decide(leader)                                             // unlocking
```

When a process runs alone before a leader is elected, it is elected and terminates after accessing the shared memory *six* times. Furthermore, all the processes that start running *after* a leader is elected terminate after three steps. The algorithm does not satisfy the disable-free shortcut property: a process that fails just before the assignment to b in line 2 or fails just before the assignment to z in line 4, may prevent other processes spinning in the *await* statement (line 7) from terminating.

7   Discussion

None of the known synchronization techniques is optimal in all cases. Despite the known weaknesses of locking and the many attempts to replace it, locking still predominates. There might still be hope for a "silver bullet", but until then, it would be constructive to also consider integration of different techniques in order to gain the benefit of their combined strengths. Such integration may involve using a *mixture* of objects which avoid locking (also called lockless objects) together with lock-based objects; and, as suggested in this paper, *fusing* lockless objects and locks together in order to create new interesting types of shared objects.

References

1. Adve, S.V., Gharachorloo, K.: Shared memory consistency models: A tutorial. IEEE Computers 29(12), 66–76 (1996)
2. Attiya, H., Guerraoui, R., Kouznetsov, P.: Computing with reads and writes in the absence of step contention. In: Fraigniaud, P. (ed.) DISC 2005. LNCS, vol. 3724, pp. 122–136. Springer, Heidelberg (2005)
3. Alur, R., Taubenfeld, G.: Results about fast mutual exclusion. In: Proceedings of the 13th IEEE Real-Time Systems Symposium, December 1992, pp. 12–21 (1992)
4. Aguilera, M.K., Toueg, S.: Timeliness-based wait-freedom: a gracefully degrading progress condition. In: Proc. 27rd ACM Symp. on Principles of Distributed Computing, pp. 305–314 (2008)
5. Bayer, R., Schkolnick, M.: Concurrency of operations on B-trees. Acta Informatica 9, 1–21 (1977)
6. Dijkstra, E.W.: Solution of a problem in concurrent programming control. CACM 8(9), 569 (1965)
7. Easton, W.B.: Process synchronization without long-term interlock. In: Proc. of the 3rd ACM symp. on Operating systems principles, pp. 95–100 (1971)
8. Ellis, C.S.: Extendible hashing for concurrent operations and distributed data. In: Proc. of the 2nd ACM symposium on Principles of database systems, pp. 106–116 (1983)
9. Fich, F.E., Luchangco, V., Moir, M., Shavit, N.N.: Obstruction-free algorithms can be practically wait-free. In: Fraigniaud, P. (ed.) DISC 2005. LNCS, vol. 3724, pp. 78–92. Springer, Heidelberg (2005)
10. Fischer, M.J., Lynch, N.A., Paterson, M.: Impossibility of distributed consensus with one faulty process. J. ACM 32(2), 374–382 (1985)
11. Fomitchev, M., Ruppert, E.: Lock-free linked lists and skip lists. In: Proc. 23rd ACM Symp. on Principles of Distributed Computing, pp. 50–59 (2004)
12. Guerraoui, R., Herlihy, M.P., Pochon, B.: Towards a theory of transactional contention managers. In: Proc. of the 24th Symp. on Principles of Dist. Computing, pp. 258–264 (2005)
13. Guerraoui, R., Kapalka, M., Kouznetsov, P.: The weakest failure detectors to boost obstruction-freedom. Distributed Computing 20(6), 415–433 (2008)
14. Harris, T.L.: A pragmatic implementation of non-blocking linked-lists. In: Welch, J.L. (ed.) DISC 2001. LNCS, vol. 2180, pp. 300–314. Springer, Heidelberg (2001)
15. Herlihy, M.P.: Wait-free synchronization. ACM TOPLAS 13(1), 124–149 (1991)
16. Herlihy, M.P., Luchangco, V., Moir, M.: Obstruction-free synchronization: Double-ended queues as an example. In: Proc. of the 23rd International Conf. on Dist. Computing Systems, pp. 522–529 (2003)
17. Herlihy, M.P., Moss, J.E.B.: Transactional memory: architectural support for lock-free data structures. In: Proc. of the 20th annual international symp. on Computer architecture, pp. 289–300 (1993)
18. Hart, T.E., McKenney, P.E., Brown, A.D.: Making lockless synchronization fast: Performance implications of memory reclamation. In: Proc. of the 20th international Parallel and Distributed Processing Symp. (2006)
19. Herlihy, M.P., Wing, J.M.: Linearizability: a correctness condition for concurrent objects. ACM Trans. on Programming Languages and Systems 12(3), 463–492 (1990)
20. Kung, H.T., Lehman, P.L.: Concurrent manipulation of binary search trees. ACM Transactions on Database Systems 5(3), 354–382 (1980)
21. Lamport, L.: A fast mutual exclusion algorithm. ACM Trans. on Computer Systems 5(1), 1–11 (1987)

22. Lamport, L.: How to make a multiprocessor computer that correctly executes multiprocess programs. IEEE Trans. on Computers 28(9), 690–691 (1979)
23. Loui, M.C., Abu-Amara, H.H.: Memory requirements for agreement among unreliable asynchronous processes. Advances in Computing Research 4, 163–183 (1987)
24. Luchangco, V., Moir, M., Shavit, N.N.: On the uncontended complexity of consensus. In: Fich, F.E. (ed.) DISC 2003. LNCS, vol. 2848, pp. 45–59. Springer, Heidelberg (2003)
25. Lehman, P.L., Yao, S.B.: Efficient locking for concurrent operations on B-trees. ACM Trans. on Database Systems 6(4), 650–670 (1981)
26. McKenney, P.E.: Memory ordering in modern microprocessors, Part I & Part II. Linux Journal, 2005(136) 2 pages, and 2005(137) 5 pages, 2005 (Revised April 2009) (2009)
27. McKenney, P.E., Michael, M.M., Walpole, J.: Why the grass not be greener on the other side: A comparison of locking vs. transactional memory. In: Proc. of the 4th workshop on Programming languages and operating systems, May 2007, pp. 1–5 (2007)
28. Moir, M., Anderson, J.: Wait-Free algorithms for fast, long-lived renaming. Science of Computer Programming 25(1), 1–39 (1995)
29. Massalin, H., Pu, C.: A lock-free multiprocessor OS kernel. Technical Report CUCS-005-91, Columbia University (1991)
30. Michael, M.M., Scott, M.L.: Simple, fast, and practical non-blocking and blocking concurrent queue algorithms. In: Proc. 15th ACM Symp. on Principles of Distributed Computing, pp. 267–275 (1996)
31. Merritt, M., Taubenfeld, G.: Computing with infinitely many processes. In: Herlihy, M.P. (ed.) DISC 2000. LNCS, vol. 1914, pp. 164–178. Springer, Heidelberg (2000)
32. Merritt, M., Taubenfeld, G.: Resilient consensus for infinitely many processes. In: Fich, F.E. (ed.) DISC 2003. LNCS, vol. 2848, pp. 1–15. Springer, Heidelberg (2003)
33. Moran, S., Wolfsthal, Y.: An extended impossibility result for asynchronous complete networks. Info. Processing Letters 26, 141–151 (1987)
34. Raynal, M.: Algorithms for mutual exclusion, 107 pages. The MIT Press, Cambridge (1986)
35. Rajwar, R., Goodman, J.R.: Speculative Lock Elision: Enabling Highly Concurrent Multithreaded Execution. In: Proc. 34th Inter. Symp. on Microarchitecture, pp. 294–305 (2001)
36. Scherer, W.N., Scott, M.L.: Advanced Contention Management for dynamic software transactional memory. In: Proc. of the 24th Symp. on Principles of Dist. Computing, pp. 240–248 (2005)
37. Shavit, N., Touitou, D.: Software transactional memory. In: Proc. 14th ACM Symp. on Principles of Distributed Computing, pp. 204–213 (1995)
38. Sundell, H., Tsigas, P.: Lock-free and practical deques using single-word compare-and-swap. In: 8th International Conference on Principles of Distributed Systems (2004)
39. Taubenfeld, G.: Efficient transformations of obstruction-free algorithms into non-blocking algorithms. In: Pelc, A. (ed.) DISC 2007. LNCS, vol. 4731, pp. 450–464. Springer, Heidelberg (2007)
40. Taubenfeld, G.: Synchronization Algorithms and Concurrent Programming, 423 pages. Pearson / Prentice-Hall, London (2006)
41. Taubenfeld, G., Moran, S.: Possibility and impossibility results in a shared memory environment. Acta Informatica 33(1), 1–20 (1996)
42. Valois, J.D.: Implementing lock-free queues. In: Proc. of the 7th International Conference on Parallel and Distributed Computing Systems, pp. 212–222 (1994)
43. Transactional memory, http://www.cs.wisc.edu/trans-memory/

Brief Announcement: Acceleration by Contention for Shared Memory Mutual Exclusion Algorithms

Michiko Inoue, Tsuyoshi Suzuki, and Hideo Fujiwara

Nara Institute of Science and Technology (NAIST), Japan

Introduction. This paper is exploring a possibility of designing distributed algorithms accelerated by high contention. We propose a mutual exclusion algorithm with such a property for asynchronous read/write shared memory systems with N processes. In a mutual exclusion algorithm, each process executes its *entry* and *exit* sections to enter its *critical* section, where **mutual exclusion:** at most one process executes its critical section at any time, and **starvation freedom:** each process that executes its entry section eventually executes its critical section, are required.

We propose an efficient mutual exclusion algorithm with respect to remote memory reference (RMR) complexity. Yang et al. [1] proposed an algorithm with the worst case RMR complexity of $O(\log N)$ and Attiya et al. [2] proved the lower bound of $\Omega(\log N)$. Though our algorithm has the worst case RMR complexity of $O(\log N)$, it becomes efficient with increasing the number of processes executing concurrently. We show the efficiency using queuing theory and simulation.

Algorithm. Our algorithm uses an arbitration tree[3] to resolve the mutual exclusion problem. An arbitration tree for N processes is an $N/2$-leaf binary tree where each node resolves 2-process mutual exclusion (2PME). A process executes the entry sections at 2PMEs from a designated leaf to the root to enter its critical section. After executing its critical section, the process executes the exit sections at 2PMEs from the root to the leaf.

In our algorithm Tree Skip (TS), some processes can skip to visit nodes in the path to the root. To realize such a mechanism, we introduce a waiting array and one additional 2PME (TOP2PME) (Fig.1). In each 2PME node, if two processes concurrently execute the entry sections, one process has to wait until the other process exits the node. In TS, such processes are added and then retrieved from the waiting array in a FIFO fashion to ensure the *starvation-freedom*. The retrieved process goes to TOP2PME to compete for the privilege to enter the critical section with a process from the arbitration tree to ensure *mutual exclusion*. Processes exclusively maintain the waiting array at the beginning of the exit section before they release the privilege of the critical section.

Each process in its entry section checks if it is added in the waiting array between 2PME nodes. If it notices that, the process just waits until it is retrieved from the waiting array. The process is waiting in the array with local spins (a checking procedure by only local memory accesses).

I. Keidar (Ed.): DISC 2009, LNCS 5805, pp. 172–173, 2009.
© Springer-Verlag Berlin Heidelberg 2009

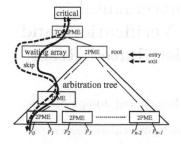

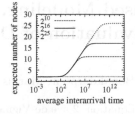

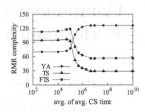

Fig. 1. Algorithm TS   **Fig. 2.** Queuing theory **Fig. 3.** Simulation result
analysis

Evaluation. In TS, every process incurs a constant number of remote memory accesses in the waiting array, and therefore, the RMR complexity of TS is proportional to the number of nodes that the process visits. This implies that the proposed TS has the worst case RMR complexity of $O(\log N)$.

We then evaluate the average case RMR complexity in the case where all the processes behave uniformly. We use $M/M/1(1)$ queuing system where we consider the interval from when a process starts the entry section of some 2PME node to when the process leaves the node as a service of the node for the process. Figure 2 shows the expected number of 2PME nodes that one process visits per one critical section entry in the case where the average service time is fixed. When the interarrival time is long (not congested case), the numbers of visited nodes are close to $\log N + 1$ and the numbers converge to 2 with reducing the interarrival time (congested case).

We also evaluate the performance of TS by simulation. In the simulation, times for the critical section, one remote memory access, one local memory access and one local operation are different among processes. Figure 3 shows the RMR complexity for Yang's algorithm (YA), our proposed algorithms Tree Skip (TS) and Fast Tree Skip (FTS). Since each process maintains the waiting array while making other processes wait in TS, it has long execution time for both entry and exit sections. FTS resolves this problem by separating the privilege to maintain the waiting array from the privilege to execute the critical section. Figure 3 shows that the RMR complexity is reduced as the average of average critical section (CS) time is longer. That is our algorithms are accelerated when the system is congested.

References

1. Yang, J., Anderson, J.: A fast, scalable mutual exclusion algorithm. Distributed Computing 9(1), 51–60 (1995)
2. Attiya, H., Hendler, D., Woelfel, P.: Tight RMR lower bounds for mutual exclusion and other problems. In: Proceedings of the Fourtieth Annual ACM Symposium on Theory of Computing, pp. 217–226 (2008)
3. Peterson, G., Fischer, M.: Economical solutions for the critical section problem in a distributed system. In: Proceedings of the Ninth Annual ACM Symposium on Theory of Computing, pp. 91–97. ACM, New York (1977)

Brief Announcement: Incremental Component-Based Modeling, Verification, and Performance Evaluation of Distributed Reset*

Ananda Basu, Borzoo Bonakdarpour, Marius Bozga, and Joseph Sifakis

VERIMAG, Centre Équation, 2 ave de Vignate, 38610 Gières, France

1 Motivation

Design and implementation of distributed algorithms often involve many subtleties due to their complex structure, nondeterminism, and low atomicity as well as occurrence of unanticipated physical events such as faults. Thus, constructing correct distributed systems has always been a challenge and often subjects to serious errors. This is essentially due to the fact that we currently lack disciplined methods for the rigorous design and correct implementation of distributed systems, mainly for two reasons: (1) formal methods are not easy to use by designers and developers; and (2) there is a wide gap between modeling formalisms and automated verification tools on one side, and practical development and deployment tools on the other side.

In this work, we apply a methodology which consistently integrates modeling, verification, and performance evaluation techniques, based on the BIP (Behavior, Interaction, Priority) component framework developed at Verimag [3,2]. BIP is based on a semantic model encompassing composition of heterogeneous components. The distributed semantics of BIP allows generating from a high-level component-based model in BIP an observationally equivalent distributed implementation [2]. BIP uses two families of composition operators for expressing coordination between components: *interactions* and *priorities*. Interactions may involve multiple components (unlike traditional point-to-point formalisms) and are expressed by combining two protocols: *rendezvous* and *broadcast*. We note that addition of interactions among components adds no extra behaviors.

We illustrate our methodology using the self-stabilizing distributed reset algorithm due to Arora and Gouda [1]. The algorithm consists of two layers: (1) the tree layer, where adjacent processes communicate in order to construct and maintain a rooted spanning tree throughout the alive processes, and (2) the wave layer, which achieves a global reset through a diffusing computation. We demonstrate how BIP allows independent modeling, verification, and analysis of the tree layer and wave layer and ultimately their safe composition in order to construct a correct model of distributed reset. This composition involves in addition to interactions, scheduling constraints expressed as dynamic priorities among interactions.

* This work is sponsored by the COMBEST European project. For all correspondence about this please contact Borzoo Bonakdarpour at borzoo@imag.fr

I. Keidar (Ed.): DISC 2009, LNCS 5805, pp. 174–175, 2009.

2 Approach and Results

Modeling. We model distributed reset according to the BIP system construction methodology: (1) designing the *behavior* of each atomic component (i.e., an automaton extended by variables, ports, and possibly C++ functionality), (2) applying synchronization mechanisms for ensuring coordination of components through *interactions* (i.e., broadcasts and rendezvous), and (3) specifying scheduling constraints by using *priorities*. We model each layer based on its normal operation in the absence of faults and self-stabilizing mechanism in the presence of faults. Each layer consists of a set of processes modeled by BIP atomic components. The notion of faults such as process failures and variable corruptions is captured by internal transitions inside components. Processes in each layer communicate through interactions constrained by priorities. Upon the occurrence of faults, components execute their recovery mechanism to reach a legitimate state within a finite number of steps using the embedded interactions.

Verification. In order to model check the distributed reset algorithm, we construct a finite representation of the overall behavior of the model as a flat labeled transition system using BIP state-space explorer. States correspond to configurations reached by the algorithm, and transitions are labeled by the interactions taken to move from one configuration to another. Our properties of interest are: *closure*, *deadlock-freedom*, and *finite reachability* of the set of legitimate states starting from any arbitrary state. To reduce the complexity of verification, we incorporate a compositional approach by showing interference-freedom between the layers and manually apply model checking techniques such as *abstraction*, *live analysis*, and *sequence simplification* on the BIP model.

Performance Analysis. The BIP toolset provides us with means for generating C++ multi-threaded code from high-level BIP models. This feature enables us to evaluate the performance of distributed algorithms described by high-level models. It allows us to evaluate the impact of changes to the high-level model without getting involved with its actual C++ code. We emphasize that the logical properties and dynamics of the C++ model conform with the high-level model and an actual C++ implementation. In this context, we measure the degree of parallelism (i.e., the number of processes working simultaneously), that the BIP scheduler allows to achieve under different parallelism policies. Moreover, we analyze the severity of different types of faults and the effect of specifying stabilizing priorities in performance of the distributed reset algorithm.

References

1. Arora, A., Gouda, M.: Distributed reset. IEEE Transactions on Computers 43, 316–331 (1994)
2. Basu, A., Bidinger, P., Bozga, M., Sifakis, J.: Distributed semantics and implementation for systems with interaction and priority. In: Formal Techniques for Networked and Distributed Systems (FORTE), pp. 116–133 (2008)
3. Basu, A., Bozga, M., Sifakis, J.: Modeling heterogeneous real-time components in BIP. In: IEEE International Conference on Software Engineering and Formal Methods (SEFM), pp. 3–12 (2006)

Local Computation of Nearly Additive Spanners

Bilel Derbel[1,*], Cyril Gavoille[2,**], David Peleg[3,***], and Laurent Viennot[4,†]

[1] Laboratoire d'Informatique Fondamentale de Lille (LIFL),
Université des Sciences et Technologies de Lille, France
`bilel.derbel@lifl.fr`
[2] Laboratoire Bordelais de Recherche en Informatique (LaBRI),
Université de Bordeaux, France
`gavoille@labri.fr`
[3] Department of Computer Science and Applied Mathematics,
The Weizmann Institute of Science, Rehovot, Israel
`david.peleg@weizmann.ac.il`
[4] INRIA, University Paris 7, France
`Laurent.Viennot@inria.fr`

Abstract. An (α, β)-spanner of a graph G is a subgraph H that approximates distances in G within a multiplicative factor α and an additive error β, ensuring that for any two nodes u, v, $d_H(u, v) \leq \alpha \cdot d_G(u, v) + \beta$. This paper concerns algorithms for the distributed deterministic construction of a sparse (α, β)-spanner H for a given graph G and distortion parameters α and β. It first presents a generic distributed algorithm that in constant number of rounds constructs, for every n-node graph and integer $k \geq 1$, an (α, β)-spanner of $O(\beta n^{1+1/k})$ edges, where α and β are constants depending on k. For suitable parameters, this algorithm provides a $(2k - 1, 0)$-spanner of at most $kn^{1+1/k}$ edges in k rounds, matching the performances of the best known distributed algorithm by Derbel et al. (PODC '08). For $k = 2$ and constant $\varepsilon > 0$, it can also produce a $(1 + \varepsilon, 2 - \varepsilon)$-spanner of $O(n^{3/2})$ edges in constant time. More interestingly, for every integer $k > 1$, it can construct in constant time a $(1 + \varepsilon, O(1/\varepsilon)^{k-2})$-spanner of $O(\varepsilon^{-k+1}n^{1+1/k})$ edges. Such deterministic construction was not previously known. The paper also presents a second generic deterministic and distributed algorithm based on the construction of small dominating sets and maximal independent sets. After computing such sets in sub-polynomial time, it constructs at its best a $(1 + \varepsilon, \beta)$-spanner with $O(\beta n^{1+1/k})$ edges, where $\beta = k^{\log(\log k/\varepsilon)+O(1)}$. For $k = 3$, it provides a $(1 + \varepsilon, 6 - \varepsilon)$-spanner with $O(\varepsilon^{-1}n^{4/3})$ edges. The additive terms $\beta = \beta(k, \varepsilon)$ in the stretch of our constructions yield the best trade-off currently known between k and ε, due to Elkin and Peleg (STOC '01). Our distributed algorithms are rather short, and can be viewed as a unification and simplification of previous constructions.

* Supported by the équipe-projet INRIA "DOLPHIN".
** Supported by the ANR-project "ALADDIN", and the équipe-projet INRIA "CÉPAGE".
*** Supported by grants from the Israel Science Foundation and the Minerva Foundation.
† Supported by the ANR-project "ALADDIN", and the équipe-projet INRIA "GANG".

I. Keidar (Ed.): DISC 2009, LNCS 5805, pp. 176–190, 2009.

1   Introduction

Applications for networks. Sparse spanners are motivated by routing protocols used in practical networks, where fast construction of a "skeleton" of the underlying network topology is crucial. As recently shown in [1], spanners and their variants can be efficiently used for routing in ad-hoc networks in view of the IETF standardized OLSR routing protocol [2].

Sparse spanners, as introduced by Peleg et al. [3,4], and implicitly used in [5], are key ingredients of various distributed applications, e.g., synchronizers [6], computing almost shortest paths in distributed networks [7,8], or distance oracles [9,10,11,12]. Spanners have also found applications in approximation algorithms for geometric spaces [13], and for solving linear systems [14]. In all of those problems, the quality of the spanners used directly impacts the quality of the solutions.

Spanners and their variants. Given an undirected unweighted graph G, let $d_G(u, v)$ denote the distance between u and v in G. An (α, β)-*spanner* of G is a spanning subgraph H of G such that $d_H(u, v) \le \alpha \cdot d_G(u, v) + \beta$ for every two nodes u, v. There are several variations on the concept of spanners. A spanning H that is not restricted to be a subgraph of G is called an (α, β)-*emulator* of G [15,16]. A subgraph H of G that must preserve distances larger than d only is called a d-*preserver* for G [17]. Other recent developments can be found in [18]. The paper will not discuss any of these variants, as well as extensions for digraphs [19].

Constructing sparse spanners. There is an abundant literature on spanners and related combinatorial objects, which is surveyed, e.g., by Pettie in [20]. It is well-known that every n-node graph has a $(2k - 1, 0)$-spanner with $O(n^{1+1/k})$ edges, which can be obtained by modification of the Kruskal's minimum spanning tree algorithm [21]. Moreover, according to Erdös-Simonovits Girth Conjecture [22,23], it is believed that every (α, β)-spanner with $\alpha + \beta < 2k + 1$ must have $\Omega(n^{1+1/k})$ edges for some worst-case graphs. The lower bound suggests that (α, β)-spanners such that $\alpha + \beta = 2k - 1$ and $\alpha < 2k - 1$ with $O(n^{1+1/k})$ edges may exist for all graphs. Indeed, for $\alpha = 1$, $(1, 2)$-spanner of size $O(n^{3/2})$ [24], and $(1, 6)$-spanner of size $O(n^{4/3})$ [25] exist for all graphs. It is not known whether $(1, 4)$-spanners with $O(n^{4/3})$ edges exist, or if $(1, O(1))$-spanner with $o(n^{4/3})$ edges can exist. Woodruff [26] proved, for every $k > 0$, that every $(1, 2k-2)$-spanner requires $\Omega(n^{1+1/k})$ edges in the worst-case, independently of the Erdös-Simonovits Girth Conjecture. For $\alpha = 1 + \varepsilon$, and for small $\varepsilon > 0$, Elkin and Peleg [27] showed that $(1 + \varepsilon, \beta)$-spanners with $O(\beta n^{1+1/k})$ edges exist, where[1] $\beta = k^{\log(\log k/\varepsilon)+O(1)}$. Thorup and Zwick [16] showed that $(1 + \varepsilon, O(1/\varepsilon)^{k-2})$-spanners with $O(kn^{1+1/k})$ edges exist. The stretch is worse than in the Elkin-Peleg construction, however it holds simultaneously for all ε. Note that their construction is not local as it possibly involves collaboration between nodes at distance $\Omega(n)$. (This occurs, for instance, for the n-node path.) Pettie [20,28] addressed the problem of constructing spanners of *linear* size. E.g., $(1, \tilde{O}(n^{9/16}))$-spanners[2] and $(O(1), \tilde{O}(1))$-spanners with $O(n)$ edges are presented in [20].

---

[1] All logarithms are in base two.

[2] The notation $\tilde{O}(f(n))$ stands for $f(n) \log^{O(1)} n$.

Distributed algorithms. Efficiently constructing sparse spanners by distributed algorithms is clearly important for network applications. Indeed, distributed algorithms for constructing $(2k-1,0)$-spanners with $O(kn^{1+1/k})$ edges exist. By the above discussion, these constructions are essentially optimal in size and stretch (distortion). A randomized algorithm achieving this performance (with guarantees on the stretch and expected size) has been presented in [29]. It has been recently shown in [30] that randomization is actually not required, and that $(2k-1,0)$-spanners with $O(kn^{1+1/k})$ edges can be constructed in k rounds. Interestingly, allowing $2k$ additional rounds, the algorithm can work without any knowledge of n, and still provide the same guarantee on the maximum spanner size.

When k tends to $\log n$, such constructions achieve $\Omega(n \log n)$ size only. A series of (randomized) constructions producing linear or near-linear size has been presented in [28]. At its sparsest level, $(1+\varepsilon, \beta)$-spanners with $n \cdot (\varepsilon^{-1} \log \log n)^{O(1)}$ edges are constructed in $O(\beta)$ time, where β is in the form $(\varepsilon^{-1} \log \log n)^{O(\log \log n)}$.

For $(1+\varepsilon, \beta)$-spanners, only few distributed constructions are known. Actually, it has been proved in [30,28] that $(1, f(k))$-spanners (for some function $f(k)$ of k), which are known to exist for $k=2$ and $k=3$, cannot be constructed quickly (say, in polylog time). So the best polylogarithmic-time distributed constructions one may hope for will yield $(1+\varepsilon, f(k))$-spanners. For $k=2$, a $(1+\varepsilon, 2)$-spanner with $O(\varepsilon^{-1} n^{3/2})$ edges is constructed in [30] in $O(\varepsilon^{-1})$ time.

There were previous attempts to devise a distributed implementation of the Elkin-Peleg construction of $(1+\varepsilon, \beta)$-spanners with $\beta = \beta(k, \varepsilon)$ and arbitrary k, ε. However, as pointed out by several authors [31,20], the resulting constructions, while achieving the goal of demonstrating the existence of sparse $(1+\varepsilon, \beta)$-spanners, can hardly serve as a basis for an efficient algorithm. (We refer the reader to [31] for a discussion on the technical reasons for the difficulty of implementing these constructions in a distributed setting.) Nevertheless, Elkin and Zhang [32] proposed a distributed implementation of $(1+\varepsilon, \beta)$-spanners (albeit through a very complicated algorithm). The trade-off for β is worse than the one of [33] by a factor of roughly $k^{\log k}$ (more precisely, in [32], $\beta = O((k \log k)/\varepsilon)^{\log k} = k^{\log k} \cdot k^{\log(\log k/\varepsilon)+O(1)})$, and the algorithm is randomized.

Our results. In this article, we come up with an alternative construction of sparse $(1+\varepsilon, \beta)$-spanners, and demonstrate that the new construction leads to significant improvements in the current state-of-the-art for the problem of computing almost shortest paths in distributed settings. It positively answers Pettie's open question [28] concerning the deterministic construction of additive spanners.

We present two algorithms. The first (in Section 2) constructs sparse spanners in *constant* time, for fixed k and ε. In the spirit of Pettie's constructions [20], our algorithm is generic. Depending on the parameters, it can achieve, for instance, a $(2k-1,0)$-spanner with $O(kn^{1+1/k})$ edges, or a $(1+\varepsilon, O(1/\varepsilon)^{k-2})$-spanner with $O(\varepsilon^{-k+1} n^{1+1/k})$ edges. More specifically, it can produce a $(1+\varepsilon, 2-\varepsilon)$-spanner with $O(\varepsilon^{-1} n^{3/2})$ edges. Note that this latter construction is optimal even in the sequential sense, since the absolute lower bound discussed above implies that $\alpha + \beta = (1+\varepsilon) + (2-\varepsilon) \geq 3$ for such a number of edges. Other trade-offs produced by our algorithm are summarized in the table of Section 2.2. Finally, it has the extra feature that it does not require the nodes to know the value of n, and still guarantees the desired size. This first contribution provides a positive answer to Pettie's open question [28].

Our second construction (Section 3) runs in sub-polynomial time, and relies on the deterministic computation of maximal independent sets, which is known to be difficult in the distributed setting [34]. Similarly to the first algorithm, it is generic and can be parameterized to produce a new family of spanners. In particular (see the table in Section 3.3 for more details), it provides a $(1+\varepsilon, \beta)$-spanner with $O(\beta n^{1+1/k})$ edges in sub-polynomial time, where $\beta = k^{\log (\log k/\varepsilon)+O(1)}$. This matches the performance of the best existential (sequential) constructions of [33]. As a particular case, our algorithm can also produce a $(1 + \varepsilon, 8 - \varepsilon)$-spanner with $O(\varepsilon^{-1}n^{4/3})$ edges, and a specific construction, with the same number of edges, actually provides a $(1 + \varepsilon, 6 - \varepsilon)$-spanner (Subsection 3.4). We also observe that using a Las Vegas algorithm for selecting a maximal independent set, our algorithms can run in poly-logarithmic time while achieving the best known stretches. Finally, our implementation is considerably simpler than that of [32].

In this paper we consider the classical $\mathcal{LOCAL}$ model of computation [35,36], where in each time unit a node can send any amount of information to its neighbors and perform any amount of local computations. Although the issue of message size may be important (see e.g., [32,28]), we do not address it in this paper, and leave open the question of deterministically constructing similar spanners with low message complexity.

Open questions. We leave open two main questions for further study. First, can the performances of the second construction be achieved deterministically in polylog time without the bottleneck of "breaking symmetry"? and with short messages? Second, do $(1+\varepsilon, f(k))$-spanners with at most $g(k)\cdot n^{1+1/k}$ edges exist for all graphs, for fixed $\varepsilon > 0$ and for some $f(k) = k^{O(1)}$? or even $f(k) = O(k)$? As far as we know, the best upper bound is $f(k) \leq k^{\log\log k+O(1)}$.

2 A Local Algorithm

2.1 Description of Algorithm LOCAL-SPAN

A *distance sequence* is a sequence of strictly positive integers. Given a distance sequence $\rho_1, \ldots, \rho_k$, denote its partial sums by

$$\rho[i,j] = \begin{cases} \rho_i + \cdots + \rho_j, & \text{if } i \leq j, \\ 0, & \text{if } i > j. \end{cases} \tag{1}$$

For every subgraph H of G, denote by $B_H(u, \rho)$ the ball of radius ρ in H centered at u. The subscript is omitted when $H = G$ is clear from the context.

The deterministic distributed algorithm LOCAL-SPAN is presented next. Informally, the algorithm operates in k iterations, during which each node u builds a cluster $R(u)$ around itself. At any stage, the subgraph H consists of all the edges selected to the spanner so far. This H enjoys the property that at any stage and for any node u, the subgraph of H induced by the nodes of the cluster $R(u)$ is connected. In iteration i, the "target radius" of the constructed cluster is $\rho[1, i]$. Every node u learns the clusters $R(v)$ of all the nodes v in its ρ_i-neighborhood, $B(u, \rho_i)$. Of those nodes, it keeps in the set $W(u)$ all the candidates to join its cluster $R(u)$. In an internal loop, it selects up to σ such candidates w from $W(u)$ and adds their clusters $R(w)$ to its own cluster $R(u)$, by adding to H a shortest path connecting w and u.

Input: a graph $G = (V, E)$, a distance sequence $\rho_1, \ldots, \rho_k$
Output: a spanner $H = \bigcup_{u \in V} H(u)$ of G
1 Set σ to any value in the range $[\max_{v \in B(u, \rho[1,k])} |B(v, \rho[1, k])|^{1/k}, n^{1/k}]$
2 $R(u) := \{u\}$ /* cluster around u */
3 $F(u) := \text{FALSE}$ /* termination flag */
4 $H(u) := (\{u\}, \varnothing)$ /* spanner edges selected by u */
5 **for** $i := 1$ *to* k **do**
6   Node u sends $R(u), F(u)$ to all nodes in $B(u, \rho_i)$,
7   and receives $R(v), F(v)$ from all $v \in B(u, \rho_i)$
8      $W(u) := B(u, \rho_i) \setminus \{v \mid F(v) = \text{TRUE}\}$ /* candidate nodes to be covered */
9      $\ell := 0$
10   **while** $\exists w \in W(u)$ *and* $\ell < \sigma$ **do**
11   (a) Pick $w \in W(u)$ such that $d_G(u, w)$ is minimal
12   (b) Add a shortest path in G from u to w to $H(u)$
13   (c) Add $R(w)$ to $R(u)$
14   (d) $W(u) := W(u) \setminus \{v \in W(u) \mid R(v) \cap R(w) \neq \varnothing\}$
15   (e) $\ell := \ell + 1$
16   **if** $W(u) = \varnothing$ **then** $F(u) := \text{TRUE}$ **else** $F(u) := \text{FALSE}$

Algorithm 1. Algorithm LOCAL-SPAN - Code for a node u

2.2 Results

Theorem 1. *Algorithm* LOCAL-SPAN *computes, for every n-node graph G and distance sequence $\rho_1, \ldots, \rho_k$, a spanner H of at most $\rho[1, k] \cdot n^{1+1/k}$ edges. The stretch of H and the time complexity of* LOCAL-SPAN *are summarized in the following table.*

stretch	size	time	parameters
$(2k - 1, 0)$	$k \cdot n^{1+1/k}$	$O(k)$	$\rho_1 = \cdots = \rho_k = 1$
$(1 + \varepsilon, 2 - \varepsilon)$	$(1 + \frac{2}{\varepsilon}) \cdot n^{3/2}$	$O(\varepsilon^{-1})$	$\rho_1 = 1, \rho_2 = 2/\varepsilon$ $\varepsilon \in (0, 2]$
$(1 + \varepsilon, 4(1 + \frac{4}{\varepsilon})^{k-2} - \varepsilon)$	$(1 + \frac{4}{\varepsilon})^{k-1} \cdot n^{1+1/k}$	$O((1 + \frac{4}{\varepsilon})^{k-1})$	$\rho_1 = 1, \rho_i = \frac{4}{\varepsilon}(1 + \frac{4}{\varepsilon})^{i-2}$ $\varepsilon \in (0, 4]$
$(5, 2^k - 4)$	$5^{k-1} \cdot n^{1+1/k}$	$O(5^k)$	$\hookrightarrow$ with $\varepsilon = 4$
$(3, 4 \cdot 3^{k-2} - 2)$	$3^{k-1} \cdot n^{1+1/k}$	$O(3^k)$	$\hookrightarrow$ with $\varepsilon = 2$

The correctness of algorithm LOCAL-SPAN and Theorem 1 are proved in the next section.

2.3 Analysis of Algorithm LOCAL-SPAN

Let $H_i(u)$, $R_i(u)$, $F_i(u)$, and $W_i(u)$ denote the values of $H(u)$, $R(u)$, $F(u)$, and $W(u)$, respectively, at the end of iteration i. The parameter u is omitted from these notations when u is clear from the context.

Proposition 1. *Algorithm* LOCAL-SPAN *has time complexity* $\rho[1,k]$ *if* n *is known to each node, and* $3\rho[1,k]$ *otherwise.*

Proof. At Step i, a node communicates with other nodes at distance at most ρ_i. So after $\rho[1,k]$ rounds the algorithm ends. If n is known, then σ can be set immediately to $n^{1/k}$. If it is not, then σ can be set to $\max_{v \in B(u,\rho[1,k])} |B(v,\rho[1,k])|^{1/k}$, and calculating this value requires $2\rho[1,k]$ extra rounds. □

Proposition 2. *The resulting spanner* H *has at most* $\rho[1,k] \cdot n^{1+1/k}$ *edges.*

Proof. Each node u adds to H, in each iteration i of its main loop, up to $\sigma = \sigma(u)$ paths of length at most ρ_i. Hence the overall contribution of u to the spanner consists of at most $\sigma \cdot \rho[1,k]$ edges. The bound follows as $\sigma \leq n^{1/k}$. □

The following proposition is proved by induction on i.

Proposition 3. *For all* $i \geq 0$, $R_i(u) \subseteq B_{H_i}(u, \rho[1,i])$.

Proposition 4. *Let* x *be a node at distance at most* ρ_i *from* u *and satisfying* $F_{i-1}(x) = $ FALSE. *If* $F_i(u) = $ TRUE *then* $d_{H_i}(u,x) \leq d_G(u,x) + 2\rho[1,i-1]$.

Proof. As $F_{i-1}(x) = $ FALSE, x is in $W(u)$ before the while loop of iteration i. As $F_i(u) = $ TRUE, i.e., $W_i(u) = \varnothing$, there must exist some $w \in W(u)$ such that $R_{i-1}(w) \cap R_{i-1}(x) \neq \varnothing$. Consider the first vertex w satisfying this (eventually $w = x$) and let $z \in R_{i-1}(w) \cap R_{i-1}(x)$. By the triangle inequality,

$$d_{H_i}(u,x) \leq d_{H_i}(u,w) + d_{H_i}(w,z) + d_{H_i}(z,x)$$
$$\leq d_{H_i}(u,w) + d_{H_{i-1}}(w,z) + d_{H_{i-1}}(z,x) \qquad (2)$$

The choice of w and step (b) in the while loop imply that $d_{H_i}(u,w) = d_G(u,w) \leq d_G(u,x)$. In addition, Proposition 3, applied to $R_{i-1}(w)$ and $R_{i-1}(x)$, implies that $d_{H_{i-1}}(w,z) \leq \rho[1,i-1]$ and $d_{H_{i-1}}(z,x) \leq \rho[1,i-1]$. Hence (2) yields $d_{H_i}(u,x) \leq d_G(u,x) + 2\rho[1,i-1]$.

In the special case $i = 1$, we indeed have $d_{H_1}(u,x) = d_G(u,x)$ since $W_1(u) = \varnothing$ implies that $R_1(u)$ contains all nodes in $B(u,\rho_1)$. Indeed, as no nodes v satisfy $R_0(v) = \varnothing$, $W(u) = B(u,\rho_1)$ before the while loop. We then obtain $d_{H_1}(u,x) \leq d_G(u,x) + 2\rho[1,0]$ as claimed because $\rho[1,0] = 0$. □

Define $\bar{R}_i(u)$ as the union of the sets $R(w)$ added to $R(u)$ during the while loop of iteration i.

Proposition 5. *If $F_i(u) = $ FALSE, then*

$$|R_i(u)| \geq |\bar{R}_i(u)| \geq \max_{v \in B(u,\rho[i+1,k])} |B(v,\rho[1,k])|^{i/k}.$$

Proof. By induction on i. The assertion is satisfied for $i = 0$ as $|R_0(u)| = 1$. Consider the sets $R_{i-1}(w)$ added to $R(u)$ in the while loop of iteration i. The inductive hypothesis implies

$$|R_{i-1}(w)| \geq \max_{v \in B(w,\rho[i,k])} |B(v,\rho[1,k])|^{(i-1)/k}$$

$$\geq \max_{v \in B(u,\rho[i+1,k])} |B(v,\rho[1,k])|^{(i-1)/k}$$

since $d_G(u,w) \leq \rho_i$. If $F_i(u) = $ FALSE, then

$$\sigma = \max_{v \in B(u,\rho[1,k])} |B(v,\rho[1,k])|^{1/k} \geq \max_{v \in B(u,\rho[i+1,k])} |B(v,\rho[1,k])|^{1/k}$$

sets are added to $R(u)$. As these sets are disjoint, the size of $\bar{R}_i(u)$ is thus at least $\max_{v \in B(u,\rho[i+1,k])} |B(v,\rho[1,k])|^{i/k}$. □

Proposition 6. *For all u, $F_k(u) = $ TRUE.*

Proof. Suppose, towards contradiction, that $F_k(u) = $ FALSE for some u. Proposition 5 then implies

$$|\bar{R}_k(u)| \geq \max_{v \in B(u,\rho[k+1,k])} |B(v,\rho[1,k])|^{k/k} = |B(u,\rho[1,k])|.$$

Moreover, Proposition 3 implies $\bar{R}_k(u) \subseteq B(u,\rho[1,k])$. We thus deduce $\bar{R}_k(u) = B(u,\rho[1,k])$. In particular, $\bar{R}_k(u)$ contains $B(u,\rho_k)$. As every node that is added to $R(u)$ is immediately removed from $W(u)$, all $B(u,\rho_k)$ is removed from $W(u)$ and necessarily $W_k(u) = \varnothing$. This is in contradiction with the fact that $F_k(u) = $ FALSE. □

Proposition 7. *For every u,v, we have*

$$d_H(u,v) \leq (1+\varepsilon) \cdot d_G(u,v) + 4\rho[1,k-1] - \varepsilon$$

where $\varepsilon = \max_{1 \leq i \leq k} \{4\rho[1,i-1]/\rho_i\}$.

Proof. We prove this by induction on $d_G(u,v)$. The claim is obviously satisfied for $d_G(u,v) = 0$. Now consider u and v at distance $\delta = d_G(u,v)$ and suppose that the property is verified for any pair of nodes u',v' such that $d_G(u',v') < \delta$. Consider a shortest path P from u to v in G. Let x_i denote the vertex at distance ρ_i from u on P (we set $x_0 = u$ for $i = 0$ and $x_i = v$ if $\rho_i \geq d_G(u,v)$). Let P_i denote the sub-path of P from u to x_i.

Consider the lowest value of i such that $F_i(y) = \text{TRUE}$ for all $y \in P_i$. (Note that $i \leq k$ by Proposition 6). Then $F_{i-1}(y) = \text{FALSE}$ for some $y \in P_{i-1}$. As $F_i(u) = \text{TRUE}$ and $F_i(x_i) = \text{TRUE}$, Proposition 4 implies $d_{H_i}(u, y) \leq d_G(u, y) + 2\rho[1, i-1]$ and $d_{H_i}(x_i, y) \leq d_G(x_i, y) + 2\rho[1, i-1]$. By the triangle inequality, $d_{H_i}(u, x_i) \leq d_{H_i}(u, y) + d_{H_i}(y, x_i) \leq d_G(u, y) + d_G(y, x_i) + 4\rho[1, i-1] \leq d_G(u, x_i) + 4\rho[1, i-1]$.

In case $x_i = v$, we thus obtain $d_H(u, v) \leq (1 + \varepsilon) \cdot d_G(u, v) + 4\rho[1, k-1] - \varepsilon d_G(u, v) \leq (1 + \varepsilon) \cdot d_G(u, v) + 4\rho[1, k-1] - \varepsilon$, since $d_G(u, v) \geq 1$.

In case $x_i \neq v$ (i.e., $d_G(u, v) > \rho_i$), we have $d_G(u, x_i) = \rho_i$ and $d_H(u, x_i) \leq \rho_i + 4\rho[1, i-1]$. By the choice of ε, $\varepsilon \geq 4\rho[1, i-1]/\rho_i$, and thus $d_H(u, x_i) \leq \rho_i + \varepsilon\rho_i = (1+\varepsilon)\rho_i$. By the induction hypothesis, $d_H(x_i, v) \leq (1+\varepsilon)\cdot(\delta-\rho_i) + 4\rho[1, k-1] - \varepsilon$; the desired inequality for u, v follows. $\quad\square$

Consider the sequence defined by $\rho_1 = 1$ and $\rho_i = \alpha\,(1+\alpha)^{i-2}$ for $i \geq 2$, which is a distance sequence for every $\alpha \geq 1$. We have

$$\rho[1, i-1] \;=\; 1 + \alpha\sum_{j=0}^{i-3}(1+\alpha)^j \;=\; 1 + \alpha\frac{(1+\alpha)^{i-2} - 1}{(1+\alpha) - 1} \;=\; (1+\alpha)^{i-2} = \rho_i/\alpha.$$

This yields $\varepsilon = \max_i \{4\rho[1, i-1]/\rho_i\} = 4/\alpha$. By Proposition 7, for every $\varepsilon \in (0, 4]$, $d_H(u, v) \leq (1 + \varepsilon) \cdot d_G(u, v) + 4\,(1 + 4/\varepsilon)^{k-2} - \varepsilon$. By Proposition 2, the number of edges of H is no more than $(1 + 4/\varepsilon)^{k-1} \cdot n^{1+1/k}$. For instance, for $\varepsilon = 2, 3$ or 4, we get for H the stretches $(2, 4 \cdot 5^{k-2} - 1)$, $(3, 4 \cdot 3^{k-2} - 2)$, and $(5, 2^k - 4)$, respectively.

We can obtain a better analysis when $\rho_1 = \cdots = \rho_{k-1}$.

Proposition 8. *If $\rho_1 = \cdots = \rho_{k-1}$, then for all u, v, we have $d_H(u, v) \leq (1 + \varepsilon) \cdot d_G(u, v) + 2\rho[1, k-1] - \varepsilon$ where $\varepsilon = \max_{1 \leq i \leq k} \{2\rho[1, i-1]/\rho_i\}$.*

Proof. In the proof of Proposition 7, consider the highest value of i such that $F_i(u) = \text{FALSE}$ and $F_i(x_1) = \text{FALSE}$. Proposition 6 implies $i < k$. In case $i = k - 1$, Proposition 4 implies $d_H(u, x_k) \leq d_G(u, x_k) + 2\rho[1, k-1]$ since $F_k(x_k) = \text{TRUE}$. In case $i < k - 1$, we have $F_{i+1}(u) = \text{TRUE}$ or $F_{i+1}(x_1) = \text{TRUE}$. Proposition 4 then implies $d_H(u, x_1) \leq d_G(u, x_1) + 2\rho[1, i]$. In both cases, we have $d_H(u, x_{i+1}) \leq d_G(u, x_{i+1}) + 2\rho[1, i]$. We can then conclude similarly to the proof of Proposition 7. $\quad\square$

Consider the distance sequence $\rho_1 = \cdots = \rho_k = 1$. Then $\rho[1, k-1] = k - 1$ and $\varepsilon = \max_{1 \leq i \leq k} \{2\rho[1, i-1]/\rho_i\} = 2(k - 1)$. By Proposition 7, it follows that $d_H(u, v) \leq (2k - 1) \cdot d_G(u, v)$. The number of edges is $k \cdot n^{1+1/k}$.

For $k = 2$, consider the distance sequence $\rho_1 = 1$ and $\rho_2 = 2/\varepsilon$, for every $\varepsilon \in (0, 2]$. We have $\max_{1 \leq i \leq k} \{2\rho[1, i-1]/\rho_i\} = \max\{2\rho[1, 0]/1, 2\rho[1, 1]/(2/\varepsilon)\} = \varepsilon$, and also $\rho[1, k-1] = 1$, which yields, for every $\varepsilon \in (0, 2]$, a stretch of $(1+\varepsilon, 2-\varepsilon)$ for $(1 + 2/\varepsilon) \cdot n^{3/2}$ edges.

3   An Algorithm Based on Independent Dominating Sets

3.1   Definitions

Let us consider a graph $G = (V, E)$. A triple (v, S, T) is called a *cluster* if $S \subseteq V$, $v \in S$, and T is a tree of G spanning[3] S. The node v is called the *center* of the cluster. Two clusters (v, S_v, T_v) and (w, S_w, T_w) are *disjoint* if $S_v \cap S_w = \varnothing$.

Let $\mathcal{C}$ be a collection of clusters of G. If the clusters of $\mathcal{C}$ are pairwise disjoint, we say that $\mathcal{C}$ is a *partition* of G. We denote by center$(\mathcal{C})$ the set of centers of all clusters of $\mathcal{C}$. For $v \in$ center$(\mathcal{C})$, denote by S_v and T_v the subset and tree such that (v, S_v, T_v) is a cluster of $\mathcal{C}$.

For two node sets S, S', let $d_G(S, S') = \min \{d_G(v, v') \mid v \in S, v' \in S'\}$. Denote by $G_\rho(\mathcal{C})$ the graph whose vertex set is center$(\mathcal{C})$, and whose edge set is the set of all pairs of centers u, v such that $d_G(S_v, S_w) \leq \rho$.

Denote by G^2 the graph obtained from G by adding an edge between every two nodes at distance 2 in G. Given a set W of nodes, let $G[W]$ denote the graph induced by W in G. Denote by IDS(G, λ) an independent λ-dominating set of G, i.e., a subset S of non-neighboring nodes such that every node v in G is at distance at most λ of S (namely, $d_G(v, S) \leq \lambda$).

3.2   Description of Algorithm DOM-SPAN

Algorithm DOM-SPAN decomposes the node set of G into increasingly denser clusters using a classical merging technique. The algorithm is formally described below. Roughly speaking, at each iteration i, sparse unmerged clusters (kept in the set L) are connected to their neighbors at distance ρ_i using few shortest paths (in the loop of line 8). Next, the dense clusters are merged together (in the loop of line 10). This process is repeated until all the clusters become sparse. Intuitively, connecting sparse neighboring clusters with long shortest paths allows us to obtain a small multiplicative stretch, but it can cause the size of the spanner to increase too much. The general idea of the algorithm is to tune the sequence ρ_i according to each iteration i so that not too many edges are added to the spanner. In fact, as the clusters become dense, the number of clusters decreases and thus we are allowed to connect clusters that lie at a large distance of each other, i.e., the denser the clusters in an iteration i, the larger the distances ρ_i we can choose.

The condition used to evaluate the sparseness of a cluster (line 4) guarantees that the size of the clusters increases exponentially. As a consequence, within a logarithmic number of iterations (in k), all clusters become sparse and all nodes are connected together in the spanner. Using an independent dominating set X on the dense clusters (in line 5) allows us to break the symmetry efficiently and to grow the clusters in parallel.

One key ingredient of our construction is to ensure that the clusters grow sufficiently in each iteration without overlapping. For that purpose, we use an

---

[3] Note that S itself is not necessarily connected, and the tree T may span also some nodes that do not belong to S.

independent dominating set to pick some independent dense clusters at distance at least 3 from one another (set X of line 5). These independent clusters can then grow in parallel. In fact, using a consistent coloring technique (in the loop of line 6), each cluster determines the cluster in the independent set to which it will be merged. Thus, at least the clusters in the neighborhood of each independent cluster can be merged together in parallel without overlap (the loop of line 10). This process of picking clusters using an independent set allows us to enlarge them sufficiently while preventing new merged clusters from overlapping.

Input: a graph $G = (V, E)$, a sequence $\rho_1, \ldots, \rho_K$ where $K = \lfloor \log k \rfloor + 1$, $\lambda \geq 1$
Output: a spanner H of G

1   $H := (V, \varnothing)$, $\mathcal{C} := \bigcup_{v \in V}(v, \{v\}, (\{v\}, \varnothing))$
2   **for** $i := 1$ *to* K **do**
3     $\mathcal{C}' := \varnothing$, $M := G_{\rho_i}(\mathcal{C})$
4     $L := \{v \in \text{center}(\mathcal{C}) \mid \deg_M(v) \leq n^{1/k} |S_v|\}$ /* sparse clusters */
5     $X := \text{IDS}(M^2[\text{center}(\mathcal{C}) \setminus L], \lambda)$ /* dominating set for the dense clusters */
6   **for** $v \in \text{center}(\mathcal{C})$ **do**
7   **if** $d_M(v, X) \leq 2\lambda$ **then** set $c(v)$ to be its closest node of X in M
       (breaking ties by identities), **else** $c(v) := \perp$
8   **for** $v, w \in \text{center}(\mathcal{C})$ *such that* v, w *are neighbors in* M *and* $c(v) = \perp$ **do**
9   Add a shortest path in G from S_v to S_w to H
10   **for** $v \in \text{center}(\mathcal{C}) \cap X$ **do**
11      $S := S_v$ and $T := T_v$
12   **for** $w \in \text{center}(\mathcal{C})$ *such that* $c(w) = v$ **do**
13   Compute a shortest path $v = x_0, x_1, \ldots, x_t = w$ in M
14   **for** $j := 1$ *to* t **do**
15   Add a shortest path in G from $S_{x_{j-1}}$ to S_{x_j} to H and to T
16   Add S_{x_j} to S, and add T_{x_j} to T
17   Add (v, S, T) to $\mathcal{C}'$
18    $\mathcal{C} := \mathcal{C}'$

Algorithm 2. Algorithm DOM-SPAN

3.3 Analysis

Our result is summarized in the following theorem. (Recall the notation (1).) Due to lack of space, the proof is omitted.

Theorem 2. *Algorithm* DOM-SPAN *is a deterministic distributed algorithm that, for all n-node graph G, integers $k, \lambda \geq 1$, and distance sequence $\rho_1, \ldots, \rho_K$ where $K = \lfloor \log k \rfloor + 1$, computes for G a spanner H of at most $\rho[1, K] \cdot (n^{1+1/k} + n)$ edges. The stretch of H and the time complexity of* DOM-SPAN *are summarized in the table below.*

In the following table, size and time complexities are stated up to a constant factor. $\text{IDS}(n, \lambda)$ denotes the complexity of computing (distributively) an independent λ-dominating set of an n-node graph. The best currently known bounds are $\text{IDS}(n, 1) = 2^{O(\sqrt{\log n})}$ [37], and $\text{IDS}(n, 2 \log n) = O(\log n)$ (cf. [36]).

stretch	size	time	parameters
$(1+\varepsilon, 8-\varepsilon)$	$\varepsilon^{-1} \cdot n^{4/3}$	$\varepsilon^{-1} + \text{IDS}(n,1)$ $\leq \varepsilon^{-1} + 2^{O(\sqrt{\log n})}$	$\rho_1 = 1, \rho_2 = 8/\varepsilon, k = 3$ $\varepsilon \in (0,8]$
$(1+\varepsilon, \beta_1)$ $\beta_1 = k^{\log(\log k/\varepsilon)+O(1)}$	$\beta_1 \cdot n^{1+1/k}$	$\beta_1 \cdot \text{IDS}(n,1)$ $\leq \beta_1 \cdot 2^{O(\sqrt{\log n})}$	$\rho_i = (9\lfloor \log k \rfloor /\varepsilon)^{i-1}$ $\varepsilon \in (0, O(\log k)]$
$(1+\varepsilon, \beta_2)$ $\beta_2 = (\log n/\varepsilon)^{O(\log \log n)}$	$\beta_2 \cdot n$	$\beta_2 \cdot \text{IDS}(n, 2\log n)$ $\leq \beta_2 \cdot \log n$	$\hookrightarrow k = \log n$ $\varepsilon \in (0, O(\log \log n)]$

For $k = 3$, the stretch can be slightly improved as shown in Subsection 3.4. Observe that an independent dominating set ($\lambda = 1$), which is nothing else than a maximal independent set, can be computed in $O(\log n)$ expected time [38], leading to better performances in our algorithm if Las Vegas algorithms are considered.

3.4   An Improved Algorithm for $k = 3$

Finally, we propose a specific construction for $k = 3$, slightly improving the stretch over the general algorithms LOCAL-SPAN and DOM-SPAN. The construction, which combines ideas from both algorithms, yields to a $(1+\varepsilon, 6-\varepsilon)$-spanner with $O(\varepsilon^{-1}n^{4/3})$ edges.

Theorem 3. *There is a deterministic distributed algorithm that, for every n-node graph and $\varepsilon \in (0,6]$, computes a $(1+\varepsilon, 6 - \varepsilon)$-spanner of $O(\varepsilon^{-1}n^{4/3})$ edges in $O(\varepsilon^{-1} + \text{IDS}(n,1)) = O(\varepsilon^{-1}) + 2^{O(\sqrt{\log n})}$ time.*

Proof. The proof is based on an ad-hoc construction obtained by merging both algorithms LOCAL-SPAN and DOM-SPAN.

Let us denote by D the set of nodes of degree at least $n^{1/3}$, the dense nodes. We first construct a small 2-dominating set X for nodes in D. More formally, we compute a set X such that for every $v \in D$, $d_G(v, X) \leq 2$. This can be done by computing distributively an MIS of $G^2[D]$ in $O(\text{IDS}(n,1))$ time, as done in Algorithm DOM-SPAN with $\lambda = 1$. We obtain a 2-dominating set X for D with $|X| \leq n^{2/3}$.

From X, we create a partition of D into "clusters", i.e., a connected subgraph $C(x)$ centered in each node x of X and of radius at most 2. This can be done in $O(1)$ time by a vote of each node of D of its closest "dominator" in X, equality being break in a consistence nanner.

For each node v of G select a set $R(v)$ composed of v and of min $\{\deg_G(v), n^{1/3}\}$ of its neighbors. This phase is similar to the first phase of Algorithm LOCAL-SPAN with $k = 3$.

The edges of the spanner H are composed of:

(1) the edges between v and $R(v)$ for each node v of G;
(2) the edges of BFS trees centered at each node $x \in X$ and spanning $C(x)$; and
(3) the edges of the shortest paths computed as follows (the next procedure is similar to the while-loop of Algorithm LOCAL-SPAN):

for each node $x \in X$, **do** (in parallel):

1. $W(x) := (B(x, \rho) \cap D) \setminus C(x)$, where $\rho = 6/\varepsilon + 2$
2. **while** $W(x) \neq \emptyset$ **do**
   (a) pick the closest $w \in W(x)$ from x;
   (b) add a shortest path in G from x to w; and
   (c) remove from $W(x)$ all nodes v such that $R(v)$ and $R(w)$ intersect.

Time: The time complexity is $O(\text{IDS}(n, 1) + \varepsilon^{-1})$, since Phase (3) involves only nodes at distance $O(\varepsilon^{-1})$.

Size: The number of edges for Phase (1) is at most $n^{4/3}$. For Phase (2) this is at most $n - |X|$ since $\{C(x)\}_{x \in X}$ is a partition of the nodes of G. For Phase (3) we observe that the instructions of the while-loop are executed at most $n/n^{1/3} = n^{2/3}$ times since:

- the w's selected at Step 2(a) have pairwise disjoint regions $R(w)$;
- once w is picked, at least all nodes of $R(w)$ are removed from G and cannot be considered any more in $W(x)$, because if $v \in R(w)$ then $R(v) \cap R(w)$ contains at least v since $v \in R(v)$;
- the size of $R(w)$ is $n^{1/3}$ since $w \in W(x) \subseteq D$.

Each path added at Step 2(b) is of length at most ρ, so Phase (3) contributes for at most $|X| \cdot n^{2/3} \cdot \rho \leq \rho \cdot n^{4/3}$ edges. In total, the number of edges of H is at most $(\rho + 1) \cdot n^{4/3} + n = O(\varepsilon^{-1} n^{4/3})$.

Stretch: The stretch analysis is similar to the one of Proposition 7. One consider two distinct nodes u, v in G, and let P be a shortest path from u to v in G. We want to show that $d_H(u, v) \leq (1 + \varepsilon) d_G(u, v) + 6 - \varepsilon$, that is H is a $(1 + \varepsilon, 6 - \varepsilon)$-spanner. We will proceed by induction, prove the result for "small distances", and then assume it holds for all distances $\delta < d_G(u, v)$.

For that, we assume that P is not wholly included in H, since otherwise $d_H(u, v) = d_G(u, v)$ and we are done. Let us first show that:

Claim. If $1 \leq d_G(u, v) \leq \rho - 2$, then $d_H(u, v) \leq d_G(u, v) + 6$.

Proof. Let $u', v' \in P$ respectively be the closest and farthest node from u that are in D. Both nodes exist otherwise P would be composed of only nodes of degree less than $n^{1/3}$ (i.e., not in D), and $P \subseteq H$: contradiction. Note that $d_H(u, u') = d_G(u, u')$ and $d_H(v, v') = d_G(v, v')$. So it suffices to prove that $d_H(u', v') \leq (1 + \varepsilon) d' + 6 - \varepsilon$, where $d' = d_G(u', v')$.

Let $x \in X$ such that $u' \in C(x)$. Such x exists, since $u' \in D$. If $v' \in C(x)$, we are done $d_H(u', v') \leq 2$. Note that $d_G(x, v') \leq d_G(x, u') + d_G(u', v') \leq 2 + d'$ that is at most ρ because $d' \leq d_G(u, v) \leq \rho - 2$ by assumption. In other words, $v' \in B(x, \rho)$. It follows that v' is in the set $W(x)$ when initialized at Step 1.

Let w be the node picked at Step 2(a) in the while-loop such that v' is removed from $W(x)$. Let P' be the shortest path added to H from x to w. We have

$R(w) \cap R(v') \neq \varnothing$ ($v' = w$ is possible). Since all the edges from a node z to all its neighbors in $R(z)$ are in H, we have $d_H(w, v') \leq 2$. In other words, there is a route from u' to v' through x and P', and through w to v' thanks to $R(w)$ and $R(v')$. Note that $d_G(x, w) \leq d_G(x, v')$ by the choice of w. Hence, the length of P' is $|P'| \leq d_G(u', w) + 2$ because $d_G(u', x) \leq 2$. So $d_H(u', v') \leq d_H(u', x) + d_H(x, v') \leq 2 + |P'| + 2 \leq d_G(u', v') + 6$, completing the proof of the claim.   □

So, if $d_G(u, v) \leq \rho - 2$, then $d_H(u, v) \leq d_G(u, v) + 6 \leq (1 + \varepsilon)d_G(u, v) + 6 - \varepsilon$ since $d_G(u, v) \geq 1$.

Assume now that $d_G(u, v) > \rho - 2$, and let $z \in P$ be such that $d_G(u, z) = \rho - r$. By definition of ρ and the choice of $\varepsilon \in (0, 6]$, $\rho - 2 \geq 1$. Therefore $u \neq z$ and Claim 3.4 applies: $d_H(u, z) \leq \rho - 2 + 6$. Observe that $\varepsilon(\rho - 2) \geq 6$, and thus $d_H(u, z) \leq \rho - 2 + \varepsilon(\rho - 2) = (1 + \varepsilon)(\rho - 2)$.

By induction hypothesis on the distance between z and v, which is $< d_G(u, v)$, we get: $d_H(z, v) \leq (1 + \varepsilon)d_G(z, v) + 6 - \varepsilon = (1 + \varepsilon)(d_G(u, v) - d_G(u, z)) + 6 - \varepsilon$. If follows that $d_H(u, v) \leq d_H(u, z) + d_H(z, v) \leq (1 + \varepsilon)(\rho - 2) + (1 + \varepsilon)(d_G(u, v) - (\rho - 2)) + 6 - \varepsilon = (1 + \varepsilon)d_G(u, v) + 6 - \varepsilon$. This completes the stretch analysis, and the proof of Theorem 3.   □

References

1. Jacquet, P., Viennot, L.: Remote spanners: what to know beyond neighbors. In: 23rd IEEE International Parallel & Distributed Processing Symposium (IPDPS), IEEE Computer Society Press, Los Alamitos (2009)
2. Adjih, C., Laouiti, A., Muhlethaler, P., Qayyum, A., Viennot, L.: The optimised routing protocol for mobile ad-hoc networks: protocol specification. Technical Report 5145, INRIA (March 2003)
3. Peleg, D., Ullman, J.D.: An optimal synchronizer for the hypercube. In: 6th Annual ACM Symposium on Principles of Distributed Computing (PODC), pp. 77–85. ACM Press, New York (1987)
4. Peleg, D., Schäffer, A.A.: Graph spanners. Journal of Graph Theory 13(1), 99–116 (1989)
5. Awerbuch, B.: Complexity of network synchronization. Journal of the ACM 32(4), 804–823 (1985)
6. Peleg, D., Ullman, J.D.: An optimal synchornizer for the hypercube. SIAM Journal on Computing 18(4), 740–747 (1989)
7. Cohen, E.: Fast algorithms for constructing t-spanners and paths with stretch t. SIAM Journal on Computing 28(1), 210–236 (1998)
8. Elkin, M., Zhang, J.: Efficient algorithms for constructing $(1 + \epsilon, \beta)$-spanners in the distributed and streaming models. Distributed Computing 18(5), 375–385 (2006)
9. Baswana, S., Goyal, V., Sen, S.: All-pairs nearly 2-approximate shortest-paths in $O(n^2 \text{polylog} n)$ time. In: Diekert, V., Durand, B. (eds.) STACS 2005. LNCS, vol. 3404, pp. 666–679. Springer, Heidelberg (2005)
10. Baswana, S., Kavitha, T.: Faster algorithms for approximate distance oracles and all-pairs small stretch paths. In: 47th Annual IEEE Symposium on Foundations of Computer Science (FOCS), pp. 591–602. IEEE Computer Society Press, Los Alamitos (2006)

11. Thorup, M., Zwick, U.: Approximate distance oracles. Journal of the ACM 52(1), 1–24 (2005)
12. Roditty, L., Thorup, M., Zwick, U.: Deterministic constructions of approximate distance oracles and spanners. In: Caires, L., Italiano, G.F., Monteiro, L., Palamidessi, C., Yung, M. (eds.) ICALP 2005. LNCS, vol. 3580, pp. 261–272. Springer, Heidelberg (2005)
13. Narasimhan, G., Smid, M.: Geometric Spanner Networks. Cambridge University Press, Cambridge (2007)
14. Spielman, D.A., Teng, S.H.: Nearly-linear time algorithms for graph partitioning, graph sparsification, and solving linear systems. In: 36th Annual ACM Symposium on Theory of Computing (STOC), pp. 81–90. ACM Press, New York (2004)
15. Dor, D., Halperin, S., Zwick, U.: All-pairs almost shortest paths. SIAM Journal on Computing 29(5), 1740–1759 (2000)
16. Thorup, M., Zwick, U.: Spanners and emulators with sublinear distance errors. In: 17th Symposium on Discrete Algorithms (SODA), January 2006, pp. 802–809. ACM/ SIAM (2006)
17. Bollobás, B., Coppersmith, D., Elkin, M.: Sparse distance preservers and additive spanners. SIAM Journal of Discrete Mathematics 19(4), 1029–1055 (2006)
18. Chechik, S., Langberg, M., Peleg, D., Roditty, L.: Fault-tolerant spanners for general graphs. In: 41st Annual ACM Symposium on Theory of Computing (STOC). ACM Press, New York (2009)
19. Roditty, L., Thorup, M., Zwick, U.: Roundtrip spanners and roundtrip routing in directed graphs. ACM Transactions on Algorithms 3(4), Article 29 (2008)
20. Pettie, S.: Low distortion spanners. In: Arge, L., Cachin, C., Jurdziński, T., Tarlecki, A. (eds.) ICALP 2007. LNCS, vol. 4596, pp. 78–89. Springer, Heidelberg (2007)
21. Althöfer, I., Das, G., Dobkin, D., Joseph, D.A., Soares, J.: On sparse spanners of weighted graphs. Discrete & Computational Geometry 9(1), 81–100 (1993)
22. Erdös, P.: Extremal problems in graph theory, pp. 29–36. Publ. House Cszechoslovak Acad. Sci., Prague (1964)
23. Erdös, P., Simonovits, M.: Compactness results in extremal graph theory. Combinatorica 2(3), 275–288 (1982)
24. Aingworth, D., Chekuri, C., Indyk, P., Motwani, R.: Fast estimation of diameter and shortest paths (without matrix multiplication). SIAM Journal on Computing 28(4), 1167–1181 (1999)
25. Baswana, S., Kavitha, T., Mehlhorn, K., Pettie, S.: New constructions of (α, β)-spanners and purely additive spanners. In: 16th Symposium on Discrete Algorithms (SODA), pp. 672–681. ACM/ SIAM (2005)
26. Woodruff, D.P.: Lower bounds for additive spanners, emulators, and more. In: 47th Annual IEEE Symposium on Foundations of Computer Science (FOCS), pp. 389–398. IEEE Computer Society Press, Los Alamitos (2006)
27. Elkin, M., Peleg, D.: $(1 + \epsilon, \beta)$-spanner constructions for general graphs. SIAM Journal on Computing 33(3), 608–631 (2004)
28. Pettie, S.: Distributed algorithms for ultrasparse spanners and linear size skeletons. In: 27th Annual ACM Symposium on Principles of Distributed Computing (PODC), pp. 253–262. ACM Press, New York (2008)
29. Baswana, S., Sen, S.: A simple linear time algorithm for computing a $(2k - 1)$-spanner of $O(n^{1+1/k})$ size in weighted graphs. In: Baeten, J.C.M., Lenstra, J.K., Parrow, J., Woeginger, G.J. (eds.) ICALP 2003. LNCS, vol. 2719, pp. 384–396. Springer, Heidelberg (2003)

30. Derbel, B., Gavoille, C., Peleg, D., Viennot, L.: On the locality of distributed sparse spanner construction. In: 27th Annual ACM Symposium on Principles of Distributed Computing (PODC), pp. 273–282. ACM Press, New York (2008)
31. Elkin, M.: Computing almost shortest paths. ACM Transactions on Algorithms 1(2), 283–323 (2005)
32. Elkin, M., Zhang, J.: Efficient algorithms for constructing $(1+\epsilon, \beta)$-spanners in the distributed and streaming models. In: 23rd Annual ACM Symposium on Principles of Distributed Computing (PODC), pp. 160–168. ACM Press, New York (2004)
33. Elkin, M., Peleg, D.: $(1 + \epsilon, \beta)$-spanner constructions for general graphs. In: 33rd Annual ACM Symposium on Theory of Computing (STOC), pp. 173–182. ACM Press, New York (2001)
34. Kuhn, F., Moscibroda, T., Wattenhofer, R.: What cannot be computed locally! In: 23rd Annual ACM Symposium on Principles of Distributed Computing (PODC), pp. 300–309. ACM Press, New York (2004)
35. Linial, N.: Locality in distributed graphs algorithms. SIAM Journal on Computing 21(1), 193–201 (1992)
36. Peleg, D.: Proximity-preserving labeling schemes. Journal of Graph Theory 33(3), 167–176 (2000)
37. Panconesi, A., Srinivasan, A.: On the complexity of distributed network decomposition. Journal of Algorithms 20(2), 356–374 (1996)
38. Luby, M.: A simple parallel algorithm for the maximal independent set problem. SIAM Journal on Computing 15(4), 1036–1053 (1986)

A Local 2-Approximation Algorithm
for the Vertex Cover Problem

Matti Åstrand, Patrik Floréen, Valentin Polishchuk, Joel Rybicki,
Jukka Suomela, and Jara Uitto

Helsinki Institute for Information Technology HIIT, University of Helsinki
P.O. Box 68, FI-00014 University of Helsinki, Finland
`firstname.lastname@cs.helsinki.fi`

Abstract. We present a distributed 2-approximation algorithm for the
minimum vertex cover problem. The algorithm is deterministic, and it
runs in $(\Delta + 1)^2$ synchronous communication rounds, where Δ is the
maximum degree of the graph. For $\Delta = 3$, we give a 2-approximation
algorithm also for the weighted version of the problem.

1 Introduction

The minimum vertex cover is one of the best-known NP-hard graph problems.
The decision version was one of Karp's [1] original NP-complete problems, and
it is the first problem in Garey and Johnson's [2] list.

In a centralised setting, the polynomial-time approximability of the vertex
cover is a long-standing open question. Finding a factor 2 approximation is easy,
and there is some evidence that the problem may be hard to approximate within
factor $2 - \epsilon$ for any constant $\epsilon > 0$ [3].

In this work, we study the approximability of the vertex cover problem in a
distributed setting. We present a deterministic distributed algorithm that finds a
2-approximation of a minimum vertex cover in $(\Delta + 1)^2$ communication rounds,
where Δ is an upper bound on the maximum degree of the graph. To our knowledge, this is the first deterministic distributed 2-approximation algorithm for
the vertex cover problem whose running time depends only on Δ and not on the
number of nodes in the graph.

Prior Work. Several distributed 2-approximation algorithms are known for the
vertex cover problem (see, e.g., Grandoni et al. [4]). In particular, any distributed
algorithm that finds a maximal matching also provides a 2-approximation algorithm for the vertex cover problem; for example, Hańćkowiak et al. [5] present a
distributed algorithm that finds a maximal matching in $O(\log^4 n)$ rounds, and
Panconesi and Rizzi's [6] algorithm finds a maximal matching on $O(\log^* n + \Delta)$
rounds. However, the running time of any such algorithm depends on n, the
number of nodes: Linial's [7] seminal result shows that even if we have unique
node identifiers, and even if the network topology is an n-cycle, it is not possible
to find a maximal matching in $o(\log^* n)$ synchronous communication rounds.

I. Keidar (Ed.): DISC 2009, LNCS 5805, pp. 191–205, 2009.
© Springer-Verlag Berlin Heidelberg 2009

In this work, we focus on *local algorithms* [8,9], in the strict meaning of the term: a local algorithm is a distributed algorithm whose running time is independent of the number of nodes. It is known that finding a constant-factor approximation to the minimum vertex cover requires $\Omega(\log \Delta / \log \log \Delta)$ communication rounds [10], and hence the best that one can hope for is a local approximation algorithm in bounded-degree graphs.

Several such algorithms are known. Kuhn et al. [11] present a local approximation scheme for covering LPs; this scheme, together with deterministic rounding [12], provides a factor $2 + \epsilon$ approximation in $O(\log \Delta / \epsilon^4)$ rounds for any $\epsilon > 0$. Moscibroda [13] gives a $(4 + \epsilon)$-approximation algorithm that uses the primal–dual schema. There is also a simple purely combinatorial 3-approximation algorithm with running time $O(\Delta)$ [14].

On the negative side, the recent work by Czygrinow et al. [15] and Lenzen and Wattenhofer [16] has settled that there is no local algorithm for the minimum vertex cover problem with the approximation factor $2 - \epsilon$ for any $\epsilon > 0$, and this holds even in the case $\Delta = 2$.

Hence for each $\epsilon > 0$, it is known that there is a local $(2 + \epsilon)$-approximation algorithm for vertex cover in bounded-degree graphs, and there is no local $(2 - \epsilon)$-approximation algorithm. However, the existence of a local 2-approximation algorithm for the problem has been open.

Contributions. Our work settles the question of the approximability of the vertex cover problem with distributed constant-time algorithms. We show that there is a local 2-approximation algorithm for the minimum vertex cover problem in bounded-degree graphs; together with the negative result [15,16] for factor $2 - \epsilon$, this provides a complete characterisation of the constant-time approximability of vertex cover.

Our algorithm does not require unique node identifiers. The only piece of symmetry-breaking information that we use is a port numbering, i.e., each node imposes an ordering on the incident edges. Our algorithm is deterministic, it runs in $(\Delta + 1)^2$ communication rounds, and the size of each message is 2 bits.

The algorithm is presented in Sect. 3. In Sect. 5, we give a different algorithm for the *weighted* vertex cover in graphs of maximum degree 3; the need for a different algorithm is justified by a lower bound construction in Sect. 4.

2   Preliminaries

Model of Distributed Computing. Let $\mathcal{G} = (V, E)$ be a simple, undirected graph. Throughout this work, $\mathcal{G}$ is the *communication graph* of a distributed system: each node $v \in V$ is a computational entity, and if $\{u, v\} \in E$ then the nodes u and v can exchange messages on each communication round. Let Δ be an upper bound on the maximum node degree in $\mathcal{G}$.

We assume that $\mathcal{G}$ is an *anonymous network with a port numbering*, i.e., a node $v \in V$ can refer to its neighbours by numbers $1, 2, \ldots, d(v)$, where $d(v)$ is the degree of v. No other symmetry-breaking information is assumed; in particular, we do not need unique node identifiers. We assume that each node $v \in V$ knows $d(v)$ and Δ.

Every node runs the same deterministic synchronous distributed algorithm. In one synchronous *communication round*, the following steps are performed, in this order: (i) each node performs local computation, (ii) each node sends a message to each of its neighbours, and (iii) each node receives a message from each of its neighbours. Finally, after T communication rounds, each node performs local computation and announces an output – in our case, the node announces whether it is part of the vertex cover or not. The number of rounds T is the running time of the algorithm.

We emphasise that the model that we use – deterministic distributed algorithms in anonymous port-numbered networks – is a very weak model of distributed computing. In particular, in this model it is not possible to break the symmetry in a symmetric network. For example, finding a maximal matching in an n-cycle is impossible, regardless of the running time T. The model that we use is strictly weaker than, for example, Linial's [7] model; if we had unique identifiers, we could easily find a port numbering, but the converse is not true. Constant-time distributed algorithms in this model provide efficient algorithms in virtually any conceivable model of distributed computing; to give one example, standard reductions [17] can be used to construct an efficient self-stabilising algorithm that stabilises in constant time.

Vertex Covers. A set of nodes $C \subseteq V$ is a *vertex cover* if each edge $e \in E$ is incident to at least one node in C. A *fractional vertex cover* is a non-negative function $x \colon V \to [0,1]$ such that $x(u) + x(v) \geq 1$ for each edge $\{u,v\} \in E$. A *minimum fractional vertex cover* minimises $\sum_v x(v)$. This is an LP relaxation of the vertex cover problem; a set of nodes $C \subseteq V$ is a vertex cover if and only if the characteristic function $\mathbf{1}_C \colon V \to \{0,1\}$ is a fractional vertex cover.

Edge Packings and Matchings. Throughout this work, we consider non-negative functions $y \colon E \to [0,+\infty)$ that assign a *weight* to each edge. For a node $v \in V$, let us write $s(y,v) = \sum_{e \in E : v \in e} y(e)$ for the total weight assigned to the edges adjacent to v. The function y is an *edge packing* if $s(y,v) \leq 1$ for each node $v \in V$. A *maximum edge packing* maximises $\sum_e y(e)$.

A node $v \in V$ is *saturated* in an edge packing y if $s(y,v) = 1$. An edge $\{u,v\}$ is saturated if u or v is saturated. An edge packing y is *maximal* if each edge is saturated; put otherwise, we cannot increase $y(e)$ for any $e \in E$ without violating a constraint. We write $S(y) = \{v \in V : s(y,v) = 1\}$ for the set of saturated nodes.

Edge packings can be interpreted as fractional matchings: a set of edges $M \subseteq E$ is a *matching* if the characteristic function $\mathbf{1}_M$ is an edge packing, and M is a *maximal matching* if $\mathbf{1}_M$ is a maximal edge packing. We use the shorthand notation $s(X,v) = s(\mathbf{1}_X, v)$ for a set of edges $X \subseteq E$, and we write $\mathcal{G}[X]$ for the subgraph induced by X. In other words, $s(X,v)$ is the degree of v in the graph $\mathcal{G}[X]$.

LP Duality. From the perspective of linear programming, the maximum edge packing problem is the dual of the minimum fractional vertex cover problem. From LP duality, one can obtain the following well-known lemma that forms the basis of our distributed algorithm.

Lemma 1. *If y is a maximal edge packing, then $S(y)$ is a 2-approximation of a minimum vertex cover.*

Lemma 1 is a simplified version of a classical result that dates back to Bar-Yehuda and Even [18]. From a modern perspective, this result can be seen as an application of the primal–dual schema to obtain an approximation algorithm for the minimum vertex cover problem [19,20].

In addition to the algorithm by Bar-Yehuda and Even [18], many other approximation algorithms can be interpreted as applications of Lemma 1 and its various generalisations and special cases. Hochbaum [12] applies Lemma 1 in the case where y is a maximum edge packing. The algorithm generally attributed to Fanica Gavril and Mihalis Yannakakis applies Lemma 1 in the case where y is the characteristic function of a maximal matching; then $S(y)$ consists of the endpoints of the edges in the matching – see, for example, Papadimitriou and Steiglitz [21]. Gonzalez [22] presents a simple algorithm that uses Lemma 1 directly. Khuller et al. [23] present a distributed algorithm that applies a relaxation of Lemma 1.

3   Algorithm

In this section, we present a distributed algorithm that finds a maximal edge packing. The algorithm is purely combinatorial; we do not need to refer to linear programming and duality in the description and analysis of the algorithm. Once we have found a maximal edge packing, we can apply Lemma 1 to find a 2-approximation of a minimum vertex cover.

Our algorithm heavily relies on *half-integral* edge packings. An edge packing y is half-integral if $y(e) \in \{0, 1/2, 1\}$ for each $e \in E$. In a half-integral edge packing we also have $s(y, v) \in \{0, 1/2, 1\}$ for each $v \in V$.

The following definition is central to our work.

Definition 1. *A half-integral edge packing y is almost saturating if the following conditions hold: If $s(y, v) = 0$ then $s(y, u) = 1$ for all neighbours u of v. If $s(y, v) = 1/2$ then $s(y, u) = 1$ for at least one neighbour u of v.*

If an edge $e = \{u, v\} \in E$ is not saturated by an almost saturating edge packing y, then $s(y, u) = s(y, v) = 1/2$; we say that e is *half-saturated* in y. Furthermore, both u and v are adjacent to saturated nodes; therefore u and v are incident to saturated edges. See Fig. 1 for an illustration.

Algorithm Overview. Our algorithm begins with the original graph $\mathcal{G}_0 = \mathcal{G}$. In each iteration $i = 0, 1, \ldots, \Delta - 1$, we find an almost saturating edge packing y_i in the graph $\mathcal{G}_i$. Then we form the subgraph $\mathcal{G}_{i+1}$ of $\mathcal{G}_i$ that is induced by the edges that are half-saturated in y_i. See Fig. 2 for an illustration.

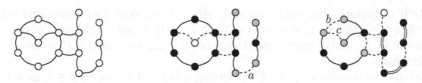

Fig. 1. A graph and two different almost saturating edge packings (see Definition 1). Double lines are edges with weight 1, single lines are edges with weight $1/2$, and dashed lines are edges with weight 0. Black circles are saturated nodes, grey circles are nodes with total weight $1/2$, and white circles are nodes with total weight 0. Edges a, b and c are half-saturated.

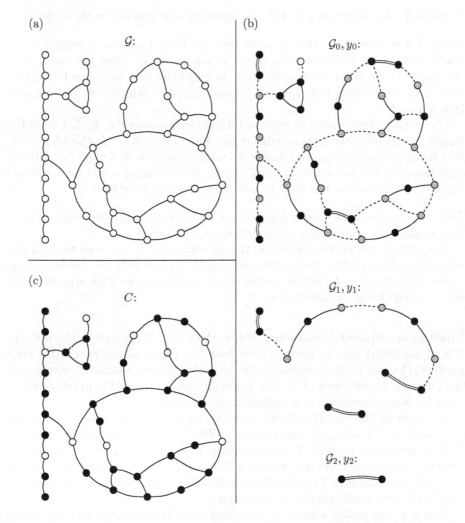

Fig. 2. Overview of the vertex cover algorithm. (a) An input graph $\mathcal{G}$. (b) The edge packings y_0, y_1, and y_2 found by the algorithm; see Fig. 1 for the notation. (c) The resulting vertex cover C.

Both endpoints of a half-saturated edge are incident to a saturated edge; therefore the maximum degree of $\mathcal{G}_{i+1}$ is strictly smaller than the maximum degree of $\mathcal{G}_i$. Since the maximum degree of $\mathcal{G}_0$ is Δ, we conclude that the graph $\mathcal{G}_\Delta$ is empty.

Extend the domain of y_i to E by setting $y_i(e) = 0$ whenever $e \in E$ is not an edge of $\mathcal{G}_i$; now each y_i is an edge packing in $\mathcal{G}$. To find a maximal edge packing in $\mathcal{G}$, construct the function

$$y = \sum_{i=0}^{\Delta-1} 2^{-i} y_i. \tag{1}$$

Lemma 2. *The function y in* (1) *is a maximal edge packing in the graph $\mathcal{G}$.*

Proof. Let us first show that y is an edge packing. Consider a node $v \in V$. Let k be the largest integer such that v is a node in $\mathcal{G}_k$. Then for each $i < k$, the node v is incident to an edge that is half-saturated in y_i, and therefore $s(y_i, v) = 1/2$. Furthermore, $s(y_k, v) \le 1$ and $s(y_i, v) = 0$ for $i > k$. We conclude that $s(y, v) \le 1$.

Let us then show that y is maximal. Consider an edge $e \in E$. Let k be the largest integer such that e is an edge in $\mathcal{G}_k$. Then for each $i < k$, the edge e was half-saturated in $\mathcal{G}_i$ by y_i, and finally it was saturated in $\mathcal{G}_k$ by y_k. Let u be an endpoint of e that was saturated in $\mathcal{G}_k$ by y_k. Then $s(y_i, u) = 1/2$ for $i < k$ and $s(y_k, u) = 1$. Therefore $s(y, u) = 1$, and the edge e is saturated in y. □

Thus we have found a maximal edge packing, and the saturated nodes form a 2-approximation of a minimum vertex cover by Lemma 1.

Naturally, in an implementation of the algorithm, we do not need to explicitly compute y. In each iteration i, the nodes with $s(y_i, v) = 0$ are discarded, the nodes with $s(y_i, v) = 1$ join the vertex cover, and the nodes with $s(y_i, v) = 1/2$ get a second chance on iteration $i + 1$.

Finding an Almost Saturating Edge Packing. To complete the description of the algorithm, we have to show how to find an almost saturating edge packing. Our algorithm is based on the idea of forming a maximal matching in the bipartite double cover of $\mathcal{G}_i$. The same idea has been used in prior work [14] to find a 3-approximation of a minimum vertex cover.

To construct the *bipartite double cover* $\mathcal{H} = \mathcal{G}_i \times K_2$ of the graph $\mathcal{G}_i$, replace each node $v \in V$ of $\mathcal{G}_i$ by two copies: a black copy v_1 and a white copy v_2. Replace each edge $\{u, v\} \in E$ by two edges: $\{u_1, v_2\}$ and $\{u_2, v_1\}$. Now $\mathcal{H}$ is a bipartite graph; more importantly, it is 2-coloured, and we can use the colours to break the symmetry in a distributed algorithm. The nodes in the graph $\mathcal{H}$ inherit the port numbering from the graph $\mathcal{G}$.

Now it is easy to find a maximal matching M in $\mathcal{H}$ by a distributed algorithm in 2Δ synchronous communication rounds [24]: For each $j = 1, 2, \ldots, \Delta$, in the round $2j - 1$, unmatched black nodes send proposals to their white neighbour number j, if any. In the round $2j$, all white nodes process the proposals; each

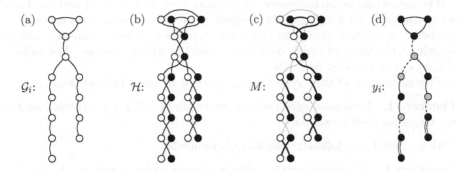

Fig. 3. Using the bipartite double cover to find an almost saturating edge packing. (a) The input graph $\mathcal{G}_i$. (b) The bipartite double cover $\mathcal{H}$ of $\mathcal{G}_i$. (c) A maximal matching M in $\mathcal{H}$. (d) An almost saturating edge packing y_i.

white node accepts the first proposal it gets, breaking the ties with port numbers. See Fig. 3 for an illustration.

Now we can construct an almost saturating edge packing y_i in $\mathcal{G}_i$ by setting

$$y_i(\{u, v\}) = \frac{\mathbf{1}_M(\{u_1, v_2\}) + \mathbf{1}_M(\{u_2, v_1\})}{2}. \tag{2}$$

Here $\mathbf{1}_M$ is the characteristic function of M.

Lemma 3. *The function y_i in (2) is an almost saturating edge packing in $\mathcal{G}_i$.*

Proof. For each node $v \in V$ we have $s(y_i, v) = (s(M, v_1) + s(M, v_2))/2$. Since $s(M, v_1) \in \{0, 1\}$ and $s(M, v_2) \in \{0, 1\}$, we have $s(y_i, v) \leq 1$, and y_i is an edge packing. Since $\mathbf{1}_M$ is integral, y_i is half-integral.

To show that y_i is almost saturating, first consider a node $v \in V$ with $s(y_i, v) = 0$. Then $s(M, v_1) = s(M, v_2) = 0$. Now let u be a neighbour of v. Since M is maximal, v_1 is not matched, and u_2 is adjacent to v_1 in $\mathcal{H}$, we must have $s(M, u_1) = 1$; similarly, $s(M, u_2) = 1$. Therefore $s(y_i, u) = 1$.

Second, consider a node $v \in V$ with $s(y_i, v) = 1/2$. Assume that $s(M, v_1) = 0$ and $s(M, v_2) = 1$; the other case is symmetric. Then there is a neighbour u of v in $\mathcal{G}_i$ such that $\{v_2, u_1\} \in M$. Furthermore, u_2 is adjacent to v_1 in $\mathcal{H}$ and v_1 is not matched; therefore u_2 must be matched in M. We have $s(M, u_1) = s(M, u_2) = 1$ and $s(y_i, u) = 1$. $\square$

Running Time and Message Complexity. Finding an almost saturating edge packing y_i in $\mathcal{G}_i$ takes $2(\Delta - i)$ synchronous communication rounds [24]. Then, in 1 communication round, each node $v \in V$ can inform its neighbours about $s(y_i, v)$; after that, each node knows its neighbours in the graph $\mathcal{G}_{i+1}$. Therefore iteration i can be completed in $2(\Delta - i) + 1$ synchronous communication rounds, and the total running time is bounded by $(\Delta + 1)^2$.

The algorithm can be implemented by using 2-bit messages. To find an almost saturating edge packing, the black copies of the nodes send 1-bit messages – 'proposal' or 'no operation' – and the white copies send 1-bit responses – 'accept' or 'reject', the latter of which doubles as a 'no operation' message. The value of $s(y_i, v)$ can be encoded in 2 bits.

The main result of this section is summarised by the following theorem.

Theorem 1. *A maximal edge packing can be found in* $(\Delta + 1)^2$ *communication rounds, using 2-bit messages.*

With Lemma 1, the following corollary is immediate.

Corollary 1. *A 2-approximation of a minimum vertex cover can be found in* $(\Delta + 1)^2$ *communication rounds, using 2-bit messages.*

4   Weighted Edge Packing

A natural question is whether the results from the previous section can be generalised to the case when each node $v \in V$ has a non-negative weight w_v. The definitions from Sect. 2 have straightforward generalisations: A minimum vertex cover $C \subseteq V$ minimises $\sum_{v \in C} w_v$, and a minimum fractional vertex cover $x: V \to [0, 1]$ minimises $\sum_v w_v x(v)$. An edge packing is a function $y: E \to [0, +\infty)$ that satisfies $s(y, v) \leq w_v$ for each $v \in V$, and $v \in V$ is a saturated node if $s(y, v) = w_v$.

Lemma 1 holds for the weighted graphs verbatim: if y is a maximal edge packing in a weighted graph, then the set of saturated nodes is a 2-approximation of a minimum vertex cover. Therefore the key question is whether there is a weighted counterpart of Theorem 1.

At first sight, there seems to be some hope. In particular, it is possible to find a maximal edge packing in a weighted 2-coloured graph in 2Δ rounds. However, the trick of using the bipartite double cover can no longer be applied. Indeed, we prove the following impossibility result. It shows that in the weighted case, the running time of *any* distributed algorithm necessarily depends on the number of nodes (or the range of the weights) and not only on the maximum degree.

Theorem 2. *There is no local algorithm that finds a maximal edge packing in weighted cycles.*

Theorem 2 holds even in Linial's [7] model: we can assume unique node identifiers, and we can allow unbounded local computation and arbitrarily large messages.

Our proof uses ideas that are similar to Czygrinow et al.'s [15] proof of the inapproximability of the maximum independent set problem. Let $\mathcal{A}$ be a local algorithm that finds a feasible edge packing y in any weighted cycle: for each edge $e = \{u, v\}$, both u and v know the value $y(e)$ when the algorithm $\mathcal{A}$ terminates. Let T be the number of synchronous communication rounds that $\mathcal{A}$ takes; w.l.o.g., we assume that T is even.

Let $n \gg T$ be a constant that we fix later; n only depends on the constant T. Let $N = \{1, 2, \ldots, n\}$. For any $H \subseteq N$, we define the n-cycle $\mathcal{C}_H = (N, E_H)$ as

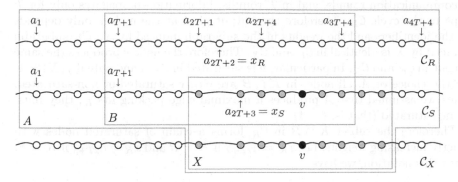

Fig. 4. Construction of $\mathcal{C}_R$ and $\mathcal{C}_S$. In this illustration, $T = 4$. The figure also illustrates the radius-T neighbourhood X of a node $v \in S \cap B$ (see the proof of Lemma 4). The output of the node v in $\mathcal{C}_S$ is identical to the output of the node v in $\mathcal{C}_X$.

follows. Let $k = |H|$. Let $H = \{h_1, h_2, \ldots, h_k\}$ and let $N \setminus H = \{j_1, j_2, \ldots, j_{n-k}\}$ with $h_1 < h_2 < \ldots < h_k$ and $j_i < j_2 < \ldots < j_{n-k}$. Then the edges of the cycle $\mathcal{C}_H$ are $E_H = \{\{h_1, h_2\}, \{h_2, h_3\}, \ldots, \{h_k, j_1\}, \{j_1, j_2\}, \ldots, \{j_{n-k}, h_1\}\}$. The following figure illustrates $\mathcal{C}_H$ in the case $n = 100$ and $H = \{2, 7, 10\}$.

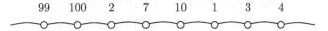

Finally, we assign the unique identifiers and node weights as follows: for each node $v \in N$, the unique identifier of v is v, and the weight of v is also v.

Let us now define a function f that assigns a label 0 or 1 to each subset $X \subset N$ with $|X| = 2T + 1$. Let $X = \{x_1, x_2, \ldots, x_{2T+1}\}$ with $x_1 < x_2 < \ldots < x_{2T+1}$. Consider the execution of $\mathcal{A}$ in the cycle $\mathcal{C}_X$. If the node x_{T+1} is saturated in the edge packing y produced by $\mathcal{A}$, we set $f(X) = 1$, otherwise we set $f(X) = 0$.

By Ramsey's theorem [25], we can choose the value of n so that the following holds, no matter how we choose the values $f(X)$: there exists a label $\ell \in \{0, 1\}$ and a subset $A \subseteq N$ with $|A| = 4T + 4$ such that $f(X) = \ell$ whenever $X \subset A$ and $|X| = 2T + 1$.

Now let $A = \{a_1, a_2, \ldots, a_{4T+4}\}$ with $a_1 < a_2 < \ldots < a_{4T+4}$. Let $R = A \setminus \{a_{2T+3}\}$ and $S = A \setminus \{a_{2T+2}\}$; see Fig. 4. Theorem 2 follows from the following lemma.

Lemma 4. *Algorithm $\mathcal{A}$ cannot produce a maximal edge packing in both $\mathcal{C}_R$ and $\mathcal{C}_S$.*

Proof. To reach a contradiction, assume that $\mathcal{A}$ produces a maximal edge packing in both $\mathcal{C}_R$ and $\mathcal{C}_S$. Define $B = \{a_{T+1}, a_{T+2}, \ldots, a_{3T+4}\}$. Let $K \in \{R, S\}$, and let y_K be the edge packing computed by $\mathcal{A}$ in $\mathcal{C}_K$.

We first show that each node $v \in K \cap B$ is saturated in by y_K. To see this, let X consist of the nodes that are within distance T from v in $\mathcal{C}_K$. By construction, $X \subseteq A$. We make the following observations. The algorithm $\mathcal{A}$ terminates after

T communication rounds, and in T rounds, information propagates only for T hops in the cycle $\mathcal{C}_K$. Therefore the output of $\mathcal{A}$ at the node v only depends on the identifiers and the weights in the subgraph induced by X. The subgraph induced by X is identical in $\mathcal{C}_K$ and $\mathcal{C}_X$. Therefore the node v produces the same output in $\mathcal{C}_K$ and $\mathcal{C}_X$. In particular, v is saturated in $\mathcal{C}_K$ if and only if $f(X) = 1$. By the choice of $\mathcal{A}$, all nodes in $K \cap B$ are either saturated or non-saturated. Since we assumed that $\mathcal{A}$ produces a maximal edge packing in $\mathcal{C}_K$, they must all be saturated (that is, $\ell = 1$).

Therefore the subset $K \cap B$ in $\mathcal{C}_K$ forms a chain of saturated nodes with strictly increasing weights. Let $x_K = a_{2T+2}$ if $K = R$ and $x_K = a_{2T+3}$ if $K = S$. With this notation, we have

$$
\begin{aligned}
y_K(\{a_{3T+3}, a_{3T+4}\}) &= a_{3T+3} - y_K(\{a_{3T+2}, a_{3T+3}\}) \\
&= a_{3T+3} - a_{3T+2} + y_K(\{a_{3T+1}, a_{3T+2}\}) = \ldots \\
&= a_{3T+3} - a_{3T+2} + \ldots \\
&\ldots + a_{2T+5} - a_{2T+4} + x_K - a_{2T+1} + \ldots \\
&\ldots + a_{T+2} - y_K(\{a_{T+1}, a_{T+2}\}).
\end{aligned}
\tag{3}
$$

Since the radius-T neighbourhoods of a_{T+1} and a_{3T+4} are identical in $\mathcal{C}_R$ and $\mathcal{C}_S$, we have

$$
\begin{aligned}
y_R(\{a_{T+1}, a_{T+2}\}) &= y_S(\{a_{T+1}, a_{T+2}\}), \\
y_R(\{a_{3T+3}, a_{3T+4}\}) &= y_S(\{a_{3T+3}, a_{3T+4}\}).
\end{aligned}
$$

This is a contradiction with (3) and $x_R \neq x_S$. □

Theorems 1 and 2 are one of the few pairs of results where the existence of weights makes a significant difference from the perspective of local algorithms. This is unlike problems such as max-min LPs [26], in which the existence of weights is provably irrelevant as far as local approximability is concerned.

5   Weighted Vertex Cover

Theorem 2 shows that we cannot directly apply the weighted version of Lemma 1 to design a local 2-approximation algorithm for the minimum-weight vertex cover problem in bounded-degree graphs. This setback suggests the possibility that there is no local 2-approximation algorithm for the problem. However, we show that the opposite is the case if $\Delta \leq 3$.

Theorem 3. *There is a local algorithm that finds a factor 2 approximation of a minimum-weight vertex cover in graphs with maximum degree 3.*

Let $\mathcal{G} = (V, E)$ be a node-weighted graph with maximum degree 3, see Fig. 5a. Let $w_v \geq 0$ denote the weight of the node $v \in V$; we call w_v the *w-weight* of v. We will now present an algorithm for finding a 2-approximation for weighted vertex cover in $\mathcal{G}$. The algorithm works in three stages. We will construct three sets, C_I, C_{II}, and C_{III}, the union of which is the vertex cover C that our algorithm outputs.

Stage I. Let $E_I = \{\{u, v\} \in E : w_u = w_v\}$ be the edges whose endpoints have the same w-weight, see Fig. 5b. Use the algorithm from Sect. 3 to find a maximal edge packing y_I in $\mathcal{G}[E_I]$. Pick the nodes saturated by y_I into the set C_I; see Fig. 5c.

Stage II. Let $E_{II} \subseteq E$ be the edges not saturated by y_I. Since the endpoints of every edge in E_{II} have different w-weights, the edges in E_{II} can be oriented according to the w-weight; see Fig. 5d. Add a dummy degree-1 neighbour to every node with even degree in $\mathcal{G}[E_{II}]$, as illustrated in Fig. 5e. The new graph is oriented and every node has an odd degree, so we can run the Naor–Stockmeyer algorithm [8,27] to find a weak 2-colouring of the nodes of the new graph; see black and white nodes in Fig. 5f. Now forget about the dummy nodes and only consider the original nodes of $\mathcal{G}[E_{II}]$; each node with an odd degree has a neighbour of a different colour.

Consider the edges $E'_{II} \subseteq E_{II}$ whose endpoints have different colours (heavy lines in Fig. 5f); the subgraph $\mathcal{G}[E'_{II}]$ is 2-coloured. The proposal–acceptance procedure for finding a maximal matching in 2-coloured graphs [24] can be modified to find a maximal edge packing: every proposing node proposes its residual weight along an edge, and every accepting node accepts its residual weight; at every proposal–acceptance round each node either saturates at least one adjacent edge or learns that at least one adjacent edge is saturated, so the algorithm completes in 2Δ rounds. Using this procedure, we can find a maximal edge packing y_{II} in $\mathcal{G}[E'_{II}]$ while giving each node v the weight $r_v = w_v - s(y_I, v)$. Pick the nodes saturated (w.r.t. r-weights) by y_{II} into the set C_{II}; see Fig. 5g. In other words, $C_I \cup C_{II}$ consists of the nodes saturated (w.r.t. w-weights) by $y_I + y_{II}$.

Stage III. Let $E_{III} \subseteq E$ be the edges not saturated by $y_I + y_{II}$; see Fig. 5h. For each degree-3 node of $\mathcal{G}$, the edge packing $y_I + y_{II}$ saturates at least one adjacent edge. Thus, $\mathcal{G}[E_{III}]$ has maximum degree at most 2, i.e., it consists of disjoint paths and cycles. Note that by Theorem 2 we cannot find a maximal edge packing in $\mathcal{G}[E_{III}]$. Instead, we will find a vertex cover in $\mathcal{G}[E_{III}]$ directly. To prove that our vertex cover is not too heavy, we exhibit a maximal edge packing with a comparable weight.

Define two new weights for the nodes of $\mathcal{G}[E_{III}]$. The *c-weight* of $v \in V$ is $c_v = w_v - s(y_I + y_{II}, v)$. The *cw-weight* of v is a pair (c_v, w_v); see Fig. 5h. Since adjacent nodes always have different w-weights, the endpoints of each edge can be ordered lexicographically according to the *cw*-weight. Hence we can partition the nodes of $\mathcal{G}[E_{III}]$ in the five sets illustrated below.

increasing *cw*-weight

The set B ("bottom") consists of degree-2 nodes that are a local minimum w.r.t. *cw*-weights, T ("top") consists of degree-2 nodes that are a local maximum

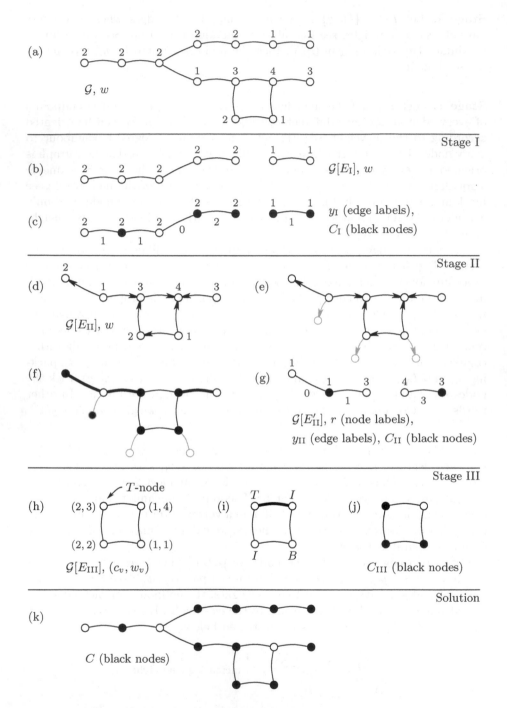

Fig. 5. Overview of the algorithm from the proof of Theorem 3

w.r.t. *cw*-weights, I ("internal") consists of the other degree-2 nodes, S ("start") consists of degree-1 nodes that are a local minimum w.r.t. *cw*-weights, and F ("finish") consists of degree-1 nodes that are a local maximum w.r.t. *cw*-weights. We use the terminology such as T-nodes to refer to the nodes in the set T, and TI-edges to refer to the edges that join a T-node and an I-node, etc.

Now let $v \in T$. If both edges incident to v are TB-edges, we say that v is a *BTB-node*. Otherwise v is incident to at least one TI-edge or TS-edge; the node v chooses (arbitrarily, using the port numbers to break the symmetry) one such edge and nominates it as a *hinge edge*. The following figure shows a BTB-node (black) and hinge edges (heavy lines); note that each node is incident to at most one hinge edge.

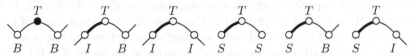

Finally, we partition the endpoints of the hinge edges into two sets. Let $\{u, v\} \in E_{III}$ be a hinge edge and let u be the node with the smaller w-weight; then we say that u is a *cheap hinge node* and v is a *costly hinge node*.

We are now ready to construct the set C_{III}. It consists of all nodes of $\mathcal{G}[E_{III}]$, except the following: (i) F-nodes, (ii) BTB-nodes, and (iii) costly hinge nodes. In the example of Fig. 5i we have chosen one hinge edge. The resulting set C_{III} is illustrated in Fig. 5j.

This completes the construction of our vertex cover. Fig. 5k illustrates the solution $C = C_I \cup C_{II} \cup C_{III}$.

Correctness. By construction, all edges in $E \setminus E_{III}$ are covered by $C_I \cup C_{II}$. Now consider an edge $e \in E_{III}$; we show that e is covered by C_{III}.

Clearly, BTB-nodes cannot be adjacent to other BTB-nodes, F-nodes, or hinge nodes. Hence if one of the endpoints of e is a BTB-node, the other endpoint must be in C_{III}. It remains to be shown that both endpoints of $e = \{u, v\}$ cannot be F-nodes or costly hinge nodes. The key observation is that there are no paths of the form (F, F), (F, T), (F, I, T), or (F, S, T). Hence F-nodes are not adjacent to other F-nodes or any kind of hinge nodes. Furthermore, there are no paths of the form (T, T), (T, I, T), (T, S, T), (T, I, I, T), (T, S, I, T), or (T, S, S, T). Hence if both u and v are hinge nodes, then e is a hinge edge and one of the nodes u, v is a cheap hinge node in C_{III}.

Approximation Ratio. We now exhibit a maximal edge packing y of $\mathcal{G}$. The set $S(y)$ of nodes saturated by y is then a 2-approximation of a minimum vertex cover. To complete the proof of Theorem 3, it is enough to show that the total w-weight of the vertex cover C constructed by our algorithm is not larger than the total w-weight of $S(y)$.

More specifically, we construct an edge packing y_{III} of $\mathcal{G}[E_{III}]$ which is maximal w.r.t. c-weights. Then $y = y_I + y_{II} + y_{III}$ is a maximal edge packing of $\mathcal{G}$ w.r.t. w-weights. We have $v \in C_I \cup C_{II}$ if and only if v is saturated by $y_I + y_{II}$; hence it is sufficient to show that the set of nodes saturated (w.r.t. c-weights) by y_{III} in $\mathcal{G}[E_{III}]$ is at least as heavy (w.r.t. w-weights) as C_{III}.

We construct y_{III} by "propagating" c-weights from S-nodes and B-nodes up towards T-nodes and F-nodes. First we process all non-hinge nodes v, from bottom to top in the order of increasing cw-weights:

- If $v \in S$, the incident edge gets the weight c_v.
- If $v \in B$, both incident edges get the weight $c_v/2$.
- If $v \in I$ and we have already assigned the weight to one incident edge, we choose the weight of the other edge so that v is saturated.

Eventually, we have chosen a weight $y_{III}(e)$ for each non-hinge edge $e \in E_{III}$. We do not exceed the capacity c_v of any non-hinge node v: if $v \in S \cup B \cup I \cup F$, this follows from the fact that we proceed in the order of non-decreasing c; if $v \in T$, then v must be a BTB-node and both incident edges get weights at most $c_v/2$. Furthermore, the weights y_{III} saturate all non-hinge nodes in $S \cup B \cup I$ (and possibly some F-nodes and BTB-nodes). Hence the total weight of non-hinge nodes in C_{III} is at most the total weight of non-hinge nodes saturated by y_{III}.

Finally, we augment y_{III} so that it saturates all hinge edges as well; now y_{III} is maximal w.r.t. c-weights. Consider a hinge edge $\{u,v\}$ with $w_u < w_v$. The edge packing y_{III} saturates u or v or both, while the set C_{III} constructed by our algorithm contains only u and not v. Hence the total weight of hinge nodes in C_{III} is at most the total weight of hinge nodes saturated by y_{III}. This completes the proof of Theorem 3.

Acknowledgements. We thank anonymous reviewers for their helpful comments. This work was supported in part by the Academy of Finland, Grants 116547 and 118653 (ALGODAN), by Helsinki Graduate School in Computer Science and Engineering (Hecse), and by the Foundation of Nokia Corporation.

References

1. Karp, R.M.: Reducibility among combinatorial problems. In: Miller, R.E., Thatcher, J.W. (eds.) Complexity of Computer Computations, pp. 85–103. Plenum Press, New York (1972)
2. Garey, M.R., Johnson, D.S.: Computers and Intractability: A Guide to the Theory of NP-Completeness. W. H. Freeman and Company, New York (1979)
3. Khot, S., Regev, O.: Vertex cover might be hard to approximate to within $2 - \epsilon$. Journal of Computer and System Sciences 74(3), 335–349 (2008)
4. Grandoni, F., Könemann, J., Panconesi, A.: Distributed weighted vertex cover via maximal matchings. ACM Transactions on Algorithms 5(1), 1–12 (2008)
5. Hańćkowiak, M., Karoński, M., Panconesi, A.: On the distributed complexity of computing maximal matchings. SIAM Journal on Discrete Mathematics 15(1), 41–57 (2001)
6. Panconesi, A., Rizzi, R.: Some simple distributed algorithms for sparse networks. Distributed Computing 14(2), 97–100 (2001)
7. Linial, N.: Locality in distributed graph algorithms. SIAM Journal on Computing 21(1), 193–201 (1992)

8. Naor, M., Stockmeyer, L.: What can be computed locally? SIAM Journal on Computing 24(6), 1259–1277 (1995)
9. Suomela, J.: Survey of local algorithms (2009, manuscript),
   http://www.iki.fi/jukka.suomela/local-survey
10. Kuhn, F., Moscibroda, T., Wattenhofer, R.: What cannot be computed locally!
    In: Proc. 23rd Symposium on Principles of Distributed Computing (PODC), pp.
    300–309. ACM Press, New York (2004)
11. Kuhn, F., Moscibroda, T., Wattenhofer, R.: The price of being near-sighted. In:
    Proc. 17th Symposium on Discrete Algorithms (SODA), pp. 980–989. ACM Press,
    New York (2006)
12. Hochbaum, D.S.: Approximation algorithms for the set covering and vertex cover
    problems. SIAM Journal on Computing 11(3), 555–556 (1982)
13. Moscibroda, T.: Locality, Scheduling, and Selfishness: Algorithmic Foundations of
    Highly Decentralized Networks. PhD thesis, ETH Zürich (2006)
14. Polishchuk, V., Suomela, J.: A simple local 3-approximation algorithm for vertex
    cover. Information Processing Letters 109(12), 642–645 (2009)
15. Czygrinow, A., Hańćkowiak, M., Wawrzyniak, W.: Fast distributed approximations
    in planar graphs. In: Taubenfeld, G. (ed.) DISC 2008. LNCS, vol. 5218, pp. 78–92.
    Springer, Heidelberg (2008)
16. Lenzen, C., Wattenhofer, R.: Leveraging Linial's locality limit. In: Taubenfeld, G.
    (ed.) DISC 2008. LNCS, vol. 5218, pp. 394–407. Springer, Heidelberg (2008)
17. Awerbuch, B., Varghese, G.: Distributed program checking: a paradigm for building
    self-stabilizing distributed protocols. In: Proc. 32nd Symposium on Foundations
    of Computer Science (FOCS), pp. 258–267. IEEE Computer Society Press, Los
    Alamitos (1991)
18. Bar-Yehuda, R., Even, S.: A linear-time approximation algorithm for the weighted
    vertex cover problem. Journal of Algorithms 2(2), 198–203 (1981)
19. Ausiello, G., Crescenzi, P., Gambosi, G., Kann, V., Marchetti-Spaccamela, A., Protasi, M.: Complexity and Approximation: Combinatorial Optimization Problems
    and Their Approximability Properties. Springer, Heidelberg (2003)
20. Vazirani, V.V.: Approximation Algorithms. Springer, Heidelberg (2001)
21. Papadimitriou, C.H., Steiglitz, K.: Combinatorial Optimization: Algorithms and
    Complexity. Dover Publications, New York (1998)
22. Gonzalez, T.F.: A simple LP-free approximation algorithm for the minimum weight
    vertex cover problem. Information Processing Letters 54(3), 129–131 (1995)
23. Khuller, S., Vishkin, U., Young, N.: A primal-dual parallel approximation technique
    applied to weighted set and vertex covers. Journal of Algorithms 17(2), 280–289
    (1994)
24. Hańćkowiak, M., Karoński, M., Panconesi, A.: On the distributed complexity of
    computing maximal matchings. In: Proc. 9th Symposium on Discrete Algorithms
    (SODA), pp. 219–225. SIAM, Philadelphia (1998)
25. Ramsey, F.P.: On a problem of formal logic. Proceedings of the London Mathematical Society 30, 264–286 (1930)
26. Floréen, P., Kaasinen, J., Kaski, P., Suomela, J.: An optimal local approximation
    algorithm for max-min linear programs. In: Proc. 21st Symposium on Parallelism
    in Algorithms and Architectures (SPAA). ACM Press, New York (2009)
27. Mayer, A., Naor, M., Stockmeyer, L.: Local computations on static and dynamic
    graphs. In: Proc. 3rd Israel Symposium on the Theory of Computing and Systems
    (ISTCS 1995), pp. 268–278. IEEE Computer Society Press, Los Alamitos (1995)

Distributed Discovery of Large Near-Cliques

Zvika Brakerski[1] and Boaz Patt-Shamir[2,*]

[1] Weizmann Institute of Science
zvika.brakerski@weizmann.ac.il
[2] Dept. of Electrical Engineering, Tel-Aviv University
boaz@eng.tau.ac.il

Abstract. Given an undirected graph and $0 \leq \epsilon \leq 1$, a set of nodes is called ϵ-near clique if all but an ϵ fraction of the pairs of nodes in the set have a link between them. In this paper we present a fast synchronous network algorithm that uses small messages and finds a near-clique. Specifically, we present a constant-time algorithm that finds, with constant probability of success, a linear size ϵ-near clique if there exists an ϵ^3-near clique of linear size in the graph. The algorithm uses messages of $O(\log n)$ bits. The failure probability can be reduced to $n^{-\Omega(1)}$ in $O(\log n)$ time factor, and the algorithm also works if the graph contains a clique of size $\Omega(n/\log^\alpha \log n)$ for some $\alpha \in (0,1)$. Our approach is based on a new idea of adapting property testing algorithms to the distributed setting.

1 Introduction

Discovering dense subgraphs is an important task both theoretically and practically. From the theoretical point of view, clique detection is a fundamental problem in the theory of computational complexity, and for distributed algorithms, computing useful constructs of the underlying communication graph is one of the central goals. Let us elaborate a little about that.

Dense graph detection has always been an important problem for clustering and hierarchical decomposition of large systems for administrative purposes, for routing and possibly other purposes [4]. Another reason to consider dense subgraphs is conflicts in radio ad-hoc networks [13]. On top of these low-level communication-related tasks, dense subgraph detection has recently also attracted considerable interest for Web analysis: as is well known, the ranking of results generated by search engines such as Google's PageRank [6] is derived from the topology of the Web graph; in particular, it can be heavily influenced by "tightly knit communities" [16], which are essentially dense subgraphs. Hence, to understand the structure of the web, it is important to be able to identify such communities. Another dimension where dense subgraphs are interesting for the Web is time: it has been observed [15] that evolution of links in blogs is, to some extent, a sequence of significant events, where significant events are characterized as dense subgraphs. Thus, considering the web as a dynamic graph, identifying large dense subgraphs is useful in understanding its temporal aspect.

---

* Supported in part by the Israel Science Foundation, grant 664/05.

I. Keidar (Ed.): DISC 2009, LNCS 5805, pp. 206–220, 2009.
© Springer-Verlag Berlin Heidelberg 2009

Our Contribution. In this paper we give an efficient randomized distributed algorithm that finds large dense subgraphs. Obviously, our algorithm does not decide whether there exists a large clique in the graph: that would be impossible to do efficiently unless P=NP. Instead, our algorithm solves a relaxed problem. First, we find near-cliques, defined as follows. Given a graph and a constant $\epsilon \geq 0$, a set of nodes D is said to be an ϵ-*near clique* if all, except perhaps an ϵ fraction of the pairs of nodes of D have an edge between them (see Section 2 for more details). For example, using this definition, a clique is 0-near clique. Second, our algorithm only identifies a large near-clique, and it is only guaranteed that the density of the output is close to the best possible. For example, given a graph G and a sufficiently small constant[1] $\epsilon > 0$ such that G contains an ϵ^3-near clique with a linear number of nodes, our algorithm finds at least one ϵ-near clique of linear size in G. (Our algorithm can also discover dense subgraphs of sublinear size for sub-constant values of ϵ.) Our algorithm is extremely frugal: the output is computed (with constant probability of success) in constant number of rounds, and all messages contain $O(\log n)$ bits.[2] Given any $q > 0$, it is possible to amplify the success probability to $1 - q$ in $O(\log(1/q))$ time factor.

In addition to the direct contribution of the algorithm, we believe that our methodology is interesting in its own right. Specifically, our work extends ideas presented in [11] in relation to property testing of the ρ-clique problem (defined below). Even though our construction does not use the property tester of [11] as a black box, our approach of deriving a distributed algorithm from graph property testers seems to be an interesting idea to consider when approaching other problems as well. In a nutshell, property testers do very little overall work but have a "random access" probing capability, namely they can probe topologically distant edges; distributed algorithms, on the other hand, can do a lot of work (in parallel), but information flow is local, i.e., an algorithm which runs for T rounds allows each node to gather information only from distance at most T. However, quite a few graph property testers exhibit some locality that can be exploited by distributed algorithms.

Related work. We are not aware of any previous distributed algorithm that finds large dense subgraphs efficiently. Maximal independent sets, which are cliques in the complement graph, can be found efficiently distributively [17,2]. In this case, there can be no non-trivial guarantee about their size with respect to the size of the largest (maximum) independent set in the graph. But on the positive side, the sets output by these algorithms are strictly independent.

Much more is known about dense subgraphs in the centralized setting. The fundamental result is that finding the largest *clique* (i.e., fully connected subset of nodes) in a graph, or even approximating its size to within a factor of $n^{1-\epsilon}$ for any constant $\epsilon > 0$, is computationally hard [14]. Problems that are closely related to ours have been studied in the centralized model and in the property testing model. In the centralized model, the Dense k-Subgraph (DkS) problem was studied. In DkS, the input consists of a graph and a positive integer k,

---

[1] We assume for our analysis that $\epsilon < 1/3$.

[2] See Section 3 for discussion of unbounded message size.

and the goal is to find a the subset of k nodes with the most number of edges between them. Feige, Peleg and Kortsarz [9] present a centralized algorithm approximating DkS within a factor of $O(n^\delta)$ for a certain $\delta < 1/3$, and it is also possible to approximate DkS to within roughly n/k [8]. Abello, Resende and Sudarsky [1] presented a heuristic for finding near-cliques (which they refer to as "Quasi-Cliques") in sparse graphs.

Property testing was defined by Rubinfeld and Sudan [22] for algebraic properties, and extended by Goldreich, Goldwasser and Ron [11] to combinatorial graph properties. The relevant concepts are the following. In the *dense graph model*, the basic action of a property tester is to query whether a pair of nodes is connected by an edge in the graph. An n-node graph is said to have the ρ-clique property if it contains a clique of size ρn, for some given parameter $0 \le \rho \le 1$. The ρ-clique tester of [11] gets an n-node graph G and constants ρ, ϵ as input, and decides, using $\tilde{O}(1/\epsilon^6)$ queries and with constant probability of being correct, whether the input graph has a ρ-clique or whether no set of ρn nodes in G is (ϵ/ρ^2)-near clique. They further present an "approximate find" algorithm that, provided that the property tester answers in the affirmative, finds an ϵ-near clique of size ρn in the graph in $O(n)$ time. Our algorithm is a new variant of the ideas of [11] and, using a new analysis, gets a better complexity result in the case of the relaxed assumption of existence of a near-clique.

This relaxation is a special case of *tolerant* property testing [20], which in our case can be defined as follows. An (ϵ_1, ϵ_2)-tolerant ρ-clique tester takes parameters ρ, ϵ_1 and ϵ_2 where $\epsilon_1 < \epsilon_2$, and decides whether the graph contains an ϵ_1-near clique or whether no set of ρn nodes is an ϵ_2-near clique. The general results of [20] imply that the property tester of [11] is in fact (ϵ^6, ϵ)-tolerant (our construction is (ϵ^3, ϵ)-tolerant). Fischer and Newman [10] prove a general result (for any property testable in $O(1)$ queries), whose implication to our case is that it is possible to find the smallest ϵ for which a graph has an ϵ-near clique of size ρn, but the query complexity is an exponent-tower of height $\mathrm{poly}(\epsilon^{-1})$.

A relation between distributed algorithms and property testers was pointed out by Parnas and Ron in [19], where it is shown for Vertex Cover how to derive a good property tester from a good distributed algorithm (the reduction goes in the direction opposite to the one we propose in this paper). Recently, techniques from property testing were used, along with other techniques by Nguyen and Onak [18], to present constant-time approximation algorithms for vertex-cover and maximum-matching in bounded-degree graphs. Their techniques also yield constant-time distributed algorithms for these problems. Saks and Seshadhri [23] show how to devise a parallel algorithm that "reconstructs" a noisy monotone function, again using ideas from property testing.

Paper organization. The problem and main results are stated in Section 2. Simple solutions are discussed in Section 3. The algorithm is presented in Section 4 and analyzed in Section 5. We conclude in Section 6. Some proofs are omitted from this extended abstract, we refer the reader to the full version [5] for more details.

2   Definitions, Model, Results

Graph concepts. In this paper we assume that we are given a simple undirected graph $G = (V, E)$. We denote $n \stackrel{\text{def}}{=} |V|$. For any given set $U \subseteq V$ of nodes, $\Gamma(U)$ denotes the set of all neighbors of nodes in U. Formally, $\Gamma(U) \stackrel{\text{def}}{=} \{v \mid \exists \, u \in U. \, (u, v) \in E\}$.

For counting purposes, we use a slightly unusual approach, and view each undirected edge $\{u, v\}$ as two anti-symmetrical directed edges (u, v) and (v, u). Using this approach, we define the following central concept.

Definition 2.1. *Let $G = (V, E)$ be a graph. A set of nodes $D \subseteq V$ is called ϵ-near clique if*

$$\Big| \{(u, v) \mid (u, v) \in D \times D \text{ and } \{u, v\} \in E\} \Big| \;\geq\; (1 - \epsilon) \cdot |D| \cdot (|D| - 1).$$

The *density* of a node set is the number of edges connecting nodes in the set divided by the number of node-pairs of the set.

Distributed Algorithms. We use the standard synchronous distributed model **CONGEST** as defined in [21]. Briefly, the system is modeled by an undirected graph, where nodes represent processors and edges represent communication links. It is assumed that each node has a unique $O(\log n)$ bit identifier. An execution starts synchronously and proceeds in rounds: in each round each node sends messages (possibly different messages to different neighbors), receives messages, and does some local computation. By the end of the execution, each processor writes its output in a local register. A key constraint in the **CONGEST** model is that the messages contain $O(\log n)$ bits, which intuitively means that each message can describe a constant number of nodes, edges, and polynomially-bounded numbers. The time complexity of the algorithm is the maximal number of rounds required to compute all output values. We note that we assume no processor crashes, and therefore any synchronous algorithm can be executed in an asynchronous environment using a synchronizer [3].

Problem Statement. In this paper we consider algorithms for finding ϵ-near clique. The input to the algorithm is the underlying communication graph and ϵ. Each node has an output register, which holds, when the algorithm terminates, either a special value "$\perp$" or a label. All nodes with the same output label are in the same ϵ-near clique, and $\perp$ means that the node is not associated with any near-clique. Note that there may be more than one near-cliques in the output.

Results. The main result of this paper is given below (see Theorem 5.1 for a detailed version).

Theorem 2.1. *Let $\epsilon, \delta > 0$. If there exists an ϵ^3-near clique $D \subseteq V$ with $|D| \geq \delta n$, then an $O(\epsilon/\delta)$-near clique D' with $|D'| = |D| \cdot (1 - O(\epsilon))$ can be found by a distributed algorithm with probability $\Omega(1)$, in $2^{O\left(\epsilon^{-4}\delta^{-1} \log(\epsilon^{-1}\delta^{-1})\right)}$ rounds, using messages of $O(\log n)$ bits.*

We stress that the message length is a function of n and is independent of ϵ, δ.

Let us list a few immediate corollaries to our result. First, for the case where there are near-cliques of linear size (i.e., $\delta = \Omega(1)$).

Corollary 2.1. *Let ϵ be a constant. If there exists an ϵ^3-near clique $D \subseteq V$ with $|D| = \Theta(n)$, then an $O(\epsilon)$-near clique D' with $|D'| = |D| \cdot (1 - O(\epsilon))$ can be found by a distributed algorithm with probability $\Omega(1)$, in $O(1)$ rounds and using messages of $O(\log n)$ bits.*

Second, for the case where there are strict cliques of (slightly) sublinear size.

Corollary 2.2. *If there exists a clique D with $|D| \geq n/\log^\alpha \log n$ for a sufficiently small constant $\alpha > 0$, then an $o(1)$-near clique D' with $|D'| \geq (1 - o(1)) \cdot |D|$ can be found by a distributed algorithm with probability $1 - o(1)$, in polylogarithmic number of rounds and using messages of $O(\log n)$ bits.*

3   Simple Approaches

In this section we consider, as a warm-up, two simplistic approaches to solving the near-clique problem, and explain why they fail.

The neighbors' neighbors algorithm. The first idea is to let each node inform all its neighbors about all its neighbors. This way, after one communication round, each node knows the topology of the graph to distance 2, and can therefore find the largest clique it is a member of. It is easy to kill cliques that intersect larger cliques (using, say, the smallest ID of a clique as a tie-breaker), and so we can output a set of locally largest cliques in a constant number of rounds. Indeed, one can develop a correct algorithm based on these ideas, but there are two show-stopper problems in this case. First, the size of a message sent in this algorithm may be very large: a message may contain all node IDs. (This is the **LOCAL** model [21].) And second, the algorithm requires each node to locally solve the largest clique problem, which is notoriously hard to compute. We thus rule out this algorithm on the basis of prohibitive computational and communication complexity.

The shingles approach. Based on the idea of shingles [7], one may consider the following algorithm. Each node picks a random ID (from a space large enough so that the probability of collision is negligible), sends it out to all its neighbors, and then selects the smallest ID it knows (among its neighbors and itself) to be its label. All nodes with the same label are said to be in the same *candidate set*. Each candidate set finds its density by letting all nodes send their degree in the set to the set leader (the namesake of the set label), and only sets with sufficient size and density survive. Conflicts due to overlapping sets are resolved in favor of the larger set, and if equal in size, in favor of the smaller label. Call this the "shingles algorithm."

Clearly, if there is a clique of linear size in the graph, then with probability $\Omega(1)$ the globally minimal ID will be selected by a node in the clique, in which case all nodes in the clique belong to the same candidate set. Unfortunately, many other nodes not in the clique may also be included in that candidate set, "diluting" it significantly. Formally, we claim the following.

Claim 3.1. *For any constant $\delta \in (0,1)$ there exists an infinite family of graphs $\{G_n\}$ such that G_n has n nodes and it contains a clique of size δn, but for all $\epsilon < \min\left\{\frac{1-\delta}{1+\delta}, 1/9\right\}$ and for sufficiently large n, the shingles algorithm cannot find an ϵ-near clique with at least $(1-\epsilon)\delta n$ nodes in G_n.*

Proof: Fix $\delta \in (0,1)$ and consider, for simplicity, n such that δn, n are even. The graph G_n is defined as follows. The nodes of G_n are partitioned into four sets denoted C_1, C_2, I_1, I_2, where $|C_1| = |C_2| = \delta n/2$, $|I_1| = |I_2| = (1-\delta)n/2$. The sets C_1, C_2 are complete subgraphs and I_1, I_2 are independent sets (see Figure 1). The pairs of sets (I_1, C_1), (C_1, C_2), (C_2, I_2) are connected with complete bipartite graphs (i.e., every node in I_1 is connected to every node in C_1 and similarly for the other pairs). The resulting graph contains a clique $C = C_1 \cup C_2$ of size δn.

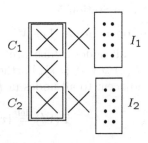

Fig. 1. *Crosses represent full connectivity*

Let $v_{\min}$ denote the node with the globally minimal ID in G_n, as drawn by the shingle algorithm. We proceed by case analysis.

Case 1: $v_{\min} \in C_1 \cup C_2$. W.l.o.g assume that $v_{\min} \in C_1$. Then $v_{\min}$'s candidate set contains exactly $C_1 \cup C_2 \cup I_1$, a set whose density is

$$\frac{\binom{|C_1|+|C_2|}{2} + |I_1| \cdot |C_1|}{\binom{|C_1|+|C_2|+|I_1|}{2}} = \frac{\binom{\delta n}{2} + \delta(1-\delta)n^2/4}{\binom{(1+\delta)n/2}{2}} = \frac{2\delta}{1+\delta},$$

and for $\epsilon < \frac{1-\delta}{1+\delta}$ the density is less than $1 - \epsilon$. Clearly in this case all other candidates are subsets of $I_1 \cup I_2$ and thus have density 0.

Case 2: $v_{\min} \in I_1 \cup I_2$. W.l.o.g assume that $v_{\min} \in I_1$. Then $v_{\min}$'s candidate set is exactly $C_1 \cup \{v_{\min}\}$ and thus has size $\delta n/2 + 1$ which is asymptotically smaller than $(1-\epsilon)\delta n$ for any constant $\epsilon < 1/2$.

Finally, consider the other candidate sets in this case. Clearly all nodes in C_2 belong to the same candidate set. Let A denote the set of vertices from $I_1 \cup I_2$ belonging to C_2's candidate set. If $|A| < \delta n/4$ then the candidate set size is $|C_2| + |A| < 3\delta n/4$ which is less than $(1-\epsilon)\delta n$ for all $\epsilon \leq 1/4$. If $|A| \geq \delta n/4$ then the candidate set density is at most

$$\frac{\binom{|C_2|}{2} + |C_2| \cdot |A|}{\binom{|C_2|+|A|}{2}} \leq 1 - \frac{1 - 4/\delta n}{3 \cdot (3 - 4/\delta n)}.$$

which is asymptotically less than $1 - \epsilon$ for any ϵ smaller than $1/9$. The remaining candidate sets are subsets of $I_1 \cup I_2$ and thus have density 0.   □

Summary. The simple approaches demonstrate the basic difficulty of the distributed ϵ-near clique problem: looking to distance 1 is not sufficient, but looking to distance 2 is too costly. The algorithm presented next finds a middle ground using sampling.

4 Algorithm

Below we present the algorithm for finding dense subgraphs. Analysis is presented in Section 5.

The basic idea. Let $V' \subseteq V$ be a set of nodes. Define $K(V')$ to be the set of all nodes which are adjacent to all other nodes in V', i.e., $K(V') \stackrel{\text{def}}{=} \{v \mid \Gamma(v) \supseteq V' \setminus \{v\}\}$. Further define $T(V')$ to be the set of nodes in $K(V')$ that are adjacent to all nodes in $K(V')$, i.e.,

$$T(V') \stackrel{\text{def}}{=} \{v \in K(V') \mid \Gamma(v) \supseteq K(V') \setminus \{v\}\} \ .$$

Our starting point is the following key observation (essentially made in [11]). If D is a clique, then $D \subseteq K(D)$, and also, by definition, $D \subseteq T(D)$. Furthermore, $T(D)$ is a clique since each $v \in T(D)$ is adjacent to all vertices in $K(D)$ and in particular those in $T(D)$.

The algorithm finds a set which is roughly $T(D)$, where D is the existing near-clique, by random sampling. Suppose that we are somehow given a random sample X of D. Consider $K(X)$: it is possible that $K(X) \not\subseteq K(D)$, because $K(X)$ is the set of nodes that are adjacent to all nodes in X, but not necessarily to all nodes in D. We therefore relax the definitions of $K(X)$ and $T(X)$ to approximate ones $K_\epsilon(X)$ and $T_\epsilon(X)$. Finally, we overcome the difficulty of inability to sample D directly (because D is unknown), by taking a random sample S of V, trying *all* its subsets $X \subseteq S$ ($|S|$ is polynomial in $1/\epsilon$), and outputting the maximal $T(X)$ found.

Description and implementation details. We now present the algorithm in detail. We shall use the following notation. Let $X \subseteq V$ be a set of nodes, and let $0 \le \epsilon \le 1$. We denote by $K_\epsilon(X)$ the set of nodes which are neighbors of all but an ϵ-fraction of the nodes in X, i.e.,

$$K_\epsilon(X) \stackrel{\text{def}}{=} \{v \in V \mid |\Gamma(v) \cap X| \ge (1 - \epsilon)|X|\} \ . \tag{1}$$

Using the notion of K_ϵ, we also define

$$T_\epsilon(X) \stackrel{\text{def}}{=} K_\epsilon(K_{2\epsilon^2}(X)) \cap K_{2\epsilon^2}(X) \ . \tag{2}$$

The algorithm, presented in Figure 2, works in stages as follows. In the **sampling stage**, a random sample of nodes S is selected; the **exploration stage**

Algorithm DistNearClique

Input: Graph $G = (V, E)$, $\epsilon > 0$, $p \in (0, 1)$.
Output: A label label$_v \in V \cup \{\perp\}$ at each node v, such that u and v are in the same near clique iff label$_v$ = label$_u \neq \perp$.

Sampling stage. Each node joins a set S with probability p (i.i.d). Let $G[S]$ denote the subgraph of G induced by S.

Exploration stage: Finding near-clique "candidates".

(1) Construct a rooted spanning tree for each connected component of $G[S]$. By the end of this step, each node $v \in S$ has a variable parent(v) that points to one of its neighbors (for the root, parent(v) = NULL).

(2) Each node in S finds the identity of all nodes in its connected component and stores them in a variable Comp(v).

(3) Each node $v \in S$ sends Comp(v) to all its neighbors $\Gamma(v)$. A node $u \in \Gamma(S)$ may receive at this step messages from several nodes, that may or may not be in different components of S. Each node $u \in \Gamma(S)$ sets a parent pointer parent$_{S_i}(u)$ for each connected component S_i of $G[S]$ that u is adjacent to (choosing arbitrarily between its neighbors from the same S_i).

(4) Let $u \in \Gamma(S)$. Let $S_1, \ldots, S_\ell$ be the different connected components which are adjacent to u. For each S_i where $1 \le i \le \ell$, the following procedure is executed.

   (4a) For *all* subsets $X \subseteq S_i$, u determines (using the information received in Step 3) if $u \in K_{2\epsilon^2}(X)$.

   (4b) u sends the results of the computations ($2^{|S_i|}$ bits) to all its neighbors, including parent$_{S_i}(u)$.

   (4c) This information is sent up to the root of S_i, summing the counts for each X along the way, so that the root of S_i knows the value of $|K_{2\epsilon^2}(X)|$ for each $X \subseteq S_i$.

   (4d) The root sends the values of $|K_{2\epsilon^2}(X)|$, for all $X \subseteq S_i$, down back to all nodes in $\Gamma(S_i)$.

   (4e) Each node $v \in \Gamma(S_i)$ notifies all its neighbors whether it is a member of $K_{2\epsilon^2}(X)$, for all $X \subseteq S_i$.

   (4f) Each node $u \in \Gamma(S_i)$ finds whether $u \in K_\epsilon(K_{2\epsilon^2}(X))$ for each $X \subseteq S_i$, and thus determines whether $u \in T_\epsilon(X)$ for each X.

Decision stage: Conflict resolution.

(1) For each connected component S_i, the size of $T_\epsilon(X)$ is computed for each $X \subseteq S_i$ similarly to Steps 4b–4c of the exploration stage. Let $X(S_i)$ be the subset that maximizes $|T_\epsilon(X)|$ over all $X \subseteq S_i$.

(2) The root of each component S_i sends $|T_\epsilon(X(S_i))|$ out to all nodes in $\Gamma(S_i)$.

(3) After receiving $|T_\epsilon(X(S_i))|$ for all relevant connected components, each node sends an "acknowledge" message to the component reporting the largest $|T_\epsilon(X(S_i))|$, breaking ties in favor of the largest root ID, and an "abort" message to all other components.

(4) If no node in $\Gamma(S_i)$ sent an "abort" message to S_i, the root sends back the result to all nodes in $T_\epsilon(X(S_i))$ (this is done by sending $X(S_i)$). The label of a node in $T_\epsilon(X(S_i))$ is the root ID of S_i, and $\perp$ otherwise.

Fig. 2. Algorithm DistNearClique.

generates near-clique candidates by considering $T_\epsilon(X)$ for all $X \subseteq S_i$ s.t. S_i is a connected component of the induced subgraph $G[S]$; and the **decision stage** resolves conflicts between intersecting candidates. A detailed explanation of the distributed implementation of Algorithm DistNearClique follows.

The **sampling stage** is trivial: each node locally flips a biased coin, so that the node enters S with probability p (p is a parameter to be fixed later). This step is completely local, and by its end, each node knows whether it is a member of S or not.

The **exploration stage** is the heart of our algorithm. To facilitate it, we first construct a spanning tree for each connected components of $G[S]$ (Step 1 of the exploration stage). This construction is implemented by constructing a BFS spanning tree of each connected component S_i, rooted at the node with the smallest ID in S_i. This is a standard distributed procedure (see, e.g., [21]), but here only the nodes in S take part, and all other nodes are non-existent for the purpose of this protocol.

In Step 2 of the exploration stage, all nodes send their IDs to the root. Once the root has all IDs, it sends them back down the tree.

In Step 3 of the exploration stage, each node in S_i sends the identity of all nodes in S_i to all its neighbors. In addition, we effectively add to each spanning tree all adjacent nodes. This is important so that we avoid over-counting later. Note that a node of S is member of a single tree (the tree of its connected component), but a node in $V \setminus S$ may have more than one parent pointer: it has exactly one pointer for each component it is adjacent to.

Step 4 of the exploration stage determines for each node its membership in $T_\epsilon(X)$ for each subset X of each connected component. Consider a node $u \in \Gamma(S_i)$. After Step 3, u knows the IDs of all members of S_i, so it can locally enumerate all $2^{|S_i|}$ subsets $X \subseteq S_i$, and furthermore, u can determine whether $u \in K_{2\epsilon^2}(X)$ for each such subset X. Thus, each such node u locally computes $2^{|S_i|}$ bits: one for each possible subset $X \subseteq S_i$. We assume that the coordinates of the resulting vector are ordered in a well known way (say, lexicographically). These vectors are sent by each node $u \in \Gamma(S_i)$ to all its neighbors, and in particular to its parent in S_i. This is done by u for each S_i it is adjacent to. Step 4c is implemented using standard convergecast on the tree spanning S_i: the vectors are summed coordinate-wise and sent up the tree, so that when the information reaches the root of S_i, it knows the size of $K_{2\epsilon^2}(X)$ for each $X \subseteq S_i$. Finally, using the size of $K_{2\epsilon^2}(X)$, and knowing which of its neighbors is in $K_{2\epsilon^2}(X)$, each node u can determine whether $u \in K_\epsilon(K_{2\epsilon^2}(X))$, and thus decide whether it is in $T_\epsilon(X)$ for each of the possible subsets X.

When the **decision stage** of Algorithm DistNearClique starts, each connected component S_i of $G[S]$ has a "candidate" near-clique and we need to choose the largest $T_\epsilon(X)$ over all X's. The difficulty is that there may be more than one set that qualifies as a near-clique, and these sets may overlap. Just outputting the union of these sets may be wrong because in general, the union of ϵ-near clique need not be an ϵ-near clique. The decision stage resolves this difficulty by allowing each node to "vote" only for the largest subset it is a member of. This vote is implemented by killing all other subsets using 'abort' messages, which are routed to the root of the spanning tree constructed in the exploration stage. This ensures that from each collection of overlapping sets, the largest one survives. Some small node sets may also have non-$\perp$ output: they can be disqualified if a lower bound on the size of the dense subgraph is known.

4.1   Wrappers

To conclude the description of the algorithm, we explain how to obtain a deterministic upper bound on the running time, and how to decrease error probability.

• *Bounding the running time.* As we argue in Section 5.1, the time complexity of the algorithm can be bounded with some constant probability. If a deterministic bound on the running time is desired, one can add a counter at each node, and abort the algorithm if the running time exceeds the specified time limit.

• *Boosting the success probability.* The way to decrease the failure probability is not simply running the algorithm multiple times. Rather, only the sampling and exploration stages are run several times independently, and then apply a single decision stage to select the output. More specifically, say we want to achieve success probability of at least $1 - q$ for some given $q > 0$. Let $\lambda \overset{\text{def}}{=} \log_{1-r} q$ (r being the original success probability). To get failure probability at most q, we run λ independent versions of the sampling and exploration stages (in any interleaving order). These λ versions are run with a deterministic time bound as explained above. When all versions terminate, a single decision stage is run, and in Step 3 of the decision stage, nodes consider candidates from all λ versions, and choose (by sending "acknowledge") only the largest of these candidates. This boosting wrapper increases the running time by a factor of λ: the sampling and exploration stages are run λ times, and the decision stage is slower by a factor of λ due to congestion on the links.

5   Analysis

In this section we sketch the analysis of Algorithm DistNearClique presented in Section 4. Many proofs are omitted from this extended abstract. They can be found in the full version [5].

5.1   Complexity

We first state the time complexity in terms of the sample size, and then bound the sample size.

Lemma 5.1. *Let S be the set of nodes sampled in the sampling stage of Algorithm* DistNearClique. *Then the round complexity of the algorithm is at most* $O\left(2^{|S|}\right)$.

Lemma 5.2. $\Pr[|S| \leq 2pn] \geq 1 - e^{-\frac{pn}{3}}$.

5.2 Correctness

In this section we prove that Algorithm DistNearClique finds a large near-clique. We note that while the algorithm appears similar to the ρ-clique algorithm in [11], the analysis of Algorithm DistNearClique is different. We need to account for the fact that the input contains a near-clique (rather than a clique), and we need to establish certain locality properties to show feasibility of a distributed implementation.

For the remainder of this section, fix $G = (V, E)$, $\epsilon > 0$, and $\delta > 0$. Let $|V| = n$. Assume that $D \subseteq V$ is an ϵ^3-near clique satisfying $|D| \geq \delta n$. Recall that $G[S]$ denotes the subgraph of G induced by S. In addition, assume that $\epsilon < \frac{1}{3}$ (larger values are meaningless, see parameters of Theorem 5.1).

Let D' denote the set of nodes output by Algorithm DistNearClique. Clearly, $D' = T_\epsilon(X)$ for some X. We first show that every $T_\epsilon(X)$ is $\frac{n}{t}\epsilon$-near clique where $t = |T_\epsilon(X)|$. In the decision stage, the algorithm selects the largest $T_\epsilon(X)$. In Lemma 5.6, we prove our main technical result, namely that with constant probability, there exists a subset $X^* \subseteq S_i$ with $|T_\epsilon(X^*)| \geq (1 - O(\epsilon))|D|$.

All large $T_\epsilon(X)$ are near-cliques. The following lemma proves that any $T_\epsilon(X)$ is a near-clique with a parameter relating to its size.

Lemma 5.3. *Let $X \subseteq V$, and denote $t = |T_\epsilon(X)|$. Then $T_\epsilon(X)$ is $\frac{n\epsilon}{t}$-near clique.*

Existence of a large $T_\epsilon(X)$. We prove the existence of a connected set $X^* \subseteq S$ such that $T_\epsilon(X^*)$ is large.

First, let C denote the set of all nodes in the ϵ^3-near clique D that are also adjacent to all but ϵ^2 fraction of D. Formally: $C \stackrel{\text{def}}{=} K_{\epsilon^2}(D) \cap D$ where D is ϵ^3-near clique.

We use the following simple property.

Lemma 5.4. $|C| \geq (1 - \epsilon)|D| - \frac{1}{\epsilon^2}$.

Second, we structure the probability space defined by the sampling stage of Algorithm DistNearClique as follows. In the algorithm, each node flips a coin with probability p of getting "heads" (i.e., entering S). We view this as a two-stage process, where each node flips *two* independent coins: coin_1 with probability $p_1 \stackrel{\text{def}}{=} p/2$ of getting "heads" and coin_2 with probability $p_2 \stackrel{\text{def}}{=} \frac{p-p_1}{1-p_1} > p/2$ of getting "heads." A node enters S iff at least one of its coins turned out to be "heads." The idea is that the net result of the process is that each node enters S independently with probability p, but this refinement allows us to define two subsets of S: let $S^{(1)}$ be the set of nodes for which coin_1 is heads, and let $S^{(2)}$ be the set of nodes for which coin_2 is heads.

Combining the notions, we define $X^* \stackrel{\text{def}}{=} S^{(1)} \cap C$, i.e., X^* is a random variable representing the set of nodes from C for which coin_1 is heads. X^* is effectively a sample of C where each node is selected with probability $p/2$. We have the following.

Lemma 5.5. X^* *resides within a single connected component of* $G[S]$ *with probability at least* $1 - e^{-\Omega(\delta pn)}$.

We now arrive at our main lemma.

Lemma 5.6. *With probability at least* $1 - \frac{1}{\epsilon^2 \delta} e^{-\Omega(\epsilon^4 \delta \cdot pn)}$ *over the selection of* S, *there exists a connected component* S_i *of* $G[S]$ *and a set* $X^* \subseteq S_i$ *s.t.* $|T_\epsilon(X^*)| \geq (1 - 7\epsilon)|D| - \epsilon^{-2}$.

Proof: Let X^* be defined as above. It remains to show that $T_\epsilon(X^*)$ is large. Intuitively, X^* is a random sample of C, and since C contains almost all of D, X^* is, in a sense, a sample of D. Thus $K_{2\epsilon^2}(X^*)$ should be very close to $K_{(\cdot)}(C)$, $K_{(\cdot)}(D)$ for appropriately selected $(\cdot)$. This would complete the proof since $T_\epsilon(C)$ contains almost all of C which, in turn, contains almost all of D. Formally, we say that X^* is *representative* if the following hold.

1. $|K_{\epsilon^2}(D) \setminus K_{2\epsilon^2}(X^*)| < \epsilon |C|$.
2. $|K_{2\epsilon^2}(X^*) \setminus K_{3\epsilon^2}(C)| < \epsilon^2 |C|$.

That is, if $K_{2\epsilon^2}(X^*)$ is almost fully contained in $K_{\epsilon^2}(D)$ and almost fully contains $K_{3\epsilon^2}(C)$.

To complete the proof, we use two claims presented below. Claim 5.7 shows that if X^* is representative, then $|C \setminus T_\epsilon(X^*)| \leq 6\epsilon \cdot |C|$. Claim 5.8 shows that X^* is representative with probability $1 - \frac{1}{\epsilon^2 \delta} e^{-\Omega(\epsilon^4 \delta pn)}$. Given these claims, the proof is completed as follows. By Lemma 5.5 and the claims, we have that with probability $1 - \frac{1}{\epsilon^2 \delta} e^{-\Omega(\epsilon^4 \delta pn)}$, X^* resides in a connected component of $G[S]$. Using also Lemma 5.4, the proof is complete, because $|T_\epsilon(X^*)| \geq (1 - 6\epsilon)|C| \geq (1 - 6\epsilon)\left((1 - \epsilon)|D| - \frac{1}{\epsilon^2}\right) \geq (1 - 7\epsilon)|D| - \frac{1}{\epsilon^2}$.   □

Claim 5.7. *If* X^* *is representative, then* $|C \setminus T_\epsilon(X^*)| \leq 6\epsilon |C|$.

Claim 5.8. $\Pr[X^* \text{ is representative}] \geq 1 - \frac{1}{\epsilon^2 \delta} \cdot e^{-\Omega(\epsilon^4 \delta pn)}$.

5.3 Summary

We summarize with the following theorem, which is the detailed version of Theorem 2.1 (in Theorem 2.1, we set $p = \frac{1}{n} \cdot O\left(\frac{\log(\frac{1}{\epsilon \delta})}{\epsilon^4 \delta}\right)$).

Theorem 5.1. *Let* $G = (V, E)$, $|V| = n$. *Let* $D \subseteq V$ *be an* ϵ^3-*near clique in* G *of size* $|D| \geq \delta n$. *Then with probability at least* $1 - \frac{1}{\epsilon^2 \delta} \cdot e^{-\Omega(\epsilon^4 \delta \cdot pn)}$, *Algorithm* DistNearClique, *running on* G *with parameters* ϵ, p, *finds, in* $O\left(2^{2pn}\right)$ *communication rounds, a subgraph* D' *such that*

(1) D' *is* $\left(\frac{1}{(1-7\epsilon)} \cdot \frac{\epsilon}{\delta}\right)$-*near clique.*[3]
(2) $|D'| \geq (1 - 7\epsilon)|D| - \epsilon^{-2}$.

---

[3] For small enough ϵ, say $\epsilon < \frac{1}{14}$, this is at most $2\frac{\epsilon}{\delta}$.

Proof: By Lemmas 5.1 and 5.2, the probability that the round complexity exceeds $2^{O(2pn)}$ is bounded by $e^{-\frac{pn}{3}}$. By Lemma 5.3, whenever assertion (2) holds, assertion (1) holds as well. Assertion (2) holds by Lemma 5.6 with probability at least $1 - \frac{1}{\epsilon^2 \delta} e^{-\Omega(\epsilon^4 \delta \cdot pn)}$. The theorem follows from the union bound.   □

It may also be interesting to analyze the computational complexity of the vertices running the algorithm. A simple analysis shows that except for step 4f of the exploration stage, the operation for each node can be implemented in poly($|S|$) computational steps (on $\log n$ bit numbers) per communication round. In step 4f, however, the nodes need to "inspect" all their neighbors in order to determine whether they reside in $T_\epsilon(X)$. It is possible to reduce the complexity in this case by selecting a sample of the neighbors and estimating, rather than determining, membership in $T_\epsilon(X)$. Thus, the computational complexity can be reduced to poly($|S|$) computational steps per round (for our purposes, $|S| \le O(\log\log n)$). The analysis of this modification is omitted.

6   Discussion

On the impossibility of finding a globally maximal ϵ-near clique. Our algorithm (when successful) finds a disjoint collection of near-cliques such that at least one of them is large. We note that it is impossible for a distributed sub-diameter time algorithm to output just one (say, the largest) clique. To see that, consider a graph containing an $n/2$-vertex clique A and an $n/4$-vertex clique B, connected by an $n/4$-long path P. The largest near-clique in this case is obviously A, and the vertices of B should output $\bot$. However, if we delete all edges in A, the largest near-clique becomes B, i.e., its output must be non-$\bot$. Since no node in B can distinguish between the two scenarios in less than $|P| = n/4$ communication rounds, impossibility follows.

Deriving distributed algorithms from property testers. Our approach may raise hopes that other property testers, at least in the dense graph model, can be adapted into the distributing setting. Goldreich and Trevisan [12] prove that any property tester in the dense graph model has a canonical form where the first stage is selecting a uniform sample of appropriate size from the graph and the second is testing the graph induced by the sample for some (possibly other) property. Thus, the following scheme may seem likely to be useful:

1. Select a uniform sample of the nodes.
2. Run a (possibly inefficient) distributed algorithm on the graph induced by the selected nodes to test it for the required property.

In the distributed setting, however, it may be the case that even testing a property for a very small graph is impossible to do quickly due to connectivity issues. As the example above shows, there exist properties which are testable in the centralized setting but do not admit a fast distributed algorithm. The general method above, therefore, can only be applied in a "black-box" manner for some testers.

Specifically, the ρ-clique tester presented in [11] does not comply with the above requirements. It can, however, be converted into a near-clique finder, in the sense defined in this work, using similar ideas and with worse parameters.

References

1. Abello, J., Resende, M.G.C., Sudarsky, S.: Massive quasi-clique detection. In: Rajsbaum, S. (ed.) LATIN 2002. LNCS, vol. 2286, pp. 598–612. Springer, Heidelberg (2002)
2. Alon, N., Babai, L., Itai, A.: A fast and simple randomized parallel algorithm for the maximal independent set problem. J. Algorithms 7, 567–583 (1986)
3. Awerbuch, B.: Complexity of network synchronization. J. ACM 32(4), 804–823 (1985)
4. Basagni, S., Mastrogiovanni, M., Panconesi, a., Petrioli, C.: Localized protocols for ad hoc clustering and backbone formation: a performance comparison. IEEE Trans. Parallel and Dist. Systems. 17(4), 292–306 (2006)
5. Brakerski, Z., Patt-Shamir, B.: Distributed discovery of large near-cliques. CoRR, abs/0905.4147 (2009)
6. Brin, S., Page, L.: The anatomy of a large-scale hypertextual web search engine. Computer Networks and ISDN Systems 30(1-7), 107–117 (1998)
7. Broder, A.Z., Glassman, S.C., Manasse, M.S., Zweig, G.: Syntactic clustering of the web. In: Selected papers from the sixth international conference on World Wide Web, Essex, UK, pp. 1157–1166. Elsevier Science Publishers Ltd., Amsterdam (1997)
8. Feige, U., Langberg, M.: Approximation algorithms for maximization problems arising in graph partitioning. J. Algorithms 41(2), 174–211 (2001)
9. Feige, U., Peleg, D., Kortsarz, G.: The dense k-subgraph problem. Algorithmica 29(3), 410–421 (2001)
10. Fischer, E., Newman, I.: Testing versus estimation of graph properties. In: Proc. 37th Ann. ACM Symp. on Theory of Computing, pp. 138–146. ACM Press, New York (2005)
11. Goldreich, O., Goldwasser, S., Ron, D.: Property testing and its connection to learning and approximation. J. ACM 45(4), 653–750 (1998)
12. Goldreich, O., Trevisan, L.: Three theorems regarding testing graph properties. Random Struct. Algorithms 23(1), 23–57 (2003); Preliminary version in FOCS 2001
13. Gupta, R., Walrand, J.: Approximating maximal cliques in ad-hoc network. In: Proc. IEEE Int. Symp. on Personal, Indoor and Mobile Radio Communications, Barcelona, September 2004, pp. 365–369 (2004)
14. Håstad, J.: Clique is hard to approximate within $n^{1-\epsilon}$. Acta Mathematica 182(1), 105–142 (1999)
15. Kumar, R., Novak, J., Raghavan, P., Tomkins, A.: On the bursty evolution of blogspace. World Wide Web 8(2), 159–178 (2005)
16. Lempel, R., Moran, S.: SALSA: the stochastic approach for link-structure analysis. ACM Trans. Inf. Syst. 19(2), 131–160 (2001)
17. Luby, M.: A simple parallel algorithm for the maximal independent set problem. SIAM J. Comput. 15(4), 1036–1053 (1986)
18. Nguyen, H.N., Onak, K.: Constant-time approximation algorithms via local improvements. In: FOCS, pp. 327–336. IEEE Computer Society Press, Los Alamitos (2008)

19. Parnas, M., Ron, D.: Approximating the minimum vertex cover in sublinear time and a connection to distributed algorithms. Theoretical Comput. Sci. 381(1-3), 183–196 (2007)
20. Parnas, M., Ron, D., Rubinfeld, R.: Tolerant property testing and distance approximation. J. Comp. and Syst. Sci. 72(6), 1012–1042 (2006); Preliminary version in STOC 2005
21. Peleg, D.: Distributed computing: a locality-sensitive approach. Society for Industrial and Applied Mathematics, Philadelphia (2000)
22. Rubinfeld, R., Sudan, M.: Robust characterizations of polynomials with applications to program testing. SIAM J. Comput. 25(2), 252–271 (1996)
23. Saks, M.E., Seshadhri, C.: Parallel monotonicity reconstruction. In: Teng, S.-H. (ed.) SODA, pp. 962–971. SIAM, Philadelphia (2008)

Distributed Fractional Packing and Maximum Weighted b-Matching via Tail-Recursive Duality

Christos Koufogiannakis and Neal E. Young[*]

Department of Computer Science, University of California, Riverside
{ckou,neal}@cs.ucr.edu

Abstract. We present efficient distributed δ-approximation algorithms for FRACTIONAL PACKING and MAXIMUM WEIGHTED b-MATCHING in hypergraphs, where δ is the maximum number of packing constraints in which a variable appears (for MAXIMUM WEIGHTED b-MATCHING δ is the maximum edge degree — for graphs $\delta = 2$). (a) For $\delta = 2$ the algorithm runs in $O(\log m)$ rounds in expectation and with high probability. (b) For general δ, the algorithm runs in $O(\log^2 m)$ rounds in expectation and with high probability.

1 Background and Results

Given a weight vector $w \in \mathbb{R}_+^m$, a coefficient matrix $A \in \mathbb{R}_+^{n \times m}$ and a vector $b \in \mathbb{R}_+^n$, the FRACTIONAL PACKING problem is to compute a vector $x \in \mathbb{R}_+^m$ to maximize $\sum_{j=1}^m w_j x_j$ and at the same time meet all the constraints $\sum_{j-1}^m A_{ij} x_j \leq b_i$ ($\forall i = 1 \ldots n$). We use δ to denote the maximum number of packing constraints in which a variable appears, that is, $\delta = \max_j |\{i|\ A_{ij} \neq 0\}|$. In the centralized setting, FRACTIONAL PACKING can be solved optimally in polynomial time using linear programming. Alternatively, one can use a faster approximation algorithm (i.e. [11]).

MAXIMUM WEIGHTED b-MATCHING on a (hyper)graph is the variant where each $A_{ij} \in \{0, 1\}$ and the solution x must take integer values (without loss of generality each vertex capacity is also integer). An instance is defined by a given hypergraph $H(V, E)$ and $b \in \mathbb{Z}_+^{|V|}$; a solution is given by a vector $x \in \mathbb{Z}_+^{|E|}$ maximizing $\sum_{e \in E} w_e x_e$ and meeting all the vertex capacity constraints $\sum_{e \in E(u)} x_e \leq b_u$ ($\forall u \in V$), where $E(u)$ is the set of edges incident to vertex u. For this problem, $n = |V|$, $m = |E|$ and δ is the maximum (hyper)edge degree (for graphs $\delta = 2$).

MAXIMUM WEIGHTED b-MATCHING is a cornerstone optimization problem in graph theory and Computer Science. As a special case it includes the ordinary MAXIMUM WEIGHTED MATCHING problem ($b_u = 1$ for all $u \in V$). In the centralized setting, MAXIMUM WEIGHTED b-MATCHING on graphs belongs to the "well-solved class of integer linear programs" in the sense that it can be solved in polynomial time [5,6,19]. Moreover, getting a 2-approximate[1] solution for MAXIMUM

---

[*] Partially supported by NSF awards CNS-0626912, CCF-0729071.
[1] Since it is a maximization problem it is also referred to as a 1/2-approximation.

I. Keidar (Ed.): DISC 2009, LNCS 5805, pp. 221–238, 2009.
© Springer-Verlag Berlin Heidelberg 2009

WEIGHTED MATCHING is relatively easy, since the obvious greedy algorithm, which selects the heaviest edge that is not conflicting with already selected edges, gives a 2-approximation. For hypergraphs the problem is NP-hard, since it generalizes SET PACKING, one of Karp's 21 NP-complete problems [10].

Our results. In this work we present efficient distributed δ-approximation algorithms for the above problems. If the input is a MAXIMUM WEIGHTED b-MATCHING instance, the algorithms produce integral solutions. The method we use is of particular interest in the distributed setting, where it is the first primal-dual extension of a non-standard local-ratio technique [13,2].

- For FRACTIONAL PACKING where each variable appears in at most two constraints ($\delta = 2$), we show a distributed 2-approximation algorithm running in $O(\log m)$ rounds in expectation and with high probability. This is the first 2-approximation algorithm requiring only $O(\log m)$ rounds. This improves the approximation ratio over the previously best known algorithm [14]. (For a summary of known results see Figure 1.)
- For FRACTIONAL PACKING where each variable appears in at most δ constraints, we give a distributed δ-approximation algorithm running in $O(\log^2 m)$ rounds in expectation and with high probability, where m is the number of variables. For small δ, this improves over the best previously known constant factor approximation [14], but the running time is slower by a logarithmic-factor.
- For MAXIMUM WEIGHTED b-MATCHING on graphs we give a distributed 2-approximation algorithm running in $O(\log n)$ rounds in expectation and with high probability. MAXIMUM WEIGHTED b-MATCHING generalizes the well studied MAXIMUM WEIGHTED MATCHING problem. For a 2-approximation, our algorithm is faster by at least a logarithmic factor than any previous algorithm. Specifically, in $O(\log n)$ rounds, our algorithm gives the best known approximation ratio. The best previously known algorithms compute a $(1 + \varepsilon)$-approximation in $O(\varepsilon^{-4} \log^2 n)$ rounds [17] or in $O(\varepsilon^{-2} + \varepsilon^{-1} \log(\varepsilon^{-1}n)) \log n)$ rounds [20]. For a 2-approximation both these algorithms need $O(\log^2 n)$ rounds.
- For MAXIMUM WEIGHTED b-MATCHING on hypergraphs with maximum hyperedge degree δ we give a distributed δ-approximation algorithm running in $O(\log^2 m)$ rounds in expectation and with high probability, where m is the number of hyperedges. Our result improves over the best previously known $O(\delta)$-approximation ratio by [14], but it is slower by a logarithmic factor.

Related work for Maximum Weighted Matching. There are several works considering distributed MAXIMUM WEIGHTED MATCHING on edge-weighted graphs. Uehara and Chen present a constant time $O(\Delta)$-approximation algorithm [22], where Δ is the maximum vertex degree. Wattenhofer and Wattenhofer improve this result, showing a randomized 5-approximation algorithm taking $O(\log^2 n)$ rounds [23]. Hoepman shows a deterministic 2-approximation algorithm taking $O(m)$ rounds [7]. Lotker, Patt-Shamir and Rosén give a randomized $(4 + \varepsilon)$-approximation algorithm running in $O(\varepsilon^{-1} \log \varepsilon^{-1} \log n)$ rounds

problem	approx. ratio	running time	where	when
	$O(\Delta)$	$O(1)$	[22]	2000
	5	$O(\log^2 n)$	[23]	2004
	2	$O(m)$	[7]	2004
	$O(1)(> 2)$	$O(\log n)$	[14]	2006
max weighted matching on graphs	$(4 + \varepsilon)$	$O(\varepsilon^{-1}\log\varepsilon^{-1}\log n)$	[18]	2007
	$(2 + \varepsilon)$	$O(\log\varepsilon^{-1}\log n)$	[17]	2008
	$(1 + \varepsilon)$	$O(\varepsilon^{-4}\log^2 n)$	[17]	2008
	$(1 + \varepsilon)$	$O(\varepsilon^{-2} + \varepsilon^{-1}\log(\varepsilon^{-1}n)\log n)$	[20]	2008
	2	$O(\log^2 n)$	[17,20] $(\varepsilon = 1)$	2008
	2	$O(\log n)$	here	2009
fractional packing with $\delta = 2$	$O(1)(> 2)$	$O(\log m)$	[14]	2006
	2	$O(\log m)$	here	2009
max weighted matching on hypergraphs	$O(\delta) > \delta$	$O(\log m)$	[14]	2006
	δ	$O(\log^2 m)$	here	2009
fractional packing with general δ	$O(1) > 12$	$O(\log m)$	[14]	2006
	δ	$O(\log^2 m)$	here	2009

Fig. 1. Distributed algorithms for FRACTIONAL PACKING and MAXIMUM WEIGHTED MATCHING

[18]. Lotker, Patt-Shamir and Pettie improve this result to a randomized $(2 + \varepsilon)$-approximation algorithm taking $O(\log\varepsilon^{-1}\log n)$ rounds [17]. Their algorithm uses as a black box any distributed constant-factor approximation algorithm for maximum weighted matching which takes $O(\log n)$ rounds (i.e. [18]). Moreover, they mention (without details) that there is a distributed $(1 + \varepsilon)$-approximation algorithm taking $O(\varepsilon^{-4}\log^2 n)$ rounds, based on the parallel algorithm by Hougardy and Vinkemeier [8]. Nieberg presents a $(1 + \varepsilon)$-approximation algorithm in $O(\varepsilon^{-2} + \varepsilon^{-1}\log(\varepsilon^{-1}n)\log n)$ rounds [20]. The latter two results give randomized 2-approximation algorithms for MAXIMUM WEIGHTED MATCHING in $O(\log^2 n)$ rounds.

Related work for Fractional Packing. Kuhn, Moscibroda and Wattenhofer show efficient distributed approximation algorithms for FRACTIONAL PACKING [14]. They first show a $(1 + \varepsilon)$-approximation algorithm for FRACTIONAL PACKING with logarithmic message size, but the running time depends on the input coefficients. For unbounded message size they show a constant-factor approximation algorithm for FRACTIONAL PACKING which takes $O(\log m)$ rounds. If an integer solution is desired, then distributed randomized rounding ([15]) can be used. This gives an $O(\delta)$-approximation for MAXIMUM WEIGHTED b-MATCHING on (hyper)graphs with high probability in $O(\log m)$ rounds, where δ is the maximum hyperedge degree (for graphs $\delta = 2$). (The hidden constant factor in the big-O notation of the approximation ratio can be relative large compared to a small δ, say $\delta = 2$).

Lower bounds. The best lower bounds known for distributed packing and matching are given by Kuhn, Moscibroda and Wattenhofer [14]. They prove that to achieve a constant or even a poly-logarithmic approximation ratio for fractional maximum matching, any algorithms requires at least $\Omega(\sqrt{\log n}/\log\log n)$ rounds and $\Omega(\log\Delta/\log\log\Delta)$, where Δ is the maximum vertex degree.

Other related work. For UNWEIGHTED MAXIMUM MATCHING on graphs, Israeli and Itai give a randomized distributed 2-approximation algorithm running in $O(\log n)$ rounds [9]. Lotker, Patt-Shamir and Pettie improve this result giving a randomized $(1 + \varepsilon)$-approximation algorithm taking $O(\varepsilon^{-3} \log n)$ rounds [17]. Czygrinow, Hańćkowiak, and Szymańska show a deterministic 3/2-approximation algorithm which takes $O(\log^4 n)$ rounds [4]. A $(1 + \varepsilon)$-approximation for MAXIMUM WEIGHTED MATCHING on graphs is in NC [8].

The rest of the paper is organized as follows. In Section 2 we describe a non-standard primal-dual technique to get a δ-approximation algorithm for FRACTIONAL PACKING and MAXIMUM WEIGHTED b-MATCHING. In Section 3 we present the distributed implementation for $\delta = 2$. Then in Section 4 we show the distributed δ-approximation algorithm for general δ. We conclude in Section 5.

2   Covering and Packing

Koufogiannakis and Young show sequential and distributed δ-approximation algorithms for general covering problems [13,12], where δ is the maximum number of covering variables on which a covering constraint depends. As a special case their algorithms compute δ-approximate solutions for FRACTIONAL COVERING problems of the form $\min\{\sum_{i=1}^{n} b_i y_i : \sum_{i=1}^{n} A_{ij} y_i \geq w_j \ (\forall j = 1..m), \ y \in \mathbb{R}_+^n\}$. The linear programming dual of such a problem is the following FRACTIONAL PACKING problem: $\max\{\sum_{j=1}^{m} w_j x_j : \sum_{j=1}^{m} A_{ij} x_j \leq b_i \ (\forall i = 1 \ldots n), \ x \in \mathbb{R}_+^m\}$. For packing, δ is the maximum number of packing constraints in which a packing variable appears, $\delta = \max_j |\{i|\ A_{ij} \neq 0\}|$.

Here we extend the distributed approximation algorithm for FRACTIONAL COVERING by [12] to compute δ-approximate solutions for FRACTIONAL PACKING using a non-standard primal-dual approach.

Notation. Let C_j denote the j-th covering constraint $(\sum_{i=1}^{n} A_{ij} y_i \geq w_j)$ and P_i denote the i-th packing constraint $(\sum_{j=1}^{m} A_{ij} x_j \leq b_i)$. Let $\mathsf{Vars}(S)$ denote the set of (covering or packing) variable indexes that appear in (covering or packing) constraint S. Let $\mathsf{Cons}(z)$ denote the set of (covering or packing) constraint indexes in which (covering or packing) variable z appears. Let $N(x_s)$ denote the set of packing variables that appear in the packing constraints in which x_s appears, that is, $N(x_s) = \{x_j | j \in \mathsf{Vars}(P_i) \text{ for some } i \in \mathsf{Cons}(x_s)\} = \mathsf{Vars}(\mathsf{Cons}(x_s))$.

Fractional Covering. First we give a brief description of the δ-approximation algorithm for fractional covering by [13,12][2]. The algorithm performs *steps* to cover non-yet-satisfied covering constraints. Let y^t be the solution after the first t steps have been performed. (Initially $y^0 = \mathbf{0}$.) Given y^t, let $w_j^t = w_j - \sum_{i=1}^{n} A_{ij} y_i^t$ be the slack of C_j after the first t steps. (Initially $w^0 = w$.) The algorithm is given by Alg. 1.

---

[2] The algorithm is equivalent to local-ratio when $A \in \{0, 1\}^{n \times m}$ and $y \in \{0, 1\}^n$ [1,2]. See [13] for a more general algorithm and a discussion on the relation between this algorithm and local ratio.

There may be covering constraints for which the algorithm never performs a step because they are covered by steps done for other constraints with which they share variables. Also note that increasing y_i for all $i \in \mathsf{Vars}(C_s)$, decreases the slacks of all constraints which depend on y_i.

Our general approach. [13] shows that the above algorithm is a δ-approximation for covering, but they don't show any result for matching or other packing problems. Our general approach is to recast their analysis as a primal-dual analysis, showing that the algorithm (Alg. 1) implicitly computes a solution to the dual packing problem of interest here. To do this we use the tail-recursive approach implicit in previous local-ratio analyses [3].

---

greedy δ-approximation algorithm for fractional covering [13,12]   alg. 1
1. Initialize $y^0 \leftarrow \mathbf{0}$, $w^0 \leftarrow w$, $t \leftarrow 0$.
2. While there exist an unsatisfied covering constraint C_s do a step for C_s:
3.   Set $t = t + 1$.
4.   Let $\beta_s \leftarrow w_s^{t-1} \cdot \min_{i \in \mathsf{Vars}(C_s)} b_i / A_{is}$.   ... *OPT cost to satisfy C_s given the* *current solution*
5.   For each $i \in \mathsf{Vars}(C_s)$:
6.   Set $y_i^t = y_i^{t-1} + \beta_s / b_i$.   ... *increase y_i inversely proportional to its cost*
7.   For each $j \in \mathsf{Cons}(y_i)$ update $w_j^t = w_j^{t-1} - A_{ij}\beta_s / b_i$.   ... *new slacks*
8. Return $y = y^t$.

After the t-th step of the algorithm, define the *residual covering problem* to be $\min\{\sum_{i=1}^n b_i y_i : \sum_{i=1}^n A_{ij} y_i \geq w_j^t \ (\forall j = 1..m), \ y \in \mathbf{R}_+^n\}$ and the *residual packing problem* to be its dual, $\max\{\sum_{j=1}^m w_j^t x_j : \sum_{j=1}^m A_{ij} x_j \leq b_i \ (\forall i = 1 \ldots n), \ x \in \mathbf{R}_+^m\}$. The algorithm will compute δ-approximate primal and dual pairs (x^t, y^{T-t}) for the residual problem for each t. As shown in what follows, the algorithm increments the covering solution x in a forward way, and the packing solution y in a "tail-recursive" manner.

Standard Primal-Dual approach does not work. For even simple instances, generating a δ-approximate primal-dual pair for the above greedy algorithm requires a non-standard approach. For example, consider $\min\{y_1 + y_2 + y_3 : y_1 + y_2 \geq 1, \ y_1 + y_3 \geq 5, \ y_1, y_2 \geq 0\}$. If the greedy algorithm (Alg. 1) does the constraints in *either* order and chooses β maximally, it gives a solution of cost 10. In the dual $\max\{x_{12} + 5x_{13} : x_{12} + x_{13} \leq 1, \ x_{12}, x_{13} \geq 0\}$, the only way to generate a solution of cost 5 is to set $x_{13} = 1$ and $x_{12} = 0$. A standard primal-dual approach would raise the dual variable for each covering constraint when that constraint is processed (essentially allowing a dual solution to be generated in an *online* fashion, constraint by constraint). That can't work here. For example, if the constraint $y_1 + y_2 \geq 1$ is covered first by setting $y_1 = y_2 = 1$, then the dual variable x_{12} would be increased, thus preventing x_{13} from reaching 1.

Instead, assuming the step to cover $y_1 + y_2 \geq 1$ is done first, the algorithm should not increase any packing variable until a solution to the residual dual problem is computed. After this step the residual primal problem is $\min\{y_1' + y_2' + y_3' : y_1' + y_2' \geq -1, \ y_1' + y_3' \geq 4, \ y_1', y_2' \geq 0\}$, and the residual dual problem is $\max\{-x'_{12} + 4x'_{13} : x'_{12} + x'_{13} \leq 1, \ x'_{12}, x'_{13} \geq 0\}$. Once a solution x' to the residual dual problem is computed (either recursively or as shown later in this section) *then* the dual variable x'_{12} for the current covering constraint should be raised maximally, giving the dual solution x for the current problem. In detail, the residual dual solution x' is $x'_{12} = 0$ and $x'_{13} = 1$ and the cost of the residual dual solution is 4. Then the variable x'_{12} is raised maximally to give x_{12}. However, since $x'_{13} = 1$, x'_{12} cannot be increased, thus $x = x'$. Although neither dual coordinate is increased at this step, the dual cost is increased from 4 to 5, because the weight of x_{13} is increased from $w'_{13} = 4$ to $w_{13} = 5$. (See Figure 2 in the appendix.) In what follows we present this formally.

Fractional Packing. We show that the greedy algorithm for covering creates an ordering of the covering constraints for which it performs steps, which we can then use to raise the corresponding packing variables. Let t_j denote the time[3] at which a step to cover C_j was performed. Let $t_j = 0$ if no step was performed for C_j. We define the relation "$C_{j'} \prec C_j$" on two covering constraints $C_{j'}$ and C_j *which share a variable* and *for which the algorithm performed steps* to indicate that constraint $C_{j'}$ was done first by the algorithm.

Definition 1. *Let $C_{j'} \prec C_j$ if $\mathsf{Vars}(C_{j'}) \cap \mathsf{Vars}(C_j) \neq \emptyset$ and $0 < t_{j'} < t_j$.*

Note that the relation is not defined for covering constraints for which a step was never performed by the algorithm. Then let $\mathcal{D}$ be the partially ordered set (poset) of all covering constraints for which the algorithm performed a step, ordered according to "$\prec$". $\mathcal{D}$ is *partially* ordered because "$\prec$" is not defined for covering constraints that do not share a variable. In addition, since for each covering constraint C_j we have a corresponding dual packing variable x_j, abusing notation we write $x_{j'} \prec x_j$ if $C_{j'} \prec C_j$. Therefore, $\mathcal{D}$ is also a poset of packing variables.

Definition 2. *A reverse order of poset $\mathcal{D}$ is an order $C_{j_1}, C_{j_2}, \ldots, C_{j_k}$ (or equivalently $x_{j_1}, x_{j_2}, \ldots, x_{j_k}$) such that for $l > i$ either we have $C_{j_l} \prec C_{j_i}$ or the relation "$\prec$" is not defined for constraints C_{j_i} and C_{j_l} (because they do not share a variable).*

Then the following figure (Alg. 2) shows the sequential δ-approximation algorithm for FRACTIONAL PACKING.

The algorithm simply considers the packing variables corresponding to covering constraints that Alg. 1 did steps for, and raises each variable maximally without violating the packing constraints. The order in which the variables are considered matters: *the variables should be considered in the reverse of the order in which steps were done for the corresponding constraints, or an order which is "equivalent" (see Lemma 1).* (This flexibility is necessary for the distributed setting.)

---

[3] In general by "time" we mean some reasonable way to distinguish in which order steps were performed to satisfy covering constraints. For now, the time at which a step was performed can be thought as the step number (line 3 at Alg. 1). It will be slightly different in the distributed setting.

---

greedy δ-approximation algorithm for fractional packing   alg. 2
1. Run Alg. 1, recording the poset $\mathcal{D}$.
2. Let T be the number of steps performed by Alg. 1.
3. Initialize $x^T \leftarrow \mathbf{0}$, $t \leftarrow T$.   ... note that t will be decreasing from T to 0
4. Let Π be some reverse order of $\mathcal{D}$.   ... any reverse order of $\mathcal{D}$ works, see
    Lemma 1
5. For each variable $x_s \in \mathcal{D}$ in the order given by Π do:
6.   Set $x^{t-1} = x^t$.
7.   Raise x_s^{t-1} until a packing constraint that depends on x_s^{t-1} is tight, that is,
        set $x_s^{t-1} = \max_{i \in \mathsf{Cons}(x_j)}(b_i - \sum_{j=1}^m A_{ij}x_j^{t-1})$.
8.   Set $t = t - 1$.
9. Return $x = x^0$.

The solution x is feasible at all times since a packing variable is increased only until a packing constraint gets tight.

Lemma 1. *Alg. 2 returns the same solution x using (at line 4) any reverse order of $\mathcal{D}$.*

Proof. Let $\Pi = x_{j_1}, x_{j_2}, \ldots, x_{j_k}$ and $\Pi' = x_{j_1}, x_{j_2}, \ldots, x_{j_k}$ be two different reverse orders of $\mathcal{D}$. Let $x^{\Pi, 1 \cdots m}$ be the solution computed so far by Alg. 2 after raising the first m packing variables of order Π. We prove that $x^{\Pi, 1 \cdots k} = x^{\Pi', 1 \cdots k}$.

Assume that Π and Π' have the same order for their first q variables, that is $j_i = j_i$ for all $i \le q$. Then, $x^{\Pi, 1 \cdots q} = x^{\Pi', 1 \cdots q}$. The first variable in which the two orders disagree is the $(q + 1)$-th one, that is, $j_{q+1} \ne j'_{q+1}$. Let $s = j_{q+1}$. Then x_s should appear in some position l in Π' such that $q + 1 < l \le k$. The value of x_s depends only on the values of variables in $N(x_s)$ at the time when x_s is set. We prove that for each $x_j \in N(x_s)$ we have $x_j^{\Pi, 1 \cdots q} = x_j^{\Pi', 1 \cdots l}$, thus $x_s^{\Pi, 1 \cdots q} = x_s^{\Pi', 1 \cdots l}$. Moreover since the algorithm considers each packing variable only once this implies $x_s^{\Pi, 1 \cdots k} = x_s^{\Pi, 1 \cdots q} = x_s^{\Pi', 1 \cdots l} = x_s^{\Pi', 1 \cdots k}$.

(a) For each $x_j \in N(x_s)$ with $x_s \prec x_j$, the variable x_j should have already been set in the first q steps, otherwise Π would not be a valid reverse order of $\mathcal{D}$. Moreover each packing variable can be increased only once, so once it is set it maintains the same value till the end. Thus, for each x_j such that $x_s \prec x_e$, we have $x_j^{\Pi, 1 \cdots q} = x_j^{\Pi', 1 \cdots q} = x_j^{\Pi', 1 \cdots l}$.

(b) For each $x_j \in N(x_s)$ with $x_j \prec x_s$, j cannot be in the interval $[j'_{q+1}, \ldots, j'_{l-1})$ of Π', otherwise Π' would not be a valid reverse order of $\mathcal{D}$. Thus, for each x_j such that $x_j \prec x_s$, we have $x_j^{\Pi, 1 \cdots q} = x_j^{\Pi', 1 \cdots q} = x_j^{\Pi', 1 \cdots l} = 0$.

So in any case, for each $x_j \in N(x_s)$, we have $x_j^{\Pi, 1 \cdots q} = x_j^{\Pi', 1 \cdots l}$ and thus $x_s^{\Pi, 1 \cdots q} = x_s^{\Pi', 1 \cdots l}$.

The lemma follows by induction on the number of edges. $\square$

The following lemma and weak duality prove that the solution x returned by Alg. 2 is δ-approximate.

Lemma 2. *For the solutions y and x returned by Alg. 1 and Alg. 2 respectively,*
$\sum_{j=1}^m w_j x_j \ge 1/\delta \sum_{i=1}^n b_i y_i$.

Proof. Lemma 1 shows that any reverse order of $\mathcal{D}$ produces the same solution, so w.l.o.g. here we assume that the reverse order Π used by Alg. 2 is the reverse of the order in which steps to satisfy covering constraints were performed by Alg. 1.

When Alg. 1 does a step to satisfy the covering constraint C_s (by increasing y_i by β_s/b_i for all $i \in \mathsf{Vars}(C_s)$), the cost of the covering solution $\sum_i b_i y_i$ increases by at most $\delta\beta_s$, since C_s depends on at most δ variables ($|\mathsf{Vars}(C_s)| \leq \delta$). Thus the final cost of the cover y is at most $\sum_{s\in\mathcal{D}} \delta\beta_s$.

Define $\Psi^t = \sum_j w_j^t x_j^t$ to be the cost of the packing x^t. Recall that $x^T = \mathbf{0}$ so $\Psi^T = 0$, and that the final packing solution is given by vector x^0, so the the cost of the final packing solution is Ψ^0. To prove the theorem we have to show that $\Psi^0 \geq \sum_{s\in\mathcal{D}} \beta_s$. We have that $\Psi^0 = \Psi^0 - \Psi^T = \sum_{t=1}^{T} \Psi^{t-1} - \Psi^t$ so it is enough to show that $\Psi^{t-1} - \Psi^t \geq \beta_s$ where C_s is the covering constraint done at the t-th step of Alg. 1.

Then, $\Psi^{t-1} - \Psi^t$ is

$$\sum_j w_j^{t-1} x_j^{t-1} - w_j^t x_j^t \tag{1}$$

$$= w_s^{t-1} x_s^{t-1} + \sum_{j\neq s}(w_j^{t-1} - w_j^t)x_j^{t-1} \tag{2}$$

$$= w_s^{t-1} x_s^{t-1} + \sum_{i\in\mathsf{Cons}(x_s)} \sum_{j\in\{\mathsf{Vars}(P_j)-s\}} A_{ij}\frac{\beta_s}{b_i}x_j^{t-1} \tag{3}$$

$$= \beta_s x_s^{t-1} \max_{i\in\mathsf{Cons}(x_s)} \frac{A_{is}}{b_i} + \sum_{i\in\mathsf{Cons}(x_s)} \sum_{j\in\{\mathsf{Vars}(P_j)-s\}} A_{ij}\frac{\beta_s}{b_i}x_j^{t-1} \tag{4}$$

$$\geq \beta_s \frac{1}{b_i}\sum_{j=1}^{m} A_{ij}x_j^{t-1} \quad \text{(for } i \text{ s.t. constraint } P_i \text{ becomes tight after raising } x_s\text{)} \tag{5}$$

$$= \beta_s \tag{6}$$

In equation (2) we use the fact that $x_s^t = 0$ and $x_j^{t-1} = x_j^t$ for all $j \neq s$. For equation (3), we use the fact that the residual weights of packing variables in $N(x_s)$ are increased. If $x_j > 0$ for $j \neq s$, then x_j was increased before x_s ($x_s \prec x_j$) so at the current step $w_j^{t-1} > w_j^t > 0$, and $w_j^{t-1} - w_j^t = \sum_{i\in\mathsf{Cons}(x_s)} A_{ij}\frac{\beta_s}{b_i}$. For equation (4), by the definition of β_s we have $w_s^{t-1} = \beta_s \max_{i\in\mathsf{Cons}(x_s)} \frac{A_{is}}{b_i}$. In inequality (5) we keep only the terms that appear in the constraint P_i that gets tight by raising x_s. The last equality holds because P_i is tight, that is, $\sum_{j=1}^{m} A_{ij}x_j = b_i$. □

The following lemma shows that Alg. 2 returns integral solutions if the coefficients A_{ij} are $0/1$ and the b_i's are integers, thus giving a δ-approximation algorithm for MAXIMUM WEIGHTED b-MATCHING.

Lemma 3. *If $A \in \{0,1\}^{n \times m}$ and $b \in \mathbb{Z}_+^n$ then the returned packing solution x is integral, that is, $x \in \mathbb{Z}_+^m$.*

Proof. Since all non-zero coefficients are 1, the packing constraints are of the form $\sum_{j \in \text{Vars}(P_i)} x_j \leq b_i$ ($\forall i$). We prove by induction that $x \in \mathbb{Z}_+^m$. The base case is trivial since the algorithm starts with a zero solution. Assume that at some point we have $x^t \in \mathbb{Z}_+^m$. Let $x_s \in \mathcal{D}$, be the next packing variable to be raised by the algorithm. We show that $x_s^{t-1} \in \mathbb{Z}_+$ and thus the resulting solution remains integral. The algorithm sets $x_s^{t-1} = \min_{i \in \text{Cons}(x_s)}\{b_i - \sum_{j=1}^{m} x_j^{t-1}\} = \min_{i \in \text{Cons}(x_s)}\{b_i - \sum_{j=1}^{m} x_j^t\} \geq 0$. By the induction hypothesis, each $x_j^t \in \mathbb{Z}_+$, and since $b \in \mathbb{Z}_+^n$, then x_s^{t-1} is also a non-negative integer. $\square$

3 Distributed Fractional Packing with $\delta = 2$

3.1 Distributed model for $\delta = 2$

We assume the network in which the distributed computation takes place has vertices for covering variables (packing constraints) and edges for covering constraints (packing variables). So, the network has a node u_i for every covering variable y_i. An edge e_j connects vertices u_i and $u_{i'}$ if y_i and $y_{i'}$ belong to the same covering constraint C_j, that is, there exists a constraint $A_{ij}y_i + A_{i'j}y_{i'} \geq w_j$ ($\delta = 2$ so there can be at most 2 variables in each covering constraint). We assume the standard synchronous communication model, where in each round, nodes can exchange messages with neighbors, and perform some local computation [21]. We also assume no restriction on message size and local computation. (Note that a synchronous model algorithm can be transformed into an asynchronous algorithm with the same time complexity [21].)

3.2 Distributed Algorithm for $\delta = 2$

Koufogiannakis and Young show a distributed implementation of Alg. 1, for (fractional) covering with $\delta = 2$ that runs in $O(\log n)$ rounds in expectation and with high probability [12]. In this section we augment their algorithm to distributively compute 2-approximate solutions to the dual fractional packing problem without increasing the time complexity. The high level idea is similar to that in the previous section: run the distributed algorithm for covering to get a partial order of the covering constraints for which steps were performed, then consider the corresponding dual packing variables in "some reverse" order raising them maximally. The challenge here is that the distributed algorithm for covering can perform steps for many covering constraints in parallel. Moreover, each covering constraint, has just a local view of the ordering, that is, it only knows its relative order among the covering constraints with which it shares variables.

Distributed Fractional Covering with $\delta = 2$. Here is a short description of the distributed 2-approximation algorithm for fractional covering (Alg. 5 in appendix from [12]). In each round, the algorithm does steps on a large subset of remaining edges (covering constraints), as follows. Each vertex (covering variable) randomly chooses to be a *leaf* or a *root*. A not-yet-satisfied edge $e_j = (u_i, u_r)$ between a leaf u_i and a root u_r with $b_i/A_{ij} \leq b_r/A_{rj}$ is *active* for the round. Each leaf u_i chooses a random *star* edge (u_i, u_r) from its active edges. These star edges form stars rooted at roots. Each root u_r then performs steps (of Alg. 1) on its star edges (in any order) until they are all satisfied.

Note that in a round the algorithm performs steps in parallel for edges not belonging to the same star. For edges belonging to the same star, their root performs steps for some of them one by one. There are edges for which the algorithm never performs steps because they are covered by steps done for adjacent edges.

In the distributed setting we define the time at which a step to satisfy C_j is done as a pair (t_j^R, t_j^S), where t_j^R denotes the round in which the step was performed and t_j^S denotes that within the star this step is the t_j^S-th one. Let $t_j^R = 0$ if no step was performed for C_j. Overloading Definition 1, we redefine "$\prec$" as follows.

Definition 3. *Let $C_{j'} \prec C_j$ (or equivalently $x_{j'} \prec x_j$) if $\mathsf{Vars}(C_{j'}) \cap \mathsf{Vars}(C_j) \neq \emptyset$ (j' and j are adjacent edges in the distributed network) and ($[0 < t_{j'}^R < t_j^R]$ or $[t_{j'}^R = t_j^R$ and $t_{j'}^S < t_j^S]$).*

The pair (t_j^R, t_j^S) is enough to distinguish which of two adjacent edges had a step to satisfy its covering constraint performed first. Adjacent edges can have their covering constraints done in the same round only if they belong to the same star (they have a common root), thus they differ in t_j^S. Otherwise they are done in different rounds, so they differ in t_j^R. Thus the pair (t_j^R, t_j^S) and relation "$\prec$" define a partially ordered set $\mathcal{D}$ of all edges done by the distributed algorithm for covering.

Lemma 4. *([12]) Alg. 5 (for FRACTIONAL COVERING with $\delta = 2$) finishes in $T = O(\log m)$ rounds in expectation and with high probability. Simultaneously, Alg. 5 sets (t_j^R, t_j^S) for each edge e_j for which it performs a step ($0 < t_j^R \leq T$), thus defining a poset of edges $\mathcal{D}$, ordered by "$\prec$".*

Distributed Fractional Packing with $\delta = 2$. Alg. 3 implements Alg. 2 in a distributed fashion. First, it runs Alg. 1 using the distributed implementation by [12] (Alg. 5) and recording $\mathcal{D}$. Meanwhile, as it discovers the partial order $\mathcal{D}$, it begins the second phase of Alg. 2, raising each packing variable as soon as it can. Specifically it waits to set a given $x_j \in \mathcal{D}$ until after it knows that (a) x_j is in $\mathcal{D}$, (b) for each $x_{j'} \in N(x_j)$ whether $x_j \prec x_{j'}$, and (c) each such $x_{j'}$ is set. In other words, (a) a step has been done for the covering constraint C_j, (b) each adjacent covering constraint $C_{j'}$ is satisfied and (c) for each adjacent $C_{j'}$ for which a step was done after C_j, the variable $x_{j'}$ has been set. Subject to these constraints it sets x_j as soon as possible. Note that some nodes will be executing the second phase of the algorithm (packing) while some other nodes are still executing the first phase (covering). This is necessary because a given node cannot know when distant nodes are done with the first phase.

Distributed 2-approximation Fractional Packing with $\delta = 2$ alg. 3

input: Graph $G = (V, E)$ representing a fractional packing problem instance with
$\quad \delta = 2$.

output: Feasible x, 2-approximately minimizing $w \cdot x$.

1. Each edge $e_j \in E$ initializes $x_j \leftarrow 0$.
2. Each edge $e_j \in E$ initializes $done_j \leftarrow$ false. ... *this indicates if x_j has been set to its final value*
3. Until each edge e_j has set its variable x_j ($done_j ==$ true), perform a round:
4.   Perform a round of Alg. 5.   ... *covering with $\delta = 2$ augmented to compute* (t_j^R, t_j^S)
5.   For each node u_r that was a root (in Alg. 5) at any previous round, consider locally at u_r all stars $\mathcal{S}_r^t$ that were rooted by u_r at any previous round t. For each star $\mathcal{S}_r^t$ perform IncreaseStar($\mathcal{S}_r^t$).

IncreaseStar(star $\mathcal{S}_r^t$):

6. For each edge $e_j \in \mathcal{S}_r^t$ in decreasing order of t_j^S:
7.   If IncreasePackingVar(e_j) $==$ UNDONE then BREAK (stop the for loop).

IncreasePackingVar(edge $e_j = (u_i, u_r)$):

8. If e_j or any of its adjacent edges has a non-yet-satisfied covering constraint return UNDONE.
9. If $t_j^R == 0$ then:
10.   Set $x_j = 0$ and $done_j =$ true.
11.   Return DONE.
12. If $done_{j'} ==$ false for any edge $e_{j'}$ such that $x_j \prec x_{j'}$ then return UNDONE.
13. Set
$$x_j = \min \left\{ (b_i - \textstyle\sum_{j'} A_{ij'} x_{j'})/A_{ij}, \quad (b_r - \textstyle\sum_{j'} A_{rj'} x_{j'})/A_{rj} \right\} \text{ and } done_j = \text{true}.$$
14. Return DONE.

All x_j's will be determined in $2T$ rounds by the following argument. After round T, $\mathcal{D}$ is determined. Then by a straightforward induction on t, within $T + t$ rounds, every constraint C_j for which a step was done at round $T - t$ of the first phase, will have its variable x_j set.

Theorem 1. *For* FRACTIONAL PACKING *where each variable appears in at most two constraints there is a distributed 2-approximation algorithm running in $O(\log m)$ rounds in expectation and with high probability, where m is the number of packing variables.*

Proof. By Lemma 4, Alg. 5 computes a covering solution y in $T = O(\log m)$ rounds in expectation and with high probability. At the same time, the algorithm sets (t_j^R, t_j^S) for each edge e_j for which it performs a step to cover C_j, and thus defining a poset $\mathcal{D}$ of edges. In the distributed setting the algorithm does not define a linear order because there can be edges with the same (t_j^R, t_j^S), that is, edges that are covered by steps done in parallel. However, since these edges must be non-adjacent, we can still think that the algorithm gives a linear order (as in the sequential setting), where ties between edges with the same (t_j^R, t_j^S) are broken arbitrarily (without changing $\mathcal{D}$). Similarly, we can analyze Alg. 3 as if it considers the packing variables in a reverse order of $\mathcal{D}$. Then, by Lemma 1 and Lemma 2 the returned solution x is 2-approximate.

We prove that the x can be computed in at most T extra rounds after the initial T rounds to compute y. First note that within a star, even though its edges are ordered according to t_j^S they can all set their packing variables in a single round if none of them waits for some adjacent edge packing variable that belongs to a different star. So in the rest of the proof we only consider the case were edges are waiting for adjacent edges that belong to different stars. Note that $1 \leq t_j^R \leq T$ for each $x_j \in \mathcal{D}$. Then, at round T, each x_j with $t_j^R = T$ can be set in this round because it does not have to wait for any other packing variable to be set. At the next round, round $T + 1$, each x_j with $t_j^R = T - 1$ can be set; they are dependent only on variables $x_{j'}$ with $t_{j'}^R = T$ which have been already set. In general, packing variables with $t_j^R = t$ can be set once all adjacent $x_{j'}$ with $t_j^R \geq t + 1$ have been set. Thus by induction on $t = 0, 1, \ldots$ a constraint C_j for which a step was done at round $T - t$ may have to wait until at most round $T + t$ until its packing variable x_j is set. Therefore, the total number of rounds until solution x is computed is $2T = O(\log m)$ in expectation and with high probability. $\square$

The following theorem is a direct result of Lemma 3 and Thm 1 and the fact that for this problem $m = O(n^2)$.

Theorem 2. *For* MAXIMUM WEIGHTED b-MATCHING *on graphs there is a distributed 2-approximation algorithm running in $O(\log n)$ rounds in expectation and with high probability.*

4   Distributed Fractional Packing with General δ

4.1   Distributed Model for General δ

Here we assume that the distributed network has a node v_j for each covering constraint C_j (packing variable x_j), with edges from v_j to each node $v_{j'}$ if C_j and $C_{j'}$ share a covering variable y_i[4]. The total number of nodes in the network is m. Note that in this model the role of nodes and edges is reversed as compared to the model used in Section 3. We assume the standard synchronous model with unbounded message size.

4.2   Distributed Algorithm

Koufogiannakis and Young [12] show a distributed δ-approximation algorithm for (fractional) covering problems with at most δ variables per covering constraint that runs in $O(\log^2 m)$ rounds in expectation and with high probability. Similar to the $\delta = 2$ case, here we use this algorithm to get a poset of packing variables which we then consider in a reverse order, raising them maximally.

---

[4] The computation can easily be simulated on a network with nodes for covering variables or nodes for covering variables and covering constraints.

Distributed covering with general δ. Here is a brief description of the distributed δ-approximation algorithm for (fractional) covering from [12]. To start each phase, the algorithm finds large independent subsets of covering constraints by running one phase of Linial and Saks' (LS) decomposition algorithm, with any k such that $k \in \Theta(\ln m)^5$ [16]. The LS algorithm, for a given k, takes $O(k)$ rounds and produces a random subset $\mathcal{R} \subseteq \{v_j | j = 1 \ldots m\}$ of the covering constraints, and for each covering constraint $v_j \in \mathcal{R}$ a "leader" $\ell(v_j) \in \mathcal{R}$, with the following properties:

- Each $v_j \in \mathcal{R}$ is within distance k of its leader: $(\forall v_j \in \mathcal{R})\ d(v_j, v_{\ell(j)}) \leq k$.
- Components do not share covering variables (edges do not cross components): $(\forall v_j, v_{j'} \in \mathcal{R})\ v_{\ell(j)} \neq v_{\ell(j')} \Rightarrow \mathsf{Vars}(v_j) \cap \mathsf{Vars}(v_{j'}) = \emptyset$.
- Each covering constraint node has a chance to be in $\mathcal{R}$: $(\forall j = 1 \ldots m)\ \Pr[v_j \in \mathcal{R}] \geq 1/cm^{1/k}$ for some $c > 1$.

Next, each node $v_j \in \mathcal{R}$ sends its information (the constraint and its variables' values) to its leader $v_{\ell(j)}$. This takes $O(k)$ rounds because $v_{\ell(j)}$ is at distance $O(k)$ from v_j. Each leader then constructs (locally) the subproblem induced by the covering constraints that contacted it and the variables of those constraints, with their current values. Using this local copy, the leader does steps until all covering constraints that contacted it are satisfied. (Distinct leaders' subproblems don't share covering variables, so they can proceed simultaneously.) To end the phase, each leader u_ℓ returns the updated variable information to the constraints that contacted v_ℓ. Each covering constraint node in $\mathcal{R}$ is satisfied in the phase.

To extend the algorithm to compute a solution to the dual packing problem the idea is similar to the $\delta = 2$ case, substituting the role of stars by components and the role of roots by leaders. With each step done to satisfy the covering constraints C_j, the algorithm records (t_j^R, t_j^S), where t_j^R is the round and t_j^S is the within-the-component iteration in which the step was performed. This defines a poset $\mathcal{D}$ of covering constraints for which it performs steps.

Lemma 5. *([12]) The distributed δ-approximation algorithm for* FRACTIONAL COVERING *finishes in $T = O(\log^2 m)$ rounds in expectation and with high probability, where m is the number of covering constraints (packing variables). Simultaneously, it sets (t_j^R, t_j^S) for each covering constraint C_j for which it performs a step $(0 < t_j^R \leq T)$, thus defining a poset of covering constraints (packing variables) $\mathcal{D}$, ordered by "$\prec$".*

Distributed packing with general δ. (sketch) The algorithm (Alg. 4) is very similar to the case $\delta = 2$. First it runs the distributed algorithm for covering, recording (t_j^R, t_j^S) for each covering constraint C_j for which it performs a step. Meanwhile, as it discovers the partial order $\mathcal{D}$, it begins computing the packing solution, raising each packing variable as soon as it can. Specifically it waits to set a given $x_j \in \mathcal{D}$ until after it knows that (a) x_j is in $\mathcal{D}$, (b) for each

---

[5] If nodes don't know a $k \in \Theta(\ln m)$, a doubling technique can be used as a workaround [12].

Distributed δ-approximation Fractional Packing with general δ   alg. 4

input: Graph $G = (V, E)$ representing a fractional packing problem instance.

output: Feasible x, δ-approximately minimizing $w \cdot x$.

1. Initialize $x \leftarrow 0$.
2. For each $j = 1 \ldots m$ initialize $done_j \leftarrow$ false. ... *this indicates if x_j has been set to its final value*
3. Until each x_j has been set ($done_j == $ true) do:
4.   Perform a phase of the δ-approximation algorithm for covering by [12], recording (t_j^R, t_j^S).
5.   For each node $v_{\mathcal{K}}$ that was a leader at any previous phase, consider locally at $v_{\mathcal{K}}$ all components that chose $v_{\mathcal{K}}$ as a leader at any previous phase. For each such component $\mathcal{K}_r$ perform IncreaseComponent($\mathcal{K}_r$).

IncreaseComponent(component $\mathcal{K}_r$):

6. For each $j \in \mathcal{K}_r$ in decreasing order of t_j^S:
7.   If IncreasePackingVar(j) $==$ UNDONE then BREAK (stop the for loop).

IncreasePackingVar(j):

8. If C_j or any $C_{j'}$ that shares covering variables with C_j is not yet satisfied return UNDONE.
9. If $t_j^R == 0$ then:
10.   Set $x_j = 0$ and $done_j = $ true.
11.   Return DONE.
12. If $done_{j'} == $ false for any $x_{j'}$ such that $x_j \prec x_{j'}$ then return UNDONE.
13. Set $x_j = \min_{i \in \mathsf{Cons}(x_j)} \left((b_i - \sum_{j'} A_{ij'} x_{j'})/A_{ij} \right)$ and $done_j = $ true.
14. Return DONE.

$x_{j'} \in N(x_j)$ whether $x_j \prec x_{j'}$, and (c) each such $x_{j'}$ is set. In other words, (a) a step has been done for the covering constraint C_j, (b) each adjacent covering constraint $C_{j'}$ is satisfied and (c) for each adjacent $C_{j'}$ for which a step was done after C_j, the variable $x_{j'}$ has been set. Subject to these constraints it sets x_j as soon as possible.

To do so, the algorithm considers all components that have been done by leaders in previous rounds. For each component, the leader considers the component's packing variables x_j in order of decreasing t_j^S. When considering x_j it checks if each $x_{j'}$ with $x_j \prec x_{j'}$ is set, and if yes, then x_j can be set and the algorithm continues with the next component's packing variable (in order of decreasing t_j^S). Otherwise the algorithm cannot yet decide about the remaining component's packing variables.

Theorem 3. *For* FRACTIONAL PACKING *where each variable appears in at most δ constraints there is a distributed δ-approximation algorithm running in $O(\log^2 m)$ rounds in expectation and with high probability, where m is the number of packing variables.*

The proof is omitted because it is similar to the proof of Thm 1; the δ-approximation ratio is given by Lemma 1 and Lemma 2, and the running time uses $T = O(\log^2 m)$ by Lemma 5.

The following theorem is a direct result of Lemma 3 and Thm 3.

Theorem 4. *For* MAXIMUM WEIGHTED *b*-MATCHING *on hypergraphs, there is a distributed δ-approximation algorithm running in $O(\log^2 m)$ rounds in expectation and with high probability, where δ is the maximum hyperedge degree and m is the number of hyperedges.*

5   Conclusions

We show a new non-standard primal-dual method, which extends the (local-ratio related) algorithms for fractional covering by [13,12] to compute approximate solutions to the dual fractional packing problem without increasing the time complexity (even in the distributed setting).

Using this new technique, we show a distributed 2-approximation algorithm for FRACTIONAL PACKING where each packing variable appears in at most 2 constraints and a distributed 2-approximation algorithm for MAXIMUM WEIGHTED b-MATCHING on graphs, both running in a logarithmic number of rounds. We also present a distributed δ-approximation algorithm for FRACTIONAL PACKING where each variable appears in at most δ constraints and a distributed δ-approximation algorithm for MAXIMUM WEIGHTED b-MATCHING on hypergraphs, both running in $O(\log^2 m)$ rounds, where m is the number of packing variables and hyperedges respectively.

References

1. Bar-Yehuda, R.: One for the price of two: A unified approach for approximating covering problems. Algorithmica 27(2), 131–144 (2000)
2. Bar-Yehuda, R., Bendel, K., Freund, A., Rawitz, D.: Local ratio: a unified framework for approximation algorithms. ACM Computing Surveys 36(4), 422–463 (2004)
3. Bar-Yehuda, R., Rawitz, D.: On the equivalence between the primal-dual schema and the local-ratio technique. SIAM Journal on Discrete Mathematics 19(3), 762–797 (2005)
4. Czygrinow, A., Hańćkowiak, M., Szymańska, E.: A fast distributed algorithm for approximating the maximum matching. In: The twelfth European Symosium on Algorithms, pp. 252–263 (2004)
5. Edmonds, J.: Paths, trees, and flowers. Canadian Journal of Mathematics 17, 449–467 (1965)
6. Edmonds, J., Johnson, E.L.: Matching: A well-solved class of integer linear programs. In: Combinatorial Structures and Their Applications, pp. 89–92 (1970)
7. Hoepman, J.H.: Simple distributed weighted matchings. Arxiv preprint cs.DC/0410047 (2004)
8. Hougardy, S., Vinkemeier, D.E.: Approximating weighted matchings in parallel. Information Processing Letters 99(3), 119–123 (2006)
9. Israeli, A., Itai, A.: A fast and simple randomized parallel algorithm for maximal matching. Information Processing Letters 22, 77–80 (1986)

10. Karp, R.M.: Reducibility among combinatorial problems. In: Miller, R.E., Thatcher, J.W. (eds.) Complexity of Computer Computations. The IBM Research Symposia Series, pp. 85–103. Plenum Press, New York (1972)
11. Koufogiannakis, C., Young, N.E.: Beating simplex for fractional packing and covering linear programs. In: The forty-eighth IEEE symposium on Foundations of Computer Science, pp. 494–504 (2007)
12. Koufogiannakis, C., Young, N.E.: Distributed and parallel algorithms for weighted vertex cover and other covering problems. In: The twenty-eighth ACM symposium on Principles of Distributed Computing (2009)
13. Koufogiannakis, C., Young, N.E.: Greedy Δ-approximation algorithm for covering with arbitrary constraints and submodular cost. In: The thirty-sixth International Colloquium on Automata, Languages and Programming. LNCS, vol. 5555, pp. 634–652. Springer, Heidelberg (2009), http://arxiv.org/abs/0807.0644
14. Kuhn, F., Moscibroda, T., Wattenhofer, R.: The price of being near-sighted. In: The seventeenth ACM-SIAM Symposium on Discrete Algorithm, pp. 980–989 (2006)
15. Kuhn, F., Wattenhofer, R.: Constant-time distributed dominating set approximation. In: The twetwenty-second ACM symposium on Principles of Distributed Computing, pp. 25–32 (2003)
16. Linial, N., Saks, M.: Low diameter graph decompositions. Combinatorica 13(4), 441–454 (1993)
17. Lotker, Z., Patt-Shamir, B., Pettie, S.: Improved distributed approximate matching. In: The 12th ACM Symposium on Parallelism in Algorithms and Architectures, pp. 129–136 (2008)
18. Lotker, Z., Patt-Shamir, B., Rosén, A.: Distributed approximate matching. In: The 26th ACM symposium on Principles Of Distributed Computing, pp. 167–174 (2007)
19. Müller-Hannemann, M., Schwartz, A.: Implementing weighted b-matching algorithms: Towards a flexible software design. In: Goodrich, M.T., McGeoch, C.C. (eds.) ALENEX 1999. LNCS, vol. 1619, pp. 18–36. Springer, Heidelberg (1999)
20. Nieberg, T.: Local, distributed weighted matching on general and wireless topologies. In: The 5th ACM Joint Workshop on the Foundations of Mobile Computing, DIALM-POMC, pp. 87–92 (2008)
21. Peleg, D.: Distributed computing: a locality-sensitive approach. Society for Industrial and Applied Mathematics (2000)
22. Uehara, R., Chen, Z.: Parallel approximation algorithms for maximum weighted matching in general graphs. Information Processing Letters 76(1-2), 13–17 (2000)
23. Wattenhofer, M., Wattenhofer, R.: Distributed weighted matching. In: The 18th international symposium on Distributed Computing, pp. 335–348 (2004)

Appendix

Alg. 5 shows the distributed 2-approximation algorithm for FRACTIONAL COVER-ING with $\delta = 2$.

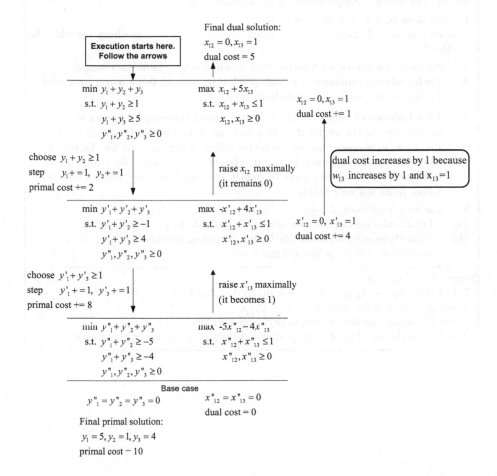

Fig. 2. Example of the execution of our greedy primal-dual algorithm (assuming constraint $y_1 + y_2 \geq 1$ is chosen first)

Distributed 2-approximation Fractional Covering with $\delta = 2$ ([12])   alg. 5

input: Graph $G = (V, E)$ representing a fractional covering problem instance with
$\delta = 2$.

output: Feasible y, 2-approximately minimizing $b \cdot y$.

1. Each node $u_i \in V$ initializes $y_i \leftarrow 0$.
2. Each edge $e_j \in E$ initializes $t_j^R \leftarrow 0$ and $t_j^S \leftarrow 0$.   ... *auxiliary variables for*
   Alg. 3

3. Until there is a vertex with unsatisfied incident edges, perform a round:
4.   Each node u_i, randomly and independently chooses to be a *leaf* or a *root*
      for the round, each with probability $1/2$.

5.   Each leaf-to-root edge $e_j = (u_i, u_r)$ with unmet covering constraint is *active*
      at the start of the round if u_i is a leaf, u_r is a root and $b_i/A_{ij} \le b_r/A_{rj}$.
      Each leaf u_i chooses, among its active edges, a random one for the round.
      Communicate that choice to the neighbors. The chosen edges form inde-
      pendent *stars* — rooted trees of depth 1 whose leaves are leaf nodes and
      whose roots are root nodes.

6.   For each root node u_r, do:
(a)   Let $\mathcal{S}_r^t$ contain the star edges sharing variable y_r (at this round t).
(b)   Until there exist an unsatisfied edge (covering constraint)
         $e_j = (u_i, u_r) \in \mathcal{S}_r^t$, perform $\mathsf{Step}(y, e_j)$.

$\mathsf{Step}(y, e_j = (u_i, u_r))$:
7. Let $\beta_j \leftarrow (w_j - A_{ij}y_i - A_{rj}y_r) \cdot \min\{b_i/A_{ij},\ b_r/A_{rj}\}$.
8. Set $y_i = y_i + \beta_j/b_i$ and $y_r = y_r + \beta_j/b_r$.
9. Set t_j^R to the number of rounds performed so far.
10. Set t_j^S to the number of steps performed by root u_r so far at this round.

Brief Announcement: Decidable Graph Languages by Mediated Population Protocols*

Ioannis Chatzigiannakis, Othon Michail, and Paul G. Spirakis

Research Academic Computer Technology Institute (RACTI), and Computer
Engineering and Informatics Department (CEID), University of Patras, 26500,
Patras, Greece
{ichatz,michailo,spirakis}@cti.gr

Abstract. We work on an extension of the Population Protocol model
of Angluin et al. [1] that allows edges of the communication graph, G, to
have *states* that belong to a *constant size set*. In this extension, the so
called Mediated Population Protocol model (MPP) [2,3], both *uniformity*
and *anonymity* are preserved. We here study a simplified version of MPP,
the Graph Decision Mediated Population Protocol model (GDM), in
order to capture MPP's ability to *decide graph languages*. We also prove
some first impossibility results both for weakly connected and possibly
disconnected communication graphs.

1 The GDM Model

A *graph decision mediated population protocol* (GDM) $\mathcal{A}$ consists of a *binary
output alphabet* $Y = \{0, 1\}$, a finite set of *agent states* Q, an *agent output function*
$O : Q \rightarrow Y$ mapping agent states to outputs, a finite set of *edge states* S, an
output instruction r, a *transition function* $\delta : Q \times Q \times S \rightarrow Q \times Q \times S$, an *initial
agent state* q_0, and an *initial edge state* s_0.

Let $\mathcal{U}$ denote a *graph universe*, that is, any set of communication graphs.
A *graph language* L is a subset of $\mathcal{U}$ containing communication graphs sharing
some common property. For example, a common graph universe is the set of all
possible directed and weakly connected communication graphs, denoted by $\mathcal{G}$,
and $L = \{G \in \mathcal{G} \mid |E(G)| \text{ is even}\}$ is a possible graph language w.r.t. $\mathcal{G}$.

A GDM protocol may run on any graph from a specified graph universe. The
graph on which the protocol runs is considered as the *input graph* of the protocol.
Note that GDM protocols have no sensed input. Instead, we require each agent
in the population to be initially in the initial agent state q_0 and each edge of the
communication graph to be initially in the initial edge state s_0. So, the initial
network configuration, C_0, of any GDM is defined as $C_0(u) = q_0$, for all $u \in V$,
and $C_0(e) = s_0$, for all $e \in E$, and any input graph $G = (V, E)$.

We say that a GDM $\mathcal{A}$ *accepts* an input graph G if in any computation of $\mathcal{A}$
on G after finitely many interactions all agents output the value 1 and continue

---

* This work has been partially supported by the ICT Programme of the European
Union under contract number ICT-2008-215270 (FRONTS).

I. Keidar (Ed.): DISC 2009, LNCS 5805, pp. 239–240, 2009.

doing so in all subsequent (infinite) computational steps. By replacing 1 with 0 we get the definition of the *reject* case. A GDM $\mathcal{A}$ *decides* a graph language $L \subseteq \mathcal{U}$ if it accepts any $G \in L$ and rejects any $G \notin L$, and a graph language is said to be *decidable* if some GDM decides it.

Theorem 1. *The class of decidable graph languages is closed under complement, union and intersection operations.*

Node and edge parity, bounded out-degree by a constant, existence of a node with more incoming than outgoing neighbors, and existence of some directed path of length at least $k = \mathcal{O}(1)$ are some examples of decidable graph languages, in the case where the graph universe is $\mathcal{G}$. Also, given that the graph universe is $\mathcal{G}$ one can prove the following.

Theorem 2. *There exists no GDM with stabilizing states to decide the graph language* $2C = \{G \in \mathcal{G} \mid G$ *has at least two nodes* u, v *s.t. both* $(u,v),(v,u) \in E(G)$ *(in other words, G has at least one 2-cycle)*$\}$.

In the case where the graph universe is $\mathcal{H}$, containing all possible directed communication graphs (i.e. also the disconnected ones), we obtain the following strong impossibility results.

Lemma 1. *For any nontrivial graph language* L *(L is nontrivial if $L \neq \emptyset$ and $L \neq \mathcal{H}$), there exists some disconnected graph G in L where at least one component of G does not belong to L or there exists some disconnected graph G' in $\overline{L}$ where at least one component of G' does not belong to $\overline{L}$ (or both).*

Theorem 3. *Any nontrivial graph language* $L \subset \mathcal{H}$ *is undecidable by GDM.*

Corollary 1. *The graph language* $C = \{G \in \mathcal{H} \mid G$ *is (weakly) connected*$\}$ *is undecidable.*

Proof. C is a nontrivial graph language and Theorem 3 applies. $\square$

A full version of this paper is available at http://fronts.cti.gr/aigaion/?TR=80

References

1. Angluin, D., Aspnes, J., Diamadi, Z., Fischer, M.J., Peralta, R.: Computation in networks of passively mobile finite-state sensors. In: 23rd Annual ACM Symposium on Principles of Distributed Computing (PODC), pp. 290–299. ACM Press, New York (2004)
2. Chatzigiannakis, I., Michail, O., Spirakis, P.G.: Mediated Population Protocols. In: 36th International Colloquium on Automata, Languages and Programming (ICALP), Rhodes, Greece, pp. 363–374, Also FRONTS Technical Report FRONTS-TR-2009-8 (2009), http://fronts.cti.gr/aigaion/?TR=65
3. Chatzigiannakis, I., Michail, O., Spirakis, P.G.: Recent Advances in Population Protocols. In: 34th International Symposium on Mathematical Foundations of Computer Science (MFCS), Novy Smokovec, High Tatras, Slovak Republic, pp. 56–76, Also FRONTS Technical Report FRONTS-TR-2009-21 (2009), http://fronts.cti.gr/aigaion/?TR=85

Brief Announcement: Towards Secured Distributed Polling in Social Networks

Rachid Guerraoui[1], Kévin Huguenin[2],
Anne-Marie Kermarrec[3], and Maxime Monod[1]

[1] EPFL, Switzerland
[2] IRISA, Université de Rennes 1, France
[3] INRIA Rennes - Bretagne Atlantique, France

Social networks are growing exponentially, and one of the most celebrated examples, Facebook, currently boasts more than 250 million users. A particularly important task in such networks is *polling*, such as the recent one about the terms of service of Facebook [1]. A defining characteristic of such networks is the one to one mapping between social network identities and real ones (as opposed to virtual world platforms such as SecondLife). Participants in social networks are *respectable*, that is they do care about their *reputation*: information related to a user is considered to reflect intimately on the associated *real* person. We claim that leveraging the fact that users of social networks are concerned over their reputation, we can achieve polling in a distributed manner in the presence of malicious users without the use of heavyweight cryptography.

The polling problem. The goal of polling is to extract some information reflecting a tendency on a given subject in a group of users out of the participants' opinions. In a typical polling application, each participant starts with a value in a predefined set of possible votes reflecting its opinion and the output of the poll is the number of users that voted for these values. With distributed polling, the output of the poll is computed in a collaborative way by the users themselves.

The main requirement that polling shares with voting is *privacy*, meaning that a user's vote must be disclosed neither by the participants nor by organizers during the process of counting. To a lesser extent, a polling algorithm must provide *accuracy* properties such as deterministic bounds on the error of its outcome. Indeed, although privacy is of the utmost importance in polling when dealing with sensitive personal topics such as politics or health, accuracy requirements can be relaxed as the goal of a poll is mainly to extract a tendency. However, security standards such as receipt freeness and universal verifiability are not relevant in polling. Finally, for practical reasons, polling must scale with the number of participants.

In addition to scalability, privacy makes decentralized solutions attractive as participants might generally not want their vote (and maybe even the result) to be known by a central entity, be it trusted or not [2], as the subject, votes and possibly the result of the poll might be very sensitive. While centralized polling is relatively easy to achieve, the design of a decentralized polling algorithm is very challenging, especially when the lack of any central entity prevents the use of asymmetric cryptography, since malicious users might try to disclose other users' votes and bias the outcome of the poll.

I. Keidar (Ed.): DISC 2009, LNCS 5805, pp. 241–242, 2009.
© Springer-Verlag Berlin Heidelberg 2009

Social networks and respectable participants. We advocate the use of an approach which, instead of masking (e.g., BFT) or preventing (e.g., cryptography) malicious behavior, leverages the users' concern over their privacy to dissuade malicious behavior. This is achieved by executing, in addition to the polling algorithm, a distributed verification protocol which tags the profiles of the participants. For instance, if the testimonies of Alice and Bob demonstrate that Mallory misbehaved in the process of counting, their profiles are tagged with "Alice and Bob jointly accused Mallory" and the profile of Mallory is tagged with "Mallory has been accused by Alice and Bob". No participant would like to be tagged as malicious (assuming the verification protocol does not wrongly accuse participants). Moreover, assuming a system with a large majority of honest participants, the risk for a participant to be caught wrongly accusing others is high. For instance, if a participant is accused only by users that are related in the social network (i.e., friends forming a coalition), the accusation would seem suspect and thus not be taken into account and this would eventually backfire on the accuser. Indeed, the very fact that profiles, and thus tags, are meant to be read by human beings makes such a coercive tagging system intrinsically resistant to false accusations. This could also be achieved by using existing automated techniques to detect suspicious patterns in the graph formed by accusations.

In this context, the behavior of users in a social network can be modelled as follows: users are either *honest* or *dishonest*, but in any case they care about their reputation. Honest users strictly follow the polling protocol and contribute to the verifications as long as their privacy is not compromised. More specifically, honest users always collaborate with verification procedures that do not require them to reveal their votes (i.e., public verifications). However, they may refuse to reveal their votes for a verification procedure (i.e., private verification). Dishonest users may misbehave either to promote their opinion or reveal the opinion of honest users. Yet, they are rational in the sense that they never behave in such a way that their reputation is tarnished with certainty, i.e., they do not perform attacks that can be detected with probability 1 by means of public verification procedures. In addition, dishonest nodes do not wrongfully blame honest nodes as it is rather easy for a human reader, when looking at other users' profiles, to distinguish between legitimate and wrongful accusations.

This model, which relies only on the fact that members of social networks are respectable, opens new perspectives for secured distributed computing. A practical application to polling based on this model is proposed in [3].

References

1. Richmond, R.: Facebook Tests the Power of Democracy. The New York Times (April 23rd, 2009)
2. Stelter, B.: Facebook's Users Ask Who Owns Information. The New York Times (Feburary 17th, 2009)
3. Guerraoui, R., Huguenin, K., Kermarrec, A.M., Monod, M.: Decentralized Polling with Respectable Participants. Research Report 6890, INRIA (March 2009)

What Can Be Observed Locally?[*]
Round-Based Models for Quantum Distributed Computing

Cyril Gavoille[1], Adrian Kosowski[1,2], and Marcin Markiewicz[3]

[1] LaBRI - University of Bordeaux
[2] Dept of Algorithms and System Modeling, Gdańsk University of Technology
[3] Institute of Theoretical Physics and Astrophysics, University of Gdańsk

Abstract. We consider the question of *locality* in distributed computing in the context of quantum information. Specifically, we focus on the round complexity of quantum distributed algorithms, with no bounds imposed on local computational power or on the bit size of messages. Linial's $\mathcal{LOCAL}$ model of a distributed system is augmented through two types of quantum extensions: (1) initialization of the system in a quantum entangled state, and/or (2) application of quantum communication channels. For both types of extensions, we discuss proof-of-concept examples of distributed problems whose round complexity is in fact reduced through genuinely quantum effects. Nevertheless, we show that even such quantum variants of the $\mathcal{LOCAL}$ model have non-trivial limitations, captured by a very simple (purely probabilistic) notion which we call "physical locality" (φ-$\mathcal{LOCAL}$). While this is strictly weaker than the "computational locality" of the classical $\mathcal{LOCAL}$ model, it nevertheless leads to a generic view-based analysis technique for constructing lower bounds on round complexity. It turns out that the best currently known lower time bounds for many distributed combinatorial optimization problems, such as *Maximal Independent Set*, bounds cannot be broken by applying quantum processing, in any conceivable way.

1 Introduction

The introduction of computational models based on quantum computing, starting from the works of Deutsch in the 1980's [11], has led to the advent of a new branch of complexity theory. Many studies have for instance focused on the complexity class BQP of problems solvable on a quantum computer in polynomial time with bounded error probability, and its relation to the classical complexity classes. One of the best known algorithmic results in this respect is Shor's polynomial-time method of integer factorization [37] based on the Quantum Fourier Transform, which has recently been partially tested in an experimental set-up for very small values of problem input. Nevertheless, application of quantum information in centralized computing scenarios still proves extremely costly and is riddled with technological difficulties resulting from quantum decoherence

---

[*] Supported by the ANR project "ALADDIN", by the INRIA équipe-project "CÉPAGE", and by the KBN Grant 4 T11C 047 25.

I. Keidar (Ed.): DISC 2009, LNCS 5805, pp. 243–257, 2009.

effects. On the other hand, in an even wider time-frame, properties of quantum-mechanical systems have proven to be of interest from the perspective of game theory [4,13,2], information theory [31,22,3], and distributed systems [4,9].

A major line of study (which we briefly look at in the related work section) concerns the application of quantum effects to reduce communication complexity, i.e., to decrease the number of communication bits required to solve a specific task performed within a system graph with several distributed agents. The influence of quantum information on the computing power of distributed systems with node anonymity and distributed systems in the presence of faults has also been studied.

This paper focuses on a different aspect of quantum distributed computing: we do not impose any bounds on the size of communicated messages, but assume that the system operates in synchronous rounds, and ask to what extent quantum effects can reduce the number of rounds required to solve combinatorial optimisation problems. The starting point for considerations is the well-established $\mathcal{LOCAL}$ model a.k.a. Linial's Free model [25,26]. We provide a comparison of the "computational power" of the quantum and non-quantum models, formalising the notion of locality in quantum distributed computing, and showing how it essentially differs from the understanding of locality in the $\mathcal{LOCAL}$ model.

1.1 Related Work

One of the most intensively studied problems related to multi-agent quantum scenarios, when expressed in the language of distributed computing, is roughly trying to address the question: *Can quantum effects be used to enhance distributed computations with messages of bounded size, i.e., in settings inspired by the $\mathcal{CONGEST}$ distributed model?* (See [35] for an introduction to the $\mathcal{CONGEST}$ model.) The quantum variant of $\mathcal{CONGEST}$, widely studied in physics, is known as the Local Operations and Classical Communication ($\mathcal{LOCC}$) model. It exploits the key quantum-mechanical concept of an entangled state (see e.g. [31]). This is achieved by altering the initialization phase of the system to allow for a starting state entangled among all the processors, which are locally given quantum computation capabilities; however, communication between processors is still restricted to the exchange of classical information, only. This application of pre-entanglement has been shown to decrease the number of communication bits required to solve certain distributed problems with output collected from one node, and consequently, to decrease the number of required communication rounds when message sizes are bounded. The first proof-of-concept example was provided in [6], where the computation of a specific function of input data distributed among three parties was shown to require at least 3 communicated bits in the classical case, but only 2 communicated bits if the system is initialized in a specific quantum entangled state. Many related results and refinements of this scenario are surveyed in e.g. [7,39].

Other works on the subject have focused on characterising the physical evolution of states attainable in the $\mathcal{LOCC}$ model [30,32,8], while other authors have dealt with the combinatorial complexity of distributing the entangled state over the whole system in the initialization phase [38]. Other modifications of the model attempt to show that a denser coding of information in transmitted messages is possible when using quantum channels, as compared to classical communication links (see e.g. [5,36]).

Very recently, some authors have begun to study the impact of quantum effects on fundamental concepts of the theory of distributed computing. An overview of this line of research is contained in the recent survey paper [9]. The advantages of applying quantum communication in games against a dynamic adversary are displayed in [1], where it is shown that a constant number of computational rounds is sufficient to solve the quantum Byzantine agreement problem for an n-node system with less than $n/3$ faulty nodes in such a dynamic setting; corresponding classical algorithms require $\Omega(\sqrt{n})$ rounds. Another especially interesting result is that the leader election problem can be solved in distributed systems with quantum links, but no pre-entanglement [40,23]. Some authors have also claimed that problems related to leader election [33,12] and distributed consensus [12,21] can be solved in distributed systems aided by quantum pre-entanglement.

1.2 Outline of the Paper

In Subsection 1.3 we briefly outline the $\mathcal{LOCAL}$ model and its extensions, obtained by modifying the initialization of the system set-up and/or adding quantum communication capabilities on the edges. Whereas this discussion is self-contained, we also provide a formal mathematical definition of the corresponding notions in an extended version of the paper [19]. Subsection 1.4 introduces some notation used when comparing computational models.

In Section 2 we compare the computational power of models based on the proposed extensions of $\mathcal{LOCAL}$. In particular, we prove that adding quantum extensions to the $\mathcal{LOCAL}$ model decreases the round complexity of certain distributed problems. This is achieved through simple proof-of-concept examples.

Most importantly, in Section 3 we introduce a probabilistic framework for proving lower bounds on the distributed time complexity of computational problems in any quantum (or other unconventional) models based on $\mathcal{LOCAL}$. This is directly applied to obtain such lower bounds for many combinatorial optimization problems, including Maximal Independent Set, Greedy Graph Coloring, and problems of spanner construction. As a side effect, the simple concept of "physical locality" formulated in this section, leads to the definition of a computational model we call $\varphi\text{-}\mathcal{LOCAL}$, which appears to be of independent interest.

Finally, in Section 4 we make an attempt to clarify issues with some of the related work on quantum distributed computing as surveyed by [9]. Making use of the framework of computational models defined in the previous sections, we explain why certain claims, saying that problems such as Leader Election or Distributed Consensus benefit from the application of quantum processing, should be approached with caution.

Section 5 contains some concluding remarks and suggests directions of future studies.

1.3   Preliminaries: Description of Computation Models

The $\mathcal{LOCAL}$ Model. The $\mathcal{LOCAL}$ model has been the subject of intensive study in the last 20 years, starting from the seminal works [25,29]. It is assumed that the distributed system consists of a set of processors V (with $|V| = n$) and operates in a sequence of synchronous rounds, each of which involves unbounded computations on the local state variables of the processors, and a subsequent exchange of messages of arbitrary size between pairs of processors which are connected by links (except for round 0, which involves local computations, only). Nodes can identify their neighbours using integer labels assigned successively to communication ports. The local computation procedures encoded in all processors are necessarily the same, and initially all local state variables have the same value for all processors, except for one distinguished local variable $x(v)$ of each processor v which encodes input data. The input of a problem is defined in the form of a labeled graph G_x, where $G = (V, E)$ is the system graph, while $x : V \to \mathbb{N}$ is an assignment of labels to processors. The output of the algorithm is given in the form of a vector of local variables $y : V \to \mathbb{N}$, and the algorithm is assumed to terminate once all variables $y(v)$ are definitely fixed. Herein we assume that faults do not appear on processors and links, that local computation procedures may be randomized (with processors having access to their own generators of random variables), and that the input labels x need not in general be distinct for all processors.

In our considerations, it is convenient to assume that the set of processors V is given *before* the input is defined. This is used for convenience of notation, and neither affects the model, nor the anonymity of nodes in the considered problems.

Extensions of System Initialization ($^+\mathcal{S}$ and $^+\mathcal{E}$). In the $\mathcal{LOCAL}$ model, it is assumed that the initial set-up of all the processors is identical. This assumption can be relaxed by allowing the processors to obtain some information from a central helper, but only before the start of the distributed process (i.e., independently of the input G_x). The initialization procedure is an integral part of the algorithm used for solving the distributed problem. Several different forms of initialization can be naturally defined; for clarity of discussion, we consider only two extensions of the model: the $^+\mathcal{S}$ extension (for *Separable* state), which allows for the most general form of initialization possible in a classical computational setting, and the more powerful $^+\mathcal{E}$ extension (for *Entangled* state), which allows for the most general form of initialization available in a quantum distributed system.

The $^+\mathcal{S}$ extension. We say that a computational model is equipped with the $^+\mathcal{S}$ *extension* if the following modifications are introduced:

- For any computational problem, the computational procedure consists of the distributed algorithm applied by all the processors during the rounds of computation, and an additional (randomized) procedure executed in a centralized way in the initialization phase. The result of the initialization procedure is an assignment $h : V \to \mathbb{N}$ of *helper* variables to the set of processors. The helper variables are independent[1] of the input G_x.

- For each processor $v \in V$, at the start of round 0, its input label $x(v)$ is augmented by the value $h(v)$, stored in a helper register of the local memory.

It is straightforward to show that the above formulation has two equivalent characterizations. From a computational perspective, we may equivalently say that for each processor v, the helper initialization value $h(v)$ encodes: (1) a unique identifier of v from the range $\{1, \ldots, n\}$, (2) the value of n, (3) the value of a random number, chosen from an arbitrarily large range, and shared by all processors. All further helper information is unnecessary, since it can be computed by the processors in round 0 of the distributed computations (simulation of the centralized assignment of further helper information can be simulated based on random bits and starting information which is common to all processors).

Alternatively, we may say that through the randomized initialization, according to some probability distribution we choose some deterministic initialization of the set of states of individual processors. This intuition precisely corresponds to the notion of a state with uncertainty in classical statistical physics, referred to in quantum-mechanical discussions as a (mixed) *separable state* of the system. It is obviously true to say that *whenever a problem is solved in a model with the ^{+}S extension, it may benefit solely from the modification of the system initialization, and not from the laws of quantum mechanics.*

The $^{+}\mathcal{E}$ extension. Unlike in classical physics, in quantum mechanics not every initialization of the system has to follow the above pattern. Consider a scenario in which we centrally create an initial global state of the whole system of processors, and spatially distribute "parts" of it to the individual processors (for example, by sharing out among the nodes a set of quantum-correlated photons). Then, each of the processors can perform operations on the "part" of the state assigned to its spatial location; by a loose analogy to processing of classical information, this is sometimes referred to as each processor "manipulating its own quantum bits (qubits)". Given a general initial state of the system, the outcome of such a physical process, as determined by the processors, may display correlations which cannot be described using any classical probabilistic framework. Initial states which can be lead to display such properties are called non-separable, or *entangled states*. Quantum entanglement is without doubt one of the predominant topics studied in quantum-mechanical literature of the last decades; we refer the interested reader to e.g. [31] for an extensive introduction to the topic.

We say that a computational model is equipped with the $^{+}\mathcal{E}$ *extension* if all processors are equipped with helper quantum information registers h, and the computational procedure used to solve a problem sets in the initialization phase in a centralized way some chosen, possibly entangled, quantum state over the set of quantum information registers h of all processors, in a way independent of the input graph G_x.

---

[1] Helper variables that do depend on the inputs are referred to in the literature as *Oracles* [16,15]. Such extensions are not discussed in this paper.

Extension of Communication Capabilities ($^+\mathcal{Q}$). Whereas the application of local quantum operations in each processor does not increase the power of the $\mathcal{LOCAL}$ model as such, the situation changes when the processors can interact with each other using quantum communication channels. Intuitively, such channels allow for the distribution of an entangled state by a processor over several of its neighbours in one communication round; such an effect cannot be achieved using classical communication links.

We say that a computational model is equipped with the $^+\mathcal{Q}$ *extension* if all communication links between processors in the system graph are replaced by quantum communication channels.

Models with the Extensions. Modifications to the initialization and communication capabilities of the system are completely independent of each other. For initialization, we can apply no extension, use a separable state ($^+\mathcal{S}$), or an entangled state ($^+\mathcal{E}$). For communication, we can apply no extension, or use quantum channels ($^+\mathcal{Q}$). Hence, we obtain 6 possible models ($\mathcal{LOCAL}$, $\mathcal{LOCAL}^+\mathcal{S}$, $\mathcal{LOCAL}^+\mathcal{E}$, $\mathcal{LOCAL}^+\mathcal{Q}$, $\mathcal{LOCAL}^+\mathcal{Q}^+\mathcal{S}$, $\mathcal{LOCAL}^+\mathcal{Q}^+\mathcal{E}$), which are discussed in the following section. (Some of these models collapse onto each other.)

1.4   Notation for Comparing the Power of Computational Models

In order to compare the computational power of different models, we introduce two basic notions: that of the *problem* being solved, and of an *outcome* of the computational process.

Definition 1. *A problem $\mathcal{P}$ is a mapping $G_x \mapsto \{y^i\}$, which assigns to each input graph G_x a set of permissable output vectors $y^i : V \to \mathbb{N}$.*

Instead of explicitly saying that we are interested in finding efficient (possibly randomized) distributed algorithms for solving problems within the considered computational models, we characterize the behavior of such procedures through the probability distribution of output vectors which they may lead to, known as an *outcome*. In fact, such a probability distribution is necessarily well defined, whereas formally describing the computational process may be difficult in some unconventional settings (see e.g. the $\varphi\text{-}\mathcal{LOCAL}$ model in Section 3).

Definition 2. *An outcome $\mathcal{O}$ is a mapping $G_x \mapsto \{(y^i, p^i)\}$, which assigns to each input graph G_x a normalized discrete probability distribution $\{p^i\}$, such that: $\forall_i \ p^i > 0$ and $\sum_i p^i = 1$, with p^i representing the probability of obtaining $y^i : V \to \mathbb{N}$ as the output vector of the distributed system.*

Definition 3. *For any outcome $\mathcal{O}$ in a computational model $\mathcal{M}$ which is a variant of $\mathcal{LOCAL}$, we will write $\mathcal{O} \in \mathcal{M}[t]$ if within model $\mathcal{M}$ there exists a distributed procedure which yields outcome $\mathcal{O}$ after at most t rounds of computation.*

We will say that an outcome $\mathcal{O}$ is a *solution* to problem $\mathcal{P}$ with probability p if for all G_x, we have: $\sum_{\{(y^i, p^i) \in \mathcal{O}(G_x) \ : \ y^i \in \mathcal{P}(G_x)\}} p_i \geq p$. When $p = 1$, we will simply call $\mathcal{O}$ a *solution* to $\mathcal{P}$ *(with certainty).*

By a slight abuse of notation, for a problem $\mathscr{P}$ we will write $\mathscr{P} \in \mathcal{M}[t]$ (respectively, $\mathscr{P} \in \mathcal{M}[t,p]$) if there exists an outcome $\mathcal{O} \in \mathcal{M}[t]$ which is a solution to problem $\mathscr{P}$ (respectively, a solution to problem $\mathscr{P}$ with probability p).

For two computational models $\mathcal{M}_1, \mathcal{M}_2$, we say that $\mathcal{M}_1$ is *not more powerful than* $\mathcal{M}_2$ (denoted $\mathcal{M}_1 \subseteq \mathcal{M}_2$) if for every problem $\mathscr{P}$, for all $t \in \mathbb{N}$ and $p > 0$, $\mathscr{P} \in \mathcal{M}_1[t,p] \implies \mathscr{P} \in \mathcal{M}_2[t,p]$. The relation $\subseteq$ induces a partial order of models which is naturally extended to say that $\mathcal{M}_1$ and $\mathcal{M}_2$ are *equivalent* ($\mathcal{M}_1 = \mathcal{M}_2$), or that $\mathcal{M}_1$ is *less powerful than* $\mathcal{M}_2$ ($\mathcal{M}_1 \subsetneq \mathcal{M}_2$).

It can easily be proved that $\mathcal{M}_1 \subseteq \mathcal{M}_2$ if and only if for every outcome $\mathcal{O}$, for all $t \in \mathbb{N}$, $\mathcal{O} \in \mathcal{M}_1[t] \implies \mathcal{O} \in \mathcal{M}_2[t]$. Such an outcome-based characterisation of models is occasionally more intuitive, since it is not explicitly parameterised by probability p.

In all further considerations, when proving that $\mathcal{M}_1 \subsetneq \mathcal{M}_2$, we will do so in a stronger, deterministic sense, by showing that there exist a problem $\mathscr{P}$ and $t \in \mathbb{N}$ such that $\mathscr{P} \in \mathcal{M}_2[t]$ and $\mathscr{P} \notin \mathcal{M}_1[t]$.

2 Hierarchy of Quantum Models

The most natural variants of $\mathcal{LOCAL}$ which are based on the extensions proposed in the previous subsection are the classical model with separable initialization ($\mathcal{LOCAL}^+\mathcal{S}$), and quantum models with pre-entanglement at initialization, quantum channels, or both ($\mathcal{LOCAL}^+\mathcal{E}$, $\mathcal{LOCAL}^+\mathcal{Q}$, and $\mathcal{LOCAL}^+\mathcal{Q}^+\mathcal{E}$, respectively). The strengths of the models can obviously be ordered as follows: $\mathcal{LOCAL} \subseteq \mathcal{LOCAL}^+\mathcal{Q} \subseteq \mathcal{LOCAL}^+\mathcal{Q}^+\mathcal{S} \subseteq \mathcal{LOCAL}^+\mathcal{Q}^+\mathcal{E}$, and $\mathcal{LOCAL} \subseteq \mathcal{LOCAL}^+\mathcal{S} \subseteq \mathcal{LOCAL}^+\mathcal{E} \subseteq \mathcal{LOCAL}^+\mathcal{Q}^+\mathcal{E}$. We now proceed to show that, whereas $\mathcal{LOCAL}^+\mathcal{E} = \mathcal{LOCAL}^+\mathcal{Q}^+\mathcal{E}$, all the remaining inclusions are in fact strict. The hierarchy of the most important models is shown in Fig. 1.

Proposition 1. $\mathcal{LOCAL} \subsetneq \mathcal{LOCAL}^+\mathcal{S}$. *Moreover, there exists a problem $\mathscr{P}$ such that $\mathscr{P} \in \mathcal{LOCAL}^+\mathcal{S}[0]$ and $\mathscr{P} \notin \mathcal{LOCAL}[t]$ for all $t \in \mathbb{N}$.*

Proof. Any problem, which can be solved when given unique node identifiers from the range $\{1, \ldots, n\}$ is clearly in $\mathcal{LOCAL}^+\mathcal{S}[0]$. On the other hand, there are many examples of such problems which are not in $\mathcal{LOCAL}$ (or require $\Omega(n)$ rounds assuming that the system graph is connected and node labels are unique), most trivially the problem $\mathscr{P}$ of assigning unique node identifiers from the range $\{1, \ldots, n\}$ to all nodes.   □

More interestingly, one can show that $\mathcal{LOCAL}^+\mathcal{S}$ benefits due to the fact that helper variables $h(v)$ can encode a value which is set in a randomized way. Consider as a simple example a problem $\mathscr{P}'$ whose input is a graph $G = (V, E)$, of sufficiently large order n, with input labels of the nodes encoding unique node identifiers $\{1, \ldots, n\}$ and the value of n; moreover, G is restricted to be the complete graph K_n minus exactly one edge. The goal is to select an edge of the graph, i.e., output y must be such that for some two nodes $u, v \in V$, with $\{u, v\} \in E$, we have $y(u) = y(v) = 1$, and for all other $w \in V$ we have $y(w) = 0$. Even

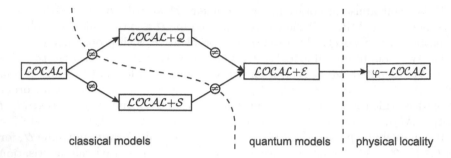

Fig. 1. Hierarchy of computational extensions to the $\mathcal{LOCAL}$ model. See Section 3 for a definition of the φ-$\mathcal{LOCAL}$ model, and Section 1.3 or the extended version [19] for definitions of all other models.

with the knowledge of node identifiers and n, in the $\mathcal{LOCAL}$ model the problem cannot be solved with high probability without communication, i.e., within 0 rounds: we have $\mathscr{P}' \notin \mathcal{LOCAL}[0, e^{-1}]$ (the proof is technical and postponed to the extended version [19]). On the other hand, within the $\mathcal{LOCAL}^+\mathcal{S}$ model this problem admits a solution in 0 rounds with probability arbitrarily close to 1 for sufficiently large n. Similar arguments can be applied to display the difference between the models for more advanced problems which simulate collaborative mobile agent scenarios, in particular variants of the cops-and-robbers problems in graphs.

We now point out the difference in power between the classical and quantum models. The proofs proceed by rephrasing one of the best established results of quantum interferometry, first introduced in the context of the so called Bell's Theorem without inequalities, for a 3-particle quantum entangled state (cf. [20] for the original paper or [34] for a contemporary exposition). We use its more algorithmic modulo-4 sum formulation, similar to that found in [41].

Theorem 1. $\mathcal{LOCAL}^+\mathcal{S} \subsetneq \mathcal{LOCAL}^+\mathcal{E}$. *Moreover, there exists a problem $\mathscr{P}$ such that $\mathscr{P} \in \mathcal{LOCAL}^+\mathcal{E}[0]$ and $\mathscr{P} \notin \mathcal{LOCAL}^+\mathcal{S}[t]$ for all $t \in \mathbb{N}$.*

Proof. Let $\mathscr{P}$ be a problem defined on a system with 3 nodes. Let the input graph be empty, and assume that input labels $x = (x_1, x_2, x_3) \in \{0,1\}^3$ of respective nodes satisfy the condition $x_1 + x_2 + x_3 \in \{0, 2\}$. An output $y = (y_1, y_2, y_3) \in \{0,1\}^3$ is considered valid for input x if and only if $2(y_1 + y_2 + y_3) \equiv (x_1 + x_2 + x_3)$ mod 4. This problem is not in $\mathcal{LOCAL}^+\mathcal{S}$, since finding a solution with certainty would imply that there exist three deterministic functions $Y_1, Y_2, Y_3 : \{0,1\} \rightarrow \{0,1\}$, such that for any input vector (x_1, x_2, x_3) satisfying the constraints of the problem, $(Y_1(x_1), Y_2(x_2), Y_3(x_3))$ is a valid output vector. It is immediate to show that this is impossible.

The situation is different when the system operates in the $\mathcal{LOCAL}^+\mathcal{E}$ model starts in an entangled state. The procedure required to obtain a valid solution is described in detail in [20]. In brief, in the initialization phase we share out to each of the processors one of 3 entangled qubits, carried e.g. by photons, which are in the entangled tripartite state known as the GHZ state (namely $\frac{1}{\sqrt{2}}(|000\rangle + |111\rangle)$ in Dirac's notation for pure states). Each of the processors then performs a simple transformation on "its own" qubit, in a way dependent only on the processor's input x_i. Finally, a measurement is performed, and it can be shown that the probability distribution of obtained output vectors (the outcome) is that stated in Table 1. Since all of the outputs are accepted as valid for the considered problem $\mathscr{P}$, this implies that $\mathscr{P} \in \mathcal{LOCAL}^+\mathcal{E}[0]$. □

Table 1. An outcome $\mathcal{O}$ which is a solution (with certainty) to the modulo-4 sum problem on the 3-node empty graph, and belongs to $\mathcal{LOCAL}^+\mathcal{E}[0]$ (see Theorem 1)

Input (x_1, x_2, x_3)	Probability p^i	Output (y_1^i, y_2^i, y_3^i)	Input (x_1, x_2, x_3)	Probability p^i	Output (y_1^i, y_2^i, y_3^i)
(0, 0, 0)	1/4	(0, 0, 0)		1/4	(1, 1, 1)
	1/4	(0, 1, 1)	(0, 1, 1)	1/4	(1, 0, 0)
	1/4	(1, 0, 1)	or (1, 0, 1)	1/4	(0, 1, 0)
	1/4	(1, 1, 0)	or (1, 1, 0)	1/4	(0, 0, 1)

Proposition 2. $\mathcal{LOCAL} \subsetneq \mathcal{LOCAL}^+\mathcal{Q}$. *Moreover, for any $t > 0$, there exists a problem $\mathscr{P}$ such that $\mathscr{P} \in \mathcal{LOCAL}^+\mathcal{Q}[t]$ and $\mathscr{P} \notin \mathcal{LOCAL}[2t-1]$.*

Proof (sketch). The proof proceeds by a modification of the argument from Theorem 1. This time, we consider a system on $n = 3k+1$ nodes, and an input graph with the topology of a uniformly subdivided star with a central node of degree 3. The modified problem $\mathscr{P}'$ consists in solving the problem from Theorem 1, when the three input and output values are put on the three leaves of the star. Within $\mathcal{LOCAL}$, this problem requires $2k$ rounds to solve, whereas within $\mathcal{LOCAL}^+\mathcal{Q}$, k rounds are sufficient. □

Whereas the time distinction between $\mathcal{LOCAL}^+\mathcal{S}$ and $\mathcal{LOCAL}^+\mathcal{E}$ given by Theorem 1 is remarkable (since it considers the feasibility of solving problems, or when discussing connected graphs, a speed-up from $\Omega(n)$ to 0 communication rounds), the situation is less clear between $\mathcal{LOCAL}^+\mathcal{Q}$ and $\mathcal{LOCAL}$. Although a speed-up factor of 2 as expressed by Proposition 2 looks like a natural limit, the authors know of no conclusive arguments to show that it cannot be increased further.

Finally, following the argumentation of [9], we observe that $\mathcal{LOCAL}^+\mathcal{E} = \mathcal{LOCAL}^+\mathcal{Q}^+\mathcal{E}$, or in other words that, given access to pre-entanglement, it is possible to simulate quantum links by means of classical ones. The effect used to achieve this is known as quantum teleportation [34]; by carefully choosing an entangled state over the whole system, it can be applied even when the communicating nodes do not yet know their neighbors' unique identifiers. The amount of pre-entanglement provided at initialization must be sufficient to allow for communication throughout all the rounds of the algorithm.

To complete a discussion of Fig. 1, we point out that $\mathcal{LOCAL}^+\mathcal{Q}$ is incomparable with $\mathcal{LOCAL}^+\mathcal{S}$. This is because the problem discussed in the proof of Proposition 1 belongs to $\mathcal{LOCAL}^+\mathcal{S}$, but not to $\mathcal{LOCAL}^+\mathcal{Q}$, and the problem discussed in the proof of Proposition 2 belongs to $\mathcal{LOCAL}^+\mathcal{Q}[1]$, but not to $\mathcal{LOCAL}^+\mathcal{S}[1]$.

The $\mathcal{LOCAL}^+\mathcal{Q}^+\mathcal{S}$ model has been left out from discussion, since it appears to be of little significance. By considering the same problems as before, we have $\mathcal{LOCAL}^+\mathcal{Q}^+\mathcal{S} \subsetneq \mathcal{LOCAL}^+\mathcal{Q}^+\mathcal{E} = \mathcal{LOCAL}^+\mathcal{E}$, so $\mathcal{LOCAL}^+\mathcal{Q}^+\mathcal{S}$ could be placed directly to the left of $\mathcal{LOCAL}^+\mathcal{E}$ in Fig. 1.

3   Lower Time Bounds Based on Physical Locality (φ-$\mathcal{LOCAL}$)

Proving lower bounds on the power of quantum models is problematic. This results, in particular, from the fact that there does not exist as yet an easy-to-use classification of entangled states, or of quantum operations (completely positive maps) which can be performed to transform one quantum state into another. However, in the context of distributed computing, it is possible to consider a more general framework of physical locality, leading to the φ-$\mathcal{LOCAL}$ model we define hereafter, which in turn can be used to bound the power of quantum models.

Within the classical $\mathcal{LOCAL}$ model, we can say that the output of any processor v after t rounds has to be computed based on the input data which can be collected from the input graph G_x by performing an exploration up to a depth of t, starting from node v; we call this the *distance-t local view* denoted by $\mathcal{V}_t(G_x, v)$. This leads to a simple characterisation of the $\mathcal{LOCAL}$ model in terms of valid outcomes (see the extended version [19] for a formalization).

In order to allow for quantum extensions to local, the assumption of classical computability needs to be relaxed, while at the same time retaining in some form the assumption of locality. Given a round-based model with interactions between nearest neighbors only, the physical understanding of locality is as follows: *Locality is violated if and only if, based on the available output data, we can conclusively verify that after t rounds some subset S of processors was affected by input data initially localized outside its view* $\mathcal{V}_t(G_x, S) := \bigcup_{v \in S} \mathcal{V}_t(G_x, v)$.

Using the above intuition, we now formalize this notion to obtain what we call the φ-$\mathcal{LOCAL}$ model, i.e., the weakest possible distributed model which still preserves physical locality. Given an output distribution $\{(y^i, p^i)\}$ acting on V, for any subset of vertices $S \subseteq V$ we define its *marginal distribution on set S*, $\{(y^i, p^i)\}[S]$, as the unique distribution $\{(\overline{y}^j, \overline{p}^j)\}$ acting on S which satisfies the condition $\overline{p}^j = \sum_{\{i \,:\, \overline{y}^j = y^i[S]\}} p^i$, where $y^i[S]$ is the restriction of output $y^i : V \to \mathbb{N}$ to nodes from subset $S \subseteq V$.

Definition 4. *An outcome $G_x \mapsto \{(y^i, p^i)\}$ belongs to φ-$\mathcal{LOCAL}[t]$ if for all subsets $S \subseteq V$, for any pair of inputs $G_x^{(a)}$, $G_x^{(b)}$ such that $\mathcal{V}_t(G_x^{(a)}, S) = \mathcal{V}_t(G_x^{(b)}, S)$, the output distributions corresponding to these inputs have identical marginal distributions on set S, i.e., $\{(y^{i(a)}, p^{i(a)})\}[S] = \{(y^{i(b)}, p^{i(b)})\}[S]$.*

Quantum relaxations of the $\mathcal{LOCAL}$ model, whether obtained through application of pre-entanglement, quantum channels, or both, lie in terms of strength "in between" the $\mathcal{LOCAL}$ and φ-$\mathcal{LOCAL}$ model. This is expressed by the following theorem, whose proof is provided in the extended version of the paper [19].

Theorem 2. $\mathcal{LOCAL}^+\mathcal{Q}^+\mathcal{E} \subseteq \varphi$-$\mathcal{LOCAL}$.

The theorem captures the property of locality of nearest-neighbor interactions in quantum mechanics, and it does not rely in any way on any other physical concepts, such as causality or speed of information in the theory of relativity.

Although it is not clear whether the containment in the above theorem is strict (we leave this as an open question), the φ-$\mathcal{LOCAL}$ model is still sufficiently constrained to preserve many important lower time bounds known from the $\mathcal{LOCAL}$ model, which are based on arguments of indistinguishability of local views of a node for different inputs. In particular, by careful analysis, it is easy to prove the following statements for the φ-$\mathcal{LOCAL}$ model.

- The problem of finding a maximal independent set in the system graph requires $\Omega(\sqrt{\frac{\log n}{\log \log n}})$ rounds to solve [24].
- The problem of finding a locally minimal (greedy) coloring of the system graph requires $\Omega(\frac{\log n}{\log \log n})$ rounds to solve [18,17].
- The problem of finding a connected subgraph with $O(n^{1+1/k})$ edges requires $\Omega(k)$ rounds to solve [10,14].

The matter is less clear in the case of the $(\Delta + 1)$-coloring problem. The proof of the famous lower bound of $\frac{1}{2} \log^* n - O(1)$ rounds [26] (and its extension to randomized algorithms [28]) does not appear to generalize from the $\mathcal{LOCAL}$ model to the φ-$\mathcal{LOCAL}$ model; we are unaware of any (even constant) bound on the number of rounds required to find a solution to $(\Delta+1)$-coloring in φ-$\mathcal{LOCAL}$. Some indication that the technique of coloring neighborhood graphs, used by Linial, may not apply in φ-$\mathcal{LOCAL}$, is that this technique can likewise be used to show a lower bound of $\lfloor \frac{n}{2} \rfloor - 1$ rounds on the time required for 2-coloring the cycle C_n, where n is even. However, in φ-$\mathcal{LOCAL}$ the same problem admits a solution in fewer rounds.

Theorem 3. *The problem of 2-coloring the even cycle C_n (given unique node labels x) belongs to φ-$\mathcal{LOCAL}[\lceil \frac{n-2}{4} \rceil]$, but does not belong to φ-$\mathcal{LOCAL}[\lceil \frac{n-2}{4} \rceil - 1]$.*

Proof (sketch). For the lower bound, consider the local view of two nodes u, v which still have disjoint views after $\lceil \frac{n-2}{4} \rceil - 1$ rounds. There are at least two nodes which belong to neither the view of u nor the view of v; hence, u and v cannot distinguish whether they are at an even or at an odd distance from each other in the cycle. This directly leads to the lower bound, since the definition condition of φ-$\mathcal{LOCAL}$ can be shown to be violated for $S = \{u, v\}$.

The upper bound is generated by on outcome $\mathcal{O}$ of the 2-coloring problem, given as follows: each of the 2 legal 2-colorings of C_n is used as the output with probability $\frac{1}{2}$. Such an outcome $\mathcal{O}$ belongs to φ-$\mathcal{LOCAL}[\lceil \frac{n-2}{4} \rceil]$. This can be easily verified, since for any subset $S \subseteq V$ we either have that S consists of exactly two antipodal nodes of C_n, or the view $\mathcal{V}_{\lceil \frac{n-2}{4} \rceil}(C_{n_x}, S)$ is simply an arc of the cycle.   □

It would be interesting to find a constructive quantum procedure for finding a 2-coloring of C_n in $\lceil \frac{n-2}{4} \rceil$ rounds. In particular, we have that 2-coloring of C_6 belongs to $\varphi\text{-}\mathcal{LOCAL}[1]$, does not belong to $\mathcal{LOCAL}^+\mathcal{S}[1]$, and do not know if it belongs to $\mathcal{LOCAL}^+\mathcal{E}[1]$.

4   Simple Problems in a Quantum Setting

In this section, we have a look at some of the related work on quantum distributed problems, as outlined in the survey [9]. Whereas the discussion in this section relies on the results and notation from the preceding sections, it can also be translated into the (not always precisely described) computational models studied in the considered related work.

Two problems which have been used to exhibit the difference between quantum models and non-quantum models are LeaderElection, where the goal is for exactly one node of the system graph to output a value of 1 whereas all other nodes output 0, and a problem which we will call BitPicking, where the goal is for all nodes to return the same output value, either 0 or 1. These discussions include the concept of *fairness*, which in the terminology of this paper means that we are asking not about the problems as such, but about obtaining specific (fair) *outcomes*. More precisely, we will say that FairLeaderElection is the outcome which puts a uniform probability distribution on the n distinct outputs valid for LeaderElection (i.e., on all possible leaders), and FairBitPicking is the outcome which puts a uniform probability distribution on the 2 distinct outputs valid for BitPicking (i.e., picking 0 or 1).

The focus of [33,12,21] is to show that FairBitPicking and FairLeaderElection belong to $\mathcal{LOCAL}^+\mathcal{E}[0]$ (even with some additional restrictions on the amount of allowed pre-entanglement), whereas they do not belong to $\mathcal{LOCAL}[0]$. This statement is correct, however, this effect is due to *the modification of initialization of the system, and not to quantum mechanics*. In fact, we can make the following obvious statement.

Proposition 3. FairBitPicking *and* FairLeaderElection *belong to the non-quantum class* $\mathcal{LOCAL}^+\mathcal{S}[0]$. *Moreover, they can be solved with only one bit of helper information per node, at initialization.*

Finally, we relate to the recent claims that the DistributedConsensus can be solved in a quantum setting without communication. Whereas these claims result from a misunderstanding of the definition [27] of DistributedConsensus, we point out that such a result is impossible in any quantum model, since it is even impossible in $\varphi\text{-}\mathcal{LOCAL}$ (a short proof is provided in the extended version of the paper [19]). We recall that in DistributedConsensus, given an assignment of input labels $(x_1, \ldots, x_n)$ to particular processors, the goal is to obtain an output vector $(y, \ldots, y)$, such that $y \in \{x_1, \ldots, x_n\}$.

Proposition 4. DistributedConsensus $\notin \varphi\text{-}\mathcal{LOCAL}[0]$.

5   Conclusions and Future Work

We have pointed out that the computational power of quantum variants of the $\mathcal{LOCAL}$ model is *strictly greater* than that of the classical $\mathcal{LOCAL}$ model, or that of the $\mathcal{LOCAL}$ model equipped with helper information such as a pool of shared random bits. It remains to be seen whether a difference can be observed for any problems of practical significance. It is potentially possible that certain combinatorial optimization problems may benefit from quantum extensions to the $\mathcal{LOCAL}$ model. However, we can say that the "view-based" limitations of the $\mathcal{LOCAL}$ model still hold in quantum models. So, one specific question which remains open is whether the $(\Delta+1)$-Coloring problem can be solved in a constant number of rounds in any of the relaxed variants of $\mathcal{LOCAL}$.

Finally, we can ask about a characterization of the limitations of quantum computability, the most natural question being to establish whether the containment $\mathcal{LOCAL}^+\mathcal{E} \subseteq \varphi\text{-}\mathcal{LOCAL}$ is strict. As a matter of fact, further studies of the $\varphi\text{-}\mathcal{LOCAL}$ model, which can be seen as the weakest distributed local model, capturing verifiability rather than computability of outcomes, appear to be of interest in their own right.

Acknowledgment. We gratefully thank Pierre Fraigniaud and Zvi Lotker for their preliminary discussions on the EPR effect and its applicability to Distributed Computing. We thank Robert Alicki and Władysław Adam Majewski for helpful discussions concerning quantum dynamic maps, and Marek Żukowski for several references on quantum information.

References

1. Ben-Or, M., Hassidim, A.: Fast quantum byzantine agreement. In: 37th Annual ACM Symposium on Theory of Computing (STOC), pp. 481–485. ACM Press, New York (2005)
2. Benjamin, S.C., Hayden, P.M.: Multiplayer quantum games. Physical Review A 64(3), 030301 (2001)
3. Bennett, C.H., Shor, P.W.: Quantum information theory. IEEE Transactions on Information Theory 44, 2724–2742 (1998)
4. Broadbent, A., Tapp, A.: Can quantum mechanics help distributed computing? ACM SIGACT News - Distributed Computing Column 39(3), 67–76 (2008)
5. Buhrman, H., Cleve, R., Wigderson, A.: Quantum vs. classical communication and computation. In: 30th Annual ACM Symposium on the Theory of Computing (STOC), pp. 63–68 (1998)
6. Cleve, R., Buhrman, H.: Substituting quantum entanglement for communication. Physical Review A 56(2), 1201–1204 (1997)
7. de Wolf, R.: Quantum communication and complexity. Theoretical Computer Science 287(1), 337–353 (2002)
8. den Nest, M.V., Dür, W., Vidal, G., Briegel, H.: Classical simulation versus universality in measurement-based quantum computation. Physical Review A 75(1), 012337 (2007)
9. Denchev, V.S., Pandurangan, G.: Distributed quantum computing: A new frontier in distributed systems or science fiction? ACM SIGACT News - Distributed Computing Column 39(3), 77–95 (2008)

10. Derbel, B., Gavoille, C., Peleg, D., Viennot, L.: On the locality of distributed sparse spanner construction. In: 27th Annual ACM Symposium on Principles of Distributed Computing (PODC), pp. 273–282. ACM Press, New York (2008)

11. Deutsch, D.: Quantum theory, the Church-Turing principle and the universal quantum computer. Proceedings of the Royal Society of London A400, 97–117 (1985)

12. D'Hondt, E., Panangaden, P.: The computational power of the W and GHZ states. Quantum Information and Computation 6(2), 173–183 (2006)

13. Eisert, J., Wilkens, M., Lewenstein, M.: Quantum games and quantum strategies. Physical Review Letters 83(11), 3077–3080 (1999)

14. Elkin, M.: A near-optimal fully dynamic distributed algorithm for maintaining sparse spanners. In: 26th Annual ACM Symposium on Principles of Distributed Computing (PODC), pp. 195–204. ACM Press, New York (2007)

15. Fraigniaud, P., Gavoille, C., Ilcinkas, D., Pelc, A.: Distributed computing with advice: Information sensitivity of graph coloring. In: Arge, L., Cachin, C., Jurdziński, T., Tarlecki, A. (eds.) ICALP 2007. LNCS, vol. 4596, pp. 231–242. Springer, Heidelberg (2007)

16. Fraigniaud, P., Ilcinkas, D., Pelc, A.: Oracle size: a new measure of difficulty for communication tasks. In: 25th Annual ACM Symposium on Principles of Distributed Computing (PODC), pp. 179–187. ACM Press, New York (2006)

17. Gavoille, C., Klasing, R., Kosowski, A., Kuszner, Ł., Navarra, A.: On the complexity of distributed graph coloring with local minimality constraints. Networks (to appear, 2009)

18. Gavoille, C., Klasing, R., Kosowski, A., Navarra, A.: Brief announcement: On the complexity of distributed greedy coloring. In: Pelc, A. (ed.) DISC 2007. LNCS, vol. 4731, pp. 482–484. Springer, Heidelberg (2007)

19. Gavoille, C., Kosowski, A., Markiewicz, M.: What can be observed locally? Round-based models for quantum distributed computing. Technical report, arXiv: quant-ph/0903.1133 (2009)

20. Greenberger, D.M., Horne, M.A., Zeilinger, A.: Going beyond Bell's Theorem. In: Bell's Theorem, Quantum Theory, and Conceptions of the Universe, pp. 69–72. Kluwer, Dordrecht (1989)

21. Helm, L.: Brief announcement: Quantum distributed consensus. In: 27th Annual ACM Symposium on Principles of Distributed Computing (PODC), p. 445. ACM Press, New York (2008)

22. Jaeger, G.: Quantum Information. An Overview. Springer, Heidelberg (2007)

23. Kobayashi, H., Matsumoto, K., Tani, S.: Fast exact quantum leader election on anonymous rings. In: 8th Asian Conference on Quantum Information Science (AQIS), August 2008, pp. 157–158 (2008)

24. Kuhn, F., Moscibroda, T., Wattenhofer, R.: What cannot be computed locally! In. In: 23rd Annual ACM Symposium on Principles of Distributed Computing (PODC), pp. 300–309. ACM Press, New York (2004)

25. Linial, N.: Distributive graph algorithms - Global solutions from local data. In: 28th Annual IEEE Symposium on Foundations of Computer Science (FOCS), pp. 331–335. IEEE Computer Society Press, Los Alamitos (1987)

26. Linial, N.: Locality in distributed graphs algorithms. SIAM Journal on Computing 21(1), 193–201 (1992)

27. Lynch, N.: Distributed Algorithms. Morgan Kaufmann Publishers, San Francisco (1997)

28. Naor, M.: A lower bound on probabilistic algorithms for distributive ring coloring. SIAM Journal on Discrete Mathematics 4(3), 409–412 (1991)

29. Naor, M., Stockmeyer, L.: What can be computed locally. SIAM Journal on Computing 24(6), 1259–1277 (1995)
30. Nielsen, M.: Conditions for a class of entanglement transformations. Physical Review Letters 83(2), 436–439 (1999)
31. Nielsen, M., Chuang, I.: Quantum Computation and Quantum Information. Cambridge University Press, Cambridge (2000)
32. Owari, M., Matsumoto, K., Murao, M.: Entanglement convertibility for infinite-dimensional pure bipartite states. Physical Review A 70(5), 1–4 (2004)
33. Pal, S.P., Singh, S.K., Kumar, S.: Multi-partite quantum entanglement versus randomization: Fair and unbiased leader election in networks. Technical report, arXiv: quant-ph/0306195v1 (June 2003)
34. Pan, J.-W., Chen, Z.-B., Żukowski, M., Weinfurter, H., Zeilinger, A.: Multi-photon entanglement and interferometry. Technical report, arXiv: quant-ph/0805.2853v1 (May 2008)
35. Peleg, D.: Proximity-preserving labeling schemes and their applications. In: Widmayer, P., Neyer, G., Eidenbenz, S. (eds.) WG 1999. LNCS, vol. 1665, pp. 30–41. Springer, Heidelberg (1999)
36. Raz, R.: Exponential separation of quantum and classical communication complexity. In: 31st Annual ACM Symposium on the Theory of Computing (STOC), pp. 358–367 (1999)
37. Shor, P.W.: Polynomial-time algorithms for prime factorization and discrete logarithms on a quantum computer. SIAM Journal on Computing 26(5), 1484–1509 (1997)
38. Singh, S.K., Kumar, S., Pal, S.P.: Characterizing the combinatorics of distributed EPR pairs for multi-partite entanglement. Technical report, arXiv: quant-ph/0306049v2 (January 2004)
39. Ta-Shma, A.: Classical versus quantum communication complexity. SIGACT News 30(3), 25–34 (1999)
40. Tani, S., Kobayashi, H., Matsumoto, K.: Exact quantum algorithms for the leader election problem. In: Diekert, V., Durand, B. (eds.) STACS 2005. LNCS, vol. 3404, pp. 581–592. Springer, Heidelberg (2005)
41. Żukowski, M.: On Bell's Theorem, quantum communication, and entanglement detection. In: Foundations of Probability and Physics 5 (August 2008)

At-Most-Once Semantics in Asynchronous Shared Memory*

Sotirios Kentros, Aggelos Kiayias,
Nicolas Nicolaou, and Alexander A. Shvartsman

Computer Science and Engineering, University of Connecticut, Storrs, USA
{skentros,aggelos,nicolas,aas}@engr.uconn.edu

Abstract. At-most-once semantics is one of the standard models for object access in decentralized systems. Accessing an object, such as altering the state of the object by means of direct access, method invocation, or remote procedure call, with at-most-once semantics guarantees that the access is not repeated more-than-once, enabling one to reason about the safety properties of the object. This paper investigates implementations of at-most-once access semantics in a model where a set of such actions is to be performed by a set of failure-prone, asynchronous shared-memory processes. We introduce a definition of the *at-most-once* problem for performing a set of n jobs using m processors and we introduce a notion of efficiency for such protocols, called *effectiveness*, used to classify algorithms. Effectiveness measures the number of jobs safely completed by an implementation, as a function of the overall number of jobs n, the number of participating processes m, and the number of process crashes f in the presence of an adversary. We prove a lower bound of $n - f$ on the effectiveness of any algorithm. We then prove that this lower bound can be matched in the two process setting by presenting two algorithms that offer a tradeoff between time and space complexity. Finally, we generalize our two-process solution in the multi-process setting with a hierarchical algorithm that achieves effectiveness of $n - \log m \cdot o(n)$, coming reasonably close, asymptotically, to the corresponding lower bound.

1   Introduction

The *at-most-once* semantic for object invocation ensures that an operation accessing and altering the state of an object is performed no more than once. This semantic is among the standard semantics for remote procedure calls (RPC) and method invocations and it provides important means for reasoning about the safety of critical applications. Uniprocessor systems may trivially provide solutions for at-most-once semantics by implementing a central schedule for operations. The problem becomes very challenging for autonomous processes in a shared-memory system with concurrent invocations on multiple objects. Although at-most-once semantics have been thoroughly studied in the context of

---

* This work is supported in part by the NSF Awards 0702670 and 0831306. The work of the first author is supported in part by the State Scholarships Foundation - Greece.

I. Keidar (Ed.): DISC 2009, LNCS 5805, pp. 258–273, 2009.

at-most-once message delivery [4, 13, 16, 23] and at-most-once process invocation for RPC [2, 14, 15, 16, 21], finding effective solutions for asynchronous shared-memory multiprocessors, in terms of how many at-most-once invocations can be performed by the cooperating processes, is largely an open problem. This paper brings the attention to the at-most-once problem in multiprocessor settings. We believe that solving this problem using only atomic memory, and without specialized hardware support, such as conditional writing, will provide a useful tool in reasoning about the safety properties of applications developed for a variety of multiprocessor systems, including those not supporting bus-interlocking instructions and multi-core systems.

We explore at-most-once implementations for asynchronous shared-memory processors that are prone to crashes. We model accesses to objects as tasks, where the correctness demands that each task is performed at-most-once. Any processor is able to perform any task and we aim to maximize the total number of performed tasks while preserving the at-most-once semantics. We define the notion of *effectiveness* used to assess the efficiency of solutions for the problem. Effectiveness measures the number of tasks performed using at-most-once semantics as a function of the number of tasks, the number of processors, and the number of crashes. We provide tight lower bounds for effectiveness, and we introduce three algorithms that solve the problem. The first two are formulated for two processors. The third algorithm is stated for an arbitrary number of processors and it uses a two-processor solution as a building block. We present rigorous analyses of the algorithms' work, space complexity, and effectiveness.

Related Work. A wide range of works study at-most-once semantics in a variety of settings. at-most-once message delivery [4, 13, 16, 23] and at-most-once semantics for RPC [2, 14, 15, 16, 21], are two areas that have attracted a lot of attention. Here the problem studied is different from the one we consider. Both in at-most-once message delivery and RPCs, we have two entities (sender/client and receiver/server) that communicate by message passing. Any entity may fail and recover and messages may be delayed or lost. In the first case one wants to guarantee that duplicate messages will not be accepted by the receiver, while in the case of RPCs, one wants to guarantee that the procedure called in the remote server will be invoked at-most-once [22].

Di Crescenzo and Kiayias in [5] demonstrate the use of the semantic in message passing systems for the sake of security. Driven by the fundamental security requirements of *one-time pad* encryption, the authors partition a common random pad among multiple communicating parties. Perfect security can be achieved only if every piece of the pad is used at most once. The authors show how the parties maintain security while maximizing efficiency by applying at-most-once semantics on pad expenditure.

One can also relate the at-most-once problem to the consensus problem [6, 9, 18, 12]; here one can view consensus as an at-most-once distributed decision.

Another related problem is the Write-All problem for the shared memory model [1, 8, 10, 11, 19]. First presented by Kanellakis and Shvartsman [10], the *Write-All* problem is concerned with performing each task at-least-once. We note that solutions to *Write-All* may be adapted to solve at-most-once, provided safeguards are in place to prevent more-than-once invocations.

Finally we note that the at-most-once problem becomes much simpler when shared-memory is supplemented by some type of read-modify-write operations. For example, one can associate a *test-and-set* bit with each task, ensuring that the task is assigned to the only processor that successfully sets the shared bit An efficient implementation can then be easily obtained from a Write-All solution, such as [1, 8, 11, 20]. Thus, in this paper we deal only with the more challenging setting where algorithms use atomic read/write registers.

Contributions. Our goal is to explore the feasibility and efficiency of solutions that satisfy the at-most-once semantic in the shared-memory model with asynchronous processors prone to crash failures. The at-most-once problem is formulated for m processors and n jobs, where any processor can perform any job, provided that no job is performed more-than-once. Note that in such a setting it is impossible to distinguish between a slow and a crashed processor, consequently it is impossible to determine whether a processor delays while performing a job or if it crashes before performing the job. This means that generally some jobs may never be performed. Our contributions are as follows.

(1) We define the *at-most-once* problem and the correctness properties to be satisfied by any solution. We introduce a complexity measure we call *effectiveness*. This measure describes the number of jobs completed (at-most-once) by an implementation, as a function of the overall number of jobs n, the number of processors m, and the number of processor crashes f. (Section 2.)

(2) We present a lower bound for the effectiveness of any at-most-once implementation. In particular, we prove that no at-most-once solution may achieve effectiveness better than $n - f$. (Section 3.)

(3) We provide two algorithms that solve the at-most-once problem for 2 processors. The algorithms use a collision-avoidance approach. The importance of these algorithms is twofold: *a*) they can be used as building blocks to construct general implementations for larger number of processors, and *b*) they achieve optimal effectiveness. The algorithms differ substantially in their space requirements and work complexity, demonstrating the trade-offs between efficiency and space. We analyse work, space, and effectiveness. (Section 4.)

(4) Finally we present a multi-processor algorithm, that employs one of our two-processor algorithms as a building block. We prove the correctness of the algorithm, and we perform rigorous analysis of its effectiveness of $n - \log m \cdot o(n)$, and its work and space complexity. (Section 5.)

The algorithms in this work are motivated by the *Write-All* algorithms from [3, 8], although the problem itself and the correctness criteria are quite different. Our work can be viewed as complementary to [5] that considers a similar problem in message-passing models. Here we use a shared-memory model in a deterministic setting.

Due to lack of space we omit some of the proofs in this manuscript. We encourage the reader to contact the authors for the detailed proofs.

2   Model, Definitions, and Efficiency

We define our model, the at-most-once problem, and measures of efficiency.

2.1   Model and Adversary

We model a multi-processor as m asynchronous, crash-prone processes with unique identifiers from some set $\mathcal{P}$. Shared memory is modeled as a collection of atomic memory cells, where the number of bits in each cell is explicitly defined. We use the *Input/Output Automata* formalism [18, 17] to specify and reason about algorithms; specifically, we use the *asynchronous shared memory automaton* formalization [18, 7]. Each process p is defined in terms of its states $states_p$ and its actions $acts_p$, where each action is of the type *input, output,* or *internal*. A subset $start_p \subseteq states_p$ contains all the start states of p. Each shared variable x takes values from a set V_x, among which there is $init_x$, the initial value of x.

We model an algorithm A as a composition of the automata for each process p. Automaton A consists of a set of states $states(A)$, where each state s contains a state $s_p \in states_p$ for each p, and a value $v \in V_x$ for each shared variable x. Start states $start(A)$ is a subset of $states(A)$, where each state contains a $start_p$ for each p and an $init_x$ for each x. The actions of A, $acts(A)$ consists of actions $\pi \in acts_p$ for each process p. A transition is the modification of the state as a result of an action and is represented by a triple (s, π, s'), where $s, s' \in states(A)$ and $\pi \in acts(A)$. The set of all transitions is denoted by $trans(A)$. Each action in $acts(A)$ is performed by a process, thus for any transition (s, π, s'), s and s' may differ only with respect to the state s_p of process p that invoked π and potentially the value of the shared variable that p interacts with during π. We also use triples $(\{vars_s\}, \pi, \{vars_{s'}\})$, where $vars_s$ and $vars_{s'}$ are subsets of variables in s and s' respectively, as a shorthand to describe transitions without having to specify s and s' completely; here $vars_s$ and $vars_{s'}$ contain only the variables whose value changes as the result of π, plus possibly some other variables of interest.

We say that states s and t in $states(A)$ are *indistinguishable* to process p if: 1) $s_p = t_p$, and 2) the values of all shared variables are the same in s and t. Now, if states s and t are indistinguishable to p and $(s, \pi, s') \in trans(A)$ for $\pi \in acts_p$, then $(t, \pi, t') \in trans(A)$, and s' and t' are also indistinguishable to p.

An *execution* fragment of A is either a finite sequence, $s_0, \pi_1, s_1, \ldots, \pi_r, s_r$, or an infinite sequence, $s_0, \pi_1, s_1, \ldots, \pi_r, s_r, \ldots$, of alternating states and actions, where $(s_k, \pi_{k+1}, s_{k+1}) \in trans(A)$ for any $k \geq 0$. If $s_0 \in start(A)$, then the sequence is called an *execution*. The set of executions of A is *execs(A)*. We say that execution α is *fair*, if α is finite and its last state is a state of A where no locally controlled action is enabled, or α is infinite and every locally controlled action $\pi \in acts(A)$ is performed infinitely many times or there are infinitely many states in α where π is disabled. The set of fair executions of A is *fairexecs(A)*. An execution fragment α' *extends* a finite execution fragment α of A, if α' begins with the last state of α. We let $\alpha \cdot \alpha'$ stand for the execution fragment resulting from concatenating α and α' and removing the (duplicated) first state of α'.

We model process crashes by action $stop_p$ in $acts(A)$ for each process p. If $stop_p$ appears in an execution α then no actions $\pi \in acts_p$ appear in α thereafter. We then say that process p *crashed*. Actions stop_p arrive from some unspecified external environment, called *adversary*. In this work we consider an *omniscient, on-line adversary* [10] that has complete knowledge of the algorithm. The adversary controls asynchrony and crashes. We allow up to $f < m$ crashes. We denote by $fairexecs_f(A)$ all fair executions of A with at most f crashes.

2.2 At-Most-Once Problem, Effectiveness and Complexity

We consider algorithms that perform a set of tasks, called *jobs*. Let A be an algorithm specified for m processes with ids from set $\mathcal{P} = [0 \ldots m-1]$, and with jobs with unique ids from set $\mathcal{J} = [0 \ldots n-1]$. We assume that there are at least as many jobs as there are processes, i.e., $n \geq m$. We model the performance of job j by process p by means of action $\text{do}_{p,j}$. For a sequence β, we let $len(\beta)$ denote its length, and we let $\beta|_\pi$ denote the sequence of elements π occurring in β. Then for an execution α, $len\left(\alpha|_{\text{do}_{p,j}}\right)$ is the number of times process p performs job j. Now we define the number of jobs performed in an execution.

Definition 1. *For execution α we denote by $J_\alpha = \{j \in \mathcal{J} \mid \text{do}_{p,j}$ occurs in α for some $p \in \mathcal{P}\}$. The total number of jobs performed in α is defined to be $Do(\alpha) = |J_\alpha|$.*

We next define the *at-most-once* problem.

Definition 2. *Algorithm A solves the at-most-once problem if for each execution α of A we have $\forall j \in \mathcal{J} : \sum_{p \in \mathcal{P}} len\left(\alpha|_{\text{do}_{p,j}}\right) \leq 1$. We call any such execution α an AO-execution (at-most-once execution).*

Measures of Efficiency. We analyze our algorithms in terms of three complexity measures: *effectiveness*, *work*, and *space*. Effectiveness counts the number of jobs performed by an algorithm in the worst case.

Definition 3. *The **effectiveness** of algorithm A is: $E_A(n,m,f) = \min_{\alpha \in fairexecs_f(A)}(Do(\alpha))$, where m is the number of processes, n is the number of jobs, and f is the number of crashes.*

A trivial algorithm can solve the at-most-once problem by splitting the n jobs in groups of size $\frac{n}{m}$ and assigning one group to each process. Such a solution has effectiveness $E(n,m,f) = (m-f) \cdot \frac{n}{m}$ (consider an execution where f processes fail at the beginning of the execution). Thus our goal is to construct algorithms that achieve higher effectiveness.

Work complexity measures the efficiency of an algorithm in terms of the total number of memory accesses.

Definition 4. *The **work** of algorithm A, denoted by W_A, is the worst case total number of bits accessed in all memory reads and writes in any execution of A.*

Space complexity measures the memory space used by the algorithm.

Definition 5. *The **space** of algorithm A is the total number of bits in shared and internal variables used by the processes of A.*

3   Lower Bound

We show that any algorithm that solves the at-most-once problem in the presence of up to f crashes has effectiveness $E \leq n - f$. While the proof is subtle, the result itself is intuitive, based on the observation that one cannot distinguish a crashed process from a slow one. If an algorithm assigns job j to process p, and the process crashes, the algorithm is unable to revoke the job and assign it to another process, since process p may simply be slow and it may ultimately perform job j, violating at-most-once semantics.

Recall that in our setting we have at least as many jobs as processes ($n \geq m > f$). (The case where $n \leq m$ is less interesting and for this reason is not presented in this paper.) For our proofs we consider only algorithms that satisfy Condition 1 below requiring that the algorithm is able to perform at least one job. Also let us denote by $F_\alpha = \{p \mid \mathsf{stop}_p \text{ occurs in } \alpha\}$ the set of crashed processes in execution α.

Condition 1. *For all infinite executions α of A, $Do(\alpha) \geq 1$ and for all finite executions α of A, there exists an execution fragment α', s.t. $\alpha \cdot \alpha' \in execs(A)$ and $Do(\alpha \cdot \alpha') \geq 1$.*

We proceed with a lemma, which shows that one may construct two executions that contain f failures and their states are indistinguishable to all correct processes, for algorithms that solve the at-most-once problem. Moreover we show that exactly f jobs are performed in the first execution, while no jobs are performed in the second one. Then we use these executions to prove the main theorem of this section, which shows that the second execution we construct from the lemma, cannot be extended to perform more than $n - f$ tasks. This implies that the effectiveness of any algorithm that solves the at-most-once problem is at most $n - f$.

Lemma 1. *If algorithm A solves the at-most-once problem in the presence of $f < m$ crashes and Condition 1 holds, then there exist finite executions $\alpha_1, \alpha_2 \in execs(A)$, s.t. $F_{\alpha_1} = F_{\alpha_2}$, $|F_{\alpha_1}| = |F_{\alpha_2}| = f$, $Do(\alpha_1) = f$, $Do(\alpha_2) = 0$, and the final states of α_1 and α_2 are indistinguishable for all processes in $\mathcal{P} - F_{\alpha_1}$.*

Proof. We prove the lemma by induction on the number of crashes f.

Base case: First we find execution α s.t. $Do(\alpha) \geq 1$ and $F_\alpha = \emptyset$. Such an execution exists by Condition 1 and the fact that crashes are determined by the adversary. Let us consider the first do event in α. Let $\mathsf{do}_{p,j}$ be that event, and let s_1 and s_2 be the states in α before and after $\mathsf{do}_{p,j}$. Since $\mathsf{do}_{p,j}$ does not change shared memory, s_1 and s_2 differ only in the state of process p and thus are indistinguishable for all processes in $\mathcal{P} - \{p\}$. Let $\alpha' = \alpha_0 \cdot (s_1, \mathsf{do}_{p,j}, s_2)$ be the prefix of α up to event $\mathsf{do}_{p,j}$. Clearly $\alpha' \in execs(A)$. We construct the executions $\alpha_1 = \alpha_0 \cdot (s_1, \mathsf{do}_{p,j}, s_2, \mathsf{stop}_p, s'_2)$ and $\alpha_2 = \alpha_0 \cdot (s_1, \mathsf{stop}_p, s'_1)$. These executions are finite, and since the crashes are controlled by the adversary $\alpha_1, \alpha_2 \in execs(A)$. Moreover $F_{\alpha_1} = F_{\alpha_2} = \{p\}$ and $Do(\alpha_1) = 1$, $Do(\alpha_2) = 0$. Since stop_p affects only the state of p, s_1, s'_1, s_2, s'_2 are indistinguishable for all processes in $\mathcal{P} - \{p\}$.

Inductive step: For $k < f$ assume that there exist finite executions $\alpha_1, \alpha_2 \in execs(A)$, s.t. $F_{\alpha_1} = F_{\alpha_2}$, $|F_{\alpha_1}| = |F_{\alpha_2}| = k$, $Do(\alpha_1) = k$, $Do(\alpha_2) = 0$ and the final states of α_1 and α_2 are indistinguishable for all processes in $\mathcal{P} - F_{\alpha_1}$. We next construct the needed executions for $k + 1$ failures.

We first take α_2. From Condition 1 there exists execution fragment α that has no crashes s.t. $\alpha_2 \cdot \alpha \in execs(A)$ and $Do(\alpha_2 \cdot \alpha) \geq 1$. Since $Do(\alpha_2) = 0$ only α has do events. Moreover since $\alpha_2 \cdot \alpha \in execs(A)$, α has only actions from processes in $\mathcal{P} - F_{\alpha_2}$. Let $\mathsf{do}_{p,j}$ be the first do event in α, where $p \in \mathcal{P} - F_{\alpha_2}$ and $j \in \mathcal{J}$, and let s_1, s_2 be the states in α before and after $\mathsf{do}_{p,j}$. Clearly s_1 and s_2 are indistinguishable for all processes in $\mathcal{P} - \{p\}$. Let us consider the prefix of $\alpha_2 \cdot \alpha$ up to event $\mathsf{do}_{p,j}$ and let us denote this as $\alpha_2 \cdot \alpha_0 \cdot (s_1, \mathsf{do}_{p,j}, s_2)$. We have that $\alpha_2 \cdot \alpha_0 \cdot (s_1, \mathsf{do}_{p,j}, s_2) \in execs(A)$.

Note that since the final states of α_1 and α_2 are indistinguishable for all processes in $\mathcal{P} - F_{\alpha_2}$, and α_0 contains only actions from process in $\mathcal{P} - F_{\alpha_2}$, the actions of the execution fragment α_0 can extend execution α_1 leading to a state s_3 that is indistinguishable for all processes in $\mathcal{P} - F_{\alpha_2}$ from state s_1. This means that there exists execution fragment α_0' that has the same sequence of actions with α_0, s.t. $\alpha_1 \cdot \alpha_0' \cdot (s_3, \mathsf{do}_{p,j}, s_4) \in execs(A)$ and s_1, s_2, s_3, s_4 are indistinguishable for all processes in $\mathcal{P} - (F_{\alpha_1} \cup \{p\})$. Since $\alpha_1 \cdot \alpha_0' \cdot (s_3, \mathsf{do}_{p,j}, s_4) \in execs(A)$, it must hold that $j \notin J_{\alpha_1}$.

We construct the executions $\alpha_2' = \alpha_2 \cdot \alpha_0 \cdot (s_1, \mathsf{stop}_p, s_1')$ and $\alpha_1' = \alpha_1 \cdot \alpha_0' \cdot (s_3, \mathsf{do}_{p,j}, s_4, \mathsf{stop}_p, s_4')$. We have that $\alpha_1', \alpha_2' \in execs(A)$, $F_{\alpha_1'} = F_{\alpha_2'} = F_{\alpha_1} \cup \{p\}$, $|F_{\alpha_1'}| = k + 1$, $Do(\alpha_1') = k + 1$, $Do(\alpha_2') = 0$, states s_1', s_4' are indistinguishable for all processes in $\mathcal{P} - F_{\alpha_1'}$.

Theorem 1. *If algorithm A solves the at-most-once problem in the presence of $f < m$ crashes, then there exists an execution $\alpha \in execs(A)$, s.t. either α is infinite and $Do(\alpha) \leq n - f$, or α is finite, and there exists no execution fragment α', s.t. $\alpha \cdot \alpha' \in execs(A)$ and $Do(\alpha \cdot \alpha') > n - f$.*

Proof. By contradiction. Assume the theorem to be false, with Condition 1 holding. Thus from Lemma 1 we can construct finite executions $\alpha_1, \alpha_2 \in execs(A)$, s.t. $F_{\alpha_1} = F_{\alpha_2}$, $|F_{\alpha_1}| = |F_{\alpha_2}| = f$, $Do(\alpha_1) = f$, $Do(\alpha_2) = 0$ and the final states of α_1 and α_2 are indistinguishable for all processes in $\mathcal{P} - F_{\alpha_1}$. Also from the assumption, there exists execution fragment α' s.t. $\alpha_2 \cdot \alpha' \in execs(A)$ and $Do(\alpha_2 \cdot \alpha') > n - f$. Since $Do(\alpha_2) = 0$, it must be that $Do(\alpha') > n - f$. Clearly α' has only actions for processes in $\mathcal{P} - F_{\alpha_2} = \mathcal{P} - F_{\alpha_1}$. Because the final states of α_1 and α_2 are indistinguishable for all processes in $\mathcal{P} - F_{\alpha_1}$ the sequence of actions in α' can extend α_1 as well. This means that there exists execution fragment α'' that has exactly the same actions as α' s.t. $Do(\alpha'') > n - f$ and $\alpha_1 \cdot \alpha'' \in execs(A)$. But $Do(\alpha_1) = f$ and $J_{\alpha_1}, J_{\alpha''} \subseteq \mathcal{J}$. Since $n = |\mathcal{J}|$ it follows by the pigeonhole principle that $J_{\alpha_1} \cap J_{\alpha''} \neq \emptyset$ and thus $\alpha_1 \cdot \alpha''$ is not an AO-execution, a contradiction.

The main result follows as a corollary to the theorem.

Corollary 1. *For all algorithms A that solve the at-most-once problem with m processes and $n \geq m$ jobs in the presence of $f < m$ crashes it holds that $E_A(n, m, f) \leq n - f$.*

4   Two Process Algorithms for At-Most-Once Problem

We present algorithms for the at-most-once problem that use a collision-avoidance approach. First we give 2-process algorithms: $AO_{2,n}$ that uses n 1-bit shared memory variables, and $AO'_{2,n}$ that uses two shared memory variables of $\log n$ bits, thus achieving lower space complexity. Both algorithms achieve optimal effectiveness. The two-process algorithms can be used as building blocks to construct algorithms for larger numbers of processes. Here we use algorithm $AO_{2,n}$ to construct an m-process algorithm for the at-most-once problem.

4.1   Algorithm $AO_{2,n}$

The algorithm, given in Fig. 1, solves the at-most-once problem for n jobs, using two processes, numbered 0 and 1, and n 1-bit shared variables. The main idea is to have the processes move towards each other, with process 0 performing jobs in the ascending order, and process 1 in the descending order. The processes avoid a *collision*, i.e., doing a job twice, by adopting a *"look ahead decide for the current"* (LA-DC) approach.

The algorithm uses n shared bit variables $x_0, \ldots, x_{n-1}$ as a bookkeeping mechanism to record progress. Initially all shared variables are set to 0. If process p performs job j using action $do_{p,j}$, then $status_p$ variable is changed to *set*. This enables action set_p that in turn sets the value of x_j to 1. The process decides whether a job can be performed in action $check_p$. Using the LA-DC approach, before a process performs job j, it decides that it is safe to do so, by checking the shared variable associated with the next job in its path, that is x_{j+1} for process 0 and x_{j-1} for process 1. If x_{j+1} (resp. x_{j-1}) is 0 then process 0 (resp. 1) proceeds to perform j; otherwise the status of the process is assigned the value *end*, and we say that the process *terminates*. The key idea is that since x_{j+1} (resp. x_{j-1}) is 0 then the competing process 1 (resp. process 0), did not yet perform the task $j + 1$ (resp. $j - 1$). Hence it cannot be performing j and collision is avoided.

To show correctness we first prove that if $cur_0 = k$ for some $k > 0$, then all shared variables "before" x_k are set to 1, and respectively that if $cur_1 = k$, then all shared variables "after" x_k are set to 1.

Lemma 2. *For any execution α of $AO_{2,n}$ and for any state s in α such that $s.cur_0 = k$ and $s.cur_1 = k'$ for $1 \leq k \leq k' \leq n - 2$, then for $i \in \{0, ..., k - 1\} \cup \{k' + 1, ..., n - 1\}$, $s.x_i = 1$, and actions $do_{*,i}$ precede s in α.*

Using Lemma 2 we prove that $AO_{2,n}$ solves the at-most-once problem.

Theorem 2. *Algorithm $AO_{2,n}$ solves the at-most-once problem.*

Shared Variables: $\mathcal{X} = \{x_0, \ldots, x_{n-1}\}$, boolean, initially all 0

Signature:

Input:	Output:	Internal:
$stop_p$, $p \in \{0,1\}$	$do_{p,j}$, $p \in \{0,1\}$, $j \in \mathcal{J}$	$next_p$, $p \in \{0,1\}$
		Read: $check_p$, $p \in \{0,1\}$
State:		Write: set_p, $p \in \{0,1\}$

$status_p \in \{check, set, do, done, end, stopped\}$, initially $check$
$cur_p \in \{0, \ldots, n-1\}$, initially $cur_0 = 0$ and $cur_1 = n-1$
$step_p \in \{-1, 1\}$, initially $step_0 = 1$ and $step_1 = -1$

Transitions of process p:

Internal Read $check_p$
Precondition:
  $status_p = check$
Effect:
  if $(cur_p + step_p) \geq 0$ AND
  $(cur_p + step_p) \leq n-1$
  then
    if $x_{cur_p + step_p} = 0$
    then $status_p \leftarrow do$
    else $status_p \leftarrow end$
  else
    $status_p \leftarrow end$

Internal $next_p$
Precondition:
  $status_p = done$
Effect:
  $cur_p \leftarrow cur_p + step_p$
  $status_p \leftarrow check$

Internal Write set_p
Precondition:
  $status_p = set$
Effect:
  $x_{cur_p} \leftarrow 1$
  $status_p \leftarrow done$

Output $do_{p,j}$
Precondition:
  $status_p = do$
  $cur_p = j$
Effect:
  $status_p \leftarrow set$

Input $stop_p$
Effect:
  $status_p \leftarrow stopped$

Fig. 1. Algorithm $\text{AO}_{2,n}$: Shared Variables, Signature, States and Transitions

4.2   Algorithm $\text{AO}'_{2,n}$

This algorithm, also uses the LA-DC idea. The difference is that we use two integer shared variables, x_{left} and x_{right}, each of $\log n$ bits, that serve as pointers to the progress of each process. Initially x_{left} and x_{right} are set to 0 and $n-1$ respectively, and thereafter each time process 0 or 1 performs a job with action $do_{*,*}$, x_{left} is incremented or x_{right} is decremented respectively at event set. The decision (made in action $check$) on whether it is safe to perform a job is based on the differences $x_{right} - cur_0$ and $cur_1 - x_{left}$ for processes 0 and 1 respectively. If the difference is greater than 1, then it is safe to perform the job. With similar arguments as in Theorem 2 the result follows.

Theorem 3. *Algorithm* $\text{AO}'_{2,n}$ *solves the at-most-once problem.*

4.3   Effectiveness, Work and Space Complexity

We now present the efficiency results for both algorithms.

Effectiveness. We show that algorithms $\text{AO}_{2,n}$ and $\text{AO}'_{2,n}$ perform $n-1$ jobs in the presence of at most one stopping failure (optimal given Corollary 1).

Theorem 4. *The effectiveness of* $\text{AO}_{2,n}$ *with* $f < 2$ *is* $E_{\text{AO}_{2,n}}(n, 2, f) = n - 1$.

Theorem 5. *The effectiveness of* $\text{AO}'_{2,n}$ *with* $f < 2$ *is* $E_{\text{AO}'_{2,n}}(n, 2, f) = n - 1$.

Work and Space: Next we asses the work and space complexity of algorithms $\text{AO}_{2,n}$ and $\text{AO}'_{2,n}$. Recall that algorithm $\text{AO}_{2,n}$ uses single bit shared variables and $\text{AO}'_{2,n}$ uses shared variables of $\log n$ bits.

Theorem 6. *Algorithm* $\text{AO}_{2,n}$ *has work* $2(n+1)$ *and space* $n+2\log n+8$ *bits.*

Theorem 7. *Algorithm* $\text{AO}'_{2,n}$ *has work* $2(n+1)\log n$ *and space* $4\log n+10$ *bits.*

5 Multiprocess Solution for the At-Most-Once problem

We now present m-process algorithm $\text{AO}_{m,n}$, given in Fig. 2, where $m = 2^h$, and the number of jobs is $n = k^h$ (non-powers are handled using standard padding techniques). The algorithm is a hierarchical generalization of algorithm $\text{AO}_{2,n}$. It uses an abstract full k-ary tree of h levels to keep track of progress and guarantee at-most-once semantics. All processes start at the root of the tree at level 0. At each node λ at level μ processes are split in two groups according to their process identifiers and look for subtrees with jobs that are safe to perform in the children of node λ. Thus at each node λ we can see the processes as two groups, group 0 and group 1, solving a sub-problem with k groups of jobs (the subtrees rooted at the children of node λ) using the approach of algorithm $\text{AO}_{2,n}$. Group 0 starts from the leftmost child of node λ and moves to the right, while group 1 starts from the rightmost child and moves to the left. Both groups use the LA-DC approach to define whether it is safe to perform a group of jobs (sub-tree rooted at a child of node λ).

We store the tree on a shared memory array by associating each node with a shared variable. Variable x_0 is associated with the root at level 0, $x_1, \ldots, x_k$ with the nodes at level 1, $x_{k+1}, \ldots, x_{k^2}$ with the nodes at level 2, and so on. In general the nodes at level $\mu \in [1 \ldots h]$ are associated with the shared variables $x_{u_\mu}, \ldots, x_{u_\mu + k^\mu - 1}$, where $u_\mu = 1 + k + k^2 + k^3 + \ldots + k^{\mu-1}$. The tree has a total of $v = u_{h+1}$ nodes. We denote by node λ the node associated with the shared variable x_λ, that has children associated with $x_{\lambda \cdot k+1}, \ldots, x_{\lambda \cdot k+k}$ and a parent associated with $x_{\lfloor \frac{\lambda-1}{k} \rfloor}$. Node $\lambda \in [0 \ldots v-1]$ is at level $\mu = \lfloor \log_k (\lambda \cdot (k-1) + 1) \rfloor$. Finally, job j is associated with leaf $x_{u_h + j}$. Next we present $\text{AO}_{m,n}$ in more detail.

Internal Variables of process p

$status_p \in \{check, set, up, down, do, done, end, stopped\}$ records the status of process p and defines its next action as follows: $down$–p can move to the children of its current node, up–p finished the current level and can move one level higher, set–p can set the shared variable associated with its current node to 1, $check$–p has to check whether it is safe to work at the current node, do–p is at a leaf and can perform the associated job, $done$–p finished working at the current node and can move to the next, end–p terminated (it is not safe for p to work on the tree), $stopped$–p crashed. All processes start at node 0, with $status_p = down$.

$pid_p[0 \ldots h]$ is a binary expansion of p into $h+1$ bits. Note that $p \in [0, 2^h - 1]$ and thus $\forall p \in \mathcal{P}, pid_p[0] = 0$.

$cur_p \in \{0, \ldots, v-1\}$ marks the node at which process p is positioned.

$left_p, right_p \in \{0, \ldots, v-1\}$ keeps the leftmost and rightmost siblings of the current node.

$lvl_p \in \{0, \ldots, h\}$ stores the level μ of the current node.

$step_p \in \{-1, 1\}$ tracks of whether process p is moving from right to left or left to right at the current level.

Actions of process p

down$_p$: Process p moves one level down. If a leaf is reached, it sets $status_p = do$ in order for the job associated with the leaf to be performed. If p is at an internal node, it checks whether $pid_p[lvl_p]$ is 0 or 1. If it is 0, then p moves to the leftmost child of node cur_p, otherwise it moves to the rightmost child. Process p sets lvl_p, cur_p, $left_p$, $right_p$ and $step_p$ accordingly. The status of p remains *down*.

check$_p$: If p works left-to-right and cur_p is the rightmost child of its parent, it sets $status_p = up$. Similarly if p works right-to-left and cur_p is the leftmost child of its parent, it sets $status_p = up$. Otherwise, p performs a look-ahead read in shared memory to determine if it is safe to work on the subtree rooted at node cur_p. If the shared variable associated with the next node ($cur_p + step_p$) is 0, it is safe to work on the subtree of node cur_p and thus sets $status_p = down$. Otherwise it sets $status_p = up$.

up$_p$: Process p moves one level up. If it is at level 1 (only root is above), it sets $status_p = end$ and terminates. If by moving up an internal node is reached, p updates its internal variables accordingly by checking the proper bit of its pid_p variable, and sets $status_p = set$.

set$_p$: Process p writes 1 to the shared variable associated with the node cur_p and sets $status_p = done$.

next$_p$: Process p moves to the next node (left or right, per value of $step_p$), and sets $status_p = check$.

do$_{p,j}$: Process p preforms job j. Then p sets $status_p = set$.

stop$_p$: Process p crashes by setting $status_p = stopped$.

Correctness. We show that algorithm $\text{AO}_{m,n}$ solves the at-most-once problem. First we prove that at any internal node λ at level μ, either only processes with $pid_p[\mu] = 0$, or only processes with $pid_p[\mu] = 1$ enter the subtree rooted at λ.

Lemma 3. *For any execution α of algorithm $\text{AO}_{m,n}$ if there exist states s, s' in α and processes $p, q \in \mathcal{P}$ s.t. $\left\lfloor \frac{s.cur_p - 1}{k} \right\rfloor = \left\lfloor \frac{s'.cur_q - 1}{k} \right\rfloor = \lambda$, for some node λ at level μ, then $pid_p[\mu] = pid_q[\mu]$.*

Proof. For node λ at level μ, if it is the leftmost child of its parent, then from the first if clause of action check$_p$, only processes with $pid_p[\mu] = 0$ may enter the subtree rooted at λ. Similarly if node λ is the rightmost child, only processes with $pid_p[\mu] = 1$ may enter the subtree rooted at λ. If node λ is between the leftmost and rightmost children of its parent $(\lambda \in [\lfloor \frac{\lambda-1}{k} \rfloor \cdot k + 2 \ldots \lfloor \frac{\lambda-1}{k} \rfloor \cdot k + k - 1])$, then processes with $pid_p[\mu] = 0$ will approach it from the left, while processes with $pid_p[\mu] = 1$ will approach it from the right. In order to get a contradiction let us assume that there exists execution α that has

Shared Variables: $\mathcal{X} = \{x_0, \ldots, x_{v-1}\}$, x_i boolean initially 0

Signature:

Input:	Output:	Internal:		
$stop_p$, $p \in \mathcal{P}$	$do_{p,j}$, $p \in \mathcal{P}$, $j \in \mathcal{J}$	$next_p$, $p \in \mathcal{P}$	*Read:*	$check_p$, $p \in \mathcal{P}$
		up_p, $p \in \mathcal{P}$	*Write:*	set_p, $p \in \mathcal{P}$
		$down_p$, $p \in \mathcal{P}$		

State:

$status_p \in \{check, set, up, down, do, done, end, stopped\}$, initially $down$

$pid_p[0 \ldots h]$, where $pid_p[i] = \left\lfloor \frac{p}{2^{h-i}} \right\rfloor$ mod 2 (the binary expansion of p to $h + 1$ bits)

$cur_p \in \{0, \ldots, v - 1\}$, initially 0 $lvl_p \in \{0, \ldots, h\}$, initially 0

$left_p \in \{0, \ldots, v - 1\}$, initially 0 $step_p \in \{-1, 1\}$, initially undefined

$right_p \in \{0, \ldots, v - 1\}$, initially 0

Transitions of process p:

Input $stop_p$
Effect:
  $status_p \leftarrow stopped$

Internal Read $check_p$
Precondition:
  $status_p = check$
Effect:
  if $(cur_p + step_p) \geq left_p$
  AND $(cur_p + step_p) \leq right_p$
  then
    if $x_{cur_p + step_p} = 0$
    then
      $status_p \leftarrow down$
    else $status_p \leftarrow up$
  else
    $status_p \leftarrow up$

Internal $next_p$
Precondition:
  $status_p = done$
Effect:
  $cur_p \leftarrow cur_p + step_p$
  $status_p \leftarrow check$

Internal up_p
Precondition:
  $status_p = up$
Effect:
  if $lvl_p = 1$ **then**
    $status_p \leftarrow end$
  else
    $lvl_p \leftarrow lvl_p - 1$
    $cur_p \leftarrow \left\lfloor \frac{cur_p - 1}{k} \right\rfloor$
    $left_p \leftarrow \left\lfloor \frac{cur_p - 1}{k} \right\rfloor \cdot k + 1$
    $right_p \leftarrow \left\lfloor \frac{cur_p - 1}{k} \right\rfloor \cdot k + k$
    if $pid_p[lvl_p] = 0$ **then**
      $step_p \leftarrow 1$
    else
      $step_p \leftarrow -1$
    $status_p \leftarrow set$

Internal Write set_p
Precondition:
  $status_p = set$
Effect:
  $x_{cur_p} \leftarrow 1$
  $status_p \leftarrow done$

Internal $down_p$
Precondition:
  $status_p = down$
Effect:
  if $lvl_p = h$ **then**
    $status_p \leftarrow do$
  else
    $lvl_p \leftarrow lvl_p + 1$
    $left_p \leftarrow cur_p \cdot k + 1$
    $right_p \leftarrow cur_p \cdot k + k$
    if $pid_{lvl_p} = 0$ **then**
      $cur_p \leftarrow left_p$
      $step_p \leftarrow 1$
    else
      $cur_p \leftarrow right_p$
      $step_p \leftarrow -1$

Output $do_{p,j}$
Precondition:
  $status_p = do$
  $cur_p = u_h + j$
Effect:
  $status_p \leftarrow set$

Fig. 2. Algorithm $\text{AO}_{m,n}$: Shared Variables, Signature, States and Transitions

states s, s' and processes p, q with $pid_p[\mu] = 0$ and $pid_q[\mu] = 1$, s.t. $\left\lfloor \frac{s.cur_p - 1}{k} \right\rfloor = \left\lfloor \frac{s'.cur_q - 1}{k} \right\rfloor = \lambda$. This means that both processes have entered the subtree rooted at node λ. For this to happen, there exist in α transitions $(\{cur_p = \lambda, status_p = check\}, check_p, \{cur_p = \lambda, status_p = down\})$ and $(\{cur_q = \lambda, status_q = check\}, check_q, \{cur_q = \lambda, status_q = down\})$, that precede s and s' respectively. Recall that p moves left-to-right and q right-to-left, and before moving to a new node at a level, they set the shared variable associated with the previous node to 1. Hence it follows that either $x_{\lambda+1} = 1$ when action $check_p$ took place or $x_{\lambda-1} = 1$ when action $check_q$ took place. If the first case is true, then the state of p becomes $\{cur_p = \lambda, status_p = up\}$ preventing p from entering the subtree rooted at λ. Otherwise the state of q becomes $\{cur_q = \lambda, status_q = up\}$ and q never enters the subtree rooted at λ. So it cannot be the case that both process p and q entered the subtree rooted at node λ in α and that completes the proof.

Lemma 4. *For any execution α of algorithm* $\text{AO}_{m,n}$ *if there exist states s, s' in α and processes $p, q \in \mathcal{P}$ s.t.* $\left\lfloor \frac{s.cur_p - 1}{k} \right\rfloor = \left\lfloor \frac{s'.cur_q - 1}{k} \right\rfloor = \lambda$, *for some node λ at level μ, then $pid_p[0 \ldots \mu] = pid_q[0 \ldots \mu]$.*

Proof. We prove this by induction on the level μ of node λ.

Base Case: Here we consider level $\mu = 0$, meaning that all processes that reach the children of the root (node 0) have the same $pid_*[0]$ bit. This holds since $\forall p \in \mathcal{P}, pid_p[0] = 0$. Thus for any execution α of $\text{AO}_{m,n}$, if there exists state s in α s.t. $\left\lfloor \frac{s.cur_p - 1}{k} \right\rfloor = 0$ for some process $p \in \mathcal{P}$, $pid_p[0] = 0$.

Induction Hypothesis: Assume that for any execution α if there exist states s, s' and processes p, q s.t. $\lfloor \frac{s.cur_p - 1}{k} \rfloor = \lfloor \frac{s'.cur_q - 1}{k} \rfloor = \lambda$, for all nodes $\lambda \in [u_\mu \ldots u_\mu + k^\mu - 1]$ at level μ, then $pid_p[0...\mu] = pid_q[0...\mu]$.

Induction Step: By Lemma 3 we show that $\forall \lambda \in [u_{\mu+1} \ldots u_{\mu+1} + k^{\mu+1} - 1]$ at level $\mu + 1$, for any execution α, if there exist states s, s' and processes p, q s.t. $\lfloor \frac{s.cur_p - 1}{k} \rfloor = \lfloor \frac{s'.cur_q - 1}{k} \rfloor = \lambda$, then $pid_p[0 \ldots \mu + 1] = pid_q[0 \ldots \mu + 1]$.

From Lemma 4 we get Corollary 2 that says, that in any execution α of $\text{AO}_{m,n}$, only one process p, if any, may reach the decision to perform job j associated with leaf $u_\mu + j$. This decision is reflected in α by a state s, where $s.cur_p = u_\mu + j, s.status_p = do$.

Corollary 2. *For any execution α of algorithm* $\text{AO}_{m,n}$ *if there exist states s, s' and processes p, q s.t. $s.cur_p = \lambda, s.status_p = do$ and $s'.cur_q = \lambda, s'.status_p = do$, for some leaf $\lambda \in [u_h \ldots u_h + k^h - 1]$, then $p = q$.*

Theorem 8. *Algorithm* $\text{AO}_{m,n}$ *solves the at-most-once problem.*

Work and Space: Next we assess work and space of algorithm $\text{AO}_{m,n}$. According to the algorithm specification, only the actions check_p and set_p perform memory accesses, and every time they do so, they access exactly one bit.

Theorem 9. *The work complexity of algorithm* $\text{AO}_{m,n}$ *is $O(n + m \log m)$.*

Proof. We observe that for each subtree rooted at an internal node λ at level μ we have a *sub-instance* of the problem for $k^{h-\mu}$ jobs and $2^{h-\mu}$ processes. All processes of such sub-instance have the same prefix at the first μ bits of their pid from Lemma 4. Let W_μ be an upper bound on work of the sub-instance. Now we consider the first level of the subtree. Processes are split in groups 0 and 1 (with $2^{h-(\mu+1)}$ processes each), according to the value of their $pid_*[\mu+1]$. Group 0 starts at the leftmost child, group 1 at the rightmost child, and they move towards each other. From Lemma 4 we have that only one of the groups, if any, will continue to the sub-instance of the next level, thus we have at most k sub-instances derived at level $\mu + 1$. From algorithm $\text{AO}_{m,n}$, we have that before a process enters a node, it does a look ahead memory read, and when it leaves a node, it sets the shared variable associated with the node to 1. This means that we have a total of $k + 2$ reads and k writes from the two groups. Since each group has $2^{h-(\mu+1)}$ processes, we get $(k + 2) \cdot 2^{h-(\mu+1)}$ reads and $k \cdot 2^{h-(\mu+1)}$ writes. From the above discussion we have the following recurrence relation: $W_\mu = k \cdot W_{\mu+1} + (2k + 2) \cdot 2^{h-(\mu+1)}$.

Also for level h (k jobs and 2 processes), we have $k + 2$ reads and k writes by Theorem 6, thus: $W_h = 2k + 2$. Combining the above we get:

$W_0 = k \cdot W_1 + (2k + 2) \cdot 2^{h-1} = (2k + 2) \cdot 2^{h-1} \cdot \sum_{i=0}^{h-1} \left(\frac{k}{2}\right)^i$.

Case $k = 2$: $(2k + 2) \cdot 2^{h-1} \cdot \sum_{i=0}^{h-1} \left(\frac{k}{2}\right)^i = 6 \cdot 2^{h-1} \cdot h = 5m \log m$

Case $k > 2$: $(2k + 2) \cdot 2^{h-1} \cdot \sum_{i=0}^{h-1} \left(\frac{k}{2}\right)^i = (2k + 2) \cdot 2^{h-1} \cdot \frac{\left(\frac{k}{2}\right)^h - 1}{\frac{k}{2} - 1} = \frac{2k+2}{k-2} \cdot$

$(n - m) \le 8(n-m)$, where the penultimate relation follows form $m = 2^h, n = k^h$.

We conclude that $W_0 = \Theta(n + m \log m)$.

Theorem 10. *The space complexity of algorithm* $\mathrm{AO}_{m,n}$ *is* $\Theta(n + m \log n)$.

Effectiveness: We now assess the effectiveness of algorithm $\mathrm{AO}_{m,n}$.

Theorem 11. *Algorithm* $\mathrm{AO}_{m,n}$ *has effectiveness* $E_{\mathrm{AO}_{m,n}}(n, m, m - 1) = (n^{\frac{1}{\log m}} - 1)^{\log m} = n - \log m \cdot o(n)$.

Proof. We observe that for each subtree rooted at an internal node λ at level μ we have a sub-instance of the problem for $k^{h-\mu}$ jobs and $2^{h-\mu}$ processes. Moreover if we consider only the first level of such a sub-instance, we have to solve a problem of k groups of jobs (with $k^{h-(\mu+1)}$ jobs each) and 2 groups of processes (with $2^{h-(\mu+1)}$ processes each). Furthermore, as we pointed out before, algorithm $\mathrm{AO}_{m,n}$ follows the same principles for solving this instance as algorithm $\mathrm{AO}_{2,n}$. Thus at each level we match the effectiveness of $\mathrm{AO}_{2,n}$ that by Theorem 4 performs $E_{\mathrm{AO}_{2,n}}(k, 2, 1) = k - 1$ jobs. If we go all the way down to level $h = \log_k n$, we have an exact instance of the 2-process problem (Section 4.1) and hence by Theorem 4 it follows that $E_{\mathrm{AO}_{m,n}}(k, 2, 1) = E_{\mathrm{AO}_{2,n}}(k, 2, 1) = k - 1$. From the above we get the following recurrence:

$$E_{\mathrm{AO}_{m,n}}(n, m, m - 1) = (k - 1) \cdot E_{\mathrm{AO}_{m,n}}\left(\frac{n}{k}, \frac{m}{2}, \frac{m}{2} - 1\right) = \cdots =$$
$$= (k - 1)^{h-1} \cdot E_{\mathrm{AO}_{m,n}}\left(\frac{n}{k^{h-1}}, \frac{m}{2^{h-1}}, \frac{m}{2^{h-1}} - 1\right) = (k - 1)^{h-1} \cdot E_{\mathrm{AO}_{m,n}}(k, 2, 1)$$

Thus $E_{\mathrm{AO}_{m,n}}(n, m, m - 1) = (k - 1)^h$.

Finally, we note that since $E_{\mathrm{AO}_{m,n}}(n, m, m - 1) = n - \log m \cdot o(n)$, the effectiveness of the algorithm comes reasonably close, asymptotically in n, to the corresponding lower bound of $n - f$.

6 Conclusions

We examined the implementation of at-most-once semantics in an asynchronous multiprocessor shared memory model. We first defined the problem, proposed a new efficiency measures, we called *effectiveness* and counts the number of jobs performed by a given implementation, and we showed that at-most-once algorithms that tolerate f failures cannot perform more than $n - f$ jobs. Then we devised and analyzed two effectiveness-optimal algorithms for 2 processors using the collision avoidance paradigm, and finally we used those algorithms as building blocks to construct an algorithm for n processors. Our results reveal an effectiveness gap as the number of processes in the system increases. Thus we challenge the discovery of more complex collision detection techniques that would achieve higher effectiveness. Finally we question the existence and efficiency of algorithms that try to implement at-most-once semantics in systems with different means of communication, such as message-passing systems.

References

[1] Anderson, R.J., Woll, H.: Algorithms for the certified write-all problem. SIAM J. Computing 26(5), 1277–1283 (1997)

[2] Birrell, A.D., Nelson, B.J.: Implementing remote procedure calls. ACM Trans. Comput. Syst. 2(1), 39–59 (1984)

[3] Buss, J.F., Kanellakis, P.C., Ragde, P., Shvartsman, A.A.: Parallel algorithms with processor failures and delays. Journal of Algorithms 20(1), 45–86 (1996)

[4] Chaudhuri, S., Coan, B.A., Welch, J.L.: Using adaptive timeouts to achieve at-most-once message delivery. Distrib. Comput. 9(3), 109–117 (1995)

[5] Di Crescenzo, G., Kiayias, A.: Asynchronous perfectly secure communication over one-time pads. In: Caires, L., Italiano, G.F., Monteiro, L., Palamidessi, C., Yung, M. (eds.) ICALP 2005. LNCS, vol. 3580, pp. 216–227. Springer, Heidelberg (2005)

[6] Fischer, M.J., Lynch, N.A., Paterson, M.S.: Impossibility of distributed consensus with one faulty process. J. ACM 32(2), 374–382 (1985)

[7] Goldman, K.J., Lynch, N.A.: Modelling shared state in a shared action model. In: Logic in Computer Science, pp. 450–463 (1990)

[8] Groote, J., Hesselink, W., Mauw, S., Vermeulen, R.: An algorithm for the asynchronous write-all problem based on process collision. Distributed Computing 14(2) (2001)

[9] Herlihy, M.: Wait-free synchronization. ACM Transactions on Programming Languages and Systems 13, 124–149 (1991)

[10] Kanellakis, P.C., Shvartsman, A.A.: Fault-Tolerant Parallel Computaion. Kluwer Academic Publishers, Dordrecht (1997)

[11] Kowalski, D.R., Shvartsman, A.A.: Writing-all deterministically and optimally using a non-trivial number of asynchronous processors. In: Proc. of the 16th annual ACM Symp. on Par. in Alg. and Arch. (SPAA 2004), pp. 311–320. ACM Press, New York (2004)

[12] Lamport, L.: The part-time parliament. ACM Trans. Comput. Syst. 16(2), 133–169 (1998)

[13] Lampson, B.W., Lynch, N.A., S-Andersen, J.F.: Correctness of at-most-once message delivery protocols. In: Proc. of the IFIP TC6/WG6.1 6th International Conference on Formal Description Techniques(FORTE 1993), pp. 385–400 (1994)

[14] Lin, K.-J., Gannon, J.D.: Atomic remote procedure call. IEEE Trans. Softw. Eng. 11(10), 1126–1135 (1985)

[15] Liskov, B.: Distributed programming in argus. Commun. ACM 31(3), 300–312 (1988)

[16] Liskov, B., Shrira, L., Wroclawski, J.: Efficient at-most-once messages based on synchronized clocks. ACM Trans. Comput. Syst. 9(2), 125–142 (1991)
[17] Lynch, N., Tuttle, M.: An introduction to input/output automata. CWI-Quarterly, 219–246 (1989)
[18] Lynch, N.A.: Distributed Algorithms. Morgan Kaufmann Publishers, San Francisco (1996)
[19] Malewicz, G.: A work-optimal deterministic algorithm for the asynchronous certified write-all problem. In: Proc. of the 22nd annual Symp. on Principles of Distributed Computing (PODC 2003), pp. 255–264. ACM Press, New York (2003)
[20] Malewicz, G.: A work-optimal deterministic algorithm for the certified write-all problem with a nontrivial number of asynchronous processors. SIAM J. Comput. 34(4), 993–1024 (2005)
[21] Panzieri, F., Shrivastava, S.: Rajdoot: A remote procedure call mechanism supporting orphan detection and killing. IEEE Transactions on Software Engineering 14(1), 30–37 (1988)
[22] Spector, A.Z.: Performing remote operations efficiently on a local computer network. Commun. ACM 25(4), 246–260 (1982)
[23] Watson, R.W.: The delta-t transport protocol: Features and experience. In: Proc. of the 14th Conf. on Local Computer Networks, pp. 399–407 (1989)

Nonblocking Algorithms and Backward Simulation

Simon Doherty[1] and Mark Moir[2]

[1] Victoria University, Wellington, New Zealand 6140
[2] Sun Microsystems Laboratories, Burlington, MA, 01803

Abstract. Optimistic and nonblocking concurrent algorithms are increasingly finding their way into practical use; an important example is software transactional memory implementations. Such algorithms are notoriously difficult to design and verify as correct, and we believe complete, formal, and machine-checked correctness proofs for such algorithms are critical. We have been studying the use of automated tools such as the PVS theorem proving system to model algorithms and their specifications using formalisms such as I/O automata, and using simulation proof techniques to show the algorithms implement their specifications. While it has been relatively rare in the past, optimistic and nonblocking algorithms often require a special flavour of simulation proof, known as *backward simulation*. In this paper, we present what we believe is by far the most challenging backward simulation proof achieved to date; this proof was developed and completely checked using PVS.

1 Introduction

Concurrent algorithms are notoriously difficult to design correctly, and nonblocking algorithms that make no use of locks even more so. Formal proofs are often too long and complicated to construct or check manually. We and others [1,5] have therefore been exploring the use of automated tools for constructing and checking complete formal proofs for such algorithms. We are particularly interested in being able to do this for complex systems such as transactional memory implementations, which have not received sufficient formal attention to date; it is critically important for these implementations to be correct if they are to deliver on their promise of making concurrent programming substantially easier.

In our work so far, we have modelled both specifications and algorithms using I/O Automata (IOAs) [8], and used *simulation* proofs to prove that the algorithm implements the specification. Simulation proofs come in two flavours: forward and backward. Backward simulations are required when we cannot tell whether an operation has taken effect until after it has done so. While backward simulations have rarely been required in the past, we have found that many nonblocking and optimistic concurrent algorithms require them ([1,4] present verifications of nonblocking algorithms using backward simulation).

For algorithms that require backward simulation, it is common to define an intermediate automaton and prove by forward simulation that the algorithm

I. Keidar (Ed.): DISC 2009, LNCS 5805, pp. 274–288, 2009.

implements the intermediate automaton and by backward simulation that the intermediate automaton implements the specification. Backward simulations are significantly more challenging than forward ones, because they have more complex proof obligations, and require us to think about program execution "backwards", which is less natural than the forward style of thinking to which we are accustomed. Therefore, it is generally desirable to keep the intermediate automaton as close as possible to the specification automaton, thus keeping the part that requires backward simulation very simple.

To our knowledge, in all previous such proofs the intermediate automaton is close to the specification automaton so the backward simulation is almost trivial. For example, in our proof of the optimistic LazyList algorithm [1], we were able to completely automate the backward simulation with a few simple strategies. Almost all previous backward simulations are manual proofs, and the few machine checked ones have generally been simple [11].

In this paper, we describe what we believe is by far the most challenging backward simulation proof completed to date. We developed this proof using the PVS theorem prover, and it is entirely machine checked. The algorithm we proved is a corrected version of the Snark [2] concurrent double-ended queue (deque) algorithm, as presented in [3]. As mentioned in [3], this proof comprises a forward simulation and a backward simulation. We briefly discuss the Snark algorithm and explain why it cannot be proved correct with just a forward simulation. The paper then focuses on the intermediate automaton we defined in order to make the backward simulation as simple as we could, and the backward simulation proof itself; these aspects of our work provide more interesting differences over previous work than the forward simulation proof showing that the corrected Snark algorithm implements the intermediate automaton.

Lamport [7] described his work using the +CAL language and the TLC model checker to identify some of the same bugs in the original Snark algorithm that were revealed by our earlier attempts to prove this algorithm correct [3]. While the automated nature of model checking is appealing, and provides an invaluable tool for quickly discovering bugs and checking putative properties of an algorithm, convincing ourselves that an algorithm is correct using model checking techniques is not as easily automatable. In some specific cases, abstraction theorems have been proved that allow an infinite-state algorithm to be proved correct by exhaustively model checking a finite-state version of it. While these are valuable directions to explore, these abstraction theorems require significant intellectual effort to prove, and apply only to a limited class of algorithms. Furthermore, both the proof of the abstraction theorem and verifying that it applies to a particular algorithm require nontrivial intellectual effort, which in general has not been mechanically checked, leaving significant room for human error. We are therefore motivated to pursue methods for constructing correctness proofs that can be checked mechanically. We do not consider that either approach subsumes the value of the other; these are complementary research directions.

In Section 2 we present background and preliminaries. Section 3 briefly describes salient features of the (corrected) Snark algorithm, explains why it requires a backward simulation, and motivates the construction of the intermediate automaton we used in our proof; this automaton is described in Section 4. In Section 5, we present the simulation relation used in this proof in detail, and describe parts of the proof showing that this relation is indeed a backward simulation relation that implies that the intermediate automaton implements the deque specification. We plan to make our proof scripts available so that interested readers can study our proof in detail and learn from our experiences. We conclude in Section 6.

2　Preliminaries

A deque deq is a triple $(deq.seq, deq.left, deq.right)$ where $deq.seq$ is a function from integers to some set V, and $deq.left$ and $deq.right$ are integers, satisfying the constraint that $deq.left < deq.right$. The value of the deque is the subsequence of values in $deq.seq$ between positions $deq.left$ and $deq.right$, not inclusive. A deque deq is empty, written $empty(deq)$, when $deq.left = deq.right - 1$.

A deque supports *push* and *pop* operations on both sides, specified by the following functions. The *push* function takes as arguments a deque value deq, a side $s \in SIDE = \{left, right\}$ and a value $v \in V$ to be pushed. It returns the deque that is the result of pushing v onto the appropriate side.[1]

$$push(deq, s, v) = \begin{cases} (deq.seq \oplus \{deq.left \mapsto v\}, \\ \qquad deq.left - 1, deq.right) & \text{if } s = left \\ (deq.seq \oplus \{deq.right \mapsto v\}, \\ \qquad deq.left, deq.right + 1) & \text{otherwise} \end{cases}$$

The *pop* function returns a new deque value as well as a *response value* in $V_\perp = V \cup \{\perp\}$ (where $\perp$ is not in V, and indicates that the deque is empty).

$$pop(deq, s) = \begin{cases} (deq, \perp) & \text{if } empty(deq) \\ ((deq.seq, deq.left + 1, deq.right), \\ \qquad deq.seq(deq.left + 1)) & \text{if } s = left \\ ((deq.seq, deq.left, deq.right - 1), \\ \qquad deq.seq(deq.right - 1)) & \text{otherwise} \end{cases}$$

I/O Automata. We briefly describe the simplified IOA model and simulation proofs used in this paper; see [9] for formal details. We omit some structure often seen in definitions of I/O automata, including features relating to the description of liveness properties. Here, we are interested only in safety properties. An *input/output automaton* is a labelled transition system, along with a signature partitioning its actions into external and internal actions. Formally, an IOA A consists of: a set $states(A)$ of states; a nonempty set $start(A) \subseteq states(A)$ of start states; a set $acts(A)$ of actions; a signature, $sig(A) = (external(A), internal(A))$, which partitions $acts(A)$; and a transition relation, $trans(A) \subseteq states(A) \times acts(A) \times states(A)$.

---

[1] $f \oplus \{x \mapsto v\}$ denotes the function that is equal to f on every element of its domain, except at x, which it maps to v.

We describe the states by a collection of state variables, and the transition relation by specifying a *precondition* and *effect* for each action. A precondition is a predicate on states, and an effect is a set of assignments showing only those state variables that change, to be performed as a single atomic action. For states s and s' and action a with precondition pre_a and effect eff_a, the transition (s, a, s') is in $trans(A)$, written $s \xrightarrow{a} s'$, if and only if pre_a holds in s (the *pre-state*) and s' (the *post-state*) is the result of applying eff_a to s.

A *(finite) execution fragment* of A is a sequence of alternating states and actions of A, $\pi = s_0, a_1, s_1, \ldots s_n$, such that $(s_{k-1}, a_k, s_k) \in trans(A)$ for $k \in [1, n]$. An *execution* is an execution fragment with $s_0 \in start(A)$. We write $trace(\pi)$ to denote the sequence of external actions in the execution fragment π. We also write $trace(\alpha)$ to denote the sequence of external actions in the sequence $\alpha \in acts(A)^*$, where $acts(A)^*$ is the set of finite sequences over $acts(A)$. For $\alpha \in acts(A)^*$, we write $s \xrightarrow{\alpha} s'$ to mean that there is an execution fragment beginning with s, ending with s', and containing exactly the actions of α. The set of *behaviours* of an automaton A is the set of traces of its executions: $traces(A) = \{trace(\pi) \mid \pi \text{ is an execution of } A\}$. For an "abstract" automaton A, modelling a specification, and a "concrete" automaton C, modelling an implementation, we say that C *implements* A iff $traces(C) \subseteq traces(A)$: every behaviour of the implementation is allowed by the specification.

One way to prove that C implements A is via *forward simulation* [9]. We consider an arbitrary execution of C and inductively construct an execution of A with the same external actions in the following fashion: Start from the initial state in C's execution, and then for each action in turn, choose a (possibly empty) sequence of actions for A to execute such that (i) the actions chosen constitute a valid execution of A, and (ii) whenever C executes an internal action, the sequence of actions chosen for A has only internal actions, and (iii) whenever C executes an external action, the sequence of actions chosen for A contains that same action, and no other external actions. In this way, we ensure that the constructed execution for A has the same trace as the given execution for C. To facilitate an inductive proof, we define a *simulation relation*, a relation R over states of C and states of A, and require that the initial states of C and A are related by R, and that the states of C and A after each induction step are similarly related by R. R captures our understanding of why C implements A; determining a relation that allows this inductive proof approach is often the most challenging part of performing a forward simulation proof.

This approach will not work if the actions of A that we should choose for some action of C depend on the *future* of the execution. In such cases, we can use a *backward simulation*, which is similar in spirit to a forward simulation, but we start at the *end* of a given execution of C and work backwards towards the initial state, thus allowing us to encode in the simulation relation information about what happens in the "future" of a given step of the given execution. A formal definition appears in Section 5.

The Abstract Automaton. The standard correctness condition for concurrent data structures is *linearisability* [6], which requires that each operation appears

$$\begin{array}{lll}
\textbf{pushInv}_\textbf{p}(\textbf{s},\textbf{v}) & \textbf{doPush}_\textbf{p}(\textbf{v}) & \textbf{pushResp}_\textbf{p} \\
\{pc_p = idle\} & \{pc_p = pushing(s,v)\} & \{pc_p = pushRPc\} \\
pc_p := pushing(s,v) & deq := push(deq,s,v), & pc_p := idle \\
& pc_p := pushRPc &
\end{array}$$

$$\begin{array}{lll}
\textbf{popInv}_\textbf{p}(\textbf{s}) & \textbf{doPop}_\textbf{p} & \textbf{popResp}_\textbf{p}(\textbf{r}) \\
\{pc_p = idle\} & \{pc_p = popping(s)\} & \{pc_p = popRPc(r)\} \\
pc_p := popping(s) & deq := \pi_1(pop(deq,s)), & pc_p := idle \\
& pc_p := & \\
& \quad popRPc(\pi_2(pop(deq,s))) &
\end{array}$$

Fig. 1. The *AbsAut* automaton. The variable p ranges over processes, v ranges over V, r ranges over $V \cup \bot$, and s ranges over $\{left, right\}$. $\pi_1(x)$ denotes the first component of the pair x and $\pi_2(x)$ denotes the second.

to take effect atomically between its invocation and its response. We capture the linearisable traces by using a *canonical automaton* [10] *AbsAut*, which models a set of processes operating on a deque. A *push* operation by process p is modelled by an external invocation action $pushIinv_p(s,v)$ for $s \in \{left, right\}$ and $v \in V$, an external response action $pushResp_p$, and an internal $doPush_p(v)$ action, $v \in V$. Similarly, *pop* operations are modelled by external $popInv_p(s)$ and $popResp_p(r)$ actions ($r \in V_\bot$), and an internal $doPop_p$ action. We use p's *program counter* pc_p to ensure that the "do" action occurs between the invocation and the response.

AbsAut is presented in Figure 1. Preconditions are defined in braces, and effects are defined using the assignment operator ":=". During a "do" action, the operation that p is executing (encoded in pc_p) is applied to the deque, and, in the case of pop operations, the outcome is encoded in pc_p. The intitial states of *AbsAut* are states in which the deque is empty and no operations are in progress: $start(A) = \{ab \mid empty(ab.deq) \land \forall p \bullet pc_p = idle\}$.

3   The Snark Algorithm

The backward simulation proof described in this paper proves that an intermediate automaton *IntAut*, described in the next section, implements *AbsAut*. Thus, the corrected Snark algorithm [3] for which we developed this proof is not directly relevant to this paper, and indeed, other deque algorithms could be proved correct by proving that they implement *IntAut*. Nonetheless, we describe some salient features of Snark, and briefly describe elements of the proof that it implements *IntAut*, in order to motivate the construction of *IntAut*. Further details of the Snark algorithm can be found in [2,3].

Snark represents the deque as a doubly-linked list of nodes, each of which contains a value. Two shared pointers, called *hats* (leftHat and rightHat) indicate the leftmost and rightmost nodes when the deque is nonempty. The "outward" pointers of the leftmost and rightmost deque nodes (e.g., the left pointer of the leftmost deque node) point to *sentinel* nodes, whose inward pointers are self pointers. Figure 2(c) shows a deque containing one value A.

When the deque is empty, `leftHat` points to a node with a left self pointer and `rightHat` points to a node with a right self pointer. These might be the same node or different nodes, so Figures 2(a) and (b) present two representations of the empty deque.

Snark uses the *double-compare-and-swap* (DCAS) synchronisation primitive, a generalisation of the well-known *compare-and-swap* (CAS) operation, that operates on two locations. DCAS allows a process to atomically compare two memory locations to respective "old" values, and to store respective "new" values to them if both comparisons succeed.

As presented in [2,3], the Snark algorithm defines four operations, `pushLeft`, `pushRight`, `popLeft` and `popRight`, that push or pop values from the appropriate side of the deque. Snark uses DCAS for both push and pop operations to atomically modify the relevant hat (`leftHat` for left-side operations, `rightHat` for right-side operations) as well as one of the pointers of the node currently indicated by that hat. For example, `pushRight` changes both the `rightHat` and the right pointer of the node it indicates to point to a newly-allocated node initialised to contain the value being pushed. Similarly, a `popRight` operation modifies the `rightHat` to point to the left neighbour of the node it currently indicates, while changing the left pointer of this node to a self pointer. This removes the rightmost node from the deque and simultaneously transforms it into the new right sentinel. Figure 2(c) shows a single-element deque containing A, and Figure 2(d) shows the deque after the DCAS of a `popRight` operation has removed this node. Note that now `leftHat` points to a node with a left self pointer, and `rightHat` points to a node with a right self pointer. Thus, the deque is empty in this state.

Observe that `leftHat` and the right pointer of the node it indicates are the same in Figures 2(c) and 2(d). Therefore, a `popLeft` operation that was poised

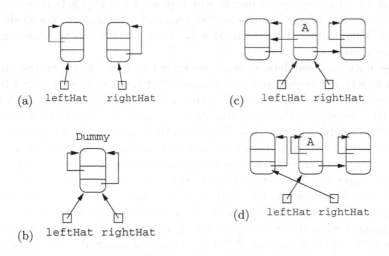

(a) leftHat   rightHat   (c) leftHat rightHat

Dummy

(b) leftHat rightHat   (d) leftHat rightHat

Fig. 2. States of the doubly-linked list

to perform its DCAS in Figure 2(c) can succeed in the state in Figure 2(d), even though the above-described popRight operation has already removed the node containing A. In the original Snark algorithm, some additional checks were used in an attempt to avoid this inconvenient situation. However, as revealed by our initial attempt to prove that algorithm correct, these checks were not sufficient, and it was still possible for two competing pop operations to believe they had removed the same node, albeit via a more complicated sequence of events than the one described above. This allowed incorrect behaviour in which both operations return A.

The corrected Snark algorithm acknowledges that this may happen (and is thus able to simplify the algorithm by eliminating the unsuccessful attempts to avoid it), and introduces an extra step to ensure that only one process successfully returns the value from a node, even if two processes believe they have removed the node from the list. In this step, the processes use CAS to atomically replace the value in the node with a special secured value, which is assumed never to be pushed onto the deque. If this succeeds, then the process has claimed the value and returns it. If it fails, then the failing process knows that another process has already claimed the value. At this point, the failing process could simply retry. However, we show that this process can in fact return "empty" immediately. Showing that this is correct complicates our proof considerably.

Why we need a backward simulation. Consider now how we might attempt to prove that the corrected Snark algorithm implements *AbsAut* using a forward simulation. Once a node has been removed from the deque, another pop operation on the same side can remove the next node from that side and return it. This requires us to consider the pop associated with the first removed node to occur before the removal of the second node. But, because two processes may have removed the first node from the deque and not yet decided which of them will return its value, we cannot decide which process's *doPop* action should be executed in *AbsAut* when the node is first removed: this requires knowledge of the future. This explains why we need a backward simulation to prove Snark implements *AbsAut*.

Because backward simulations work backward in time, when we encounter an action in which a process removes a node from the deque, we can tell from the state whether the process removing the node successfully claims the value (later in the execution). However, if a process thinks it removes a node that has actually already been removed from the other end, we cannot consider its pop operation to occur when it does the removal, as many other operations may have been completed since the node was removed for the first time. In this case, although we know *which* process pops the value, we need to determine *when* the pop can be considered to take effect. It turns out that, even in this case, before executing its DCAS to remove the node from the deque, it reads the relevant hat at a moment when the node it points to is indeed in the deque. Because the value was at the appropriate end of the deque at that moment, we can consider the pop to have occurred then. In essence, every time a pop operation reads the hat when it points to a deque element, it is safe to consider the pop operation to

pushInv$_\mathbf{p}$(s, v)
$\{pc_p = idle\}$
$pc_p := pushing(s, v)$

doPushK$_\mathbf{p}$(k)
$\{pc_p = pushing(s, v) \wedge k \notin used\}$
$pc_p := pushRPc,$
$used := used \cup \{k\},$
$kVal := kVal \oplus \{k \mapsto v\},$
$(left, right) := pushidx(left, right, s),$
$keys := keys \oplus \{idx(left, right, s) \mapsto k\}$

pushResp$_\mathbf{p}$
$\{pc_p = pushRPc\}$
$pc_p := idle$

Fig. 3. The *push* actions of the automaton *IntAut*. The assignment $(left, right) := pushidx(left, right, s)$ subtracts one from *left* or adds one to *right*, depending on the side s. The expression $idx(l, r, s)$ equals $l + 1$ or $r - 1$, depending on the side s.

have occurred at that point, provided the operation subsequently removes the node from the deque (or thinks it has even though another process already has) *and* successfully secures the value from the node. Although we cannot tell if this will happen in the future in a forward simulation proof, we can tell that this is a safe point to consider the pop to occur if does happen.

In the next section we present the intermediate automaton *IntAut*, which allows processes to "observe" that a value it will attempt to remove is at the appropriate end of the deque. When it succeeds in removing a value from the deque (or thinks it does), the point at which it previously observed this value at the appropriate end of the deque is a valid point to consider it to have been removed. Because the proof that *IntAut* implements *AbsAut* is a backward simulation, when we encounter such an observe action, we can determine whether the process executing it successfully removes the observed value in the future, and thus decide whether to consider its pop to have occurred at that point.

4 The Intermediate Automaton

In this section, we describe the intermediate automaton. *IntAut* is presented in Figures 3 and 4. *IntAut* associates each value pushed to the deque with a unique *key*; the *doPushK* action takes a previously unused key, marks it as used, associates the value being pushed with the key, and pushes the key onto the appropriate end of a sequence *keys*, whose domain is specified by the *left* and *right* variables.

The actions related to pop operations are more interesting. When process p invokes a pop operation, pc_p becomes $popping(s)$, where s is the side on which the pop operation is invoked. While in this state, p can execute multiple $observe_p$ actions, which record in key_p the key at the appropriate end of *keys*.

Having observed a key at the appropriate end of the deque, p can execute a *popNonEmpty* action in order to remove that key from (the relevant portion of) *keys* by modifying *left* or *right* as appropriate, provided it is still there (or perhaps is again there). In this case, p records that this key has been popped and that its value is ok to return. Having done so, pc_p becomes *deciding*, so p can

popInv$_p$(s)
$\{pc_p = idle\}$
$pc_p := popping(s)$
$key_p := \bot$

popResp$_p$(r)
$\{pc_p = popRPc(r)\}$
$pc_p := idle$

observe$_p$
$\{pc_p = popping(s) \wedge$
$left < right - 1\}$
$key_p :=$
$\quad keys(idx(left, right, s))$

popEmpty$_p$
$\{pc_p = popping(s) \wedge$
$left = right - 1\}$
$pc_p := popRPc(\bot)$

contend$_p$
$\{pc_p = popping(s) \wedge$
$left = right - 1 \wedge$
$popped(key_p) \wedge$
$key_p \neq \bot\}$
$pc_p := deciding(s)$

popNonEmpty$_p$
$\{pc_p = popping(s) \wedge$
$left < right - 1 \wedge$
$key_p =$
$\quad keys(idx(left, right, s))\}$
$pc_p := deciding(s),$
$valOk := valOk \cup \{key_p\},$
$popped := popped \cup \{key_p\},$
$(left, right) :=$
$\quad popidx(left, right, s)$

secureVal$_p$
$\{pc_p = deciding(s) \wedge$
$key_p \in valOk\}$
$pc_p := popRPc(kVal(key_p))$
$valOk := valOk \setminus \{key_p\}$

loseVal$_p$
$\{pc_p = deciding(s) \wedge$
$key_p \notin valOk\}$
$pc_p := popRPc(\bot)$

Fig. 4. The *pop* actions of the automaton *IntAut*. The assignment $(left, right) := popidx(left, right, s)$ adds one to *left* or subtracts one from *right*, depending on the side.

then "secure" the value associated with the key it popped from *keys*, provided the value is still ok to return (*secureVal* action). In this case, it sets pc_p in preparation for returning that value, and removes the key from the *valOk* set, indicating that it is no longer ok to return this value. Thus only one process can perform a *secureVal* action for a given key.

A process that has observed a key at the appropriate end of *keys* can also attempt to secure the value from it if the process successfully executes a *contend* action when the key sequence is empty. (As for *popNonEmpty*, *contend* sets pc_p to *deciding*.) If p is *deciding*, because it has executed either a *popNonEmpty* action or a *contend* action, and its key is no longer in *valOk* (implying that another process has already secured it), then p can execute a *loseVal* action, in which case it prepares to return $\bot$ from the pop operation. When $pc_p = popping$ and *keys* is empty, p can execute a *popEmpty* action, and then return $\bot$.

5   Verification

We cannot hope to describe all of the details of our proof in the space available. Instead, we explain how backward simulation proofs work, present the backward simulation relation used by our proof, and describe in detail a few proofs steps that illustrate important and interesting aspects of our proof. For readers interested in additional detail, we are making our proof script available[2] and preparing a more detailed description of our proof.

[2] These can be downloaded from http://ecs.victoria.ac.nz/Main/SunVUW/

$$(\forall\, is_0 \in start(IntAut), as \bullet$$
$$R(is, as) \Rightarrow as \in start(AbsAut)) \quad (1)$$

$$(\forall\, is \bullet (\exists\, as \bullet R(is, as))) \quad (2)$$

$$(\forall\, is, is', as', a \bullet$$
$$R(is', as') \wedge is \xrightarrow{a} as' \Rightarrow$$
$$(\exists\, as, \beta \bullet \quad (3)$$
$$R(is, as) \wedge as \xrightarrow{\beta} as' \wedge$$
$$trace(\beta) = trace(\langle a \rangle))$$

Fig. 5. A relation $R \subseteq states(IntAut) \times states(IntAut)$ is a *backward simulation* from *IntAut* to *AbsAut* if these conditions hold, where $is_0 \in start(intaut)$; $as_0 \in start(AbsAut)$; $is, is' \in states(IntAut)$; $as, as' \in states(AbsAut)$; $a \in acts(IntAut)$; $\beta \in acts(AbsAut)^*$

Figure 5 presents the definition of backward simulation, applied to the automata *IntAut* and *AbsAut*. The definition asserts properties of a relation $R \subseteq states(IntAut) \times states(AbsAut)$. The existence of such a relation allows us to inductively construct, for any (finite) execution of *IntAut*, an execution of *AbsAut* with the same trace, as follows. We start from the final state of the execution of *IntAut* (call it *is*) and construct a final state for the abstract execution (call it *as*) such that $R(is, as)$. Property 2 guarantees that this is possible. Then, working backwards along the execution, for each transition $is \xrightarrow{a} is'$ of *IntAut*, we choose 1) a corresponding sequence of actions β and 2) a state *as* of *AbsAut*, satisfying two properties: $as \xrightarrow{\beta} as'$ where as' is the abstract poststate related to is'; and if a is external then β contains the action a and no other external actions. Property 3 guarantees that this is possible. Finally, Property 1 guarantees that when we reach the first transition of the execution, the *AbsAut* state we choose is a start state; thus we have constructed an execution of *AbsAut* with the same trace as the *IntAut* execution, as required.

Thus, it suffices to construct a simulation relation satisfying Properties 1–3. Our simulation relation is the conjunction of the three predicates *SeqOk*, *WinnerUnique*, and *CorrespondenceOk*, which we describe below.

SeqOk *and* WinnerUnique. *SeqOk* describes the relationship between the abstract deque and *IntAut*'s key sequence. We first consider a simple assertion that *fails* to adequately describe this relationship. The variables *keys* and *kVal* of the intermediate automaton together yield a sequence of values, thus:

$$\sigma(is) = \lambda\, i \bullet is.kVal(is.keys(i)) \quad (4)$$

It may be tempting to build a simulation relation around a simple relationship between this sequence and the *deq* variable of the abstract automaton, i.e.,

$$as.deq.seq = \sigma(is) \wedge is.left = as.deq.left \wedge is.right = as.deq.right \quad (5)$$

However, consider a process p executing a pop operation on the left side of the deque, that takes a *contend$_p$* action followed by a *secureVal$_p$* action, finishing its operation with an action of the form *popResp$_p$(v)* with $v \neq \bot$. It is possible, given the transition relation of *IntAut*, that the value v is not the leftmost value

$$SeqOk(as, is, m) \triangleq \exists\, m\, \bullet$$

$$\forall\, i \bullet as.deq.left < i < as.deq.right \Rightarrow$$

$$is.left < m(i) \wedge m(i) < is.right \wedge \tag{6}$$

$$\sigma(is)(m(i)) = as.deq.seq(i) \wedge \tag{7}$$

$$\neg WinnerExists(as, is, is.keys(m(i)))) \tag{8}$$

$$\wedge$$

$$(\forall\, i, j \bullet as.deq.left < i < j < as.deq.right \Rightarrow$$

$$m(i) < m(j)) \wedge \tag{9}$$

$$(\forall\, i \bullet is.left < i < is.right \Rightarrow$$

$$InMatchRange(as, m, i) \vee \tag{10}$$

$$WinnerExists(as, is, is.keys(i))) \tag{11}$$

$$WinnerUnique(as, is) \triangleq$$

$$\forall\, p, q \bullet as.pc_p = popRPc(v_1) \wedge$$

$$as.pc_p = popRPc(v_2) \wedge is.key_p = is.key_q \wedge$$

$$v_1 \neq \bot \wedge v_2 \neq \bot \Rightarrow p = q \tag{12}$$

Fig. 6. The *SeqOk* and *WinnerUnique* predicates

of σ during any of these actions. (The key associated with the value v may be removed from *keys* when the key is rightmost, and then secured by a process popping from the left.) The only point in the execution of p's operation at which v must be the leftmost value is when p takes its *observe$_p$* transition. However, this action does not modify σ, and so we cannot make *observekey$_p$* transitions correspond to the abstract *doPop$_p$* action, while preserving property 5.

We need a weaker property that allows the key sequence in the intermediate automaton to contain values that have been removed from the abstract deque, so that we can (at least under some conditions) choose *doPop$_p$* for transitions labelled by *observe$_p$*. The predicate *SeqOk*, presented in Figure 6, defines such a property. *SeqOk* describes states of *AbsAut* and *IntAut* and an existentially quantified *match* function $m : \mathbb{Z} \to \mathbb{Z}$, that associates indexes between the limits of the abstract deque with indexes between the limits of *IntAut* (Clause 6). For any i between the limits *as.deq.left* and *as.deq.right*, this function satisfies $\sigma(is)(m(i)) = as.deq.seq(i)$. Thus, m takes each abstract index to an intermediate index that is associated with the same value.

We want to allow values to be "already popped" in the abstract automaton, but remain in the intermediate automaton. Not all indexes of σ between *is.left* and *is.right* are in the range of the function m. Each index between these limits not in the range of m is associated by *keys* with a key k that has already been observed by some process p during a transition that corresponds to a *doPop$_p$* transition. If p has executed such an *observe$_p$* action at some earlier point in the intermediate execution, then we say that p has *won* the key k. For each index in the range of m, no process has won the associated key (Clause 8). For a key k,

$WinnerExists(as, is, k) \triangleq$

$\quad \exists p \bullet as.pc_p = popRPc(r) \wedge$

$\qquad r \neq \bot \wedge is.key_p = k$

$OtherDeciderExists(is, p) \triangleq$

$\quad \exists q, s \bullet q \neq p \wedge$

$\qquad is.key_p = is.key_q \wedge$

$\qquad is.pc_q = deciding(s)$

$InMatchRange(as, m, i) \triangleq$

$\quad \exists j \bullet as.deq.left < j < as.deq.right \wedge$

$\qquad m(i) = j$

Fig. 7. Auxilliary predicates

$CorrespondenceOk(as, is) \triangleq$

$\quad \forall p \bullet IdleOk(as, is, p) \vee$

$\qquad PushOk(as, is, p) \vee$

$\qquad FinishedPopOk(as, is, p) \vee$

$\qquad LosingPopOk(as, is, p) \vee$

$\qquad WinningPopOk(as, is, p) \vee$

$\qquad StartingPopOk(as, is, p)$

$IdleOk(as, is, p) \triangleq$

$\quad as.pc_p = is.pc_p = idle$

$PushOk(as, is, p) \triangleq$

$\quad as.pc_p = is.pc_p = pushing(s, v) \vee$

$\quad as.pc_p = is.pc_p = pushRPc$

$FinishedPopOk(as, is, p) \triangleq$

$\quad as.pc_p = is.pc_p = popRPc(r)$

$StartingPopOk(as, is, p) \triangleq$

$\quad as.pc_p = is.pc_p = popping(s)$

Fig. 8. *CorrespondenceOk*, and subpredicates

WinnerExists asserts that some process has observed k during a transition that corresponds to a *doPop* transition (Figure 7).

Clause 9 asserts that m preserves the order of its domain. The final conjunct of *SeqOk* constrains the properties of indexes in the intermediate automaton. Each index between *is.left* and *is.right* is either in the range of m (Figure 7), or is associated with a key that has already been won. *WinnerUnique* (Figure 6) asserts that at most one process wins each key. This property ensures that at most one *pop* operation can return the value pushed by each *push* operation.

CorrespondenceOk requires each process p to satisfy one of six mutually exclusive predicates, which track the progress of p through its operations. For example, if *IdleOk(as, is, p)* holds, then in both the abstract state *as* and the intermediate state *is*, process p is not executing any operation. *PushOk(as, is, p)* holds if p is executing a *push* operation, and there are two disjuncts requiring p to be at the same stage (either about to apply its operation, or about to return from it) in both the intermediate and abstract states. The remaining predicates capture the more interesting relationship between stages of pop operations in the two automata, which arises because an abstract *doPop* action corresponds to different actions of the intermediate automaton in different cases.

Figure 8 presents *FinishedPopOk* and *StartingPopOk*. *FinishedPopOk* asserts that a process p has completed its pop operation in both abstract and

$WinningPopOk(as, is, p) \hat{=}$

$\quad (is.key_p \neq \perp$ (13)

$\quad\quad as.pc_p =$

$\quad\quad\quad popRPc(is.kVal(is.key_p)) \wedge$ (14)

$\quad\quad is.pc_p = deciding(s) \wedge$ (15)

$\quad\quad is.key_p \in is.popped \wedge$ (16)

$\quad\quad is.key_p \in is.valOk)$ (17)

$\quad \vee$ (18)

$\quad (is.key_p \neq \perp \wedge$ (19)

$\quad\quad is.pc_p = popping(s) \wedge$ (20)

$\quad\quad as.pc_p =$

$\quad\quad\quad popRPc(is.kVal(is.key_p)) \wedge$ (21)

$\quad\quad (is.key_p \notin is.popped \vee$

$\quad\quad\quad is.key_p \in is.valOk))$ (22)

$LosingPopOk(as, is, p) \hat{=}$

$\quad (as.pc_p = popRPc(\perp) \wedge$ (23)

$\quad\quad is.pc_p = deciding(s) \wedge$ (24)

$\quad\quad is.key_p \neq \perp \wedge$ (25)

$\quad\quad (is.key_p \in is.valOk \Rightarrow$

$\quad\quad\quad WinnerExists(as, is, k) \wedge$ (26)

$\quad\quad\quad OtherDeciderExists(is, p)))$

$\quad \vee$

$\quad (as.pc_p = popping(s) \wedge$ (27)

$\quad\quad is.pc_p = deciding(s) \wedge$ (28)

$\quad\quad is.key_p \neq \perp \wedge$ (29)

$\quad\quad (is.key_p \in is.valOk \Rightarrow$

$\quad\quad\quad WinnerExists(as, is, k)))$ (30)

Fig. 9. *WinningPopOk* and *LosingPopOk*

intermediate states and is waiting to return. *StartingPopOk* asserts that a process p has just begun its pop operation in both abstract and intermediate states. We choose abstract transitions and prestates for the pop actions so that any process executing a pop operation satisfies *FinishedPopOk* at the end of the operation (prior to returning), and *StartingPopOk* at the beginning. For example, we make intermediate transitions labelled by $popEmpty_p$ correspond to the $doPop_p$ action. Then p satisfies *FinishedPopOk* in the poststate of the action, and *StartingPopOk* in the prestate. The situation is more complicated when a process executing a pop operation does not take the $popEmpty_p$ action.

As we "walk back" across the execution of a successful pop operation of a process p, we eventually encounter a $secureVal_p$ action. We cannot linearize the operation at this point: we need to linearize it earlier in the execution, when the secured value is at the appropriate end of the deque. The only such point is at an $observe_p$ action. So, we do not make the $secureVal_p$ transition correspond to any abstract action, and instead show that p satisfies the first disjunct of *WinningPopOk* for the intermediate prestate and abstract state. This enables us to prove that $CorrespondenceOk(is, as')$, where is is the intermediate prestate and as' is the abstract state related to the intermediate poststate. Below we explain how the *WinningPopOk* predicate ensures that we arrive at an appropriate $observe_p$ action before we encounter the $popInv_p$ action of the operation.

As we continue walking back, we know from the transition relation of *IntAut* that we will encounter either a $popNonEmpty_p$ or a $contend_p$ action, and furthermore, we may encounter *contend* actions of other processes. Such *contend* actions can occur only when *IntAut*'s key sequence is empty. We can prove using *SeqOk* that when this sequence is empty, the abstract deque is empty in related states. Therefore, we can linearize any number of failing pop operations at *contend* actions. We find it convenient to make each transition labelled by a *contend*$_p$ action correspond to a sequence containing all eligible *doPop* actions: that is, actions *doPop*$_q$ where *key*$_q$ = *key*$_p$ in the intermediate states, and *pc*$_q$ = *popRPc*($\perp$) in the abstract poststate. Note that we do not linearize successful pop operations at a *contend* action. If a process p has *pc*$_p$ = *popRPc*(v), for some $v \in V$, in the abstract poststate, then its *doPop* action is not included in the abstract action sequence.

The second disjunct of *WinningPopOk* becomes true for p as we go back past a *popNonEmpty*$_p$ or *contend*$_p$ action, and is preserved as we continue walking back. This implies that *is.key*$_p$ $\neq \perp$. Therefore, we cannot encounter a *popInv*$_p$ action (because *is.key*$_p$ = $\perp$ in the poststate of such an action) before we encounter an *observe*$_p$ action that observes p's key. At this point, we can finally choose a *doPop*$_p$ abstract action, because p's key is at the appropriate end of *IntAut*'s key sequence. We construct the abstract prestate so that the value eventually returned by this pop operation appears at the appropriate end of the abstract deque.

Totality lemma. Property 2 in the definition of backward simulation requires that, for every reachable intermediate state, we can construct a related abstract state. We do this in such a way that the abstract and intermediate states satisfy the simple relationship defined by (5) near the beginning of this section. Let *is* be the reachable intermediate state. We construct a related abstract state *ws*, by setting *ws.deq.seq* = σ(*is*), *ws.deq.left* = *is.left* and *ws.deq.right* = *is.right*.

To satisfy *SeqOk*, we need to ensure that there is no process p, such that *ws.pc*$_p$ = *popRPc*(v) for some $v \in V$, while *is.key*$_p$ has not yet been removed from the key sequence. We achieve this by setting *ws.pc*$_p$ = *is.pc*$_p$ whenever *is.pc*$_p$ $\neq$ *deciding*. (It can be shown that in any reachable intermediate state *is* in which *is.pc*$_p$ = *deciding*, *is.key*$_p$ is not in the key sequence.)

To satisfy *CorrespondenceOk*, we need to construct *ws* so that each process with *is.pc*$_p$ = *deciding* satisfies either *WinningPopOk* or *LosingPopOk* (those are the only disjuncts of *CorrespondenceOk* in which *pc*$_p$ = *deciding* is possible). For each key k such that there is some process p where *is.key*$_p$ = k and *is.pc*$_p$ = *deciding*, we choose an arbitrary such process, denoted *winner*(k), to serve as the "winner" of the key. Now, for each process p, if *is.pc*$_p$ = *deciding*, *is.key*$_p$ $\in$ *is.valOk* and p = *winner*(*is.key*$_p$) we set *ws.pc*$_p$ = *popRPc*(*is.kVal*(*is.key*$_p$)). This enables us to prove that each *winner*(k) satisfies *WinningPopOk*. Otherwise, if *is.pc*$_p$ = *deciding* we set *ws.pc*$_p$ = *popRPc*($\perp$). Then we can prove that each such process satisfies *LosingPopOk*.

Proving the totality lemma was surprisingly difficult, compared to the analogous initial state requirement of forward simulation proofs, which are usually very simple. We naively left this until last, and had to amend our simulation relation and redo parts of the proof to enable us to prove the totality lemma.

The backward simulation definition does not require us to prove that the abstract state *ws* is reachable. Thus, we cannot use invariants of *AbsAut* in our proof: we cannot assume at each step that the abstract poststate is reachable. We did not find this restriction problematic, and were glad to avoid the onerous task of proving the reachability of ws. (Note that the constructed abstract execution implies that ws *is* a reachable state, but we did not have to prove it directly.)

6   Concluding Remarks

We have presented what we believe is the most challenging backward simulation proof to date; it was developed using the PVS theorem proving system, and is entirely machine checked. This proof is interesting because it is significantly more complicated than simple ones presented in the literature to date. We believe that proofs in this style are increasingly important as more and more optimistic and nonblocking concurrent algorithms makes their way into practical use, and especially because, despite disagreement on many design issues between transactional memory researchers, there is near-univeral agreement that optimistic read sharing is necessary for acceptable performance; such mechanisms will also require backward simulation proofs.

References

1. Colvin, R., Groves, L., Luchangco, V., Moir, M.: Formal verification of a lazy concurrent list-based set algorithm. In: Ball, T., Jones, R.B. (eds.) CAV 2006. LNCS, vol. 4144, pp. 475–488. Springer, Heidelberg (2006)
2. Detlefs, D., Flood, C.H., Garthwaite, A., Martin, P., Shavit, N.N., Steele Jr., G.L.: Even better DCAS-based concurrent deques. In: Proceedings of the 14th International Conference on Distributed Computing, pp. 59–73. IEEE Computer Society Press, Los Alamitos (2000)
3. Doherty, S., Detlefs, D., Groves, L., Flood, C., Luchangco, V., Martin, P., Moir, M., Shavit, N., Steele Jr., G.L.: DCAS is not a silver bullet for nonblocking synchronization. In: Proceedings of the Sixteenth ACM Symposium on Parllelism in Algorithms and Architectures. ACM Press, New York (2004)
4. Doherty, S., Groves, L., Luchangco, V., Moir, M.: Formal verification of a practical lock-free queue algorithm. In: de Frutos-Escrig, D., Núñez, M. (eds.) FORTE 2004. LNCS, vol. 3235, pp. 97–114. Springer, Heidelberg (2004)
5. Gao, H., Groote, J., Hesselink, W.H.: Lock-free resizable hash-tables with open addressing. Distributed Computing 18(1) (July 2005)
6. Herlihy, M.P., Wing, J.M.: Linearizability: A correctness condition for concurrent objects. ACM Transactions on Programming Languages and Systems 12(3), 463–492 (1990)
7. Lamport, L.: Checking a multithreaded algorithm with +CAL. In: Dolev, S. (ed.) DISC 2006. LNCS, vol. 4167, pp. 151–163. Springer, Heidelberg (2006)
8. Lynch, N., Tuttle, M.: Hierarchical correctness proofs for distributed algorithms. In: Proceedings of the Sixth Annual ACM Symposium on Principles of Distributed Computing, pp. 137–151. ACM Press, New York (1987)
9. Lynch, N., Vaandrager, F.: Forward and backward simulations, i: Untimed systems. Information and Computation 121(2), 214–233 (1995)
10. Lynch, N.A.: Distributed Algorithms. Morgan Kaufmann Publishers Inc., San Francisco (1996)
11. Søgaard-Andersen, J.F., Garland, S.J., Guttag, J.V., Lynch, N.A., Pogosyants, A.: Computer-assisted simulation proofs. In: Courcoubetis, C. (ed.) CAV 1993. LNCS, vol. 697, pp. 305–319. Springer, Heidelberg (1993)

Brief Announcement: Efficient Model Checking of Fault-Tolerant Distributed Protocols Using Symmetry Reduction*

Péter Bokor, Marco Serafini, Neeraj Suri, and Helmut Veith

Technische Universität Darmstadt, Germany
{pbokor,marco,suri,veith}@cs.tu-darmstadt.de

Motivation. Fault-tolerant (FT) distributed protocols represent fundamental building blocks behind many practical systems. A rigorous design of these protocols is desired given the complexity of manual proofs. The application of *model checking* (MC) [2] for protocol verification is attractive with its full automation and rich property language. However, being an exhaustive exploration method, its scalability is limited by the number of different system states. Although *FT distributed protocols* usually display a high degree of symmetry which stems from permuting different processes, MC efforts targeting their automated verification often disregard this symmetry. Therefore, we propose to leverage the framework of symmetry reduction [6] and improve on existing applications of it. Our secondary contribution is to define a high-level description language (called FTDP) to ease the symmetry-aware specification of FT distributed protocols.

Preliminary: Symmetry Reduction with Scalarsets. Formally, *symmetry* is a permutation π acting on all reachable system states satisfying that for every state s and its successor s' it holds that $\pi(s')$ is a successor of $\pi(s)$ [6]. For example, a state s of a distributed system where two processes assume different local states is symmetric with another state $\pi(s)$ where these two local states are swapped. Symmetry reduction eases model checking by exploring a single (or some) representative states within each set of symmetric states. This method preserves CTL* temporal logic properties [2] if the property under verification does not distinguish symmetric states. Unfortunately, the detection of symmetries is in general prohibitively complex. Therefore, we take the approach of creating symmetric models *by construction*. In order to indicate symmetries in the model the designer uses a special data type called *scalarset* with a set of restricted operations [3]. The restrictions guarantee that any permutation of scalarset values results in symmetric states.

Role-based Symmetry Reduction. FT distributed protocols can be often defined through r many *roles*, i.e., different types of independent processes having non-intersecting states whose state transitions are activated by non-intersecting sets of incoming messages or internal events. Assume that n_i is the number of

* Research supported in part by Microsoft Research, IBM Faculty Award.

I. Keidar (Ed.): DISC 2009, LNCS 5805, pp. 289–290, 2009.
© Springer-Verlag Berlin Heidelberg 2009

process *instances* in role i. In real implementations a protocol is executed by n physical nodes. Every node is a parallel composition of role instances with at most one role instance per node. We observe that it is unnecessary to explicitly model nodes if the properties of the protocol specify roles rather than nodes. Therefore, in our *role-based* approach we define each role as a new scalarset of size n_i. This enables us to permute role instances of the same role even if they are physically located on different nodes.

Role-based symmetries differ from node-based ones (commonly used for systems with replicated components) where a single scalarset of size n is used. The node-based approach only allows the permutation of entire nodes together with all hosted role instances. To compare the maximum achievable reduction assume that $n_i = n$ for all i. The reduction in the number of states of the state graph using role-based symmetries compared to the unreduced graph can be a factor of up to $(n!)^r$. This reduction is exponentially higher than the best case benefit of the node-based approach, which is up to $n!$.

The FTDP Language. The FTDP language supports automatic verification of finite FT distributed protocols. First of all, FTDP allows the definition of roles and forces (using the scalarset approach) that symmetry is not violated. Furthermore, FTDP syntactically enriches low-level specification languages. FTDP differs from existing algorithm description languages such as +CAL [5] in providing built-in abstractions for (a) synchronous and asynchronous message-passing and (b) a variety of fault types. FTDP supports the specification of safety and liveness properties (specified in CTL*). In fact, FTDP specifications closely resemble the pseudocode of common distributed protocols.

Evaluation. We have used our approach to analyze (debug and verify) real protocols, e.g., Paxos [4]. The Paxos protocol uses three roles: leader, acceptor, and learner. Our prototype FTDP implementation extends the SS language of the Murφ symmetry reduction model checker [3]. The experiments reveal that (1) the state graph obtained through role-based reduction contains up to twenty times less states than the unreduced model, (2) the benefit of this reduction approaches the theoretical maximum of $(n!)^r$, and (3) the node-based approach visits up to ten times more states than the role-based one. More details about the role-based approach and the FTDP language can be found in [1].

References

1. Bokor, P., Serafini, M., Suri, N., Veith, H.: Practical Symmetry Reduction of FT Distributed Protocols. TR-TUD-DEEDS-04-04-2009 (2009)
2. Clarke, E., Grumberg, O., Peled, D.: Model Checking. MIT Press, Cambridge (2000)
3. Ip, C.N., Dill, D.L.: Better Verif. Through Symmetry. FMSD 9(1-2), 41–75 (1996)
4. Lamport, L.: The Part-Time Parliament. ACM TOCS 16(2), 133–169 (1998)
5. Lamport, L.: Checking a Multithreaded Alg. with +CAL. DISC, 151–163 (2006)
6. Miller, A., et al.: Symmetry in Temporal Logic MC. ACM C. Surv. 38(3), 8 (2006)

Brief Announcement: Dynamic FTSS in Asynchronous Systems: The Case of Unison*

Swan Dubois, Maria Gradinariu Potop-Butucaru, and Sébastien Tixeuil

LIP6 - UMR 7606, Université Pierre et Marie Curie - Paris 6/INRIA

Context. The advent of ubiquitous large-scale distributed systems advocates that tolerance to various kinds of faults and hazards must be included from the very early design of such systems. *Self-stabilization* [1] is a versatile technique that permits forward recovery from any kind of *transient* fault, while *Fault-tolerance* [2] is traditionally used to mask the effect of a limited number of *permanent* faults. The seminal works of [3,4] define *FTSS* protocols as protocols that are both *Fault Tolerant and Self-Stabilizing*, *i.e.* able to tolerate a few crash faults as well as arbitrary initial memory corruption. In [3], some impossibility results in asynchronous systems are presented. In [4], a general transformer is presented for synchronous systems. The transformer of [4] was proved impossible to transpose to asynchronous systems in [5] due to the impossibility of tight synchronization in the FTSS context. It turns out that FTSS possibility results in fully *asynchronous* systems known to date are restricted to *static* tasks, *i.e.* tasks that require eventual convergence to some global fixed point (tasks such as naming or vertex coloring fall in this category).

In this work, we consider the more challenging problem of *dynamic* tasks, *i.e.* tasks that require both eventual safety and liveness properties (examples of such tasks are clock synchronization and token passing). Due to the aforementioned impossibility of tight clock synchronization, we consider the *unison* problem, that can bee seen as a *local* clock synchronization problem. In the unison problem [6], each node is expected to keep its digital clock value within one time unit of every of its neighbors' clock values (weak synchronization), and increment its clock value infinitely often. Note that in synchronous completely connected systems where clocks have discrete time unit values, unison induces tight clock synchronization. Several self-stabilizing solutions exist for this problem, both in synchronous and asynchronous systems, yet none of those can tolerate crash faults. As a matter of fact, there exists a number of FTSS results for *dynamic* tasks in *synchronous* systems. In particular, clock synchronization is well-studied. The reader can find more references in [7].

Contributions. In this work, we tackle the open issue of FTSS solutions to *dynamic* tasks in *asynchronous* systems, using the unison problem as a case study.

Our first negative results show that whenever two or more crash faults may occur, FTSS unison is impossible in any asynchronous setting. The remaining case of one crash fault drives the most interesting results.

---

* This work was funded in part by ANR project SHAMAN.

I. Keidar (Ed.): DISC 2009, LNCS 5805, pp. 291–293, 2009.

We first extract two key properties satisfied by all previous self-stabilizing asynchronous unison protocols: *minimality* and *priority*. Minimality means that nodes maintain no extra variables but the digital clock value. Priority means that whenever incrementing the clock value does not break the local safety predicate between neighbors, the clock value is actually incremented in a finite number of activations, even when no neighbor modifies its clock value.

Then, depending on the fairness properties of the scheduling of nodes, we provide various results with respect to the possibility or impossibility of unison. When the scheduling is *unfair* (only global progress is guaranteed), FTSS unison is impossible. When the scheduling is *weakly fair* (a processor that is continuously enabled is eventually activated), then it is impossible to solve FTSS unison by a protocol that satisfies either minimality or priority. The case of *strongly fair* scheduling (a processor that is activated infinitely often is eventually activated) is similar whenever the maximum degree of the graph is at least three. Our negative results still apply when the clock variable is unbounded and the scheduling is central (*i.e.* a single processor is activated at any time).

On the positive side, we propose a FTSS protocol for connected networks of maximum degree at most two (*i.e.* rings and chains), that satisfies both minimality and priority properties. This protocol makes minimal system hypotheses with respect to the aforementioned impossibility results (maximum degree, scheduling, etc.) and is optimal with respect to the containment radius that is achieved (*no* correct processor is *ever* prevented from incrementing its clock).

The table above provides a summary of the main results of the work. More details about this work are available in [7].

| | Unfair | Weakly fair | | Strongly fair | | |
| | | Minimal | Priority | $\Delta \geq 3$ | | $\Delta \leq 2$ |
				Minimal	Priority	
$f = 1$	Imp.	Imp.	Imp.	Imp.	Imp.	Pos.
$f \geq 2$	Imp.					

Perspectives. Future works follow: fix the remaining open cases, give results with bounded clocks, and deal with malicious nodes instead of crashes.

References

1. Dijkstra, E.W.: Self-stabilizing systems in spite of distributed control. Commun. ACM 17, 643–644 (1974)
2. Fischer, M.J., Lynch, N.A., Paterson, M.: Impossibility of distributed consensus with one faulty process. J. ACM 32(2), 374–382 (1985)
3. Anagnostou, E., Hadzilacos, V.: Tolerating transient and permanent failures (extended abstract). In: WDAG, pp. 174–188 (1993)

4. Gopal, A.S., Perry, K.J.: Unifying self-stabilization and fault-tolerance (preliminary version). In: PODC, pp. 195–206 (1993)
5. Beauquier, J., Kekkonen-Moneta, S.: Fault-tolerance and self stabilization: impossibility results and solutions using self-stabilizing failure detectors. Int. J. Systems Science 28, 1177–1187 (1997)
6. Misra, J.: Phase synchronization. Inf. Process. Lett. 38(2), 101–105 (1991)
7. Dubois, S., Potop Butucaru, M., Tixeuil, S.: Dynamic FTSS in Asynchronous Systems: the Case of Unison. Research Report arXiv:0904.4615, INRIA (April 2009)

Dynamics in Network Interaction Games

Martin Hoefer[1,*] and Siddharth Suri[2]

[1] Department of Computer Science, RWTH Aachen University, Germany
mhoefer@cs.rwth-aachen.de
[2] Yahoo! Research, New York, USA
suri@yahoo-inc.com

Abstract. We study the convergence times of dynamics in games involving graphical relationships of players. Our model of local interaction games generalizes a variety of recently studied games in game theory and distributed computing. In a local interaction game each agent is a node embedded in a graph and plays the same 2-player game with each neighbor. He can choose his strategy only once and must apply his choice in each game he is involved in. This represents a fundamental model of decision making with local interaction and distributed control. Furthermore, we introduce a generalization called 2-type interaction games, in which one 2-player game is played on edges and possibly another game is played on non-edges. For the popular case with symmetric 2×2 games, we show that several dynamics converge in polynomial time. This includes arbitrary sequential better response dynamics, as well as concurrent dynamics resulting from a distributed protocol that does not rely on global knowledge. We supplement these results with an experimental comparison of sequential and concurrent dynamics.

1 Introduction

In this paper we examine convergence of dynamics in a fundamental model for distributed decision making with local interactions movtivated by distributed computer systems and social networks. We introduce two game-theoretic models, one a generalization of the other, that combine strategic interaction with the notion of graph-based locality. This extends a variety of game-theoretic settings that have been studied intensively in the literature. In our model of a *local interaction game* there is a graph G along with a 2-player symmetric game, Γ. Players are the nodes, and the graph models the local interaction possibilities. In particular, Γ is played along each edge of G, and each player plays the same strategy against each of their neighbors. The payoff of a player is simply the sum of the payoffs earned from playing each neighbor. Local interaction games are a basic framework to capture many different types of real-world phenomena, e.g., when a person is trying to coordinate with as many of his or her neighbors as possible. Similarly, the graph could encode antipathies and actors could

---

* This author was supported by a fellowship within the Postdoc-Program of the German Academic Exchange Service (DAAD) and by DFG through UMIC Research Center at RWTH Aachen University.

I. Keidar (Ed.): DISC 2009, LNCS 5805, pp. 294–308, 2009.
© Springer-Verlag Berlin Heidelberg 2009

strive to anti-coordinate with their neighbors. This is the general incentive in many computational resource sharing environments like channel assignment in wireless networks, where nodes try to choose a frequency that minimizes the number of spatially close nodes using the same frequency. It is thus not surprising that a large number of specific local interaction games have been studied in the literature [8, 27, 29, 34].

We also introduce a generalization of local interaction games called *2-type interaction games*. Intuitively, a 2-type interaction game is a graph where one 2-player symmetric game is played on the edges, and another 2-player symmetric game is played on the non-edges. Whereas local interaction games model the restricted interaction *possibilities* of players through the topology of the graph, 2-type interaction games also model different *types* of interactions that occur between players. This is a natural assumption when considering e.g. social networks, as they do not necessarily indicate restrictions of interactions, but rather show that there is a special relationship, which is likely to alter the incentives of the involved actors. Our model allows one to specify for example how one person treats a friend differently than a stranger. In addition, it is possible to study distributed graph clustering problems (such as, e.g., correlation clustering [21]) within this framework.

In many applications that can be modeled with our games there is a crucial lack of central coordination. Our main interest is thus how the set of players can quickly arrive at a stable set of decisions – a Nash equilibrium of the game – using distributed decision making policies. Our main result is that myopic sequential better response dynamics converge in polynomial time to a Nash equilibrium. This also holds for a payoff-relative concurrent protocol without central coordination. These results hold for local interaction games based on arbitrary symmetric 2 × 2 games and arbitrary graphs, which encompasses the vast majority of cases considered previously in related work. For the more general model of 2-type interaction games with symmetric 2 × 2 games and arbitrary graphs, we can also show polynomial time convergence of sequential dynamics. While sequential better response has a natural and intuitive appeal, our concurrent policy is carefully designed. It exhibits a number of favorable properties, such as respecting player incentives and relying only on local information. Designing such policies that yield provably rapid convergence is a major concern in wireless networks and distributed control systems (see, e.g. [16, 30]), and our results contribute to this research agenda. As a byproduct, our dynamics yield efficient algorithms to compute a Nash equilibrium, which stands in sharp contrast to other game-theoretic models of restricted (graphical) interaction [12, 26].

The comparison of convergence times for sequential and concurrent dynamics in local interaction games without dominant strategy reveals that the lack of central control can result in concurrent dynamics being slower than sequential ones. This, however, is a worst-case result, and we indicate that in coordination games concurrent dynamics resulting from our protocol can be significantly faster. This does not necessarily hold for anti-coordination games, and here a simple adjustment of our concurrent dynamics to a fixed choice μ for the migration probability can yield better results. However, the choice of this value is delicate, as resulting dynamics might abruptly drown in oscillation. It remains an interesting open problem to find improved analytical bounds for expected convergence times in specific classes of local interaction games.

The rest of the paper is structured as follows. We revisit related work in Section 1.1 and define the model in Section 1.2. Sequential dynamics are treated in Section 2, concurrent dynamics in Section 3. In Section 4 we compare sequential and concurrent convergence times in simple local interaction games. Finally, Section 5 concludes the paper. Most details and proofs are omitted due to space constraints and will be given in the full version.

1.1 Related Work

This paper fits into a recent stream of works that study subclasses of local interaction games. For example, our model of local interaction games generalizes a game considered by Bramoullé [8], which concentrates on the subclass of symmetric 2×2 anti-coordination games on the edges and does not have any games on the non-edges. A special class of anti-coordination game derived from the MaxCut problem has been used in [14]. It was studied by Christodoulou et al. [11] in terms of convergence time to Nash equilibria and social welfare of states obtained after a polynomial number of best response steps.

Variants of local interaction games with coordination games are central in the study of threshold phenomena, cascading dynamics, and information diffusion in networks [29]. Closest to our focus is a recent paper by Montanari and Saberi [34] who consider local interaction games with 2×2 symmetric coordination games and a class of noisy best response dynamics called logit-response, heat bath, or Glauber dynamics. For potential games, in the long run, the time this process spends at a state scales proportional to the potential value and the noise level. For small noise levels the dynamics thus remain exclusively at global potential maximizers. For coordination games this is a state in which all players use the same strategy. The results of [34] are complementary to ours in the sense that they consider the hitting time of a *global* potential maximizer in a significantly more restrictive model. They show that convergence times increase from polynomial to exponential time when the graph becomes more well-connected. This contrasts our polynomial time bounds for all graphs and arbitrary symmetric 2×2 games when only convergence to *local* potential maximizers is required. In a related work, Kearns and Tan [28] design a voting protocol with polynomial time convergence in a similar 2-strategy coordination scenario. In contrast to our work they also require collective unity of choices.

While in our model the graph is fixed and specified in advance, there are several works on games with network formation. In particular, 2×2 anti-coordination games on endogenous graphs were studied in [9]. Much more work [6, 10, 13, 36] has been done on network formation and 2×2 coordination games. These games are classes of local interaction games with network creation, i.e., they allow only connected players to interact. There has been no focus on duration of dynamics, social welfare, and computation of Nash equilibria and optimal states. Instead, properties of the network structure and payoff properties in Nash equilibria were analyzed [4], or stochastically stable states were characterized [23, 24].

In the graphical model of evolutionary game theory introduced by Kearns and Suri [27] all players play a 2-player symmetric game with a randomly chosen neighbor. The authors characterize evolutionary equilibria in terms of the graph structure. However, they give no notion of dynamics that converge to equilibrium.

Our concurrent dynamics are closely related to recent work on protocols for concurrent strategy updating in potential games for distributed control in networks [30, 31], some of which are inspired by evolutionary game theory [1, 16, 17]. In addition, there is a large body of related work on strategic learning [20, 37], various forms of dynamics such as calibrated [18] or regret learning [5, 32, 38] or best response/ficticious play [2, 11, 14, 19, 33], and a variety of equilibrium concepts such as correlated Nash [3] or sink equilibria [15, 22].

1.2 Model and Notation

We begin by giving the formal definition of a 2-type interaction game.

Definition 1. *A 2-type interaction game is a graph $G = (V, E)$ together with two, possibly different, 2-player symmetric games Γ^c and Γ^d, where the set of strategies is the same in both games.*

Intuitively, on each edge $e \in E$ connected players play a 2-player symmetric game Γ^c. In addition, for each non-edge the pair of disconnected players play a possibly different symmetric 2×2 game, Γ^d. Each player plays the same strategy in all games he is participating. In this work, we restrict Γ^c and Γ^d to be 2×2 symmetric games with strategies 1 and 2, and payoffs for Γ^c and Γ^d are denoted as shown in Figure 1.

Next we introduce some notation that will allow us to define the utility function for each player in a 2-type interaction game. We will let $\Gamma_p = \{\Gamma^c, \Gamma^d\}$. We denote by $n = |V|$ the number of players, $m = |E|$ the number of edges, $\deg(v)$ the degree of player v. Let $S = \{1,2\}^n$ be the set of states of the game and $s = (s_v)_{v \in V} \in S$ a state, where $s_v \in \{1, 2\}$ is the strategy of player v. For a state s the set of players playing strategy 1 is denoted V_1, their number $n_1 = |V_1|$. For a player v the number $\deg_1(v)$ denotes the number of her neighbors playing 1, and n_1^{-v} the number of players except v that play strategy 1. V_2, n_2, $\deg_2(v)$,

Γ^c	1	2		Γ^d	1	2
1	a,a	d,c		1	e,e	h,g
2	c,d	b,b		2	g,h	f,f

Fig. 1. Payoffs in the Games

and n_2^{-v} are defined similarly for strategy 2. The size of the cut of a state s, which is the number of edges connecting players that play different strategies, is denoted by m_{12}. A player v has utility for strategy 1

$$\text{util}_v(1, s_{-v}) = [\text{a} \cdot \deg_1(v) + \text{d} \cdot \deg_2(v)] + [\text{e} \cdot (n_1^{-v} - \deg_1(v)) + \text{h} \cdot (n_2^{-v} - \deg_2(v)))]$$

while for strategy 2 he has utility

$$\text{util}_v(2, s_{-v}) = [\text{c} \cdot \deg_1(v) + \text{b} \cdot \deg_2(v)] + [\text{g} \cdot (n_1^{-v} - \deg_1(v)) + \text{f} \cdot (n_2^{-v} - \deg_2(v))].$$

Note that symmetric 2×2 games are known to be potential games [6, 36], and the potential is given as follows:

$$\Phi^c = \begin{pmatrix} \text{a} - \text{c} & 0 \\ 0 & \text{b} - \text{d} \end{pmatrix} \qquad \Phi^d = \begin{pmatrix} \text{e} - \text{g} & 0 \\ 0 & \text{f} - \text{h} \end{pmatrix}. \qquad (1)$$

Here the potential for two players playing strategies i and j respectively, where $i, j \in \{1, 2\}$, is $\Phi^c(i, j)$ for Γ^c and $\Phi^d(i, j)$ for Γ^d. Note that each game has a potential function $\Phi(s)$ defined as sum of the corresponding potential values Φ^c and Φ^d of the 2-type interaction games.

2 Sequential Dynamics

In this section, our goal is to examine the duration of sequential iterative better response dynamics. We provide an analysis of the potential function, whichs yield polynomial convergence times in 2-type interaction games.

Theorem 1. *For every 2-type interaction game every sequence of better response moves from any initial state terminates in a pure Nash equilibrium after at most $(n + 1)(m + 1)^2$ steps.*

Proof. Our proof relies on a more insightful characterization for the potential function. We will simplify the games by subtracting **c** and **g** from every entry of the Γ^c and Γ^d, respectively. This does not alter payoff differences for the players and preserves the incentives. We can, in turn, derive yet another game equivalent to this one which has the doubly symmetric form described by Figure 2. We use $A = \text{a}$, $B = \text{b} - \text{d}$, $E = \text{e}$, and $F = \text{f} - \text{h}$. As shown in Chapters 1 and 2 of [35] the new game exhibits the same potential and Nash Equilibria as the original game. Note that this game is not equivalent in terms of social welfare, as we alter the total payoffs in some of the states.

We analyze the underlying characteristic function more closely and denote by $S = A + B$, $T = E + F$, and $\Delta A = A - E$. The potential function of Γ_p is

$$\Phi(s) = \sum_{v \in V_1} \deg_1(v)A + (n_1 - 1 - \deg_1(v))E + \sum_{v \in V_2} \deg_2(v)B + (n_2 - 1 - \deg_2(v))F$$

$$= n(n - 1)F + 2m(B - F) + Tn_1^2 - (2(n - 1)F + T)n_1 + (T - S)m_{12}$$

$$+ (T - S + 2\Delta A) \sum_{v \in V_1} \deg(v)$$

Γ^c	1	2
1	A, A	0, 0
2	0, 0	B, B

Γ^d	1	2
1	E, E	0, 0
2	0, 0	F, F

Fig. 2. Payoffs in games transformed to be doubly symmetric

It is possible to drop the constant terms $n(n-1)\mathsf{F} + 2m(\mathsf{B}-\mathsf{F})$ from every state and derive a characteristic function $\Psi(s)$ given by

$$\Psi(s) = \mathsf{T}n_1^2 - (2(n-1)\mathsf{F} + \mathsf{T})n_1 + (\mathsf{T} - \mathsf{S})m_{12} + (\mathsf{T} - \mathsf{S} + 2\Delta\mathsf{A}) \sum_{v \in V_1} \deg(v). \quad (2)$$

This function depends - in addition to the payoffs - only on three parameters: the number n_1 of players playing strategy 1, their degrees $\sum_{v \in V_1} \deg(v)$ and the cut size m_{12}. $\Psi(s)$ becomes a potential for all 2×2 games by plugging in the payoffs of the games Γ^c and Γ^d into parameters A, B, E and F as described above. Then if we let $\mathsf{S} = \mathsf{a} + \mathsf{b} - \mathsf{d}$, $\mathsf{T} = \mathsf{e} + \mathsf{f} - \mathsf{h}$ and $\Delta\mathsf{A}_p = \mathsf{a} - \mathsf{e}$, we get a potential function

$$\Psi_p(s) = \mathsf{T}n_1^2 - ((n-1)(2\mathsf{f} - 2\mathsf{h}) + \mathsf{T})n_1 + (\mathsf{T} - \mathsf{S})m_{12} + (\mathsf{T} - \mathsf{S} + 2\Delta\mathsf{A}_p) \sum_{v \in V_1} \deg(v). \quad (3)$$

For the proof of the theorem observe that n_1 can range from 0 to n, which constitutes the factor $n + 1$ in the guarantee. Note that m_{12} and $\sum_{v \in V_1} \deg(v)$ can take at most $m + 1$ different values each. Hence, the total number of possible combinations for these parameters yields a total of $(n + 1)(m + 1)^2$ different values for Φ. As each better response iteration must strictly increase Φ in each step, every such sequence takes at most this number of iterations to reach a local optimum of Φ, from any starting state. This proves the theorem. $\quad\Box$

The main technique in the previous proof is transforming any game to an equivalent doubly symmetric game with only four different payoff values. The main outcome of this is the function Ψ in Equation 2. By using the correct payoff values, it becomes Ψ_p, a potential function for our original game with an insightful representation.

The basis of the previous proof is a simple argument that can be applied somewhat more generally. Suppose every pair of players plays an exact potential game, each player can pick his strategy only once for all games, and the payoffs he receives are summed up. Then the whole game has an exact potential function. Consider a local interaction game in which each pair of players plays a $k \times k$ potential game with constant k. We can classify edges into $O(k^2)$ classes depending on the current state of the game on the edge. This yields only a polynomial number of different combinations and potential values. The same holds if we generalize 2-type interaction games to a constant number of different $k \times k$ potential games with constant k. On the other hand, if we allow on each edge a different game, then even with $k = 2$ we can encode local search in instances of weighted MaxCut, and therefore worst-case convergence time becomes necessarily exponential. Similarly, in a local interaction game with $k \times k$ games and $k \leq n$, it is possible to encode an instance of weighted MaxCut simultaneously into payoff matrix and graph structure for a subgraph of $k/2$ nodes. Thus, for $k = \Omega(n)$ strategies this yields games, in which convergence time is necessarily exponential. A deeper characterization along these lines is left for future work.

3 Concurrent Dynamics

In this section we consider round-based concurrent dynamics, in which in each round all players simultaneously update their strategy choices. A simple approach, which is considered frequently in the area of information diffusion in networks [29], is to allow all players simultaneously play their best responses to the current state of the game. This approach converges rapidly if all players have dominant strategies. In fact, we would reach the dominant strategy equilibrium after the first round, which speeds up the convergence time by a factor of n over the sequential process considered previously. One might think that concurrent dynamics should always yield a speed-up of $\Theta(n)$ due to the possibility of simultaneous updates. However, due to the absence of global coordination, these dynamics can easily get stuck in oscillations. The main design challenge proves to be to avoid oscillation and to obtain reasonable convergence times. In order to do this we follow the idea of [16] and design a policy in order to increase the potential function in expectation in each round. The challenge here is to enlarge migration probabilities to converge quickly, yet to guarantee potential increase in expectation.

To guarantee convergence we introduce the notion of inertia. Suppose each player independently at random migrates to a better response with a probability less than 1. This allows for the construction of a Markov chain on the states, where migration probabilities of the players yield transition probabilities between states. Note that, due to inertia, with a possibly tiny probability the concurrent process can resemble any sequential better response dynamics. Thus, the only absorbing states of the Markov chain are the pure Nash equilibria, to which the process must converge with probability 1 in the limit (see, e.g., [31]). The bounds on the convergence time that can be derived from this argument, however, are usually extremely large.

Subsequently, we analyze a protocol with migration probabilities proportional to the relative payoff increase. For technical reasons, we here assume that all payoffs are non-negative integer numbers, i.e. $\mathsf{a}, \mathsf{b}, \mathsf{c}, \mathsf{d}, \mathsf{e}, \mathsf{f}, \mathsf{g}, \mathsf{h} \in \mathbb{N}$. Afterwards, we consider several preprocessing steps to adjust the payoff values such that the incentives of players are preserved and convergence is obtained in expected polynomial time.

In a state s a player v considers changing from strategy $x \in \{1, 2\}$ to strategy $y = 3 - x$ if $\mathrm{util}_v(y, s_{-v}) - \mathrm{util}_v(x, s_{-v}) > 0$. If this is the case, she migrates with migration probability that depends on her relative payoff increase (see the

Algorithm 1. Relative Migration Protocol (RMP), repeatedly executed by all players in parallel.

1: For player v let $x \leftarrow s_v$ and $y \leftarrow 3 - x$.
2: **if** $\mathrm{util}_v(y, s_{-v}) > \mathrm{util}_v(x, s_{-v})$ **then**
3:    with probability

$$\mu_{xy} = \frac{1}{\lambda} \cdot \frac{\mathrm{util}_v(y, s_{-v}) - \mathrm{util}_v(x, s_{-v})}{\mathrm{util}_v(y, s_{-v})}$$

   migrate from strategy x to y.
4: **end if**

Relative Migration Protocol (RMP), Algorithm 1). If every player updates his strategy choices using the RMP, a new state s' evolves. We define a vector $\Delta s = (s'(v) - s(v))_{v \in V}$.

Lemma 1. *If* a = b *and* e = f *in games of the form shown in Figure 1, then as long as the 2-type interaction game is not in a Nash equilibrium, it holds that* $\mathbb{E}[\Phi(s + \Delta s)] > \Phi(s)$.

Say player v could improve his utility by switching to a new strategy. He decides to switch with a probability based on the action profile of his neighbors. At the same time as v changes strategy, his neighbors might do so as well. Thus this proof works by bounding the error in how much v expects to gain before switching versus how much v actually gains after switching.

Proof. For a state s and a vector Δs consider a player v. Let $y = s(v)$ denote v's current strategy and let $x = s(v) + \Delta s(v)$ denote v's strategy after migration. The change in v's utility after migration, assuming no other players change their strategy is denoted $\Delta \mathrm{util}_v(s_{-v}) = \mathrm{util}_v(y, s_{-v}) - \mathrm{util}_v(x, s_{-v})$. Let the *virtual potential gain* be defined as $VP(s, \Delta s) = \sum_{v \in V} \Delta \mathrm{util}_v(s_{-v})$. The virtual potential simply sums all the presumed payoff increases of all players that chose to migrate. The real potential gain $\Phi(s + \Delta s) - \Phi(s)$ can be different if more than a single player moves. In this case the simultaneous migration of players u and v creates an error $F^{u,v}(s, \Delta s)$. Thus,

$$\Phi(s + \Delta s) - \Phi(s) = VP(s, \Delta s) - \sum_{u,v \in V} F^{u,v}(s, \Delta s). \tag{4}$$

In order to show that $\mathbb{E}[\Phi(s + \Delta s)] - \Phi(s) > 0$, and conclude the proof of Lemma 1, we will relate expected virtual potential gain and expected error, which are the two terms on the right hand side of Equation 4.

Lemma 2. *For any constant* $\lambda > 1$ *it holds that* $\mathbb{E}[\Phi(s + \Delta s)] - \Phi(s) \geq \frac{\lambda - 1}{\lambda} \cdot \mathbb{E}[VP(s, \Delta s)]$.

Proof. We will show that the error terms $\sum_{u,v \in V} \mathbb{E}[F^{u,v}(s, \Delta s)]$ are at most a constant fraction of $\mathbb{E}[VP(s, \Delta s)]$, and the lemma will follow by taking the expection of Eqn. (4). We will relate the expected virtual potential gain between each pair of nodes $u, v \in V$ to the expected error of the potential gain between u and v. For simplicity we drop the indices s, Δs and s_{-v}. Note that

$$\mathbb{E}\left[VP\right] = \sum_{v \in V} \mu_{xy}^v \cdot \Delta \mathrm{util}_v = \frac{1}{\lambda} \sum_{v \in V} \frac{(\Delta \mathrm{util}_v)^2}{\mathrm{util}_v(y)},$$

where μ_{xy} is defined in Algorithm 1. We split this expected virtual potential gain into parts denoted $VP^{u,v}$, which are accounted towards the pair (u, v) of players, for every $u \neq v$, $u, v \in V$. For a player v we account a fraction of his gain depending on the payoff that the game with player u contributes to $\mathrm{util}_v(y)$.

The following analysis is done for a player v with $s(v) = x = 1$ that migrates to strategy $y = 2$ and pairs of neighboring players. The arguments can be repeated similarly for a switch from 2 to 1 and/or disconnected players. We first consider a neighbor u with $s(u) = 2$. For player v we account a fraction of

$$\frac{\mathrm{b}}{\mathrm{util}_v(2)} \cdot \mu_{12}^v \cdot \Delta \mathrm{util}_v = \mathrm{b} \cdot \frac{1}{\lambda} \cdot \left(\frac{\Delta \mathrm{util}_v}{\mathrm{util}_v(2)}\right)^2$$

of the expected virtual potential gain to the edge (u, v). Similarly, for u we account a fraction

$$\frac{\mathrm{a}}{\mathrm{util}_u(1)} \cdot \mu_{21}^u \cdot \Delta \mathrm{util}_u = \mathrm{a} \cdot \frac{1}{\lambda} \cdot \left(\frac{\Delta \mathrm{util}_u}{\mathrm{util}_u(1)}\right)^2$$

to (u, v). Thus, using $\mathrm{a} = \mathrm{b}$ we have $\mathbb{E}\left[VP^{u,v}\right] = \mathrm{a} \cdot \frac{1}{\lambda} \cdot \left(\left(\frac{\Delta \mathrm{util}_u}{\mathrm{util}_u(1)}\right)^2 + \left(\frac{\Delta \mathrm{util}_v}{\mathrm{util}_v(2)}\right)^2\right)$.

The expected error is calculated as follows. Player v presumes a change in payoff of $\mathrm{b} - \mathrm{c}$, player u presumes $\mathrm{a} - \mathrm{d}$. However, if both players migrate their combined change in payoff is 0. Thus, the error is $\mathrm{a} + \mathrm{b} - (\mathrm{c} + \mathrm{d}) = 2\mathrm{a} - (\mathrm{c} + \mathrm{d})$, using $\mathrm{a} = \mathrm{b}$. Hence, the expected error is

$$\mathbb{E}\left[F^{u,v}\right] = \mu_{21}^u \mu_{12}^v \cdot (2\mathrm{a} - (\mathrm{c} + \mathrm{d})) = (2\mathrm{a} - (\mathrm{c} + \mathrm{d})) \cdot \frac{1}{\lambda^2} \cdot \left(\frac{\Delta \mathrm{util}_u}{\mathrm{util}_u(1)} \cdot \frac{\Delta \mathrm{util}_v}{\mathrm{util}_v(2)}\right),$$

with $\mathrm{a}, \mathrm{c}, \mathrm{d} \geq 0$ we again observe $\mathbb{E}\left[VP^{u,v}\right] \geq \lambda \cdot \mathbb{E}\left[F^{u,v}\right]$. The case for a neighbor u with $s(u) = 1$ follows similarly. The same argument can be repeated for all pairs of players and all possible strategy constellations. Finally, we see that $\mathbb{E}\left[VP\right] \geq \lambda \cdot \sum_{u,v \in V} \mathbb{E}\left[F^{u,v}\right]$. This combined with Equation 4 proves Lemma 2.   □

Note that, as long as at least one payoff value of $\mathrm{a}, \mathrm{b}, \mathrm{c}, \mathrm{d}$ is strictly positive, we make a strictly positive increase in the potential function whenever a player moves. This proves Lemma 1.   □

In the following we will adjust local interaction games such that we preserve the incentives of players and the dynamics resulting from the RMP converge to a Nash equilibrium in expected polynomial time. There is a simple adjustment for any 2-type interaction game to ensure that $\mathrm{a} = \mathrm{b}$ and $\mathrm{e} = \mathrm{f}$ without harming the incentives of players and at most doubling the maximum payoff. In addition, for any local interaction game we can find an equivalent game with the same player preferences and payoffs are integers in $[-2n^2, 2n^2]$. When using the RMP with suitably perturbed payoffs we can show the following.

Theorem 2. *For local interaction games the dynamics resulting from the perturbed RMP converge to a Nash equilibrium in expected polynomial time.*

The complete proof will be given in full version. We strongly believe that a similar reduction to polynomial payoff values is also possible in the case of 2-type interaction games. The technical details are quite tedious and an analysis of this case is omitted. It is, however, straightforward to argue that if an 2-type interaction game has payoffs polynomial in n, i.e., in $O(n^k)$ for some constant k, then the perturbed RMP yields an expected potential increase of $\Omega(n^{-k})$ in each iteration. As in this case the maximum potential value is in $O(n^{k+2})$, we have the following corollary.

Corollary 1. *For 2-type interaction games with payoffs bounded by $O(n^k)$ with a constant k the dynamics resulting from the perturbed RMP converge to a Nash equilibrium in expected polynomial time.*

4   Comparison of Convergence Times

The bound on convergence times presented in previous sections hold in general for any 2-type interaction game. However, there are significant differences between different types of games. We will exhibit these differences experimentally using the simpler local interaction games. In dominant strategy games concurrent dynamics have an obvious advantage, because there is no error when allowing players to migrate. In particular, by appropriately adjusting payoffs to 0 and 1 we can ensure that in the RMP every player migrates with probability 1 to the dominant strategy. The details are left as exercise to the reader.

If there is no (weakly) dominant strategy, the game Γ_p is either a coordination game with A, B > 0, or an anti-coordination game with A, B < 0. For simplicity we restrict to *elementary* games, in which a, b, c, d $\in \{0, 1\}$. For such games it is possible to show a time bound of $O(n^2)$ for sequential dynamics, and of $O(n^3)$ for concurrent dynamics resulting from the RMP, which will will call *RMP dynamics*.

4.1   Coordination Games

First we consider elementary coordination games with a = b = 1 and c = d = 0. The worst-case upper bound for the convergence time of RMP dynamics is a factor of $\Theta(n)$ larger. It is left as an exercise to design a game matching this difference, i.e. a game in which the RMP dynamics are a factor of $\Omega(n)$ slower than any sequential better response dynamics. In fact, there is a game in which *every* concurrent dynamics are at least as slow as *any* sequential dynamics. We contrast these worst-case results with the average-case behavior on random graphs generated according to the $G_{n,p}$ model, as is done in the work of [25, 27]. We will observe similar behavior also on random unit disk graphs below. It turns out that in these games aggressive concurrent dynamics can make very rapid progress in initial stages.

Theorem 3. *Let $0 \leq c < 1$ be a constant and $\frac{1}{n^c} \leq p \leq \frac{1}{2}$, and let G be generated via $G_{n,p}$. Consider a state in the elementary coordination game with at least $(1/2 + \delta)n$ nodes playing strategy 1 and at most $(1/2 - \delta)$ nodes playing strategy 2, where $1/2 \geq \delta \geq 0$ is a constant. After 1 round of concurrent best response dynamics all but $o(n)$ nodes will be playing strategy 1.*

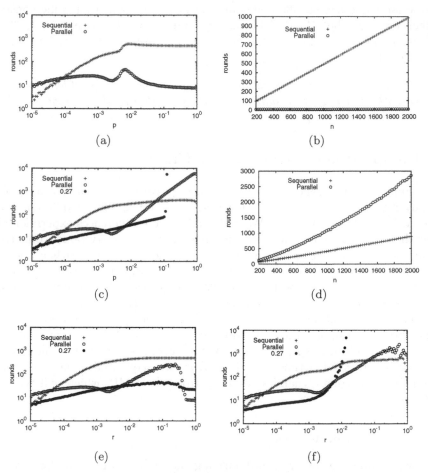

Fig. 3. Running times of sequential and concurrent dynamics. (a) Coordination games on $G_{n,p}$ with $n = 1000$ and varying p. (b) Coordination games on $G_{n,p}$ with $p = \log^{-1}(n)$ and varying n. (c) Anti-coordination games on $G_{n,p}$ with $n = 1000$ and varying p. (d) Anti-coordination games on $G_{n,p}$ with $p = \log^{-1}(n)$ and varying n. (e) Coordination games on random unit disk graphs with $n = 1000$ and varying radius r. (f) Anti-coordination games on random unit disk graphs with $n = 1000$ and varying radius r.

If the dynamics are sequential instead of concurrent, one can show by a similar argument to the above that after n rounds all but $o(n)$ nodes will be playing strategy 1.

Next, we show a number of experimental results in Fig. 3. For each value of n and p we generated 10 random graphs, and on each random graph we chose 25 starting states uniformly at random. From each starting state we initiated 25 runs of RMP dynamics. For the sequential dynamics we deterministically chose in each round one player that yields the largest payoff gain. The constant λ was set to $\lambda = 1.1$ throughout. Fig. 3(a) shows the average number of rounds for $n = 1000$ and p increasing exponentially between 10^{-5} and 1. When the large component forms (around $p = 0.005$) the sequential times are close to $n/2$, while the RMP dynamics converge rapidly in a constant number of runs.

Although Theorem 3 does not directly bound the convergence time to Nash equilibria, it provides the main intuition for the explanation of the results. After random initialization there are close to $n/2$ players playing each strategy. Afterwards, due to similar neighborhoods and coordination structure of the game, nearly all players accumulate on one strategy. Although this does not happen in one step, it still occurs quite rapidly, as each player migrating to a predominant strategy increases the probability for others to follow. Thus, in essence the behavior of the RMP dynamics is characterized by the insights from Theorem 3.

The intuition follows similarly for the sequential case, see Fig. 3(b). It depicts running times on graphs with increasing n and $p = \log^{-1}(n)$. Observe that RMP dynamics yield rapid convergence times that increase only very slightly. Sequential dynamics need roughly $\Theta(n)$ rounds until a Nash equilibrium is reached.

4.2 Anti-coordination Games

The elementary anti-coordination game is the MaxCut game with $\mathbf{a} = \mathbf{b} = 0$ and $\mathbf{c} = \mathbf{d} = 1$. For this game the worst-case results are similar to the coordination case. More specificaly, RMP dynamics are be a factor of $\Omega(n)$ slower than any sequential better response dynamics, and the game reveals that every concurrent dynamics are at least as slow as any sequential dynamics. We complement this lower bound with experimental results in Fig. 3. Fig. 3(c) and 3(d) are generated using the same parameters as for Fig. 3(a) and 3(b), respectively. While for small p the behavior of both dynamics is similar to the coordination case, it changes when $p \geq \frac{1}{n^c}$ for $c < 1$ which corresponds to roughly $p \geq 10^{-2}$ in Fig. 3(c). Observe the linear increase in running time with growing p for the RMP dynamics, which for large p leads even to worse convergence times than for sequential dynamics. A linear dependence on p is also supported by Fig. 3(d), as here $p = \log^{-1}(n)$, and the time growth for the RMP dynamics is proportional to $n \log n$. In fact, the linear dependence is a result from the RMP dynamics being too passive. Unlike in the coordination case, players do not accumulate on one strategy choice. In most iterations there is no significant majority playing one strategy. Payoff differences remain small, so with degrees growing linear in p, migration probabilities μ^v drop to a level proportional to $1/p$. The expected time until a player migrates then grows linearly in p. This effect is present until

p is very close to 1, in which case the convergence times of sequential dynamics drop to 0, as uniformly random initialization yields an almost stable profile. Furthermore, for almost complete graphs, the RMP dynamics yield a sequential process with high probability. This is because, in very dense graphs almost all players have the same neighborhood and experience the same changes in payoff. The migration probabilities in the RMP dynamics of roughly $1/n$ are balanced by the $\Theta(n)$ players that are willing to migrate in each round, so there is a roughly constant number of player migrating in each round.

Large running times are due to the payoff-relative update rule of the RMP. With different choices it is possible to achieve much more rapid convergence. Fig. 3(c) also depicts the convergence times of concurrent dynamics on graphs with $n = 1000$ and varying p where all migration probabilities μ^v are chosen as a fixed value $\mu = 0.27$, other values yield similar results. The increased migration significantly decreases the expected running times below the sequential times. At some point, however, the dynamics rather abruptly hit an "oscillation barrier" and convergence times start growing exponentially. Characterizing this barrier and providing further analytical insights on suitable choices of migration probabilities in concurrent dynamics remains a fascinating open problem.

Finally, we note that the key observations hold similarly for the case of random unit-disk graphs, which are a popular model for interference in distributed networks. We generated graphs by placing n points uniformly at random in the unit square. An edge was created between two points if the distance under the maximum norm was at most r. For each graph we chose 25 starting states uniformly at random, and from each state we initiated 25 runs of the dynamics. We provide average running times in Figure 3(e) and 3(f).

5   Conclusion

We have studied distributed decision making in a fundamental class of network interaction games with various applications in distributed systems and social networking. Our results concern the convergence time of sequential and concurrent better response dynamics. The analysis reveals polynomial convergence times for sequential dynamics in both local interaction games and 2-type interaction games. For concurrent dynamics resulting from the RMP there is polynomial convergence time in local interaction games, and in 2-type interaction games with polynomially bounded payoffs. In these games a local potential maximizer – i.e. a pure Nash equilibrium – can be obtained efficiently using distributed protocols, and thus efficient distributed decision making is possible. This stands in contrast to noisy better response dynamics and global potential maximizers, which are NP-hard to compute in anti-coordination games. Even for coordination games, in which computation is trivial, noisy better response dynamics can take exponential time [34].

While our results establish a general upper bound, the actual convergence times differ significantly based on the type of interaction and the underlying network. Using experiments we have shed some light on the influence of incentives and the degree of connectedness. More work is needed to obtain analytical characterizations for specific games and graph classes of interest.

Acknowledgment. The first author would like to thank Ulrik Brandes and Simon Fischer for discussion about the results in this work.

References

1. Ackermann, H., Berenbrink, P., Fischer, S., Hoefer, M.: Concurrent imitation dynamics in congestion games. In: Proc. 28th Symposium on Principles of Distributed Computing, PODC 2009 (to appear, 2009)
2. Ackermann, H., Röglin, H., Vöcking, B.: On the impact of combinatorial structure on congestion games. J. ACM 55(6) (2008)
3. Aumann, R.: Subjectivity and correlation in randomized strategies. Journal of Mathematical Economics 1, 67–96 (1974)
4. Berninghaus, S., Vogt, B.: Network formation in symmetric 2×2 games. Homo Oeconomicus 23(3/4), 421–466 (2006)
5. Blum, A., Mansour, Y.: Learning, regret minimization, and equilibria. In: Nisan, N., Roughgarden, T., Tardos, É., Vazirani, V. (eds.) Algorithmic Game Theory, ch. 4. Cambridge University Press, Cambridge (2007)
6. Blume, L.: The statistical mechanics of strategic interaction. Games and Economic Behavior 5, 387–424 (1993)
7. Bollobás, B.: Random Graphs, 2nd edn. Cambridge University Press, Cambridge (2001)
8. Bramoullé, Y.: Anti-coordination and social interactions. Games and Economic Behavior 58(1), 30–49 (2007)
9. Bramoullé, Y., López-Pintado, D., Goyal, S., Vega-Redondo, F.: Network formation and anti-coordination games. Intl. J. Game Theory 33(1), 1–19 (2004)
10. Brock, W., Durlauf, S.: Discrete choice with social interactions. Review of Economic Studies 68(2), 235–260 (2001)
11. Christodoulou, G., Mirrokni, V., Sidiropoulos, A.: Convergence and approximation in potential games. In: Durand, B., Thomas, W. (eds.) STACS 2006. LNCS, vol. 3884, pp. 349–360. Springer, Heidelberg (2006)
12. Daskalakis, C., Goldberg, P., Papadimitriou, C.: The complexity of computing a Nash equilibrium. In: Proc. 38th Symposium on Theory of Computing (STOC 2006), pp. 71–78 (2006)
13. Ellison, G.: Learning, local interaction, and coordination. Econometrica 61(5), 1047–1071 (1993)
14. Fabrikant, A., Papadimitriou, C., Talwar, K.: The complexity of pure Nash equilibria. In: Proc. 36th Symposium on Theory of Computing (STOC 2004), pp. 604–612 (2004)
15. Fabrikant, A., Papadimitriou, C.: The complexity of game dynamics: BGP oscillations, sink equilibria, and beyond. In: Proc. 19th Symposium on Discrete Algorithms (SODA 2008), pp. 844–853 (2008)
16. Fischer, S.: Dynamic Selfish Routing. PhD thesis, Lehrstuhl für Algorithmen und Komplexität, RWTH Aachen (2007)
17. Fischer, S., Räcke, H., Vöcking, B.: Fast convergence to Wardrop equilibria by adaptive sampling mehtods. In: Proc. 38th Symposium on Theory of Computing (STOC 2006), pp. 653–662 (2006)
18. Foster, D., Vohra, R.: Calibrated learning and correlated equilibrium. Games and Economic Behavior 21, 40–55 (1997)

19. Fudenberg, D., Levine, D.: Consistency and cautious ficticious play. Journal of Economic Dynamics and Control 19, 1065–1090 (1995)
20. Fudenberg, D., Levine, D.: The theory of learning in games. MIT Press, Cambridge (1998)
21. Giotis, I., Guruswami, V.: Correlation clustering with a fixed number of clusters. Theory of Computing 2(1), 249–266 (2006)
22. Goemans, M., Mirrokni, V., Vetta, A.: Sink equilibria and convergence. In: Proc. 46th Symposium on Foundations of Computer Science (FOCS 2005), pp. 142–154 (2005)
23. Goyal, S., Vega-Redondo, F.: Network formation and social coordination. Games and Economic Behavior 50, 178–207 (2005)
24. Jackson, M., Watts, A.: On the formation of interaction networks in social coordination games. Games and Economic Behavior 41, 265–291 (2002)
25. Kakade, S., Kearns, M., Ortiz, L., Pemantle, R., Suri, S.: Economic properties of social networks. In: Proc. 8th Conf. Neural Information Processing Systems (2004)
26. Kearns, M.: Graphical games. In: Roughgarden, T., Tardos, É., Nisan, N., Vazirani, V. (eds.) Algorithmic Game Theory, ch. 7, Cambridge University Press, Cambridge (2007)
27. Kearns, M., Suri, S.: Networks preserving evolutionary equilibria and the power of randomization. In: Proc. 7th Conference on Electronic Commerce (EC 2006), pp. 200–207 (2006)
28. Kearns, M., Tan, J.: Biased voting and the democratic primary problem. In: Papadimitriou, C., Zhang, S. (eds.) WINE 2008. LNCS, vol. 5385, pp. 639–652. Springer, Heidelberg (2008)
29. Kleinberg, J.: Cascading behavior in netwoks: Algorithmic and economic issues. In: Nisan, N., Roughgarden, T., Tardos, É., Vazirani, V. (eds.) Algorithmic Game Theory, ch. 24. Cambridge University Press, Cambridge (2007)
30. Marden, J.: Learning in Large-Scale Games and Cooperative Control. PhD thesis, UCLA, Los Angeles (2007)
31. Marden, J., Arslan, G., Shamma, J.: Joint strategy fictitious play with inertia for potential games. IEEE Transactions on Automatic Control 54(2), 208–220 (2009)
32. Mas-Colell, A., Hart, S.: A simple adaptive procedure leading to correlated equilibrium. Econometrica 68(5), 1127–1150 (2000)
33. Monderer, D., Shapley, L.: Potential games. Games and Economic Behavior 14, 1124–1143 (1996)
34. Montanari, A., Saberi, A.: Convergence to equilibrium in local interaction games. In: Proc. 50th Symposium on Foundations of Computer Science, FOCS 2009 (2009)
35. Weibull, J.: Evolutionary Game Theory. MIT Press, Cambridge (1995)
36. Young, H.P.: Individual Strategy and social structure. Princeton University Press, Princeton (1998)
37. Young, H.P.: Strategic Learning and its Limits. Oxford University Press, Oxford (2004)
38. Zinkevich, M.: Online convex programming and generalized infinitesimal gradient ascent. In: Proc. 20th Intl. Conf. Machine Learning (ICML 2003), pp. 928–936 (2003)

Brief Announcement: Cloud Computing Games: Pricing Services of Large Data Centers

Ashraf Al Daoud[1], Sachin Agarwal[2], and Tansu Alpcan[2]

[1] Department of Electrical and Computer Engineering, Boston University, USA
[2] Deutsche Telekom Laboratories, Technische Universität Berlin, Germany

Organizations opt to reduce costs by contracting their day-to-day computing needs to service providers who offer large-scale data centers and cloud computing services. Like other computing commodities, data centers provide paid services that require careful pricing. Using a Stackelberg game formulation, we present a demand-based pricing model for maximizing revenue of data center providers that serve clients who aim to maximize their utilities.

Problem Formulation: Let d_i denote the demand of client i from the data center quantified by the number of units of processing power per unit time. The service provider (data center) charges the client an amount λ_i per unit demand. So when serving N clients, the revenue of the service provider is $R(\boldsymbol{\lambda}, \mathbf{d}) = \sum_{i=1}^{N} \lambda_i d_i$, where $\boldsymbol{\lambda} = (\lambda_i : i = 1, \ldots, N)$ and $\mathbf{d} = (d_i : i = 1, \ldots, N)$. Clients share the computing resources of the data center. Therefore, the quality of service for one client in terms of processing delay at the data center is affected by the demand of the others. We define the quality-of-service factor of the ith client by $\gamma_i(\mathbf{d}) = L\frac{d_i}{\sum_{k=1, k \neq i}^{N} d_k}$, where $L \geq 1$ is a job decoupling factor which is higher for service providers who provide sufficient computing resources to separate demands of the different clients from affecting each other. If client's utility is logarithmic in the quality of service achieved, then the *net* utility for user i can be given by $U_i(\mathbf{d}, \lambda_i) = \alpha_i log\left(1 + \gamma_i(\mathbf{d})\right) - \lambda_i d_i$, where the constant $\alpha_i > 0$ converts utility to currency.

We consider selfish clients where each is interested in maximizing his net utility. Namely, if client i is charged λ_i per unit demand, and given the demand of the other clients (denoted by d_{-i}), the client's objective is to find d_i^* that solves

$$\textit{Client's problem:} \quad \max_{d_i \geq 0} \ U_i(d_i, d_{-i}, \lambda_i) \ \forall i.$$

Given this behavior, the service provider aims to maximize his revenue by imposing optimal prices. The problem can be formulated as a Stackelberg game where the service provider sets prices and consequently the clients update demands (required units of processing power per unit time) to maximize their utilities. Let $\mathbf{d}^*(\boldsymbol{\lambda}) = (d_i^*(\boldsymbol{\lambda}) : i = 1, \ldots, N)$, the service provider's objective is to solve

$$\textit{Service provider's problem:} \quad \max_{\boldsymbol{\lambda} > 0} \ R(\boldsymbol{\lambda}, \mathbf{d}^*(\boldsymbol{\lambda})).$$

Methodology and Main Results: We use a backward induction technique to find Nash Equilibrium (NE) point(s) where neither the service provider nor

I. Keidar (Ed.): DISC 2009, LNCS 5805, pp. 309–310, 2009.

any of the clients have the incentive to unilaterally deviate. We start with the clients' game and solve for the NE as a function of the price vector $\boldsymbol{\lambda}$. It can be shown that the game of the clients admits a unique NE for any set of prices $\boldsymbol{\lambda} > 0$. In particular, as in [1], index the clients such that if $\frac{\alpha_i}{\lambda_i} < \frac{\alpha_j}{\lambda_j}$ then $i > j$ with the ordering to be picked randomly if $\frac{\alpha_i}{\lambda_i} = \frac{\alpha_j}{\lambda_j}$. Let $M^*(\boldsymbol{\lambda})$ be the largest integer M for which the following condition is satisfied: $\frac{\alpha_M}{\lambda_M} > \frac{1}{L+M-1} \sum_{j=1}^{M} \frac{\alpha_j}{\lambda_j}$. The equilibrium demands of the first $M^*(\boldsymbol{\lambda})$ clients are positive and obtained by $d_i^*(\boldsymbol{\lambda}) = \frac{L}{L-1} \left(\frac{\alpha_i}{\lambda_i} - \frac{1}{(L+M^*(\boldsymbol{\lambda})-1)} \sum_{j=1}^{M^*(\boldsymbol{\lambda})} \frac{\alpha_j}{\lambda_j} \right)$, where $d_i(\boldsymbol{\lambda})^* = 0$ for $i \geq M^*(\boldsymbol{\lambda}) + 1$. We follow on this and solve for the service provider's problem. Namely, let the indexing of the clients be done such that $\sqrt{\alpha_i} < \sqrt{\alpha_j} \implies i > j$, with the ordering to be picked arbitrarily if $\sqrt{\alpha_i} = \sqrt{\alpha_j}$. If the following condition is satisfied for all $M \in \{1, \cdots, N\}$

$$\sqrt{\alpha_M} > \frac{1}{L + M - 1} \sum_{j=1}^{M} \sqrt{\alpha_j}, \tag{1}$$

then the Stackelberg game admits an infinite number of NE points $(\boldsymbol{\lambda}^*, \mathbf{d}^*)$ where

$$\frac{\lambda_i^*}{\sqrt{\alpha_i}} = \frac{\lambda_j^*}{\sqrt{\alpha_j}}, \quad \forall i, j = 1, \cdots, N. \tag{2}$$

The corresponding demand levels are non-zero and given by

$$d_i^* = \frac{L}{(L-1)} \frac{1}{\lambda_i^*} \left(\alpha_i - \frac{\sqrt{\alpha_i}}{(L+N-1)} \sum_{j=1}^{N} \sqrt{\alpha_j} \right).$$

We give a proof of this result in an analogous setup in [2]. Formula (2) devises prices that are optimal over the set of prices that result in all the clients to have non-zero demand levels. It has a proportional structure that suggests charging more the clients that are more willing to pay for their utilities, i.e. higher α's. Here, if L is large enough, then condition (1) is satisfied for all $M \in \{1, \cdots, N\}$. Intuitively, the higher the decoupling factor L is, the better the quality of service for the client and the lesser the external effect due to the other clients' demands. Therefore, there is an incentive for the clients to have non-zero demand levels. We can also show that if condition (1) is satisfied, it is suboptimal for the service provider to drop any of the clients by imposing a sufficiently high price. In other words, under that condition, the suggested prices in (2) are optimal over the set $\boldsymbol{\lambda} > 0$.

References

1. Alpcan, T., Basar, T., Srikant, R., Altman, E.: CDMA Uplink Power Control as a Noncooperative Game. Wireless Networks 8(6), 659–670 (2002)
2. Al Daoud, A., Alpcan, T., Agarwal, S., Alanyali, M.: A Stackelberg Game for Pricing Uplink Power in Wide-Band Cognitive Radio Networks. In: Proc. of 47th IEEE Conference on Descision and Control, pp. 1422–1427 (2008)

On the Existence of Weakest Failure Detectors for Mutual Exclusion and k-Exclusion

(Extended Abstract)

Vibhor Bhatt and Prasad Jayanti

Dartmouth College, Hanover, NH, USA

Abstract. Research over the past two decades has identified the weakest failure detectors for several important problems in fault-tolerant distributed computing. A recent work has shown that, for a certain definition of the term "problem," every problem that is solvable using failure detectors has a weakest failure detector. In sharp contrast to these results, we prove that a fundamental problem in concurrent computing—FCFS Mutual Exclusion—is solvable using failure detectors, but has no weakest failure detector in the shared memory model. To the best of our knowledge, this is the first problem that is proved not to have a weakest failure detector. We also show that, if the FCFS requirement is dropped, the mutual exclusion problem has a weakest failure detector. In fact, we present the weakest failure detector for the more general problem of starvation-free k-exclusion, for any k.

1 Introduction

Several basic problems in fault-tolerant distributed computing are known to be unsolvable in asynchronous systems. The unsolvability is often due to the inability of a process, when it does not hear from another process p, to distinguish between whether p has crashed or p is merely being slow. To circumvent such impossibility results, failure detectors, which augment asynchronous systems, are proposed [5]. A failure detector is a distributed oracle, with one module at each process that, when queried, responds with a value that reveals some information about the failures in the system.

Research on failure detectors was spurred [5,4] by the unsolvability of *consensus* [10], a fundamental problem in distributed computing. Chandra and Toueg showed that a surprisingly weak failure detector Ω is sufficient to solve consensus [5]. A later result by Chandra et al. proves that Ω is the *weakest* failure detector to solve consensus in the sense that, if any failure detector D is good enough to solve consensus, then it is possible to implement Ω from D [4]. Since then, weakest failure detectors have been identified for several other basic problems in fault-tolerant distributed computing (e.g., non-blocking atomic commit [6], uniform reliable broadcast [1], implementing an atomic register in a message-passing system [6], mutual exclusion [7,3], boosting obstruction-freedom [12], set consensus [16,11], etc.). Going beyond specific problems, for a certain definition of the term "problem", it is recently shown that every problem that is solvable using failure detectors has a weakest failure detector [13].

The main result of this paper runs counter to this overwhelming evidence that all natural distributed computing problems have weakest failure detectors. Specifically, we

I. Keidar (Ed.): DISC 2009, LNCS 5805, pp. 311–325, 2009.
© Springer-Verlag Berlin Heidelberg 2009

prove that *FCFS Mutual Exclusion*, although solvable using failure detectors, has no weakest failure detector in the asynchronous shared-memory model.

In Mutual Exclusion, which is a fundamental problem in distributed computing [8], each process repeatedly cycles through four sections of code—Try Section, Critical Section (CS), Exit Section, and Remainder Section. In the classical version, processes are assumed not to fail and the task is to design the code for the Try and Exit Sections satisfying: (1) the *mutual exclusion property*, which states that at most one process is in the CS at any time, and (2) some liveness property, for instance, *starvation freedom*, which requires a process in the Try Section to eventually enter the CS and a process in the Exit Section to eventually enter the Remainder Section (on the assumption that no process stays in the CS forever). When solving this problem in the shared memory model, an additional desirable property is the First-Come-First-Served (FCFS) fairness property proposed by Lamport [14]. This property requires that (1) the Try Section begins with a code segment, called the doorway, that can always be completed within a bounded number of steps by any process, and (2) if a process p completes the doorway before a process q enters the doorway, then q does not enter the CS before p.

In the *fault-tolerant version* of the problem [7], if a process crashes in the CS, another process is allowed to enter the CS: multiple processes can be in the CS simultaneously provided that at most one of them is alive and the others have already crashed. Thus, the classical mutual exclusion property is revised to state that at most one *live* process is in the CS at any time. The starvation freedom property is revised to guarantee the progress of only the correct processes: every *correct* process in the Try Section eventually enters the CS and every *correct* process in the Exit Section eventually enters the Remainder Section (on the assumption that no *correct* process stays in the CS forever). Finally, the FCFS property is revised to state that, if p completes the doorway before q enters the doorway, then q does not enter the CS before p while p is alive. In other words, q may enter the CS before p only after p fails.

Our second result is that if the FCFS requirement is dropped and the only properties required are mutual exclusion and starvation-freedom, then a weakest failure detector exists. In fact, we consider the more general problem of k-exclusion [9], where up to k live processes are allowed to be in the CS simultaneously. The starvation-freedom property for this problem states that every correct process in the Try Section eventually enters the CS even if at most $k-1$ correct processes stay in the CS forever. We present a weakest failure detector for this problem in an arbitrary environment where any process may fail at any time.

1.1 Explaining the Apparent Contradiction

Our result that there is no weakest failure detector for FCFS Mutual Exclusion appears to contradict the result in [13] that every problem, which is solvable using failure detectors, has a weakest failure detector. There is, however, no contradiction because FCFS Mutual Exclusion is outside the class of problems for which the [13] result applies, as we now explain.

Some problems have the following characteristic: their requirements are such that (1) given a run, it is possible to determine whether the problem requirements are met in the run, and (2) an algorithm is considered to solve the problem if every run of the algorithm meets the problem requirements. Consensus, for example, is such a problem: if every run of an algorithm meets the Validity, Agreement, and Termination conditions, then the algorithm is correct. The result in [13] applies only to this class of problems. But some problems, e.g., FCFS Mutual Exclusion, do not fall into this class. To see why, consider the doorway condition that some $b \in \mathbb{N}$ must exist such that the length of the doorway is bounded by b in *all* runs. It is easy to propose algorithms where for each run there is a bound, but no single bound applies to all runs. For example, consider the following change to Lamport's Bakery Algorithm: each process picks a natural number b non-deterministically once at the start of a run and, each time the process enters the Try Section, it performs b useless steps before executing the Bakery Algorithm's Try Section. Each run of this algorithm looks acceptable (because the length of the doorway in that run is bounded), but the algorithm does not meet the FCFS requirement as there is no universal bound that applies to all runs.

Another pertinent difference between [13] and this paper concerns the definition of "implementing a failure detector." According to the prevalent definition, the implementation of a failure detector D should maintain an output variable $output_p$ at each process p such that the values of these output variables, over time, are consistent with some failure detector history of D. This was the definition proposed in the original failure detector papers [5,4] and all of the failure detector papers we know of, with the exception of [13], use this definition. [13] proposes an alternative definition based on linearizability where, instead of interacting via the output variable, each process interacts with the implementation by initiating a query and later receiving a response from the implementation. This paper uses the first definition. It is an interesting open question whether a weakest failure detector exists for FCFS Mutual Exclusion under the second definition of implementation.

1.2 Related Work

The mutual exclusion problem was stated and solved in a seminal paper by Dijkstra [8]. The FCFS property and the Bakery algorithm that realizes the property were proposed by Lamport [14]. The surveys by Raynal [15] and Anderson [2] describe the work on many facets of this problem. Fischer et al. stated and solved the k-exclusion problem [9]. Delporte *et al.* studied the fault-tolerant version of mutual exclusion [7]. They proposed a failure detector, which they called the *trusting failure detector* T, and showed that it is both necessary and sufficient to solve the starvation-free mutual exclusion problem in an environment where a majority of processes is correct [7]. To solve the problem in an arbitrary environment in the message passing model, Bhatt *et al.* [3] showed that it is both necessary and sufficient to augment the trusting failure detector with a certain quorum failure detector. To the best of our knowledge, this submission is the first to investigate the weakest failure detectors for exclusion problems in the shared memory model.

2 The Model

We consider the asynchronous shared memory model augmented with failure detectors based on [5]. The model assumes the existence of a discrete global clock; the range of this clock's ticks is $\mathbb{N}$. The system we consider has $\Pi = \{1, 2, \ldots, n\}$ processes that communicate through atomic shared registers. Processes are subject to *crash failures*. A *failure pattern* is a function $F : \mathbb{N} \to 2^{\Pi}$, where $F(t)$ is the set of processes that have crashed through time t. A process p is *live* at time t if $p \notin F(t)$; *correct*(F) is the set of processes that don't fail in F. An *environment* is a set of failure patterns. The *arbitrary environment* is the environment that consists of all possible failure patterns. A *failure detector history* describes the behavior of a failure detector during an execution. Formally, it is a function $H : \Pi \times \mathbb{N} \to \{0, 1\}^*$, where $H(p, t)$ is the value output by the failure detector module of process p at time t.

A *failure detector* D is a function that maps every failure pattern F to a nonempty set of failure detector histories. $D(F)$ is the set of all possible failure detector histories that may be output by D when the failure pattern is F.

A *run of algorithm* $\mathcal{A}$ *using failure detector* D *in environment* $\mathcal{E}$ is a tuple $R = (F, H, I, S, T)$ where F is a failure pattern in $\mathcal{E}$, H is a failure detector history in $D(F)$, I is an input vector, S is a sequence of steps of algorithm $\mathcal{A}$ (S is called a *schedule*, and $S[i]$ denotes the i-th step in S), T is a sequence of times in $\mathbb{N}$ (intuitively, $T[i]$ is the time when step $S[i]$ is taken), such that F, H, I, S, and T satisfy the standard conditions. A step by a process p can be a local computation, read or write operation on some shared register or a query to its failure detector module D_p, which we also assume to be atomic.

Let $\mathcal{A}$ be an algorithm, $\mathcal{P}$ be a problem, D a failure detector, and $\mathcal{E}$ an environment.

- $\mathcal{A}$ *solves* $\mathcal{P}$ *using* D *in* $\mathcal{E}$ if and only if the set of runs of $\mathcal{A}$ using D in $\mathcal{E}$ satisfy the specification of $\mathcal{P}$.
- D *can be used to solve* $\mathcal{P}$ *in* $\mathcal{E}$ if and only if there is an algorithm that solves $\mathcal{P}$ using D in $\mathcal{E}$.

2.1 Implementing a Failure Detector

Our notion of implementation is exactly the same as described in [5,4]. Let a variable *output* be maintained at each process in A. Denote the history of *output* in run R of A by *output*^{R}, *i.e.* *output*$^R(p, t)$ is equal to the value of *output* at process p at time t. Now we define the notion of a reduction algorithm $T_{D \to D'}$ which uses failure detector D to implement failure detector D'.

$T_{D \to D'}$ implements failure detector D' in environment $\mathcal{E}$ if it maintains an variable *output* at every process such that, in every run R of $T_{D \to D'}$ in failure pattern $F \in \mathcal{E}$, *output*$^R \in D'(F)$. Informally, $T_{D \to D'}$ can implement D' using D if it can maintain a valid output for D' in any failure pattern $F \in \mathcal{E}$.

2.2 Comparing Failure Detectors

We say that a failure detector D' is *at most as strong as* D in environment $\mathcal{E}$ if there is a reduction algorithm $T_{D \to D'}$ that D' in $\mathcal{E}$. We denote this by $D' \preceq_{\mathcal{E}} D$.

For the special case when $\mathcal{E}$ is the arbitrary environment (one that contains all possible failure patterns), we write $D' \preceq D$ as a shorthand for $D' \preceq_{\mathcal{E}} D$.

We say a failure detector W is the *weakest failure detector for a problem* P in an environment $\mathcal{E}$ if (1) W can be used to solve the problem in $\mathcal{E}$, and (2) if a failure detector D' can be used to solve P in $\mathcal{E}$, then $W \preceq_{\mathcal{E}} D$.

3   FCFS Mutual Exclusion Has No Weakest Failure Detector

In an FCFS Mutual Exclusion Algorithm, each process repeatedly executes five sections of code: doorway, waiting room, CS, exit section, and remainder section. An algorithm $\mathcal{A}$ solves the *FCFS Mutual Exclusion Problem* using a failure detector D in an environment $\mathcal{E}$ if there is a $b \in \mathbb{N}$ such that the following conditions are met in every run of $\mathcal{A}$ using D where the failure pattern F is from $\mathcal{E}$:

- *Mutual Exclusion*: At most one live process is in the CS at any time.
- *Starvation Freedom*: If every correct process that enters the CS eventually leaves the CS, then every correct process in the doorway eventually enters the CS. Further, every correct process in the exit section eventually enters the remainder section.
- *Bounded Doorway*: Each execution of the doorway by a process completes within b steps of that process. (We say b is the length of the doorway.)
- *FCFS*: If a process p completes the doorway before a process q enters the doorway, then either q does not enter the CS before p or p fails before q enters the CS.

We define the *arbitrary environment* as the environment that contains all failure patterns. Informally, in an arbitrary environment, any process can crash at any time. We now state and prove the main result of this paper.

Theorem 1. *There is no weakest failure detector for the FCFS Mutual Exclusion problem in the arbitrary environment.*

Proof. The proof is by contradiction and proceeds as follows. Assume that a weakest failure detector $\mathcal{W}$ exists for FCFS Mutual Exclusion. Let $\mathcal{A}$ be an algorithm that solves FCFS Mutual Exclusion using $\mathcal{W}$. We derive a contradiction by defining a family of failure detectors $\mathcal{D}_k$, $k \in \mathbb{N}$, with three properties:

($P1$). Failure detectors in the family are good enough to solve FCFS Mutual Exclusion. More precisely, for all $k \in \mathbb{N}$, FCFS Mutual Exclusion can be solved using the failure detector $\mathcal{D}_k$. Since $\mathcal{W}$ is a weakest failure detector for FCFS Mutual Exclusion, it follows that $\mathcal{W} \preceq \mathcal{D}_k$, for all $k \in \mathbb{N}$.

($P2$). Each failure detector in the family is strictly weaker than the preceding ones. More precisely, for all $k \in \mathbb{N}$, $\mathcal{D}_{k+1} \preceq \mathcal{D}_k$ and $\mathcal{D}_k \npreceq \mathcal{D}_{k+1}$.

($P3$). $\mathcal{D}_b \preceq \mathcal{W}$, where b is the length of algorithm $\mathcal{A}$'s doorway.

We prove the above three properties in Lemmas 1, 2, and 3. Since $\mathcal{D}_b \preceq \mathcal{W}$ (by $P3$) and $\mathcal{W} \preceq \mathcal{D}_{b+1}$ (by $P1$), by the transitivity of $\preceq$, it follows that $\mathcal{D}_b \preceq \mathcal{D}_{b+1}$, which contradicts $P2$. Hence, we have the theorem.

In the rest of this section, we define $\mathcal{D}_k$ and establish the properties $P1$, $P2$, and $P3$.

3.1   Definition of the Failure Detector $\mathcal{D}_k$

Consider the failure detector $\mathbb{P}$, which is a variation of the perfect failure detector introduced by Chandra and Toueg [5]. $\mathbb{P}$'s output at any process p at any time t is a set of processes that p suspects to have failed by time t. $\mathbb{P}$ satisfies two properties:

- Accuracy: A process is not suspected before it fails.
  In contrast, the accuracy property of Chandra and Toueg's perfect failure detector makes a weaker statement that a process is not suspected unless it is faulty. Thus, their property allows a faulty process to be suspected before it fails.
- Completeness: A faulty process is eventually permanently suspected by all correct processes.

The failure detector $\mathcal{D}_k$ that we define below is similar to, but weaker than, $\mathbb{P}$. Unlike $\mathbb{P}$ where all failures are accurately detected, $\mathcal{D}_k$ can be unreliable on how it reports about processes that fail within the first k units of time. In particular, if a process q fails at or before time k, all of the following behaviors are possible with $\mathcal{D}_k$: (1) q's failure is never suspected by any correct process, (2) q is suspected even before it fails, or (3) correct processes repeatedly add and remove q from their list of suspects. However, failures that occur after time k are detected equally well by $\mathcal{D}_k$ and $\mathbb{P}$. More precisely, the failure detector $\mathcal{D}_k$ is defined as follows:

Definition 1. *For all failure patterns F, $H \in \mathcal{D}_k(F)$ if and only if $H(p,t) \subseteq \Pi$ for all $p \in \Pi$ and $t \in \mathbb{N}$, and satisfies:*

- *k-Accuracy: Unless a process fails by time k, it is not suspected before it fails.*

$$\forall p, q \in \Pi, t \in \mathbb{N} : (q \notin F(k) \wedge q \in H(p,t)) \implies q \in F(t)$$

- *k-Completeness: Unless a faulty process fails by time k, it is eventually permanently suspected by all correct processes.*
  $\forall p, q \in \Pi, t \in \mathbb{N}, \exists \tau \in \mathbb{N} : (q \notin F(k) \wedge q \notin correct(F) \wedge p \in correct(F) \wedge,$
  $t > \tau) \implies q \in H(p,t)$

3.2 Proof of Property $P3$

Recall that $\mathcal{W}$ is a weakest failure detector for the FCFS Mutual Exclusion problem; $\mathcal{A}$ is an algorithm that solves FCFS Mutual Exclusion using $\mathcal{W}$; and b is the length of $\mathcal{A}$'s doorway. The lemma below proves Property P3.

Lemma 1. $\mathcal{D}_b \preceq \mathcal{W}$

Proof. Since $\mathcal{W}$ is a weakest failure detector for FCFS Mutual Exclusion, it follows that for all failure detectors D that can be used to solve FCFS Mutual Exclusion, we have $\mathcal{W} \preceq D$. Instantiating D with $\mathcal{W}$, we have $\mathcal{W} \preceq \mathcal{W}$. This means that there is some algorithm $\mathcal{R}$ that implements $\mathcal{W}$ from $\mathcal{W}$. Let $\mathcal{R}(p)$ denote a process p's program in algorithm $\mathcal{R}$; $output_p$ denote the output variable maintained by $\mathcal{R}(p)$; and $init_p$ denote the initial value assigned by $\mathcal{R}$ to $output_p$. Since $\mathcal{R}$ implements $\mathcal{W}$ from $\mathcal{W}$, in any run R (of $\mathcal{R}$ using $\mathcal{W}$) with failure pattern F, the values of $output_p$, for all $p \in \Pi$, are consistent with a failure detector history $H \in \mathcal{W}(F)$.

The rest of the proof of Lemma 1 consists of two definitions and two claims. Specifically, we define a failure detector $\mathcal{W}'$ and an algorithm $\mathcal{R}'$ such that two claims hold: (1) $\mathcal{R}'$ implements $\mathcal{W}'$ from $\mathcal{W}$, and (2) $\mathcal{D}_b \preceq \mathcal{W}'$. Note that Claim (1) implies $\mathcal{W}' \preceq \mathcal{W}$. This fact, together with Claim (2) and the transitivity of $\preceq$, implies the lemma. We now present the two definitions and the two claims.

Informally, the failure detector W' is obtained by limiting the failure detector W to only those histories where the failure detector's value at each process p remains constant at $init_p$ for the first b units of time. More precisely, W' is defined as follows:

Definition 2. *For all failure patterns* F, $H \in W'(F)$ *if and only if*

$$H \in W(F) \quad and \quad \forall p \in \Pi, t \in \mathbb{N} : (t \leq b) \implies (H(p,t) = init_p)$$

Since the algorithm $\mathcal{A}$ solves FCFS Mutual Exclusion using W and since $W'(F) \subseteq W(F)$ for all failure patterns F, it follows that $\mathcal{A}$ must solve FCFS Mutual Exclusion also using W'. The next proposition states this fact.

Proposition 1. *Algorithm* $\mathcal{A}$ *solves FCFS Mutual Exclusion using* W'.

Next we define the algorithm $\mathcal{R}'$. In $\mathcal{R}'$ each process first executes b null steps and then executes the same code as in algorithm $\mathcal{R}$. More precisely:

Definition 3. *The algorithm* $\mathcal{R}'$ *is defined by the following two rules:*

- $\mathcal{R}'$ *assigns the same initial values to output variables as* $\mathcal{R}$: *for all* $p \in \Pi$, $\mathcal{R}'$ *initializes* output$_p$ *to* init$_p$.
- $\mathcal{R}'(p)$—*process* p's *program in algorithm* $\mathcal{R}'$—*consists of* b NOP *operations followed by* $\mathcal{R}(p)$, *which is* p's *program in algorithm* $\mathcal{R}$. *More precisely, for all* $p \in \Pi$, *we have:*

$\mathcal{R}'(p)$ {
   for $i = 1$ *to* b
      NOP
   $\mathcal{R}(p)$
}

Claim. Algorithm $\mathcal{R}'$ implements W' from W.

Proof. Consider an arbitrary run R of the algorithm $\mathcal{R}'$ using W, and let F be the failure pattern in R. We prove the claim by showing that there is a history $H \in W'(F)$ such that for all $p \in \Pi$, $t \in \mathbb{N}$, $H(p,t) = output_p(t)$, where $output_p(t)$ is the value of $output_p$ at time t in run R.

First we observe that $\mathcal{R}'$ implements W from W. This observation follows from two facts: (1) $\mathcal{R}$ implements W from W, and (2) the only difference between $\mathcal{R}'$ and $\mathcal{R}$ is the NOPs at the start of $\mathcal{R}'$ and their only effect is to introduce some initial delay, which is possible even without NOPs because of asynchrony.

Since $\mathcal{R}'$ implements W from W, it follows that the output of $\mathcal{R}'$ in run R is consistent with some history $H \in W(F)$: i.e., for all $p \in \Pi$, $t \in \mathbb{N}$, $H(p,t) = output_p(t)$. Further, since the first b steps of each process p are NOPs, it follows that $output_p$ remains at its initial value of $init_p$ for at least the first b units of time: i.e., $\forall p \in \Pi, t \in \mathbb{N} : (t \leq b) \implies (H(p,t) = init_p)$. Thus, we have: (1) $H \in W(F)$, and (2) $\forall p \in \Pi, t \in \mathbb{N} : H(p,t) = output_p(t)$ and, if $t \leq b$, $H(p,t) = init_p$. Therefore, by definition of W', $H \in W'(F)$. Hence, we have the claim.

As an immediate consequence of the above claim, we have:

Corollary 1. $\mathcal{W}' \preceq \mathcal{W}$.

Claim. $\mathcal{D}_b \preceq \mathcal{W}'$

Proof. The proof is structured as follows. We prove the claim by exhibiting an algorithm $\mathcal{T}$ that implements $\mathcal{D}_b$ using $\mathcal{W}'$. We design $\mathcal{T}$ as a collection of $n(n-1)$ co-routines, one for each ordered pair of processes. The co-routine $D_q(p)$ is a program that p runs to detect q's failure, and it guarantees two key properties: (A1) unless q fails by time b, p does not suspect q before q fails, and (A2) unless q fails by time b, if p is correct and q is faulty, then p eventually permanently suspects q. In the algorithm $\mathcal{T}$, each process p concurrently runs $n-1$ programs—namely, the programs $D_q(p)$ for all $q \in \Pi - \{p\}$—and combines their outputs to output a set of suspects. Since each $D_q(p)$ guarantees Properties A1 and A2, it follows that $\mathcal{T}$'s output satisfies the b-Accuracy and b-Completeness properties of $\mathcal{D}_b$, thereby establishing the claim. In the rest of this proof, we describe the program $D_q(p)$ and argue that it satisfies properties A1 and A2.

Recall Proposition 1, which states that algorithm $\mathcal{A}$ solves FCFS Mutual Exclusion using $\mathcal{W}'$. Let $\{r_1, r_2, \ldots, r_m\}$ be the set of all shared registers used by algorithm $\mathcal{A}$. Consider the initial configuration C_0 of $\mathcal{A}$, where all processes are in the remainder section and the shared registers $r_1, r_2, \ldots, r_m$ have their initial value. Consider a solo-run of process q from configuration C_0 until q completes its doorway. Since the length of $\mathcal{A}$'s doorway is b, this solo-run will consist of b steps where, in each step, q samples the failure detector value, reads or writes a shared register r_i, and changes its local state. On the assumption that each time q samples the failure detector it gets the same value of $init_q$, compute the values $v_1, v_2, \ldots, v_m$ of the shared registers $r_1, r_2, \ldots, r_m$ at the end of q's solo-run of b steps. Given this setup, we are ready to describe the program $D_q(p)$. Recall that $D_q(p)$ is not a distributed algorithm; it is a program that p alone runs to make inferences about q's failure. The program $D_q(p)$ is described as follows:

- $D_q(p)$ maintains variables $r_1', r_2', \ldots, r_m'$ locally at p. These variables are initialized to $v_1, v_2, \ldots, v_m$, respectively.
- $\mathcal{A}(p)$ denotes p's program in algorithm $\mathcal{A}$. Let $\mathcal{A}'(p)$ denote the program obtained by replacing each reference in $\mathcal{A}(p)$ to a shared register r_i, with a reference to the variable r_i' (for all $1 \le i \le m$). Thus, for example, if "read r_5" is an instruction in $\mathcal{A}(p)$, the corresponding instruction in $\mathcal{A}'(p)$ will be "read r_5'".
- The program $D_q(p)$ consists of b NOP instructions, followed by the code of $\mathcal{A}'(p)$. Initially, p's program counter points to the first NOP instruction.
- In $D_q(p)$, when p's program counter points to Critical Section, p permanently suspects q; until then p does not suspect q.

Consider an arbitrary run R of the program $D_q(p)$ using the failure detector $\mathcal{W}'$. Let F be the failure pattern in run R, and $H \in \mathcal{W}'(F)$ be the failure detector history in run R. We now show that if q does not fail by time b in F, then the following statements hold in run R: (A1) p does not suspect q before q fails, and (A2) if p is correct and q is faulty, then p eventually permanently suspects q.

Assume that q does not fail by time b in F. Let $t_1, t_2, \ldots$ denote the sequence of time values when p executes the instructions of $\mathcal{A}'(p)$ in run R. Since p executes b NOPs before executing the first instruction of $\mathcal{A}'(p)$, it follows that $t_1 > b$. Based on the run R (of the program $D_q(p)$ using $\mathcal{W}'$), in the following we construct a run R' of algorithm $\mathcal{A}$ using $\mathcal{W}'$, and make some observations about this run.

- The failure pattern in R' is F, the same failure pattern as in R.
- The failure detector history in R' is H, the same failure detector history as in R.
- In R', q performs b steps of its doorway during the first b units of time.
  These steps by q are possible because of our assumption that q does not fail by time b in F. Further, in these steps, when q samples the failure detector, it always gets the same value of $init_q$ because, by definition of $\mathcal{W}'$, $H(q, t) = init_q$ for all $t \leq b$. Consequently, at time b in run R' (i.e., soon after q completes its doorway in R'), the values of the shared registers $r_1, r_2, \ldots, r_m$ are $v_1, v_2, \ldots, v_m$, respectively.
- In R', p performs the steps of $\mathcal{A}(p)$ at times $t_1, t_2, \ldots$ (i.e., at the same times that p performs the steps of $\mathcal{A}'(p)$ in the run R).
  Since the failure detector history is the same in both runs, the sequence of failure detector values that p sees in R' is the same as in R. Further, by the conclusion made in the previous bullet point, for all $1 \leq i \leq m$, r_i and r_i' have the same value v_i just before p starts taking steps in the runs R' and R, respectively. Consequently, modulo the name difference between r_i' and r_i, p cannot distinguish the run R from the run R'. In particular, p enters the Critical Section in run R at time t if and only if p enters the Critical Section in run R' at time t.

To verify that $D_q(p)$ satisfies Property A1, suppose that p suspects q at time t in run R. Since p suspects q only when p is in the Critical Section, it follows that p is in the Critical Section at time t in run R. Then, by the conclusion reached above, p is in the Critical Section at time t in run R' (of algorithm $\mathcal{A}$ using $\mathcal{W}'$). In run R', q completes the doorway before p enters the doorway, and q does not take any steps after completing the doorway. So, by the specification of FCFS Mutual Exclusion, if p is in the Critical Section at time t in R', then q must have failed before time t in R'. Since R and R' have the same failure pattern F, it follows that q fails before time t also in R. Hence, $D_q(p)$ satisfies Property A1.

To verify that $D_q(p)$ satisfies Property A2, suppose that in the failure pattern F of the runs R and R', p is correct and q is faulty. Since q is faulty in R' and all processes other than p and q are in the remainder sections forever, it follows from the starvation-freedom property of Mutual Exclusion that p eventually enters the Critical Section in run R'. Since we already concluded that p enters the Critical Section in R' if and only if it enters the Critical Section in R, it follows that p enters the Critical Section in R as well. Once p enters the Critical Section, by the design of $D_q(p)$, p suspects q forever, which establishes Property A2. This concludes the proof of the claim.

Lemma 1 follows immediately from Claim 3.2, Corollary 1, and the transitivity of $\preceq$.

3.3   Proof of Property $P2$

Lemma 2. *For all $k \in \mathbb{N}$, $\mathcal{D}_{k+1} \preceq \mathcal{D}_k$ and $\mathcal{D}_k \npreceq \mathcal{D}_{k+1}$*

Proof. $\mathcal{D}_{k+1} \preceq \mathcal{D}_k$ is true by the definition of $\mathcal{D}_k$. We prove $\mathcal{D}_k \npreceq \mathcal{D}_{k+1}$ by contradiction. Suppose there exists a reduction algorithm $\mathcal{R}$ which implements $\mathcal{D}_k$ from $\mathcal{D}_{k+1}$. Consider two scenarios a, b ; in a all processes are correct, and in b, process q crashes at time $k + 1$ and rest of the processes are correct. Also assume that in both the scenarios $\mathcal{D}_{k+1}$ outputs ϕ forever at all the processes; this is a valid history of $\mathcal{D}_{k+1}$. Now take some run R^b of $\mathcal{R}$ in scenario b. By k-*Completeness*, output of $\mathcal{R}$ in R^b will eventually include q at every correct process permanently. Let p be the first process where the output of $\mathcal{R}$ includes q and say this happens at time t. Take a run R^a in scenario a, such that all processes take the same steps as in R^b till t; this is a valid run of $\mathcal{R}$ in scenario a. As p cannot distinguish between R^a and R^b, q will be included in p's output at t. This violates k-*Accuracy* property of $\mathcal{D}_k$, a contradiction.

3.4   Proof of Property P1

Lemma 3. *The algorithm $\mathcal{M}$ given in figure 1 solves FCFS mutual exclusion using $\mathcal{D}_k$.*

Proof omitted from this version.

Initialization
$token_p \leftarrow 0$
$choosing[p] \leftarrow false$

```
1    for i ← 1 to k
2        NOP
3    choosing[p] ← true
4    token_p ← 1 + max_{∀q≠p}(token_q)
5    choosing[p] ← false
6      for ∀q ≠ p
7        wait till (¬choosing[q] ∨ q ∈ D_k)
8        wait till (token_q = 0 ∨ (token_q, q) > (token_p, p) ∨ q ∈ D_k)
9    Critical-Section
10   token_p ← 0
```

Fig. 1. $\mathcal{M}$: a *FCFS* mutual exclusion algorithm using $\mathcal{D}_k$- process p

4   Weakest Failure Detector for k-Exclusion

The k-exclusion problem is a generalization of mutual exclusion introduced in [9]. Like mutual exclusion, processes cycle through four sections of the code ; try, CS, exit and remainder section. An algorithm $\mathcal{A}$ solves the k-*Exclusion Problem* using a failure detector D in an environment $\mathcal{E}$ if the following conditions are met in every run of $\mathcal{A}$ using D where the failure pattern F is from $\mathcal{E}$:

1. k-*exclusion*: At most k live processes are in the CS at any time.
2. *Starvation Freedom*: If at most $k - 1$ correct processes are in CS forever, then every correct process in the try section enters the CS eventually. Furthermore, every correct process in the exit section eventually enters the remainder section.

Note that 1-exclusion has the same properties as the starvation-free mutual exclusion. Now we define the failure detector Γ^k, which is our candidate for the weakest failure detector to solve k-exclusion in the arbitrary environment.

4.1 Definition of Γ^k

Failure detector $\Gamma^k = (Trust, Bad)$. $Trust \in \{T, F\}$ and $Bad \subseteq U_p^k$, where $U^k = \{S | S \subset \Pi, |S| = k\}$.

- **Self trusting** : If $p \in correct(F)$ then, eventually $Trust_p = true$ forever.
- **Accuracy** : If $S \in Bad_p$ at time t then at least one process in S has crashed by time t.
- **Completeness** : If $p \in correct(F)$, $S \in U^k$, $p \notin S$ such that $S \cap Faulty(F) \neq \phi$ and $\forall q \in S$, $Trust_q = true$ at some time t, then eventually $S \in Bad_p$ forever.

Failure detector Γ^k in some way is an extension of the trusting failure detector $\mathcal{T}$ [7], which was shown to be sufficient to solve (in message passing model) mutual exclusion when majority of the processes are correct. The same result also showed that $\mathcal{T}$ is necessary for mutual exclusion in the arbitrary environment. Our reduction algorithm described below, uses some ideas from that result.

4.2 Γ^k Is Necessary

Let $\mathcal{A}$ be an algorithm which solves starvation free k-exclusion using failure detector D in the arbitrary environment. Figure 2 shows the reduction algorithm $\mathcal{R}_{D \to \Gamma^k}$ which implements Γ^k using $\mathcal{A}$ and D. In $\mathcal{R}_{D \to \Gamma^k}$, at each process p, the output corresponding to Γ^k is maintained in the pair of single-writer multi-reader registers $Trust_p$ and Bad_p which are initialized to *false* and ϕ respectively. In addition to these registers, $\mathcal{R}_{D \to \Gamma^k}$ uses a collection of $|U^k| = \binom{n}{k}$ co-routines of $\mathcal{A}$, each of them corresponding to a set $s \in U^k$ and denoted by $\mathcal{A}_s$.

   Processes use these instances of $\mathcal{A}$ to *spy* on the correctness of sets of size k in the following way : process p in the beginning, tries to enter CS of all the instance $\mathcal{A}_s$ for which $p \in s$ (line 3). Once p gets in CS of $\mathcal{A}_s$, it never exits. Also any other process q which is not in s does not *try* in $\mathcal{A}_s$ till p sets $Trust_p$ to *true* . Hence if p is correct, it will enter the CS of all instances $\mathcal{A}_s$ for which $p \in s$ and set $Trust_p$ to *true* (line 14). This because of the fact mentioned above and starvation freedom of $\mathcal{A}$, thus output of R satisfies *self-trusting* property of Γ^k. To spy on the other processes, p first waits till all the processes in $s' \in U^k$, $p \notin s'$, have set their $Trust$ bit to *true* (line 6). If they have, it means that all processes in s' have entered the CS in $\mathcal{A}_{s'}$. Now p tries to enter CS of $\mathcal{A}_{s'}$ (line 8), if p successfully enters (line 11) or finds some other process $q \notin s'$ to have entered it (line 9), it can assert that some process in s' has crashed. Hence it can add s' to Bad_p (line 9,16). So one can see that the output of $\mathcal{R}_{D \to \Gamma^k}$ also satisfies the *accuracy* and *completeness* property of Γ^k. Now we formally prove these claims.

Initialization

$Trust_p \leftarrow false$	SWMR register
$Bad_p \leftarrow \phi$	SWMR register
$\forall s \in U^k, in\text{-}CS[s] \leftarrow false$	local variable
$\forall s \in U^k, spied[s] \leftarrow false$	local variable

$\mathcal{A}_s, \forall s \in U^k$ are instances of the $\mathcal{A}$ using D

```
1  begin

2    for ∀s ∈ U^k, p ∈ s              11  upon A_s.crit
3    A_s.try()                        12    in-CS[s] ← true
4    repeat forever                   13    if ∀s ∈ U^k, p ∈ s, in-CS[s] = true
5      for ∀s ∈ U^k, p ∉ s            14      Trust_p ← true
6        if(¬ spied[s] ∧_{q∈s} Trust_q) 15    if p ∉ s
7          spied[s] ← true            16      Bad_p ← Bad_p ∪ s
8          A_s.try()
9        Bad_p ← Bad_p ∪_{q∈Π} Bad_q
10   end repeat
```

Fig. 2. Reduction algorithm $\mathcal{R}_{D \to \Gamma^k}$ - process p

Theorem 2. *Let $\mathcal{A}$ be an algorithm which solves k-exclusion using D, then $\Gamma^k \preceq D$.*

Proof. We prove this theorem by showing that $\mathcal{R}_{D \to \Gamma^k}$ given in fig. 2 is a valid reduction from D to Γ^k in the arbitrary environment. Let F be a failure pattern and R be any run of $\mathcal{R}_{D \to \Gamma^k}$ in F. We will show that in R, *Trust* and *Bad* registers at any process satisfy the properties of Γ^k. First we make the following simple proposition.

Proposition 2. *If a process $r \notin s$ executes $\mathcal{A}_s.try()$ at some time t (line 8), then $\forall q \in s, t' \geq t, Trust_q = true$.*

Now we will show that the output registers ($Trust_p, Bad_p$) at any process p satisfy all the three properties of Γ^k.

- **Self trusting:** Say it is violated, that means $p \in correct(F)$ but there is no time after which $Trust_p$ is *true* forever. Let $s \in U^k$ such that $p \in s$. As $Trust_p = false$ forever, so by proposition 2 only processes in s execute $\mathcal{A}_s.try()$ in R (line 3). As $|s| = k$ and $\mathcal{A}$ satisfies starvation freedom, p will execute $\mathcal{A}_s.crit$ (line 11) eventually. Hence p executes $\mathcal{A}_s.crit, \forall s \in U^k, p \in s$ and $Trust_p = true$ forever (line 14), a contradiction.
- **Accuracy:** Say $s \in Bad_p$ at time t', which means that either it was added to Bad_p at line 9 or line 16. In either case one can see that $p \notin s$ and there is some process $q \notin s$ which executed $\mathcal{A}_s.try$ (line 8) and later executed $\mathcal{A}_s.crit$ say at time $t < t'$. By proposition 2, $\forall r \in s, Trust_r = true$ before time t, which means all processes in s entered ($in\text{-}CS[s] = true$) CS of $\mathcal{A}_s$ before time t. But as q entered the CS of $\mathcal{A}_s$ at t, by *k-exclusion* property of $\mathcal{A}$ it means that some process in s has crashed by time $t < t'$.

- **Completeness:** Let $s \in U^k$ such that $s \cap faulty(F) \neq \phi$ and $\forall q \in s, Trust_q = true$ at some time t_q. One can clearly see from the algorithm that once a $Trust_p = true$, it stays T forever, hence $\forall q \in s, t \geq t', Trust_q = true$ for some t'. Which means that all the processes from $correct(F)/s$ will eventually execute $\mathcal{A}_s.try()$ (line 8). As s contains a faulty process, by starvation freedom of $\mathcal{A}$, some process in $r \in correct(F)/s$ will eventually get in CS of $\mathcal{A}_s$ and add s to its Bad set (line 16). Then every other process in $correct(F)/s$ eventually add s to its Bad set (line 9).

4.3 Γ^k Is Sufficient

In the fig. 3 we present algorithm $\mathcal{M}^k$ which solves starvation free k-exclusion in the arbitrary environment using Γ^k. This algorithm is inspired by Lamport's bakery algorithm [14]. Below we informally describe some ideas of the algorithm.

Each process p first waits till Γ_p^k outputs $Trust_p = true$. By the self-trusting property of Γ^k, this will eventually happen for all correct processes. Then p gets a token which is higher than tokens taken by other processes and then it waits (in the "waiting room") till it believes it is safe to enter the critical section. In this waiting room, process p maintains a set (called conflict set) of processes which possibly have better priority than p, i.e., those processes who are currently getting their token or whose token is smaller than p. Following rule is used to compare tokens of any two different process q and r, $(token_q, q) < (token_r, r) \Leftrightarrow token_q < token_r \vee (token_q = token_r \wedge q < r)$. In order to properly maintain the conflict set, p first adds all the other processes to this set and then it goes over all processes $q \in \Pi$ repeatedly and removes q if any one of the following cases is true :

- q that has obtained a token greater than p's token.
- q has exited the critical section after p has got its token. It this case p knows q does not pose any danger as if it tries for critical section again, it will get a bigger token than p.
- q's token is equal to zero, this means q is in remainder section.

Processes p will exit the waiting loop when the size of the conflict set is less than k or it is sure that there are at most k live processes in it. To determine the latter p uses the routine $Safe\text{-}set$ (line 17). This routine takes a set S as an input and checks if all k-sized subsets of it are included in the Bad_p. By the accuracy property of Γ^k, if all such subsets are in Bad_p, then it means there is no k sized subset in S with all live processes, hence S has at most $k - 1$ live processes.

To implement the above ideas, each process uses two single-writer multi-reader registers ; $token_p$ and $choosing_p$. The register $token_p$ as the name suggests stores the current token (or priority) of p to enter the critical section. While getting the token flag $choosing_p$ is set to true. Apart from these registers every process has a single-writer single-reader register $bypass$. Process p uses this register to inform other processes that it is done with its critical section.

Now we are ready to describe the code of process p. In line 1 p waits for the $Trust_p$ to become $true$. The flag $choosing$ is set to $true$ in line 2. p grabs the token greater than all other processes in line 3. The variable $bypass[p, q]$ is set to $false$ in line 4, so

Initialization
$token_p \leftarrow 0$ SWMR register
$choosing_p \leftarrow false$ SWMR register
$\forall q \neq p, bypass[p, q] \leftarrow false$ SWSR register

```
 1   wait till Trust_p
 2   choosing_p ← true
 3   token_p ← 1 + max_{q∈Π}(token_q)
 4   for ∀q ≠ p, bypass[p, q] ← false
 5   choosing_p ← false
 6   C_p ← Π − {p}
 7   repeat
 8     for ∀q ≠ p
 9       if (¬choosing_q ∨ bypass[p, q])
10         if (token_q = 0 ∨ (token_q, q) > (token_p, p))
11           C_p ← C_p − {q}
12     till ( |C_p| < k ∨ Safe-set(C_p) )
13   Critical-Section
14     for ∀q ≠ p, bypass[q, p] ← true
15   token_p ← 0
```

```
16   Safe-set(S)
17     if (∀S' ⊆ S, |S'| = k, S' ∈ Bad_p)
18       return true
19     else
20       return false
```

Fig. 3. $\mathcal{M}^k$: a *starvation free* k-exclusion algorithm using Γ^k

if p later observes that $bypass[p, q]$ is $true$, it knows that q finished its critical section. p sets *choosing* to *false* in line 5 and initializes the conflict set (local variable C_p) to all other processes. In the waiting room (lines 7-12), p removes any process q from C_p if any of the following cases is true (1) $bypass[p, q] = true$: this means that q was in exit section after p got its token, (2) $choosing_q = false$ and $token_q = 0$ in this case q is in remainder section and (3) $choosing_q = false$ and $(token_q, q) > (token_p, p)$, here again q has a bigger token than p, so it poses no threat. p then waits till $|S_p| < k$ or *Safe-set*(S_p) returns $true$ (line 12) before going to critical section. After the critical section (line 13), p sets all $bypass[q, p]$ to $true$ (line 14), so that if process q is in waiting room it will know that p has finished its critical section and hence can remove p from its conflict set C_q. In the last line p sets its token back to zero (line 15). The formal proof of correctness is omitted form this version.

References

1. Aguilera, M.K., Toueg, S., Deianov, B.: Revisiting the weakest failure detector for uniform reliable broadcast. In: Jayanti, P. (ed.) DISC 1999. LNCS, vol. 1693, pp. 19–34. Springer, Heidelberg (1999)
2. Anderson, J.H., Kim, Y.j.: Shared-memory mutual exclusion: Major research trends since 1986. Distributed Computing 16, 2003 (2001)
3. Bhatt, V., Christman, N., Jayanti, P.: Extracting quorum failure detectors. In: PODC 2009: Proceedings of the 28th ACM symposium on Principles of distributed computing, ACM Press, New York (2009)

4. Chandra, T.D., Hadzilacos, V., Toueg, S.: The weakest failure detector for solving consensus. Journal of the ACM 43(4), 685–722 (1996)
5. Chandra, T.D., Toueg, S.: Unreliable failure detectors for reliable distributed systems. Journal of the ACM 43(2), 225–267 (1996)
6. Delporte-Gallet, C., Fauconnier, H., Guerraoui, R., Hadzilacos, V., Kouznetsov, P., Toueg, S.: The weakest failure detectors to solve certain fundamental problems in distributed computing. In: PODC 2004: Proceedings of the twenty-third annual ACM symposium on Principles of Distributed Computing, pp. 338–346. ACM Press, New York (2004)
7. Delporte-Gallet, C., Fauconnier, H., Guerraoui, R., Kouznetsov, P.: Mutual exclusion in asynchronous systems with failure detectors. Journal of Parallel and Distributed Computing 65(4), 492–505 (2005)
8. Dijkstra, E.W.: Solution of a problem in concurrent programming control. Commun. ACM 8(9), 569 (1965)
9. Fischer, M.J., Lynch, N.A., Burns, J.E., Borodin, A.: Resource allocation with immunity to limited process failure. In: SFCS 1979: Proceedings of the 20th Annual Symposium on Foundations of Computer Science, Washington, DC, USA, pp. 234–254. IEEE Computer Society Press, Los Alamitos (1979)
10. Fischer, M.J., Lynch, N.A., Paterson, M.S.: Impossibility of distributed consensus with one faulty process. Journal of the ACM 32(2), 374–382 (1985)
11. Gafni, E., Kuznetsov, P.: The weakest failure detector for solving k-set agreement. In: PODC 2009: Proceedings of the 28th ACM symposium on Principles of distributed computing. ACM Press, New York (2009)
12. Guerraoui, R., Kapałka, M., Kouznetsov, P.: The weakest failure detectors to boost obstruction-freedom. In: Dolev, S. (ed.) DISC 2006. LNCS, vol. 4167, pp. 399–412. Springer, Heidelberg (2006)
13. Jayanti, P., Toueg, S.: Every problem has a weakest failure detector. In: PODC 2008: Proceedings of the 27th ACM symposium on Principles of distributed computing, pp. 75–84. ACM Press, New York (2008)
14. Lamport, L.: A new solution of Dijkstra's concurrent programming problem. Commun. ACM 17(8), 453–455 (1974)
15. Raynal, M., Beeson, D.: Algorithms for mutual exclusion. MIT Press, Cambridge (1986)
16. Zielinski, P.: Anti-omega: the weakest failure detector for set agreement. In: PODC 2008: Proceedings of the twenty-seventh ACM symposium on Principles of distributed computing, pp. 55–64. ACM Press, New York (2008)

Crash-Quiescent Failure Detection*

Srikanth Sastry, Scott M. Pike, and Jennifer L. Welch

Department of Computer Science and Engineering
Texas A&M University
College Station, TX 77843-3112, USA
{sastry,pike,welch}@cse.tamu.edu

Abstract. A distributed algorithm is *crash quiescent* if it eventually
stops sending messages to crashed processes. An algorithm can be made
crash quiescent by providing it with either a crash notification service or
a reliable communication service. Both services can be implemented in
practical environments with *failure detectors*. Therefore, crash-quiescent
failure detection is fundamental to system-wide crash quiescence. We
establish necessary and sufficient conditions for crash-quiescent failure
detection in partially synchronous environments where a bounded, but
unknown, number of consecutive messages can be arbitrarily late or lost.
Without a correct majority of processes, not even the weakest oracle
for fault-tolerant consensus, $\Diamond \mathcal{W}$, can be implemented crash quiescently.
With a correct majority, however, the eventually perfect failure detector,
$\Diamond \mathcal{P}$, is possible. Our $\Diamond \mathcal{P}$ algorithm is correct in all runs, but improves
performance via crash quiescence in any run with a correct majority. We
also present a refinement of our $\Diamond \mathcal{P}$ algorithm to mitigate the overhead
of achieving crash quiescence; the resulting bit complexity per utilized
link is asymptotically better than or equal to that of non-crash-quiescent
counterparts.

1   Introduction

A distributed algorithm is called *crash quiescent*, if, in all runs, correct processes
eventually stop sending messages to crashed processes. Depending on the system
model, crash quiescence may be straightforward, non-trivial, or even impossible.
For example, crash quiescence is straightforward with reliable communication,
even for purely asynchronous systems: every message received generates an ack,
and each process can have at most k unacknowledged messages per process at
any time. Crashed processes — which permanently halt without warning — stop
sending acks, so after the final such ack is delivered, each correct process will
become crash quiescent once k subsequent messages go unacknowledged.

By contrast, crash quiescence with unreliable communication is far more challenging due to inherent limitations on process coordination in the presence of
both crash faults and message loss. For example, consider any application where

* This work was supported in part by Texas Higher Education Coordinating Board
  grants ARP-00512-0007-2006 and ARP-00512-0130-2007, and by NSF grant 0500265.

I. Keidar (Ed.): DISC 2009, LNCS 5805, pp. 326–340, 2009.

some correct process i requires acknowledged delivery of a message m to each correct process. With lossy communication, i must re-send m sufficiently many times until the corresponding acks are received from each correct process; otherwise, the application program will be incorrect. For each crashed process, however, i must eventually stop re-sending m; otherwise, crash quiescence will be violated. In such systems, correct processes are committed to distinctly different (and contradictory) communication behaviors, depending on whether messages are sent to correct or faulty processes.

Since each message can be dropped (due to message loss), or never sent (due to process crashes), or just late (due to asynchrony), crash-quiescent algorithms must navigate an intersection of uncertainties. Fortunately, in systems with both crashes and native message loss, application-layer algorithms can be made crash quiescent relative to underlying system services for crash detection. As such, crash-quiescent failure detection is fundamental to system-wide crash quiescence.

A *failure detector* [1] can be viewed as a distributed oracle that can be queried for (potentially unreliable) information about process crash faults. Despite such unreliability, failure detectors can solve many problems that are *not* solvable in pure asynchrony [2]: most notably, crash-tolerant consensus [1]. As system services, failure detection oracles decouple distributed algorithms from explicit commitments to lower-level timing parameters; more theoretically, such oracles function as proxies for various degrees of partial or even full synchrony.

One oracle — the eventually perfect failure detector $\Diamond \mathcal{P}$ — is particularly useful for enabling crash-quiescent applications. Informally, $\Diamond \mathcal{P}$ suspects all crashed processes and eventually trusts all correct processes permanently. As such, $\Diamond \mathcal{P}$ can suspect correct processes only finitely many times. In an asynchronous system augmented with $\Diamond \mathcal{P}$, applications can become crash quiescent (despite message loss) as follows: so long as the recipient remains trusted by $\Diamond \mathcal{P}$, re-send each (new or buffered) message sufficiently many times until an acknowledgment is received; otherwise, buffer outbound messages while the recipient is suspected.

The foregoing protocol essentially provides quiescent reliable communication among correct processes, which is the approach taken by [3] as well. The same paper proves that — among oracles that output a list of suspected processes — $\Diamond \mathcal{P}$ is actually the weakest failure detector for quiescent reliable communication. Nonetheless, a fundamental problem remains: *for system-wide crash quiescence, it is essential that any underlying oracles are crash quiescent as well.*

Contribution. We prove necessary and sufficient conditions for crash-quiescent failure detection in partially synchronous environments where a bounded, but unknown, number of consecutive messages can be arbitrarily late or lost. Without a correct majority of processes, not even the weakest oracle for fault-tolerant consensus, $\Diamond \mathcal{W}$, can be implemented crash quiescently. With a correct majority, however, $\Diamond \mathcal{P}$, is possible. Our $\Diamond \mathcal{P}$ algorithm is correct in all runs, but improves performance via crash quiescence in any run with a correct majority. We also present a refinement of our $\Diamond \mathcal{P}$ algorithm to mitigate the overhead of achieving crash quiescence; the resulting bit complexity per utilized link is asymptotically better than or equal to that of non-crash-quiescent counterparts.

2   Definitions

System Model. We consider partially-synchronous systems subject to bounded intervals of message loss and delay. We start with the canonical model $\mathcal{M}_1$ from [4,1], and we weaken channel reliability and synchrony guarantees to allow an infinite number of messages to be lost or arbitrarily delayed. Specifically, we assume that communication takes place on ADD channels [5]. We informally describe the system model, which we denote E_{CLPS} (for Communication-Lossy Partially-Synchronous Environment — pronounced "eclipse"), next.

The system consists of a finite fixed set Π of n processes. We assume that the set Π is known to all processes. Each process's local program is represented as an action system consisting of a finite set of guarded commands. At each step of a process, the process can receive at most one message from one of its incoming message buffers, update its local state, and send at most one message to each process. Each process' action system includes a special *crash* action. The crash action can be executed at most once and permanently disables the guards of all the program actions, thereby halting the process.

Processes communicate with each other by sending messages over a fully connected communication topology. A send statement by process i causes the indicated message to be added to the channel from i to the recipient process j. When a message m is in the channel from i to j, a *deliver* action is enabled whose effect is to remove m from the channel and place it in the incoming message buffer at j for sender i.[1]

Starting from a system state in which channels are empty and local program variables have specified initial values, a *run* of an algorithm consists of a potentially infinite sequence of enabled actions (or steps). Each action in the run is either a local program action of a process, a crash action, or a deliver action of a channel. If the run is finite, then no program action should be enabled at the end of the run. A process that has not (yet) crashed is called *live*. Processes that never crash are called *correct*, and processes that crash are called *faulty*.

In a given run, each step is associated with a non-negative integer, which is the real time when it occurs; times assigned to steps in a run must be non-decreasing, but no two steps by the same process may have the same time. This common way of modeling runs enforces an upper bound on *absolute* process speed[2], but processes can decelerate indefinitely subject to the following restriction on *relative* process speeds: there exists $\Phi \in \mathbb{N}$ such that if (1) processes i and j are both live during a time interval, and (2) i takes at least Φ steps in the interval, then j takes at least one step in the interval. The bound Φ is not necessarily known to the processes and can vary for different runs of the system.

We assume that the actions of each process are locally scheduled by a First-Come-First-Serve (FCFS) scheduler which executes program actions in the order

---

[1] Our impossibility result holds even if incoming message buffers are infinite, while our algorithm works with a one-slot buffer whose contents are overwritten by the execution of each deliver event.

[2] This assumption is necessary to implement eventually reliable timeouts using only action-time clocks [6].

in which they were enabled. Note that such scheduling fairness applies only to program actions and not to crash actions, which are a modeling device. Thus, the crash action is always enabled at a correct process but never executed, while it is continuously enabled at a faulty process until the action is executed.

Each channel guarantees that some subset of the messages sent on it will be delivered in a timely manner and such messages are not too sparsely distributed in time, i.e., it is an ADD channel [5]. In more detail, consider the channel from process i to process j. The (real-time) *delay* of a message is the time elapsed between the step in which the message is sent and the deliver event for the message; if there is no deliver event, then the delay is infinite. For each run, there exist constants $\Delta \in \mathbb{N}$ and $B \in \mathbb{N}$ and a subset S_p of the set of messages sent over the channel (the *privileged* messages) satisfying the following: (1) The delay of each message in S_p is at most Δ. (2) For all intervals of time in which i sends at least B messages to j, at least one of the messages sent over the channel in that interval is in S_p. The bounds Δ and B and the set S_p are not necessarily known to the processes and can be different in different runs of the system.[3]

As consequences of our model definition, the following properties hold:

Property 1. The maximum number of steps taken by a process during the time that a privileged message is in transit in a channel is Δ.

Property 2. For every pair of processes i and j, the maximum number of steps taken by i during a time period in which j takes s steps is $(\Phi \cdot s)$.

Eventually Perfect Failure Detector. The *eventually perfect failure detector* $\Diamond\mathcal{P}$ satisfies the following two properties in each run [1]:

- **Strong Completeness:** Every crashed process is eventually and permanently suspected by every correct process.
- **Eventual Strong Accuracy:** There exists a time after which no correct process is suspected by any correct process.

$\Diamond\mathcal{P}$ is a particularly attractive oracle. First, it is sufficiently powerful to solve many fundamental problems including fault-tolerant consensus [1], stable leader election [7], and wait-free dining [8]. Additionally, it is realistically implementable: in contrast to other relatively powerful oracles — such as Perfect [1], Strong [1], and Trusting [9] — $\Diamond\mathcal{P}$ is actually implementable in classic models of partial synchrony[4].

---

[3] If the bound B is known, then implementing $\Diamond\mathcal{P}$ in E_{CLPS} with an arbitrary number of crash faults is straightforward. Simply take a standard ping-ack implementation of $\Diamond\mathcal{P}$ for reliable channels, and instead of sending a single ping or a single ack, send B pings or B acks, respectively.

[4] This claim is based on: (a) the many implementations of $\Diamond\mathcal{P}$ in recent works (cf. [1, 10, 11, 12, 13, 7, 14, 15]), and (b) the results from [16], where Larrea, *et al.*, prove that failure detectors with perpetual accuracy (including $\mathcal{P}$, and $\mathcal{S}$) cannot be implemented in classic models of partial synchrony [1,4].

Crash Quiescence. Algorithm $\mathcal{A}$ is said to be *crash quiescent* if, for every run of $\mathcal{A}$, there exists a time after which no correct process sends messages to any crashed process.

3   Impossibility of Crash-Quiescent $\Diamond\mathcal{P}$ in E_{CLPS}

In this section we show that it is impossible to implement $\Diamond\mathcal{P}$ crash quiescently in E_{CLPS} without a correct majority of processes. We start by showing that it is impossible to implement the *eventually weak failure detector* $(\Diamond\mathcal{W})$ [1], a weaker failure detector than $\Diamond\mathcal{P}$, in E_{CLPS} crash-quiescently if at most $\lceil\frac{n}{2}\rceil$ processes may crash. The oracle $\Diamond\mathcal{W}$ satisfies *weak completeness*, which states that every crashed process is eventually and permanently suspected by *some* correct process, and *eventual weak accuracy*, which states that *some* correct process is eventually and permanently trusted by all correct processes. Since every implementation of $\Diamond\mathcal{P}$ is also an implementation of $\Diamond\mathcal{W}$, the impossibility result for $\Diamond\mathcal{W}$ holds for $\Diamond\mathcal{P}$ as well.

Theorem 3. *It is impossible to implement a deterministic crash-quiescent* $\Diamond\mathcal{W}$ *in* E_{CLPS} *if up to* $\lceil\frac{n}{2}\rceil$ *processes may crash.*

Proof. For the purpose of contradiction, assume there is an algorithm $\mathcal{A}$ that implements crash-quiescent $\Diamond\mathcal{W}$ in E_{CLPS}. Partition the set of processes into two sets X and Y such that $|X| = \lfloor\frac{n}{2}\rfloor$ and $|Y| = \lceil\frac{n}{2}\rceil$.

Consider a run α_X in which all processes in X are correct and execute in synchronous rounds, all processes in Y crash initially, and all messages are received (by correct processes) in the next round after they are sent. By the assumed correctness of $\mathcal{A}$, there exists a round r_X after which each process in Y is permanently suspected by some process in X, and all processes in X stop sending messages to processes in Y. Let m_X denote the maximum number of messages sent by any process $x \in X$ to any process $y \in Y$ during execution α_X.

Let α_Y be a run that is the same as α_X except that the roles of X and Y are reversed; define r_Y and m_Y analogously to r_X and m_X.

Let L_{part} be the set of communication links that go between processes in X and processes in Y.

Now consider a run α in which all processes are correct and execute in synchronous rounds. All messages sent over links in L_{part} through round $r = \max(r_X, r_Y)$ are lost, and all other messages (those sent over the other links and those sent over L_{part} after round r, if any) are delivered with delay of one round. It can be shown using standard arguments that α_X and α are indistinguishable to all processes in X through round r, and thus each process in X is quiescent with respect to all processes in Y at the end of round r of α. Similarly, α_Y and α are indistinguishable to all processes in Y through round r, and thus each process in Y is quiescent with respect to all processes in X at the end of round r of α. The processes in X remain quiescent with respect to the processes in Y and each process in Y is permanently suspected by at least one process in X.

Similarly, the processes in Y remain quiescent with respect to the processes in X and each process in X is permanently suspected by at least one process in Y.

The link behavior in α conforms to the ADD channel specification with $B = \max(m_X, m_Y)$. Since $\mathcal{A}$ is supposed to work correctly in α but every correct process is permanently suspected by at least one other correct process (violating the specification of $\diamond\mathcal{W}$), we have a contradiction.   □

$\diamond\mathcal{P}$ *implementation for each process* $i \in \Pi$

    constant n *Total number of processes in* Π

    constant $intermission_i \in \mathbb{N}^+$ *Min. interval between sending heartbeat pulses*

    integer $next\text{-}pulse_i$ $:= 0$ *Countdown timer to send next heartbeat pulse*

    integer $estimate_{ij}$ $:= 1$ *Predicted interval between heartbeats from* j

    integer $deadline_{ij}$ $:= 1$ *Countdown timer to receive next heartbeat from* j

    $\Pi \times \Pi$ **boolean matrix** S_i *Suspect matrix:* $S_i(j,k) = $ true *implies* j *suspected* k

$\diamond\mathcal{P}_i \stackrel{\text{def}}{=} \{\forall j \in \Pi : S_i(i,j) = true : j\}$ $\diamond\mathcal{P}$ *output when queried by* i

$Q_i \stackrel{\text{def}}{=} \{\forall j, k \in \Pi : S_i(i,k) \land count(\neg S_i(i,j) \land S_i(j,k)) > \lfloor \frac{n}{2} \rfloor : k\} \cup \{i\}$ *Quiescence Set*

---

1 : $\{next\text{-}pulse_i = 0\} \longrightarrow$ Action 1: Send Pulse

2 :   **foreach** $(j \notin Q_i)$ **send** $\langle \diamond\mathcal{P}_i \rangle$ **to** j *Send suspected ids in pulse*

3 :   **foreach** $(k \in \Pi)$ **do** $S_i(i,k) := (deadline_{ik} = 0)$ *Update local suspect list*

4 : $next\text{-}pulse_i := intermission_i - 1$ *Schedule next heartbeat pulse*

---

5 : $\{$**receive** $\langle hb \rangle$ **from** $j\} \longrightarrow$ Action 2: Receive Heartbeats

6 :   **if**$(S_i(i,j) = $ **true**$)$ *Detect a false-positive mistake*

7 : $S_i(i,j) := $ **false**   *Remove* j *from local suspect list*

8 : $estimate_{ij} := estimate_{ij} + 1$ *Increase predicted interval for* j

9 :   **foreach** $(k \in \Pi)$ **do** $S_i(j,k) := (k \in hb)$ *Update suspect matrix row for* j

10 : $deadline_{ij} := estimate_{ij}$ *Set next heartbeat deadline for* j

---

11 : $\{$**true**$\} \longrightarrow$ Action 3: Decrement Timers

12 : $next\text{-}pulse_i := max(0, next\text{-}pulse_i - 1)$

13 :   **foreach** $(j \in \Pi)$ **where** $(j \neq i)$ **do** $deadline_{ij} := max(0, deadline_{ij} - 1)$

Alg. 1. Implementation of $\diamond\mathcal{P}$ that is correct in all runs and crash quiescent in any run with a correct majority of processes. Initial values for the suspect matrix can be arbitrary. Note that $deadline_{ii}$ is initially positive and is never decremented, so each process i will eventually trust itself permanently.

Corollary 4. *It is impossible to implement a crash-quiescent* $\diamond\mathcal{P}$ *in* E_{CLPS} *if up to* $\lceil \frac{n}{2} \rceil$ *processes may crash.*

4   Crash-Quiescent $\diamond\mathcal{P}$ in E_{CLPS} with Majority Correct

In contrast to the previous result, we now show that it is possible to implement crash-quiescent $\diamond\mathcal{P}$ in E_{CLPS} if a majority of the processes are correct; furthermore, the implementation is correct, although not crash-quiescent, without a correct majority of processes.

Alg. 1 presents one such $\Diamond \mathcal{P}$ implementation in E_{CLPS}. It is a heartbeat-based implementation that gains extra information by exchanging suspect lists with other processes. This extra information is used to achieve crash quiescence. Specifically, each process i relays its entire suspect list by including it in heartbeat messages sent to other processes at regular intervals (Action 1, line 2). The intervals are measured by a step timer $next\text{-}pulse_i$ which is decremented in Action 3 to send the heartbeat messages. Every time $next\text{-}pulse_i$ expires (counts down to zero), the process sends heartbeats with its current suspect list to a subset of processes (Action 1, line 2), determined by a method explained later.

Process i expects to receive heartbeats from each live neighbor at regular intervals. The upper bound on the inter-arrival time of the heartbeats may be unknown. Hence, i has an adaptive step timer $deadline_{ij}$ with respect to each process j that is initialized to the value of $estimate_{ij}$ and is decremented in Action 3. If the timer $deadline_{ij}$ expires (counts down to zero) before i receives a heartbeat from j (Action 1, line 3), then i suspects j. Every time i receives a heartbeat from a process j, i trusts j (Action 2) and restarts the timer $deadline_{ij}$ (Action 2, line 10). However, if j was previously suspected by i, then i also increases the timer value $estimate_{ij}$ (Action 2, line 8).

Recall that processes send their suspect lists in each heartbeat. When a process i receives a heartbeat from process j, it records the list of processes suspected by j, as communicated in that heartbeat (Action 2, line 9), in the jth row of the suspect matrix S_i. Every time $next\text{-}pulse_i$ expires, process i determines the set of processes that it will not send a heartbeat to as follows: If a process j is currently suspected by i, and among the processes that i trusts, more than $\lfloor \frac{n}{2} \rfloor$ suspect j (as communicated through the latest heartbeats received by i), then i adds j to the quiescence set Q_i (as per the definition of Q_i in Alg. 1), and i does not send a heartbeat to j. Also, note that i is always in Q_i. The set Q_i is dynamically defined every time $next\text{-}pulse_i$ expires, so it is possible for i to send a heartbeat to j in some instances of Action 1 in a run and not in others.

4.1 Proof of Correctness

Theorem 5. *Alg. 1 satisfies strong completeness: every crashed process is eventually and permanently suspected by all correct processes.*

Proof. Upon crashing, each faulty process j stops sending heartbeats. Thus, each correct process i stops receiving heartbeats from j. Since Action 3 at i is always enabled and executed infinitely often, eventually $estimate_{ij}$ is permanently 0. After such time, all executions of Action 1 at i suspect j, and j is never trusted again because no heartbeats from j are received. ☐

We prove eventual strong accuracy (eventually no correct process is suspected by any correct process) through the following lemmas:

Lemma 6. *The values taken on by variable $estimate_{ij}$ are non-decreasing, and every time a process j is taken off a process i's suspect list, the value of $estimate_{ij}$ is increased.*

Proof. Inspection of Alg. 1 reveals that $estimate_{ij}$ is never decremented. Furthermore, the only action at i that takes a process j off the suspect list is Action 2 (in line 6–9). However, the same action also increments the value of $estimate_{ij}$ by 1 (in line 9) after j is taken off the suspect list.   □

Since the action system at each process contains $n + 1$ actions and the local scheduler is FCFS, we get:

Lemma 7. *For each correct process i, the maximum number of steps executed by i between the time that an action a is enabled at i and the earliest time thereafter that the action a is executed is n.*

Let INT denote the largest $intermission_i$ over all processes $i \in \Pi$.

Lemma 8. *Within every interval in which process i takes $n \cdot INT$ steps, i executes Action 1 at least once.*

Proof. Inspection of Alg. 1 shows that $next\text{-}pulse_i$ is always non-negative, it is set to a value not exceeding $INT - 1$ in Action 1, and it is decremented by 1 in Action 3. If Action 3 is executed $INT - 1$ times, then $next\text{-}pulse_i$ is guaranteed to be decremented to 0, enabling Action 1. Since Action 3 is always enabled, by Lemma 7, we know that within $n \cdot (INT - 1)$ steps by i, Action 1 is enabled at i. Applying Lemma 7 again, we know that Action 1 will be executed within the next n steps at i.   □

Lemma 9. *If processes i and j are correct and i sends a heartbeat to j infinitely often, then j sends a heartbeat to i infinitely often.*

Proof. If process i sends heartbeats to process j infinitely often, then j receives heartbeats from i infinitely often. From Action 2, we know that j trusts i upon receiving a heartbeat from i. Process j continues to trust i until the next execution of Action 1, guaranteed to occur by Lemma 8. This execution of Action 1 will send a heartbeat to i.   □

Lemma 10. *If processes i and j are correct and i sends a heartbeat to j infinitely often, then i and j eventually trust each other permanently.*

Proof. If i sends heartbeats to j infinitely often, then by Lemma 9 j sends heartbeats to i infinitely often as well. Consequently, i and j trust each other infinitely often. By Lemma 6 we know that every time i (falsely) suspects j, the value of $estimate_{ij}$ increases in the future when i trusts j again. Similarly, every time j (falsely) suspects i, the value of $estimate_{ji}$ increases in the future when j trusts i again.

We now show that after i and j suspect each other finitely many times, either i and j trust each other permanently (thus vacuously satisfying eventual strong accuracy), or the values of $estimate_{ij}$ and $estimate_{ji}$ grow sufficiently large such that: in an infinite suffix, i and j always receive heartbeats from each other before timers $deadline_{ij}$ and $deadline_{ji}$ (which are reset to $estimate_{ij}$ and $estimate_{ji}$, respectively) expire. Therefore, i and j eventually and permanently trust each other.

Let $M \stackrel{\text{def}}{=} B \cdot n \cdot INT + \Delta + \Phi(n + B \cdot n \cdot INT) + \Delta + n$. Consider a time t_{suf} at which: (a) either i permanently trusts j or $estimate_{ij}$ exceeds M, and (b) either j permanently trusts i or $estimate_{ij}$ exceeds M.

Consider any time t_f (subscript f for *final*) after t_{suf} at which i receives a heartbeat from j by executing Action 2. Thus, i trusts j at time t_f and $deadline_{ij}$ is reset to $estimate_{ij}$. By Lemma 8 we know that in the next $B \cdot n \cdot INT$ steps at i, process i executes Action 1 at least B times. Since $estimate_{ij}$ exceeds M, which is greater than $B \cdot n \cdot INT$, i continues to trust j for B executions of Action 1, and therefore, B heartbeats are sent to j. Note that at least one heartbeat among the B is privileged. Let m_1 be one such heartbeat.

From the system model definitions, the message delay for m_1 is at most Δ time ticks. By Property 1, the maximum number of steps taken by i while m_1 is in transit is Δ. Delivery of m_1 at j enables Action 2 at j (if it had not been enabled already).

By Lemma 7, the maximum number of steps by j between the delivery of m_1 and the receipt of a heartbeat from i is n. The same argument as above shows that after j receives a heartbeat from i, j trusts i and within $B \cdot n \cdot INT$ steps (at j) process j sends a privileged message, m_2, to i. Thus, by Property 2 the maximum number of steps taken by i during the time that j is waiting to take delivery of a heartbeat from i and to send the B heartbeats (including m_2) to i is $\Phi(n + B \cdot n \cdot INT)$.

A symmetric argument shows that the maximum number of steps taken by i while m_2 is in transit to i and some heartbeat from j is received by i is $\Delta + n$.

In aggregate, we see that within $(B \cdot n \cdot INT + \Delta + \Phi(n + B \cdot n \cdot INT) + \Delta + n) = M$ steps of i after time t_f, i gets another heartbeat from j. Since $estimate_{ij} > M$, i has been continuing to trust j throughout this interval. Applying the same argument iteratively, it follows that i never suspects j after time t_f.

Reversing the roles of i and j shows that j never suspects i after time t_f.   □

Lemma 11. *If processes i and j are correct and i sends only finitely many heartbeats to j, then j sends only finitely many heartbeats to i, and i and j suspect each other eventually and permanently.*

Proof. Let i and j be two correct processes such that i sends only finitely many heartbeats to j. By the contra-positive of Lemma 9, j sends only finitely many heartbeats to i as well.

Let t_x be the latest time at which a heartbeat from i to j, or from j to i, is received. After t_x, process i never executes Action 2 with respect to j, and j never executes Action 2 with respect to i. Consequently, timers $deadline_{ij}$ and $deadline_{ji}$ are never increased, but since Action 3 at both i and j is continuously enabled, the timers are decremented infinitely often. Eventually, these timers reach 0 and when i and j execute their respective Action 1 after such time, i suspects j, and *vice versa*. Since no more heartbeats are received by i or j from each other, processes i and j suspect each other permanently.   □

Lemma 12. *If process i is correct, then its suspect list stops changing.*

Proof. From Theorem 5 we know that eventually all crashed processes are permanently suspected. From Lemmas 10 and 11 we know that i either eventually and permanently trusts a correct process j, or i eventually and permanently suspects a correct process j. That is, i's suspect list eventually stops changing.   □

Theorem 13. *Alg. 1 satisfies eventual strong accuracy whereby every correct process is eventually and permanently trusted by all correct processes.*

Proof. From Lemma 12 we know that the suspect list at each correct process stops changing eventually. Consider a run α of Alg. 1. Let t_{stable} be the time after which the suspect list at each correct process stops changing and all faulty processes have crashed.

Let i and j be two correct processes in run α. If i sends infinitely many heartbeats to j, then from Lemma 10 we know that i eventually and permanently trusts j. However, if i sends only finitely many heartbeats to j, then from Lemma 11 we know i and j eventually and permanently suspect each other. We will now show that the latter is impossible.

For the purposes of contradiction, let us assume that i sends only finitely many heartbeats to j. By Lemma 11, i and j eventually and permanently suspect each other and stop sending heartbeats to each other. By Lemma 12, the suspect lists of all correct processes eventually stop changing. Hence, eventually, i and j receive unchanging heartbeats (if at all) from other correct processes in the system. In other words, eventually, the suspect matrices S_i and S_j stay constant.

Since i eventually stops sending heartbeats to j, it implies that $j \in Q_i$ eventually and permanently. That is, i trusts a majority of processes, and therefore, a majority of processes trust i (follows from Lemma 10 and the fact that i sends heartbeats in Action 1 to such trusted processes infinitely often). Also, a majority of processes suspect j. This suspicion information is relayed to i in the contents of the heartbeats from the trusted processes.

Reversing the roles of i and j in the arguments above, we know that a majority of processes suspect i for j to stop sending heartbeats to i.

The above arguments establish that a correct majority of processes trust i permanently for i to stop sending heartbeats to j, but a correct majority of processes also suspect i permanently for j to stop sending heartbeats to i. This is a contradiction! Hence, it follows that i and j send heartbeats to each other infinitely often. Lemma 10 implies that i eventually and permanently trusts j.

Thus, every correct process is eventually and permanently trusted by all correct processes.   □

Theorem 14. *Alg. 1 is crash quiescent if a majority of processes are correct.*

Proof. From Theorem 5, we know that every crashed process is suspected by every correct process. From Theorem 13, we know that every correct process eventually and permanently trusts every correct process. Hence, every correct process receives suspect lists from all correct processes infinitely often. Since eventually every correct process permanently suspects every crashed process, the following is eventually and permanently true: for all pairs of processes (i, k) where i and k are correct, $S_k(i, j)$ is true for all crashed processes j.

Therefore, in all runs where a majority of processes are correct, eventually for every correct process i, every crashed process j is permanently in the set Q_i. In other words, every correct process i eventually and permanently stops sending heartbeats to any crashed process.   □

Communication Complexity. Next, we analyze the communication complexity of our algorithm, both in terms of the number of messages and the number of bits sent. Since processes send messages periodically, and correct processes never cease doing so, we focus on the number of messages (and bits) sent in each period (the same approach is used in, for instance, [12]). In every run of a non-crash-quiescent implementation of $\Diamond\mathcal{P}$ using heartbeats, eventually all faulty processes have crashed and every correct process periodically sends heartbeats to all the processes, resulting in $\mathcal{O}(c \cdot n)$ messages per period, where c is the number of correct processes. By contrast, in runs of Alg. 1 where $c > \lfloor \frac{n}{2} \rfloor$, eventually $\mathcal{O}(c^2)$ messages are sent per period. Thus, Alg. 1 offers improved message complexity in majority-correct runs, and this improvement has no penalty in message complexity for runs where half or more processes crash.

Ironically, the bit complexity of Alg. 1 is greater than that of its non-crash-quiescent counterparts in all runs. Since the receipt of a "dummy" heartbeat message devoid of any payload may be sufficient to establish the liveness of the sender, each heartbeat message in a non-crash-quiescent algorithm requires just $\mathcal{O}(\log n)$ bits (for encoding the sender and recipient). But each message in Alg. 1 requires $\Theta(n)$ bits (to encode the suspect list and the sender and recipient addresses). Thus the total periodic bit complexity of Alg. 1 is $\Theta(c^2 \cdot n)$ as compared to $\mathcal{O}(c \cdot n \cdot \log n)$ for the non-crash-quiescent version. Thus for instance, if c is a constant fraction of n, as will be the case if processes have a fixed probability of failure, the bit complexity of Alg. 1 is asymptotically worse than that of the non-crash-quiescent version. Yet the purpose of crash-quiescence is to reduce the overall communication complexity. We address this next.

5   Improving the Communication Bit Complexity

Algorithm. We improve the communication bit complexity of Alg. 1 by inserting a communication sub-layer between Alg. 1 and the communication infrastructure. This communication sub-layer sends and receives two types of heartbeats: *heavyweight heartbeats* and *lightweight heartbeats*. The heavyweight heartbeats contain the entire suspect list sent by the process, whereas the light-weight heartbeats merely contain 'i-am-alive' information.

Alg. 2 implements such a communication sub-layer. In the action system, each process maintains, in the variable $prev\_hb_{ij}$, the suspect list that the $\Diamond\mathcal{P}$ module sent to process j in the previous heartbeat. If the contents of the current heartbeat to be sent are different from the contents of the previous heartbeat sent, then the action system generates a new sequence number (Action 1, line 3)

---

set $prev\_hb_{ij} := \emptyset$ *The previous heartbeat sent by the local $\Diamond\mathcal{P}$-module to process j*
message $msg_{ij} := \langle 0, null, 0 \rangle$ *The actual heartbeat (HB) sent to j*
integer $seq\_num_{ij} := 0$ *The current sequence number for heartbeats to j*
integer $max\_seq_{ij} := 0$ *The highest sequence number received from j*
integer $latest\_ack_{ij} := 0$ *The latest ack sent to j*
message $hb_{ij} := \emptyset$ *The heartbeat (suspect list) sent to the local $\Diamond\mathcal{P}$ module*

```
 1 : {upon exec(◇P−send ⟨hb⟩ to j)} ⟶                    Action 1: Send a heartbeat
 2 :     if (hb ≠ prev_hb_ij)                    Check if the suspect list has changed
 3 :         increment seq_num_ij by 1     A new sequence number for new suspect list
 4 :         prev_hb_ij := hb              Update local record of the latest heartbeat
 5 :         msg_ij := ⟨seq_num_ij, hb, latest_ack_ij⟩     Construct HB (piggybacked ack)
 6 :     if (j ∉ hb) send ⟨msg_ij⟩ to j       Send constructed HB if j is trusted
 7 :     else send ⟨0, null, 0⟩ to j                  Else send a lightweight HB
```

```
 8 : {upon receive ⟨seq, hb, ack⟩ from j} ⟶        Action 2: Receive a heartbeat
 9 :     if (ack = seq_num_ij)           Check if the ack is for latest local suspect list
10 :         msg_ij := ⟨0, null, seq⟩    Construct a lightweight HB (with piggybacked ack)
11 :     latest_ack_ij := seq              Record the ack to be sent in the next HB
12 :     if (seq > max_seq_ij)           Check if the suspect list from j is newer
13 :         hb_ij := hb                     Update hb_j with the new suspect list
14 :         max_seq_ij := seq           Update the max sequence number received from j
15 :         exec(◇P−receive ⟨hb_ij⟩ from j)   Send suspect list to the local ◇P-module
```

Alg. 2. Bit-complexity optimizer for the $\Diamond\mathcal{P}$ algorithm in Alg. 1

and constructs a heavyweight heartbeat (Action 1, line 5). However, it sends the heavyweight heartbeat only if the recipient is not currently suspected (Action 1, line 6)[5]; otherwise it sends a lightweight heartbeat (Action 1, line 7). Alg. 2 stores the sequence number of the latest heartbeat received from each process j in the variable $latest\_seq_{ij}$ (Action 2, line 11) and piggybacks, in the next heartbeat sent, the sequence number as the ack for the latest heartbeat received (Action 1, line 5 and Action 2, line 10). The action system continues to send heavyweight heartbeats until it receives an ack from the recipient process for the new heavyweight heartbeat (Action 2, lines 9–10). After the ack for the new heavyweight heartbeat is received, the action system starts sending lightweight heartbeats until the suspect list changes again.

At the receiver, the communication sub-layer maintains the latest suspect list received so far from each process j (in the variable hb_{ij}). Upon receiving a heavyweight heartbeat with a suspect list that is newer than the latest one on record (Action 2, line 12), the communication sub-layer updates its local information (Action 2, lines 13–14). It then sends the latest heartbeat on record (stored in the variable hb_{ij}) to the local $\Diamond\mathcal{P}$ module (Action 2, line 15).

---

[5] The condition for trusting a recipient to send a heavyweight heartbeat ensures that in non-crash-quiescent runs, a correct process does not send an infinite number of heavyweight heartbeats to a crashed process.

Correctness. We show that the proof of correctness in Sect. 4.1 applies to Alg. 1 + 2 as well. Inspection of the action system in Alg. 2 shows that the communication sub-layer does not change the number of messages sent or received in the system. It also ensures that the end-to-end communication delay for privileged messages is bounded in the number of action clock ticks (because messages are sent or received in a single atomic step).

Additionally, the heartbeat that is sent to the local $\Diamond\mathcal{P}$-module is always a valid suspect list. This fact follows from the observation that the value of hb_{ij} is initialized to a valid suspect list, and the only modification of hb_{ij} is in lines 12–13. This change to hb_{ij} could result in an invalid suspect list (*viz.*, the value *null*) only when a lightweight heartbeat is received. However, all lightweight heartbeats are sent with sequence number 0, and hence, do not overwrite the existing (valid) suspect list. Consequently, the heartbeat sent to the local $\Diamond\mathcal{P}$-module is always a valid suspect list.

Strong Completeness. The proof for Theorem 5 is agnostic to the contents of the heartbeats and is therefore applicable to Alg. 1 + 2 as well. Thus, by Theorem 5, Alg. 1 + 2 satisfies *strong completeness*.

Eventual Strong Accuracy. The proofs for Lemmas 6 through 12 are agnostic to the heartbeat content. Hence, these lemmas are applicable to Alg. 1 + 2 too.

Inspection of the proof for Theorem 13 reveals that the argument for eventual strong accuracy is made in the suffix in which all faulty processes have crashed and the suspect lists at all correct processes have stopped changing (by Lemma 12). Since Lemma 12 holds for Alg. 1 + 2 as well, every run of Alg. 1 + 2 has a suffix in which all faulty processes have crashed and the suspect lists at all correct processes have stopped changing. In such a suffix, each pair (i,j) of correct processes either (a) trust each other permanently, or (b) suspect each other permanently (by Lemmas 10 and 11).

In the former case, processes i and j send heavyweight heartbeats for the final change in their suspect lists until the acks for the reception of such a heavyweight heartbeat are received; after the reception of these acks, the jth row in i's suspect matrix is the same as j's suspect list, and *vice versa*. In the latter case, i and j stop sending heartbeats to each other (Lemma 11). Thus, in this suffix, the suspect matrices S_i and S_j stay constant. The same arguments in the proof for Theorem 13 show that processes i and j always send heartbeats to each other infinitely often. Then Lemma 10 implies *eventual strong accuracy*.

Crash Quiescence. From the eventual strong accuracy property we know that every correct process is eventually and permanently trusted by all correct processes. Thus, the last change in the suspect list at each correct process is successfully communicated to all other correct processes in the system by Alg. 2. This allows us to apply the proof for Theorem 14 to Alg. 1 + 2, thus showing that Alg. 1 + 2 is crash quiescent in majority-correct runs.

5.1 Communication Bit Complexity

Alg. 2 uses sequence numbers in the heartbeats. Hence, in a finite prefix of the execution, heartbeat size may be unbounded. However, as we show next, eventually the processes send only lightweight heartbeats of size $\mathcal{O}(\log(n))$ bits.

Consider an infinite suffix of any run of Alg. 1 + 2 that starts after (a) all processes that crash in the run have already crashed, (b) all correct processes have started permanently suspecting crashed processes, and (c) no correct process is suspected by any correct process. In this suffix, the local suspect list at each process stops changing.

The finite number of heartbeats that were sent before the start of the suffix are either dropped or delivered in finite time. Subsequently, all heartbeats in transit in the system are ones that are sent during the suffix. Since a process continues to send heavyweight heartbeats until the sending process receives an ack for the latest change in the suspect list, sufficiently many heavyweight heartbeats for the final change in the suspect list are guaranteed to be sent. This ensures that these heartbeats are delivered to their recipients, and the acks for these heavyweight heartbeats are received by the senders.

Thus, eventually all processes have received acks for the last change in their suspect list from all correct processes. Consequently, eventually all processes send only lightweight heartbeats, and hence the piggyback acks are only for lightweight heartbeats as well. In other words, eventually the heartbeats sent by all correct processes are lightweight heartbeats with sequence number 0 and ack number 0. Such heartbeats require $\mathcal{O}(\log(n))$ bits (including the bits needed to encode the sender and the recipient identifier information).

In majority-correct runs, since the asymptotic message complexity is $\mathcal{O}(c^2)$, the communication bit complexity is $\mathcal{O}(c^2 \log(n))$. Similarly, in runs where half or more processes crash, since the asymptotic message complexity is $\mathcal{O}(n \cdot c)$, the communication bit complexity is $\mathcal{O}(n \cdot c \log(n))$.

The asymptotic communication bit complexity of Alg. 1 + 2 for majority-correct runs is lower than its non-crash-quiescent counterparts, and in runs where half or more processes crash, the asymptotic bit complexity is no worse than its non-crash-quiescent counterparts. Thus, we have achieved crash-quiescence for $\Diamond \mathcal{P}$ in E_{CLPS} in majority-correct runs with improved message complexity and (importantly) improved bit complexity.

6 Conclusion

We have proposed a new property of distributed algorithms called crash quiescence. An algorithm is said to be crash quiescent if all correct processes eventually stop sending messages to any crashed process. We have motivated the importance of crash quiescence in the context of the eventually perfect failure detector $\Diamond \mathcal{P}$. We have shown that in some partially-synchronous environments where a bounded, but unknown, number of consecutive messages may be arbitrarily late or lost, it is impossible to achieve crash quiescence for even $\Diamond \mathcal{W}$ — the weakest failure detector in the Chandra-Toueg hierarchy. However, in such partially synchronous environments, we have presented an implementation of $\Diamond \mathcal{P}$ that is correct in all runs and that is crash quiescent in runs where a majority of processes are correct. Furthermore, we have presented a refinement of our $\Diamond \mathcal{P}$ algorithm to optimize the message size so that the resulting bit complexity per utilized link is asymptotically better than or equal to that of non-crash-quiescent counterparts.

References

1. Chandra, T.D., Toueg, S.: Unreliable failure detectors for reliable distributed systems. Journal of the ACM 43(2), 225–267 (1996)
2. Mostefaoui, A., Mourgaya, E., Raynal, M.: An introduction to oracles for asynchronous distributed systems. Future Gener. Comput. Syst. 18(6), 757–767 (2002)
3. Aguilera, M.K., Chen, W., Toueg, S.: On quiescent reliable communication. SIAM Journal on Computing 29(6), 2040–2073 (2000)
4. Dwork, C., Lynch, N., Stockmeyer, L.: Consensus in the presence of partial synchrony. Journal of the ACM 35(2), 288–323 (1988)
5. Sastry, S., Pike, S.M.: Eventually perfect failure detection using ADD channels. In: Proceedings of the 5th International Symposium on Parallel and Distributed Processing and Applications, pp. 483–496 (2007)
6. Sastry, S., Pike, S.M., Welch, J.L.: Crash fault detection in celerating environments. In: Proceedings of the 23rd IEEE International Parallel and Distributed Processing Symposium, pp. 1–12 (2009)
7. Aguilera, M.K., Delporte-Gallet, C., Fauconnier, H., Toueg, S.: Stable leader election. In: Proceedings of the 15th International Symposium on Distributed Computing, pp. 108–122 (2001)
8. Pike, S.M., Song, Y., Sastry, S.: Wait-free dining under eventual weak exclusion. In: Proceedings of the 9th International Conference on Distributed Computing and Networking, pp. 135–146 (2008)
9. Delporte-Gallet, C., Fauconnier, H., Guerraoui, R., Kouznetsov, P.: Mutual exclusion in asynchronous systems with failure detectors. Journal of Parallel and Distributed Computing 65(4), 492–505 (2005)
10. Mostéfaoui, A., Mourgaya, E., Raynal, M.: Asynchronous implementation of failure detectors. In: Proceedings of the 33rd International Conference on Dependable Systems and Networks, pp. 351–360 (2003)
11. Bertier, M., Marin, O., Sens, P.: Implementation and performance evaluation of an adaptable failure detector. In: Proceedings of the 32nd International Conference on Dependable Systems and Networks, pp. 354–363 (2002)
12. Larrea, M., Arévalo, S., Fernández, A.: Efficient algorithms to implement unreliable failure detectors in partially synchronous systems. In: Proceedings of the 13th International Symposium on Distributed Computing, pp. 34–49 (1999)
13. Fetzer, C., Raynal, M., Tronel, F.: An adaptive failure detection protocol. In: Proceedings of the 7th Pacific Rim International Symposium on Dependable Computing, pp. 146–153 (2001)
14. Fetzer, C., Schmid, U., Süsskraut, M.: On the possibility of consensus in asynchronous systems with finite average response times. In: Proceedings of the 25th International Conference on Distributed Computing Systems, pp. 271–280 (2005)
15. Larrea, M., Lafuente, A.: Communication-efficient implementation of failure detector classes $\Diamond \mathcal{P}$ and $\Diamond \mathcal{Q}$. In: Proceedings of the 19th International Symposium on Distributed Computing, pp. 495–496 (2005)
16. Larrea, M., Fernández, A., Arévalo, S.: On the implementation of unreliable failure detectors in partially synchronous systems. IEEE Transactions on Computers 53(7), 815–828 (2004)

The Price of Anonymity: Optimal Consensus Despite Asynchrony, Crash and Anonymity

François Bonnet and Michel Raynal

IRISA, Université de Rennes 1, France
fbonnet@irisa.fr, raynal@irisa.fr

Abstract. This paper addresses the consensus problem in asynchronous systems prone to process crashes, where additionally the processes are anonymous (they cannot be distinguished one from the other: they have no name and execute the same code). To circumvent the three computational adversaries (asynchrony, failures and anonymity) each process is provided with a failure detector of a class denoted ψ, that gives it an upper bound on the number of processes that are currently alive (in a non-anonymous system, the classes ψ and $\mathcal{P}$ -the class of perfect failure detectors- are equivalent).

The paper first presents a simple ψ-based consensus algorithm where the processes decide in $2t + 1$ asynchronous rounds (where t is an upper bound on the number of faulty processes). It then shows one of its main results, namely, $2t + 1$ is a lower bound for consensus in the anonymous systems equipped with ψ. The second contribution addresses early-decision. The paper presents and proves correct an early-deciding algorithm where the processes decide in $\min(2f + 2, 2t + 1)$ asynchronous rounds (where f is the actual number of process failures). This leads to think that anonymity doubles the cost (wrt synchronous systems) and it is conjectured that $\min(2f + 2, 2t + 1)$ is the corresponding lower bound.

The paper finally considers the k-set agreement problem in anonymous systems. It first shows that the previous ψ-based consensus algorithm solves the k-set agreement problem in $R_t = 2\left\lfloor \frac{t}{k} \right\rfloor + 1$ asynchronous rounds. Then, considering a family of failure detector classes $\{\psi_\ell\}_{0 \le \ell < k}$ that generalizes the class $\psi(= \psi_0)$, the paper presents an algorithm that solves the k-set agreement in $R_{t,\ell} = 2\left\lfloor \frac{t}{k-\ell} \right\rfloor + 1$ asynchronous rounds. This last formula relates the cost $(R_{t,\ell})$, the coordination degree of the problem (k), the maximum number of failures (t) and the the strength (ℓ) of the underlying failure detector. Finally the paper concludes by presenting problems that remain open.

1 Introduction

Anonymous systems. In a somewhat restrictive way, the aim of a real-time system is to master *on time computing*, and the main aim of parallelism is to obtain *efficient* algorithms. Similarly we can say that the central issue of distributed computing consists in *mastering uncertainty*. This uncertainty has first appeared under the form of asynchrony, failure occurrences, and the multiplicity of loci of

I. Keidar (Ed.): DISC 2009, LNCS 5805, pp. 341–355, 2009.
© Springer-Verlag Berlin Heidelberg 2009

control (also referred as locality). More recently, new facets of uncertainty (such as dynamicity, scalability and mobility) have appeared and made distributed computing even more challenging.

Among the many facets of uncertainty that distributed computing has to cope with, *anonymity* is particularly important. It occurs when the computing entities (processes, agents, sensors, etc.) have no name, and consequently cannot distinguish the ones from the others. It is worth noticing that, from a practical point of view, anonymity is a first class property as soon as one is interested in guaranteeing privacy.

One of the very first works (to our knowledge) that addressed anonymous systems is from D. Angluin [2]. In that paper, considering message passing systems, she was mainly interested in computability issues, namely answering the question "which functions can be computed in presence of asynchrony and anonymity?" The leader election problem is a simple example of a problem that is unsolvable in such a setting (intuitively, this because symmetry cannot be broken in presence of asynchrony and anonymity). Failure-free message passing anonymous systems have also been investigated in [34,35] where is given a characterization of problems solvable in this context according to which amount on information about network attributes are initially known by the processes.

Failure-free asynchronous shared memory systems have been studied in the context of anonymity. A characterization of the problems (tasks) that can be solved in this setting (when additionally the number of processes is not known) is given in [3]. The use of randomization to cope with crash-prone anonymous shared memory systems has been addressed in [31], where a randomized wait-free naming algorithm is given that solves the naming problem when each atomic register is a single-writer/multi-reader register. Recently, wait-free algorithms implementing snapshot and weak counters have been proposed for anonymous asynchronous shared memory systems prone to process crash [18]. *Wait-free* means that every non-faulty process has to terminate its snapshot or counter operations, whatever the number of failures and and the concurrency pattern [21].

Consensus in anonymous shared memory systems. Consensus is one of the most famous distributed computing problem. It is a coordination problem defined as follows: each process proposes a value, and each non-faulty process has to decide a value (termination), such that no two processes decide different values (agreement) and the decided value is a proposed value (validity). While it has a very simple statement and can be trivially solved in (anonymous or not) failure-free systems where the number of processes is known, and has simple solutions in (anonymous or not) crash-prone synchronous systems, the consensus problem has no solution in asynchronous non-anonymous failure-prone systems, as soon as (even only) one process can be faulty, be the failure a simple crash and the communication system a reliable shared memory system [24], or a reliable message passing system [16]. Trivially, the problem cannot be solved either if anonymity is added to asynchrony and failures.

An approach based on randomization is presented in [7] to circumvent the previous impossibility in anonymous crash-prone shared memory systems. As noticed in [18], this shows that producing unique identifiers is harder than consensus.

Another approach to circumvent the previous impossibility consists in considering a weaker version of the problem. Taking such an approach, [18] looks for obstruction-free consensus algorithms. *Obstruction-freedom* is a termination property weaker than wait-freedom. While wait-freedom requires that every non-faulty process always decides (see above), obstruction-freedom requires that, whatever the failure pattern, each non-faulty process p decides when the concurrency pattern is such that p can execute "long enough" without concurrency. (From a practical point of view, "long enough" means the time to execute its algorithm.) An obstruction-free consensus algorithm for anonymous shared memory systems is described in [18]. This algorithm requires $O(n)$ binary atomic registers (where n is the total number of processes).

Content of the paper. As far as we know, the consensus problem has not been investigated in anonymous crash-prone *message passing* systems. This is the topic addressed in this paper. Several contributions are presented. The first is a failure detector-based algorithm that solves the consensus problem despite the net effect of asynchrony, crash failures and anonymity. The second (and, to our view, a main contribution) is a lower bound on the number of rounds required by any algorithm that solves consensus in such an uncertainty context. The third contribution is an early-deciding algorithm, while the last contribution is the investigation of the k-set agreement problem in anonymous systems.

As consensus cannot be solved in presence of process crashes and asynchrony in a message passing systems [16], these systems have to be enriched with additional power in order the problem becomes solvable. Failure detectors are a well-known approach proposed to provide processes with such an additional power [8]. Informally, a failure detector provides each process with information on failures. As we are interested in the most efficient asynchronous message passing algorithm that solves consensus despite crashes and anonymity (and not in the weakest Ω-like [9] failure detector to face anonymity), we consider here the failure detector class denoted ψ. That failure detector class is the strongest of a family of failure detector classes that has been introduced in [28,29]. When queried by a process, such a failure detector returns an over-estimate of the number of alive processes. Interestingly, ψ and the class $\mathcal{P}$ of perfect failure detectors are equivalent in asynchronous non-anonymous systems. (A failure detector of the class $\mathcal{P}$ provides each process with a set that does not contain the id of a process before it crashes and eventually contains the ids of all the crashed processes.)

The paper first presents an asynchronous anonymous ψ-based algorithm that solves the consensus problem in $2t + 1$ rounds, where t is an upper bound on the number of processes that are allowed to crash in a run ($1 \leq t \leq n - 1$). Then the paper presents one of its results, namely, a proof that, whatever the crash failure pattern, $2t + 1$ is a lower bound on the number of rounds required to solve the consensus problem in the proposed round-based model. While $t + 1$ is a lower bound on the number of rounds to solve consensus in both synchronous message passing systems [1,15,23], and asynchronous message passing systems equipped with a perfect failure detector [20], we show that $2t + 1$ is the corresponding lower bound for anonymous systems. This is a noteworthy feature of anonymity as it shows that, when one wants to solve consensus deterministically despite anonymity, an additional price of t rounds has to be paid.

The paper then considers early decision in anonymous systems enriched with ψ. It presents an algorithm where the processes decide and halt by $\min(2f + 2, 2t + 1)$ rounds (where f is the actual number of faulty processes, $0 \le f \le t$). This leads to think that $\min(2f + 2, 2t + 1)$ could be the lower bound on the number of rounds for solving consensus in these asynchronous systems.

Finally, the paper focuses on the k-set agreement problem [10] that extends consensus in the sense it allows up to k values to be decided. It first shows that the previous ψ-based algorithm (designed for consensus) solves k-set agreement in $2 \lfloor \frac{t}{k} \rfloor + 1$ rounds. As k-set agreement is a weaker problem than consensus, a failure detector weaker than ψ should be able to solve it. To investigate this idea, a family of failure detector classes, denoted $\{\psi_\ell\}_{0 \le \ell < n}$, is introduced; ψ_0 is ψ, and $\psi_{\ell+1}$ is weaker than ψ_ℓ (ℓ is the maximal number of alive processes that can be falsely suspected to have crashed). It is shown that $\ell < k$ is a sufficient requirement to solve k-set agreement with the help of ψ_ℓ. Moreover a ψ_ℓ-based k-set agreement is presented that requires $R = 2 \lfloor \frac{t}{k-\ell} \rfloor + 1$ rounds. Interestingly, this formula relates the cost (R), the coordination degree of the problem (k), and the strength (ℓ) of the underlying failure detector. It also clearly exhibits the point until which the failure detector class can be weakened while still solving k-set agreement, namely ℓ should be lesser than k (the threshold value $\ell = k$, i.e. the value from which ψ_ℓ is too weak to solve k-set agreement, corresponds to a division by 0 in the formula).

Roadmap. The paper is made up of 7 sections. Section 2 presents the system model which includes the failure detector class ψ. Section 3 presents and proves correct a simple ψ-based algorithm that solves consensus despite asynchrony, process crashes and anonymity. Then, Section 4 proves a main theorem of the paper: $(2t + 1)$ is a lower bound on the number of rounds for any algorithm that solves the consensus problem in that computation model. Then, Section 5 addresses early decision, and Section 6 focuses on the k-set agreement problem. Finally, Section 7 concludes the paper giving a list of related open problems.

2   Computation Model

2.1   Base Model

Process model. The system is made up of a fixed number n of processes, denoted $p_1, \ldots, p_n$. The value of the system parameter n is not known by the processes. Moreover, the process p_i does not know its index i, which means that indexes are only used for a presentation purpose. Processes are anonymous in the sense that they have no name and execute the same algorithm. They are asynchronous in the sense that there is no assumption on their respective speeds.

Failure model. Up to t processes can crash in a run, $0 \le t \le n - 1$. A process executes correctly its algorithm until it possibly crashes. A crash is a premature stop; after it has crashed, a process executes no step. The value of the system parameter t is know by the processes. A process that does not crash in a run is *correct* in that run. Otherwise, it is *faulty* in that run. Until it crashes (if ever it does), a process is *alive*.

Communication. The processes communicate by exchanging messages through reliable channels. These channels are asynchronous, which means that there is no assumption on the speed of messages on channels, except that it is positive (eventually every message arrives).

   The processes are provided with a brodcast() communication primitive that allows the invoking process to send the same message to all the processes (including itself). The brodcast() primitive is not reliable in the sense that, if a process p_i crashes while broadcasting a message, that message can be received by an arbitrary subset of processes. When it receives a message, a process cannot determine the sender of the message. Moreover, given any set of messages it has received, a process cannot determine if these messages are from the same sender or from different senders.

Round-based model. The processes execute asynchronous rounds. During each round, a process broadcasts a message, receives messages sent during the very same round and executes local computation. This means that, as in the asynchronous models described in [4,17,25], the rounds are communication-closed.

Notation. The previous computation model is denoted $\mathcal{AARS}_{n,t}^{cl}[\emptyset]$. $\mathcal{AARS}$ stands for *A*nonymous *A*synchronous *R*ound-based *S*ystem, with communication-*cl*osed rounds, while $\emptyset$ means there is no additional assumption.

2.2   The Failure Detector Class ψ

As indicated in the introduction this failure detector class has been introduced in [28,29]. The class ψ is the equivalent of the class of perfect failure detectors $\mathcal{P}$, when we consider non-anonymous systems ("equivalent" means that, if we associate distinct names with each process of an anonymous system, we have the following: given a failure detector of any one class it is possible to build a failure detector of the other class. (In [5] appears a bounded transformation from ψ to $\mathcal{P}$.).

Definition. Let f denote the number of processes that crash in a given run $(0 \le f \le t)$, and f^τ denote the number of processes that have crashed up to time τ. A failure detector of the class ψ provides each process p_i with a positive integer denoted aal_i (approximate number of *a*live processes) that satisfies the following properties (where aal_i^τ denotes the value of aal_i at time τ):

- Safety: $\forall \tau : aal_i^\tau \ge n - f^\tau$.
- Liveness: $\exists \tau : \forall \tau' \ge \tau : aal_i^{\tau'} = n - f$.

The safety property states that $aa\ell_i$ is always an over-estimate of the number of processes that are still alive, while the liveness property states that it eventually converges to its exact value[1].

2.3 The Computation Model $\mathcal{AARS}_{n,t}^{cl}[\psi]$

This computation model is $\mathcal{AARS}_{n,t}^{cl}[\emptyset]$ enriched with ψ and where, in each round, the number of messages received by a process p_i is determined by the current value of $aa\ell_i$. More precisely, for each process p_i, the algorithms have the canonical form described on Fig. 1. The local variable r_i is the current round number of p_i. Each process p_i execute asynchronous rounds until some condition is satisfied. During its round r_i, p_i broadcast a message tagged r_i, waits until it has received $aa\ell_i$ messages tagged r_i, and executes local computation. ($aa\ell_i$ is repeatedly read until the wait statement terminates.) Before proceeding to the next round, the process p_i increases r_i. (As the model is asynchronous it is up to each process p_i to manage its round number).

```
r_i ← 1;
while (¬ condition) do
    begin asynchronous round
    broadcast a msg tagged (r_i, −);
    wait until (aaℓ_i msgs tagged r_i have been received);
    Local computation;
    r_i ← r_i + 1
    end asynchronous round
end while;
Local computation.
```

Fig. 1. Canonical form of algorithms

Misleading notification. Let us consider Fig. 2 where the rounds $r-1$, r and $r+1$ are represented, the processes p_a crashes during the round $r-1$ (a crash is represented by a cross in the figure), and the process p_b crashes after it has broadcast its round r message (in the figure, the corresponding crash appears during the round $r+1$). The asynchronous notification of each crash appears at p_i as a decrease of $aa\ell_i$; each is indicated with a dotted line. As p_a crashes during the round $r-1$, it will not send round r messages, and so, during the round r, p_i has to wait for at least 3 messages ($aa\ell_i = 3$). Differently, p_i is notified of the crash of p_b (i.e., $aa\ell_i$ is decreased to 2) while it is waiting for round r messages. As a result p_i waits for only two messages and, as it has received two round r messages (from p_b and itself), it terminates its participation to the round r. Such an early failure notification is called a *misleading* notification, and

---

[1] In [28], n is known and ψ provides each process p_i with an integer anc_i such that $n = aa\ell_i + anc_i$.

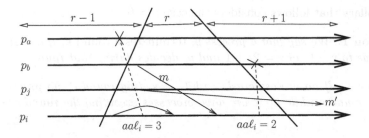

Fig. 2. Misleading notification

the message m sent by the corresponding crashed process is called a misleading message. More precisely, a message m sent at round r is *misleading* if it allows its receiver to terminate its round r, while the corresponding sender has crashed after or during the broadcast of m. These misleading notifications/messages come from the independence between the asynchronous communication-closed rounds on one side, and the crash notifications supplied by failure detector ψ on the other side (it is such an independence that makes the system different from a synchronous system).

The theorem that follows is central to the $\mathcal{AARS}^{cl}_{n,t}[\psi]$ model. It characterizes exactly the synchronization power of ψ.

Theorem 1. *If x processes crash while they execute the round r, no process can proceed to the round $r + 1$ while there are still $(x + 1)$ processes that are alive and execute the round $r - 1$.*

Proof. let τ be the time at which the first process (say p_i) progresses from the round r to the round $r + 1$. Moreover, let $A(\tau)$ be the number of processes that are alive at time τ, and $R(\tau, r)$ be the number of processes that, at time τ, have entered a round $r' \geq r$. We have $R(\tau, r) = RA(\tau, r) + RC(\tau, r)$ where $RA(\tau, r)$ is the number of processes that, at τ, are alive and execute a round $r' \geq r$ (notice that only p_i starts executing $r' = r + 1$, the other processes of $RA(\tau, r)$ are executing r), and $RC(\tau, r)$ is the number of processes that have started executing the round r and have crashed by time τ).

- It follows from the safety property of ψ that, when the process p_i progresses from the round r to the round $r + 1$, we have $aa\ell_i(\tau) \geq A(\tau)$. Moreover, during the round r, p_i receives and processes only messages sent during the same round r, from which we conclude that $R(\tau, r) \geq aa\ell_i(\tau)$, and by transitivity we obtain $R(\tau, r) \geq A(\tau)$.
- At time τ, there are $A(\tau) - RA(\tau, r)$ alive processes that have not yet entered the round r. As $RA(\tau, r) = R(\tau, r) - RC(\tau, r)$ and $0 \leq RC(\tau, r) \leq x$, we conclude that there are at most $A(\tau) - R(\tau, r) + x$ alive processes that have not yet entered the round r.

Finally, as, at time τ, there are at most $A(\tau) - R(\tau, r) + x$ alive processes that have not yet entered the round r, and $R(\tau, r) \geq A(\tau)$, we conclude that $A(\tau) - R(\tau, r) + x \leq x$, which completes the proof of the theorem. $\qquad\square$

The corollary that follows considers the case $x = 0$.

Definition 1. *We say that a process p_i terminates a round r, if $r < 2t + 1$ and p_i proceeds to $r + 1$, or $r = 2t + 1$ and p_i decides during that round.*

Corollary 1. *If no process crashes while executing round r, no process terminates the round r while there are alive processes executing the round $r - 1$.*

3   Solving Consensus in $\mathcal{AARS}^{cl}_{n,t}[\psi]$

A consensus algorithm for the $\mathcal{AARS}^{cl}_{n,t}[\psi]$ model is described in Fig. 3. This algorithm is a simple enrichment of the skeleton described in the previous section that adapts to $\mathcal{AARS}^{cl}_{n,t}[\psi]$ the classical flood set consensus algorithm designed for synchronous system [4,25,32].

A process p_i invokes propose(v_i) where v_i is the value it proposes to the consensus. It terminates when it executes the return(est_i) statement (line 10) where est_i is the value it decides. The processes execute $(2t + 1)$ asynchronous rounds (line 02). In each round, each process p_i broadcasts its current estimate (denoted est_i and initialized to v_i) of the decision value and updates it (by taking the minimum on the values it has received and taken into account up to now, lines 05-06).

```
operation propose(v_i):
(01)   est_i ← v_i; r_i ← 1;
(02)   while (r_i ≤ 2t + 1) do
(03)       begin asynchronous round
(04)       brodcast EST(r_i, est_i);
(05)       wait until( aaℓ_i messages EST(r_i, −) have been received);
(06)       est_i ← min(est values received at the previous line);
(07)       r_i ← r_i + 1;
(08)       end asynchronous round
(09)   end while;
(10)   return(est_i).
```

Fig. 3. Anonymous consensus in $\mathcal{AARS}^{cl}_{n,t}[\psi]$

Remark. If n is known by the processes, the algorithm can be improved to reduce the number of rounds in the particular case where $t = n - 1$ (wait-free case). Instead of $(2t + 1)$ rounds, the processes can then execute only $2t$ rounds.

Theorem 2. *The algorithm described in Fig. 3 solves the consensus problem in $(2t + 1)$ rounds in the $\mathcal{AARS}^{cl}_{n,t}[\psi]$ model.*

Proof of the algorithm. Due to pages limitation, the proof appears in [5].

4 $(2t + 1)$ Is a Lower Bound

Assuming $t < n - 1$, this section shows that $(2t+1)$ is a lower bound on the number of rounds to solve the consensus problem in both the model $\mathcal{AARS}^{cl}_{n,t}[\psi]$ and the model $\mathcal{AARS}^{op}_{n,t}[\psi]$ described in the next section devoted to early decision (the main difference is that $\mathcal{AARS}^{op}_{n,t}[\psi]$ is not round communication-closed).

The proof is by contradiction. Assuming that there is an algorithm A that solves the binary consensus problem in $2t$ rounds, it shows that such an algorithm cannot be designed. (In the binary consensus problem, only the values 0 and 1 can be proposed by the processes. It is easy to see that considering only binary consensus can be done without loss of generality.)

Structure of the proof. The structure of the proof is as in [1,16]. The contradiction follows from the following lemmas. The first lemma shows that a configuration of A after $2(t - 1)$ rounds is univalent. The second lemma shows that there is a configuration of A that, after $2(t - 1)$ rounds, is bivalent. That lemma uses the fact that, assuming the existence of an algorithm A that solves the binary consensus problem, there is an initial bivalent configuration.

The proof does not consider all the possible runs of A. It relies only on the runs of A in which no process crashes in odd rounds, and there is at most one process crash per even round. As the algorithm described in Fig. 3 needs $2t + 1$ rounds, the $2t + 1$ bound proved for these runs is a tight lower bound (Theorem 4). Due to pages limitation, the proof appears in [5]. (As for Theorem 2, for $t = n - 1$, it is possible to show that $2t$ rounds are necessary and sufficient.)

Theorem 3. *Let $t < n - 1$. There is no consensus algorithm that always terminates in at most $2t$ rounds in the $\mathcal{AARS}_{n,t}[\psi]$ model.*

The following theorem is an immediate consequence of the previous theorem and Theorem 2.

Theorem 4. *Let $t < n - 1$. The algorithm described in Fig. 3 is optimal (for the number of rounds) in the $\mathcal{AARS}_{n,t}[\psi]$ model.*

5   Early Decision and Halting

5.1   Early Decision

The aim is here to allow the processes to decide before the round $2t + 1$ when there are few failures. Let f $(0 \leq f \leq t)$ be the actual number of faulty processes. The corresponding consensus lower bound is $\min(t + 1, f + 2)$ rounds in non-anonymous asynchronous systems equipped with a perfect failure detector [12] and in non-anonymous synchronous systems [4,23,25,32]. What is the lower bound in $\mathcal{AARS}^{cl}_{n,t}[\psi]$?

Compared to the previous systems, the new difficulty we have to cope with in $\mathcal{AARS}^{cl}_{n,t}[\psi]$ lies in the fact that, due misleading messages, during a round a process can miss messages from processes that have not crashed. Providing early decision in such a context is a real challenge. Our intuition is that early decision in $\mathcal{AARS}_{n,t}^{cl}[\psi]$ requires the processes to decide simultaneously during the very same round. The simultaneous agreement problem, introduced in [13,14], has been shown to be strongly related to the "common knowledge" theory [19], and has received some attention in the literature (e.g., [26,27]). So, we conjecture that early decision and halting in $\mathcal{AARS}_{n,t}^{cl}[\psi]$ requires simultaneous agreement and should be attained in $2t + 1 - D$ rounds where D $(0 \leq D \leq t)$ is parameter defined from the actual failure pattern [14].

5.2   The System Model $\mathcal{AARS}_{n,t}^{op}[\psi]$

This paper addresses early decision in a model, denoted $\mathcal{AARS}_{n,t}^{op}[\psi]$(where op stands for $open$), derived from, and less constraining than, $\mathcal{AARS}_{n,t}^{cl}[\psi]$. This model, that assumes that each process knows initially t and n, is round-based but not round communication-closed. During any round r, in addition to the messages tagged r, a process can send or receive and process a round-free message, i.e., a message that is not tagged by a round number. This model allows the behavior of a process to be defined by two tasks: a round-based task $T1$, and a task $T2$ that processes the round-free messages. Both $\mathcal{AARS}_{n,t}^{cl}[\psi]$ and $\mathcal{AARS}_{n,t}^{op}[\psi]$ assume that t is known by each process. Additionnally $\mathcal{AARS}_{n,t}^{op}[\psi]$ assumes also that n is known.

It is interesting to recall that, differently from what can be done in the round-based synchronous model, a lot of "round-based" asynchronous algorithms do actually assume a model similar to $\mathcal{AARS}_{n,t}^{op}[\psi]$. This is the case, for example, of the round-based consensus algorithms that assume an underlying failure detector such as the eventual leader Ω. Before deciding, a process broadcasts a DECIDE() that allows its receiver to stop executing its round-based task, and decide immediately (e.g., [8,9,30]).

5.3   An Early Deciding Algorithm for $\mathcal{AARS}_{n,t}^{op}[\psi]$

An algorithm that solves the consensus problem in $\min(2t + 1, 2f + 2)$ rounds in the $\mathcal{AARS}_{n,t}^{op}[\psi]$ model is described in Figure 4. As announced, it is made up of two tasks. The task $T2$ is to prevent deadlock: when a process early decides (line N5), it broadcasts a round-free DECIDE() message and, if a process p_i has not yet decided when it receives such a message, it forwards it and returns the decided value (and stops accordingly).

The main task $T1$ is a round-based task partly similar to the the behavior described in Figure 3. The lines common to both algorithms have the same number. M is appended to the number of a line that is modified, while the new lines are numbered N1, N2, etc.

Each process p_i manages the following additional local variables: $early_i$ initialized to $false$ (its meaning will be explained later), rec_i that counts the number of messages received during the current round (line N1), and a variable k whose current value is such that $r_i = 2k + 1$ in odd rounds and $r_i = 2k + 2$ in even rounds (line N2). Moreover, a round message now carries the additional boolean value $early_i$ (line 04M).

```
operation propose(v_i):
task T1:
(01M) est_i ← v_i; r_i ← 1; early_i ← false;
(02)   while (r_i ≤ 2t + 1) do
(03)      begin asynchronous round
(04M)     brodcast EST(r_i, est_i, early_i);
(05)      wait until ( aaℓ_i messages EST(r_i, −, −) have been received );
(06)      est_i ← min(est values received at the previous line);
(N1)      let rec_i[r_i] = number of messages received at line 05;
(N2)      let k = ⌊(r_i−1)/2⌋;
(N3)      if   (r_i is even) ∧ (rec_i[r_i] = n − k)
(N4)        ∧ (each EST(r_i, −, early) received is such that early = true)
(N5)            then brodcast DECIDE(est_i); return(est_i) end if;
(N6)      if (r_i + 1 is even) then early_i ← (rec_i[r_i] = n − k) end if;
(07)      r_i ← r_i + 1
(08)   end asynchronous round
(09)   end while;
(10)   return(est_i).
==============================================
task T2: when DECIDE(est) is received : brodcast DECIDE(est); return(est).
```

Fig. 4. Early deciding anonymous consensus in $\mathcal{AARS}^{op}_{n,t}[\psi]$ (n and t are known)

The core of the early decision is at lines N3-N6, namely a process p_i early decides during the round r if the following round-dependent predicate is satisfied: the round is even, exactly $n - k = n - \lfloor\frac{r-1}{2}\rfloor$ messages EST$(r, -, -)$ have been received and each carries the value *true* (lines N3-N4). As we will see in the proof, when satisfied, this locally evaluable predicate says that p_i knows (1) the minimal value (v) of the est_j variables of the set of the processes p_j that started the round $2k + 1$, and (2) that all the processes p_j that started the round $2k + 2$, know that value v. It follows that the est_j values of all the processes that started the round $2k + 2$ are equal to v, and consequently no other value can be decided. The boolean $early_j$ is used by a process p_j to indicate (line 04) if, during an odd round $r = 2k + 1$, it has received $n - k = n - \lfloor\frac{r-1}{2}\rfloor$ round r messages (line N6).

Theorem 5. *The algorithm described in Figure 4 solves the consensus problem in* $\min(2f + 2, 2t + 1)$ *rounds in the* $\mathcal{AARS}^{op}_{n,t}[\psi]$ *model (where f denotes the actual number of process crashes).*

Proof of the early deciding algorithm. Due to pages limitation, the proof appears in [5].

6   From Consensus to k-Set Agreement

This section considers the k-set agreement problem in anonymous asynchronous crash-prone message passing systems.

The k-set agreement problem. The k-set agreement problem has been introduced in [10] to study how the number of choices (k) allowed to the processes is related to the maximum number of faulty processes (t). It is defined by the same validity and termination properties as the consensus problem, and the following agreement property: at most k different values can be decided (so, consensus is 1-set agreement). The k-set agreement problem cannot be solved in non-anonymous asynchronous crash-prone systems as soon as $k \leq t$ [6,22,33]. Differently, it can always be solved in round-based synchronous systems where $\lfloor \frac{t}{k} \rfloor + 1$ is a lower bound on the number of rounds [11].

6.1   Solving k-Set Agreement in $\mathcal{AARS}_{n,t}^{cl}[\psi]$ with $t \leq n - k$

The algorithm described in Fig. 3, where $2t + 1$ is replaced by $2 \lfloor \frac{t}{k} \rfloor + 1$ solves the k-set agreement in $\mathcal{AARS}_{n,t}^{cl}[\psi]$. The assumption $t \leq n - k$ generalizes the assumption $t \leq n - 1$ associated with the consensus problem. Due to pages limitation, the proof appears in [5].

Theorem 6. *The algorithm described in Figure 3 (where $(2t + 1)$ is replaced by $2 \lfloor \frac{t}{k} \rfloor + 1$) solves the k-set agreement problem in $2 \lfloor \frac{t}{k} \rfloor + 1$ rounds in the $\mathcal{AARS}_{n,t}^{cl}[\psi]$ model where $t \leq n - k$.*

6.2   Solving the k-Set Agreement with Weaker Failure Detectors

The failure detector class ψ_ℓ. As, when $k > 1$, the k-set agreement problem is weaker than consensus, it should be possible to use a failure detector weaker than ψ in order to solve it. So, let us consider the class of failure detectors, denoted ψ_ℓ, $0 \leq \ell < n$, that is a simple generalization of ψ. It is defined as follows (the notation is the same as in Section 2.2):

- Safety: $\forall \tau : aal_i^\tau \geq n - f^\tau - \ell$.
- Liveness: $\exists \tau : \forall \tau' \geq \tau : n - f - \ell \leq aal_i^{\tau'} \leq n - f$.

From this definition, we obtain a family of failure detector classes $\{\psi_\ell\}_{0 \leq \ell < n}$. It is easy to see that ψ_0 is ψ and ψ_ℓ is weaker than $\psi_{\ell-1}$.

A k-set algorithm for $\mathcal{AARS}_{n,t}^{cl}[\psi_\ell]$. Interestingly, when the number of rounds $2t + 1$ is replaced by $2 \lfloor \frac{t}{k-\ell} \rfloor + 1$, the algorithm described in Fig. 3 solves the k-set agreement problem in $\mathcal{AARS}_{n,t}^{cl}[\psi_\ell]$ (assuming $t \leq n - k + \ell$ and $\ell < k$). As we can see, the ψ-based consensus algorithm described in Figure 3 and its ψ-based k-set agreement variant (described in the previous section), are two particular instances of the general ψ_ℓ-based algorithm. These instances consider $\ell = 0$, i.e., the strongest class in the failure detector family $\{\psi_\ell\}_{0 \leq \ell < n}$. Due to pages limitation, the proof appears in [5].

Theorem 7. *Let $k \leq t \leq n - k$ and $0 \leq \ell < k$. The algorithm described in Fig. 3, where $(2t + 1)$ is replaced by $2 \lfloor \frac{t}{k-\ell} \rfloor + 1$, solves the k-set agreement problem in $2 \lfloor \frac{t}{k-\ell} \rfloor + 1$ rounds in the $\mathcal{AARS}_{n,t}^{cl}[\psi_\ell]$ model.*

Discussion. Let us consider the instance of the general ψ_ℓ-based algorithm where the number of rounds is fixed to a predetermined value R (instead of $2\lfloor t/(k-\ell)\rfloor+1$.

- Then, that algorithm instance solves the k-set agreement problem where k is the smallest value such that $R \geq 2\lfloor t/(k-\ell)\rfloor + 1$.
- From a different point of view, the weakest failure detector class ψ_ℓ for which that instance can solve the k-set agreement problem in R rounds is defined by the greatest value of $\ell < k$ such that $R \geq 2\lfloor t/(k-\ell)\rfloor + 1$ (if such a value does exist[2]).

This clearly shows how the algorithm captures and links its cost (measured by its time complexity R), the power of the failure detector the system is equipped with (this power is defined by ℓ, the greater ℓ, the weaker the power of the underlying failure detector), and the difficulty of the considered set agreement problem (measured by the coordination degree k: k'-set agreement is more difficult than k-set agreement if $k' < k$). Solving a more difficult problem requires either more rounds, or a more powerful failure detector class than solving an easier problem. In the $\mathcal{AARS}_{n,t}[\psi_\ell]$ model, the three critical parameters R, k and ℓ are related by the simple formula $R = 2\lfloor \frac{t}{k-\ell}\rfloor + 1$.

7 Open Problems

This work leaves open problems for future research. Among them there are the following ones.

- Design a simultaneous consensus algorithm in the $\mathcal{AARS}_{n,t}^{cl}[\psi]$ model.
- Prove (or disprove) that $\min(2f + 2, 2t + 1)$ rounds is the lower bound for early decision in the $\mathcal{AARS}_{n,t}^{op}[\psi]$ model.
- Investigate the question of the weakest failure detector class for solving consensus despite asynchrony, anonymity and failures. (An introductory view of this problem appears in [5].)
- Assuming $k < t \leq n - k$, show (or disprove) that there is a ψ_ℓ-based k-set agreement algorithm in the $\mathcal{AARS}_{n,t}^{cl}[\psi]$ model if and only if $0 \leq \ell < k$.
- Design an early deciding k-set agreement algorithm for the $\mathcal{AARS}_{n,t}^{op}[\psi]$ model.

References

1. Aguilera, M.K., Toueg, S.: A Simple Bivalency Proof that t-Resilient Consensus Requires $t + 1$ Rounds. Information Processing Letters 71, 155–178 (1999)
2. Angluin, D.: Local and Global Properties in Networks of Processes. In: Proc. 12th Symposium on Theory of Computing (STOC 1980), pp. 82–93. ACM Press, New York (1980)

---

[2] Let us notice that there are cases where such an integer ℓ does not exist. As an example, let us take $t = 3$, $k = 1$ and $R = 2$. It is easy to see that there is no $\ell < 1$ such that $R = 2 \geq 2\lfloor\frac{3}{1-\ell}\rfloor + 1$. This means that to solve consensus ($k = 1$) in $\mathcal{AARS}_{n,t}^{cl}[\psi_\ell]$, we need $\ell = 0$ and this entails $R = 2\lfloor\frac{3}{1}\rfloor + 1 = 7$ rounds.

3. Attiya, H., Gorbach, A., Moran, S.: Computing in Totally Anonymous Asynchronous Shared Memory Systems. Inf. and Comp. 173(2), 162–183 (2002)
4. Attiya, H., Welch, J.: Distributed Computing, Fundamentals, Simulation and Advanced Topics, 2nd edn. Wiley Series on Parallel and Distributed Computing, 414 page (2004)
5. Bonnet, F., Raynal, M.: The Price of Anonymity: Optimal Consensus despite Asynchrony, Crash and Anonymity. Tech. Report, #1918, IRISA, Université de Rennes (France) (December 2008)
6. Borowsky, E., Gafni, E., Generalized, F.L.P.: Impossibility Results for t-Resilient Asynchronous Computations. In: Proc. 25th ACM Symposium on Theory of Computation (STOC 1993), pp. 91–100 (1993)
7. Buhrman, H., Panconesi, A., Silvestri, R., Vityani, P.: On the Importance of Having an Identity or Is Consensus Really Universal? Distributed Computing 18(3), 167–175 (2006)
8. Chandra, T., Toueg, S.: Unreliable Failure Detectors for Reliable Distributed Systems. Journal of the ACM 43(2), 225–267 (1996)
9. Chandra, T., Hadzilacos, V., Toueg, S.: The Weakest Failure Detector for Solving Consensus. Journal of the ACM 43(4), 685–722 (1996)
10. Chaudhuri, S.: More Choices Allow More Faults: Set Consensus Problems in Totally Asynchronous Systems. Information and Computation 105, 132–158 (1993)
11. Chaudhuri, S., Herlihy, M., Lynch, N., Tuttle, M.: Tight Bounds for k-Set Agreement. Journal of the ACM 47(5), 912–943 (2000)
12. Delporte-Gallet, C., Fauconnier, H., Helary, J.-M., Raynal, M.: Early Stopping in Global Data Computation. IEEE Transactions Parallel Distributed Systems 14(9), 909–921 (2003)
13. Dolev, D., Reischuk, R., Strong, R.: Early Stopping in Byzantine Agreement. Journal of the ACM 37(4), 720–741 (1990)
14. Dwork, C., Moses, Y.: Knowledge and Common Knowledge in a Byzantine Environment: Crash Failures. Information and Computation 88(2), 156–186 (1990)
15. Fischer, M.J., Lynch, N.A.: A Lower Bound on the Time to Assure Interactive Consistency. Information Processing Letters 14(4), 183–186 (1982)
16. Fischer, M.J., Lynch, N.A., Paterson, M.S.: Impossibility of Distributed Consensus with One Faulty Process. Journal of the ACM 32(2), 374–382 (1985)
17. Gafni, E.: Round-by-round Fault Detectors: Unifying Synchrony and Asynchrony. In: Proc. 17th ACM Symposium on Principles of Distributed Computing (PODC 2000), pp. 143–152. ACM Press, New York (1998)
18. Guerraoui, R., Ruppert, E.: Anonymous and Fault-tolerant Shared Memory Computing. Distributed Computing 20(3), 165–177 (2007)
19. Halpern, J.Y., Moses, Y.: Knowledge and Common Knowledge in a Distributed Environment. Journal of the ACM 37(3), 549–587 (1990)
20. Hélary, J.-M., Hurfin, M., Mostefaoui, A., Raynal, M., Tronel, F.: Computing Global Functions in Asynchronous Distributed Systems with Perfect Failure Detectors. IEEE Trans. on Parallel and Distributed Systems 11(9), 897–909 (2000)
21. Herlihy, M.P.: Wait-Free Synchronization. ACM Transactions on Programming Languages and Systems 13(1), 124–149 (1991)
22. Herlihy, M.P., Shavit, N.: The Topological Structure of Asynchronous Computability. Journal of the ACM 46(6), 858–923 (1999)
23. Keidar, I., Rajsbaum, S.: A Simple Proof of the Uniform Consensus Synchronous Lower Bound. Information Processing Letters 85, 47–52 (2003)
24. Loui, M.C., Abu-Amara, H.: Memory Requirements for Agreement Among Unreliable Asynchronous Processes. Advances in Computing research 4, 163–183 (1987)

25. Lynch, N.A.: Distributed Algorithms, 872 pages. Morgan Kaufmann, San Francisco (1996)
26. Moses, Y., Raynal, M.: Revisiting Simultaneous Consensus with Crash Failures. Journal of Parallel and Distributed Computing 69(4), 400–409 (2009)
27. Moses, Y., Tuttle, M.R.: Programming Simultaneous Actions Using Common Knowledge. Algorithmica 3, 121–169 (1988)
28. Mostefaoui, A., Rajsbaum, S., Raynal, M., Travers, C.: On the Computability Power and the Robustness of Set Agreement-oriented Failure Detector Classes. Distributed Computing 21(3), 201–222 (2008)
29. Mostefaoui, A., Rajsbaum, S., Raynal, M., Travers, C.: The Combined Power of Conditions and Information on Failures to Solve Asynchronous Set Agreement. SIAM Journal of Computing 38(4), 1574–1601 (2008)
30. Mostefaoui, A., Raynal, M.: Leader-Based Consensus. Parallel Processing Letters 11(1), 95–107 (2001)
31. Panconesi, A., Papatriantafilou, M., Tsigas, P., Vityani, P.: Randomized Naming Using Wait-free Shared Variables. Distributed Computing 11(3), 113–124 (1998)
32. Raynal, M.: Consensus in Synchronous Systems: a Concise Guided Tour. In: Proc. 9th IEEE Pacific Rim Int'l Symposium on Dependable Computing (PRDC 2002), pp. 221–228. IEEE Computer Society Press, Los Alamitos (2002)
33. Saks, M., Zaharoglou, F.: Wait-Free k-Set Agreement is Impossible: The Topology of Public Knowledge. SIAM Journal on Computing 29(5), 1449–1483 (2000)
34. Yamashita, M., Kameda, T.: Computing on Anonymous Networks: Part I - Characterizing the Solvable Cases. IEEE Transactions on Parallel Distributed Systems 7(1), 69–89 (1996)
35. Yamashita, M., Kameda, T.: Computing on Anonymous Networks: Part II - Decision and Membership Problems. IEEE Transactions on Parallel Distributed Systems 7(1), 90–96 (1996)

Brief Announcement: On Implementing Omega Efficiently in the Crash-Recovery Model*

Mikel Larrea[1] and Cristian Martín[2]

[1] The University of the Basque Country, 20018 San Sebastián, Spain
mikel.larrea@ehu.es
[2] Ikerlan Research Center, 20500 Arrasate-Mondragón, Spain
cmartin@ikerlan.es

Abstract. This work focuses on implementing Omega in the crash-recovery model. Previously proposed algorithms either use stable storage or have a permanent all-to-all communication pattern. We propose a more efficient algorithm which does not use stable storage, and in which eventually, among correct processes, only one keeps sending messages.

1 Motivation

Omega provides an eventual leader election functionality, i.e., eventually all processes agree on a common process [1]. Previously proposed algorithms for Omega in the crash-recovery model [3,4] either use stable storage or have an all-to-all communication pattern, i.e., periodically every process sends a message to the rest of processes. We propose here a more efficient algorithm in which eventually only one correct process, i.e., the leader, sends a message periodically to the rest.

2 The Algorithm

The algorithm, presented in Figure 1, works under the following assumptions on communication reliability and synchrony: (i) for every correct process p, there is an eventually timely link from p to every correct and every unstable process, and (ii) for every unstable process u, there is a fair lossy link from u to every correct process. A detailed description of the algorithm can be found in [2].

With this algorithm, unstable processes are allowed to disagree with correct processes. In practice, it is interesting that eventually all the processes that are up, either correct or unstable, agree on a common and correct leader process. We propose in [2] an adaptation of the algorithm that makes unstable processes not trust any process upon recovery, i.e., output a special value $\perp$, until either they trust the leader or crash. The adaptation assumes a majority of processes in the system to be correct.

---

* Research partially supported by the Spanish Research Council, under grants TIN2007-67353-C02-02 and TIN2006-15617-C03-01, and the Comunidad de Madrid, under grant S-0505/TIC/0285.

I. Keidar (Ed.): DISC 2009, LNCS 5805, pp. 356–357, 2009.

procedure *update_leader*()
    leader_p ← process in *Candidates_p* with smallest associated counter in *Recovered_p*

Initialization:
    $leader_p \leftarrow p$
    $Candidates_p \leftarrow \{p\}$
    for all $q \in \Pi$ except p:
        $Timeout_p[q] \leftarrow \eta$
        $Recovered_p[q] \leftarrow 0$
    $Recovered_p[p] \leftarrow 1$
    send ($RECOVERED$, p) to all processes except p
    start tasks 1, 2 and 3

Task 1:
    repeat forever every η **time units**
        if $leader_p = p$ **then**
            send ($LEADER$, p, $Recovered_p$) to all processes except p
Task 2:
    upon reception of message ($RECOVERED$, q) **or** message ($LEADER$, q, $Recovered_q$) **do**
        if message is of type $RECOVERED$ **then**
            $Recovered_p[q] \leftarrow Recovered_p[q] + 1$
        else
            for all $r \in \Pi$:
                $Recovered_p[r] \leftarrow \max\{Recovered_p[r], Recovered_q[r]\}$
            $Timeout_p[q] \leftarrow \max\{Timeout_p[q], Recovered_p[p]\}$
        $Candidates_p \leftarrow Candidates_p \cup \{q\}$
        update_leader()
        reset $timer_p(q)$ to $Timeout_p[q]$
Task 3:
    upon expiration of $timer_p(q)$ **do**
        $Timeout_p[q] \leftarrow Timeout_p[q] + 1$
        $Candidates_p \leftarrow Candidates_p - \{q\}$
        update_leader()

Fig. 1. Efficient Omega algorithm in the crash-recovery model. Code for process p

Using message relaying it is possible to relax the assumptions on communication reliability and synchrony of the algorithm, which would work under the following weaker assumptions: (i') for every correct process p, there is an eventually timely *path* from p to every correct and every unstable process, and (ii') for every unstable process u, there is a fair lossy link from u to *some* correct process. A consequence of the use of relaying is that the algorithm is no longer efficient.

References

1. Chandra, T., Hadzilacos, V., Toueg, S.: The weakest failure detector for solving consensus. Journal of the ACM 43(4), 685–722 (1996)
2. Larrea, M., Martín, C.: Optimal Leader Election in Crash-Recovery Systems. Technical Report EHU-KAT-IK-10-08, The University of the Basque Country (December 2008), http://www.sc.ehu.es/acwlaalm/
3. Martín, C., Larrea, M.: Eventual leader election in the crash-recovery failure model. In: Proceedings of the 14th Pacific Rim International Symposium on Dependable Computing (PRDC 2008), Taipei, Taiwan, December 2008, pp. 208–215 (2008)
4. Martín, C., Larrea, M., Jiménez, E.: Implementing the Omega failure detector in the crash-recovery failure model. Journal of Computer and System Sciences 75(3), 178–189 (2009)

Brief Announcement:
The Minimum Failure Detector for Non-Local Tasks in Message-Passing Systems*

Carole Delporte-Gallet[1], Hugues Fauconnier[1], and Sam Toueg[2]

[1] LIAFA, University Paris Diderot, France
[2] University of Toronto, ON, Canada

Abstract. This paper defines the basic notions of local and non-local tasks, and determines the minimum information about failures that is necessary to solve any non-local task in message-passing systems. It also introduces a natural weakening of the well-known set agreement task, and show that, in some precise sense, it is the weakest non-local task in message-passing systems.

We investigate the following question: *What is the minimum information about failures that is necessary to solve* any *non-local task in message-passing systems?*

To understand this question, we must first explain what we mean here by "non-local task". Roughly speaking, an (input/output) task is a relation between the input and the output values of processes [1]. In this paper, we consider *one-shot* tasks where each process has a single input value drawn from a finite number of possible input values, and each process outputs a single value. To classify a task as being local or non-local, we consider its input/output requirement in simple systems with no failures. Intuitively, a task is *local* if, in systems with no failures, every process can compute its output value locally by applying some function on its own input value. A task is *non-local* if it is not local.

To illustrate the concept of task locality, consider the trivial "identity" task which requires that every process simply outputs a copy of its input. Intuitively, this task is local: every process can compute its output locally, without any message exchange. Now consider the binary consensus task. This task is not local, in the sense that at least one process cannot compute its output from its individual input only (this holds even in a system where all processes are correct). So consensus is a non-local task.

To determine the minimum information about failures that is necessary to solve non-local tasks, we use the abstraction of failure detectors [2]. Failure detectors have been used to solve several basic problems of fault-tolerant distributed computing and to capture the minimum information about failures that is necessary to solve these problems (e.g., consensus, set agreement, non-blocking atomic commit, mutual exclusion, uniform reliable broadcast, boosting obstruction-freedom to wait-freedom, implementing an atomic register in a message-passing system, etc.).

---

* Work partially supported by supported by the ANR verso Shaman and the National Science and Engineering Research Council of Canada.

I. Keidar (Ed.): DISC 2009, LNCS 5805, pp. 358–359, 2009.

In this paper, we show that there is a non-trivial failure detector, denoted $\mathcal{FS}^*$, that is necessary to solve non-local tasks in message-passing systems. By this we mean that $\mathcal{FS}^*$ can be extracted from *any* failure detector that can be used to solve *any* non-local task in such systems. We also show that $\mathcal{FS}^*$ is the strongest failure detector with this property. More precisely, we prove that:

1. NECESSITY: $\mathcal{FS}^*$ is necessary to solve non-local tasks, i.e., if a failure detector $\mathcal{D}$ can be used to solve a non-local task $\mathcal{T}$ then $\mathcal{FS}^*$ is weaker than $\mathcal{D}$, and
2. MAXIMALITY: if a failure detector $\mathcal{D}^*$ is necessary to solve non-local tasks, then $\mathcal{D}^*$ is weaker than $\mathcal{FS}^*$.

So, intuitively, $\mathcal{FS}^*$ is the greatest lower bound of the set of failure detectors that solve non-local tasks, and it captures the minimum information about failures necessary for solving such tasks in message-passing systems.

$\mathcal{FS}^*$ is a very weak failure detector, so one may ask wether it is too weak to solve any interesting problem. We show that this is not the case: $\mathcal{FS}^*$ can be used to solve a natural weakening of the well-known *set agreement* task, that we call *weak set agreement (WSA)*. In fact, we prove that $\mathcal{FS}^*$ is the weakest failure detector for solving this task. Our results imply that, in some precise sense, WSA is the weakest non-local task for message-passing systems: for *any* non-local task $\mathcal{T}$, if $\mathcal{T}$ is solvable using a failure detector $\mathcal{D}$, then WSA is also solvable with $\mathcal{D}$.

Finally, we compare $\mathcal{FS}^*$ to two closely related failure detectors, namely, $\mathcal{L}$ and anti-Ω, which are the weakest failure detectors to solve set agreement in message-passing and shared memory systems, respectively. We prove that anti-Ω is strictly weaker than $\mathcal{FS}^*$ and $\mathcal{FS}^*$ is strictly weaker than $\mathcal{L}$, in message-passing systems.

The failure detector $\mathcal{FS}^*$ and the weak set agreement task WSA that we introduce in this work are both very simple. Intuitively, failure detector $\mathcal{FS}^*$ outputs GREEN or RED at each process such that (1) if *all* processes are correct, then $\mathcal{FS}^*$ outputs GREEN forever at some process, and (2) if *exactly one* process is correct, then there is a time after which $\mathcal{FS}^*$ outputs RED at this process. Weak set agreement is like set agreement, except that the condition that there are at most $n - 1$ distinct decision values is required *only for failure-free runs*.

A preliminary version of the full paper, which includes a discussion of related results, is in [3].

References

1. Biran, O., Moran, S., Zaks, S.: A combinatorial characterization of the distributed 1-solvable tasks. J. Algorithms 11(3), 420–440 (1990)
2. Chandra, T.D., Toueg, S.: Unreliable failure detectors for reliable distributed systems. Journal of the ACM 43(2), 225–267 (1996)
3. Delporte-Gallet, C., Fauconnier, H., Toueg, S.: The minimum failure detector for non-local tasks in message-passing systems. Technical Report hal-00401844, LIAFA - Laboratoire d'Informatique Algorithmique: Fondements et Applications (June 2009)

Brief Announcement: Weak Synchrony Models and Failure Detectors for Message Passing (*k*-)Set Agreement*

Martin Biely, Peter Robinson, and Ulrich Schmid

Technische Universität Wien, Embedded Computing Systems Group (E182/2)
{biely,robinson,s}@ecs.tuwien.ac.at

Motivation. In recent years, the quest for weak system assumptions, which add just enough synchrony resp. failure information to purely asynchronous systems to circumvent impossibility results, has been an active research topic in distributed computing. Most work in this area has been devoted to (1) identifying weak(est) failure detectors (FDs), and (2) identifying synchrony assumptions just strong enough to implement these weak FDs.

Due to the FLP impossibility result [1], the first focus of this research has been the *consensus* problem. More recently, *k-set agreement* (termed set agreement for $k = n-1$) has been identified as a promising target for further exploring the solvability border in asynchronous systems. As for (1), *anti-Ω* [2] was shown to be the weakest FD for set agreement in shared memory systems: Whereas Ω (the weakest FD for solving consensus [3]) outputs the id of one *correct* process infinitely often, anti-Ω outputs the id of one *correct* process only finitely often. Subsequently, a generalization called anti-Ω_k that returns $n-k$ processes has been shown to be the weakest FD for *k*-set agreement in shared memory system [4,5]. For message passing systems, only the weakest FD for set agreement is known, namely, the "loneliness" failure detector $\mathcal{L}$ [6]. Concerning (2), a class of shared memory models for implementing anti-Ω_k was presented in [7].

Contributions. In the full paper [8], we generalize $\mathcal{L}$, the weakest FD for $(n-1)$-set agreement, to the $(n-k)$-*loneliness detector* $\mathcal{L}(k)$ that allows to solve *k*-set agreement for any *k*. Like $\mathcal{L}$, $\mathcal{L}(k)$ outputs either TRUE or FALSE: While $\mathcal{L}$ is required to perpetually output FALSE on at least one process, $\mathcal{L}(k)$ is required to do so on $n-k$ processes. Moreover, when *k* or more processes crash, $\mathcal{L}(k)$ detects these crashes by outputting TRUE on at least one correct process, just like $\mathcal{L}$ for $n-1$ crashes. We prove that $\mathcal{L}(k)$ does not allow to solve $(k-1)$-set agreement, and give an algorithm that implements *k*-set agreement using $\mathcal{L}(k)$ even in anonymous systems, i.e., without unique identifiers (in contrast to the algorithm for $\mathcal{L}$ provided in [6]). We also provide a detailed analysis of the relationship between $\mathcal{L}(k)$ and the limited scope failure detector $\mathcal{S}_{n-k+1}$ [9].

* This research was supported by the Austrian BM:vit's FIT-IT programme (proj. no. 812205) and by Austrian Science Foundation (FWF) (proj. no. P20529).

I. Keidar (Ed.): DISC 2009, LNCS 5805, pp. 360–361, 2009.

Moreover, we introduce two system models with weak synchrony requirements that still allow to implement $\mathcal{L}$. The first model $\mathcal{M}^{\text{sink}}$ is related to the aforementioned weak timely link models: Instead of a timely source, it is based on the idea of a *sink*, i.e., a process with a moving incoming timely link. The other model $\mathcal{M}^{\text{anti}}$ is a query-response based model that is, processes send queries to all their peers from time to time, and wait for responses. $\mathcal{M}^{\text{anti}}$ requires the existence of one specific process whose round-trips with itself are never the fastest. To the best of our knowledge, our models are the first message passing models where set agreement is solvable but consensus is not.

References

1. Fischer, M.J., Lynch, N.A., Paterson, M.S.: Impossibility of distributed consensus with one faulty process. JACM 32, 374–382 (1985)
2. Zieliński, P.: Automatic classification of eventual failure detectors. In: Pelc, A. (ed.) DISC 2007. LNCS, vol. 4731, pp. 465–479. Springer, Heidelberg (2007)
3. Chandra, T.D., Hadzilacos, V., Toueg, S.: The weakest failure detector for solving consensus. JACM 43(4), 685–722 (1996)
4. Gafni, E., Kuznetsov, P.: The weakest failure detector for solving k-set agreement. In: ACM Symposium on Principles of Distributed Computing (2009)
5. Delporte Gallet, C., Fauconnier, H., Guerraoui, R., Tielmann, A.: Brief announcement: The Disagreement Power of an Adversary. In: ACM Symposium on Principles of Distributed Computing (2009)
6. Delporte-Gallet, C., Fauconnier, H., Guerraoui, R., Tielmann, A.: The weakest failure detector for message passing set-agreement. In: Taubenfeld, G. (ed.) DISC 2008. LNCS, vol. 5218, pp. 109–120. Springer, Heidelberg (2008)
7. Aguilera, M.K., Delporte-Gallet, C., Fauconnier, H., Toueg, S.: Partial synchrony based on set timeliness. In: ACM Symposium on Principles of Distributed Computing, PODC 2009 (to appear, 2009)
8. Biely, M., Robinson, P., Schmid, U.: Weak synchrony models and failure detectors for message passing (k-)set agreement. Research Report 182-51/2009, Inst. f. technische Informatik, TU Wien (2009),
http://www.vmars.tuwien.ac.at/php/pserver/docdetail.php?DID=2657 &viewmode=paper
9. Mostéfaoui, A., Raynal, M.: Unreliable failure detectors with limited scope accuracy and an application to consensus. In: Foundations of Software Technology and Theoretical Computer Science, pp. 329–340 (1999)

Brief Announcement
Zab: A Practical Totally Ordered Broadcast Protocol

Flavio P. Junqueira and Benjamin C. Reed

Yahoo! Research

At Yahoo!, we have developed a fault-tolerant coordination service called *ZooKeeper* [4] that allows large scale applications to implement coordination tasks such as leader election, status propagation, and rendezvous. ZooKeeper forgoes locks [2] and instead implements simple wait-free data objects [3] along with a consistency model that guarantees linearizable updates and FIFO order for client operations. We have found the service to be flexible with performance that meets the production demands of the Web-scale applications of Yahoo!.

The ZooKeeper service comprises n ZooKeeper replicas ($n \geq 2f + 1$, f is a threshold on the number of faulty replicas). Among these replicas, there is a distinguished, elected replica: the *leader*. The remaining replicas are *followers*. Clients of the ZooKeeper service can connect and submit requests through any ZooKeeper replica. If this request reads the state of ZooKeeper, the replica serves this request locally. Otherwise, it forwards the request to the leader. The leader receives ZooKeeper requests and transforms them into *idempotent transactions*. The transformation corresponds to generating the state modifications for the given request, as with primary-backup protocols [1]. The leader then sends transactions as messages using atomic broadcast. As a leader can crash, there must be an additional leadership election protocol. To elect a leader, ZooKeeper requires at least $\lceil (n + 1)/2 \rceil$ non-faulty replicas.

The failure model and leader-based operation of ZooKeeper makes Paxos [5] a good option for our atomic broadcast implementation. We found, however, that for Zab we could simplify some aspects of the protocol. One particular issue we found difficult to handle with Paxos is the following. Failures or false suspicions of the leader may cause multiple values to be proposed to a given instance, and violate the order clients expect. For example, suppose the following case:

- There are two proposers due to failures or false suspicions;
- A client c_1 submits operations A and B in this order, and a client c_2 submits C and D in this order. Neither client waits for the previous operation to return to submit the next one.

In such a scenario, replicas might end up executing A followed by D, which is not a behavior that typical applications expect. Of course, we could have a client submitting one operation at time. Such a choice would drastically reduce the performance of a client as we cannot pipeline several requests under such a design. Having multiple outstanding requests, however, is quite important in

I. Keidar (Ed.): DISC 2009, LNCS 5805, pp. 362–363, 2009.

some concrete cases, such as when a new primary is elected and needs to read and reconstruct the metadata of its application as part of the fail-over process.

Highlights of Zab. We assume an unbounded sequence of slots identified by a transaction id (zxid), and replicas agree on a proposal for each slot. A zxid is a pair $\langle e, c \rangle$, where e is an epoch number and c is the counter for epoch e. An execution of Zab therefore proceeds in epochs. An epoch starts when a new leader is elected and ends upon the election of another leader. To broadcast an operation, the leader of an epoch proposes the operation with a given zxid (counter c is incremented upon every proposal), replicas acknowledge the proposal, and the leader commits once a quorum has acknowledged. The following properties also hold for Zab:

Single leader per epoch: We use a leader election primitive to elect the leader of an epoch. An epoch has at most one leader, and we enforce it by guaranteeing that a replica only exercises the role of leader in an epoch once it has the support of a quorum of replicas. Moreover, a replica can support the leadership of at most one replica for a given epoch. Because a quorum has to support a leader for the leader to be active, we can have at most one active epoch at any time;

Highest transaction identifier: Our leader election algorithm elects the replica that has accepted the highest zxid among all replicas that initially support the new leader;

Skipping instances: Because the leader has the highest transaction identifier among all replicas in the quorum that supports it and by the intersection of quorums, the leader must have seen all previously committed proposals. Consequently, any message it has not seen can be safely skipped;

TCP channels: We use TCP channels between the leader and the followers. By using TCP channels, we guarantee that there are no gaps in the sequence of delivered messages and messages are delivered in order for a given channel;

Multiple outstanding requests: Because of TCP channels and pipelined processing in all replicas, we guarantee that a prefix of requests of a leader will be committed even if a leader has multiple operations outstanding.

In our experience, Zab has been simple to implement and maintain in a production environment, and yet it provides the performance necessary for demanding Web-scale applications, such as the Yahoo! Crawler.

References

1. Budhiraja, N., et al.: The primary-backup approach. In: Mullender, S. (ed.) Distributed Systems, vol. 8, pp. 199–216. Addison-Wesley, Reading (1993)
2. Burrows, M.: The chubby lock service for loosely-coupled distributed systems. In: OSDI 2006, pp. 335–350 (2006)
3. Herlihy, M.: Wait-free synchronization. ACM Trans. Program. Lang. Syst. 13(1), 124–149 (1991)
4. Zookeeper project (2008), http://hadoop.apache.org/zookeeper
5. Lamport, L.: The part-time parliament. ACM Trans. Comput. Syst. 16(2), 133–169 (1998)

Compact Multicast Routing

Ittai Abraham[1], Dahlia Malkhi[1], and David Ratajczak[2]

[1] Microsoft Research, Silicon Valley Center
ittaia@microsoft.com, dalia@microsoft.com
[2] Computer Science Department, UC Berkeley
dratajcz@eecs.berkeley.edu

Abstract. In a distributed network, a *compact multicast scheme* is a routing scheme that allows any source to send messages to any set of targets. We study the trade-off between the *space* used to store the routing table on each node and the *stretch* factor of the multicast scheme – the maximum ratio over all sets of nodes between the cost of the multicast route induced by the scheme and the cost of a steiner tree between the same set of target nodes. We obtain results in several variants of the problem: *labeled* – in which the designer can choose polylogarithmic node names, *name-independent* – in which nodes have arbitrarily chosen names, *dynamic* – an online version of the problem in which nodes dynamically join and leave the multicast service and the goal is to minimize both the cost of the multicast tree at each stage and the total cost of control messages needed to update the tree.

1 Introduction

As the Internet becomes increasingly used for wide-scale broadcast of information, the ability to send packets to large fractions of the Internet at near-optimal cost may be the vital step that will allow the Internet to replace traditional broadcast media. For large multicast groups, there are substantial inefficiencies that result from using unicast to send messages to many recipients, both from the standpoint of the sender, and from the standpoint of wasted aggregate bandwidth. However, present-day routers cannot possibly incorporate full global information about all possible multicast sets, nor can they store the complete network graph and calculate the minimum spanning tree (MST) or minimum Steiner tree on the set of destinations. Therefore, it is absolutely crucial that memory is efficiently utilized within the routing fabric.

In this paper, we initiate the study of *compact multicast routing*. Informally, the multicast routing problem it to determine the memory held for routing by each network node, and to devise a routing algorithm that delivers a packet with multiple targets to its destinations. A routing scheme is *compact* if it is memory efficient. Its goodness is measured by its *stretch*, the total network distance it utilizes, compared with the shortest multicast path available. Precise problem definition and performance measures are provided below, and are among the contributions of this paper. Additionally, we provide multicast routing schemes whose memory/stretch tradeoffs are comparable to the unicast case.

I. Keidar (Ed.): DISC 2009, LNCS 5805, pp. 364–378, 2009.
© Springer-Verlag Berlin Heidelberg 2009

There is a very extensive literature on compact unicast routing [10,12]. Suppose we are given a set of n vertices V with distinct labels from $\{1, \ldots, n\}$, and a weighted, undirected graph G on those vertices. A routing scheme is a distributed algorithm that produces a path in G between $u, v \in V$. The *stretch* of the scheme is defined as the maximum, over all choices of $u, v \in V$, of the length of the produced path between u and v divided by the length of the shortest such path. The *memory* of the scheme is the maximum amount of information the algorithm requires to be stored at a node for the node to locally produce the next hop of any routing path. The *header size* of the scheme is the amount of information the scheme requires to be included in each packet to be routed. The challenge is to produce *compact routing schemes* that use $o(n)$ memory and poly-log sized headers, while producing $O(1)$ stretch.

Much is known about these tradeoffs. When nodes are allowed to be renamed, it is known that producing stretch $2k - 1$ requires $\widetilde{O}(n^{1/k})$ memory [12], and this matches the lower bound known for $k = 3, 5$. For trees, routing requires $O(\log^2 n / \log \log n)$ memory and header size, and this is known to be optimal [6]. When nodes are given fixed labels, it is known that a stretch 3 scheme exists requiring $\widetilde{O}(n^{1/2})$ memory [2], and a stretch $O(k)$ scheme exists with memory $\widetilde{O}(kn^{1/k})$ [1].

We propose the existence of *compact multicast routing schemes*, which are distributed algorithms to deliver a packet from any node $u \in V$ to any set of target nodes $A \subseteq V$. The *memory* of the scheme is defined as in the unicast problem, but stretch is now defined as the maximum, over all choices of u and A, of the total weight of edges used by the algorithm to deliver the packet to all nodes of A, divided by the weight of the minimum Steiner tree with $A \cup \{u\}$ as targets. We allow headers to be $\widetilde{O}(|A|)$ bits in size, so that the packets can include a list of all destinations, but are similarly restrained, as in the unicast case, from including full path information.

At first sight, the problem seems daunting. There are $2^n - 1$ possible destination subsets. So a complete information scheme should maintain at each node the next step(s) of the shortest spanning tree, for all possible subsets. So it might appear that an optimal solution that locally determines how to forward a packet to each possible target set requires exponential memory. Fortunately, this is not so, as the entire graph can be stored using $\widetilde{O}(n^2)$ memory (more precisely, using $\widetilde{O}(|E|)$ memory), from which a 2-approximation of the optimal solution can be derived in reasonable computation. Therefore, from here on, we refer to any solution that stores $o(|E|)$ as compact multicast routing. We are also interested in the total space consumption of a scheme, and desire to have $o(n \times |E|)$.

Contributions. Our contributions include the following.

1. A formulation of the *compact multicast routing problem* and its performance measures.
2. A labeled multicast routing scheme whose memory requirement at each node is $\widetilde{O}(n^{1/k})$, uses labels of size $\widetilde{O}(n^{1/k})$, employs headers of size $\widetilde{O}(n^{1/k})$, whose stretch is $4k - 2$.

3. A name-independent multicast routing scheme whose total memory is $\widetilde{O}(kn^{1+1/k} \log \Delta)$ with stretch $O(k)$.
4. A name-independent multicast routing scheme for growth bounded networks whose memory is $\widetilde{O}(kn^{1/2+1/k})$ per node with stretch $O(k)$.
5. A definition of the *dynamic multicast routing problem*, allowing destinations to be added and removed incrementally to the multicast path.
6. A dynamic multicast scheme that adapts to online node joins with polylogarithmic memory per node and $O(\log^2 n)$ competitive ratio.
7. A dynamic multicast scheme that adapts to online node joins and leaves with polylogarithmic memory per node and $O(\log^3 n)$ competitive ratio.

Related work. Our constructions uses building blocks from compact unicast routing schemes. Among them we use: the labelled tree routing of Thorup & Zwick [12] and Fraigniaud & Gavoille [6], the distance oracles of Thorup and Zwick [12,13], the sparse partitions of Awerbuch and Peleg [4]. We details these results in Section A.

The non-distributed dynamic multicast problem is related to the online steiner tree problem [8,5] in which a similar join-only problem (without leave events) is studied in a centralized model. In contrast our problem concerns a distributed setting and requires nodes to leave the services at a competitive cost. Awerbuch, Bartal and Fiat study the distributed file allocation problem [3]. The join-only dynamic multicast problem can be viewed as a variation of their problem limited to read only requests and serving each request by creating a copy at the reader. In their setting, they achieve a $O(\log^3 n)$ competitive ratio, while our join-only scheme achieves an $O(\log^2 n)$ ratio. Jia et al. [9] propose a single source *universal* scheme in which a *single* tree provides a $O(\log^4 / \log\log n)$ competitive steiner tree for *any* target set. Gupta et al. [7] claim to improve the bound to $O(\log^2 n)$. We use a construction based on [7] in our dynamic join-leave problem. Our scheme implicitly builds a universal tree for *every* target in a non-trivial manner while storing only a polylogarithmic number of bits per node. Moreover, our resulting scheme is *oblivious*, the path from the source to a given target is irrespective of the current set of other targets. We utilize this fact to efficiently handle leave events.

2   Preliminaries

Let $G = (V, E, \omega)$ be an undirected graph with $n = |V|$ nodes and non-negative weight function $\omega : E \to \Re^+$. For an edge set $P \subseteq E$ let $G(P)$ be the subgraph of G induced by the nodes in P. Let the cost of an edge set be the sum of weights of it edges, for a set of nodes $S \subset V$ let $d_G(S)$ be their *Steiner tree* cost, the cost of the minimum cost edge set P such that S is connected in $G(P)$ (this must be a tree). When G is clear from the context we omit it from the notation and write $d(S)$. When $|S| = 2$, we write $d(u, v)$ as the cost of the minimal cost path between u and v. When $S = V$ then $d(S)$ is the cost of a minimal cost spanning tree on G. Let Δ be the ratio between $\max d(u, v)$ and $\min d(u, v)$ (also called the *aspect ratio* of G).

Consider a subset $A \subseteq V$ of 'target' nodes, and an origin node s. We denote by $S = \{s\} \cup A$ the set containing both origin and target nodes. Let $m = |S|$. Our focus is on the following problems:

- **Labeled compact multicast routing scheme.** This consists of a labeling of nodes and a routing function. The source gets a list of all targets and needs to create a multicast tree.
- **Name-independent compact multicast routing scheme.** This consists of a routing function. The source gets a list of all targets and needs to create a multicast tree. In this model the names of the nodes are chosen arbitrarily as a permutation of $\{1, \ldots, n\}$.
- **Dynamic compact multicast routing scheme.** This consists of a labeling of nodes and a routing function. The source gets an arbitrary sequence join and leave events in an online manner. For each join event it receives the label of the new target and it adds edges to the multicast to connect the target.

We measure the performance of a compact multicast scheme based on the following criteria:

Label size: The maximum number of bits of the label assigned to each node.
Header size: The maximum number of bits sent in a message header.
Total space: The total number of bits used used to store the routing tables.
Max space: The maximum number of bits used at any node to store its routing table.
Stretch: The worst-case ratio, over all sets of destinations, of the sum of the weights of edges used in multicasting to the destinations to the optimal such tree.

In Section 6 we give additional competitive measures for the dynamic online version of the problem.

3   Labeled Compact Multicast Routing

Our first approach builds a multicast route using a Steiner-tree approximation over an approximation of the graph induced by a distance labeling scheme.

Theorem 1. *Let G be a weighted, undirected graph. There is a compact multicast routing scheme for G whose memory requirement at each node is $\widetilde{O}(n^{1/k})$, uses labels of size $\widetilde{O}(n^{1/k})$, employs headers of size $\widetilde{O}(n^{1/k})$, whose stretch is $4k - 2$.*

The scheme makes use of the distance labels and handshake routing scheme of Lemma 9.

Labeling. The labels of nodes and the routing tables are the ones induced by Lemma 9, i.e., node v is specified by its label TZlabel(v).

Storage. Each node v maintains the routing table information TZtable(v) induced by Lemma 9.

Routing. For any two nodes u, v let DO(u, v) be the distance estimation induced by the labels. Let H be a weighted graph on nodes S such that weights between nodes $u, v \in S$ is DO(u, v). Let T be a minimum cost tree on H whose cost is $d_H(S)$. The source computes T in $O(m^2)$ time, and creates a header that contains a *current* node (initially set to s) and the tree T, where each node u of T is designated using its label TZlabel(u).

A node u that receives such a header does the following: If u is the current node of the header then it finds all the edges in T that u needs to send along. For each such edge (TZlabel(u), TZlabel(v)), it creates a header with current node v and forwards it using the handshake routing mechanism and the header information.

Otherwise, if u is not the current node then using the handshake routing scheme, u forwards to the next hop towards the current destination.

Analysis. The storage and header sizes of the scheme are immediate from Lemma 9. We prove the stretch below.

Lemma 1. *The stretch of the multicast routing scheme above is* $4k - 2$

Proof. Let $\bar{H}$ be a weighted graph on S such that weights between nodes $u, v \in S$ is $d(u, v)$. It is well known that minimum cost tree on $\bar{H}$ is a 2 approximation[1] of the cost of the steiner tree of S on G, $d_{\bar{H}}(S) \leq 2d_G(S)$. Hence we only need to show that $d_H(S) \leq (2k - 1)d_{\bar{H}}(S)$.

Let $\bar{T}$ be a minimum cost tree on $\bar{H}$ whose cost is $d_{\bar{H}}(S)$. Using the fact that $d_H(u, v) \leq (2k - 1)d_{\bar{H}}(u, v)$ for any u, v, we have that the cost of the tree $\bar{T}$ on H is at most $(2k - 1)d_{\bar{H}}(S)$. Since T is a minimum cost tree on H then its cost is also at most $(2k - 1)d_{\bar{H}}(S)$.

4   Name-Independent Compact Multicast Schemes

The construction in the previous section may require labels of size $\Omega(n^{1/k} \log n)$ per node. In this section, we remove the use of labels. That is, we assume that an origin s is given the set of targets $A = \{t_1, \ldots, t_m\}$ using their original network names (for example, taken out of $\{1, \ldots, n\}$). Hence, this solution variant is called *name-independent*. As a consequence of name-independence, we also avoid the need to carry around lengthy labels in packet headers. Headers in our name-independent schemes below are of size proportional to the target list, $\widetilde{O}(m)$.

We remark that a trivial compact name independent multicast scheme can be derived by requiring each node to maintain the distance oracle of Lemma 9. Then employ it to map the set of unlabeled destination into a labeled set, and

---

[1] There exist better approximations (e.g., see [11]), which may shave off a factor of almost two from our scheme. However, our stress in this exposition is on clarity, rather than optimal constants.

use the labeled scheme of Section 3 above. The memory requirement at each node is $\widetilde{O}(n^{1+1/k})$. Although this is indeed a compact solution (compared with $\widetilde{O}(|V|+|E|)$ memory per node), the memory at every node is super-linear, which might be prohibitive for large networks. We can bring down the total memory consumption by storing information selectively at key points in the network, and looking it up when needed.

Theorem 2. *Let G be a weighted, undirected graph with aspect ratio Δ. There is a name-independent compact multicast routing scheme for G whose total memory requirement is $\widetilde{O}(kn^{1+1/k}\log\Delta)$, uses the original network labels (of size $\widetilde{O}(1)$), employs headers of size $\widetilde{O}(m)$, whose stretch is $20k - 10$.*

The rest of this section is devoted to the proof of Theorem 2. We use the sparse partitions building block given in Theorem 10: Let $I = \{0, 1, 2, \ldots, \lceil\log\Delta\rceil\}$. The bundle $\mathcal{B}_k$ consists for $i \in I$ of $\mathcal{TC}_{k,2^i}(G)$, a sparse cover of radius 2^i with parameter k.

For every $T \in \mathcal{TC}_{k,2^i}(G)$, denote by $c(T)$ its center node (the center is the seed node from which the cluster was grown). For any node v and index $i \in I$, denote by $T_i(v)$ the tree in $\mathcal{TC}_{k,2^i}(G)$ that contains $B(v, 2^i)$.

Storage

1. Each $v \in V$ stores TZlabel($c(T_i(v))$) for all $i \in I$, where TZlabel($\cdot$) is given by Lemma 9.
2. Each $v \in V$ stores the routing table information TZtable(v).
3. For each $i \in I$ and $T \in \mathcal{TC}_{k,2^i}(G)$, node $c(T)$ stores the mapping $v \longrightarrow$ TZlabel(v), from node names to labels, for each node $v \in T$.

Lemma 2. *The total storage used by all nodes is $\widetilde{O}(kn^{1+1/k})$ bits.*

Proof. By Lemma 10, for every $i \in I$, every node v belongs to at most $2kn^{1/k}$ cover-sets of $\mathcal{TC}_{k,2^i}(G)$. According to Lemma 9, a label label(v) has size $\widetilde{O}(n^{1/k})$. Therefore, the total memory used for label-maps by all $c(T)$, where $T \in \mathcal{TC}_{k,2^i}(G)$ is at most $n \cdot 2kn^{1/k} \cdot O(n^{1/k}) = O(kn^{1+1/k})$. The total memory over all $|I|$ radii is $O(kn^{1+1/k}\log\Delta)$. In addition, each node v stores $O(\log\Delta)$ labels of size $\widetilde{O}(kn^{1/k})$ each. The total memory consumption of $\widetilde{O}(kn^{1+1/k})$ bits.

Routing. We need to devise a strategy for an origin s to obtain the labels of the multicast targets without going too far. This is achieved as follows.

Observe that $c = c(T_i(s))$ is at distance at most $k2^i$ from s, and c stores label mappings for all $v \in B(s, 2^i)$. Therefore, with cost $O(k2^i)$, s can send S to $c(T_i(s))$, and let $c(T_i(s))$ compute the required multicast route. By repeatedly trying for increasing distances 2^i, s can find the appropriate $c(T_i(s))$ at a competitive cost.

The multicast strategy is as follows. Node s iteratively sends a request for help containing the target list S to nodes $c(T_i(s))$ for $i \in I$, until it reaches a node $c = c(T_i(s))$ such that c stores the labels of every node in S. Then node c computes the header as in Theorem 1.

Lemma 3. *The stretch of the multicast routing scheme is $20k - 10$.*

Proof. Let j be the index such that $2^{j-1} < \max_{a \in A} d(s, a) \leq 2^j$. Then clearly $S \subseteq T_j(s)$ and $2^j < 2d(S)$. Since the radius of a level 2^i cover is $(2k - 1)2^i$ then the cost of going from s to $T_i(s)$ and back is at most $2(2k - 1)2^i$. And the total cost to reach $T_j(s)$ is

$$\sum_{1 \leq i \leq j} 2(2k - 1)2^i \leq 4(2k - 1)2^j \leq 8(2k - 1)d(S)$$

In addition, the cost of the multicast scheme of Theorem 1 is at most $(4k-2)d(S)$. ☐

5   Balanced Name Independent Compact Multicast Routing for Growth Bounded Networks

In this section we provide a balanced scheme for growth bounded networks. Formally, for a node $v \in V$ and $i \in \mathbb{N}$ let $N_v(i)$ denote the i closest nodes to v with ties broken by lexicographical order.

We assume the network is δ-*growth bounded*, for $\delta \geq 2$, such that

$$\mathrm{diam}(N_v(2i)) \geq \delta \cdot \mathrm{diam}(N_v(i)) \ .$$

The Single Source Directory Scheme (SSD)

We begin by building a single source directory (SSD) scheme. For a network of n nodes and a parameter k, the scheme requires each node to store $\widetilde{O}(n^{1/2+1/k})$ bit of storage. The scheme allows a fixed source c to find all the labels of a set A of target nodes with cost that is proportional to the farthest node in A from c. The result is stated in the following lemma:

Lemma 4 (Single-Source Directory (SSD)). *Let $F = (V, E, \omega)$ be a weighted graph, $|V| = n, c \in V$ a given source node. There exists a multi-node lookup scheme as follows.*

- *Given a set of target nodes $A \subseteq V$, the source c can find the labels TZlabel(a) of all nodes $a \in A$, where TZlabel(a) is determined as in Lemma 9.*
- *The scheme requires each node to store $\widetilde{O}(kn^{1/2+1/k})$ bits.*
- *The length of the path used for finding the labels in A is at most $4 \max_{a \in A} d(c, a)$.*

SSD Storage. Let c be the source node. Let $\Gamma = \sqrt{n}$. Enumerate the nodes in $N_c(\Gamma)$ arbitrarily $w_1, w_2, \ldots, w_\Gamma$. For any integer $i < \log \Gamma$ let the nodes $w_{2^i}, w_{2^i+1}, \ldots, w_{2^{i+1}-1}$ store the labels of all the nodes in $(N_c(\Gamma 2^{(i+1)}) \backslash N_c(\Gamma 2^i))$. Note that each w_j stores $\sqrt{n}$ labels. Node c itself stores the labels of $N_c(\Gamma 2^0)$, i.e., of the $\sqrt{n}$ nodes closest to it.

SSD Lookup. It is left to show how to obtain the labels of targets with a competitive cost. This is done as follows.

1. If $A \subseteq N_c(\Gamma)$, then c has all the labels already.
2. Otherwise, set $i = 0$, and set $A_0 = A \setminus (A \cap N_c(\Gamma))$. That is, A_0 contains the remaining targets for which c does not have labels yet. Repeat for $i = 0, 1, 2, \ldots$, until A_i is empty:
   - Node c queries from $w_{2^i}, w_{2^i+1}, \ldots, w_{2^{i+1}-1}$ the labels of any target nodes in A_i. Note that in response, c should obtain the labels of all nodes in $A_i \cap N_c(\Gamma 2^{i+1})$.
   - Then set $A_{i+1} = A_i \setminus N_c(\Gamma 2^{i+1})$, set $i = i + 1$, and repeat.

SSD Analysis

Proof (Proof of Lemma 4). let $d = \operatorname{diam}(N_c(\Gamma))$. An invariant maintained in the algorithm is as follows. At step i, there is a target $a \in (A \setminus N_c(\Gamma 2^i))$. Hence, if step i is reached, there is a target $a \in A_i$ whose distance from c is at least $\operatorname{diam}(N_c(\Gamma 2^i))$. By the growth bound,

$$\operatorname{diam}(N_c(\Gamma 2^i)) \geq 2^i d .$$

Therefore, $\max_{a \in A} d(c, a) \geq 2^i d$. The total cost of steps $j = 1, \ldots, i$ is a geometric series, whose sum is bounded by $\sum_{j=0..i} 2 \times 2^j \leq 4 \times 2^i$. This yields that the total distance of lookups is at most $4 \max_{a \in A} d(c, a)$.

The Full Scheme

As in the un-balanced name-independent multicast scheme of Section 4, we make use of sparse partitions as given in Theorem 10.

Storage

1. Each $v \in V$ stores TZlabel$(c(T_i(v)))$ for all $i \in I$.
2. Each $v \in V$ stores the routing table information TZtable(v).
3. For each $i \in I$ and $T \in \mathcal{TC}_{k,2^i}(G)$, employ the scheme of Lemma 4 with T the graph, and $c(T)$ the source node. (Recall that this allows $c(T)$ to look up the labels TZlabel(a) of any set of targets A, such that $a \in A$, with cost at most $4\operatorname{diam}(T)$.

Lemma 5. *The total storage used by any node is $\widetilde{O}(kn^{1/2+1/k})$.*

Routing. Given a set of targets A, s computes a Steiner graph spanning A in two steps: First, it obtains the labels of all the nodes in A; then it computes an approximate Steiner graph as in the labeled scheme of Section 3.

We need to devise a strategy for an origin s to obtain the labels of the multicast targets without going too far. This is achieved as follows.

Observe that $c = c(T_i(s))$ is at distance at most $(2k - 1)2^i$ from s. By Lemma 4, from origin c a lookup of label mappings for all $v \in B(s, 2^i)$ has a cost bounded by $4 \times (2k - 1)2^i$. Therefore, with cost $O(k2^i)$, s can send A to $c(T_i(s))$, and let $c(T_i(s))$ return the required labels. By repeatedly trying for increasing distances 2^i, s can find the appropriate $c(T_i(s))$ at a competitive cost.

The multicast strategy is as follows. Node s iteratively sends a request for help containing the target list A to nodes $c(T_i(s))$ for $i \in I$, until it reaches a node $c = c(T_i(s))$ such that c can find the labels of every node in A. Then node c computes the header as in Theorem 1.

Lemma 6. *The stretch of the multicast routing scheme is $36k - 18$.*

Proof. Let j be the index such that $2^{j-1} < \max_{a \in A} d(s, a) \leq 2^j$. Then clearly $S \subseteq T_j(s)$ and $2^j < 2d(S)$. For every $i \leq j$, since the radius of a level 2^i cover is $(2k - 1)2^i$ then the cost of going from s to $c(T_i(s))$ and back is at most $2(2k - 1)2^i$. The cost of searching for label mappings in $T_i(s)$ is bounded according to Lemma 4 by $2(2k-1)2^i$. Hence, the total cost to collect all required label mappings is:

$$\sum_{1 \leq i \leq j} 4(2k - 1)2^i \leq 8(2k - 1)2^j \leq 16(2k - 1)d(S)$$

Finally, the cost of the Steiner tree computed using these labels is bounded according to Lemma 1 by an additional $(4k - 2)d(S)$.

6 Dynamic Compact Multicast Routing Schemes

A weakness of all the solutions above is that the multicast dissemination path must be re-computed each time a target wants to join or eave the multicast service. In a highly dynamic setting in which the multicast set is constantly changing rebuilding the multicast tree from scratch after each change may be unacceptable.

Consider a source node s and a sequence of node join and node leave events. In such a dynamic setting there are two measures one would like to minimize. The first is the *communication-cost*, namely, the total cost of the edges used during the algorithm while building the multicast trees of the various stages. The second is the *multicast-cost*, which for each stage is the cost of the current multicast tree.

We now explain why communication-cost alone does not suffice to bound the cost of a multicast scheme. In order to understand this, consider a simple-path graph $s = v_1 - v_2 - \dots - v_n$, and suppose that the sequence of joins/leaves is the following: $\text{join}(v_n)$, $\text{join}(v_{n-1})$, ..., $\text{join}(v_2)$, $\text{join}(v_1)$, $\text{leave}(v_n)$, $\text{leave}(v_{n-1})$, ..., $\text{leave}(v_2)$. If we consider only the total communication cost, we need not ever remove edges from the multicast path, which is the whole graph in this case. In the end, we may be left with a very inefficient multicast graph containing v_1 and v_2, but the communication cost measure does not capture this. Therefore, we must also consider the efficiency of the current multicast path at every step, which is precisely captured by multicast-cost.

In order to formally bound theses measures, we make use of *online analysis*. Specifically we compare both costs to an optimal off-line algorithm. The off-line algorithm knows the sequence of joins/leaves in advance, and has no extraneous communication cost in setting up the multicast overlay. The communication-cost for the online algorithm is therefore the total cost of edges used for the optimal Steiner trees at different steps.

An on-line algorithm is (α, β) competitive for the dynamic multicast problem if for any source and for any sequence of join/leave events the total cost of the set of edges used is at most α times that of the total cost of the set of edges used by the optimal algorithm and at *each* stage the cost of the current multicast tree is at most β times that of the cost of the current optimal algorithm.

Let A be the set of all nodes that joined during a sequence. Then any algorithm must pay at least $d(A \cup \{s\})$ for communication-cost, and if A' is the current set of nodes of a given stage then any algorithm must pay $d(A' \cup \{s\})$ multicast-cost for this stage.

In this extended abstract we handle the labeled variant of this problem in which nodes are labeled and the sequence of join/leave events are given in an online manner to the source. In the full paper we will show how to extend these ideas for a name-independent variant of the problem.

We begin by presenting our first scheme that only allows join events to the multicast service over time (but no leave events). We prove it is $(O(\log^2 n), O(\log^2 n))$ competitive. This may be appropriate in settings where once a node joins a multicast service it will not leave until the multicast is complete. Our second scheme handles both join and leave events at a cost of a being $(O(\log^3), O(\log^3))$ competitive.

6.1   Dynamic Compact Multicast Routing Schemes for Join-Only Events

Assume the sequence of node joins is $A = \{a_1, a_2, \ldots\}$. The scheme employs a bundle $\mathcal{B}_k = \{\mathcal{TC}_{k,2^i}(G) \mid i \in I\}$ of Sparse Covers of Lemma 10 with $k = \log n$. For a node v, denote by $\mathcal{B}(v)$ the set of all covers T in the bundle $\mathcal{B}_k$ such that $v \in T$.

Labelling. The label SPlabel(v) stores the label $\lambda(T, c(T))$ given by Lemma 9 for each $T \in \mathcal{B}(v)$. Note that the label size is $O(\log^3 n \log \Delta / \log \log n)$.

Storage. Each node v stores tree routing information $\mu(T, v)$ for all the trees in its own label SPlabel(v) (recall that SPlabel(v) consists of $\lambda(T, c(T))$ for every tree-cover $T \in \mathcal{B}$ containing v). The total storage is $O(\log^3 n \log \Delta / \log \log n)$.

Multicast-graph Construction. The construction of the multicast graph is done in steps. At step j, node a_j is brought into the multicast graph. This entails informing all relevant nodes in the graph who should become their new neighbors.

For convenience, we denote by $A_j = \{s, a_1, \ldots, a_j\}$. The key is to maintain for each $i \in I$ a set $U_i \subset A_j$ such that if $u, v \in U_i$ then $d(u, v) \geq 2^i$ and for any $v \in A_j$ there exists $u \in U_i$ such that $T_i(u) \in \mathcal{B}(v)$.

Initially $U_i = \{s\}$ for all $i \in I$. Given a new node a with label SPlabel(a), let i^* be the maximal index i such that $\mathcal{B}(a) \cap \{T_i(u) \mid u \in U_i\} = \emptyset$ then we connect a to the existing multicast tree by a route from a to $c(T_{i^*+1}(u))$ and from $c(T_{i^*+1}(u))$ to u where $u \in U_{i^*+1}$ and $T_{i^*+1}(u) \in \mathcal{B}(a)$. We update the sets by adding a to U_i for all $i \in \{0, 1, 2, \ldots, i^*\}$. Note that it suffices for s to store the tuple $(u, c(T_{i^*+1}(u)), \text{TZlabel}(T_{i^*+1}(u), a))$ for the multicast route to be able to reach a.

Analysis. It is immediate to see that for each $i \in I$ the set U_i maintains the property that for any $v \in A_j$ there exists $u \in U_i$ such that $T_i(u) \in \mathcal{B}(v)$. To see that if $u, v \in U_i$ then $d(u, v) \geq 2^i$ note that if $d(a, u) < 2^i$ for some $u \in U_i$ then it must be that $a \in T_i(u)$ so $T_i(u) \in \mathcal{B}(a)$ and thus a will not be added to U_i.

Since the model allows only join events the communication cost and the multicast cost are both bounded by the cost of the Steiner tree on the set of current nodes.

Lemma 7. *The dynamic multicast algorithm for joins is $O(\min\{\log n, \log \Delta\} \log n)$ competitive both in communication cost and in multicast cost.*

Proof. In the case of joins only, the communication cost and multicast cost of the off-line algorithm are the same, namely, the cost of optimal Steiner tree of all targets. For each $i \in I$ for which $|U_i| > 1$ any algorithm must pay at least $|U_i|2^{i-1}$ since the balls of radius 2^{i-1} around members of U_i are disjoint. On the other hand our algorithm pays at most $|U_i|2^i \cdot 2\log n \cdot 2$ for connecting nodes in U_i.

Let d be the diameter of A then for each $i \leq \log d \in I$ we pay at most $4\log n$ times the optimal. If $\log \Delta$ is large we note that it is actually enough to look at the $4\log n$ levels $\{\log d, \log d - 1, \ldots, \log d - 4\log n\}$, as the cost of all the edges of the lower levels will add only a constant factor to the overall cost.

6.2 Fully Dynamic Compact Multicast Routing Scheme

Consider a finite sequence of node join and node leave events. For each stage j let A_j be the current set of multicast targets. Note that at each stage either one node joins or one node leaves, so $|A_{j+1} \ominus A_j| = 1$ (where $X \ominus Y$ is the set of all nodes x such that either $x \in X$ or $x \in Y$ but not both). Let A be the set of all nodes that joined the multicast service.

Recall the following definition from Gupta et al. [7].

Definition 1 (α-padded nodes). *Given a hierarchical decomposition $P = (P_i)_{i=0}^h$, a node $v \in V$ is α-padded in P if for all $i \in [0, h]$, the ball $B(v, \alpha 2^i)$ is contained in some cluster of P_i.*

We use the Theorem 2.2 of Gupta et al. [7] to get a set of $O(\log n)$ hierarchical decompositions $\mathcal{P}$ such that for node u there exists $P \in \mathcal{P}$ such that u is $\Omega(1/\log n)$-padded in P. We denote the decomposition by $P^{(u)}$. If there exists several such $P \in \mathcal{P}$ then define $P^{(u)}$ as the lexicographically first.

Recall that a hierarchical decomposition P induces a dominating tree $T(P)$ simply by associating each cluster with the center node of the cluster and the edge between a cluster and its parent cluster is simply the shortest path between the two cluster's centers. Routing on such a dominating tree can be done using Lemma 8 for deciding which "tree-edge" to take. Each tree edge between a node $u \in T$ that corresponds to a cluster in P_i and a node $v \in T$ that corresponds to a cluster in P_{i+1} induces a path in the graph that is part of a shortest path tree emanating from v and spanning all the nodes corresponding to the cluster in P_{i+1}. Hence we use Lemma 8 again for routing on the shortest path in G from u to v.

A major property of the construction of the multicast graph is that it is *oblivious*. The path from the source to a given target is irrespective of the current set of other targets.

The path of a target a is simply the path induced on G by the path on the tree $T(P^{(a)})$ from a to the source. Note that it is possible to route along this path using Lemma 8 while routing on a shortest path from each node in the sequence to its neighbor in the sequence.

Due to obliviousness, when other nodes join and leave the multicast service this does not effect the path taken to a. When a leaves the source simply stops sending along the edges that are not required any more. This can be implemented by maintaining a simple reference counter on the edges.

Analysis. For any hierarchical decomposition P and scale i, let $X_{P,i}$ be a $2^{i-6}/\log n$-net of the nodes $(A \cup \{s\}) \cap P_i$ (an r-net is a maximal set of nodes whose distance from each other is at least r). For any P and i, even the optimal offline solution must pay $|X_{P_i}|2^{i-7}/\log n$. We will now show that the total cost of edges between clusters of P_{i+1} to clusters of P_{i+2} is at most $|X_{P,i}|2^{i+3}$. Summing over all $\log \Delta$ scales and all $O(\log n)$ trees (each tree is induced by a hierarchical decomposition $P \in \mathcal{P}$) gives a competitive ratio of $O(\log^2 n \min\{\log \Delta, \log n\})$. To see that the total cost of edges between the centers of clusters of P_{i+1} to centers of clusters of P_{i+2} is at most $|X_{P,i}|2^{i+3}$, consider any $a \in A$ that uses P to reach the souse (hence $P^{(a)} = P$). By definition there exists $x \in X_{P,i}$ such that $d(x,a) \leq 2^{i-6}/\log n$. Let $C(x)$ be the cluster in P_{i+1} that contains x. Since x is fully padded then $a \in C(x)$. Hence the path from a to s and the path from x to s both meet at the center of $C(x)$ so the total cost of the path from the center of $C(x)$ to its parent cluster center in P_{i+2} for all $a \in C(x)$ is at most 2^{i+3}.

7   Conclusions

We have initiated the study of distributed compact multicast routing schemes. No lower bounds are known (other than the known ones for unicast routing). It is an interesting open question to find the optimal trade-offs between storage and space for the various problems considered in this paper.

References

1. Abraham, I., Gavoille, C., Malkhi, D.: Routing with Improved Communication-Space Trade-off. In: Guerraoui, R. (ed.) DISC 2004. LNCS, vol. 3274, pp. 305–319. Springer, Heidelberg (2004)
2. Abraham, I., Gavoille, C., Malkhi, D., Nisan, N., Thorup, M.: Compact name-independent routing with minimum stretch. In: SPAA 2004: Proceedings of the sixteenth annual ACM symposium on Parallelism in algorithms and architectures, pp. 20–24. ACM Press, New York (2004)
3. Awerbuch, B., Bartal, Y., Fiat, A.: Distributed paging for general networks. In: SODA 1996: Proceedings of the seventh annual ACM-SIAM symposium on Discrete algorithms, Philadelphia, PA, USA, pp. 574–583. Society for Industrial and Applied Mathematics (1996)
4. Awerbuch, B., Peleg, D.: Sparse partitions. In: 31th Annual IEEE Symposium on Foundations of Computer Science (FOCS), pp. 503–513. IEEE Computer Society Press, Los Alamitos (1990)
5. Berman, P., Coulston, C.: On-line algorithms for steiner tree problems (extended abstract). In: STOC 1997: Proceedings of the twenty-ninth annual ACM symposium on Theory of computing, pp. 344–353. ACM Press, New York (1997)
6. Fraigniaud, P., Gavoille, C.: Routing in trees. In: Orejas, F., Spirakis, P.G., van Leeuwen, J. (eds.) ICALP 2001. LNCS, vol. 2076, pp. 757–772. Springer, Heidelberg (2001)
7. Gupta, A., Hajiaghayi, M.T., Räcke, H.: Oblivious network design. In: SODA 2006: Proceedings of the 17th annual ACM-SIAM symposium on Discrete algorithm, pp. 970–979. ACM Press, New York (2006)
8. Imase, M., Waxman, B.M.: Dynamic steiner tree problem. SIAM J. Disc. Math. 4, 369–384 (1991)
9. Jia, L., Lin, G., Noubir, G., Rajaraman, R., Sundaram, R.: Universal approximations for tsp, steiner tree, and set cover. In: STOC 2005: Proceedings of the 37th annual ACM symposium on Theory of computing, pp. 386–395. ACM Press, New York (2005)
10. Peleg, D.: Distributed Computing: A Locality-Sensitive Approach. SIAM Monographs on Discrete Mathematics and Applications (2000)
11. Robins, G., Zelikovsky, A.: Improved steiner tree approximation in graphs. In: SODA 2000: Proceedings of the 11th annual ACM-SIAM symposium on Discrete algorithms, Philadelphia, PA, USA, pp. 770–779. Society for Industrial and Applied Mathematics (2000)
12. Thorup, M., Zwick, U.: Compact routing schemes. In: 13th Annual ACM Symposium on Parallel Algorithms and Architectures (SPAA), Hersonissos, Crete, Greece, pp. 1–10. ACM Press, New York (2001)
13. Thorup, M., Zwick, U.: Compact routing schemes. In: 13th Annual ACM Symposium on Parallel Algorithms and Architectures (SPAA), pp. 1–10. ACM Press, New York (2001)

A   Building Blocks

Our schemes make use of several graph partitioning and routing techniques. For clarity, we group them in this section.

Labelled tree routing of Thorup & Zwick [12] and Fraigniaud & Gavoille [6]:

Lemma 8. [6,12] *For every weighted tree T with n nodes there exists a labeled routing scheme that, given any destination label, routes optimally on T from any source to the destination. The storage per node in T, the label size, and the header size are $O(\log^2 n/\log\log n)$ bits. Given the information of a node and the label of the destination, routing decisions take constant time.*

For a tree T containing a node v, we let $\mu(T,v)$ denote the routing information of node v and $\lambda(T,v)$ denote the destination label of v in T as required from Lemma 8.

Distance oracles of Thorup and Zwick [12,13]:
We use their distance labels, handshake routing scheme and distance oracles. The following are simple variations of their results.

Lemma 9 ([12](3.4),(3,1), [13](4.1)). *Let G be a weighted graph with aspect ratio Δ. Let $1 \le k \le \log n$ be an integer.*

1. *It is possible to assign to each point $v \in V$ an $O(n^{1/k}\log^{1-1/k} n\log(n\Delta))$-bit label, denoted TZlabel(v), such that given TZlabel(u) and TZlabel(v), for any two points $u,v \in V$, it is possible to compute, in $O(k)$ time, an approximation to the distance $d(u,v)$ with stretch of at most $2k-1$.*
2. *It is possible to assign each node a $\widetilde{O}(kn^{1/k})$ bit routing table, denoted TZtable(v), such that given TZlabel(v) any source u can extract $o(\log^2)$ bits and use them as a header to route from the source to u with cost that equals the cost of the distance estimation obtained by TZlabel(u) and TZlabel(v) via item (1).*
3. *It is possible to create a data structure with size $O(kn^{1/k}\log(n\Delta))$ bits, such that distance queries can be answered with the same cost of the distance estimation of item (1). Given TZlabel(u) and TZlabel(v) it is possible to extract $o(\log^2 n)$ bits such that routing from source to target will also have the same cost.*

Sparse partitions of Awerbuch and Peleg [4]:

Lemma 10. [4] *For every weighted graph $G = (V,E,\omega)$, $|V| = n$ and integers $k,\rho \ge 1$, there exists a polynomial algorithm that constructs a collection of rooted trees $\mathcal{TC}_{k,\rho}(G)$ such that:*

1. *(Cover) For all $v \in V$, there exists $T \in \mathcal{TC}_{k,\rho}(G)$ such that $B(v,\rho) \subseteq T$.*
2. *(Sparse) For all $v \in V$, $|\{T \in \mathcal{TC}_{k,\rho}(G) \mid v \in T\}| \le 2kn^{1/k}$.*
3. *(Small radius) For all $T \in \mathcal{TC}_{k,\rho}(G)$, there is a root node $r \in T$ such that $\mathrm{rad}(T) \le (2k-1)\rho$, where $\mathrm{rad}(T) = \max_u\{d_T(r,u)\}$.*

Denote by $I = \{0, 1, \ldots, \lceil \log \Delta(G) \rceil\}$. Usually, we make use of a *bundle* $\mathcal{B}_k = \{\mathcal{TC}_{k,2^i}(G) \mid i \in I\}$ of covers and in some cases we make use of a bundle $\mathcal{B}_k^\sigma = \{\mathcal{TC}_{k,\sigma^i}(G) \mid i \in \{0, 1, \ldots, \log_\sigma \Delta(G)\}\}$.

For every $T \in \mathcal{TC}_{k,2^i}(G)$, denote by $c(T)$ its center node (the center is the seed node from which the cluster was grown). For any node v and index $i \in I$, denote by $T_i(v)$ the tree in $\mathcal{TC}_{k,2^i}(G)$ that contains $B(v, 2^i)$.

Compact Routing in Power-Law Graphs

Wei Chen[1], Christian Sommer[2], Shang-Hua Teng[3], and Yajun Wang[1]

[1] Microsoft Research Asia, Beijing, China
[2] The University of Tokyo and National Institute of Informatics, Tokyo, Japan
[3] Department of Computer Science, University of Southern California, CA, USA

Abstract. We adapt the compact routing scheme by Thorup and Zwick to optimize it for power-law graphs. We analyze our adapted routing scheme based on the theory of unweighted random power-law graphs with fixed expected degree sequence by Aiello, Chung, and Lu. Our result is the first theoretical bound coupled to the parameter of the power-law graph model for a compact routing scheme. In particular, we prove that, for stretch 3, instead of routing tables with $\tilde{O}(n^{1/2})$ bits as in the general scheme by Thorup and Zwick, expected sizes of $O(n^\gamma \log n)$ bits are sufficient, and that all the routing tables can be constructed at once in expected time $O(n^{1+\gamma} \log n)$, with $\gamma = \frac{\tau-2}{2\tau-3} + \varepsilon$, where $\tau \in (2,3)$ is the power-law exponent and $\varepsilon > 0$. Both bounds also hold with probability at least $1 - 1/n$ (independent of ε). The routing scheme is a labeled scheme, requiring a stretch-5 handshaking step and using addresses and message headers with $O(\log n \log \log n)$ bits, with probability at least $1 - o(1)$. We further demonstrate the effectiveness of our scheme by simulations on real-world graphs as well as synthetic power-law graphs. With the same techniques as for the compact routing scheme, we also adapt the approximate distance oracle by Thorup and Zwick for stretch 3 and obtain a new upper bound of expected $\tilde{O}(n^{1+\gamma})$ for space and preprocessing.

1 Introduction

Message routing is a fundamental service in communication networks. When routing a message from a source to a destination in the network, to decide where to forward the message to, a node may only use its local information, which includes its local routing table, the destination address, and a message header. A routing scheme is expected to route messages between all source-destination pairs along shortest or approximate shortest paths. A key measure of the quality of a routing scheme is its worst-case multiplicative *stretch*, which is defined as the maximum ratio of the length of the message route between a pair of nodes s and t by the scheme and the actual shortest path length between s and t, among all s-t pairs in the network.

Routing schemes address the tradeoff between stretch and routing table size. A trivial stretch-1 routing scheme is one in which every node stores for every destination in the network where to forward the message to. However, for a network with n nodes, this approach requires unscalable $\Omega(n \log n)$-bit routing tables for every node [20]. A *compact* routing scheme is only allowed to have routing tables with sizes sublinear in n and message header sizes polylogarithmic in n. There are two classes of compact routing schemes: *Labeled* schemes are allowed to add labels to node addresses to encode useful

I. Keidar (Ed.): DISC 2009, LNCS 5805, pp. 379–391, 2009.

information for routing purposes, where each label has length at most polylogarithmic in n. *Name-independent* schemes do not allow the renaming of node addresses, instead they must function with all possible addresses.

Both labeled and name-independent compact routing schemes have been studied extensively. Universal schemes work for all network topologies [3,4,5,14,28,29]. It has been shown that with $\tilde{O}(n^{1/k})$-bit routing tables (as usual, we abbreviate $O(f(n) \cdot \log^t n)$ for some constant t by $\tilde{O}(f(n)))$ one can achieve a stretch of $O(k)$, and that this tradeoff is essentially tight due to a girth conjecture by Erdős.

Due to these impeding lower bounds for general graphs, specialized schemes were designed for various families of network topologies, including trees [18,23,29], planar graphs [19,25], fixed-minor-free graphs [2], or graphs with low doubling dimension [1,21,22]. These topology-specific schemes achieve significant improvements on the stretch-space tradeoff over universal routing schemes.

Power-law graphs [27] constitute an important family of networks appearing in various real-world scenarios such as the Internet, the World Wide Web, collaboration networks, and social networks [12,17]. In a power-law graph, the number of nodes with degree x is proportional to $x^{-\tau}$, for some constant τ. The power-law exponent τ for many real-world networks is in the range between 2 and 3. Power-law graphs do not seem to belong to any of the well-studied network families such as trees, planar graphs or low doubling dimension graphs mentioned above.

Despite their high relevance in practice, the family of power-law graphs has not received much attention from the compact routing community. There are experimental studies of compact routing in power-law graphs and Internet-like graphs. Krioukov et al. [24] evaluate the universal routing scheme of Thorup and Zwick (*TZ*) [29] on random power-law graphs [6] and provide experimental evidence of much better performance (both in terms of stretch and table sizes) than the theoretical worst-case bound. However, they do not provide a theoretical bound of the TZ scheme on power-law graphs for neither stretch nor table size. Enahescu et al. [15] propose a landmark selection scheme that adapts the TZ scheme and they show empirically that their adaptation achieves good stretch and table sizes for power-law graphs and Internet Autonomous System (AS) graphs. Unfortunately, their theoretical analysis is for Erdős-Rényi random graphs [16] instead of power-law graphs. Brady and Cowen [8] give a compact routing scheme tailored for power-law graphs with additive stretch d and header and table sizes $O(e \log^2 n)$, where both d and e depend on the graph, and they show experimentally that these values are reasonably small for certain random power-law graphs [6]. However, there is no rigorous analysis connecting d and e to the parameter τ of power-law graphs.

Our contribution. In this paper, we bridge the gap in the study of compact routing schemes for power-law graphs. We provide the first theoretical analysis that directly links the power-law exponent τ of a random power-law graph to the bound on the routing table sizes.

More specifically, we adapt the labeled universal compact routing scheme of Thorup and Zwick [29] to optimize it for unweighted, undirected power-law graphs. Our adaptations include (a) selecting nodes with the largest degrees as the landmarks instead of random sampling, and (b) directly encoding shortest paths in node labels and message headers instead of relying on a tree routing scheme.

Our complexity analysis of the routing scheme is based on the random power-law graph model with expected degree sequence proposed by Aiello, Chung and Lu [6,10,11] with some minor simplifications. We assume the power-law exponent τ to lie in the range of $(2, 3)$, which is the so called "finite mean infinite variance" region of the power-law degree distribution, where most practical power-law networks are assumed to be in.

We prove that for a stretch upper bound of 3, instead of tables of size $\tilde{O}(n^{1/2})$ shown to be optimal up to a polylogarithmic factor for general graphs [29], expected sizes of $O(n^\gamma \log n)$ bits are sufficient, and that the routing tables can be constructed at once in expected time $O(n^{1+\gamma} \log n)$, with $\gamma = \frac{\tau-2}{2\tau-3} + \varepsilon$ and $\varepsilon > 0$ (which implies $\varepsilon < \gamma < 1/3 + \varepsilon$). Both bounds also hold with probability at least $1 - 1/n$ (independent of ε). This means that for all $\tau \in (2, 3)$, we have an upper bound of $\tilde{O}(n^{1/3+\varepsilon})$ on the routing table sizes, which is better than the optimal bound of $\tilde{O}(n^{1/2})$ for general graphs. For values of τ close to 2, for example for $\tau = 2.1$, which is the exponent that fits the power-law distribution well to the degree distribution of the actual Internet inter-domain graph [17,24], our bound is $O(n^{1/12+\varepsilon})$. The routing scheme requires a stretch-5 handshaking (similar to [29, Sec. 4]), and uses addresses and message headers of size $O(\log n \log \log n)$, with probability at least $1 - o(1)$. The efficient encoding using $O(\log n \log \log n)$ bits in addresses and headers relies on specific distance properties of power-law graphs. Our scheme is a *fixed-port* scheme, meaning that it works for any permutation of port number assignments on any node.

We provide simulation results for both random power-law graphs and actual router-level networks, which demonstrate the effectiveness of our adapted compact routing scheme. With the same techniques as for the compact routing scheme, we also adapt the approximate distance oracle by Thorup and Zwick for stretch 3 and obtain a new upper bound of $\tilde{O}(n^{1+\gamma})$ for space and preprocessing of random power-law graphs. Complete proofs of the results in this paper as well as the detailed distance oracle results can be found in a technical report [9].

2 Preliminaries

We adapt the random graph model for fixed expected degree sequence as defined by Aiello, Chung, and Lu [6,10,11] using the definition from [10, Section 2]. We refer to the original random graph distribution using the expression Fixed Degree Random Graph (**FDRG**).

Definition 1. *For a constant $\tau \in (2, 3)$, the random power-law graph distribution* **RPLG**(n, τ) *is defined as follows. Let the sequence of generating parameters $w = \{w_1, w_2, \ldots, w_n\}$ obey a power law, that is $w_k = \left(\frac{n}{k}\right)^{1/(\tau-1)}$ for $k \in \{1, 2, \ldots n\}$. The edge between v_i and v_j is inserted into the random graph with probability* $\min\{w_i w_j \rho, 1\}$*, where $\rho = \frac{1}{\sum_k w_k}$.*

Note that we adapt the original model by deterministically inserting edges if $w_i w_j > \sum_k w_k$, since in the **FDRG** model it is required that $\forall i, j : w_i w_j < \sum_k w_k$, which, without modification, rules out the values for τ we consider in this paper. In the **FDRG** model, the value w_i corresponds to the expected degree of vertex v_i, and they refer to w as the *expected degree sequence*. In our adaptation, the graph is sampled due to the generating parameter values w_i. Let D_i be the random variable denoting the degree of node v_i. In our model, the expected degree $E[D_i]$ of node v_i is smaller than or equal to the generating parameter w_i.

We require that $n = |V(G)|$ is sufficiently large, specifically, that

$$n^{\frac{\varepsilon(2\tau-3)}{\tau-1}} \geq \frac{2(\tau-1)}{\tau-2} \ln n. \tag{1}$$

Our results do not have any other implicit dependencies on ε.

The *core* of a graph consists of nodes having large degrees. Let $\gamma = \frac{\tau-2}{2\tau-3} + \varepsilon$ for some $\varepsilon > 0$ and $\gamma' = \frac{1-\gamma}{\tau-1}$.

Definition 2. *For a power-law degree sequence w and a graph G with n nodes, the core with degree threshold $n^{\gamma'}$, $\gamma' \in (0,1)$, is defined as follows.*

$$\text{core}_{\gamma'}(w) := \{v_i : w_i > n^{\gamma'}\},$$
$$\text{core}_{\gamma'}(G) := \{v_i : \deg_G(v_i) > n^{\gamma'}/4\},$$

where $\deg_G(v_i)$ is the degree of v_i in G.

For each vertex u of a graph G, we define its ball relative to the core as $B_G(u) := \{v \in V(G) : d(u,v) < \min_{v' \in \text{core}_{\gamma'}(G)} d(u,v')\}$.

3   The Adapted Compact Routing Scheme

Let the unweighted graph $G = (V, E)$ model the network. Each node v in the network has a unique $\lceil \log_2 n \rceil$-bit static name. Whenever we write v in a routing table, a message header, or a node address, we mean its $\lceil \log_2 n \rceil$-bit static name representation. Each node v has $\deg(v)$ ports connecting it with its neighbors. These ports are numbered by $0, 1, \ldots, \deg(v) - 1$, and thus each port number of v requires $\lceil \log_2 \deg(v) \rceil$ bits. For every packet, the routing scheme needs to decide which port the packet is to be forwarded to. Our scheme is a fixed-port scheme, that is, it works with arbitrary permutations of port number assignments.

The routing algorithm is inspired by and based on [14,29]. We also use a set of landmarks $A \subseteq V$, but different from [14,29], we use $\text{core}_{\gamma'}(G)$ as landmarks instead of nodes sampled at random. For each node u in G, let $\ell(u)$ denote u's closest landmark, that is, $\ell(u) := \arg \min_{v \in \text{core}_{\gamma'}(G)} d(u,v)$. The local targets of node u are defined as the elements of its *ball* $B_G(u)$. Similar to the second scheme in [29], each node u stores the ports to route messages along the shortest paths to all landmarks and to its local targets. If the target v is neither a landmark nor a local target of u, the message is routed to v's closest landmark $\ell(v)$ and from there to the target v.

The scheme is a labeled scheme. For a node u to know $\ell(v)$ of any target v, the address of node v contains an encoding of $\ell(v)$. Moreover, for a node w on the shortest path from $\ell(v)$ to v ($w \neq \ell(v)$ and $w \neq v$), v may not be in $B_G(w)$ and thus w may not know the port to route messages to v. To resolve this issue, we further extend the address of v by *encoding* the shortest path from the landmark $\ell(v)$ to v.

Let $(s = u_0, u_1, \ldots, u_m = t)$ denote the sequence of nodes on a shortest path from s to t. Let $SP(s,t)$ be the encoding of this shortest path as an array with m entries, wherein $SP(s,t)[i]$ denotes the port to route from u_i to u_{i+1} for all $i = 0, 1, \ldots, m-1$. Thus $SP(s,t)$ can be encoded with $\sum_{i=0}^{m-1} \log_2 \lceil \deg(u_i) \rceil$ bits. We now provide the precise definitions of addresses, message headers, and local routing tables.

Definition 3

– *The address of node u is* $\mathtt{addr}(u) := (u, \ell(u), SP(\ell(u), u))$.
– *The header of a message from node s to node t is in one of the following formats:*
  1. $\mathtt{header} = (route, s, t)$, *where* $route = \mathtt{local}$,
  2. $\mathtt{header} = (route, s, addr)$, *where* $route = \mathtt{toLandmark}$ *and* $addr = \mathtt{addr}(t)$,
  3. $\mathtt{header} = (route, s, t, pos, SP)$, *where* $route \in \{\mathtt{fromLandmark}, \mathtt{direct}\}$, *pos is a non-negative integer that may be modified along the route, and* $SP = SP(s,t)$ *if route =* $\mathtt{direct}$ *or* $SP = SP(\ell(t), t)$ *if route =* $\mathtt{fromLandmark}$,
  4. $\mathtt{header} = (route, s, t, SP)$, *where* $route = \mathtt{handshake}$ *and* SP *is a reversed shortest path from t to s to be encoded along the path from s to t.*
– *The local routing table for each node u consists of the information about routes to the core and the information about local routes:*
  $\mathtt{tbl}(u) := \{(v, \mathtt{port}_u(v)) : v \in \mathtt{core}_{\gamma'}(G)\} \cup \{(v, \mathtt{port}_u(v)) : v \in B_G(u)\}$,
  where $\mathtt{port}_u(v)$ *is the local port of u to route messages towards node v along some shortest path from u to v.*

The routing procedure is described in Algorithm 1. It includes pseudocode for the source node s to determine the method of sending a message to target t (Lines 1–10), based on whether t is local or not and whether a shortest path to t is known due to an earlier handshake or not. It also includes pseudocode for an intermediate node u to determine whether to forward the message using its local routing table (Lines 20 and 26), or to forward the message using the shortest path encoded in the header (Lines 22–24), or to switch the routing direction from towards the landmark $\ell(t)$ to towards the target t (Lines 16–18). The correctness of the algorithm is based on the simple observation that if $t \in B_G(s) \cup \mathtt{core}_{\gamma'}(G)$ (and thus t is in the routing table of s), then, for all nodes w on the shortest path from s to t, we also have $t \in B_G(w) \cup \mathtt{core}_{\gamma'}(G)$.

An additional handshake protocol (Algorithm 2) handles the special case when $t \notin B_G(s)$ but $s \in B_G(t)$. In this case, the basic LANDMARKBALLROUTING scheme only achieves worst-case stretch 5 instead of 3. However, t knows the reverse path from t to s. Since the graph is undirected, t can send a special handshake message back to s (Line 2), and each node along the path encodes the reverse port number such that, in the end, s knows the shortest path from s to t (Lines 3–10). For simplicity of exposition we use the reasonable assumption [3] that node u knows the port q on which the message is received. If this assumption does not hold, our handshake protocol can be adapted accordingly (see [9]). The performance of Algorithms 1 and 2 is evaluated in the following theorem, which is proven in the next section.

Theorem 1. LANDMARKBALLROUTING *together with the handshake protocol is a routing scheme with the following properties: (1) the worst-case stretch is 5 without handshaking, (2) the worst-case stretch is 3 after handshaking, and (3) every routing decision takes constant time. In addition, for random graphs sampled from* **RPLG**(n, τ),

---

Algorithm 1. LANDMARKBALLROUTING on node u, with source s, target $t \neq s$, and header header.

1: **if** $u = s$ **then**
2:　　**if** $t \in B_G(s)$ **then**
3:　　　　send packet with header $= (\texttt{local}, s, t)$ using $\text{port}_s(t)$ stored in $\text{tbl}(s)$
4:　　**else if** u knows $SP(s, t)$ /* due to handshake */ **then**
5:　　　　send packet with header $= (\texttt{direct}, s, t, 0, SP(s, t))$ using port $SP(s, t)[0]$
6:　　**else**
7:　　　　send packet with header $= (\texttt{toLandmark}, s, \text{addr}(t))$ using $\text{port}_s(\ell(t))$ stored in $\text{tbl}(s)$
8:　　**end if**
9:　　**exit**
10: **end if**
11: /* $u \neq s$ */
12: **if** $u = \text{header}.t$ **then**
13:　　**exit** as the packet arrived.
14: **end if**
15: **if** header.$route = \texttt{toLandmark}$ **then**
16:　　**if** $u = \text{header}.addr.\ell(t)$ **then**
17:　　　　header.$route \leftarrow \texttt{fromLandmark}$; header.$pos \leftarrow 0$; header.$SP \leftarrow$ header.$addr.SP(\ell(t), t)$;
18:　　　　forward packet with the new header using port header.$SP[0]$
19:　　**else**
20:　　　　forward the packet to $\text{port}_u(\text{header}.addr.\ell(t))$ stored in $\text{tbl}(u)$
21:　　**end if**
22: **else if** header.$route \in \{\texttt{fromLandmark}, \texttt{direct}\}$ **then**
23:　　header.$pos \leftarrow$ header.$pos + 1$
24:　　forward the packet using port header.$SP[\text{header}.pos]$
25: **else if** header.$route = \texttt{local}$ **then**
26:　　forward the packet using $\text{port}_u(\text{header}.t)$ stored in $\text{tbl}(u)$
27: **end if**

---

the following properties hold: (4) the expected maximum table size is $O(n^\gamma \log n)$ bits; this bound also holds with probability at least $1 - 1/n$, (5) address length and message header size are $O(\log n \log \log n)$ bits with probability $1 - o(1)$, and (6) addresses and routing tables can be generated efficiently in expected time $O(n^{1+\gamma} \log n)$ and this bound also holds with probability at least $1 - 1/n$.

4 Analysis

Stretch. The proofs use the triangle inequality as in [14,29].

Random Power-Law Graphs and their Cores and Balls. We first prove some properties of the adapted random power-law graph model. Let G be a random graph sampled from **RPLG**(n, τ). For a set of nodes S, define its *volume* $Vol(S)$ as the sum of all its nodes' w_i, that is, $Vol(S) := \sum_{v_i \in S} w_i$. We abbreviate $Vol(G) = Vol(V(G))$. Note that $Vol(G) = 1/\rho$. Let $vol(S)$ denote the sum of the nodes' degrees in the actual graph G, $vol(S) := \sum_{v_i \in S} \deg_G(v_i)$. The following lemma proves that $Vol(G)$ is linear in n.

Algorithm 2. Handshake protocol on node u upon the receipt of a packet from a port q with header header.

1: **if** header.$route$ = fromLandmark **and** u = header.t **and** header.$s \in B_G(u) \cup$ core$_{\gamma'}(G)$ **then**

2:    send packet with header = (handshake, u, header.s, Nil) using port$_u$(header.s) stored in tbl(u).

3: **else if** header.$route$ = handshake **then**

4:    header.$SP = q \cdot$ header.SP /* prepend the port q as part of the reverse path */

5:    **if** header.$t = u$ /* reach handshake destination */ **then**

6:       store $SP(u, \text{header}.s)$ = header.SP locally for later use (see Line 4 of LAND-MARKBALLROUTING.)

7:    **else**

8:       forward packet with the new header to port$_u$(header.t) stored in tbl(u).

9:    **end if**

10: **end if**

Lemma 1. *Let G be a random graph sampled from* **RPLG**(n, τ). *The volume $Vol(G)$ satisfies $n < Vol(G) \leq \frac{\tau-1}{\tau-2}n$.*

In the following, we show concentration results for the actual degree of a vertex and for the volume of a set of vertices in the adapted **RPLG**(n, τ) model. The basic idea to prove the results for the **RPLG**(n, τ) model is to split the random variable for the degree D_i of node v_i into deterministic and random edges and then bound both parts individually.

Lemma 2. *Let $n \geq 4^{\frac{\tau-1}{(\tau-2)^2}}$. For a random graph sampled from* **RPLG**(n, τ), *if $w_i \geq 32 \ln n$, for vertex v_i, the degree D_i satisfies the following:* $\Pr[w_i/4 \leq D_i \leq 3w_i] > 1 - 2/n^4$.

Lemma 3. *Let G be a random graph sampled from* **RPLG**(n, τ). *For a subset of vertices S satisfying $Vol(S) \geq 192 \ln n$, it holds with probability at least $1 - 2/n^3$ that $Vol(S)/8 \leq vol(S) \leq 4\,Vol(S)$.*

Corollary 1. *The number of edges of a random graph sampled from* **RPLG**(n, τ) *is at most $vol(G)/2 \leq \frac{4(\tau-1)}{\tau-2}n$ with probability at least $1 - 1/n^2$.*

There is an edge between two nodes v_i, v_j with probability proportional to w_i and w_j. This is generalized for sets of nodes $S, T \subseteq V(G)$ in the following and holds for both **FDRG**(w) and **RPLG**(n, τ).

Lemma 4 ([10, Lem. 3.3]). *For any two disjoint subsets S and T with $Vol(S) \cdot Vol(T) > c \cdot Vol(G)$, we have $\Pr[d(S, T) > 1] \leq e^{-c}$.*

Core size. To compute the size of core$_{\gamma'}(w)$, we solve the inequality $w_k > n^{\gamma'}$ and obtain $k < n^{\gamma'(1-\tau)+1}$. As $\gamma' = \frac{1-\gamma}{\tau-1}$, we have $|\text{core}_{\gamma'}(w)| = \lceil n^{\gamma'(1-\tau)+1} \rceil - 1 = \lceil n^{\gamma} \rceil - 1$. Even if the same degree threshold $n^{\gamma'}$ is used for core$_{\gamma'}(w)$ and core$_{\gamma'}(G)$, the two sets of nodes may differ. For a slightly smaller degree threshold $n^{\gamma'}/4$ (as in Definition 2), the core of the actual graph contains core$_{\gamma'}(w)$ with high probability (apply Lemma 2).

Lemma 5. *Let G be a random graph sampled from* **RPLG**(n, τ). *With probability at least $1 - 1/n^2$ it holds that* $\mathrm{core}_{\gamma'}(\boldsymbol{w}) = \{v_i : w_i > n^{\gamma'}\} \subseteq \{v_i : \deg(v_i) > n^{\gamma'}/4\} = \mathrm{core}_{\gamma'}(G)$.

Lemma 6. *Let G be a random graph sampled from* **RPLG**(n, τ). *With probability at least $1 - 1/n^2$, $|\mathrm{core}_{\gamma'}(G)| = \Theta(n^{\gamma})$.*

Ball sizes.

Lemma 7. *Let $\beta = \gamma'(\tau - 2) + \frac{(2\tau - 3)\varepsilon}{\tau - 1}$ be a constant. Assume Equation (1) is satisfied. For a random graph G sampled from* **RPLG**(n, τ), *with probability at least $1 - 3/n^2$, it holds that for all $u \in V(G)$,*

$$|B_G(u)| = |\{u' \in V(G) : d(u, u') < d(u, \mathrm{core}_{\gamma'}(\boldsymbol{w}))\}| = O(n^{\beta}),$$
$$|E(B_G(u))| = O(n^{\beta} \log n),$$

where $E(B_G(u))$ is the set of internal edges among vertices in $B_G(u)$.

Since for **RPLG**(n, τ) the edges are independent, in our analysis, the existence of every edge in random graph G is only determined when it is needed, and before that it is treated as a probability distribution as defined in our random graph model. We call the determination of the existence of an edge according to its probability distribution *revealing* the edge.

For a given vertex $u \in V(G)$, we define a sequence of balls as follows: Let $V' = V \setminus \mathrm{core}_{\gamma'}(\boldsymbol{w})$. Now define $B_0 = \{u\}$ and $B_i = \{v : d_G(u, v) \leq i\}$. We also define the circles $C_i = B_i \setminus B_{i-1}$ for $i \geq 0$ with $B_{-1} = \emptyset$. Let E_i be the number of edges between C_i and $C_i \cup C_{i+1}$.

Lemma 8. *For circle C_i, the following holds with probability at least $1 - 2/n^3$: If $Vol(C_i) < 192 \ln n$, then $E_i \leq 4 \cdot 192 \ln n$, and if $Vol(C_i) \geq 192 \ln n$, then $E_i \leq 4 \, Vol(C_i)$.*

Since there are at most n circles, Lemma 8 holds for all circles with probability at least $1 - 2/n^2$.

Table Sizes and Computations. The core $\mathrm{core}_{\gamma'}(G)$ has size $\Theta(n^{\gamma})$ with probability at least $1 - 1/n^2$ (Lemma 6) and all balls $B_G(u)$ have size $O(n^{\gamma})$ with probability at least $1 - 3/n^2$ (Lemma 7). Therefore, we have the following result.

Lemma 9. *For a random graph G sampled from* **RPLG**(n, τ), *for all $u \in V(G)$, the expected table size is at most $|\mathrm{tbl}(u)| = O(n^{\gamma})$ and all tables can be generated in expected time at most $O(n^{1+\gamma} \log n)$. These bounds also hold with probability at least $1 - 1/n$.*

Proof. Note that each entry of $\mathrm{tbl}(u)$ has $O(\log n)$ bits. Thus the total table size per node is $O(n^{\gamma} \log n)$ bits. Our algorithm is deterministic. The expected time (space) complexity is the average running time (space) of our algorithm over all graphs from the random graph distribution **RPLG**(n, τ).

Given a graph G with n nodes and m edges, our algorithm computes the core $\text{core}_{\gamma'}(G)$ of G with time complexity $O(m + n \log n)$. It runs a complete breadth-first search for each node of the core in time $O(m)$. Let $B_G(u)$ be the ball computed in our algorithm for vertex u. Let $T(B_G(u))$ denote the time to compute $B_G(u)$. Therefore, the time complexity TC and space complexity SC of our algorithm are at most

$$TC(G) = O\left(m \cdot |\text{core}_{\gamma'}(G)| + \sum_{v \in V(G)} T(B_G(u))\right), \tag{2}$$

$$SC(G) = O\left(n \cdot |\text{core}_{\gamma'}(G)| + \sum_{v \in V(G)} |B_G(u)|\right). \tag{3}$$

We now know that with probability at least $1 - 5/n^2$, all of the following conditions are true: (1) $m = \Theta(n)$ (Corollary 1); (2) $|\text{core}_{\gamma'}(G)| = \Theta(n^{\gamma})$ (Lemma 6); (3) $|B_G(u)| = O(n^{\beta})$ for all vertices u (Lemma 7); (4) $T(B_G(u)) = O(n^{\beta} \log n)$ for all vertices u (Lemma 7). Therefore, from Equations (2) and (3), we know that with probability at least $1 - 5/n^2$, the space complexity of our algorithm is $O(n^{1+\gamma} + n^{1+\beta})$ and the time complexity is $O(n^{1+\gamma} + n^{1+\beta} \log n)$.

Finally, we fix the parameters to obtain a balanced scheme. In a balanced scheme, the core size and the expected ball sizes are asymptotically equivalent, that is, $\beta = \gamma$. Together with $\beta = \gamma'(\tau - 2) + \frac{(2\tau - 3)\varepsilon}{\tau - 1}$ and $\gamma' = \frac{1 - \gamma}{\tau - 1}$, we have $\gamma = \frac{\tau - 2}{2\tau - 3} + \varepsilon$. Therefore, assuming that Equation (1) is satisfied, the space requirement per node is $O(n^{\gamma} \log n)$ bits and the preprocessing time is bounded by $O(n^{1+\gamma} \log n)$, which holds with probability at least $1 - 1/n$. □

Address Lengths. We now bound the number of bits for the address of each vertex. For one vertex u, its address contains the encoding of the shortest path $SP(u, \ell(u))$ from u to its landmark $\ell(u)$. We need to bound the diameter of a random power-law graph and the diameter of its core. The proofs in [10] on diameters can be carried over to our adapted model.

Lemma 10 (Chung and Lu [10, Claim 4.4]). *For a random graph sampled from* **RPLG**(n, τ)*, with probability at least $1 - o(1)$, the diameter of its largest connected component is $\Theta(\log n)$.*

By Lemma 10, the length of $SP(u, \ell(u))$ is at most $O(\log n)$ asymptotically almost surely. Therefore, $SP(s, t)$ can be encoded with $O(\log^2 n)$ bits. This bound can be improved to $O(\log n \log \log n)$, as proven in the following lemma.

Lemma 11. *For a random graph G sampled from* **RPLG**(n, τ)*, with probability at least $1 - o(1)$, it holds that for all $s, t \in V(G)$, $SP(s, t)$ can be encoded with $O(\log n \log \log n)$ bits.*

The proof is split into several claims from [10]. We first extend the core.

Definition 4. *The* extended core *of a random graph from* **RPLG**(n, τ) *contains all nodes v_i with w_i at least $n^{1/\log \log n}$, that is, $\text{core}^+(\boldsymbol{w}) = \{v_i \in V : w_i \geq n^{1/\log \log n}\}$.*

Note that, as τ is a constant, $1/\log\log n \leq \gamma'$ for large enough n, and thus $\mathrm{core}^+(\boldsymbol{w}) \supseteq \mathrm{core}_{\gamma'}(\boldsymbol{w})$. The following lemma constitutes a bound for the diameter of the core.

Lemma 12 (Chung and Lu [10, Claim 4.1]). *Let G be a random graph sampled from* **RPLG**(n, τ). *The diameter of the subgraph induced by* $\mathrm{core}^+(\boldsymbol{w})$ *in G is $O(\log\log n)$ with probability at least $1 - 1/n$.*

Lemma 13 (Chung and Lu [10, Claim 4.2]). *Let G be a random graph sampled from* **RPLG**(n, τ). *There exists a constant C, such that each vertex v_i with $w_i \geq \log^C n$ is at distance $O(\log\log n)$ from the* extended core, *with probability at least $1 - 1/n^2$.*

Corollary 2 (Corollary of Lemma 13). *Let G be a random graph sampled from* **RPLG**(n, τ). *Let C be the constant in Lemma 13. With probability at least $1 - 1/n$, the distance between any two vertices v_i, v_j with $w_i \geq \log^C n$ and $w_j \geq \log^C n$ is $O(\log\log n)$.*

Proof (of Lemma 11). Let v_i and v_j be the first and the last vertex in $SP(s, t)$ from s to t such that w_i and w_j both are greater than $\log^C n$, where C is the constant from Lemma 13. By Corollary 2, with probability $1 - 1/n$, the portion of the shortest path $SP(s, t)$ between v_i and v_j has length at most $O(\log\log n)$. Therefore, this portion of the shortest path can be encoded with $O(\log n \log\log n)$ bits, with probability $1 - 1/n$.

For the rest of the shortest path, each node has w_i at most $\log^C n$. By Lemma 2, all such nodes have degree at most $3\log^C n$ with probability at least $1 - 2/n^3$. To encode the next neighbor in the shortest path, at most $O(\log\log n)$ bits are necessary. Since $SP(s, t)$ contains $O(\log n)$ nodes with probability $1 - o(1)$ (Lemma 10), the rest of the shortest path can also be encoded with $O(\log n \log\log n)$ bits, with probability $1 - o(1)$. $\qquad\square$

5   Experiments

Real-world graphs. The most important application scenario for a compact routing scheme is arguably a communication network. The router-level topology of a portion of the Internet, measured by CAIDA [13], is an undirected, unweighted graph with $190, 914$ nodes and $607, 610$ edges.

Random Power-Law Graphs. We extracted the largest connected component from the random power-law graphs generated by Brady and Cowen [8] (pre-generated graphs, $N = 10,000$ and $\tau \in (2, 3)$). In addition, we generated graphs of 10,000 nodes with the tool BRITE [26] using the configurations for the Barabási [7] and Waxman [30] models for an Autonomous System Topology (AS) and a Router Topology (RT). The edge weights were ignored and the links interpreted as undirected. Note that for all the random graphs considered, the generation process does not exactly match the **RPLG**(n, τ).

Routing schemes. In the specification of our routing scheme LANDMARKBALLROUT-ING, we use $n^{\gamma'}/4$ as a degree threshold (Definition 2) and obtain a core of size $\Theta(n^{\gamma})$. The largest connected components of the graphs generated by Brady and Cowen [8] and

Table 1. Table sizes: mean and standard deviation

Graph	CAIDA [13]	ASBarabasi	RTBarabasi	ASWaxman	RTWaxman
random, $p = n^{-1/2}$	929.84±95.40	204.03±25.57	208.32±22.21	221.95± 24.73	217.75± 28.00
highdeg, $\lceil n^\gamma \rceil$	173.68±55.80	32.16±41.30	44.95±58.21	139.45±142.94	130.65±131.78
Graphs [8]	$\tau = 2.1$	$\tau = 2.2$	$\tau = 2.3$	$\tau = 2.4$	$\tau = 2.5$
random, $p = n^{-1/2}$	74.90±37.96	74.94±44.78	77.49±50.56	79.74± 55.50	82.54± 60.17
highdeg, $\lceil n^\gamma \rceil$	55.20±67.48	48.50±54.57	42.20±42.94	43.28± 40.10	43.55± 38.37
Graphs [8]	$\tau = 2.6$	$\tau = 2.7$	$\tau = 2.8$	$\tau = 2.9$	
random, $p = n^{-1/2}$	86.88±69.69	85.56±71.35	84.69±73.87	76.65± 71.71	
highdeg, $\lceil n^\gamma \rceil$	45.59±39.59	50.24±46.08	56.48±56.26	46.85± 46.65	

Table 2. Stretch: mean and standard deviation

Graph	CAIDA [13]	ASBarabasi	RTBarabasi	ASWaxman	RTWaxman
random	1.28±0.16	1.38±0.28	1.38±0.25	1.37±0.25	1.38±0.16
highdeg, $\lceil n^\gamma \rceil$	1.12±0.14	1.15±0.21	1.20±0.22	1.36±0.26	1.35±0.24
Graphs [8]	$\tau = 2.1$	$\tau = 2.2$	$\tau = 2.3$	$\tau = 2.4$	$\tau = 2.5$
random, $p = n^{-1/2}$	1.34±0.24	1.35±0.24	1.35±0.25	1.34±0.26	1.34±0.26
highdeg, $\lceil n^\gamma \rceil$	1.30±0.24	1.26±0.23	1.23±0.23	1.21±0.23	1.18±0.22
Graphs [8]	$\tau = 2.6$	$\tau = 2.7$	$\tau = 2.8$	$\tau = 2.9$	
random, $p = n^{-1/2}$	1.33±0.28	1.31±0.28	1.29±0.29	1.25±0.28	
highdeg, $\lceil n^\gamma \rceil$	1.16±0.22	1.15±0.22	1.15±0.24	1.11±0.22	

the graphs generated using BRITE [26] do not contain nodes with such a high degree. Therefore, for the experiments with our routing scheme, the algorithm selects the $\lceil n^\gamma \rceil$ nodes with the highest degrees as landmarks. We compare our high-degree selection strategy with the random selection with probability $n^{-1/2}$, which is *similar* to Thorup and Zwick [29] for $k = 2$. Recall that their scheme is not optimized for power-law graphs but works for general, weighted graphs as well. We also compare our scheme with the values obtained by Brady and Cowen [8].

Settings and results. For the graphs generated by Brady and Cowen [8], the high-degree selection and the random sampling process were executed five times for each of the ten graphs per value of τ, which gives a total of $5 \cdot 10 \cdot 9 \cdot 2 = 900$ routing scheme constructions. For each of the remaining graphs (Barabási, Waxman, CAIDA), both schemes were constructed at least 10 times. We report the table sizes (mean and standard deviation) in Table 1. For each instance, 200 random (s, t) pairs were generated and packets routed. The stretch (the length of the route divided by the length of a shortest path) is reported in Table 2.

In our experiments, the strategy of selecting few high-degree nodes as landmarks always produces significantly smaller routing tables compared to a large number of landmarks selected at random. The best results are achieved for the graphs stemming from the Barabási model, for which the high-degree-based tables are roughly 5 times smaller than their random-based counterpart. The average table size for the randomly selected landmarks is close to $\sqrt{n}$, which means that most balls are actually (almost) empty. As predicted by our analysis, this indicates that, for power-law graphs, the optimal balance for randomly selected landmarks may be smaller than $O(\sqrt{n})$.

The average stretch is surprisingly consistent among different datasets. Even though there are fewer landmarks, the average stretch is better if high-degree nodes are selected as landmarks. Brady and Cowen [8] claim average stretch 1.18–1.25 for the scheme by Thorup and Zwick [29]. Our experiments do not confirm this claim: randomly selected nodes (similar to TZ) did not achieve this stretch. Brady and Cowen also claim average stretch 1.11–1.22 for their scheme and small values for $\tau \in \{2.1, 2.2, 2.3\}$. Our scheme, except for the graphs of the Waxman model and for small values of $\tau \leq 2.2$, also achieves these average stretch values.

6 Conclusion

Our analysis provides theoretical justification that high-degree nodes in power-law graphs are indeed very important for finding shortest paths in such networks, and thus are effective in improving the performance of shortest-path-related computations. With the ubiquity of power-law networks, our result suggests that, when designing network algorithms, optimizing for power-law graphs rather than dealing with general graphs, may lead to significantly better algorithm performance in real-world networks.

Perhaps the most intriguing question is whether even polylogarithmic tables would suffice to route with small stretch in power-law graphs. It also remains open whether the scheme by Thorup and Zwick for general k can be optimized for power-law graphs and whether similar techniques can be applied to the name-independent scheme by Abraham et al. [5]. An average-case analysis of the actual scheme by Thorup and Zwick would be interesting as well as a rigorous analysis of the scheme by Brady and Cowen [8]. Furthermore, the analysis for other random power-law graphs models is an interesting topic.

Acknowledgments. The second author thanks Mikkel Thorup for helpful comments and interesting discussions.

References

1. Abraham, I., Gavoille, C., Goldberg, A.V., Malkhi, D.: Routing in networks with low doubling dimension. In: Proceedings of the 26th International Conference on Distributed Computing Systems (2006)
2. Abraham, I., Gavoille, C., Malkhi, D.: Compact routing for graphs excluding a fixed minor. In: Fraigniaud, P. (ed.) DISC 2005. LNCS, vol. 3724, pp. 442–456. Springer, Heidelberg (2005)
3. Abraham, I., Gavoille, C., Malkhi, D.: On space-stretch trade-offs: lower bounds. In: SPAA, pp. 207–216 (2006)
4. Abraham, I., Gavoille, C., Malkhi, D.: On space-stretch trade-offs: upper bounds. In: SPAA, pp. 217–224 (2006)
5. Abraham, I., Gavoille, C., Malkhi, D., Nisan, N., Thorup, M.: Compact name-independent routing with minimum stretch. ACM Transactions on Algorithms 4(3) (2008)
6. Aiello, W., Chung, F.R.K., Lu, L.: A random graph model for massive graphs. In: STOC, pp. 171–180 (2000)

7. Barabási, A.-L., Albert, R.: Emergence of scaling in random networks. Science 286(5439), 509–512 (1999)
8. Brady, A., Cowen, L.: Compact routing on power law graphs with additive stretch. In: Proc. of the 9th Workshop on Algorithm Eng. and Exper., pp. 119–128 (2006)
9. Chen, W., Sommer, C., Teng, S.-H., Wang, Y.: A compact routing scheme and approximate distance oracle for power-law graphs. Technical Report MSR-TR-2009-84, Microsoft Research (July 2009)
10. Chung, F., Lu, L.: The average distances in random graphs with given expected degrees. Internet Mathematics 99, 15879–15882 (2002)
11. Chung, F., Lu, L.: Complex Graphs and Networks. American Mathematical Society (2006)
12. Clauset, A., Shalizi, C.R., Newman, M.E.J.: Power-law distributions in empirical data. arXiv:0706.1062 (2007)
13. Cooperative Association for Internet Data Analysis. CAIDA's router-level topology measurements (2003), http://www.caida.org/tools/measurement/skitter/router_topology/file:itdk0304_rlinks_undirected.gz
14. Cowen, L.: Compact routing with minimum stretch. J. Algorithms 38(1), 170–183 (2001)
15. Enachescu, M., Wang, M., Goel, A.: Reducing maximum stretch in compact routing. In: INFOCOM, pp. 336–340 (2008)
16. Erdős, P., Rényi, A.: On the evolution of random graphs. Magyar Tudományos Akadémia Matematikai Kutató Intézetének Közleményei 5, 17–61 (1960)
17. Faloutsos, M., Faloutsos, P., Faloutsos, C.: On power-law relationships of the Internet topology. In: SIGCOMM: Proceedings of the conference on applications, technologies, architectures, and protocols for computer communication, pp. 251–262 (1999)
18. Fraigniaud, P., Gavoille, C.: Routing in trees. In: Orejas, F., Spirakis, P.G., van Leeuwen, J. (eds.) ICALP 2001. LNCS, vol. 2076, pp. 757–772. Springer, Heidelberg (2001)
19. Gavoille, C., Hanusse, N.: Compact routing tables for graphs of bounded genus. In: Wiedermann, J., Van Emde Boas, P., Nielsen, M. (eds.) ICALP 1999. LNCS, vol. 1644, pp. 351–360. Springer, Heidelberg (1999)
20. Gavoille, C., Perennes, S.: Memory requirements for routing in distributed networks (extended abstract). In: PODC, pp. 125–133 (1996)
21. Konjevod, G., Richa, A.W., Xia, D.: Optimal-stretch name-independent compact routing in doubling metrics. In: PODC, pp. 198–207 (2006)
22. Konjevod, G., Richa, A.W., Xia, D., Yu, H.: Compact routing with slack in low doubling dimension. In: PODC, pp. 71–80 (2007)
23. Korman, A.: Improved compact routing schemes for dynamic trees. In: PODC, pp. 185–194 (2008)
24. Krioukov, D.V., Fall, K.R., Yang, X.: Compact routing on internet-like graphs. In: INFOCOM (2004)
25. Lu, H.-I.: Improved compact routing tables for planar networks via orderly spanning trees. In: Proc. of the 8th Int. Computing and Combinatorics Conference, pp. 57–66 (2002)
26. Medina, A., Lakhina, A., Matta, I., Byers, J.W.: Brite: An approach to universal topology generation. In: 9th International Workshop on Modeling, Analysis, and Simulation of Computer and Telecommunication Systems, p. 346 (2001)
27. Mitzenmacher, M.: A brief history of generative models for power law and lognormal distributions. Internet Mathematics 1(2) (2003)
28. Peleg, D., Upfal, E.: A trade-off between space and efficiency for routing tables. J. ACM 36(3), 510–530 (1989)
29. Thorup, M., Zwick, U.: Compact routing schemes. In: SPAA, pp. 1–10 (2001)
30. Waxman, B.M.: Routing of multipoint connections. IEEE Journal on Selected Areas in Communications 6(9), 1617–1622 (1988)

Virtual Ring Routing Trends

Dahlia Malkhi[1], Siddhartha Sen[2], Kunal Talwar[1], Renato F. Werneck[1],
and Udi Wieder[1]

[1] Microsoft Research Silicon Valley
{dalia,kunal,renatow,uwieder}@microsoft.com
[2] Princeton University
sssix@cs.princeton.edu

Abstract. Virtual Ring Routing (VRR) schemes were introduced in the
context of wireless ad hoc networks and Internet anycast overlays. They
build a network-routing layer using ideas from distributed hash table
design, utilizing randomized virtual identities along a ring. This makes
maintenance practical when nodes may enter or leave.

Previously, VRR was evaluated over a small wireless network and
through medium-scale simulations, exhibiting remarkably good performance. In this paper, we provide a formal analysis of a family of VRR-
like schemes. The analysis provides insight into a variety of issues, e.g.,
how well does VRR perform compared with brute force shortest paths
routing? What properties of an underlying network topology make VRR
work well?

Our analysis is backed by extensive simulation over a variety of topologies. Whereas previous works evaluated VRR over fairly small networks
(up to 200 nodes), we are interested in scaling the simulations so as to
exhibit asymptotic trends. Simulating network sizes beyond 2^{20} results
in a memory explosion: In some of the topologies of interest, such as
a 2-dimensional plane, the total memory taken up by routing tables is
$\Omega(N^{3/2})$ for an N-node network. We devise a simulation strategy that
builds necessary information on the fly using a Luby and Rackoff pseudo-
random permutation, leading to simulations at a scale of 2^{32} nodes.

1 Introduction

Virtual Ring Routing (VRR) schemes were deployed for wireless ad hoc networks [4], for anycast Internet routing [5], and for scaling Ethernet [8]. Deviat-
ing drastically from any known method of compact routing [7], these practical
systems borrow ideas from distributed hash table overlays, and use virtual addresses (aka flat labels) for routing. The vision behind these schemes is to have
node identities that contain no structural information about the network. Hence,
they support mobility naturally, and impose less administrative burden in assigning addresses. Additionally, they are easy to maintain, in that adding and
removing nodes from the network is efficient, and incurs updates in only a small
fraction of the nodes. In contrast to the well-founded theory of compact routing,
there exists no rigorous analysis of VRR schemes. This paper tackles the formal
analysis of a family of VRR schemes and provides insight into a variety of issues.

I. Keidar (Ed.): DISC 2009, LNCS 5805, pp. 392–406, 2009.
© Springer-Verlag Berlin Heidelberg 2009

DHT overlays assign virtual identities (e.g., in the range [0..1], or integers) to nodes and maintain connections between nodes based on their virtual id's. When used for forming a network layer, DHT overlay techniques must be modified for the following reason. In an overlay network, a node p simply stores the name of each overlay neighbor q in a local overlay routing table; the lower-level networking layer facilitates the connection between p and q. However, in the absence of a network layer, it is not enough for p to remember q's name in order to connect to it.

VRR schemes such as [4,5] resolve this issue by maintaining routing information between p and q along an entire physical path between them. This means that every node along a physical path from p to q has a routing table entry with the destination q in it, storing the next hop toward q. We note that other techniques that adapt DHT routing to the network layer exist, but are of no relevance here, e.g., write an entire path on the packet header at p [11], or route through landmark gateways [12,10,6].

To prevent confusion between routes at the different layers, we introduce some conventions.

Glossary: The entire node-by-node path determined by a routing scheme is called the *actual routing path*. It is induced by a sequence of hops, each hop between *virtual neighbors* in the virtual overlay. The physical path toward a virtual neighbor is carried along a *physical segment*, potentially composed of multiple nodes.

Routing efficiency is measured by its *stretch*: Given a pair of nodes, their routing stretch is the ratio between their actual routing path length and their shortest path length.

The overlay topology utilized in [4,5] is a simple ring. Hence, overlay paths may take a linear number of virtual hops from a source to a destination. For example, say that we have a ring of nodes numbered [1..30]. The virtual ring route from node 5 to 15 goes through nodes $5, 6, ..., 15$ in succession. Each of these virtual hops is carried along a physical segment in the network. Thus, routing toward a virtual destination using overlay virtual hops could incur a linear stretch.

Fortunately, VRR allows *greedy hops* which considerably improve the routing efficiency. Imagine going along a physical path from node 5 to 6 in the above virtual path. Quite likely, this path crosses other physical paths, say 10 to 11, 20 to 21 and 28 to 29. When we reach the node en-route from 5 to 6 which is on the path from 10 to 11, VRR greedily chooses to route toward 11 instead of continuing toward 6.

Thus far, the advantage of using path intersection in greedy routing in this manner was evaluated over a small wireless network and through medium-scale simulations, exhibiting remarkably good performance.

1.1 Technical Approach

The high-level intuition provided in [4] for constant expected stretch of VRR in a two-dimensional space with uniformly scattered nodes is as follows. The

routing table at each node is populated with expected $O(\sqrt{N})$ randomly selected destinations. Hence, a greedy hop to the final target is expected after
visiting $O(\sqrt{N})$ physical nodes. Unfortunately, this intuition is not easily turned
into a rigorous analysis because of the subtle dependencies between the routing
tables of neighboring nodes in the topology. Rather, our analysis builds from
the fundamental probability of path intersection. For example, consider the Euclidean grid of dimension d. For reasonable selection of shortest paths between
randomly chosen endpoints, intersection occurs with probability in $O(N^{-\frac{d-2}{d}})$.
For the two-dimensional grid, this is constant. We call this the *intersection coefficient*, and denote it by p.

Two factors contribute to bound the routing path length. First, consider the
last $2c/\sqrt{p}$ virtual identities preceding the target, for some constant c. They
determine a collection of $c/\sqrt{p}$ physical segments with disjoint endpoints, that
are hence independently assigned in the network. Any additional independently
chosen segment intersects one of the segments in the collection with probability
$1 - (1-p)^{(c/\sqrt{p})}$. A collection of $c/\sqrt{p}$ additional, independently selected, segments intersects the first collection with probability $1 - \left((1-p)^{(c/\sqrt{p})}\right)^{(c/\sqrt{p})} \approx$
$1 - e^{-c^2}$, hence the expected collection size until intersection is in $O(1/\sqrt{p})$.
Intuitively, this bounds the number of physical segments that are traversed to
completion in the actual routing path to expected $O(1/\sqrt{p})$. A more precise argument, which considers the inter-dependencies among virtual hops in a routing
path, is given in the body of the paper; it gives $O(\log N/\sqrt{p})$ expected number
of completed physical segments.

So far, we have bounded the expected number of virtual hops that are made
to completion in an actual routing path. We did not count the nodes in physical
segments that are interrupted by greedy steps. Here, intuition suggests that a
greedy step shortens the virtual distance to the target by an expected factor of
two. However, we were unable to provide a formal proof for this property, due
to the intricate dependency between the conditions imposed by a path traversed
up to some point and the possible remaining virtual identity mappings.

Instead, we slightly modify the scheme to assist with the analysis. We modified
the VRR scheme to allow a greedy hop only when, indeed, it reduces the virtual
distance to the target by at least a constant factor α. Extensive simulation
indicates that the modification has marginal (and even somewhat negative) effect
on the actual routing complexity, e.g., for $\alpha = 2$. We can then bound the number
of physical segments which terminate with a greedy hop by $O(\log_\alpha(N))$. Proving
this for the original VRR scheme remains an open challenge.

1.2 Contribution

Leveraging the analysis we highlight above, we make the following contributions.

- Our analysis relates the path intersection coefficient p with an expected overall routing stretch of $O(\log N/\sqrt{p})$. We prove that this is tight up to a logarithmic factor, with a matching lower bound of $\Omega(1/\sqrt{p})$. Using this insight,

one can predict the stretch of VRR schemes over any network topology, as the physical network topology determines path intersection probability p. For example, in a two-dimensional grid, two pairs of randomly selected endpoints have intersecting shortest paths with constant probability. The expected stretch in the two dimensional grid is in $O(\log N)$.

More generally, for the Euclidean grid of dimension d, intersection occurs with probability in $O(N^{-\frac{d-2}{d}})$, and the expected stretch is in $O(N^{\frac{d-2}{2d}} \log n)$.

- We readily determine the relationship between the overall routing table memory and the stretch. The network topology determines the expected number of overlay paths that pass through a certain node, and thus, the expected routing table size at a node. For example, in a d-dimensional grid, routing tables size is in $O(N^{1/d})$.

Memory-stretch tradeoffs have been studied extensively in the theory of compact routing, and we can draw a comparison with VRR here. Methods were suggested that can achieve better characteristics: [1] gives a $O(k)$-stretch name-independent routing with $O(k^2 N^{1/k} \log^3 N)$ routing table resources per node for arbitrary graphs, and [2] gives a name-independent scheme for planar graphs with constant stretch and only polylogarithmic memory at each node. The advantage of VRR schemes is their simplicity and maintainability.

- We also extend our experiments to two overlay variants, using the same VRR methodology. One is a ring where each node has outgoing links to its k ring-successors, for a parameter k. The other is the ring with $k - 1$ successors, and a k-th neighbor is selected from the virtual ring using a "small-world" distribution.

Our analysis is backed by extensive simulation over the two, three and four dimensional grids. Whereas previous works evaluated VRR over fairly small networks (up to 200 nodes), we are interested in scaling the simulations so as to exhibit asymptotic trends. However, directly simulating network sizes beyond 2^{20} results in a memory explosion: In some of the topologies of interest, such as a 2-dimensional plane, the total memory taken up by routing tables is $\Omega(N^{3/2})$ for an N-node network. Rather, we devise a simulation strategy that builds necessary information on the fly using a Luby-Rackoff pseudo-random permutation, leading to simulations at a scale of 2^{32} nodes.

2   Problem Description

We describe the VRR scheme in greater detail. The system is modeled as an undirected graph $G = (V, E)$. V is a set of $|V| = N$ nodes. Edges $(u, v) \in E$ indicate that u and v know each other, are physically connected and can communicate directly.

In VRR, every node v has a unique identifier $id(v)$ drawn uniformly at random from a range $R \gg N$ of integers. This defines a natural order on the identifiers and for the rest of the paper, we assume the identifiers simply define a permutation on $[N]$. The node to id mapping is known to all nodes in the system.

Define the *successor* of a node v, denoted $succ(v)$, as the node u whose identity is $(id(u) + 1) \mod N$.

Virtual routes are maintained from every node to its k successors in the identity space, where k is a parameter of the scheme. In our analysis to simplify things we assume that $k = 1$, i.e. the virtual topology is just the ring. For identities i, j, define $dist(i, j)$ to be the number of edges in the shortest path from i to j in this virtual overlay network. Thus for the ring case $k = 1$, $dist(i, j)$ is $j - i$ if $i < j$, and $N - (i - j)$ otherwise. In the simulations we tested the case of larger k.

The virtual topology induces a virtual path between every two nodes. These paths are realized in the physical network via a set of predetermined physical segments between each node u and $succ(u)$. These actual physical paths are ideally shortest paths but are not necessarily so. Denote the nodes in this physical path as $PS(u, succ(u))$. Now, every node v has a local *routing table* with entries $\langle dst, nxt \rangle$ for each path $PS(w, succ(w))$ that contains v (with $dst = succ(w)$), such that nxt is the next hop after v in the segment $PS(w, succ(w))$. The method in which these paths are chosen and maintained is not within the scope of this paper. The work in [4],[5] suggests ways of choosing these paths and argues they are easy to maintain in the face of insertions and deletions.

VRR employs a *greedy routing* (GR) strategy over the virtual identity space. When a message with destination T is injected at a source S, an initial packet header $\langle target : T, intermediate\_target : succ(S) \rangle$ is formed.

When a node u receives a packet with header $\langle T, IT \rangle$, it performs the following:

- If u has a routing-table entry $\langle T', h' \rangle$, such that T' is closer to T than IT (in the virtual distance $dist(\cdot, T)$), then u modifies the header by overwriting intermediate-target with T'. If there is more than one such T', u picks the one closest to T. It forwards the packet to h'.
- Otherwise, u forwards to h, where $\langle IT, h \rangle$ appears in u's routing table.

The entire node-to-node routing path is called the *actual routing path*. In this work, we are interested in analyzing the expected length of the actual routing path, over the choices of identities for a variety of initial graphs.

3   Stretch Analysis

We first give some intuition on the routes generated by GR. Suppose that GR is invoked from s to t. The first routing table lookup performed by GR at s finds an intermediate target m_0 with identity between s and t. This intermediate target may be $(s + 1)$ or some node u such that s lies on a path $PS(u, succ(u))$ and $dist(u, t) < dist(s + 1, t)$. In this case, s chooses the routing table entry corresponding to target $succ(u)$.

In this case GR continues to the next table lookup, which is invoked at a node w following s en route to m_0. Note that w must have m_0 in its routing table, or w is m_0 itself. Therefore, GR continues with an intermediate target no farther than m_0. However, a change of intermediate target may occur. First, if

w is m_0, then it will find among $m_0 + 1, m_0 + 2, ..., m_0 + k$ an intermediate target m_1 closer to t. We call this a *non-greedy transition*. Second, w may find in its routing table an entry m_1 closer than m_0 to t. Again, this happens when w is on a path leading to such m_1. In this case, GR moves to a route leading towards m_1. We call this a *greedy transition*.

The route to m_1 may get interrupted again, and so on. Finally, a route to the target t itself will be found, at which point the intermediate target becomes fixed.

More formally, we have the following definition. For source-destination pair (s, t), let $D(s, t)$ denote $m_0, m_1, ..., m_c = t$ the sequence of intermediate targets set by GR. We say that a transition from m_i to m_{i+1} is *non-greedy* if it was set at m_i from amongst $m_i + 1, ..., m_i + k$, and it is *greedy* otherwise.

We will upper bound the actual routing path length by bounding the size of $D(s, t)$ in a conservative way: if $Diam$ is the diameter of the network, the length of the actual routing path between s and t is at most $Diam \cdot |D(s, t)|$.

Generally, a greedy hop at step j may depend on the first j hops. Obviously, it must be caused by a route toward a target closer to the destination than the intermediate target at step $j - 1$ is. Additionally, it must be caused by a route that does not go through any of the first $j - 1$ hops. In order to handle these weak dependencies, we introduce a slight generalization of the GR procedure called GR'. The idea in GR' is to choose a greedy hop only if this change is a significant improvement. We do this by introducing a parameter α to the first routing rule as follows:

- If u has a routing-table entry $\langle T', h' \rangle$, such that T' is closer to T than IT **by factor of α or more**, i.e. $dist(T', T)/dist(IT, T) < \alpha^{-1}$, then u modifies the header by overwriting intermediate-target with T'. If there is more than one such T', u picks the one closest to T. It forwards the packet to h'.

Note that GR corresponds to special case of GR' with $\alpha = 1$. We now prove some bounds on the expected actual path length of GR'. First we observe that the number of greedy virtual hops is at most logarithmic.

Lemma 1. *For any source s and target t, the number of greedy transitions in $GR'(s, t)$ is $O(\log_\alpha(N))$.*

Proof. We bound the number of greedy transitions by observing that in a greedy transition from m_i to m_{i+1}, the destination m_{i+1} is closer to t by a factor α. Hence, after at most $\log_\alpha(dist(s, t))$ greedy transitions we reach the target.

It remains to bound the number of non-greedy transitions. Recall that $D(s, t)$ denotes the total number of intermediate targets seen by the algorithm and that we bound the path length by bounding the size of $D(s, t)$. The key observation in this section is that the bound is parameterized by the likelihood of path intersection, formally defined below.

First recall the definition of intersection coefficient. We refer to a physical segment between two points chosen uniformly at random as a *random virtual hop*.

Definition 1. *Let $p = p(N)$ be such that two independent random virtual hops intersect with probability p. We say that the intersection coefficient of the set of paths is p.*

Now suppose that we were concerned about the probability that a random virtual hop intersects at least one of l other independent random virtual hops. The following definition defines conditions under which such probabilities can be estimated.

Definition 2. *A set of virtual hops $(s_1, t_1), \ldots, (s_l, t_l)$ are said to be almost mutually exclusive if for a random virtual hop (s, t), the probability that $PS(s, t)$ intersects one of the paths $PS(s_i, t_i)$ is at least $\frac{1}{2}lp$.*

Note that the expected number of i's such that $PS(s, t)$ intersects $PS(s_i, t_i)$ is in fact lp. However, these events are not independent, and not mutually exclusive.

Definition 3. *Let $p = p(N)$ be such that for a constant c and for any $l \in [1, \frac{1}{cp}]$, the probability that l random virtual hops are not almost mutually exclusive is at most polynomially small in the size of the network. Then we say that the group intersection coefficient is p.*

Lemma 2. *With high probability, for all pairs s, t it holds that $|D(s, t)|$ can be bounded by $O(\frac{\alpha \log(1/p) + \log_\alpha N}{\sqrt{p}})$, where the probability is taken over the choice of mapping id's to nodes.*

Proof. We first give some intuition for the proof. The number of greedy hops is clearly at most $O(\log_\alpha N)$. Consider the $\frac{1}{\sqrt{p}}$ virtual hops $(t - j - 1, t - j)$ for $j \in [1, \frac{1}{\sqrt{p}}]$ closest to the destination t in the ring. If we reached one of these virtual hops within the first $\frac{1}{\sqrt{p}}$ non-greedy hops in the routing, then we would get a bound of $O(\frac{1}{\sqrt{p}} + \log_\alpha N)$ on $|D(s, t)|$. What is the likelihood that the first $\frac{1}{\sqrt{p}}$ non-greedy hops in $D(s, t)$ do not reach this set? For this to happen, each of the $\frac{1}{\sqrt{p}}$ completed non-greedy hops must avoid hitting one of the $\frac{1}{\sqrt{p}}$ virtual hops close to the destination. Since this gives us $O(\frac{1}{p})$ pairs of virtual hops, and each pair intersects with probability p, this avoidance is unlikely. Of course there are dependencies to be taken care of and we formalize the argument below.

For any r, call the virtual hops $(t - j - 1, t - j)$ for $j \in [1, r]$ the *r-last hops*. Let k, l be parameters to be chosen later. We will argue that with high probability, within l virtual hops when routing from s to t, the current intermediate target is within distance αk in the virtual space.

Let $m_0, m_1, \ldots, m_l$ be the sequence of first l routing destinations set by GR. Of these, some $r < \log_\alpha N$ are chosen due to a greedy hop, let these be $m_{i_1}, \ldots, m_{i_r}$. Let a configuration C be defined by a set of at most $\log_\alpha N$ indices $i_1, \ldots, i_r$. For a fixed configuration C, we shall bound the probability that any sequence $m_0, m_1, \ldots, m_l$ has not hit the αk-last hops.

Let $D'(s, t)$ be the list of m_i's such that $i \notin \{i_j, i_j - 1, i_j + 1\}$. Let $l' = \lfloor \frac{1}{2}|D'(s, t)| \rfloor$. Clearly, $l' > \frac{l}{3} - 3\log_\alpha N$. $D'(s, t)$ contains at least l' disjoint pairs $(m_i, m_i + 1)$ such that $m_i - 1, m_i, m_i + 1, m_i + 2$ are all in $D(s, t)$.

The k-last hops consists of $k/2$ disjoint virtual hops. Thus except with poly-nomially small probability, these $k/2$ virtual hops are almost-mutually exclusive. Thus the virtual hop (m_i, m_{i+1}) intersects one of the k-last hops with proba-bility at least $kp/4$ (k is taken to be smaller than $\frac{1}{cp}$). Moreover, this event for (m_i, m_{i+1}) depends only on the random assignment of the virtual identifies m_i and m_{i+1} to physical nodes, and is therefore independent of the corresponding event for $(m_j, m_j + 1)$, for any $j : |j - i| > 1$.[1] Thus the probability that for a fixed configuration C, a prefix $m_0, \ldots, m_l$ exists that satisfies C but does not intersect the k-last hops is bounded by

$$(1 - \frac{kp}{4})^{l'}$$

Unless the prefix $m_0, \ldots, m_l$ has already hit the αk-last hops, any intersection with the k-last hops is a greedy step that GR' would have taken. Thus the above bounds the probability that for a fixed C, the prefix $m_0, \ldots, m_l$ defined by C has not reached the αk-last hops.

We next bound the number of configurations. There are $\binom{l}{r}$ ways of choosing the indices $i_1, \ldots, i_r$, and since $r \leq \log_\alpha N$, the number of configurations is at most

$$\log_\alpha N \binom{l}{\log_\alpha N}.$$

On the other hand, for $|D(s, t)|$ to be greater than $l + \alpha k$, the prefix $m_0, \ldots, m_l$ must not hit the αk-last hops. Thus the probability

$$Pr[|D(s, t)| > l + \alpha k)] \leq \log_\alpha N \binom{l}{\log_\alpha N} (1 - \frac{lp}{4})^{l/3 - 3 \log_\alpha N}.$$

The claim follows by plugging in the value of $l = O(\frac{\log_\alpha N}{\sqrt{p}})$ and $k = O(\frac{\log(1/p)}{\sqrt{p}})$. $\square$

Properties of the d-dimensional Grid

In this section we identify the intersection coefficient of the grid for a natural set of paths. Consider a d-dimensional grid with n^d nodes, each node can be identified by a d-dimensional vector in $[0, n - 1]^d$. Let $s = (s_1, \ldots, s_d)$ and $t = (t_1, \ldots, t_d)$ be two nodes. There are many shortest paths between them. Natural candidates for a collection of paths are paths that follow more or less the l_2 shortest path between the points. The paths we analyze, and use to drive the simulation are crude approximations. We randomly sample an intermediate node $w = (w_1, \ldots, w_d)$ where each w_i is uniformly sampled in $[s_i, t_i]$ and then route through w as follows: first route from from s to w by fixing the coordinates one after the other, i.e. first go to $(w_1, s_2, \ldots, s_d)$ and so on. Once w is reached, route

---

[1] There is in fact a small dependency here: since the mapping is a permutation, m_i cannot be mapped to the same location as m_j. However, this excludes at most $O(l)$ locations for m_i and m_{i+1}, and hence conditioning changes the probabilities by at most a $(1 - \frac{l}{N})$ factor, which is negligible and ignored for the rest of the proof.

to t by fixing the coordinates in reverse order, i.e. first go to $(w_1, w_2, \ldots, t_d)$ and so on. The node w is called the *intermediate routing node* of the path. Denote by $p(c) = cn^{-(d-2)}$. The next bound states that there is a way to chose c as a function of d such that p is the intersection coefficient of the network.

Lemma 3. *For every d there is c such that for every n, the intersection coefficient of the n^d grid is $p = cn^{-(d-2)}$.*

Proof. The proof is by induction on d. For $d = 2$, $p(c) = c$ so we need to show that the probability two virtual hops intersect is at least a constant independent of n. Intuitively this should hold because with constant probability both paths are roughly diagonals in the two-dimensional grid and thus intersect. A formal (and rather crude) argument is as follows: say the first source–target pair is $(s_1^{(1)}, s_2^{(1)})$ and $(t_1^{(1)}, t_2^{(1)})$. Similarly the second pair is $(s_1^{(2)}, s_2^{(2)})$ and $(t_1^{(2)}, t_2^{(2)})$. With probability 3^{-6} it holds that $s_1^{(1)}, s_2^{(1)} \leq n/3$ and $t_1^{(1)}, t_2^{(1)} \geq 2n/3$, and their intermediate node $(w_1^{(1)}, w_2^{(1)})$ satisfies that $w_1^{(1)}, w_2^{(1)} \in [n/3, 2n/3]$. In other words the path $s^{(1)} \to t^{(1)}$ is a diagonal. Similarly with probability 3^{-6} the path $s^{(2)} \to t^{(2)}$ is the crossing diagonal, i.e. $s_1^{(2)}, t_2^{(2)} \leq n/3$ and $t_1^{(2)}, s_2^{(2)} \geq 2n/3$, and $w_1^{(2)}, w_2^{(2)} \in [n/3, 2n/3]$. If both these events occur then the paths intersect.

Now assume $d > 2$. Let $w^{(1)}$ and $w^{(2)}$ denote the intermediate hops. If $w^{(1)}$ and $w^{(2)}$ agree in the first $(d-2)$ co-ordinates, then the probability of intersection is at least c using the two-dimensional case. Since $w^{(1)}$ and $w^{(2)}$ are drawn from the same probability distribution, the probability that they agree on the first $(d-2)$ co-ordinates is at least $n^{-(d-2)}$: the collision probability for a distribution is maximized when it is uniform, in which case we get the $n^{-(d-2)}$ bound. Moreover, it is easy to check that the collision probability is at least $(an)^{-(d-2)}$ for a constant a. The claim follows.   □

Lemma 4. *For every d there is c such that for every n, the group intersection coefficient of the n^d grid is $p = cn^{-(d-2)}$.*

Proof. The proof is very similar to the previous lemma. For $d = 2$, there is nothing to prove since l is at most 1.

Now assume $d > 2$. Let $w^{(1)}, \ldots, w^{(l)}$ denote the intermediate hops of the l virtual hops, and let $w^{(*)}$ denote the intermediate hop for (s, t). If $w^{(*)}$ agrees with one of the $w^{(i)}$'s in the first $(d-2)$ co-ordinates, then the probability of intersection is at least c using the two-dimensional case. Since $w^{(1)}, \ldots, w^{(l)}$ are drawn from the same probability distribution and $l < \frac{1}{cp}$ they span at least $l/2$ different values for the first $(d-2)$ co-ordinates with high probability. The claim follows.   □

Lower Bound

Lemma 5. *If $dist(s, t) = \frac{1}{10\sqrt{p}}$ then with probability at least 0.99 the size of $D(s, t)$ is at least $\frac{1}{10\sqrt{p}}$.*

Proof. We calculate the probability there is a greedy hop in the path. In total there are $\frac{1}{100p}$ pairs of paths. Each of them intersects with probability p so on expectation there are $1/100$ intersections. Markov's inequality implies that the probability there is at least one greedy hop is at most 0.01.   □

We can also show the following result, the proof of which is omitted from this extended abstract:

Lemma 6. *For* $1 < s < t < N - 1$, *we have*

$$E[D(s, t+1)] \geq \min\{E[D(s,t)], \frac{1}{10\sqrt{p}}\}.$$

The above two lemmas imply that for randomly chosen s and t the expected size of $D(s,t)$ is $\Omega(\frac{1}{\sqrt{p}})$. Thus our upper bound is tight up to logarithmic factors.

4 Simulation

We simulate a family of VRR schemes over d-dimensional grids. The challenging aspect of our simulation is scaling. In order to demonstrate asymptotic trends, we want to test networks of considerable sizes. This cannot be done naively. The fundamental routing step in VRR scheme involves a routing-table lookup. Naively simulated, this requires maintaining $O(n \times$ routing table size) information. For some of the topologies we consider, this prohibits simulating networks beyond 2^{20} nodes ($\approx 2^{30}$ entries $\approx$ 8GB memory). Though this is already quite sizable, we devised a simulation technique that can scale even higher. We first describe the simulation technique, and then present the result.

4.1 Simulation Framework

The underlying (physical) networks in our simulation are d-dimensional grids with n nodes on each side (and $N = n^d$ nodes in total). Nodes have integral physical identifiers from 0 to $n^d - 1$, assigned so as to allow a node's position in the grid to be easily retrieved from its identifier (and vice-versa).

In our simulation, we take $sp(u, v)$, a shortest path, as the physical segment $PS(u, v)$ between neighboring nodes u and v in the virtual space. In general, these paths are not unique in a d-dimensional cube; we pick paths that we analyzed in the previous section.

Suppose we are computing the route to a (virtual) target t and let v be the current vertex. VRR schemes need to examine v's routing table and find the intermediate target t' that is the closest (in the virtual space) predecessor of t in the ring.

Memory constraints prevent us from storing the routing tables explicitly when simulating very large networks. Instead, we check all possible candidates for t' (starting at t, then $t - 1$, then $t - 2$, and so on) until we find one that would actually be an intermediate target in v's routing table. For each candidate t', we must check if there is a physical segment that crosses v. Such a segment would have as endpoints t' and a virtual neighbor of t', denoted by s'. Let $S(t')$ be the set of virtual sources s' such that (s', t') is a physical segment. Note that $S(t')$ is just $\{t' - 1\}$ in a simple ring, but in other overlay topologies we experiment with, it is a set. For each $s' \in S(t')$, we can check in $O(d)$ time whether v belongs to the physical segment from s' to t'. If it does, we can stop: t' is the best entry in v's routing table.

Implicit mapping. Even storing the mapping of nodes to virtual identities (with quick reverse lookup) is quite costly for sizable networks, and we avoid that. Our simulation picks as the virtual identifiers a (pseudo-)random permutation of $[0, n^d - 1]$. We do not maintain the permutation explicitly in memory. Instead, we keep it implicitly with the Luby-Rackoff scheme [9], which works as follows.

Assume node identifiers have exactly $2k$ bits (i.e., $N = 2^{2k}$). We must define a permutation $\pi : \{0, 1\}^{2k} \rightarrow \{0, 1\}^{2k}$, so that a node with physical identifier x has virtual identifier $\pi(x)$. An identifier $x = (L, R)$ can be seen as the concatenation of its first k bits (L) and last k bits (R). Define $\pi(x)$ as $\pi(L, R) = (R, f(R) \oplus L)$, where $f : \{0, 1\}^k \rightarrow \{0, 1\}^k$ is an auxiliary pseudorandom function. It is easy to see that $\pi(x)$ produces a permutation of all $2k$-bit strings. When f is sampled from a family of one-way functions, Luby and Rackoff proved that it suffices to iterate π four times, sampling a fresh function each time, to obtain a pseudo-random permutation. Therefore, to convert a physical identifier x into the corresponding virtual identifier, we simply compute $\pi^*(x) = \pi(\pi(\pi(\pi(x))))$. To convert a virtual identifier to a physical identifier, we use the inverse function $\pi^{-1}(x) = \pi^{-1}(L, R) = (f(L) \oplus R, L)$, also iterated four times.

To determine $f(X)$ (where X is a k-bit string), our implementation concatenates X with a user-defined 32-bit seed s, calculates the 128-bit MD5 hash of the resulting string, and discards all but the first k bits of the result. These operations (in particular the MD5 computation) are costly in practice. To speed up the simulation, we use two levels of caching. We remember the first C pairs $(x, \pi^*(x))$ that we evaluate, as well as the result of every $f(X)$ computation we ever perform (the corresponding table, with $\sqrt{N}$ entries, is small enough to fit in memory). We used $C = 2.5 \cdot 10^8$ in our experiments.

4.2   Results

We start our experiments with the most basic version of VRR, in which each vertex has a single virtual neighbor in the ring (i.e., $|S(v)| = 1$ for every v). Table 1 shows the results obtained for grids with 2, 3, and 4 dimensions and various sizes. Every entry in the table was computed from 1000 routes. The endpoints of each route are two nodes picked uniformly at random. Each route uses a different pseudorandom mapping between physical and virtual nodes.

For each instance size, we report the average shortest path length and the average actual routing path length. The ratio between these two is the *aggregate stretch*, which is our main performance measure and is reported in the last column. For reference, we also report the 99th percentile of the actual path length (over all 1000 routes).

Table 1. Simple ring simulation results. Columns are: Grid dimensionality; network size; average nodes on shortest path; average nodes on actual routing path; 99th percentile of nodes on actual routing path; 99th percentile stretch; aggregate stretch.

DIM	NODES	SHRT. PATH	NODES AVG	99TH	STRETCH 99TH	AGGR.
2	2^{24}	2685	7679	18548	18.75	2.86
	2^{26}	5539	15494	37511	26.37	2.80
	2^{28}	10720	31141	70889	23.36	2.90
	2^{30}	22113	61979	141664	21.80	2.80
	2^{32}	43456	120237	300127	23.02	2.77
3	2^{12}	16	94	212	34.01	5.83
	2^{18}	65	736	1714	51.00	11.35
	2^{24}	255	5797	13986	112.76	22.75
	2^{30}	1031	45180	111140	270.81	43.82
4	2^{20}	42	1316	3200	118.05	31.23
	2^{24}	86	5295	12844	301.34	61.86
	2^{28}	170	21087	49399	504.08	123.89
	2^{32}	342	85614	193431	1002.67	250.10

Recall that the intersection coefficient is $p \in O(N^{-\frac{d-2}{d}})$, and the expected stretch is proportional to $1/\sqrt{p}$. Hence, for the two-dimensional case, the expected stretch is constant; for $d = 3$, when we grow N by a factor of 2^6, we expect the average stretch to grow by a factor $(2^6)^{1/6} = 2$; and for $d = 4$, when growing N by factor 2^4, the stretch is expected to grow by factor $(2^4)^{1/4} = 2$. Table 1 indeed demonstrates these trends.

Other Overlay Structures. We considered two variations of the simple VRR ring. As suggested in the original VRR work, we vary the number c of ring successors to which each node maintains connections.

Additionally, we considered a variation in which the overlay topology has sublinear hop diameter. The idea here is that even without the effect of path intersection and greedy hops, the stretch is bounded by the routing complexity of the overlay network. Specifically, we introduce a small change, one that would not impair the spirit and practical value of VRR scheme. Borrowing from *small world* extensions of ring overlays [3], we replace the c-th neighbor of a node v with $v - 2^j$, where j is an integer picked uniformly at random from the range $[\lceil \log_2 c \rceil, (\log_2 N) - 1]$.

Table 2 shows the average aggregate stretch (over 1000 seeds) for the various topologies.

Increasing the size of virtual neighborhoods reduces the average stretch, since the intersection coefficient increases correspondingly. The asymptotic trends remain the same with increased neighborhood sizes (on a simple ring). The effect of small world links become noticeable only with four dimensions, and fairly large network size. This is when the polylogarithmic effect of small world routing starts dominating the simple ring stretch of $O(N^{d-2/2d}) = O(N^{1/4})$.

Table 2. Simulation results with varying overlay topologies, with 1, 2, and 5 virtual neighbors. The small world variations are denoted with a '$*$'

NETWORK		NEIGHBORHOOD SIZE				
DIM	NODES	1	2	2*	5	5*
2	2^{24}	2.86	2.24	2.25	1.73	1.68
	2^{26}	2.80	2.16	2.16	1.76	1.66
	2^{28}	2.90	2.24	2.29	1.82	1.74
	2^{30}	2.80	2.23	2.20	1.78	1.72
	2^{32}	2.77	2.20	2.23	1.80	1.74
3	2^{12}	5.83	3.72	3.99	2.47	2.42
	2^{18}	11.35	6.90	7.45	4.01	3.99
	2^{24}	22.75	13.34	13.72	7.30	7.21
	2^{30}	43.82	26.42	24.10	12.51	12.69
4	2^{20}	31.23	18.55	17.72	8.98	8.81
	2^{24}	61.86	34.56	27.70	16.46	15.46
	2^{28}	123.89	69.58	42.73	31.93	27.27
	2^{32}	250.10	136.60	66.98	63.12	48.26

Table 3. Average aggregate stretch with different α values

NETWORK		GREEDY FACTOR (α)		
DIM	NODES	20	2	1
2	2^{24}	3.67	2.95	2.86
	2^{26}	3.62	2.86	2.80
	2^{28}	3.65	2.96	2.90
	2^{30}	3.69	2.92	2.80
	2^{32}	3.54	2.80	2.77
3	2^{12}	8.31	6.10	5.83
	2^{18}	18.14	12.63	11.35
	2^{24}	38.63	25.14	22.75
	2^{30}	77.17	49.97	43.82
4	2^{20}	55.14	34.11	31.23
	2^{24}	108.56	68.85	61.86
	2^{28}	218.14	138.10	123.89
	2^{32}	426.98	279.61	250.10

Modified Greedy Routing. Finally, we examine the effect of modifying the greedy hop criterion as suggested in our analysis section above. We introduce into the VRR scheme a parameter α, and allow a greedy hop to occur only when the intermediate routing target is improved by a factor α. When $\alpha = 1$ (as in the experiments reported so far), the routing algorithm performs every greedy step it can. For larger values of α, a greedy step (i.e., a change of the intermediate target) happens only if the gap to the final target (in the virtual space) is reduced by factor α.

Table 3 shows the average aggregate stretch (over 1000 routes) for three values of α: 20, 2, and 1. The results show that setting α to 2 has little effect on the performance of the routing algorithm.

As a final note, while running the experiments above, we observed that in a typical path most of the hops in a route are close (in the virtual space) to the target. Let the *median target* of a route with h nodes be the intermediate target of the algorithm when the $(h/2)$-th node is visited. With $\alpha = 1$, on average the median target was less than $\log_2 N$ hops away from the target in two dimensions. Even in higher dimensions, the average gap was always smaller than $\log^2 N$.

5 Conclusions

We have theoretically and empirically analyzed Virtual Ring Routing. We show that for a 2-dimensional grid, VRR indeed gives expected path length which is at most $O(\log N)$ times the diameter. On the other hand, for a d-dimensional grid, we show that the expected path length is at least $\Omega(N^{\frac{d-2}{2d}})$ times the diameter of the graph. We note that for the two-dimensional case, our bound only shows a bound of $O(Diam \cdot \log N)$ on the routing path length. Empirically, VRR does not seem to exhibit good *locality* properties. It would be interesting to investigate this question further.

References

1. Abraham, I., Gavoille, C., Malkhi, D.: On space-stretch trade-offs: Upper bounds. In: ACM Symposium on Parallel Algorithms and Architectures (SPAA) (July 2006)
2. Abraham, I., Gavoille, C., Malkhi, D.: Compact routing for graphs excluding a fixed minor. In: Fraigniaud, P. (ed.) DISC 2005. LNCS, vol. 3724, pp. 442–456. Springer, Heidelberg (2005)
3. Barrière, L., Fraigniaud, P., Kranakis, E., Krizanc, D.: Efficient routing in networks with long range contacts. In: Welch, J.L. (ed.) DISC 2001. LNCS, vol. 2180, pp. 270–284. Springer, Heidelberg (2001)
4. Caesar, M., Castro, M., Nightingale, E.B., O'Shea, G., Rowstron, A.: Virtual ring routing: Network routing inspired by DHTs. In: ACM annual conference of the Special Interest Group on Data Communication (SIGCOMM), pp. 351–362 (2006)
5. Caesar, M., Condie, T., Kannan, J., Lakshminarayanan, K., Stoica, I., Shenker, S.: ROFL: Routing on flat labels. In: ACM annual conference of the Special Interest Group on Data Communication (SIGCOMM) (September 2006)
6. Cheng, B.-N., Yuksel, M., Kalyanaraman, S.: Orthogonal rendezvous routing protocol for wireless mesh networks. In: IEEE International Conference on Network Protocols (2006)
7. Gavoille, C.: Routing in distributed networks: Overview and open problems. ACM SIGACT News - Distributed Computing Column 32(1), 36–52 (2001)
8. Kim, C., Caesar, M., Rexford, J.: Floodless in SEATTLE: a scalable ethernet architecture for large enterprises. In: ACM annual conference of the Special Interest Group on Data Communication (SIGCOMM), pp. 3–14 (2008)
9. Luby, M., Rackoff, C.: How to construct pseudorandom permutations and pseudo-random functions. SIAM J. Comput. 17, 373–386 (1988)

10. Mao, Y., Wang, F., Qiu, L., Lam, S.S., Smith, J.M.: S4: Small state and small stretch routing protocol for large wireless sensor networks. In: 4th USENIX Symposium on Networked Systems Design and Implementation (NSDI) (2007)
11. Pucha, H., Das, S.M., Hu, Y.C.: Imposed route reuse in ad hoc network routing protocols using structured peer-to-peer overlay routing. IEEE Transactions on Parallel and Distributed Systems (2006)
12. Westphal, C., Kempf, J.: A compact routing architecture for mobility. In: MobiArch 2008: Proceedings of the 3rd international workshop on Mobility in the Evolving Internet Architecture, pp. 1–6. ACM Press, New York (2008)

A New Self-stabilizing Minimum Spanning Tree Construction with Loop-Free Property

Lélia Blin[1], Maria Potop-Butucaru[1], Stephane Rovedakis[2], and Sébastien Tixeuil[1]

[1] Univ. Pierre & Marie Curie - Paris 6,
LIP6-CNRS UMR 7606, France
{lelia.blin,maria.gradinariu,sebastien.tixeuil}@lip6.fr
[2] Université d'Evry, IBISC, CNRS FRE 3190, France
stephane.rovedakis@ibisc.univ-evry.fr

Abstract. The minimum spanning tree (MST) construction is a classical problem in Distributed Computing for creating a globally minimized structure distributedly. Self-stabilization is versatile technique for forward recovery that permits to handle any kind of transient faults in a unified manner. The loop-free property provides interesting safety assurance in dynamic networks where edge-cost changes during operation of the protocol.

We present a new self-stabilizing MST protocol that improves on previous known approaches in several ways. First, it makes fewer system hypotheses as the size of the network (or an upper bound on the size) need *not* be known to the participants. Second, it is loop-free in the sense that it guarantees that a spanning tree structure is always preserved while edge costs change dynamically and the protocol adjusts to a new MST. Finally, time complexity matches the best known results, while space complexity results show that this protocol is the most efficient to date.

1 Introduction

Since its introduction in a centralized context [25,22], the minimum spanning tree (or MST) construction problem gained a benchmark status in distributed computing thanks to the influential seminal work of [13]. Given an edge-weighted graph $G = (V, E, w)$, where w denotes the edge-weight function, the MST problem consist in computing a tree T spanning V, such that T has minimum weight among all spanning trees of G.

One of the most versatile techniques to ensure forward recovery of distributed systems is that of *self-stabilization* [6,7]. A distributed algorithm is self-stabilizing if after faults and attacks hit the system and place it in some arbitrary global state, the system recovers from this catastrophic situation without external (*e.g.* human) intervention in finite time. A recent trend in self-stabilizing research is to complement the self-stabilizing abilities of a distributed algorithm with some additional *safety* properties that are guaranteed when the permanent and intermittent failures that hit the system satisfy some conditions. In addition to being self-stabilizing, a protocol could thus also tolerate a limited number of topology changes [9], crash faults [15,2], nap faults [10,23], Byzantine faults [11,3], and sustained edge cost changes [4,20].

This last property is especially relevant when building spanning trees in dynamic networks, since the cost of a particular edge is likely to evolve through time. If an MST

I. Keidar (Ed.): DISC 2009, LNCS 5805, pp. 407–422, 2009.
© Springer-Verlag Berlin Heidelberg 2009

protocol is *only* self-stabilizing, it may adjust to the new costs in such a way that a previously constructed MST evolves into a disconnected or a looping structure (of course, in the abscence of new edge cost changes, the self-stabilization property guarantees that *eventually* a new MST is constructed). Of course, if edge costs change unexpectedly and continuously, an MST cannot be maintained at all times. Now, a packet routing algorithm is *loop free* [14,12] if at any point in time the routing tables are free of loops, despite possible modification of the edge-weights in the graph (*i.e.*, for any two nodes u and v, the actual routing tables determines a simple path from u to v, at any time). The *loop-free* property [4,20] in self-stabilization guarantees that, a spanning tree being constructed (not necessarily an MST), then the self-stabilizing convergence to a "minimal" (for some metric) spanning tree maintains a spanning tree at all times (obviously, this spanning tree is not "minimal" at all times). The consequence of this safety property in addition to that of self-stabiization is that the spanning tree structure can still be used (e.g. for routing) while the protocol is adjusting, and makes it suitable for networks that undergo such very frequent dynamic changes.

Related works. Gupta and Srimani [18] have presented the first self-stabilizing algorithm for the MST problem. It applies on graphs whose nodes have unique identifiers, whose edges have integer edge weights, and a weight can appear at most once in the whole network. To construct the (unique) MST, every node performs the same algorithm. The MST construction is based on the computation of all the shortest paths (for a certain cost function) between all the pairs of nodes. While executing the algorithm, every node stores the cost of all paths from it to all the other nodes. To implement this algorithm, the authors assume that every node knows the number n of nodes in the network, and that the identifiers of the nodes are in $\{1, \ldots, n\}$. Every node u stores the weight of the edge $e_{u,v}$ placed in the MST for each node $v \neq u$. Therefore the algorithm requires $\Omega(\sum_{v \neq u} \log w(e_{u,v}))$ bits of memory at node u. Since all the weights are distinct integers, the memory requirement at each node is $\Omega(n \log n)$ bits.

Higham and Lyan [19] have proposed another self-stabilizing algorithm for the MST problem. As in [18], their work applies to undirected connected graphs with unique integer edge weights and unique node identifiers, where every node has an upper bound on the number of nodes in the system. The algorithm performs roughly as follows: every edge aims at deciding whether it eventually belongs to the MST or not. For this purpose, every non tree-edge e floods the network to find a potential cycle, and when e receives its own message back along a cycle, it uses information collected by this message (*i.e.*, the maximum edge weight of the traversed cycle) to decide whether e could potentially be in the MST or not. If the edge e has not received its message back after the time-out interval, it decides to become tree edge. The core memory of each node holds only $O(\log n)$ bits, but the information exchanged between neighboring nodes is of size $O(n \log n)$ bits, thus only slightly improving that of [18].

To our knowledge, *none* of the self-stabilizing MST construction protocols is loop-free. Since the aforementioned two protocols also make use of the knowledge of the global number of nodes in the system, and assume that no two edge costs can be equal, these extra hypoteses make them suitable for static networks only.

Relatively few works investigate merging self-stabilization and loop free routing, with the notable exception of [4,20]. While [4] still requires that a upper bound on the

Table 1. Distributed Self-Stabilizing algorithms for the MST and loop-free SP problems

	metric	size known	unique weights	memory usage	loop-free
[18]	**MST**	yes	yes	$O(n \log n)$	no
[19]	**MST**	upper bound	yes	$O(n \log n)$	no
[4]	SP	upper bound	**no**	$\Theta(\log n)$	**yes**
[20]	SP	**no**	**no**	$\Theta(\log n)$	**yes**
This paper	**MST**	**no**	**no**	$O(\log n)$	**yes**

network diameter is known to every participant, no such assumption is made in [20]. Also, both protocols use only a reasonable amount of memory ($O(\log n)$ bits per node). However, the metrics that are considered in [4,20] are derivative of the shortest path (*a.k.a.* SP) metric, that is considered a much easier task in the distributed setting than that of the MST, since the associated metric is *locally optimizable* [17], allowing essentially locally greedy approaches to perform well. By contrast, some sort of *global optimization* is needed for MST, which often drives higher complexity costs and thus less flexibility in dynamic networks.

Our contributions. We describe a new self-stabilizing algorithm for the MST problem. Contrary to previous self-stabilizing MST protocols, our algorithm does not make any assumption about the network size (including upper bounds) or the unicity of the edge weights. Moreover, our solution improves on the memory space usage since each participant needs only $O(\log n)$ bits[1], and node identifiers are not needed.

In addition to improving over system hypotheses and complexity, our algorithm provides additional safety properties to self-stabilization, as it is loop-free. Compared to previous protocols that are both self-stabilizing and loop-free, our protocol is the first to consider non-monotonous tree metrics.

The key techniques that are used in our scheme include fast construction of a spanning tree, that is continuously improved by means of a pre-order construction over the nodes. The cycles that are considered over time are precisely those obtained by adding one edge to the evolving spanning tree. Considering solely that type of cycles reduces the memory requirement at each node compared to [18,19] because the latter consider all possible paths connecting pairs of nodes. Moreover, constructing and using a pre-order on the nodes allows our algorithm to proceed in a completely asynchronous manner, and without any information about the size of the network, as opposed to [18,19]. The main characteristics of our solution are presented in Table 1, where a boldface denotes the most useful (or efficient) feature for a particular criterium.

2   Model and Notations

We consider an undirected weighted connected network $G = (V, E, w)$ where V is the set of nodes, E is the set of edges and $w : E \to \mathbb{R}^+$ is a positive cost function. Nodes

---

[1] Note that one may use the techniques proposed in [1] in order to construct a self-stabilizing MST starting from non-stabilizing solutions. This technique would increase the memory complexity.

represent processors and edges represent bidirectional communication links. Additionally, we consider that $G = (V, E, w)$ is a network in which the weight of the communication links may change value. We consider anonymous networks (i.e., the processors have no IDs), with one distinguished node, called the *root*[2]. Throughout the paper, the root is denoted r. We denote by $\deg(v)$ the number of v's neighbors in G. The $\deg(v)$ edges incident to any node v are labeled from 1 to $\deg(v)$, so that a processor can distinguish the different edges incident to a node.

The processors asynchronously execute their programs consisting of a set of variables and a finite set of rules. The variables are part of the shared register which is used to communicate with the neighbors. A processor can read and write its own registers and can read the shared registers of its neighbors. Each processor executes a program consisting of a sequence of guarded rules. Each *rule* contains a *guard* (boolean expression over the variables of a node and its neighborhood) and an *action* (update of the node variables only). Any rule whose guard is *true* is said to be *enabled*. A node with one or more enabled rules is said to be *privileged* and may make a *move* executing the action corresponding to the chosen enabled rule.

A *local state* of a node is the value of the local variables of the node and the state of its program counter. A *configuration* of the system $G = (V, E)$ is the cross product of the local states of all nodes in the system. The transition from a configuration to the next one is produced by the execution of an action at a node. A *computation* of the system is defined as a *weakly fair, maximal* sequence of configurations, $e = (c_0, c_1, \ldots c_i, \ldots)$, where each configuration c_{i+1} follows from c_i by the execution of a single action of at least one node. During an execution step, one or more processors execute an action and a processor may take at most one action. *Weak fairness* of the sequence means that if any action in G is continuously enabled along the sequence, it is eventually chosen for execution. *Maximality* means that the sequence is either infinite, or it is finite and no action of G is enabled in the final global state.

In the sequel we consider the system can start in any configuration. That is, the local state of a node can be corrupted. Note that we don't make any assumption on the bound of corrupted nodes. In the worst case all the nodes in the system may start in a corrupted configuration. In order to tackle these faults we use self-stabilization techniques.

Definition 1 (self-stabilization). *Let $\mathcal{L}_A$ be a non-empty legitimacy predicate[3] of an algorithm A with respect to a specification predicate $Spec$ such that every configuration satisfying $\mathcal{L}_A$ satisfies $Spec$. Algorithm A is self-stabilizing with respect to $Spec$ iff the following two conditions hold:*

---

[2] Observe that the two self-stabilizing MST algorithms mentioned in the Previous Work section assume that the nodes have distinct IDs with no distinguished nodes. Nevertheless, if the nodes have distinct IDs then it is possible to elect one node as a leader in a self-stabilizing manner. Conversely, if there exists one distinguished node in an anonymous network, then it is possible to assign distinct IDs to the nodes in a self-stabilizing manner [8]. Note that it is not possible to compute deterministically an MST in a fully anonymous network (i.e., without any distinguished node), as proved in [18].

[3] A legitimacy predicate is defined over the configurations of a system and is an indicator of its correct behavior.

(i) Every computation of $\mathcal{A}$ starting from a configuration satisfying $\mathcal{L}_{\mathcal{A}}$ preserves $\mathcal{L}_{\mathcal{A}}$ (closure).

(ii) Every computation of $\mathcal{A}$ starting from an arbitrary configuration contains a configuration that satisfies $\mathcal{L}_{\mathcal{A}}$ (convergence).

We define bellow a *loop-free* configuration of a system as a configuration which contains paths with no cycle between any couple of nodes in the system. Given two nodes $u, v \in V$, we note $P(u, v)$ the path between u and v.

Definition 2 (Loop-Free Configuration). *Let $Cycle(u, v)$ be the following predicate defined for two nodes $u, v \in V$ on configuration C: $Cycle(u, v) \equiv \exists P(u, v), P(v, u) : P(u, v) \cap P(v, u) = \emptyset$.*
A loop-free configuration is a configuration of the system which satisfies: $\forall u, v \in V, Cycle(u, v) = false$.

We use the definition of a loop-free configuration to define a *loop-free stabilizing* system.

Definition 3 (Loop-Free Stabilization). *A distributed system is called loop-free stabilizing if and only if it is self-stabilizing and there exists a non-empty set of configurations such that the following conditions hold: (i) Every computation starting from a loop-free configuration reaches a loop-free configuration (closure). (ii) Every computation starting from an arbitrary configuration contains a loop-free configuration (convergence).*

In the sequel we study the loop-free self-stabilizing LoopFreeMSTproblem. The legitimacy predicate $\mathcal{L}_{\mathcal{A}}$ for the LoopFreeMSTproblem is the conjunction of the following two predicates: (i) a tree T spanning the network is constructed. (ii) T is a minimum spanning tree of G (i.e., $\forall T', W(T) \leq W(T')$, with T' be a spanning tree of G and $W(S) = \sum_{e \in S} w(e)$ be the cost of the subgraph S).

3   The Algorithm LoopFreeMST

In this section, we describe our self-stabilizing algorithm for the MST problem. We call this algorithm LoopFreeMST. Let us begin by an informal description of LoopFreeMST aiming at underlining its main features.

3.1   High Level Description

LoopFreeMST is based on the red rule. That is, for constructing an MST, the algorithm successively deletes the edges of maximum weight within every cycle. For this purpose, a spanning tree is maintained, together with a pre-order labeling of its nodes. Given the current spanning tree T maintained by our algorithm, every edge e of the graph that is not in the spanning tree creates an unique cycle in the graph when added to T. This cycle is called *fundamental cycle*, and is denoted by C_e. (Formally, this cycle depends on T; Nevertheless no confusion should arise from omitting T in the notation of C_e). If $w(e)$ is not the maximum weight of all the edges in C_e, then, according to the red rule, our algorithm swaps e with the edge f of C_e with maximum weight . This swapping procedure is called an *improvement*. A straightforward consequence of the red rule is that if no improvements are possible then the current spanning tree is a minimum one.

Algorithm LoopFreeMST can be decomposed in three procedures: (i) Tree construction, (ii) Token label circulation, (iii) Cycle improvement.

The latter procedure (Cycle improvement) is in fact the core of our contribution. Indeed, the two first procedures are simple modifications of existing self-stabilizing algorithms, one for building a spanning tree, and the other for labelling its nodes. We will show how to compose the original procedure "Cycle improvement" with these two existing procedures. Note that "Cycle improvement" differs from the previous self-stabilizing implementation of the improvement swapping in [19] by the fact that it does not require any a priori knowledge of the network, and it is loop-free.

LoopFreeMST starts by constructing a spanning tree of the graph, using the self-stabilizing loop-free algorithm "Tree construction" described in [21]. The two other procedures are performed concurrently. A token circulates along the edges of the current spanning tree, in a self-stabilizing manner. This token circulation uses algorithms proposed in [5,24] as follows. A non-tree-edge can belong to at most one fundamental cycle, but a tree-edge can belong to several fundamental cycles. Therefore, to avoid simultaneous possibly conflicting improvements, our algorithm considers the cycles in order. For this purpose, the token labels the nodes of the current tree in a DFS order (pre-order). This labeling is then used to find the unique path between two nodes in the spanning tree in a distributed manner, and enables computing the fundamental cycle resulting from adding one edge to the current spanning tree.

We now sketch the description of the procedure "Cycle improvement" (see Figure 1). When the token arrives at a node u in a state Done, it checks whether u has some incident edges not in the current spanning tree T connecting u with some other node v with smaller label. If it is the case, then enters state Verify. Let $e = \{u, v\}$. Node u then initiates a traversal of the fundamental cycle C_e for finding the edge f with maximum weight in this cycle. If $w(f) = w(e)$ then no improvement is performed. Else an improvement is possible, and u enters State Improve. Exchanging e and f in T results in a new tree T'. When the improvement is terminated u enters in State end. The key issue here is to perform this exchange in a loop-free manner. Indeed, one cannot be sure that

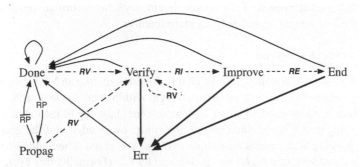

Fig. 1. Evolution of the node's state in cycle improvement module. Rule R_D is depicted in plain. Rule R_{Err} is depicted in bold.

two modifications of the current tree (i.e., removing f from T, and adding e to T) that are applied at two distant nodes will occur simultaneously. And if they do not occur simultaneously, then there will be a time interval during which the nodes will not be connected by a spanning tree. Our solution for preserving loop-freedomless relies on a sequence of successive local and atomic changes, involving a single variable. This variable is a pointer to the current parent of a node in the current spanning tree. To get the flavor of our method, let us consider the example depicted on Figure 2. In this example, our algorithm has to exchange the edge $e = \{10, 12\}$ of weight 9, with the edge $f = \{7, 8\}$ of weight 10 (Figure 2(a)). Currently, the token is at node 12. The improvement is performed in two steps, by a sequence of two local changes. First, node 10 switches its parent from 8 to 12 (Figure 2(b)). Next, node 8 switches its parent from 7 to 10 (Figure 2(c)). A spanning tree is preserved at any time during the execution of these changes.

Note that any modification of the spanning tree makes the current labeling globally inaccurate, i.e., it is not necessarily a pre-order anymore. However, the labeling remains a pre-order in the portion of the tree involved in the exchange. For instance, consider again the example depicted on Figure 2(c). When the token will eventually reach node A, it will label it by some label $\ell > 12$. The exchange of $e = \{10, 12\}$ and $f = \{7, 8\}$ has not changed the pre-order for the fundamental cycle including edge $\{A, 12\}$. However, when the token will eventually reach node B and label it $\ell' > \ell$, the exchange of $e = \{10, 12\}$ and $f = \{7, 8\}$ has changed the pre-order for the fundamental cycle including edge $\{B, 9\}$: the parent of node labeled 10 is labeled 12 whereas it should have a label smaller than 10 in a pre-order. When the pre-order is modified by an exchange, the inaccurately labeled node changes its state to Err, and stops the traversal of the fundamental cycle. The token is then informed that it can discard this cycle, and carry on the traversal of the tree.

3.2 Detailed Level Description

We now enter into the details of Algorithm LoopFreeMST. First, let us state all variables used by the algorithm. Later on, we will describe its predicates and its rules.

Variables. For any node $v \in V(G)$, we denote by $N(v)$ the set of all neighbors of v in G. Algorithm LoopFreeMST maintains the set $N(v)$ at every node v. We use the following notations:

- parent$_v$: the parent of v in the current spanning tree;
- label$_v$: the integer label assigned to v;
- d_v: the distance (in hops) from v to the root in the current spanning tree;
- state$_v$: the state of node v, with values in {Done, Verify, Improve, End, Propag, Err}[4];
- DefCycle$_v$: Let C_e the current fundamental cycle with $e = \{x, y\}$, DefCycle$_v$ = (x, y) .
- VarCycle$_v$: a pair of variables: the first one is the maximum edge-weight in the current fundamental cycle; the second one is a (boolean) variable in {Before, After};[5]
- suc$_v$: the successor of v in the current fundamental cycle.

---

[4] The state Propag is detailed in Consistency rules.
[5] For details see paragraph 3.2 Cycle improvement rules.

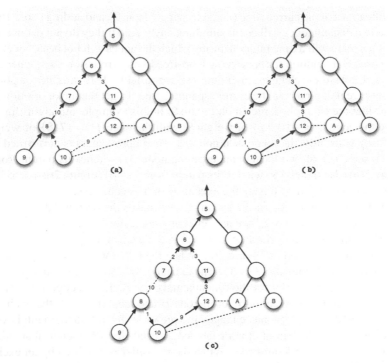

Fig. 2. Example of a loop-free improvement of the current spanning tree. The direction of the edges indicates the parent relation. Edges in the spanning tree are depicted as plain lines; Edges not in the spanning tree are denoted by dotted lines.

Consistency rules. The first task executed by **LoopFreeMST** is to check the consistency of the variables of each node see Figure 1. Done is the standard state of a node when this node does not have the token, or is not currently visited by the traversal of a fundamental cycle. When the variables of a node are detected to be not coherent, the state of the node becomes Err thanks to rule R_{Err}. There is one predicate in R_{Err} for each state, except for state Propag, to check whether the variables of the node are consistent (see Figure 3). The rule R_D allows the node to return to the standard state Done. More precisely, rule R_D resets the variables, and stops the participation of the node to any improvement.

R_{Err}: **(Bad label)**
    If CoherentCycle(v) $\land$ Error(v) $\land$ DefCycle$[0]_v \neq$ label$_v$ $\land$ EndPropag(v)
    then state$_v :=$ Err;
R_D: **(Improvement consistency)**
    If $\neg$CoherentCycle(v) $\land$ EndPropag(v)
    then state$_v :=$ Done; DefCycle$_v :=$ (label$_v$, done); VarCycle$_v :=$ (0, Before);
        suc$_v := \emptyset$;

Tree construction. **LoopFreeMST** starts by constructing a spanning tree of the graph, using the self-stabilizing loop-free algorithm "Tree construction" described in [21].

$\text{CoherentCycle}(v) \equiv \text{Coherent\_Done}(v) \lor \text{Coherent\_Verify}(v) \lor \text{Coherent\_Improve}(v) \lor$
$\qquad\qquad\qquad \text{Coherent\_End}(v) \lor \text{Coherent\_Error}(v)$

$\text{Coherent\_Done}(v) \equiv \text{state}_v = \text{Done} \land \text{suc}_v = \emptyset \land \text{DefCycle}_v = (\text{label}_v, \text{done}) \land$
$\qquad\qquad\qquad \text{VarCycle}_v = (0, \text{Before})$

$\text{Coherent\_Verify}(v) \equiv \text{state}_v = \text{Verify} \land \text{suc}_v = \text{Succ}(v) \land [(\text{Init}(v) \land$
$\qquad\qquad\qquad \text{VarCycle}_x = (0, \text{Before})) \lor \text{Nds\_Verify}(v)]$

$\text{Coherent\_Improve}(v) \equiv \text{state}_v = \text{Improve} \land \text{suc}_v = \text{Succ}(v) \land$
$\qquad\qquad\qquad \text{DefCycle}_v = \text{DefCycle}_{\text{parent}_v} \land \text{VarCycle}_v = \text{VarCycle}_{\text{parent}_v}$

$\text{Coherent\_End}(v) \equiv \text{state}_v = \text{End} \land \text{DefCycle}_v = \text{DefCycle}_{\text{parent}_v} \land (\text{NdDel}(v) \lor$
$\qquad\qquad\qquad \text{Ask\_EI}(v))$

$\text{Coherent\_Error}(v) \equiv \text{state}_v = \text{Err} \land (\text{suc}_v = \text{Succ}(v) = \emptyset \lor \text{Ask\_E}(v)) \land$
$\qquad\qquad\qquad \text{DefCycle}_v = \text{DefCycle}_{\text{Pred}(v)}$

$\text{CoherentTree}(v)^{\,a} \equiv (v = r \land \text{d}_v = 0 \land st_v = N) \lor (v \neq r \land \text{d}_v = \text{d}_{\text{parent}_v} + 1 \land st_v = N$
$\qquad\qquad\qquad \land rw_v = \text{d}_v) \lor \text{state}_{\text{parent}_v} = \text{Improve} \lor \text{state}_{\text{parent}_v} = \text{Propag}$

$\text{Ask\_V}(v) \equiv \text{state}_{\text{Pred}(v)} = \text{Verify}$

$\text{Ask\_I}(v) \equiv (\text{state}_{\text{Pred}(v)} = \text{Improve} \land \text{VarCycle}[1]_{\text{Pred}(v)} = \text{Before}) \lor$
$\qquad\qquad\qquad (\text{state}_{\text{suc}_v} = \text{Improve} \land \text{VarCycle}[1]_{\text{suc}_v} = \text{After})$

$\text{Ask\_EI}(v) \equiv (\exists u \in N(v), \text{parent}_u = v \land \text{state}_u = \text{End} \land \text{DefCycle}_u = \text{DefCycle}_v)$

$\text{Ask\_E}(v) \equiv \text{suc}_v \neq \emptyset \land \text{state}_{\text{suc}_v} = \text{Err} \land \text{DefCycle}_v = \text{DefCycle}_{\text{suc}_v}$

$\text{Tree\_Edge}(v, u) \equiv \text{parent}_v = u \lor \text{parent}_u = v$

$\text{C\_Ancestor}(v) \equiv \text{parent}_v \neq \text{suc}_v \land \text{parent}_v \neq \text{Pred}(v)$

$\text{Init}(v) \equiv \text{DFS\_F}(v) \land \text{DefCycle}[0]_v = \text{label}_v$

$\text{Nds\_Verify}(v) \equiv [(\text{Ask\_V}(v) \land \text{VarCycle}_v = (\text{Max\_C}(v), \text{Way\_C}(v))) \lor \text{Ask\_I}(v)] \land$
$\qquad\qquad\qquad \text{DefCycle}_v = \text{DefCycle}_{\text{Pred}(v)}$

$\text{NdDel}(v) \equiv \text{state}_{\text{parent}_v} \neq \text{Done} \land \text{state}_{\text{parent}_v} \neq \text{Propag} \land \neg \text{Improve}(v)$

---

^{a} In [21], variable st_v indicates if v propagates a new distance (state P) or not (state N), and rw_v is used to propagate the new distance in the tree.

Fig. 3. Corrections predicates used by the algorithm

This algorithm constructs a BFS, and uses two variables *parent* and *distance*. During the execution of our algorithm, these two variables are subject to the same rules as in [21]. After each modification of the spanning tree, the new distance to the parent is propagated in sub-trees by Rules R_P and $\bar{R}_P$.

R_P: **(Distance propagation)**
$\quad$ If $\text{Coherent\_Done}(v) \land \neg \text{Ask\_V}(v) \land \text{suc}_v \neq \text{parent}_v \land \text{Pred}(v) \neq \text{parent}_v \land$
$\qquad \text{d}_v \neq \text{d}_{\text{parent}_v} + 1 \land (\text{state}_{\text{parent}_v} = \text{Improve} \lor \text{state}_{\text{parent}_v} = \text{Propag})$
$\quad$ then $\text{state}_v := \text{Propag}; \text{d}_v := \text{d}_{\text{parent}_v} + 1;$

$\bar{R}_P$: **(End distance propagation)**
$\quad$ If $\text{state}_v = \text{Propag} \land \text{EndPropag}(v)$
$\quad$ then $\text{state}_v := \text{Done}; \text{DefCycle}_v := (\text{label}_v, \text{done}); \text{VarCycle}_v := (0, \text{Before});$
$\qquad \text{suc}_v := \emptyset;$

Token circulation and pre-order labeling. LoopFreeMST uses the algorithm described in [5] to provide each node v with a label label$_v$. Each label is unique in the network traversed by the token. This labeling is used to find the unique path between two nodes in the spanning tree, in a distributed manner. For this purpose, we use the snap-stabilizing algorithm described in [24] for the circulation of a token in the spanning tree (a snap-stabilizing algorithm stabilizes in 0 steps thus algorithm in [24] allows to always have a correct token circulation). We have slightly modified this algorithm because LoopFreeMST stops the token circulation at a node during the "Cycle improvement" procedure. A node v knows if it has the token by applying predicate Init(v) (Predicate DFS_F(v) is true at node v if the token was forwarded by its parent). Rule R$_{DFS}$ guides the circulation of the token. The token carries on its tree traversal if one of the following three conditions is satisfied: (i) there is no improvement which could be initiated by the node which holds the token, (ii) an improvement was performed in the current cycle, or (iii) inconsistent node labels were detected in the current cycle. The latter is under the control of Predicate ContinueDFS(v).

R$_{DFS}$: **(Continue DFS token circulation)**
    If CoherentCycle$(v) \wedge$ Init$(v) \wedge$ ContinueDFS(v)
    then state$_v$:= Done; DefCycle$[1]_v$ = done;

Cycle improvement rules. The procedure "Cycle improvement" is the core of LoopFreeMST. Its role is to avoid disconnection of the current spanning tree, while successively improving the tree until reaching an MST. The procedure can be decomposed in four tasks: (1) to check whether the fundamental cycle of the non-tree edge has an improvement or not, (2) perform the improvement if any, (3) update the distances, and (4) resume the token circulation.

Let us start by describing the first task. A node u in state Done changes its state to Verify if its variables are in consistent state, it has a token, and it has identified a candidate (i.e., an incident non-tree edge $e = \{u, v\}$ whose other extremity v has a smaller label than the one of u). The latter is under the control of Predicate InitVerify(v), and the variable VarCycle$_v$ contains the label of u and v. If the three conditions are satisfied, then the verification of the fundamental cycle C_e is initiated from node u, by applying rule R$_V$. The goal of this verification is twofold: first, to verify whether C_e exists or not, and, second, to save information about the maximum edge weight and the location of the edge of maximum weight in C_e. These information are stored in the variable Way_C(v). In order to respect the orientation in the current spanning tree, the node u or v that initiates the improvement depends on the localization of the maximum weight edge f in C_e. More precisely, let r be the least common ancestor of nodes u and v in the current tree. If f occurs before r in T in the traversal of C_e from u starting by edge (u, v), then the improvement starts from u, otherwise the improvement starts from v. To get the flavor of our method, let us consider the example depicted on Figure 2. In this example, f occurs after the least common ancestor (node 6). Therefore node 10 atomically swaps its parent to respect the orientation. However, if one replaces in the same example the weight of edge $\{11, 6\}$ by 11 instead of 3, then f would occur before r, and thus node 12 would have to atomically swaps its parent. The relative places of f and r in the cycle is indicated by Predicate Way_C(v) that

$\mathsf{Pred}(v) \equiv \arg\min\{\mathsf{label}_u : u \in N(v) \wedge \mathsf{state}_u \neq \mathtt{Done} \wedge \mathsf{state}_u \neq \mathtt{Propag} \wedge \mathsf{suc}_u = v\}$
if u exists, $\emptyset$ otherwise

$\mathsf{MaxLab}(v,x) \equiv \arg\max\{\mathsf{label}_s : s \in N(v) \wedge \mathsf{label}_s < x\}$

$$\mathsf{Succ}(v) \equiv \begin{cases} \mathsf{VarCycle}[0]_v & \text{if } \mathsf{DefCycle}[1]_v = \mathsf{label}_v \\ \mathsf{parent}_v & \text{if } (\mathsf{label}_v > \mathsf{DefCycle}[1]_v \wedge \mathsf{state}_v = \mathtt{Verify}) \vee \\ & (\mathsf{label}_v < \mathsf{DefCycle}[1]_v \wedge \\ & (\mathsf{state}_v = \mathtt{Improve} \vee \mathsf{state}_v = \mathtt{End})) \\ \mathsf{MaxLab}(v, \mathsf{DefCycle}[1]_v) & \text{if } (\mathsf{label}_v < \mathsf{DefCycle}[1]_v \wedge \mathsf{state}_v = \mathtt{Verify}) \\ \mathsf{MaxLab}(v, \mathsf{label}_v) & \text{if } (\mathsf{label}_v > \mathsf{DefCycle}[1]_v \wedge \\ & (\mathsf{state}_v = \mathtt{Improve} \vee \mathsf{state}_v = \mathtt{End})) \end{cases}$$

$\mathsf{Max\_C}(v) \equiv \max\{\mathsf{VarCycle}[0]_{\mathsf{Pred}(v)}, w(v, \mathsf{Pred}(v))\}$

$$\mathsf{Way\_C}(v) \equiv \begin{cases} \mathtt{After} & \text{if } \mathsf{VarCycle}[0]_v \neq \mathsf{VarCycle}[0]_{\mathsf{Pred}(v)} \wedge \mathsf{label}_v > \mathsf{label}_{\mathsf{Pred}(v)} \\ \mathsf{VarCycle}[1]_{\mathsf{Pred}(v)} & \text{otherwise} \end{cases}$$

$\mathsf{LabCand}(v) \equiv \min\{\mathsf{label}_u : u \in N(v) \wedge \mathsf{label}_u < \mathsf{label}_v \wedge \neg\mathsf{Tree\_Edge}(v,u) \wedge$
$\qquad\qquad \mathsf{label}_u \succ \mathsf{DefCycle}[1]_v\}^a$ if u exists, end otherwise

---

[a] $\succ$ order on neighbor labels for which 'end' is the biggest element and 'done' is the smallest one.

Fig. 4. Predicates used by the algorithm

returns two different values: **Before** or **After**. During the improvement of the tree, the fundamental cycle is modified. It is crucial to save information about this cycle during this modification. In particular, the successor of a node w in a cycle, stored in the variable suc_w, must be preserved. Its value is computed by Predicate $\mathsf{Succ}(v)$ which uses node labels to identify the current examined fundamental cycle. Each node is able to compute its predecessor in the fundamental cycle by applying Predicate $\mathsf{Pred}(v)$. The state of a node is compared with the ones of its successor and predecessor to detect potential inconsistent values. At the end of this task, the node u learns the maximum weight of the cycle C_e and can decide whether it is possible to make an improvement or not. If not, but there is another non-tree edge e' that is candidate for potential replacement, then u verifies $C_{e'}$. Otherwise the token carries on its traversal, and rule $\bar{\mathsf{R}}_\mathsf{P}$ is applied.

R_V: (Verify rule)
    If $\mathsf{CoherentCycle}(v) \wedge \neg\mathsf{Error}(v) \wedge (\mathsf{InitVerify}(v) \vee [\neg\mathsf{Init}(v) \wedge (\mathsf{Coherent\_Done}(v) \vee$
    $\mathsf{state}_v = \mathtt{Propag}) \wedge \mathsf{Ask\_V}(v)])$
    then $\mathsf{state}_v := \mathtt{Verify}$;
        If $\mathsf{DFS\_F}(v)$ **then** $\mathsf{DefCycle}[1]_v := \mathsf{LabCand}(v)$;
        Else $\mathsf{DefCycle}_v := \mathsf{DefCycle}_{\mathsf{Pred}(v)}$; $\mathsf{VarCycle}_v := (\mathsf{Max\_C}(v), \mathsf{Way\_C}(v))$;
        $\mathsf{suc}_v := \mathsf{Succ}(v)$;

If C_e can yield an improvement, then rule R_I is executed. By this rule, a node enters in state $\mathtt{Improve}$, and changes its parent to its predecessor if $\mathsf{VarCycle}[1]_v = \mathsf{Before}$ (respectively to its successor if $\mathsf{VarCycle}[1]_v = \mathsf{After}$). For this purpose, it uses the variable suc_v and the predicate $\mathsf{Pred}(v)$.

R_l: **(Improve rule)**

　　If $\mathsf{CoherentCycle}(v) \wedge \neg\mathsf{Error}(v) \wedge \mathsf{Coherent\_Verify}(v) \wedge \mathsf{Improve}(v)\wedge$
　　　　$\neg\mathsf{C\_Ancestor}(v) \wedge [(\mathsf{DFS\_F}(v) \wedge \mathsf{Ask\_V}(v)) \vee \mathsf{Ask\_I}(v)]$
　　then $\mathsf{state}_v := \mathtt{Improve};$
　　If $\mathsf{DFS\_F}(v) \vee \mathsf{state}_{\mathsf{Pred}(v)} = \mathtt{Improve}$ **then** $\mathsf{VarCycle}_v := \mathsf{VarCycle}_{\mathsf{Pred}(v)}$
　　If $(\mathsf{DFS\_F}(v) \wedge \mathsf{VarCycle}[1]_v = \mathsf{Before}) \vee \neg\mathsf{DFS\_F}(v)$ **then** $\mathsf{parent}_v := \mathsf{Pred}(v);$
　　If $\mathsf{state}_{\mathsf{suc}_v} = \mathtt{Improve}$ **then** $\mathsf{VarCycle}_v := \mathsf{VarCycle}_{\mathsf{suc}_v}; \mathsf{parent}_v := \mathsf{suc}_v;$
　　If $w(v, \mathsf{suc}_v) \geq \mathsf{VarCycle}[0]_v$ **then** $\mathsf{suc}_v = \mathsf{Succ}(v)$
　　$d_v := d_{\mathsf{parent}_v} + 1;$

At the end of an improvement, it is necessary to inform the node holding the token that it has to carry on its traversal. This is the role of rule R_E. It is also necessary to inform all nodes impacted by the modification that they have to update their distances to the root (see Section 3.2).

R_E: **(End of improvement rule)**

　　If $\mathsf{CoherentCycle}(v) \wedge \neg\mathsf{Error}(v) \wedge \mathsf{End\_Improve}(v) \wedge \mathsf{EndPropag}(v)$
　　then $\mathsf{state}_v := \mathtt{End};$

Module composition. All the different modules presented, except the tree construction parts of the correction module, need the presence of a spanning tree in G. Thus, we must execute the tree construction rules first if an incoherency in the spanning tree is detected. To this end, these rules are composed using the level composition defined in [16], i.e., if Predicate $\mathsf{CoherentTree}(v)$ (see Fig. 3) is not verified then the tree construction rules are executed, otherwise the other modules can be executed. The token circulation algorithm and the naming algorithm are composed together using the conditional composition described in [5], i.e., the naming algorithm is executed when a logical expression (based on guards of token circulation algorithm) is true. Finally, we compose the token circulation algorithm and the cycle improvement module with a conditional composition using Predicate $\mathsf{ContinueDFS}(v)$ (see Fig. 5). This allows to execute the token circulation algorithm only if the cycle improvement module does not need the token on a node. Figure 6 shows how the modules are composed together.

$\mathsf{Candidate}(v) \equiv \mathsf{LabCand}(v) \neq \mathsf{end}$
$\mathsf{InitVerify}(v) \equiv \mathsf{Init}(v) \wedge \mathsf{Candidate}(v) \wedge (\mathsf{Coherent\_Done}(v) \vee [\mathsf{Coherent\_Verify}(v)\wedge$
　　　　　　$\neg\mathsf{Improve}(v) \wedge \neg\mathsf{C\_Ancestor}(v) \wedge \mathsf{Ask\_V}(v)])$
$\mathsf{ImproveF}(v, x) \equiv \neg\mathsf{Tree\_Edge}(v, x)) \wedge \max(\mathsf{VarCycle}[0]_v, \mathsf{VarCycle}[0]_x) > w(v, x)$
$\mathsf{Improve}(v) \equiv \mathsf{ImproveF}(v, \mathsf{Pred}(v)) \vee \mathsf{ImproveF}(v, \mathsf{suc}_v)$
$\mathsf{End\_Improve}(v) \equiv \mathsf{Coherent\_Improve}(v) \wedge (\mathsf{NdDel}(v) \vee \mathsf{Ask\_EI}(v))$
$\mathsf{ContinueDFS}(v) \equiv (\mathsf{Init}(v) \wedge [([\mathsf{Coherent\_Done}(v) \vee (\mathsf{Coherent\_Verify}(v)\wedge$
　　　　　　$\neg\mathsf{ImproveF}(v, \mathsf{Pred}(v)) \wedge \mathsf{Ask\_V}(v))] \wedge \neg\mathsf{Candidate}(v))\vee$
　　　　　　$\mathsf{Coherent\_End}(v) \vee \mathsf{Error}(v)]) \vee \neg\mathsf{DFS\_F}(v)$
$\mathsf{Error}(v) \equiv \mathsf{state}_v \neq \mathtt{Done} \wedge \mathsf{state}_v \neq \mathtt{Err} \wedge (\mathsf{suc}_v = \mathsf{Succ}(v) = \emptyset \vee \mathsf{Ask\_E}(v))$
$\mathsf{EndPropag}(v) \equiv (\forall u \in N(v), \mathsf{parent}_u = v \wedge \mathsf{state}_u = \mathtt{Done} \wedge d_u = d_v + 1)$

Fig. 5. Predicates used by the algorithm

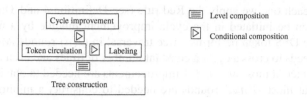

Fig. 6. Composition of the presented modules

3.3 Complexity

Definition 4 (Red Rule). *If C is a cycle in $G = (V, E)$ with no red edges then color in red the maximum edge weight in C.*

Theorem 1 (Tarjan et al. [26]). *Let G be a connected graph. If it is not possible to apply Red Rule then the set of not colored edges forms a minimum spanning tree of G.*

Lemma 1. *Starting from a configuration where an arbitrary spanning tree is constructed, in at most $O(mn)$ rounds the cycle improvement module produces a minimum spanning tree of G, with respectively m and n the number of edges and nodes of the network G.*

Proof. In a given network $G = (V, E)$, if a spanning tree of G is constructed then there are exactly $m - (n - 1)$ fundamental cycles in G since there are $n - 1$ edges in any spanning tree of G. Thus, a tree edge can be contained in at most $m - n + 1$ fundamental cycles. Consider a configuration where a spanning tree T of G is constructed and a tree edge e_0 is contained in $m - n + 1$ fundamental cycles and all tree edges have a weight equal to 1, except e_0 of weight $w(e_0) > 1$. Suppose that T is not a minimum spanning tree of G such that $\forall e_i \in E, i = 1, \ldots, m - n + 1, w(e_{i-1}) > w(e_i)$ with $e_0 \in T$ and $\forall i = 1, \ldots, m - n + 1, e_i \notin T$ and $w(e_i) > 1$ (see the graph of Figure 7(a)). Consider the following sequence of improvements: $\forall i, i = 1, \ldots, m - n + 1$, exchange the tree edge e_{i-1} by the not tree edge e_i (see a sequence of improvements in Figure 7). In this sequence, we have exactly $m - n + 1$ improvements and this is the maximum number of improvements to obtain a minimum spanning tree since there are $m - n + 1$ fundamental

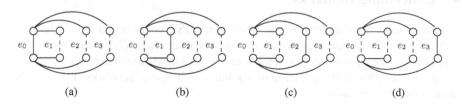

| (a) | (b) | (c) | (d) |

Fig. 7. (a) a spanning tree with plain lines in a graph with $m - n + 1$ improvements, (b) the spanning tree obtained after the first improvement, (c) the spanning tree obtained after the second improvement, (d) the minimum spanning tree of the graph obtained after the third improvement

cycles and for each one we apply the Red rule (see Definition 4 and Theorem 1). An improvement can be initiated in the cycle improvement module by a node with the DFS token. The DFS token performs a tree traversal in $O(n)$ rounds. Moreover, each improvement needs to cross a cycle a constant number of times and each cross requires $O(n)$ rounds. Since at most $m - n + 1$ improvements are needed to obtain a minimum spanning tree, at most $O(mn)$ rounds are needed to construct a minimum spanning tree.

Lemma 2. *Starting from a legitimate configuration, after a weight edge modification the system reaches a legitimate configuration in at most $O(mn)$ rounds.*

Proof. After a weight edge change the system is no more in a legitimate configuration in the following cases: (1) the weight of a not tree edge is less than the weight of the heaviest tree edge in its fundamental cycle, or (2) the weight of a tree edge is greater than the weight of a not tree edge in one of the fundamental cycles including the tree edges. In each case above, the algorithm must verify if improvements must be performed to reach again a legitimate configuration, otherwise the system is still in a legitimate configuration. Thus, in case (1) it is only sufficient to verify if an improvement must be performed in the fundamental cycle associated to the not tree edge (i.e. to apply the Red rule a single time). To this end, its fundamental cycle must be crossed at most three times: the first time to verify if an improvement is possible, a second time to perform the improvement and a last time to end the improvement, each one needs at most $O(n)$ rounds. Case (2) is more complicated, indeed the weight of a tree edge can change which leads to a configuration where at most $m - n + 1$ improvements must be performed to reach a legitimate configuration, since a tree edge can be contained in at most $m - n + 1$ fundamental cycles as described in proof of Lemma 1. Since each improvement phase needs $O(n)$ rounds (see case (1)) at most $O(mn)$ rounds are needed to reach a legitimate configuration. The complexity of case (2) dominates the complexity of the first case. Therefore, after a weight edge change at most $O(mn)$ rounds are needed to reach a legitimate configuration.

Note that the presented algorithm uses only a constant number of variables of size $O(\log n)$. Therefore, $O(\log n)$ bits of memory are needed at each node to execute the algorithm. Moreover, due to space constraints correctness proof are given in [27].

4   Concluding Remarks

We presented a new solution to the distributed MST construction that is both self-stabilizing and loop-free. It improves on memory usage from $O(n \log n)$ to $O(\log n)$, yet doesn't make strong system assumptions such as knowledge of network size or unicity of edge weights, making it particularly suited to dynamic networks. Two important open questions are raised:

1. For depth first search tree construction, self-stabilizing solutions that use only constant memory space do exist. It is unclear how the obvious constant space lower bound can be raised with respect to metrics that minimize a global criterium (such as MST).

2. Our protocol pionneers the design of self-stabilizing loop-free protocols for *non* locally optimizable tree metrics. We expect the techniques used in this paper to be useful to add loop-free property for other metrics that are only globally optimizable, yet designing a generic such approach is a difficult task.

References

1. Katz, S., Perry, K.J.: Self-stabilizing extensions for message-passing systems. Distributed Computing 7, 17–26 (1993)
2. Anagnostou, E., Hadzilacos, V.: Tolerating transient and permanent failures (extended abstract). In: Schiper, A. (ed.) WDAG 1993. LNCS, vol. 725, pp. 174–188. Springer, Heidelberg (1993)
3. Ben-Or, M., Dolev, D., Hoch, E.N.: Fast self-stabilizing byzantine tolerant digital clock synchronization. In: Bazzi, R.A., Patt-Shamir, B. (eds.) PODC, pp. 385–394. ACM Press, New York (2008)
4. Cobb, J.A., Gouda, M.G.: Stabilization of general loop-free routing. J. Parallel Distrib. Comput. 62(5), 922–944 (2002)
5. Datta, A.K., Gurumurthy, S., Petit, F., Villain, V.: Self-stabilizing network orientation algorithms in arbitrary rooted networks. Stud. Inform. Univ. 1(1), 1–22 (2001)
6. Dijkstra, E.W.: Self-stabilizing systems in spite of distributed control. Commun. ACM 17(11), 643–644 (1974)
7. Dolev, S.: Self-stabilization. MIT Press, Cambridge (2000)
8. Dolev, S.: Self-Stabilization. MIT Press, Cambridge (2000)
9. Dolev, S., Herman, T.: Superstabilizing protocols for dynamic distributed systems. Chicago J. Theor. Comput. Sci. (1997)
10. Dolev, S., Welch, J.L.: Wait-free clock synchronization. Algorithmica 18(4), 486–511 (1997)
11. Dolev, S., Welch, J.L.: Self-stabilizing clock synchronization in the presence of byzantine faults. J. ACM 51(5), 780–799 (2004)
12. Gafni, E.M., Bertsekas, P.: Distributed algorithms for generating loop-free routes in networks with frequently changing topology. IEEE Transactions on Communications 29, 11–18 (1981)
13. Gallager, R.G., Humblet, P.A., Spira, P.M.: A distributed algorithm for minimum-weight spanning trees. ACM Trans. Program. Lang. Syst. 5(1), 66–77 (1983)
14. Garcia-Luna-Aceves, J.J.: Loop-free routing using diffusing computations. IEEE/ACM Trans. Netw. 1(1), 130–141 (1993)
15. Gopal, A.S., Perry, K.J.: Unifying self-stabilization and fault-tolerance (preliminary version). In: PODC, pp. 195–206 (1993)
16. Gouda, M.G., Herman, T.: Adaptive programming. IEEE Trans. Software Eng. 17(9), 911–921 (1991)
17. Gouda, M.G., Schneider, M.: Stabilization of maximal metric trees. In: Arora, A. (ed.) WSS, pp. 10–17. IEEE Computer Society Press, Los Alamitos (1999)
18. Gupta, S.K.S., Srimani, P.K.: Self-stabilizing multicast protocols for ad hoc networks. J. Parallel Distrib. Comput. 63(1), 87–96 (2003)
19. Higham, L., Liang, Z.: Self-stabilizing minimum spanning tree construction on message-passing networks. In: Welch, J.L. (ed.) DISC 2001. LNCS, vol. 2180, pp. 194–208. Springer, Heidelberg (2001)
20. Johnen, C., Tixeuil, S.: Route Preserving Stabilization. In: Huang, S.-T., Herman, T. (eds.) SSS 2003. LNCS, vol. 2704, pp. 184–198. Springer, Heidelberg (2003)
21. Johnen, C., Tixeuil, S.: Route preserving stabilization. In: Self-Stabilizing Systems, pp. 184–198 (2003)

22. Kruskal, J.B.: On the shortest spanning subtree of a graph and the travelling salesman problem. Proc. Amer. Math. Soc. 7, 48–50 (1956)
23. Papatriantafilou, M., Tsigas, P.: On self-stabilizing wait-free clock synchronization. Parallel Processing Letters 7(3), 321–328 (1997)
24. Petit, F., Villain, V.: Optimal snap-stabilizing depth-first token circulation in tree networks. J. Parallel Distrib. Comput. 67(1), 1–12 (2007)
25. Prim, R.C.: Shortest connection networks and some generalizations. Bell System Tech. J., 1389–1401 (1957)
26. Sleator, D.D., Tarjan, R.E.: A data structure for dynamic trees. J. Comput. Syst. Sci. 26(3), 362–391 (1983)
27. Blin, L., Potop-Butucaru, M.G., Rovedakis, S., Tixeuil, S.: A new self-stabilizing minimum spanning tree construction with loop-free property. Research Report, inria-00384041, INRIA (2009)

Euler Tour Lock-In Problem
in the Rotor-Router Model[*]
I Choose Pointers and You Choose Port Numbers

Evangelos Bampas[1,3], Leszek Gąsieniec[2,**], Nicolas Hanusse[3], David Ilcinkas[3],
Ralf Klasing[3], and Adrian Kosowski[3,4]

[1] School of Elec. & Comp. Eng., National Technical University of Athens, Greece
ebamp@cs.ntua.gr
[2] Dept of Computer Science, Univ. of Liverpool, UK
L.A.Gasieniec@liverpool.ac.uk
[3] LaBRI, CNRS / INRIA / Univ. of Bordeaux, France[***]
{nicolas.hanusse,david.ilcinkas,ralf.klasing}@labri.fr
[4] Dept of Algorithms and System Modeling, Gdańsk Univ. of Technology, Poland
adrian@kaims.pl

Abstract. The *rotor-router model*, also called the *Propp machine*, was
first considered as a deterministic alternative to the random walk. It is
known that the route in an undirected graph $G = (V, E)$, where $|V| = n$
and $|E| = m$, adopted by an agent controlled by the rotor-router mecha-
nism forms eventually an Euler tour based on arcs obtained via replacing
each edge in G by two arcs with opposite direction. The process of ush-
ering the agent to an Euler tour is referred to as the *lock-in problem*. In
recent work [11] Yanovski et al. proved that independently of the initial
configuration of the rotor-router mechanism in G the agent locks-in in
time bounded by $2mD$, where D is the diameter of G.

In this paper we examine the dependence of the lock-in time on the
initial configuration of the rotor-router mechanism. The case study is
performed in the form of a game between a player $\mathcal{P}$ intending to lock-in
the agent in an Euler tour as quickly as possible and its adversary $\mathcal{A}$
with the counter objective. First, we observe that in certain (easy) cases
the lock in can be achieved in time $O(m)$. On the other hand we show
that if adversary $\mathcal{A}$ is solely responsible for the assignment of ports and
pointers, the lock-in time $\Omega(m \cdot D)$ can be enforced in any graph with m
edges and diameter D. Furthermore, we show that if $\mathcal{A}$ provides its own
port numbering after the initial setup of pointers by $\mathcal{P}$, the complexity of
the lock-in problem is bounded by $O(m \cdot \min\{\log m, D\})$. We also propose
a class of graphs in which the lock-in requires time $\Omega(m \cdot \log m)$. In the
remaining two cases we show that the lock-in requires time $\Omega(m \cdot D)$ in
graphs with the worst-case topology. In addition, however, we present
non-trivial classes of graphs with a large diameter in which the lock-in
time is $O(m)$.

[*] This work was done during the visit of the second author in Bordeaux.
[**] Partially funded by the Royal Society International Joint Project, IJP - 2007/R1.
[***] Additional support by the ANR projects ALADDIN and IDEA and the INRIA
project CEPAGE.

I. Keidar (Ed.): DISC 2009, LNCS 5805, pp. 423–435, 2009.
© Springer-Verlag Berlin Heidelberg 2009

1   Introduction

A graph is a fundamental combinatorial concept used for modeling complex systems in various application domains including communication, transportation and computer networks, manufacturing, scheduling, molecular biology, and peer-to-peer networks. Certain models based on graphs, very often classified as *alternative models of computation*, rely on the use of mobile entities called *agents*. An agent can be, e.g., a robot servicing a hazardous environment or a software process navigating the Internet in search of information.

The family of *anonymous graphs* provides foundations for a model that has found its application in network communication, graph exploration and stabilisation of distributed processes. In principle, due to minimalistic assumptions, any solution provided in this model constitutes also a valid solution in any other communication graph-based model. Another important rationale for the use of anonymous graphs is the intention to study border cases (limits of computation) in the field of distributed computing.

The *rotor-router mechanism* was introduced as a deterministic alternative to the random walk and studied in the context of a wide selection of network problems, including work on load balancing problems in [6, 5], graph exploration [7,2,8], and stabilisation of distributed processes [9,3,11]. The rotor-router mechanism is represented by an undirected anonymous graph $G = (V, E)$, where $|V| = n$ and $|E| = m$. The nodes in V bear no names, however, the endpoints of edges in E, called *ports*, are arranged in a *cyclic order* at each node. Furthermore, each node is equipped with a *pointer* that indicates the current exit port to be adopted by an agent on the conclusion of the next visit to this node. The rotor-router mechanism guarantees that after each consecutive visit at a node its pointer is moved to the next port in the cyclic order. Due to a limited number of configurations in a graph G of a bounded size it is intuitive that a walk of the agent controlled by the rotor-router mechanism must be locked-in in a loop eventually. Rather surprisingly, however, Priezzhev et al. [9] proved that an agent traversing a finite graph gets locked-in in an Euler tour based on arcs obtained by replacing each edge in G with two arcs having opposite directions. Later, Bhatt et al. [3] proved that the lock-in time is bounded by $O(m \cdot n)$. This bound was further improved by Yanovski et al. in [11] to $2mD$, where D is the diameter of G. Related models of traversal in undirected graphs were studied in [4].

1.1   Our Contribution and Outline of the Paper

In this paper we examine the influence of the initial configuration of pointers and port numbers on the time needed to lock-in the agent in an Euler tour. The case study is performed in the form of a competition between a *player* $\mathcal{P}$ intending to lock-in the agent in an Euler tour as quickly as possible and its *adversary* $\mathcal{A}$ having the counter objective. We assume that both the player $\mathcal{P}$ and its adversary $\mathcal{A}$ have unlimited computational power, i.e., we do not take into account the cost of computation of the initial configuration of ports and pointers to be adopted by $\mathcal{P}$ and $\mathcal{A}$. The results of our studies are asymptotically tight in terms of the worst-case choice of the graph topology and the initial location of the agent.

We start our analysis with border cases. In the case $\mathcal{P}$-*all* where the player $\mathcal{P}$ is in charge of the initial arrangement of port numbers and pointers we observe that the lock-in in an Euler tour can be obtained in time $O(m)$. Also the case $\mathcal{A}(\circlearrowleft)\mathcal{P}(f)$, where $\mathcal{P}$ sets the pointers after the port numbers are assigned by $\mathcal{A}$, reduces to the border case where $\mathcal{P}$ is solely in charge of the initial configuration. On the other hand, in the case $\mathcal{A}$-*all* where the adversary $\mathcal{A}$ solely decides about the initial configuration, we show that in any graph with m edges and diameter D the adversary $\mathcal{A}$ is able to enforce the lower bound $\Omega(m \cdot D)$ for the lock-in matching the upper bound from [11].

Furthermore, we show that if $\mathcal{A}$ provides its own port numbering after the initial setup of pointers by $\mathcal{P}$, case $\mathcal{P}(f)\mathcal{A}(\circlearrowleft)$, the complexity of the lock-in problem is bounded by $O(m \cdot \min\{\log m, D\})$. We also propose a respective class of graphs in which the lock-in requires time $\Omega(m \cdot \min\{\log m, D\})$. At the same time we point out that, e.g., in Hamiltonian graphs the lock-in is obtained in time $O(m)$.

We conclude with the proof that in the remaining two cases the lock-in requires time $\Omega(m \cdot D)$ in graphs with the worst-case topology. In the case $\mathcal{A}(f)\mathcal{P}(\circlearrowleft)$ where $\mathcal{P}$ responds by appropriate port assignment to initial setup of pointers by $\mathcal{A}$, we show that there exist graphs for which the lock-in requires time $\Omega(m \cdot D)$. At the same time, we present a non-trivial class of graphs with an arbitrarily large diameter in which an appropriate choice of port numbers leads to the lock-in in time $O(m)$. Finally, in the case $\mathcal{P}(\circlearrowleft)\mathcal{A}(f)$ where $\mathcal{A}$ sets the pointers after the assignment of ports is revealed by $\mathcal{P}$, the lower bound $\Omega(m \cdot D)$ argument for the lock-in follows directly from the previous case. Also, here we propose a non-trivial class of graphs, this time with an arbitrary diameter $D \leq \sqrt{n}$, in which the lock-in is feasible in time $O(m)$. Our results are summarised in Table 1.

Table 1. Minimum and maximum values of the lock-in time in considered cases

Scenario	Worst case	Best case
Case $\mathcal{P}$-*all*	$\Theta(m)$	$\Theta(m)$
Case $\mathcal{A}(\circlearrowleft)\mathcal{P}(f)$	$\Theta(m)$	$\Theta(m)$
Case $\mathcal{P}(f)\mathcal{A}(\circlearrowleft)$	$\Theta(m \cdot \min\{\log m, D\})$	$\Theta(m)$
Case $\mathcal{A}(f)\mathcal{P}(\circlearrowleft)$	$\Theta(m \cdot D)$	$\Theta(m)$
Case $\mathcal{P}(\circlearrowleft)\mathcal{A}(f)$	$\Theta(m \cdot D)$	$\Theta(m)$ for all $D \leq \sqrt{n}$
Case $\mathcal{A}$-*all*	$\Theta(m \cdot D)$	$\Theta(m \cdot D)$

1.2   The Euler Tour Lock-In Problem Revisited

In this section we provide basic definitions and we recall known facts in relation to performance of the rotor-router mechanism in anonymous graphs. Recall that $G = (V, E)$ is an input graph in which the starting node is denoted by s.

Definition 1. *For any m and D, $D \leq m$, let $\mathcal{G}_{m,D}$ denote the class of graphs with diameter between D and $4D$ and a number of edges between m and $4m$.*

Definition 2. *For any $v \in V$ let $E_G(v)$ denote the set of edges of G that are incident to node v.*

Definition 3. *Let $H = (X, C)$ be a connected subgraph of G induced by some $C \subseteq E$. We denote by $N_G(H)$ the subgraph of G induced by the set $\bigcup_{v \in X} E_G(v)$.*

Definition 4 (port assignment). *A port assignment to the nodes of graph G is a collection of bijective functions between $E_G(v)$ and $\{1, \ldots, \deg(v)\}$, one for each $v \in V$.*

Definition 5 (pointer assignment). *An initial pointer assignment to the nodes of an undirected graph $G = (V, E)$ is a function $f : V \to E$, s.t., for all $v \in V$, $f(v) \in E_G(v)$.*

Definition 6. *A node becomes saturated when all its incident edges are traversed in both directions for the first time.*

Note that when a node becomes saturated, its pointer returns to the initial position for the first time.

Lemma 1 ([3]). *Let $G = (V, E)$ be a graph with a starting node $s \in V$, an assignment of ports and pointers. The Euler tour lock-in in G is performed in phases $\{P_i\}_{i \geq 1}$. Each phase starts when the mobile agent leaves s via edge $f(s)$ indicated by the initial assignment of pointers and continues until the agent traverses all edges incident to s in both directions. The following properties hold:*

- *While the agent is visiting nodes saturated in some earlier phase, it retraces the route of phase P_{i-1}.*
- *If the agent encounters a node u that has been visited but not saturated in an earlier phase, it suspends the retracing of the tour of phase P_{i-1}. A new tour starts at u and ends there. Node u is now saturated. The tour of phase P_{i-1} is resumed (via port $f(s)$).*
- *Every edge is traversed at most once in each direction during each phase.*

Eventually all nodes in G get saturated. In other words, there exists integer $j \geq 1$, s.t., starting from the phase P_j the agent adopts the same (Euler) tour in G.

One can conclude from Lemma 1 that during each phase P_i the agent gets locked-in in a subgraph G_i of G where (1) G_0 contains a single node s; (1) each G_i is a subgraph of G_{i+1}; and (2) all edges in G that are incident to nodes in G_i are present in G_{i+1}, i.e., $N_G(G_i) \subseteq G_{i+1}$. Since the number of edges in each G_i is bounded by m the following theorem follows.

Theorem 1 ([11]). *For any graph, any starting node, and any initial pointer and port assignments, the lock-in (which is equivalent with exploration of all edges in G) is achieved in time $O(m \cdot D)$.*

2   Case Study of the Lock-In Problem

In this section we study the game between $\mathcal{P}$ and $\mathcal{A}$ in detail.

2.1   Border Cases

In this section we briefly discuss border cases in which for any graph G the complexity of the lock-in problem is either $\Theta(m)$ or $\Theta(mD)$.

Cases with Lock-in Time $\Theta(m)$. Consider first the case $\mathcal{P}$-*all* where the player $\mathcal{P}$ is solely responsible for the initial setup of port numbers and pointers. Since we assume unbounded computational power of $\mathcal{P}$ clearly the player can choose a configuration that locks-in the agent in an Euler tour right from the beginning. Similarly, also in the case $\mathcal{A}(\circlearrowright)\mathcal{P}(f)$, after the adversary $\mathcal{A}$ sets port numbers, $\mathcal{P}$ can respond with an appropriate assignment of pointers that leads to an Euler tour instantly for any input graph G. Thus in those two cases the agent visits all edges in G locking-in itself in an Euler tour in time $O(m)$.

Case with Lock-in Time $\Theta(m \cdot D)$. At the other end of the spectrum, in the case $\mathcal{A}$-*all* where the adversary $\mathcal{A}$ is solely responsible for the initial configuration of port numbers and pointers the proof of the complexity $\Theta(m \cdot D)$ is more complex. We start with the following lemma.

Lemma 2. *Given an input graph $G = (V, E)$ with a starting node $s \in V$. For any subset $C \subseteq E$, s.t. C contains at least $E_G(s)$ and also induces a connected subgraph $H = (X, C)$ of G, there exists an assignment of ports and pointers, s.t., the first phase of the exploration of G traverses all edges in C in both directions, and only these edges.*

Proof. Let $\mathcal{C}$ be an Euler cycle in H. Fix the corresponding sequence of edge traversals $e_1, \ldots, e_{2|C|}$, s.t. e_1 is an edge incident to s (each undirected edge in C is traversed exactly twice by $\mathcal{C}$, once in each direction). We now define a port assignment and an assignment of pointers f to the nodes of G.

For any node $v \in V$, let $e_{v_1}, \ldots, e_{v_k}$ be the order in which its incident edges are traversed in $\mathcal{C}$, going *out* of v. It can happen that $k < \deg_G(v)$ if v has incident edges in $E \setminus C$, or even $k = 0$ if $v \notin X$. Define the port assignment for the node v, s.t., for any $i \le k$, edge e_{v_i} is the port with number i. If $k < \deg_G(v)$, extend this port assignment, s.t., edges in $E \setminus C$ receive higher port numbers than edges in C. Finally, define $f(v)$ to be the edge e_{v_1} if $k \ge 1$, otherwise, define $f(v)$ to be an arbitrary edge in $E_G(v)$.

Now, let $\mathcal{E}$ be the sequence of edges traversed by the agent in the first phase of the exploration of G starting from s. For every node $v \in V$ and every i, consider the i-th time that $\mathcal{E}$ visits v. The edge followed then by $\mathcal{E}$ is e_{v_i}, which coincides with the edge that $\mathcal{C}$ followed during the i-th visit at v. It follows that $\mathcal{E}$ coincides with $\mathcal{C}$ and therefore $\mathcal{E}$ traverses all edges of C in both directions, and only these edges. $\square$

Lemma 3. *Let $G = (V, E)$ be an undirected graph with a starting node $s \in V$, a given port assignment, and a pointer assignment f for each node of G. Let $\mathcal{E}$ be the sequence of edges traversed by the agent in the first i phases of exploration, for some $i \geq 1$. Let $H = (X, C)$ be the subgraph of G induced by the edges traversed in $\mathcal{E}$ (not necessarily in both directions). The ports and pointers of nodes in $V \setminus X$ can be modified, s.t., during Phase $i + 1$ of exploration the agent traverses all edges of $N_G(H)$ in both directions, but it traverses no further edges in G.*

Proof. Let $N_G(H) = (Y, D)$. Clearly, $Y \supseteq X$ and $D \supseteq C$. Phase $i + 1$ of the exploration will saturate all nodes that were visited during the first i phases. This implies that all edges incident to nodes in X are traversed in both directions during the second phase. Therefore all edges in D will be traversed in both directions.

To ensure that no other edges will be traversed, we modify the port assignment of nodes in $Y \setminus X$ as follows. For each $v \in Y \setminus X$, all edges connecting v to nodes in X receive smaller port numbers than all edges connecting v to nodes in $V \setminus X$. Furthermore, we set $f(v)$ to be the edge with port number 1, for all $v \in Y \setminus X$.

To prove the claim, assume for the sake of contradiction that during Phase $i + 1$ the agent traverses some edges in $E \setminus D$. Let e be the first such edge. The edge e must have been traversed on the way out from some node $v \in Y \setminus X$. But, due to the port numbering scheme defined above, the cyclic distance between the port number of e and the first pointer at node v is greater than the number of edges that connect v to nodes in X, which implies that at least one of these edges was traversed at least twice in the same direction (toward v) during Phase $i + 1$. This leads to a contradiction, since an edge is never traversed twice in the same direction during the same phase. □

Theorem 2. *For any graph $G = (V, E)$ in $\mathcal{G}_{m,D}$ there exists a starting node s, and a port and pointer assignment in G, s.t., the lock-in requires time at least $\frac{1}{4} \cdot mD$.*

Proof. Let T be the BFS tree of G rooted in an arbitrary node $u \in V$. Let $r \geq \frac{D}{2}$ be the height of T. Finally, let H be the subgraph of G induced by the nodes of the lowermost $\frac{r}{2}$ levels of T, and let $H_1 = (X, C)$ be a connected component of H that contains at least one node from the r-th level of T (Figure 1).

If H_1 contains at least $\frac{m}{2}$ edges, then pick an arbitrary starting node s in H_1 and set the ports and pointers, s.t., the first phase of the exploration starting from s explores exactly $G_1 = H_1$. This is feasible due to Lemma 2. Furthermore, arrange ports and pointers so that for any $i \geq 2$, $G_i = N_G(G_{i-1})$, where G_i denotes the graph induced by the edges traversed during phase P_i of the exploration. This is feasible by multiple applications of Lemma 3. In this case, the exploration from s will require at least $2 \cdot \frac{m}{2} \cdot \frac{r}{2} \geq \frac{1}{4} \cdot mD$ edge traversals before visiting all nodes.

Otherwise, the subgraph H_2 induced on G by the edge set $E \setminus C$ must contain at least $\frac{m}{2}$ edges. Pick a starting node s in H_2 and set the ports and pointers, s.t., $G_1 = H_2$ and for any $i \geq 2$, $G_i = N_G(G_{i-1})$. The exploration will again require at least $\frac{1}{4} \cdot mD$ edge traversals before visiting all nodes. □

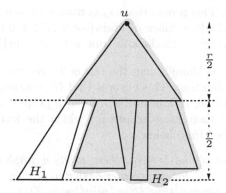

Fig. 1. The partition of G into subgraphs that is described in the proof of Theorem 2. Either subgraph H_1 or subgraph H_2 contains at least half of the edges of G.

2.2   Almost Linear Lock-In – Case $\mathcal{P}(f)\mathcal{A}(\circlearrowleft)$

In this section we discuss the case where the player $\mathcal{P}$ chooses pointers first and the adversary $\mathcal{A}$ responds with the worst-case assignment of ports.

Theorem 3. *For any graph $G = (V, E)$ in $\mathcal{G}_{m,D}$ and any starting point s there exists a pointer assignment, s.t. for any port assignment the lock-in can be obtained in time $O(m \cdot \min\{\log m, D\})$.*

Proof. We show that the player can find an assignment of pointers, s.t. the lock-in is obtained in G_i, for some $i \leq \min\{\log m, D\}$.

Take an arbitrary BFS tree T in G rooted in s. For every node in T compute a *rank* according to the following rules. Each leaf in T acquires rank 0. For each internal node v (including the root s) we look at the rank of its children. If the top rank r belongs to only one child the node v adopts r as its own rank. Otherwise, i.e., when the top rank is shared by at least two children the node v adopts the rank $r + 1$. One can prove that the rank ρ of the root s is the largest and it does not exceed $\log m$. It does not exceed D either, because we chose a BFS tree. The rank of the root is known as the *Strahler number*, a numerical measure of branching complexity of the tree T [10]. Note that the nodes with the same rank form a collection of *downward chains* in T.

After the ranks are introduced to T, the pointer at each node in T is assigned to the port leading towards a child with the largest rank. This is to ensure that G_i contains all nodes in T with ranks $\leq \rho - i + 1$. And indeed G_1 contains all nodes with rank ρ since as soon as the traversal process is initiated the agent is forced to visit all nodes with the highest rank (and possibly some others). Assume now inductively that all nodes with ranks $\leq \rho - i + 1$ belong to G_i. These include the nodes that are connected to downward chains with rank $\rho - i$ with nodes still not present in G_i. But note that due to Lemma 1 all edges incident to nodes in G_i are present in G_{i+1} which means that each downward chain with rank $\rho - i$ will be accessed and all of their nodes will be traversed when G_{i+1} is formed. This proves that G_ρ contains all nodes from G and $G_{\rho+1}$ contains all nodes and edges. Since $\rho \leq \min\{\log m, D\}$ and the number of edges in each G_i is bounded by m, the lock-in time is $O(m \cdot \min\{\log m, D\})$.   □

Note finally, that if G is Hamiltonian the player $\mathcal{P}$ can arrange pointers so that they form a Hamiltonian tour. This ensures that G_2 contains all edges in G and that the complexity of the lock-in problem in such graphs is $O(m)$.

We now show that there exist graphs for which the lock-in upper bound is asymptotically matched from below.

Theorem 4. *For any m and $D \leq m$, there exists a graph $G = (V, E)$ in $\mathcal{G}_{m,D}$ with a starting node s, s.t., for any pointer assignment there is a port assignment for which the lock-in requires time $\Omega(m \cdot \min\{\log m, D\})$.*

Proof. Consider a graph formed of a complete graph K with $\Omega(m)$ edges and $O(\sqrt{m})$ nodes connected by a path of length $\max\{1, D - \log m\}$ with a complete binary tree B of height $\min\{\log m, D\}$. This is to ensure that G_2 contains all the edges from K. Consider now the arrangement of pointers in each node of B. We show that independently of the assignment of the pointer at an internal node v, if i is the smallest integer such that v belongs to G_i, then one of its children is not present in G_i.

And indeed, assume that G_i is the first graph in which v is visited by the agent. There are three ports associated with v. One port leads to its parent and two towards its children. If the player $\mathcal{P}$ decides to assign the pointer to the port leading towards the parent of v after the agent arrives in v (forming a part of G_i) it immediately returns back to the parent of v. Since each edge in G_i is visited exactly once in each direction, see Lemma 1, the next visit at v must occur in G_{i+1}. Thus none of its children can be present in G_i.

Now assume that the pointer is assigned to a port k leading to one of the children c_1 of v. Since the port numbers available at v are 1,2 and 3, the adversary $\mathcal{A}$ assigns number $(k \bmod 3) + 1$ (that follows k in the cyclic order) to the port leading to the parent of v. This is to ensure that after the agent comes back from c_1 it immediately returns to the parent of v. Since each edge in G_i is visited exactly once in each direction, see Lemma 1, the next visit at v must occur in G_{i+1}. This proves that the other child of v does not belong to G_i. Thus there is a path from the root of B to some leaf on which neither of two consecutive nodes belong to the same G_i.

Finally, since the height of B is $\Omega(\min\{\log m, D\})$ and each G_i, for $i \leq 2$, contains at least m edges the lock-in requires time $\Omega(m \cdot \min\{\log m, D\})$.   □

2.3   The Two Remaining Cases

In the last part of the paper we discuss two cases with the worst-case complexity $\Omega(m \cdot D)$. We show, however, that here, in contrast to the border case $\mathcal{A}$-*all*, there exist non-trivial classes of graphs with a lock-in time of $O(m)$.

Case $\mathcal{A}(f)\mathcal{P}(\circlearrowleft)$. In the case where the player responds by a port assignment to the adversary's initial pointer assignment, we demonstrate a family of graphs in which locking-in requires time $\Omega(mD)$, matching the general worst-case upper bound from Theorem 1. We also demonstrate a non-trivial family of graphs in which for any choice of starting point the lock-in is achieved in time $O(m)$.

Theorem 5. *For any m and $D \leq m$, there is a graph $G = (V, E)$ in $\mathcal{G}_{m,D}$ with starting node s, and a pointer assignment, s.t. for any port assignment the lock-in requires time $\Omega(mD)$.*

Proof. Let G be a lollipop graph obtained by connecting a complete graph K_a to a path P_D with D nodes via a bridging edge. The diameter of G is $D + 1$ and it is always possible to pick $a = \Theta(\sqrt{m})$, s.t., the number of edges of G is between m and $4m$. Thus $G \in \mathcal{G}_{m,D}$. Let s be a node of K_a different from the node connecting K_a to P_D, and let the pointers within K_a point towards s (the pointer of s can initially be on an arbitrary port). Finally, set the pointers at each node of P_D towards K_a.

It is clear that, no matter which port assignment is chosen by the player, during the first phase of the exploration initiated in s the agent traverses the edges connecting s to its neighbors in the clique in both directions, thus visiting all nodes in K_a. During the second phase the agent will traverse all $\Theta(m)$ edges of K_a in both directions, and it will return to K_a by the first pointer of P_D. During subsequent phases of exploration the agent will progress along the path at a rate of one edge per phase, until the last node of the path is reached. Therefore, D phases are required, each of which retraces at least the $\Theta(m)$ edges in K_a; the lower bound of $\Omega(m \cdot D)$ for the lock-in time follows. □

Theorem 6. *For any m and $D \leq m$, there is a graph $G = (V, E)$ in $\mathcal{G}_{m,D}$, s.t., for any starting node s and for any pointer assignment, there exists a port assignment for which the lock-in is achieved in time $\leq 24m$.*

Proof. Let $G = (V, E)$ be a chain of length D of complete bipartite graphs $K_{2,2}$. The number of edges in G is equal to $4D \leq 4m$. In the case where $4D < m$, append to G a star consisting of $m - 4D + 2$ edges, as illustrated in Figure 2. In both cases, the diameter of G is either D or $D + 2$ and the number of edges is between m and $4m$, thus $G \in \mathcal{G}_{m,D}$. Let $s \in V$ be the starting node in G, and f be the pointer assignment supplied by the adversary $\mathcal{A}$. Denote the set of

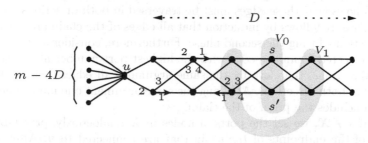

Fig. 2. The construction described in the proof of Theorem 6

nodes of the chain of complete bipartite graphs by X, and the central node of the appended star by u (if it exists).

For the time being, assume also that $s \in X$ and s' is the node on the opposite to s side in the chain (i.e., the node that has exactly the same neighbors as s). Furthermore, let V_i denote the subset of X that contains nodes at distance i from s ($i \geq 0$), with the exception that s' belongs not to V_2 but to V_0. We adopt a port assignment for the nodes of G as follows (refer to Figure 2 for illustration):

- For the special case of s and s', arrange the port numbers arbitrarily.
- For the node u, assign port 1 to $f(u)$. If $f(u)$ connects u to the chain, assign port number $\deg(u)$ to the other edge that connects u to the chain, and the rest of the ports arbitrarily. Otherwise, assign port numbers $\deg(u) - 1$ and $\deg(u)$ to the edges connecting u to the chain, and set the rest of the port numbers arbitrarily.
- For a node $v \in X$ at the endpoint of the chain, if v is not connected to u then set ports arbitrarily. If v is connected to u, then assign port 1 to $f(v)$ and assign the smallest possible port to the edge connecting v to u (if it is not $f(v)$).
- For any other $v \in X$, port 1 is always assigned to $f(v)$. Let $i \geq 1$ be the distance of v from s, thus $v \in V_i$. If $f(v)$ connects v to V_{i-1}, assign ports 2 and 3 to the edges connecting v to V_{i+1}, and port 4 to the remaining edge that connects v to V_{i-1}. Otherwise, assign port 2 to the remaining edge connecting v to V_{i+1} and ports 3 and 4 to the edges connecting v to V_{i-1}.

We claim that during the second phase of exploration the agent traverses all edges in both directions. In order to prove this claim, we first observe that during the first phase of exploration the agent must visit all the nodes in V_1. Therefore, during the second phase all the edges connecting V_0 to V_1 are traversed in both directions. Now, for some $i \geq 1$, assume that during the second phase of exploration the agent traverses all edges connecting V_i to V_{i-1} in both directions. According to the port assignment scheme defined above, for any $v \in V_i$ there is an incident edge e with port number 4 that connects it to some node in V_{i-1}. By assumption, e is traversed in both directions during the second phase. But before the tour of the second phase can use edge e on the way out of v, it is forced to use all other edges incident to v also on the way out of v, and in particular the edges that connect v to V_{i+1}. Since this property holds for all $v \in V_i$, and since the edges connecting V_i to V_{i+1} constitute a cut that disconnects s from V_{i+1}, it follows that these edges must be traversed in both directions during the second phase. It follows by induction that all edges of the chain are traversed in both directions during the second phase. Furthermore, consider any node $v \in X$ that is connected to u. The edge with the highest port number at v is traversed in both directions, therefore by the same argument all edges incident to v are traversed in both directions. Applying the same argument one more time for the node u concludes the proof of the claim.

Now, if $s \notin X$, we set the ports of nodes in X analogously, pretending that s is one of the endpoints of the chain that are connected to u. After at most two phases of exploration the agent traverses all edges of the star centered at u, and thus it visits the two endpoints of the chain connected to u. Then, by an analogous argument, during the third phase the agent traverses all edges in G in both directions.

We have proved that for any starting point and any pointer assignment, after at most three phases of exploration the agent traverses all edges in G in both directions. Since during each phase at most $4m$ edges are traversed in each direction, the upper bound of $24m$ for the lock-in time follows. $\square$

Case $\mathcal{P}(\circlearrowleft)\mathcal{A}(f)$. In the case where the adversary $\mathcal{A}$ responds by a pointer assignment to player $\mathcal{P}$'s initial port assignment, we first prove existence of a family of graphs in which locking-in requires time $\Omega(mD)$, matching the general worst-case upper bound from Theorem 1.

Theorem 7. *For any m and $D \leq m$, there is a graph $G = (V, E)$ in $\mathcal{G}_{m,D}$ with a starting node $s \in V$, s.t. for any port assignment there exists a pointer assignment under which the lock-in time in G is $\Omega(mD)$.*

Proof. Follows immediately from Theorem 5. $\square$

We show, however, that there is also a non-trivial class of graphs with diameter $O(\sqrt{n})$ in which the lock-in time is $O(m)$ in this case.

Theorem 8. *For any $D \leq \sqrt{n}$, there is a graph $G = (V, E)$ in $\mathcal{G}_{m,D}$, s.t., for any starting node s, there is a port assignment, s.t., for any possible pointer assignment the lock-in time is $O(m)$.*

Proof. For any a, let $G_a = (V, E)$ be the graph consisting of a chain of length a of complete bipartite graphs $K_{a,a}$. We will show that for any starting node s, there is a port assignment, s.t., for any possible pointer assignment the lock-in time in G_a is bounded by $8m$, where $m = |E|$.

Let $s \in V$ be a starting node with eccentricity ϵ. Let V_0 be the subset of nodes on the same level of the chain as s, and let V_i, $1 \leq i \leq \epsilon$, be the subset of $V \setminus V_0$ that contains all nodes at distance i from s. Moreover, let E_i denote the set of edges connecting V_i to V_{i+1}.

Consider an arbitrary node $v \in V_i$, for some i. The degree of this node is $2a$. Exactly a edges in E_i connect v to nodes in the set V_{i+1}; call these the *outward* edges of v. Moreover, exactly a of these edges connect v to nodes in the set V_{i-1}; call these the *inward* edges of v. We define a port assignment as follows. For any node v, its outward edges receive the odd port numbers $1, 3, \ldots, 2a - 1$, and its inward edges receive the even port numbers $2, 4, \ldots, 2a$. The ports of nodes in V_0 are assigned arbitrarily.

Regardless of the adversary's initial pointer assignment f, during the first phase of the exploration the agent visits at least all neighbors of s, i.e., at least all nodes in V_1. Therefore, during the second phase of exploration all nodes in V_1 become saturated which implies that all edges in E_0 and in E_1 are traversed in both directions.

For the remaining part of the proof we consider only nodes and edges on the side of V_0 that contains V_ϵ. The proof for the other side is analogous. We claim that during the second phase of exploration the agent will visit at least one node in V_ϵ. For the sake of the proof, first observe that for any node and during any phase of exploration, if x of the node's inward edges are traversed on the way out of v then, due to the alternating port assignment we adopted, at least $x-1$ outward edges will be traversed also on the way out of v. Now, for any $i \geq 1$ let y_i be the number of edges in E_i that are traversed in the direction $(V_i \rightarrow V_{i+1})$ during the second phase of exploration. Since E_i separates s from the nodes in V_{i+1}, y_i edges in E_i must be also traversed in the direction $(V_{i+1} \rightarrow V_i)$ during the second phase. By the previous observation, at least $y_i - a$ edges of E_{i+1} will be traversed in the direction $(V_{i+1} \rightarrow V_{i+2})$. Therefore, $y_{i+1} \geq y_i - a$. We have already established that $y_1 = a^2$. This recurrence boils down to $y_i \geq a^2 - (i-1)a$, which implies that for $i \leq \epsilon \leq a$ we have $y_i \geq a$. Thus, during the second phase of exploration the agent visits at least one node at the end-point of the chain.

It follows that every node in the graph is at distance at most 1 from some node visited during the second phase of exploration. Therefore, during the third phase the agent visits all nodes in the graph, and in the fourth phase it traverses all edges of the graph in both directions, achieving the Euler tour lock-in. Since during each phase the agent traverses at most m edges, each at most once in each direction, the upper bound of $8m$ for the lock-in time follows.   □

3   Further Work and Open Problems

Herein we have shown that it is advantageous to be in charge of pointer assignment in the rotor-router model. In all cases where the player $\mathcal{P}$ is responsible for pointer assignment the complexity of the lock-in problem is either linear or close to linear. In contrast, in all remaining cases where the adversary $\mathcal{A}$ controls assignment of pointers the worst-case complexity of the lock-in problem is always $\Omega(m \cdot D)$, i.e., the worst possible in view of Theorem 1.

In view of results from Subsection 2.3 a detailed study on the lock-in problem in more specific classes of graphs such as 2D-grids, planar or random graphs would be highly appreciated. This could be accompanied by a comparative study with the random walk procedure. Indeed, the lock-in time of a Propp machine is, in all the studied scenarios, equal up to constant factors to the time required to visit all the edges of the graph (its edge cover time). For example, in the $\mathcal{A}$-all scenario, the edge cover time using the Propp machine is precisely $\Theta(mD)$. This compares interestingly to the expected edge cover time of a graph when using random walk, which can be bounded as $O(mD \log m)$. Whereas our bound for the Propp machine is tight for any graph, the bound for random walks is not; indeed, for a 2D-grid on $k \times k$ nodes we have a worst-case edge cover time of $\Theta(k^3)$ using the Propp machine, and an expected edge cover time of $\Theta(k^2 \log^2 k)$ using random walk [1].

One could also imagine a game in which a player and its adversary choose assignments of ports and pointers in consecutive nodes visited by the agent in alternative turns. What is the complexity of such a game?

Acknowledgement

We would like to thank Shay Kutten and Tomasz Radzik for several inspiring discussions during the early stages of this work.

References

1. Aldous, D., Fill, J.: Reversible Markov Chains and Random Walks on Graphs (2001), http://stat-www.berkeley.edu/users/aldous/RWG/book.html
2. Afek, Y., Gafni, E.: Distributed Algorithms for Unidirectional Networks. SIAM Journal on Computing 23(6), 1152–1178 (1994)
3. Bhatt, S., Even, S., Greenberg, D., Tayar, R.: Traversing Directed Eulerian Mazes. Journal of Graph Algorithms and Applications 6(2), 157–173 (2002)
4. Cooper, C., Ilcinkas, D., Klasing, R., Kosowski, A.: Derandomizing Random Walks in Undirected Graphs Using Locally Fair Exploration Strategies. In: Albers, S., Marchetti-Spaccamela, A., Matias, Y., Niko-letsea, S. (eds.) ICALP 2009. LNCS, vol. 5556, pp. 411–422. Springer, Heidelberg (2009)
5. Cooper, J.N., Spencer, J.: Simulating a random walk with constant error. Combinatorics, Probability and Computing 15, 815–822 (2006)
6. Doerr, B., Friedrich, T.: Deterministic Random Walks on the Two-Dimensional Grid. Combinatorics, Probability and Computing 18(1-2), 123–144 (2009)
7. Fraenkel, A.S.: Economic traversal of labyrinths. Mathematics Magazine 43, 125–130 (1970)
8. Gąsieniec, L., Radzik, T.: Memory efficient anonymous graph exploration. In: Broersma, H., Erlebach, T., Friedetzky, T., Paulusma, D. (eds.) WG 2008. LNCS, vol. 5344, pp. 14–29. Springer, Heidelberg (2008)
9. Priezzhev, V.B., Dhar, D., Dhar, A., Krishnamurthy, S.: Eulerian walkers as a model of selforganized criticality. Physics Review Letters 77, 5079–5082 (1996)
10. Strahler, A.N.: Hypsometric (area-altitude) analysis of erosional topography. Geological Society of America Bulletin 63(11), 1117–1142 (1952)
11. Yanovski, V., Wagner, I.A., Bruckstein, A.M.: A Distributed Ant Algorithm for Efficiently Patrolling a Network. Algorithmica 37, 165–186 (2003)

Optimum Simultaneous Consensus for General Omissions Is Equivalent to an NP Oracle

Yoram Moses

Department of Electrical Engineering, Technion, Haifa 32000 Israel
moses@ee.technion.ac.il

Abstract. The general omissions failure model, in which a faulty process may omit both to send *and* to receive messages is inherently more complex than the more popular sending omissions model. This fact is exemplified in tasks involving simultaneous decisions, such as the simultaneous consensus (SC) problem. While efficient polynomial protocols for SC that are optimal in all runs are known for the sending omissions model, they do not exists for general omissions. It has been shown that such a protocol must perform at least NP-hard computations (in the number of processes n) between rounds. In fact, the best previously known SC protocol that is optimal in all runs in this model performs PSPACE (in n) computations between rounds. The current paper closes this twenty-year old gap by presenting such an optimal SC protocol that performs P^{NP} computations (polynomial-time computations using an oracle for NP; in fact, a constant number of accesses to the oracle are needed per round.) The result is based on a new characterization of common knowledge in the general omissions failure model.

Keywords: Simultaneous Consensus, synchronous systems, general omissions failure model, simultaneous action, common knowledge, NP Oracles.

1 Introduction

Fault-tolerant systems often require a means by which independent processes or processors can arrive at an exact mutual agreement of some kind. As a result, reaching consensus is one of the most fundamental problems in fault-tolerant distributed computing, dating back to the seminal work of Pease, Shostak, and Lamport [21]. In the early consensus algorithms, decisions were reached in the same round of communication by all correct processes. It was soon discovered, however, that allowing decisions to be made in different rounds at different sites ("eventual agreement") gives rise to simpler protocols in which the processes can often decide much faster than they would if we insist that decisions be simultaneous [5]. In many cases, eventual agreement suffices: In recording the outcomes of transactions, for example. In some instances, however, a simultaneous decision or action may be beneficial or even necessary: E.g., when one distributed algorithm ends and another one begins, and the two may interfere with each other if executed concurrently. Similarly, many synchronous algorithms are designed assuming that all sites start participating in the same round of communication. Finally, simultaneity may be motivated by the fact that a distributed system interacts

I. Keidar (Ed.): DISC 2009, LNCS 5805, pp. 436–448, 2009.

with the outside world, and these interactions may need to be simultaneously consistent. A non-simultaneous announcement to financial (stock) markets may enable unfair arbitrage trading, for example. The simultaneous version of consensus is defined as follows (cf. [17]):

Simultaneous Consensus (SC). Given is a set $\mathbb{P} = \{1,\ldots,n\}$ of processes, each starting out with an *initial value* $v_i \in \{0,1\}$. Desired is a protocol that will satisfy the following properties in each of its runs.

- Decision. Every nonfaulty process i decides on some value d_i.
- Validity. Every value d_i decided on is one of the initial values.
- Agreement. All nonfaulty processes decide on the same value.
- Simultaneous decision. All nonfaulty processes decide at the same time.

Simultaneous Consensus has been studied in a variety of failure models: crash [6], omission [17,20,19,13,14], and malicious failures [15,12]. One observation from these analyses (emphasized already in [6]) is that simultaneous consensus admits solutions satisfying a very strong notion of optimality: protocols that decide in the smallest number of rounds possible in each and every instance. More formally, let the *operating environment* σ of a run consist of the vector of initial values, the identity of the faulty processes, and the pattern of their faulty behavior. For a deterministic protocol P, we denote by $P(\sigma)$ the unique run resulting from executing P with the operating environment σ. With respect to a given failure model, we define

Definition 1. *An SC protocol P is optimal in all runs (or optimum) in a given failure model if, for every SC protocol P' and every operating environment σ, the decision (by the last correct process to decide) in $P(\sigma)$ takes place at least as early as in $P'(\sigma)$.*

Interestingly, as shown in [17], no protocol can be optimal in all runs for the *Eventual Consensus* problem—in which Decision, Validity and Agreement are required, but Simultaneity need not hold.

Moreover, there is a significant gap in the computational requirements for optimality in all runs between two closely related failure models: sending omissions and general omissions (see [17]). Roughly speaking, under *sending* omissions, a faulty process may fail to send an arbitrary subset of its prescribed messages in any given round. Under *general* omissions, a faulty process may fail both to receive *and* to send arbitrary subsets of its incoming and outgoing messages in every round.

There are very efficient polynomial-time SC protocols that are optimal in all runs for the crash and the sending omissions failure models [6,13,16,17]. In the case of general omissions, however, the most efficient known SC protocol that is optimal in all runs requires the processes to perform PSPACE computations between rounds [17]. Moreover, we have

Proposition 1 (Moses and Tuttle 88). *If $P{\neq}NP$ then there exists no polynomial-time SC protocol that is optimal in all runs for general omissions.*

Intuitively, the jump in the computational difficulty between sending and general omissions comes from the uncertainty regarding who to blame for a missing message in the case of general omissions. In the sending omissions model, a missing message indicates that the intended sender is faulty. With general omissions, it implies that (at least) one of the sender and receiver is faulty, without necessarily determining which of them is faulty.

For general omissions, as well as for more malicious failure models, failure detection and fault tolerance are facilitated by the construction of a *conflict graph* [1,7,17,18]. Intuitively, this is a graph whose nodes are process names, and where an edge between two process names implies that at least one of them must be faulty. (In our case, this edge will correspond to a missed message between the two processes.) The faulty processes must at all times form a vertex cover of the conflict graph. Using this observation, the proof of Proposition 1 in [17] reduces a variant of vertex cover to the problem of computing whether or not to "decide" in an optimum SC protocol for general omissions. Roughly speaking, the processes must simultaneously decide at a given time iff a particular vertex cover of the conflict graph does not exist. As a result, the computation performed by a process in an optimum protocol can be used to implement an oracle for NP. The gap between the NP-hardness lower bound and the PSPACE upper bound for general omissions has been open for over twenty years.

The analysis of simultaneous consensus is facilitated by knowledge-based reasoning. Dwork and Moses proved that *common knowledge* about the existence of particular initial values is a necessary and sufficient condition for deciding in an SC protocol [6]. The optimum protocols that have been designed for crash and sending omissions are based on a computationally efficient characterization of such common knowledge. These techniques for computing common knowledge in the crash and sending omissions model did not extend to general omissions. In this paper we present a new construction that characterizes common knowledge for general omissions using P^{NP} computations (polynomial-time computations with access to an NP oracle). The main contributions of this paper are:

- A new characterization of common knowledge in the general omissions modelis presented;
- An SC protocol is derived that is optimal in all runs for general omissions, in which processes perform computations in P^{NP} between rounds. This improves on the previous PSPACE solution, and closes a complexity gap that has been open for more than twenty years;
- The characterization can be used to optimally solve the more general continuous consensus at the same complexity cost, improving results of [15] for this model; and
- While all of the protocols that we are concerned with here are intractable, the analysis of optimum behavior and reachability in general omissions is expected to lead to further insight into the fundamental structure of fault tolerant computation, and the differences between failure models. Moreover, we expect our techniques and construction to be applicable to the authenticated Byzantine model, and perhaps extensible to the (pure) Byzantine model.

This paper is organized as follows: In the next section we define the model. Section 3 briefly introduces the bit of knowledge theory required for relating SC and common knowledge for our analysis. In Section 4 we motivate and present a new construction characterizing common knowledge in the general omissions model. Finally, Section 5 discusses further implications of this work, possible future extensions, and some conclusions.

2 Model and Preliminary Definitions

Following [17], this paper analyzes protocols in the standard round-synchronous model, with a set $\mathbb{P} = \{1,2,\ldots,n\}$ of $n \geq 2$ possibly unreliable processes, and a bound on the number of failures. The processes share a discrete global clock that starts out at time 0 and advances by increments of one. Communication in the system proceeds in a sequence of *rounds*, with round $k+1$ taking place between time k and time $k+1$. Each pair of processes is connected by a two-way communication channel. Depending on the failure pattern, discussed below, a channel is either blocked or not blocked in a given round. If the channel is blocked, messages sent over it are lost. In a round in which it is not blocked, messages sent over the channel are delivered, unaltered.

Benign Failure Patterns. Our focus in this paper is on general omission failures, which are instances of benign failures. Intuitively, a benign failure pattern specifies which channels are blocked in any given round. Define the set $\mathbb{V} = \mathbb{P} \times \mathbb{N}$ of *process-time nodes* (or *nodes*, for short). A node $(i,k) \in \mathbb{V}$ serves to refer to process i at time k. We denote by $\mathbb{V}(k)$ the set $\mathbb{P} \times \{k\} \subset \mathbb{V}$ of all time k nodes; moreover, for $k \leq \ell \leq \infty$, we define $\mathbb{V}[k,\ell] = \{(i,h) | i \in \mathbb{P} \ \& \ k \leq h \leq \ell\}$.[1]

A *failure pattern* (for benign failures) is a function $\varphi : \mathbb{V} \to 2^{\mathbb{P}}$. The set $\varphi(i,k)$ lists the processes to which messages sent by i in round $k+1$ will not be delivered. In other words, a message sent by i to j in round $k+1$ will be delivered iff $j \notin \varphi(i,k)$.[2] In this paper we assume for ease of exposition that a process (implicitly) sends a message to itself in every round, and its "channel" to itself is never blocked. Thus, formally, $i \notin \varphi(i,k)$ for all φ, $i \in \mathbb{P}$ and $k \geq 0$. We identify a failure pattern φ with a *communication graph*[3] $G^{\varphi} = (\mathbb{V}, E^{\varphi})$, where $E^{\varphi} = \{ \langle (i,k),(j,k+1) \rangle : j \notin \varphi(i,k) \}$. Notice that φ uniquely determines G^{φ} and vice-versa. For a node $v = (i,k) \in \mathbb{V}$, we denote by $G^{\varphi}(i,k)$—or $G^{\varphi}(v)$—the subgraph of G^{φ} generated by v and all nodes $w \in \mathbb{V}$ such that there is a directed path from w to v in G^{φ}. This subgraph, illustrated in Figure 1, captures the potential "causal past" of v under φ: all nodes by which v can be affected via communication, either directly or indirectly. Given a set of nodes $S \subseteq \mathbb{V}$, we denote by $G^{\varphi}(S)$ the subgraph of G^{φ} obtained by taking the union of the graphs $G^{\varphi}(v)$, taken over all $v \in S$. By definition, $G^{\varphi}(\emptyset)$ is the empty graph, with no nodes and no edges.

Runs and Protocols. We think of each process $i \in \mathbb{P}$ as receiving a message from the environment at time 0, consisting of its *initial value* $v_i \in \{0,1\}$. The vector $(v_1,\ldots,v_n) \in \{0,1\}^n$ of initial values is called the *input vector* and is denoted by I. A *run* is determined by a tuple $r = (\text{Faults}_r, \varphi_r, I_r, \lambda_r, \mu_r)$, where $\text{Faults}_r \subseteq \mathbb{P}$ is the set of faulty processes, φ_r is a failure pattern, I_r is an input vector, λ_r assigns a local state to every

---

[1] There are no nodes (i,h) with $h < 0$. We will find it convenient to refer to the set $\mathbb{V}(-1) = \emptyset$.

[2] Somewhat in the spirit of [3], we treat benign failure patterns as focusing on message loss or blocked channels, without implying who is to blame for such failures. For problems such as SC, which are specified in terms of the behavior of the correct processes, however, the set of faulty processes in a given run must be well-defined. Our definition of a run below will indeed have a separate component Faults_r defining the set of faulty processes in the run.

[3] Communication graphs were first used, informally, in the analysis of consensus by Merritt [11]. They were formalized in [17,8]. Our modeling is taken from the latter.

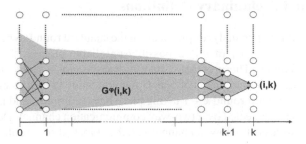

Fig. 1. Subgraph $G^{\varphi}(i,k)$ of the communication graph G^{φ}

node of $\mathbb{V}$, and μ_r assigns a message (or $\bot$, standing for "no message") to every edge of G^{φ_r} (i.e., to every channel not blocked by φ_r). Finally, a (joint) protocol is a sequence $P = (P_1, \ldots, P_n)$, where every P_i determines process i's outgoing messages and local state at a node of $\mathbb{V}$ as a deterministic function of its previous local state and the messages on its incoming channels. We consider r to be a *run of* P if λ_r and μ_r are consistent with P, I_r and φ_r.

t-bounded general omission faults. In the general omissions model, the only source of failures are process failures. Faults_r defines the set of faulty processes in the run r. Intuitively, a faulty process may fail to send or to receive arbitrary sets of messages. More formally, this means that if $i \in \mathsf{Faults}_r$ then an arbitrary subset of both incoming and outgoing channels to and from nodes (i,k) can be blocked. It is convenient to define the *(potential) conflict graph* of a failure pattern φ to be an undirected graph $\mathsf{ConfG}(\varphi) = (\mathbb{P}, \mathsf{E_C})$ whose nodes are the processes, and $\{i,j\} \in \mathsf{E_C}$ iff there is some time h for which at least one of $j \in \varphi(i,h)$ or $i \in \varphi(j,h)$ holds. We say that r is a run in the *general omissions failure model* if the processes in Faults_r form a Vertex Cover of $\mathsf{ConfG}(\varphi_r)$. Let $\Phi_{\mathrm{go}}(t)$ denote the set of patterns φ for which $\mathsf{ConfG}(\varphi)$ has a vertex cover of size $\leq t$.

We represent a protocol P in the t-bounded general omissions model by the set $\mathcal{R}(P,t)$ of all runs of P in which there are at most t faulty processes. Notice that $\mathcal{R}(P,t)$ contains exactly one run for every pair (φ, I) where $\varphi \in \Phi_{\mathrm{go}}(t)$ and $I \in \{0,1\}^n$ is an input vector. We remark that having Faults_r be an explicit component of a run r allows a specification such as SC, requiring nonfaulty processes to behave in a prescribed way, to be well-defined. A failure pattern φ determines the blocked channels in a run, and so it does not uniquely determine the faulty processes in the case of general omissions. Sometimes, however, φ forces a process to be faulty. With respect to a given bound t, we will say that φ *condemns* i if i belongs to *every* vertex cover of size t of $\mathsf{ConfG}(\varphi)$. This may happen, for example, if i conflicts with more than t other processes.

3 Simultaneous Consensus and Common Knowledge

Knowledge theory, and specifically the notion of common knowledge, are central to the study of simultaneously coordinated actions. This connection has been developed and described in [10,6,8,17,19,20,14]. For a more complete exposition of knowledge theory see [8]. Knowledge is analyzed within the context of a *system* $\mathcal{R} = \mathcal{R}(P,t)$. A pair (r,k) where r is a run and k is a time is called a *point*. We say that i *cannot distinguish* (r,k) from (r',k) if i has the same local state at both points, i.e., if $\lambda_r(i,k) = \lambda_{r'}(i,k)$. For $b \in \{0,1\}$, we denote by '$\exists b$' the basic fact that *"at least one of the initial values is b"*. We consider knowledge formulas to be true or false at a given point (r,k) in the context of a system $\mathcal{R}$. In the standard definition [8], process i knows a fact such as $\exists b$ at (r,k) if $\exists b$ holds at all points that i cannot distinguish from (r,k).

For every property X of runs or points we denote by $C(X)$ the fact that X is common knowledge, which intuitively means that everybody knows X, everybody knows that everybody knows X, and so on ad infinitum. We define common knowledge formally in the following way, which can be shown to capture this intuition in a precise sense (see [17]). We define a *reachability relation* $\sim$ among points of $\mathcal{R}$ to be the least relation satisfying that $(r,k) \sim (r',k)$ if either:

1. $\lambda_r(i,k) = \lambda_{r'}(i,k)$ holds for some process $i \notin (\text{Faults}_r \cup \text{Faults}_{r'})$, or
2. for some $r'' \in \mathcal{R}$, both $(r,k) \sim (r'',k)$ and $(r'',k) \sim (r',k)$.

In other words, define the *similarity graph* over $\mathcal{R}$ to be an undirected graph whose nodes are the points of $\mathcal{R}$, and where two points are connected by an edge if there is a process, nonfaulty at both points, that cannot distinguish between them. Then $(r,k) \sim (r',k)$ if both points are in the same *connected component* of the similarity graph over $\mathcal{R}$. Notice that $\sim$ is an equivalence relation.

We write $(\mathcal{R},r,k) \models C(X)$ to state that X is common knowledge to the correct processes at time k in r. We formally define:

$$(\mathcal{R},r,k) \models C(X) \quad \text{if } X \text{ is true at } (r',k) \text{ for every } r' \in \mathcal{R} \text{ such that } (r,k) \sim (r',k).$$

The Validity property guarantees that processes cannot decide on a value b unless $\exists b$ holds. An essential observation of [6] is that deciding in simultaneous consensus requires *common knowledge* of $\exists b$:

Theorem 1 ([6,17]). *Let P be an SC protocol for general omissions, and let $r \in \mathcal{R} = \mathcal{R}(P,t)$. If the nonfaulty processes decide on the value b at the end of round k in r, then $(\mathcal{R},r,k) \models C(\exists b)$.*

Analyzing Common Knowledge via Failure Patterns

While Theorem 1 shows that common knowledge is a necessary condition for deciding in simultaneous consensus, common knowledge has also proved to be a sufficient condition for such decision. This suggests an approach to solving SC by deciding *as soon as some initial value becomes common knowledge*. Interestingly, common knowledge is reached in the fastest possible way in all runs of *full information* protocols [6,17]. In fact, it turns out that the round in which initial values become common knowledge in a full-information protocol depends only on the failure pattern. To simplify the technical development we now define a notion of reachability at the level of failure patterns.

Definition 2 (Pattern Similarity). *Fix t and $\ell \geq 0$. We define '$\approx_\ell$' to be the least binary relation over $\Phi_{go}(t)$ satisfying that $\varphi \approx_\ell \varphi'$ if:*

1. $G^\varphi(i, \ell) = G^{\varphi'}(i, \ell)$ *and neither φ nor φ' condemns i, or*
2. *for some $\varphi'' \in \Phi_{go}(t)$, both $\varphi \approx_\ell \varphi''$ and $\varphi'' \approx_\ell \varphi'$.*

As in the case of $\sim$, the $\approx_\ell$ relation is an equivalence relation. We can use $\approx_\ell$ to determine that certain facts cannot be common knowledge, because, in a precise sense, reachability at the level of failure patterns refines reachability among points:

Lemma 1. *Let $r, r' \in \mathcal{R}(P, t)$ be runs with the same input vector $I_r = I_{r'}$. Then $\varphi_r \approx_\ell \varphi_{r'}$ implies $(r, \ell) \sim (r', \ell)$. Moreover, if P is a full-information protocol then $\varphi_r \approx_\ell \varphi_{r'}$ is equivalent to $(r, \ell) \sim (r', \ell)$.*

4   The CK Construction

We now turn to characterizing the $\approx_\ell$ relation among failure patterns in $\Phi_{go}(t)$. Given the definition of common knowledge, and Lemma 1, this will determine the earliest time at which common knowledge of facts about the input and failure pattern is attained, for each failure pattern. Thus, by Theorem 1, this will allow us to obtain tight bounds on when a decision in simultaneous consensus can be performed, for every individual failure pattern. Indeed, since common knowledge is related to many additional simultaneous tasks, such as the firing squad problem and continuous consensus, the characterization will yield similar bounds for these tasks as well.

Definition 3 (Shut Out and Silenced Nodes). *The node $v = (i, k)$ is said to be* shut out *in φ if $\varphi(i, k) = \mathbb{P} \setminus \{i\}$, so that i's adjacent channels are all blocked in round $k + 1$. We say that the node $v = (i, k)$ is* silenced *in φ if (i, h) is shut out in φ for all $h \geq k$.*

We say that φ and ψ *agree on* a set $W \subseteq \mathbb{V}$ if $\varphi(w) = \psi(w)$ holds for all $w \in W$. For a pattern φ and a node $v \in \mathbb{V}$ we define $^{(v)}\varphi$ to be the pattern that shuts out the node v and that agrees with φ on all other nodes. Recall that a node is shut out if all of its outgoing channels, in the round immediately following the node, are blocked. Similarly, we denote by $^{\langle\!\langle v \rangle\!\rangle}\varphi$ the failure pattern in which v is silenced, and agrees with φ on all remaining nodes.

Intuition and motivation for the construction. Roughly speaking, if $\varphi \approx_\ell {}^{\langle\!\langle v \rangle\!\rangle}\varphi$, so that the node v can be silenced at a reachable pattern, then information available only at v in φ cannot be common knowledge, since $^{\langle\!\langle v \rangle\!\rangle}\varphi \approx_\ell {}^{\langle\!\langle v \rangle\!\rangle}\psi$, where in $^{\langle\!\langle v \rangle\!\rangle}\psi$ this information is not true. Examples of such local information are initial values, if v is a time 0 node, or the set of blocked channels leading into v. The first construction characterizing common knowledge was presented in [17] for the **sending** omissions model. It is based on an analysis showing, essentially, that if k processes are discovered to be faulty by time ℓ in φ, then it is possible to silence every time h nodes in the range $\ell - (t - k) \leq h \leq \ell$, "unblock" all incoming channels to these nodes, and then revive the nodes. (Reviving a node v in this case means moving from $^{\langle\!\langle v \rangle\!\rangle}\psi$ to the pattern ψ in which none of v's outgoing channels is blocked.) In fact, the same can also be done to the time $\ell - (t - k) - 1$ nodes belonging to processes that the nonfaulty processes in φ know are faulty. If φ' is the result of performing such a silencing-then-reviving step on φ, then the number of faulty processes in φ' is no larger than in φ. If it is strictly smaller, then we can perform another such step, this time with respect to φ'. Clearly, after at most k steps, the number of failures cannot be further reduced, and performing such a step will yield $\varphi' = \varphi$. The resulting pattern is a fixed point of this process. All nodes that can be silenced in this process cannot contain information that is common knowledge at time ℓ. Interestingly, it was shown that all nodes that remain and cannot be silenced in this way at the fixed point pattern, appears in all $\approx_\ell$-reachable patterns. Consequently, local information available at these nodes can become common knowledge.

Extending to general omissions. Following the work of [6] for the crash failure model, the construction of [17] made essential use of the fact that a missing message implicates the sender as being faulty. This is no longer the case in the general omissions model. As a result, the set of time $\ell - (t - k) - 1$ nodes that should be silenced-then-revived cannot be uniquely determined. The new construction, which handles general omissions, is inspired by a recent improvement of the construction of [17] that appeared in [14]. The latter construction was still designed for a variant of sending omissions. It required major modifications to apply correctly to general omissions. The main technical difference is that the construction is not based on what the set of nonfaulty processes know. Rather, there is a careful definition of *maskable* nodes—essentially the silenceable nodes discussed above. While failures are not uniquely determined by the missing messages, a lower bound on their number is obtainable based on the pattern's conflict graph. In a precise sense, this now depends not on the view of the elusive set of nonfaulty processes, but rather on the view available at the nodes not yet shown to be maskable. We proceed as follows.

Definition 4 (Maskable Nodes). *Let* $\psi \in \Phi_{go}(t)$ *and let* $0 \le k < \ell$. *The set of maskable nodes in* ψ *is:*

$$Mask(\psi) = \mathbb{V}(\ell) \cup \{v = (i,k) : {}^{(v)}\psi \in \Phi_{go}(t + k - \ell + 1)\}.$$

In other words, a node $v = (i,k)$ is maskable in ψ w.r.t. time ℓ if shutting out v creates a pattern whose conflict graph has a vertex cover of size $t + k - \ell + 1$. The definition of maskable nodes is of interest because, for every node v maskable in φ, the pattern ${}^{\langle\!\langle v \rangle\!\rangle}\varphi$ obtained by silencing v in φ is reachable from φ:

Lemma 2. *If* $v \in Mask(\varphi)$ *then* $\varphi \approx_\ell {}^{\langle\!\langle v \rangle\!\rangle}\varphi$.

Another useful property of maskable nodes is

Lemma 3. *If* $(i,k) \in Mask(\varphi)$ *then* $\mathbb{V}[k+1,\ell] \subseteq Mask(\varphi)$.

Lemma 3 implies that the transition from maskable to unmaskable nodes is abrupt: In a given pattern, there is always one time instant after which all nodes are maskable. All nodes at earlier times are not maskable. The following definition captures this transition point:

$$k_\varphi = \min\{h \ge -1 : \mathbb{V}(h+1) \subseteq Mask(\varphi)\}.$$

We denote $Mask(\varphi, h) = Mask(\varphi) \cap \mathbb{V}(h)$, the set of maskable time h nodes. By Lemma 3 we have that if $h > k_\varphi$ then $Mask(\varphi, h) = \mathbb{V}(h)$, while $Mask(\varphi, h) = \emptyset$ for $h < k_\varphi$. We are interested in the *view* of the unmaskable time k_φ nodes. We define this set of nodes by:

Definition 5. *Let* $\psi \in \Phi_{go}(t)$, *and* $\ell \geq 0$. *Then* $U[\psi] = (\mathbb{V}(k_\psi) \setminus Mask(\psi, k_\psi))$.

Observe that if $\mathbb{V}[0, \ell] \subseteq Mask(\psi)$ then $k_\psi = -1$, and since $\mathbb{V}(-1) = \emptyset$ we obtain that $U[\psi] = \emptyset$. If $k_\psi \neq -1$ then $Mask(\psi, k_\psi) \neq \mathbb{V}(k_\psi)$ and thus $U[\psi] = \mathbb{V}(k_\psi) \setminus Mask(\psi, k_\psi) \neq \emptyset$.

We will characterize common knowledge in the general omissions model using a construction that makes use of the sets $U[\psi]$ for a sequence of patterns ψ. By Lemma 2 we have that nodes in the complement $Mask(\psi, k_\psi)$ of $U[\psi]$ can be silenced. Roughly speaking, once they are silenced, information that they have about blocked channels can be discarded, and the channels can be unblocked. For the resulting pattern ψ' we will have that $Mask(\psi) \subseteq Mask(\psi')$ and possibly $U[\psi'] \neq U[\psi]$. Intuitively, the construction will consist of repeating the process of computing maskable nodes, eliminating incriminating evidence that *only they* hold, and obtaining a new, improved, pattern. The latter step is based on the following operation:

Definition 6 ($\varphi \bmod A$). *Let* $A \subseteq \mathbb{V}$. *Then* '$\varphi \bmod A$' *is the pattern* ψ *defined, for all* $(i, h) \in \mathbb{V}$, *by*

$$\psi(i, h) = \{j \in \varphi(i, h) : (j, h+1) \text{ appears in } G^\varphi(A)\}.$$

Thus, a channel $i \rightarrow j$ is blocked in a given round $h + 1$ according to $\psi = (\varphi \bmod A)$ if and only if $G^\varphi(A)$ records this channel as being blocked in that round. Channels about which $G^\varphi(A)$ contains no information, as well as ones that the graph records as unblocked, are not blocked in $\varphi \bmod A$. We note that in the extreme case of $A = \emptyset$, we have that $\psi \bmod \emptyset = \odot$, where $\odot$ is the failure-free pattern. Note that the pattern $\varphi \bmod A$ is a function of the graph $G^\varphi(A)$. In the sequel, the mod operation will be applied only to sets $A \subseteq \mathbb{V}(k)$ for some k, so that all nodes of A come from the same time slice in $\mathbb{V}$.

The CK Construction, depicted in Figure 2, is a fixed-point construction in the spirit of the Moses and Tuttle construction in [17]. It accepts as input the values of n and t, and a point (φ, ℓ), and outputs a communication graph. The construction consists of a set of iterations, each creating a new pattern $\hat{\varphi}$, with potentially fewer blocked channels, attempting to increase the set of maskable nodes. Once an iteration no longer reduces the set of blocked channels, the construction ends, and returns $G^\varphi(U[\hat{\varphi}])$, for the final pattern $\hat{\varphi}$ obtained when the construction ends.

In the full paper we show that the CK construction is guaranteed to terminate:

The **CK_Construction**(n, t, φ, ℓ):
(01) $\hat{\varphi} \leftarrow \varphi \bmod \mathbb{V}(\ell)$;
(02)   **while** $\hat{\varphi} \neq \varphi \bmod U[\hat{\varphi}]$
(03)   **do** $\hat{\varphi} \leftarrow \varphi \bmod U[\hat{\varphi}]$
(04)   **return** $G^\varphi(U[\hat{\varphi}])$

Fig. 2. Computing the subgraph characterizing common knowledge

Lemma 4. *If* $\varphi \in \Phi_{go}(t)$ *and* $t < n - 1$ *then the CK construction on input* (n, t, φ, ℓ) *terminates.*

We denote by $\hat{G}_{ck}[\varphi, \ell]$ the communication graph returned by the construction on input (n, t, φ, ℓ). A careful analysis of the construction, whose details are beyond the scope of this abstract, we are able to show that the construction completely characterizes $\approx_\ell$ reachability:

Theorem 2. *Let* $\varphi, \psi \in \Phi_{go}(t)$ *and* $\ell \geq 0$. *Then* $\varphi \approx_\ell \psi$ *iff* $\hat{G}_{ck}[\varphi, \ell] = \hat{G}_{ck}[\psi, \ell]$.

Based on Theorem 2 we will be able to show that the results of the CK construction completely characterize decision in optimum SC protocols. Fix t, and for every $\varphi \in \Phi_{go}(t)$ denote by dec-time(φ) the first time ℓ for which $\hat{G}_{ck}[\varphi, \ell]$ is nonempty. For a lower bound, we have:

Lemma 5. *For every* $\varphi \in \Phi_{go}(t)$, *a correct SC protocol* P *never decides before time* dec-time(φ) *in runs with pattern* φ.

More importantly, the CK construction enables us to design a relatively efficient optimum SC protocol for general omissions. Observe that the CK construction is performed on a run's failure pattern up to time ℓ. This is a global computation, which cannot be directly simulated by individual processes, because a process does not have access to the whole failure pattern. We can, however, use the construction to derive a protocol in the following manner. First, as in [17], we can define a protocol in which the local state of a process i at time k a run with pattern φ consists of the graph $G^\varphi(i, k)$, and where the time 0 nodes are labeled by their initial values. As a result, local states have size $O(n^2)$. Moreover, this can be done with small messages of size $O(n^2)$ and amortized size of $O(n)$. Since process i has access to $G^\varphi(i, k)$ at time k, it can easily construct the pattern $\varphi \mathrm{mod}(i, k)$, in which all channels about which it has no information are not blocked. We can show:

Lemma 6. *Let* $\varphi \in \Phi_{go}(t)$, *and let* $\varphi_i = \varphi \mathrm{mod}(i, \ell)$. *If* φ *does not condemn* i, *then* $\hat{G}_{ck}[\varphi_i, \ell] = \hat{G}_{ck}[\varphi, \ell]$.

This lemma combined with Theorem 2 and Lemma 1 imply that the initial values that label the time 0 nodes of $\hat{G}_{ck}[\varphi, \ell]$ are common knowledge. This observation enables us to reduce the problem of optimum SC to the problem of computing $\hat{G}_{ck}[\varphi, \ell]$ given the graph $G^\varphi(\ell)$. Based on the CK construction, we no longer need PSPACE computations for this. Indeed, we can show:

Theorem 3. *There is an optimum SC protocol* Opt-go *for general omissions in which computations between rounds of communication are in* $P^{NP}(n)$.

Proof. Given that there are well-known SC protocols that terminate in exactly $t + 1$ rounds, we have by Lemma 5 that dec-time(φ) $\leq t + 1$, and so $\ell \leq t + 1 < n$.

We first describe how to compute $\hat{G}_{ck}[\varphi, \ell]$ from $G^\varphi(\mathbb{V}[0, \ell])$ in $P^{NP}(n)$. Since $\ell < n$, there are $O(n^2)$ nodes in $\mathbb{V}[0, \ell]$. It is easy to compute a pattern $\hat{\varphi} \mathrm{mod} A$ given $\hat{\varphi}$ and a set $A \subseteq \mathbb{V}(k)$. It remains to show how to compute the sets $A = U[\hat{\varphi}]$. The first step is to compute $k_{\hat{\varphi}}$, which is a time k satisfying that ConfG($\hat{\varphi}$) has a vertex cover of size

$t + k - \ell + 2$ but not one of size $t + k - \ell + 1$. This can be obtained by guessing $k = \mathsf{k}_{\hat{\varphi}}$ and a VC of size $t + k - \ell + 2$, and verifying that it has no cover of size $t + k - \ell + 1$. Denote $A = \mathsf{Mask}(\hat{\varphi}, \mathsf{k}_{\hat{\varphi}})$, and recall that it is nonempty. We can now guess A and verify with a single NP query (a co-VC test) that each node in A is not maskable, and by a VC test that every node in $\mathbb{V}(\mathsf{k}_{\hat{\varphi}}) \setminus A$ is maskable. Thus, with $O(n)$ queries we can compute $\varphi \bmod \mathsf{U}[\hat{\varphi}]$. Since there are at most $O(n \cdot \ell) = O(n^2)$ iterations, it follows that $\hat{\mathsf{G}}_{\mathsf{ck}}[\varphi, \ell]$ can be computed in P^{NP}, as desired.

The Opt-go protocol maintains local states consisting of the local communication graph as done in [17] and discussed above. In particular, process i's local state at time ℓ at a run of Opt-go$_i$ with pattern φ maintains $\mathsf{G}^{\varphi}(i, \ell)$. The Opt-go$_i$ protocol computes $\varphi_i = \varphi \bmod \{(i, \ell)\}$ and obtains $\hat{\mathsf{G}}_{\mathsf{ck}}[\varphi_i, \ell]$ by the P^{NP} computation just described. It has process i *not decide* at time ℓ if $\hat{\mathsf{G}}_{\mathsf{ck}}[\varphi_i, \ell]$ is empty. If $\hat{\mathsf{G}}_{\mathsf{ck}}[\varphi_i, \ell]$ is nonempty, then process i decides on a value $d_i = 0$ if at least one of the initial values recorded an initial node of $\hat{\mathsf{G}}_{\mathsf{ck}}[\varphi_i, \ell]$ is 0, it decides $d_i = 1$ otherwise. Lemma 5 and the fact that i is nonfaulty imply that the values that appear in $\hat{\mathsf{G}}_{\mathsf{ck}}[\varphi_i, \ell]$ appear in $\hat{\mathsf{G}}_{\mathsf{ck}}[\varphi_j, \ell]$ for every other nonfaulty process j as well. Hence, under Opt-go, all nonfaulty processes decide at time dec-time(φ), in a manner that satisfies the four requirements of SC.   ■

A closer inspection of the P^{NP} computation described in the proof of Theorem 3 shows that the $O(n^3)$ guesses can all be generated in parallel, and consequently the computation of $\hat{\mathsf{G}}_{\mathsf{ck}}[\varphi, \ell]$ can be obtained using two queries to the NP Oracle: One to verify the VC claims, and one to verify the co-VC claims.

5   Extensions and Conclusions

Moses and Tuttle showed in [17] that there are simultaneous consensus protocols that are optimal in all runs in the sending omissions and in the general omissions models. The protocol for sending omissions is computationally efficient—performing polynomial time (in n) computations between rounds, while the one for general omissions makes use of PSPACE computations between rounds. An accompanying lower bound showed that any optimum SC protocol for general omissions must require processes to perform NP-hard computations between rounds. Indeed, this result immediately implies that an NP oracle can be reduced to the computation performed between two rounds (from the second round on) in such a protocol. The current paper closes the gap left by [17], presenting an optimum SC protocol that makes use of P^{NP} computations.

Our SC protocol is based on a new characterization of common knowledge in the general omissions model. As done for crash and omissions models in [17,13], this characterization can be used to solve other simultaneous decision problems such as *Firing Squad* [2,4]. Indeed, the characterization readily provides a solution to the much more general problem of *continuous consensus* (CC) as done in [13] for crash and sending omissions models. It therefore improves the results of [15], in which P^{NP} computations were used to design fast, but not optimum, protocols for continuous consensus for general omissions. A continuous consensus service is a perpetual service, for which the global bound of t on the number of failures is ultimately inappropriate. More appropriate is the (m, t) interval-bounded fault assumption, in which it is assumed that at most t

processes fail in every interval of m rounds, which was considered for sending omissions in [14]. It is still an open problem to combine our construction with techniques from [14], in order to handle the (m,t) assumption with general omissions.

The complexity gap between sending and general omissions comes from the ambiguity in the latter model concerning the identity of the faulty process that caused an observed failure. In crash and sending omissions, a missing message proves that the intended sender is faulty. Similar phenomena are observed in the more malicious authenticated Byzantine failure model. In this case, when one process claims that another process did not send it a required message, all that can be concluded is that one of them is faulty. We believe that the techniques developed in the current paper can be extended to provide a characterization of common knowledge for the authenticated Byzantine model. Indeed, we expect similar P^{NP} computations to be necessary and sufficient for optimum SC and CC protocols in this case.

Ambiguity regarding the identity of faulty processes is commonplace also in the purely malicious case of (non-authenticated) Byzantine failures. It is an interesting open problem to extend our work to the Byzantine model. An initial attempt at applying common knowledge to solving SC in this model was made in [12]. In the Byzantine model we have both a bound of $n > 3t$ on the ratio between the number of processes and the number of faulty processes [21], and a bound of $t + 1$ rounds on the worst case for consensus. Both results are based on reachability arguments (cf. [9]), although the proofs are very different. An interesting open problem is whether extensions of the techniques developed in this paper and in [14] can be used to obtain both bounds for consensus in the Byzantine model in a unified manner.

References

1. Berman, P., Garay, J.A.: Cloture Votes: n/4-Resilient Distributed Consensus in $t + 1$ Rounds. Math. Syst. Theo. 26(1), 3–19 (1993); SIAM J. Comput. 27(1), 247–290 (1998)
2. Burns, J.E., Lynch, N.A.: The Byzantine Firing Squad Problem. Technical Report MIT/LCS/TM-275 (1985)
3. Charron-Bost, B., Schiper, A.: The Heard-of Model: Computing in Distributed Systems with Benign Faults. Distributed Computing (published online) (July 2009)
4. Coan, B.A., Dolev, D., Dwork, C., Stockmeyer, L.J.: The Distributed Firing Squad Problem. SIAM J. Comput. 18(5), 990–1012 (1989)
5. Dolev, D., Reischuk, R., Strong, H.R.: Eventual is Earlier than Immediate. In: Proc. 23rd IEEE Symp. on Foundations of Computer Science, pp. 196–203 (1982)
6. Dwork, C., Moses, Y.: Knowledge and Common Knowledge in a Byzantine Environment: Crash failures. Information and Computation 88(2), 156–186 (1990)
7. Garay, J.A., Moses, Y.: Fully Polynomial Byzantine Agreement for $n > 3t$ Processors in $t + 1$ Rounds. SIAM J. Comput. 27(1), 247–290 (1998)
8. Fagin, R., Halpern, J.Y., Moses, Y., Vardi, M.Y.: Reasoning about Knowledge. MIT Press, Cambridge (1995 revised 2003)
9. Fischer, M.J., Lynch, N.A., Merritt, M.: Easy Impossibility Proofs for Distributed Consensus Problems. J. ACM 34(1), 98–115 (1987)
10. Halpern, J.Y., Moses, Y.: Knowledge and Common Knowledge in a Distributed Environment. J. ACM 37(3), 549–587 (1990)
11. Merritt, M.J.: Unpublished notes on the Dolev-Strong lower bound for Byzantine Agreement (1984)

12. Michel, R.: A Categorical Approach to Distributed Systems Expressibility and Knowledge. In: Proc. 8th Symp. Princ. Dist. Comp. (PODC), pp. 129–143 (1989)
13. Mizrahi, T., Moses, Y.: Continuous Consensus via Common Knowledge. Distributed Computing 20(5), 305–321 (2008)
14. Mizrahi, T., Moses, Y.: Continuous consensus with failures and recoveries. In: Taubenfeld, G. (ed.) DISC 2008. LNCS, vol. 5218, pp. 408–422. Springer, Heidelberg (2008)
15. Mizrahi, T., Moses, Y.: Continuous Consensus with Ambiguous Failures. In: Proc. ICDCN, pp. 73–85 (2008)
16. Moses, Y., Raynal, M.: Revisiting Simultaneous Consensus with Crash Failures. J. Par. Dist. Comp. 69, 400–409 (2009)
17. Moses, Y., Tuttle, M.R.: Programming simultaneous actions using common knowledge. Algorithmica 3, 121–169 (1988)
18. Moses, Y., Waarts, O.: Coordinated Traversal: $(t+1)$-round Byzantine Agreement in Polynomial Time. J. Algorithms 17(1), 110–156 (1994)
19. Neiger, G., Bazzi, R.A.: Using Knowledge to Optimally Achieve Coordination in Distributed Systems. Theor. Comput. Sci. 220(1), 31–65 (1999)
20. Neiger, G., Tuttle, M.R.: Common Knowledge and Consistent Simultaneous Coordination. Distributed Computing 6(3), 181–192 (1993)
21. Pease, M., Shostak, R., Lamport, L.: Reaching Agreement in the Presence of Faults. Journal of the ACM 27(2), 228–234 (1980)

On the Number of Synchronous Rounds Sufficient for Authenticated Byzantine Agreement

Matthias Fitzi* and Jesper Buus Nielsen

¹ ETH Zurich, Switzerland
² Aarhus University, Denmark

Abstract. Byzantine agreement is typically considered with respect to either a fully synchronous network or a fully asynchronous one. In the synchronous case, $t + 1$ communication rounds are necessary for deterministic protocols whereas all known probabilistic protocols require an *expected* large number of rounds. In this paper we examine the question of how many initial synchronous rounds are required for Byzantine agreement in the *worst case* if we allow to switch to asynchronous operation afterward. Let $n = h + t$ be the number of parties where h are honest and t are corrupted. As the main result we show that, in the model with a public-key infrastructure and signatures (aka authenticated Byzantine agreement), $d + O(1)$ deterministic synchronous rounds are sufficient where d is the minimal integer such that $n - d > 3(t - d)$. This improves over the $t + 1$ necessary deterministic rounds for almost all cases, and over the exact expected number of rounds in the non-deterministic case for many cases.

1 Introduction

Two standard timing models are typically considered for the communication among parties in distributed tasks such as Byzantine agreement or general multi-party computation. In the synchronous model, the parties operate in synchronous clock cycles where messages being sent at the beginning of a given clock cycle are guaranteed to have arrived by the end of the same cycle. In the asynchronous model, messages being sent at a certain point in time are only guaranteed to be delivered eventually.

In contrast, Dwork, Lynch, and Stockmeyer [9] considered an initially asynchronous network that will become synchronous only eventually — at some unknown point in time. They showed that, for authenticated Byzantine agreement among n parties with t active corruptions in their model, $n > 3t$ is necessary. Dutta and Gerraoui [8], and, Alistarh, Gilbert, Gerraoui, and Travers [1], for essentially the same model with f crash corruptions, showed that an eventual window of $f + 2$ synchronous rounds is necessary and sufficient for consensus.

---

* Supported by the Swiss National Science Foundation.

I. Keidar (Ed.): DISC 2009, LNCS 5805, pp. 449–463, 2009.
© Springer-Verlag Berlin Heidelberg 2009

Recently, with respect to multi-party computation, Beerliova, Hirt, and Nielsen [3] studied the somehow converse problem of an initially synchronous network that will eventually be switched to asynchronous operation — the motivation being to try to minimize the synchronicity requirements by going asynchronous as soon as possible. Indeed, they were able to show that one single initial synchronous round of broadcast (followed by asynchronous communication) is sufficient to achieve multi-party computation secure against a faulty minority. In this paper, we address a similar question with respect to Byzantine agreement itself: what is the worst-case number of initial synchronous rounds required in order to eventually achieve Byzantine agreement in an asynchronous environment? Combined with the solution in [3] this would in particular characterize the worst-case number of initial synchronous rounds required in order to achieve general multiparty computation; but we find the question intriguing in its own right. Let n be the number of parties, t the number of corrupted parties, and $h = n - t$ the number of honest parties. We show that, for any $n > t$, $t - h/2 + O(1)$ initial synchronous rounds are sufficient. For many parameters this improves over the straight-forward approach of using a protocol where all rounds are synchronous — where $t + 1$ is optimal for deterministic protocols [6], and some large constant number of expected rounds is necessary (but not even guaranteed) for probabilistic protocols [10,12,11]. Note that, in contrast to [9,8,1], this "converse" model does neither restrict resiliency ($n > t$ can be achieved as in the fully synchronous model) nor typically require t rounds of synchronous communication.

Finally, our technique also improves over a result by Garay et al. [11] who considered Byzantine agreement in the standard synchronous-network model in presence of $t = h + k$ (i.e., a surplus of k) dishonest parties. We show how to achieve this task in $O(k)$ rounds as opposed to $\Omega(k^2)$ rounds in [11].

1.1   Model

We consider a complete network of pairwise secure channels among n parties of which t are corrupted by a Byzantine adversary and $h = n - t$ parties are honest. The parties additionally share a public-key infrastructure (PKI) that allows them to sign messages and verify signatures from other parties (authenticated Byzantine agreement). Note that such a "PKI" can in general allow for unconditionally secure signatures [13] and thus for unconditionally secure Byzantine agreement. First, communication proceeds in a synchronous manner for a fixed number of rounds. All succeeding communication is fully asynchronous.

1.2   Motivation, Result, and Comparison

Whereas asynchronous communication is easy to achieve, synchronous communication is either extremely slow (one day of delay might be necessary to guarantee delivery under any circumstances) or very hard (if not impossible) to implement on a wide-area scale with reasonable speed. Furthermore, asynchronous communication can still be optimistically expected to be very fast in most cases. It is thus a reasonable mode of operation to first run a protocol with a minimal number of initial synchronous rounds and then switch to asynchronous communication as soon as agreement can be guaranteed.

We show that Byzantine agreement can be achieved in $\lceil \frac{2t-h+1}{2} \rceil + 5$ deterministic synchronous rounds followed by a reasonable amount of asynchronous communication — for any $n > t$ (and even one round less if $n > 2t$). This stands in contrast to:

- A lower bound of $t + 1$ synchronous rounds for *deterministic* protocols for any $n > t$ [5,7]. For example, our protocol requires strictly less synchronous rounds than any deterministic protocol as long as there are at least $h = n - t > 10$ honest parties involved.
- An expected large number of $O(1)$ synchronous rounds for *probabilistic* protocols if $n > 2t - O(1)$, e.g., 56 in [12] for $n > 2t$. For example, our protocol requires less synchronous rounds than any probabilistic protocol for all parametrizations where $n < 210$.
- Expected $\Theta(k^2)$ synchronous rounds for the *probabilistic* case if $t = h+k$ [11]. In this case, our protocol requires only $O(k)$ synchronous rounds and does not require any asynchronous extension, i.e., strictly improves over the prior result.

Additionally, when compared to the probabilistic protocols, our synchronous-round complexities are worst-case in contrast to average-case in the probabilistic case.

2 The Protocol

Definition 1 (Broadcast). *A protocol among n parties $P = \{p_1, \ldots, p_n\}$ where a sender $p_s \in P$ inputs $x_s \in \{0, 1\}$ and each party p_i computes an output $y_i \in \{0, 1\}$ achieves broadcast if the following conditions are satisfied:*

1. *(Validity). If p_s is honest then each honest party p_i computes $y_i = x_i$.*
2. *(Consistency). All honest parties compute the same output value.*

Definition 2 (Consensus). *A protocol among n parties $P = \{p_1, \ldots, p_n\}$ where each party p_i inputs $x_i \in \{0, 1\}$ and each party p_i computes an output $y_i \in \{0, 1\}$ achieves consensus if the following conditions are satisfied:*

1. *(Validity). If every honest party p_i holds the same input value $x_i = b$ then every honest p_i computes $y_i = b$.*
2. *(Consistency). All honest parties compute the same output value.*

2.1 Overview

With n parties $P = \{p_1, \ldots, p_n\}$ of which $t < n/2$ are corrupted, one can achieve broadcast in $\lceil t/2 \rceil + 4$ synchronous rounds followed by a fully asynchronous protocol. In general, $d + 4$ synchronous rounds are sufficient for d such that $3(t - d) < n - d$. When $t \geq n/2$ we need $d + 5$ rounds.

The synchronous part is an n-party protocol that either achieves agreement or wherein, alternatively, all honest parties detect a common set of some d parties that are corrupted, similar to a single phase in the protocols by Bar-Noy *et al.* [2]. We call this protocol CORRECT-OR-DETECT BROADCAST, d-CoD. We will choose d such that $n - d > 3(t - d)$, i.e., that out of the $N = n - d$ remaining non-detected parties at most $T = t - d < N/3$ are corrupted.

Since the commonly detected set of parties is not commonly known (locally, a larger set can be detected), the d-CoD protocol is followed by a protocol constructing proofs of participation, called the PoP protocol. There exists a verification algorithm ver which takes as input a bit string pop and party id p_j and outputs ver(pop, p_j) $\in \{0, 1\}$. Below we write pop$_j$ to mean that pop is a bit string for which ver(pop, p_j) = 1 and we call such a pop$_j$ a PROOF OF PARTICIPATION for p_j. After the execution of PoP all honest parties will hold some pop$_j$ for all other honest p_j. Furthermore, no pop$_j$ will ever be constructed for a commonly detected p_j. For p_j which is not honest nor commonly detected some honest parties might hold a pop$_j$ and some might not. In addition the proofs pop$_j$ are transferable. I.e., they can be sent along with messages in the asynchronous phase and will be accepted by the recipient. The PoP protocol adds one extra synchronous rounds when $t \geq n/2$.

After the PoP protocol follows the asynchronous part, which is a consensus protocol where the parties only consider messages from parties for which they saw a proof of participation. This will have the effect that the *commonly* detected parties will be no more powerful than being fail-stop corrupted. Thus, if d-CoD achieves common detection of d parties then the asynchronous part basically is a consensus protocol among $N = n - d$ parties with $T = t - d < N/3$ active corruptions or, alternatively, among n parties with T active corruptions and where d parties are fail-stop corrupted (crashed) from the beginning, and where $n > 3T + d$. We refer to the latter case as the *pre-crash model*. Note that, typically, the parties will not agree on whether agreement or common detection happened. The asynchronous part will also guarantee termination even when t parties are actively corrupted but all honest parties hold the same input. So, if the initial d-CoD does not achieve common detection of d parties, then it will achieve agreement, which will still ensure that the asynchronous part terminates.

We now proceed as follows. We give a protocol for synchronous d-CoD in Section 2.2. In Section 2.3 we describe the construction of proofs of participation and describe how to use them to implement the pre-crash model with T active corruptions and where d parties are fail-stop corrupted from the beginning of the protocol. In Section 2.4 we then give an asynchronous consensus protocol for the pre-crash model: we call this protocol *pre-crash consensus, PCC*. This protocol uses a coin-flip protocol described in Section 2.5. In Section 2.6, we finally show how to combine d-CoD with PCC.

2.2   Correct-or-Detect Broadcast (CoD)

Definition 3 (d-CoD). *A protocol among n parties $P = \{p_1, \ldots, p_n\}$ where a sender $p_s \in P$ inputs $x_s \in \{0, 1\}$ and each party p_i outputs a triplet*

$(y_i, \mathcal{F}_i, \det_i) \in \{0, 1\} \times 2^P \times \{C, D\}$ *achieves* CORRECT-OR-DETECT BROAD-CAST WITH d (d-CoD) *if the following conditions are satisfied:*

1. ($\mathcal{F}$-SOUNDNESS) *An honest party's set $\mathcal{F}_i$ only contains corrupted parties.*
2. (C-CORRECTNESS) *If any honest party computes $\det_i = C$ then the protocol achieves broadcast (Def. 1) with respect to input x_s and outputs y_i. If broadcast is achieved we say that* THE PROTOCOL IS CORRECT. *Furthermore, if p_s is honest then $\det_i = C$ for every honest party p_i.*
3. (D-SOUNDNESS) *If any honest party computes $\det_i = D$ then $\left| \bigcap_{p_j \in H} \mathcal{F}_j \right| \geq d$, where H is the set of honest p_j. In the case of such common detection of d parties we say that* THE PROTOCOL HAS DETECTION.

Let the given instance of the final broadcast protocol to be achieved be defined by ID number id. The protocol below is a $(d+4)$-round construction for d-CoD. The protocol basically proceeds like the first $d + 4$ rounds of the protocol in [7] for synchronous broadcast. In the first round, if the input is $x_s = 1$, the sender creates a signature on id and sends it to all parties — input 0 is communicated by sending nothing. The first time when a party, during some round $r - 1$, receives a chain of $r - 1$ different signatures then he accepts the respective input value, appends his own signature, and sends the new chain to all parties in round r. Let r_i be the first round where party p_i receives such a set of signatures where $r_i = d + 4$ may also stand for "there is no such round." Depending on r_i party p_i decides in the following way.

r_i	$\leq d+1$	$d+2$	$d+3$	$d+4$
$(y_i, \det_i)$	$(1, C)$	$(1, D)$	$(0, D)$	$(0, C)$

It is easy to see that $|r_i - r_j| \leq 1$ for all honest p_i, p_j. It will also be easy to see that the parties can commonly detect d corrupted parties if some honest p_i has $r_i \in \{d+2, d+3\}$. Furthermore, as can be seen in the table above, if the honest parties disagree on y_i, then (by $|r_i - r_j| \leq 1$) all honest p_l have $r_l \in \{d+2, d+3\}$. In Protocol 1, we use the following notions:

- A party p_i's signature on a value z is denoted by $\sigma_{p_i}(z)$.
- A 1-CHAIN is a triplet (id, s, σ_s) where σ_s is a valid signature by p_s on id. An ℓ-CHAIN is a tuple $(id, p_{i_1}, \sigma_{i_1}, \ldots, p_{i_{\ell-1}}, \sigma_{i_{\ell-1}}, p_{i_\ell}, \sigma_{i_\ell})$ where $C_{\ell-1} = (id, p_{i_1}, \sigma_{i_1}, \ldots, p_{i_{\ell-1}}, \sigma_{i_{\ell-1}})$ is an $(\ell - 1)$-chain and σ_{i_ℓ} is a valid signature by p_{i_ℓ} on $C_{\ell-1}$, and where the parties $p_{i_1}, \ldots, p_{i_\ell}$ are distinct.
- An ℓ-CHAIN WITH RESPECT TO p_i is an ℓ-chain with $i_\ell = i$.

Protocol 1: d-CoD

- Round 1:
  - p_s: if the input is $x_s = 1$ then p_s sends 1-chain $C_1 = (id, p_s, \sigma_s)$ to all parties and outputs $(y_s = 1, \mathcal{F}_s = \emptyset, \det_s = C)$. Otherwise, p_s sends nothing and outputs $(y_s = 0, \mathcal{F}_s = \emptyset, \det_s = C)$.
  - p_i ($i \neq s$): $r_i = d + 4$ (sentinel).

- Rounds $2 \leq r \leq d + 4$:
  - p_i $(i \neq s)$: If an $(r-1)$-chain $C_{r-1} = (id, p_{j_1}, \sigma_{j_1}, \ldots, p_{j_{r-1}}, \sigma_{j_{r-1}})$ was received during round $r - 1$ (the previous round) then:
    * If $r_i = d + 4$ then $r_i := r - 1$ (mark first round where a sufficiently large chain was received)
    * For one such chain C_{r-1}, send r-chain $C_r = (C_{r-1}, p_i, \sigma_{p_i}(C_{r-1}))$ to all parties.
- Epilogue:
  - p_i $(i \neq s)$:
    * If $r_i \leq d + 2$ then $y_i := 1$. If $d + 2 \leq r_i \leq d + 3$ then $\det_i := D$ else $\det_i = C$.
    * For each received ℓ-chain $(id, p_{j_1}, \sigma_{j_1} \ldots, p_{j_\ell}, \sigma_{j_\ell})$ add $p_{j_1}, \ldots, p_{j_{r_i}-1}$ to $\mathcal{F}_i$.   ◇

Let $\mathcal{F}_i^0 = \mathcal{F}_i$. For a party p_i with $r_i < d + 4$ we define $\mathcal{F}_i^1$ to contain exactly the first $r_i - 2$ parties that appear in the $(r_i + 1)$-chain it redistributed during round $r_i + 1$, $\mathcal{F}_i^1 = \{p_{j_1}, \ldots, p_{j_{r_i}-2}\}$. If $r_i = d + 4$, we define $\mathcal{F}_i^1 = \emptyset$.

Lemma 1. *The given protocol efficiently achieves d-CoD in $d + 4$ rounds.*

Proof. If $\det_i = C$ for some honest party p_i then either $r_i \leq d + 1$ or $r_i = d + 4$. In the former case, every honest p_j has $r_j \leq d + 2$ and thus $y_i = y_j = 1$. In the latter case, every honest p_j has $r_j \geq d + 3$ and thus $y_i = y_j = 0$. Finally, if the sender p_s is honest then $y_i = x_s$ and $\det_i = C$ since the adversary cannot forge signatures. This gives the C-correctness. By construction, no honest p_j signs a chain in round r_j or earlier. Since p_i knows that $r_j \geq r_i - 1$ for all honest p_j, party p_i knows that no honest p_j signed a chain in round $r_i - 1$ or earlier. So, if p_i sees a chain signed by parties $p_{j_1}, \ldots, p_{j_\ell}$, then p_i knows that the parties $p_{j_1}, \ldots, p_{j_{r_i}-1}$ are corrupted. This implies $\mathcal{F}$-soundness. From $r_j \geq r_i - 1$, the party p_i knows that when an honest p_j saw this chain, then p_j added at least the parties in $\mathcal{F}_i^1$ to $\mathcal{F}_j^0$, i.e., $\mathcal{F}_i^1 \subseteq \mathcal{F}_j^0$ for all honest p_j. Since p_i only sets $\det_i = D$ if $r_i \in \{d + 2, d + 3\}$, it follows that $|\mathcal{F}_i^1| \geq r_i - 2 \geq d$, which implies D-soundness.   □

2.3 Proofs of Participation (PoP), Minority Case

After running CoD, the parties construct proofs of participation. This construction depends on whether $t < n/2$ or $t \geq n/2$. We give the simple construction for $t < n/2$. To not interrupt the flow of presentation of the overall protocol, we defer the description of the construction for $t \geq n/2$ to Section 2.7.

When $t < n/2$ a proof of participation pop_l for p_l is a collection of $n - t$ signatures on (id, part, p_l) from distinct parties. These proofs are clearly transferable. They are constructed asynchronously as follows. Let $\mathcal{P}_i^0 = \{p_1, \ldots, p_n\} - \mathcal{F}_i^0$ and $\mathcal{P}_i^1 = \{p_1, \ldots, p_n\} - \mathcal{F}_i^1$. Each p_i will for each $p_l \in \mathcal{P}_i^1$, send a signature on (id, part, p_l) to p_j. Since $\mathcal{P}_j^0 \subseteq \mathcal{P}_i^1$, p_j knows that all $n - t$ honest p_i will send a signature on (id, part, p_l) for all $p_l \in \mathcal{P}_j^0$. Therefore p_j can wait for $n - t$ such signatures for all $p_l \in \mathcal{P}_j^0$ and thus get a pop_l for all $p_l \in \mathcal{P}_j^0$, which includes the honest parties. No honest party signs (id, part, p_l) for any commonly detected p_l so, since $t < n - t$, no pop_l is constructed for a commonly detected p_l.

2.4   Asynchronous Pre-Crash Consensus (PCC)

Recall that the commonly detected parties during CoD will be ignored by all honest parties and thus will be treated as having crashed. Also, recall that there are d commonly detected parties if CoD has not already reached agreement. The following assumptions model this situation.

Among the n parties, we now assume T to be actively corrupted and d to have crashed already before the execution of the protocol, and $n > 3T + d$. We call the $N = n - d$ parties that have not crashed before the execution the PARTICIPATING PARTIES IN PCC. In particular, we have $N > 3T$ among the participating parties. In this section, we are allowed to make the following assumptions:

- All honest parties accept each other as participating, i.e., do not detect each other as being corrupted — as follows from PoP.
- Once an honest p_i accepts p_l as participating, all other honest parties accept p_l as participating before they receive their next message from p_i — we can simply make the honest parties ignore p_i's messages until p_i's (transferable) PoP for p_l has arrived.

As usual we assume the adversary to fully control the actively corrupted parties. From the crashed parties the adversary is allowed to learn their internal states but the crashed parties send no messages during the PCC-protocol. The honest parties do not know the identities of the crashed or the actively corrupted parties.

This model is implemented by relaying all newly received proofs of participation pop_l with the next outgoing message to each of the other parties and ignoring all messages from parties p_l for which no pop_l was yet received.

Our PCC protocol is inspired by the protocol in [4]. Some changes have been made to deal with the fact that we cannot use threshold signature schemes in our setting (the excluded parties can still create signature shares, lending the corrupted parties an unfair advantage). Other changes have been made to simplify the protocol. The well-known standard structure stays the same: repeating rounds over a weak form of agreement (committed crusader consensus) followed by a weak coin-flip protocol.

Definition 4 (Committed Crusader Consensus (CCC)). *A protocol among n parties $P = \{p_1, \ldots, p_n\}$ where every party p_i inputs $x_i \in \{0,1\}$ and outputs a value $y_i \in \{0, \perp, 1\}$ is called* COMMITTED CRUSADER CONSENSUS (CCC) *if the following conditions are satisfied:*

1. (VALIDITY) *If all honest parties have the same input x then every honest party p_i outputs $y_i = x$.*
2. (CONSISTENCY) *If some honest party p_i outputs $y_i = 0$ then no honest party p_j outputs $y_j = 1$.*
3. (COMMITMENT) *As soon as some honest party p_i terminates the protocol, a value $y \in \{0,1\}$ is fixed such that no honest party p_j can terminate the protocol with output $y_j = y$.*
4. (TERMINATION) *All honest parties terminate the protocol.*

Note that the commitment property defends against the adversary adapting the crusader-consensus outcome to its following coin-flip outcome. This might be possible since the protocol is asynchronous.

Protocol 2: Committed Crusader Consensus — CCC (local code of p_i)

1. Send a signature on (id, vote, x_i) to all parties.
2. Wait for signatures from $N - T$ *participating* parties and pick $u_i \in \{0, 1\}$ to be the value for which $N - 2T$ signatures on (id, vote, u_i) was received. Then send u_i to all parties along with the $N - 2T$ signatures.
3. Wait for $N - T$ *participating* parties p_j to send u_j along with $N - 2T$ signatures on (id, vote, u_j) from *participating* parties.
   ○ If all u_j are identical then let v_i be the common value and send ok to all parties.
   ○ Otherwise, let $v_i = \bot$, pick $N - 2T$ of the signatures on $(id, \mathsf{vote}, 0)$ and $N - 2T$ of the signatures on $(id, \mathsf{vote}, 1)$ and combine them to a PROOF OF DISAGREEMENT, and send this proof to all parties.[1]
4. Wait to receive ok or a proof of disagreement from $N - T$ *participating* parties. If all sent ok, then let $y_i = v_i$. Otherwise, let $y_i = \bot$. Then send done to all parties.
5. Wait for $N - T$ *participating* parties to send done, and then terminate with output y_i.   ◇

Lemma 2. *The above protocol achieves CCC.*

Proof.

1. (VALIDITY). Straight forward.
2. (CONSISTENCY). Assume that p_i is honest and that $y_i = b \in \{0, 1\}$. Then p_i received $N - T$ votes u_j on b. At least $N - 2T$ of these votes were sent by honest parties, so any other honest p_k sees at least one vote u_j on b and thus outputs b or $\bot$.
3. (COMMITMENT). Assume that some honest party terminated. This means that it saw $N - T$ parties send done. Hence at least $N - 2T$ honest parties sent done. We consider these $N - 2T$ parties and distinguish two cases:
   − Assume that one of the considered parties had $v_i = b \in \{0, 1\}$. In this case it is easy to see that $v_j = 1 - b$ is impossible for all other honest parties p_j. Since $y_j = 1 - b$ implies $v_j = 1 - b$, it follows that $v_j = 1 - b$ is impossible for each honest party p_j.
   − Assume that $v_i = \bot$ for the at least $N - 2T$ considered honest parties. Then these $N - 2T$ parties sent a proof of disagreement to all parties. Therefore every honest party p_j receives at least one proof of disagreement and thus outputs $y_j = \bot$, making both values $y_k \in \{0, 1\}$ impossible for every honest party p_k.
4. (TERMINATION). Straight forward.   □

---

[1] A proof of disagreement shows that at least one honest party had input 0 and that at least one honest party had input 1.

We can now combine CCC with an unpredictable coin-flip protocol. We assume a coin-flip protocol where the parties input $(id, \texttt{flip}, r)$ to flip coin number r and where they receive an outcome $(C_r \in \{0, 1\}, g \in \{0, 1\})$. We assume that if $N - T$ honest parties input $(id, \texttt{flip}, r)$, then they eventually all receive an outcome (v, g). The outcome should guarantee that if some honest party has outcome $(v, 1)$, then all honest parties have outcome $(v, 1)$ or $(v, 0)$. Furthermore, a fraction p of the coins should have the property that all parties output $(C_r, 1)$ and that C_r cannot be predicted with probability negligibly better than $\frac{1}{2}$ until the first honest party gets input $(id, \texttt{flip}, r)$. We call such a coin GOOD. See Section 2.5 for the implementation of such a coin.

Protocol 3: Pre-Crash Consensus — PCC (local code of p_i)

1. Let $r = 1$ and let x_i be the input.
2. Run CCC on input x_i to get an output z_i.
3. Input $(id, \texttt{flip}, r)$ to the coin-flip protocol and wait for an output (C_r, g).
4. If $z_i = C_r$ and $g = 1$, then $y_i := z_i$ but *do not terminate*.
5. If $z_i = \perp$ then $x_i = C_r$ else $x_i = z_i$.
6. Let $r := r + 1$ and go to Step 2.   ⬦

Lemma 3. *The above protocol achieves pre-crash consensus (except for termination) in expected $2/p$ "rounds".*

Proof. The protocol has the following properties and thus fulfills the claims:

1. (PERSISTENCE: *If the honest parties agree on the x_i at the beginning of round r, then they will all have $y_i = x_i$ and will end up with the same x_i in round $r + 1$*). This follows from validity of CCC.
2. (VALIDITY). Follows from persistence.
3. (MATCHING COIN: *If no honest party receives output $z_i = z \in \{0, 1\}$ from the CCC protocol and coin C_r is good, then with probability negligibly close to $\frac{1}{2}$, the coin produces $C_r = 1 - z$ and $g = 1$ for all parties*). When the first honest party p_i inputs $(id, \texttt{flip}, r)$ to the coin-flip protocol, at least p_i terminated the CCC protocol. Therefore there exists $z \in \{0, 1\}$ such that no honest party can end up with $z_i = z$. Since C_r is unpredictable until the first honest party inputs $(id, \texttt{flip}, r)$ there is probability negligibly close to $\frac{1}{2}$ that $C_r = 1 - z$.
4. (CONSISTENCY). By the matching-coin condition, all honest parties eventually end up with the same value y_i.
5. (CONSISTENCY DETECTION: *When an honest party p_i sees that $z_i = C_r$ and $g = 1$ then p_i knows that all honest parties p_j will finally compute output $y_j = z_i$*). If this happens then, after Step 5 of the same iteration, all honest parties will agree on $x_j = z_i$ which will persist by the persistence condition.
6. (NUMBER OF "ROUNDS"). Follows from the properties of the coin.   □

As of now, the protocol runs forever. Allowing all honest parties to terminate in a constant number of rounds can be achieved by adding the following rules to the above protocol.

- After computing y_i in Step 4, send a signature on $(id, \texttt{result}, y_i)$ to all parties.
- On receiving a valid signature on $(id, \texttt{result}, y)$ by any party, send it to all parties.
- If for some $y \in \{0,1\}$ and $h = N - T$ distinct participating parties p_j a valid signature on $(id, \texttt{result}, y)$ by p_j has been (received and re)sent to all parties, terminate.

Theorem 1. *The above protocol together with the given termination augmentation achieves pre-crash consensus among n parties with d pre-crashes and T actively corrupted parties when $n > 3T + d$. The protocol terminates in $2/p$ expected rounds where p is the unpredictability of the coin.*

Proof. Follows from Lemma 3 and the above discussion. $\square$

2.5   The Coin

We describe a generic construction that can be based on any existing coin protocol in order to get a coin for the pre-crash model that can be set up during the last synchronous round and opened during the asynchronous part of the protocol. The coin itself is pre-shared by some designated party p_i and is reliable when p_i is honest. The iterations of pre-crash consensus can then be done with respect to different designated parties. The advantage of this approach is that 1 synchronous round is sufficient and that it can be described generically. The disadvantage is that expected $O(t)$ asynchronous "rounds" will be required in order to hit a reliable matching coin.[2]

Generic Construction. We let each party P_i prepare a coin C_i in the last synchronous round, by picking $C_i \in \{0,1\}$ uniformly at random and secret sharing C_i. In asynchronous round i, the parties then try to reconstruct C_i. To get ℓ coins, each p_i prepares ℓ/n coins and the coins of p_i are used in rounds $i+nq$. We pick ℓ large enough that the PCC protocol will have terminated after ℓ phases except with negligible probability when there is detection (and thus $N > 3T$). If the parties run out of coins, they conclude that there was not detection, but agreement already in CoD. In the following, we let $\mathcal{P}_i = \{1, \ldots, n\} - \mathcal{F}_i$.

Protocol 4: Coin Flip
- A coin of p_i is prepared as follows:
  ∘ Last synchronous round: p_i picks C_i uniformly at random and creates a Shamir sharing of C_i among n parties with degree T. Let C_{ij} denote the share of p_j. For $p_j \in \mathcal{F}_i$ it deletes C_{ij}. For $p_j \in \mathcal{P}_i$ it signs $(id, \texttt{flip}, i, j, C_{ij})$ and sends it securely to p_j.

---

[2] We also have a protocol to produce a coin along the lines of Katz and Koo [12] solely based on digital signatures (and a PKI). The advantage of this construction is that only an expected constant number of asynchronous "rounds" will be required to hit a reliable matching coin. However, more than 1 synchronous round is required to set it up (but still $O(1)$).

- The flipping of the coin proceeds as follows:
  - p_j: On input $(id, \texttt{flip}, r = i + nq)$, send the signed $(id, \texttt{flip}, r, j, C_{ij})$ to all p_k, if it was received, and otherwise sign and send $(id, \texttt{flip}, r, j, \perp)$.
  - p_k: Wait for $N - T$ participating parties p_j from $\mathcal{P}_k$ to send either $(id, \texttt{flip}, r, j, C_{ij})$ signed by p_i or $(id, \texttt{flip}, r, j, \perp)$ signed by p_j. If $N - 2T$ participating parties sent a signed $(id, \texttt{flip}, r, j, \perp)$, collect the signatures to a PROOF THAT p_i IS CORRUPT,[3] and send the proof to all parties. Otherwise, if $N - 2T$ participating parties sent a signed $(id, \texttt{flip}, i, j, C_{ij})$, then interpolate a degree T polynomial $f(\texttt{X})$ with $f(j) = C_{ij}$ for all $N - 2T$ values, let $C_i = f(0)$ and collect the $N - 2T$ signed values to a PROOF THAT $C_i = f(0)$ IS JUSTIFIED, and send the proof to all parties along with a signature on $(id, \texttt{flip}, r, f(0))$.
  - p_j: Wait for $N - T$ participating parties p_k to send a message as required above. If one of them sent a proof that p_i is corrupt, store this proof. Otherwise, if one of them sent a proof that $C_i = 0$ is justified and one of them sent a proof that $C_i = 1$ is justified, pool these proofs to a PROOF THAT p_i IS CORRUPT. Otherwise, the $N - T$ parties all sent a PROOF THAT $C_i = v$ IS JUSTIFIED for the same v. Collect the corresponding $N - T$ signatures on $(id, \texttt{flip}, r, v)$ to a PROOF THAT $C_i = v$ IS UNIQUELY JUSTIFIED.[4] In both cases, send the obtained type of proof to all parties.
  - p_k: Wait for $N - T$ participating parties p_j to send a proof that p_i is corrupt or that some v is uniquely justified. If all $N - T$ parties sent a proof that v is uniquely justified, then output $(v, 1)$. If at least one party sent a proof that v is uniquely justified, then output $(v, 0)$. Otherwise, output $(0, 0)$

It is straight-forward to see that at most one value v will have a proof that it is uniquely justified. Furthermore, all pairs of parties receive a message from at least one common honest party in the last step. So, as p_j having output $(v, g = 1)$ implies that it received a proof that v is uniquely justified from all parties, it knows that all other honest parties received at least one such value, and therefore has output $(v, \cdot)$. Ergo output $(v, 1)$ implies that all parties agree on the coin. Finally, if p_i is honest, no proof that p_i is corrupt will be constructed. Hence all parties will have output $(C_i, 1)$. So, all coins prepared by honest parties are good, and they make up a fraction $p = (n - t)/n$ of all coins.

2.6   The Final Protocol: Putting Things Together

We now demonstrate how to combine synchronous d-CoD with asynchronous pre-crash consensus (PCC).

Let $h = n - t$ be the number of honest parties. Pick $T < h/2$, let $d = t - T$ and let $N = n - d$. We first run Protocol d-CoD with respect to n and t. Protocol d-CoD is either correct or has detection. The difficulty now is that the parties

---

[3] At least one honest party is claiming that it did not get a signed share from p_i.

[4] At least $N - 2T$ honest parties signed for v and no honest party signs for both 0 and 1. Therefore at most one value v will have such a proof.

do not necessarily agree on their values det $\in \{C, D\}$ that stands for knowing that correctness or detection was achieved. Therefore we always unconditionally append Protocol Pre-Crash Consensus (PCC) which is run among all n parties and with respect to d crashes and $T < N/3$ active corruptions. However, only the parties p_i with $\det_i = D$ will adopt the output of PCC, whereas the parties with $\det_i = C$ already accept their outputs from d-CoD. In more detail:

Protocol 5: Broadcast (local code of p_i)

1. Run the d-CoD on input x_i and let $(v_i, \mathcal{F}_i, \det_i)$ be p_i's output.
   <FROM NOW ON EVERYTHING IS ASYNCHRONOUS>
2. If $\det_i = C$ then output $y_i = v_i$ but *do not terminate*.
3. Run PoP to create proofs of participation and use these to simulate a pre-crash model, where all parties without a proof of participation are considered crashed.
4. Run PCC on input v_i in the simulated pre-crash model; if $\det_i = D$ then let y_i be the output of PCC.   ◇

The final protocol has the following properties:

1. If $\det_i = C$ for all honest p_i then all honest parties eventually output some y_i and the outputs y_i are correct.

   Proof. When $\det_i = C$ for all honest p_i all honest p_i have $y_i = v_i$, where v_i is the output of d-CoD, which is correct since $\det_i = C$ for some honest P_i.

2. If $\det_i = D$ for some honest p_i, then the asynchronous BA eventually terminates with some common output y which is equal to some v_i held by an honest party p_i.

   Proof. Even a party with $\det_i = C$ will run the asynchronous PCC protocol. Therefore the asynchronous PCC is run by *all* honest parties, but as if all parties without a proof of participation were crashed before the protocol began. The only malicious thing a party without a proof of participation can do is therefore to leak his secrets to the corrupted parties which do have proof of participation. Therefore the PCC protocol is essentially run in a pre-crash model with N being the number of parties with a proof of participation and T being the number of corrupted parties with a proof of participation. When $\det_i = D$ for some honest p_i, then $N > 3T$ as no commonly detected party gets a proof of participation and all honest parties get a proof of participation. Since $N > 3T$, it follows from the properties of PCC that it eventually terminates with some common output y which is equal to some v_i held by an honest party p_i.

3. If $\det_i = D$ for all honest p_i, then all parties eventually output some y and the output y is correct.

   Proof. When $\det_i = D$ for all honest p_i, then all honest p_i take the output y_i of PCC to be the output of the final protocol. If p_s is honest, then no honest p_i has $\det_i = D$, so when $\det_i = D$ for all honest p_i, then p_s is corrupted and any common output $y_i = y$ is correct. It is therefore sufficient that PCC has termination and consistency. This follows from Property 2.

4. If $\det_i = C$ for some honest p_i and $\det_j = D$ for some honest p_j then all honest parties eventually output some y and the output y is correct.

Proof. From $\det_j = D$ for some honest p_j it follows from Property 2 that PCC eventually terminates with some common output y, which is equal to some v_i held by an honest party. By $\det_i = C$ for some honest p_i it follows that the v_i held by the honest parties are the same, meaning that each honest p_i gets output $y_i = v_i$ from PCC where v_i is his output from d-CoD. Hence every honest p_i will output v_i which is correct as p_s must be corrupted.   □

Theorem 2. *The above protocol achieves broadcast for n parties secure against $t < n/2$ actively corrupted parties in*

- $\lceil \frac{2t-h+1}{2} \rceil + 4 \leq \lceil t/2 \rceil + 4$ *deterministic synchronous rounds followed by an expected-$O(t)$-"round" asynchronous protocol when using the generic coin.*
- $t - h/2 + O(1)$ *deterministic synchronous rounds followed by an expected-$O(1)$-"round" asynchronous protocol when using the specific coin.*

Proof. From Property 1, Property 3 and Property 4 it follows that the protocol achieves broadcast. The rest can be verified by inspection.   □

2.7   Proofs of Participation (PoP), Majority Case

We now describe the construction of proofs of participation for the case $t \geq n/2$. The first modification is that we run CoD for one more round and let the parties decide as follows.

r_i	$\leq d+2$	$d+3$	$d+4$	$d+5$
$(y_i, \det_i)$	$(1, C)$	$(1, D)$	$(0, D)$	$(0, C)$

I.e., just run $(d+1)$-CoD. For the $(r_i + 1)$-chain sent in round $(r_i + 1)$, p_i adds $p_{i_1}, \ldots, p_{i_{r_i-3}}$ to a set $\mathcal{F}_i^2$. In all rounds, for all incoming chains, it adds $p_{i_1}, \ldots, p_{i_{r_i-2}}$ to a set $\mathcal{F}_i^1$ and adds $p_{i_1}, \ldots, p_{i_{r_i-1}}$ to a set $\mathcal{F}_i^0$. Except in the last round, it then relays the chain, which will make other parties p_j see the chain and do the same, possibly using $r_j = r_i - 1$. It can be seen that this results in sets with $\mathcal{F}_i^2 \subseteq \mathcal{F}_j^1 \subseteq \mathcal{F}_k^0$ for all honest p_i, p_j, p_k. The output of this modified d-CoD is taken to be $\mathcal{F}_i = \mathcal{F}_i^2$. We call $\mathcal{P}_i^b = \{1, \ldots, n\} - \mathcal{F}_i^b$ the b-PARTICIPATING PARTIES (seen by p_i) and we have that $\mathcal{P}_i^0 \subseteq \mathcal{P}_j^1 \subseteq \mathcal{P}_k^2$ for all honest p_i, p_j, p_k. We need that $N > 3T$ for all sets $\mathcal{P}_j^l$ when an honest p_i has $\det_i = D$. This follows from $r_i \geq d+3$.

Now, for $b = 2, 1, 0$ we define a b-PROOF OF PARTICIPATION FOR p_l (from the viewpoint of p_i) to be $2T + 1$ signatures on $(id, \mathtt{part}, p_l)$ from parties in $\mathcal{P}_i^b$.

Invariant. We will maintain the invariant that if there exists any b-proof of participation for p_l, then at least one honest party did not exclude p_l initially (we say p_i excluded p_l if $p_l \notin \mathcal{P}_i^2$). In particular, there will exist no b-proof of participation for a commonly detected party p_l. Furthermore, all honest parties will initially hold a 0-proof of participation for all other honest parties, and 0-proofs of participation will be transferable. Therefore 0-proofs of participation can be used to simulate the pre-crash model, as desired.

Establishing the invariant. Every p_i sends a signature on (id, part, p_l) for all $p_l \in \mathcal{P}_i^0$ to all p_j. Below we call a signature on (id, part, p_l) a SIGNATURE OF PARTICIPATION FOR p_l. Since all honest parties are in all $\mathcal{P}_i^0$, and there are at least $N - T$ honest parties, all honest p_j can wait to collect a 0-proof of participation for all $p_l \in \mathcal{P}_j^1$, which includes all honest parties. Furthermore, if all honest parties excluded p_l, then less than $N - T$ signatures of participation are constructed for p_l, so no b-proof of participation is constructed for a commonly detected party.

Upgrading. To build transferability, we first observe that if p_j holds a 1-proof of participation for p_l, it can upgrade it to a 0-proof of participation: It sends the 1-proof of participation to all p_k. Any p_k receiving it will see the $N - T$ signatures from $\mathcal{P}_j^1$. Since $\mathcal{P}_j^1 \subset \mathcal{P}_k^2$, this will be a 2-proof of participation for p_l to p_k. Therefore p_k knows, by the invariant, that at least one honest party did not exclude p_l initially. Hence p_k can safely sign (id, part, p_l) and send the signature to p_j. All honest p_k will eventually do this. Since all honest parties are in $\mathcal{P}_j^0$, p_j will eventually receive $N - T$ signatures on (id, part, p_l) from parties in $\mathcal{P}_j^0$. These signatures p_j collects to a 0-proof of participation for p_l.

Transfer. Assume now that p_i holds a 0-proof of participation for p_l. It can send this to all p_j, who will see it at least as a 1-proof of participation, as $\mathcal{P}_i^0 \subseteq \mathcal{P}_j^1$. Therefore p_j can upgrade it to a 0-proof of participation for p_l. This gives transferability.

Theorem 3. *The above protocol achieves broadcast for n parties secure against $t < n$ actively corrupted parties where d is the minimal integer for which $n - d > 3(t - d)$*

- *in $\lceil \frac{2t-h+1}{2} \rceil + 5$ deterministic synchronous rounds followed by an expected-$O(t)$- "round" asynchronous protocol when using the generic coin.*
- *in $t - h/2 + O(1)$ deterministic synchronous rounds followed by an expected-$O(1)$- "round" asynchronous protocol when using the specific coin.*

Proof. The theorem follows along the lines of the proof of Theorem 2 and the above discussion.   □

3   Observations

Multi-Valued Broadcast. Above, our protocols were stated with respect to a binary value domain. We note that, for arbitrary value domains $\mathcal{D}$, the protocol can be adapted such that the number of synchronous rounds stays the same whereas the number of asynchronous rounds remains of same order (one additional round per coin flip).

Fully Synchronous Byzantine Agreement with a PKI. We observe that our approach can also be used to improve over the result in [11]. There it was shown how to achieve Byzantine agreement in the fully synchronous model among $t = h + k$ parties (with a minority of h honest parties) in expected $\Omega(k^2)$ rounds. Applying our approach together with the specific coin from [12] directly to the fully synchronous case yields a protocol that requires only expected $k + O(1)$ rounds. In this case, the coin does not have to be pre-shared as described in Section 2.5 but the leader can simply dictate it on the spot. Hence the protocol only relies on signatures and a PKI and works for any value domain.

References

1. Alistarh, D., Gilbert, S., Guerraoui, R., Travers, C.: How to solve consensus in the smallest window of synchrony. In: Taubenfeld, G. (ed.) DISC 2008. LNCS, vol. 5218, pp. 32–46. Springer, Heidelberg (2008)
2. Bar-Noy, A., Dolev, D., Dwork, C., Strong, H.R.: Shifting gears: Changing algorithms on the fly to expedite Byzantine agreement. Inf. Comput. 97(2), 205–233 (1992)
3. Beerliova-Trubiniova, Z., Hirt, M., Nielsen, J.B.: Almost-asynchronous mpc with faulty minority. Cryptology ePrint Archive, Report 2008/416 (2008), http://eprint.iacr.org/
4. Cachin, C., Kursawe, K., Shoup, V.: Random oracles in constantinople: Practical asynchronous Byzantine agreement using cryptography. J. Cryptology 18(3), 219–246 (2005)
5. DeMillo, R.A., Lynch, N.A., Merritt, M.J.: Cryptographic protocols. In: Proceedings of the 14th Annual ACM Symposium on Theory of Computing (STOC 1982), pp. 383–400 (1982)
6. Dolev, D., Reischuk, R., Strong, H.R.: Early stopping in Byzantine agreement. J. ACM 37(4), 720–741 (1990)
7. Dolev, D., Strong, H.R.: Authenticated algorithms for Byzantine agreement. SIAM Journal on Computing 12(4), 656–666 (1983)
8. Dutta, P., Guerraoui, R.: The inherent price of indulgence. Distributed Computing 18(1), 85–98 (2005)
9. Dwork, C., Lynch, N.A., Stockmeyer, L.J.: Consensus in the presence of partial synchrony. J. ACM 35(2), 288–323 (1988)
10. Feldman, P., Micali, S.: An optimal probabilistic protocol for synchronous Byzantine agreement. SIAM Journal on Computing 26(4), 873–933 (1997)
11. Garay, J.A., Katz, J., Koo, C.-Y., Ostrovsky, R.: Round complexity of authenticated broadcast with a dishonest majority. In: FOCS, pp. 658–668. IEEE Computer Society, Los Alamitos (2007)
12. Katz, J., Koo, C.-Y.: On expected constant-round protocols for byzantine agreement. In: Dwork, C. (ed.) CRYPTO 2006. LNCS, vol. 4117, pp. 445–462. Springer, Heidelberg (2006)
13. Pfitzmann, B., Waidner, M.: Information-theoretic pseudosignatures and Byzantine agreement for t > = n/3. Technical Report RZ 2882 (#90830), IBM Research (1996)

From Almost Everywhere to Everywhere: Byzantine Agreement with $\tilde{O}(n^{3/2})$ Bits

Valerie King[1],[*] and Jared Saia[2],[**]

[1] Dept. of Computer Science, University of Victoria
P.O. Box 3055, Victoria, BC, Canada V8W 3P6
val@uvic.ca
[2] Department of Computer Science, University of New Mexico
Albuquerque, NM 87131-1386
saia@cs.unm.edu

Abstract. We address the problem of designing distributed algorithms for large scale networks that are robust to Byzantine faults. We consider a message passing, full information synchronous model: the adversary is malicious, controls a constant fraction of processors, and can view all messages in a round before sending out its own messages for that round. Furthermore, each corrupt processor may send an unlimited number of messages. The only constraint on the adversary is that it must choose its corrupt processors at the start, without knowledge of the processors' private random bits. To the authors' best knowledge, there have been no protocols for such a model that compute Byzantine agreement without all-to-all communication, even if private channels or cryptography are assumed, unless corrupt processors' messages are limited.

In this paper, we give a polylogarithmic time algorithm to agree on a small representative committee of processors using only $\tilde{O}(n^{3/2})$ total bits which succeeds with high probability. This representative set can then be used to efficiently solve Byzantine agreement, leader election, or other problems. This work extends the authors' work on scalable almost everywhere agreement.

1 Introduction

Increases in frequency, speed and severity of attacks on the Internet have led to a resurgence of interest in the Byzantine fault model for very large networks, see for example [3,14]. The goal of this work is to address the problem of designing distributed algorithms for large scale networks that are robust to Byzantine faults.

Our paper concerns the well-studied message-passing model: n processors are in a fully connected network and a malicious adversary with full information controls less than a $1/3 - \epsilon$ fraction of these processors, where ϵ is any positive constant. Our main contribution is to show that randomization can be used to

---

[*] This research was supported by NSERC.
[**] This research was partially supported by NSF CAREER Award 0644058 and NSF CCR-0313160 Award.

I. Keidar (Ed.): DISC 2009, LNCS 5805, pp. 464–478, 2009.

break the 1985 $\Omega(n^2)$ barrier [4] for message and bit complexity for Byzantine agreement in the deterministic synchronous model, if we assume the adversary's choice of bad processors is made at the start of the protocol, i.e., independent of processors' private coinflips. Our techniques lead to solutions with $\tilde{O}(n^{3/2})$ bit complexity for leader election and universe reduction. Our protocols are polylog-arithmic in time and, except for leader election, succeed with high probability.

We overcome the lower bound of [4] by allowing for a small probability of error. In particular, the lower $\Omega(n^2)$ lower bound on the number of messages to compute Byzantine agreement deterministically implies that any randomized protocol which computes Byzantine agreement with $o(n^2)$ messages must err with some probability $\rho > 0$, since with probability $\rho > 0$, an adversary can guess the random coinflips and cause the protocol to fail when those coinflips occur. Thus, any randomized algorithm achieving $o(n^2)$ messages must necessarily be a Monte Carlo algorithm.

In 2006, the authors [12] showed that almost everywhere Byzantine agreement, where $(1 - 1/\log n)$ fraction of the good processors come to agreement on a good processor's input bit, could be computed with high probability in polylogarithmic time with a polylogarithmic number of bits of communication per processor. It is easy to see that one round suffices to go from almost everywhere agreement to everywhere agreement with $n(n-1)$ additional bits of communication. Each processor sends every other processor its bit, and each processor decides on the majority. Is there a way to avoid this last high cost round?

The difficulty of achieving $o(n^2)$ messages is illustrated by showing what goes wrong with the obvious approach: each processor randomly selects $O(\log n)$ processors to poll and decides a value equal to the majority of their responses. The problem with this protocol is *flooding*. That is, bad processors may all bombard every processor for requests and no processor will be able to respond to all the requests without incurring a cost of $\Theta(n^2)$ messages. Previous to this paper we did not know of any technique of flood avoidance other than to design a protocol in which each processor predetermines (perhaps using private random bits) at the start of each round the list of processors it is willing to listen to. That is, this list does not depend on the list of processors who actually send. This paper uses a novel technique to deal with flooding that may be of independent interest.

1.1   Model

We assume a fully connected network of n processors, whose IDs are common knowledge. Each processor has a private coin. Communication channels are au-thenticated, in the sense that whenever a processor sends a message directly to another, the identity of the sender is known to the recipient, but we other-wise make no cryptographic assumptions. We assume a *nonadaptive* (sometimes called *static*) adversary. That is, the adversary chooses the set of t bad processors at the start of the protocol, where t is a constant fraction, namely, $1/3 - \epsilon$ for any positive constant ϵ of the number of processors n. The adversary is *malicious*: it chooses the input bits of every processor, bad processors can engage in any kind of deviations from the protocol, including false messages and collusion, or crash failures, while the remaining processors are good and follow the protocol. Bad processors can send *any* number of messages.

We consider both synchronous and asynchronous models of communication. In the *synchronous* model, communication proceeds in rounds; messages are all sent out at the same time at the start of the round, and then received at the same time at the end of the same round; all processors have synchronized clocks. The time complexity is given by the number of rounds. In the *asynchronous* model, each communication can take an arbitrary and unknown amount of time, and there is no assumption of a joint clock as in the synchronous model. The adversary can determine the delay of each message and the order in which they are received. We follow [1] in defining the running time of an asynchronous protocol as the time of execution, assuming the maximum delay of a message between the time it is sent and the time it is processed is assumed to be one unit.

We assume *full information*: in the synchronous model, the adversary is *rushing*, that is, it can view all messages sent by the good processors in a round before the bad processors send their messages in the same round. In the asynchronous model, the adversary can view any sent message before its delay is determined.

1.2 Problems

One of the most well studied problems in distributed computing is the *Byzantine agreement* problem. In this problem, each processor begins with either a 0 or 1. An execution of a protocol is *successful* if all processors terminate and, upon termination, agree on a bit held by at least one good processor at the start. The *leader election* problem is the problem of all processors agreeing on a good processor [12]. The *universe reduction* problem [9] is to bring processors to agreement on a small subset of processors with a fraction of bad processors close to the fraction for the whole set. I.e., the protocol terminates and each good processor outputs the same set of processor ID's such that this property holds. For each of these problems, we say the protocol solves the problem with probability ρ if, given any worst case adversary behavior, including choice of initial inputs, the probability of success of any execution over the distribution of private random coin tosses is at least ρ.

Almost everywhere Byzantine agreement, universe reduction, and leader election is the modified version of each problem where instead of bringing all good processors to agreement, a large majority, but not necessarily all, good processors are brought to agreement.

1.3 Results

We use the phrase *with high probability* (*w.h.p.*) to mean that an event happens with probability at least $1 - 1/n^c$ for every constant c and sufficiently large n. For readability, we treat $\log n$ as an integer throughout. We show:

Theorem 1. [BYZANTINE AGREEMENT] *Let n be the number of processors in a synchronous full information message passing model with a nonadaptive, rushing* *adversary that controls less than $1/3 - \epsilon$ fraction of processors, for any positive constant ϵ. Then, there exists a protocol which w.h.p. computes Byzantine agreement, runs in polylogarithmic time, and uses $\tilde{O}(n^{3/2})$ bits of communication.*

This result follows easily from the solution to the universe reduction problem (see the next section) which we present here:

Theorem 2. [UNIVERSE REDUCTION] *Let ϵ be any positive constant and let n be the number of processors in a synchronous fully connected message passing network with a nonadaptive malicious rushing adversary in the full information model which controls less than $1/3 - \epsilon$ fraction of processors. For any positive constant $\epsilon' < \epsilon$, there exists a protocol which uses $\tilde{O}(n^{3/2})$ number of bits of communication per processor and polylogarithmic number of rounds, such that w.h.p., all good processors output the same subset of processors, the "representative set" of size polylogarithmic in n such that $2/3 + \epsilon'$ fraction of its elements are good.*

1.4 Techniques

Our results build on the almost everywhere universe reduction protocol of [12]:

Theorem 3. *[12] [ALMOST EVERYWHERE UNIVERSE REDUCTION] Let ϵ be any positive constant and let n be the number of processors in a synchronous fully connected message passing network with a nonadaptive, rushing adversary in the full information model which controls less than $1/3 - \epsilon$ fraction of processors. For any positive constant $\epsilon' < \epsilon$, there exists a protocol which uses polylogarithmic number of bits of communication per processor and polylogarithmic number of rounds, such that w.h.p. $1 - O(1/\log n)$ fraction of good processors output a subset of processors of size polylogarithmic in n such that $2/3 + \epsilon'$ fraction of its elements are good.*

Our protocol first runs the protocol for almost everywhere universe reduction in [12] to achieve w.h.p. almost everywhere universe reduction. The technical challenge is to go from almost everywhere universe reduction to everywhere universe reduction in $o(n^2)$ bits. It is straightforward to go from everywhere universe reduction to everywhere agreement for Byzantine agreement and leader election (see [12]). The idea is to notice that any "representative" subset of processors can run a standard Byzantine agreement protocol or leader election protocol (using their own input bits, in the case of Byzantine agreement) and the outcome for the representative subset is a solution to the problem for the whole set. The representative set need only communicate its results to the other processors, which determine the correct answer by taking the message sent by the majority.

We actually prove a stronger result than necessary to prove Theorems 1 and 2 from Theorem 3. That is, we can go from almost everywhere universe reduction to everywhere universe reduction even in the case where (1) only $1/2 + \epsilon$ fraction of good processors are in agreement on the representative subset; (2) up to a $1/2 - \epsilon$ fraction of the processors are controlled by the adversary; and (3) communication is in the asynchronous model. Specifically, we show:

Theorem 4. [ALMOST EVERYWHERE TO EVERYWHERE UNIVERSE REDUCTION]
*Let ϵ be any positive constant and assume n processors are connected in the full
information, asynchronous, message passing communication model, with a nonadaptive adversary. Further, suppose there are $(1/2+\epsilon)n$ good processors that agree
on a subset C of processors containing a majority of good processors. Then there is
a $O(n^{3/2} \log^3 n |C|)$ bit protocol which runs in $O(\log n/ \log \log n)$ time steps after
which w.h.p. all good processors agree on C.*

We give the Almost Everywhere to Everywhere Universe Reduction Protocol
in Section 3; its proof of correctness in Section 4; and include a sketch of the
Almost Everywhere Universe Reduction Protocol in the Appendix.

2   Related Work

In a 2006 paper, the authors (and collaborators) present a polylogarithmic time
protocol with polylogarithmic bits of communication per processor for almost everywhere Byzantine agreement, leader election, and universe reduction in the synchronous full information message passing model with a nonadaptive rushing adversary [12]. Also in 2006, [8,2] give logarithmic time protocols which use $\Omega(n^2)$
bits of communication for Byzantine agreement in the same model with different
techniques. The algorithm in [2] also solves universe reduction and leader election.

In the asynchronous version of the same model, in a 2008 paper [11], the authors give a polynomial time protocol for Byzantine agreement, leader election,
and universe reduction. While this protocol uses $\tilde{\Theta}(n^2)$ messages (and polynomial time), its structure is very similar to the almost everywhere agreement
protocols [12,13], and we believe it can be implemented as an almost everywhere
agreement protocol with polylogarithmic bits of communication.

In the *gossip problem* each process starts with an initial value called a rumor and
attempts to learn all the other rumors. In this literature, one concern is the number of messages sent between processors. A 2008 paper [7] presents a protocol to
solve the gossip problem in the asynchronous model with crash failures rather than
Byzantine failures, with an oblivious adversary which sets the timing and crashes
in advance and an assumption of private channels. The protocol in [7] was adapted
to solve the consensus problem using $O(n^{7/4} \log^2 n)$ messages. The adversary in [7]
is weaker than ours in several respects, though it is stronger in the sense that the
adversary can set delays in communication, so our results seem incomparable.

Almost everywhere agreement in sparse networks has been studied since 1986.
See [12,13] for references. The problem of almost everywhere agreement for secure
multiparty computation on a partially connected network was defined and solved
in 2008 in [6].

In a 2006 paper [13], the authors give a sparse network implementation of their
protocols from [12]. It is easy to see that everywhere agreement is impossible in a
sparse network where the number of faulty processors t is sufficient to surround
a good processor. To see this, one can use an observation from [10]. Let t be the
number of bad processors. Then any Byzantine agreement protocol where all
$n - t$ good processors have their input bits set to 1 must result in an output of

1. And this must be true even if the bad processors act like good processors that have a 0. Moreover, it must be the case that when bad processors act like good processors that have a 1 and t or fewer good processors have a 0, the output must be a 1 as well. If a processor is surrounded by bad processors, then all communication with the processor can be made to simulate any execution of the protocol consistent with that processor's input bit. Hence if a single processor has an input bit of 0, and it is surrounded by bad processors, it will be unable to distinguish between the case where it must output a 0 because all good processors have a 0, or a 1 because fewer than t processors have a 0.

A protocol in which processors use $o(n)$ bits may seem as vulnerable to being isolated as in a sparse network, but the difference is that without access to private random bits, the adversary can't anticipate at the start of the protocol where communication will occur. In [10], it is shown that even with private channels, if a processor must pre-specify the set of processors it is willing to listen to at the start of a round, where its choice in each round can depend on the outcome of its random coin tosses, at least one processor must send $\Omega(n^{1/3})$ messages to compute Byzantine agreement with probability at least $1/2 + 1/\log n$. Hence the only hope for a protocol where every processor sends $o(n^{1/3})$ messages is to design outside this constraint. Note that the protocol here does NOT fall within this restrictive model, only because of line 8 in our Almost Everywhere to Everywhere protocol, where the decision of whether a message is listened to (or acted upon) depends on how many messages are received so far.

3   The Almost Everywhere to Everywhere Universe Reduction Protocol

In this section, we describe the algorithm that satisfies Theorem 4 by going from almost everywhere committee election to everywhere committee election.

Precondition: Each processor p starts with an hypothesis of the membership of C, C_p; this hypothesis may or may not be equal to C or may be empty. However, the following two assumptions are critical. First, there exists a subset of the processors, C, of polylogarithmic size, with a majority of good processors. Second, there is a set S of at least $(1/2 + \epsilon)n$ good processors, such that for all $p \in S$, $C_p = C$.

Overview of Algorithm: The main idea of this protocol is for each processor p to randomly select $c \log n$ processors to poll as to the membership of C. Unfortunately, if these requests are made directly from p, the adversary can flood the network with "fake" requests so that the good processors are forced to send too many responses. Thus, the polling request are made through the set C, which counts the messages received from each processor to enforce that that total number of polling requests sent out is not too large.

Unfortunately, this approach introduces a new problem: processor p may have an incorrect guess about the membership of C. We solve this by having p send a (type 1) message containing its poll-list ($Poll_p$) to $List_p$, a set of $c\log n\sqrt{n}$ randomly sampled processors. Processor p hopes that at least one processor in the set $List_p$ will have a correct guess about C and will thus be able to forward a (type 2) message containing $Poll_p$ to C. To prevent these processors $q \in List_p$ from being flooded, each such processor q only forwards a type 2 message from a processor p if p appears in the set $Forward_q$, which is a set of $\sqrt{n}$ processors that are randomly sampled in advance. Upon receiving a $< Poll_p, p >$ (type 2) message from any processor q, a processor in C then sends a (type 3) request with p's ID to each member $s \in Poll_p$. More precisely, a processor in C only processes the first $\sqrt{n}$ such type 2 messages that it receives from any given processor q: this is the crucial filtering that ensures that the total number of requests answered is not too large. Upon receiving a type 3 request, $< p, 3 >$ from a majority of C, s sends C_s to p, a (type 4) message.

There are two remaining technical problems. First, since a confused processor, p, can have a C_p equal to a mostly corrupt set C', C' can overload every confused processor. Hence we require that any processor, p, who receives an overload (more than $\sqrt{n}\log^2 n$) of type 3 requests wait until their own C_p is verified before responding. Second, the processors in C handle many more requests than the other processors. The adversary can conceivably exploit this by bombarding confused processors which think they are in C with type 2 requests. Thus, the algorithm begins with a verification of membership in C. Each processor p sends a request message to a randomly selected sample ($Poll_p$) which is responded to by a polled processor q if and only if $p \in C_q$.

Example: An example run of our algorithm is shown in Figure 1. This figure follows the technically challenging part of our protocol, steps 6-10, which are

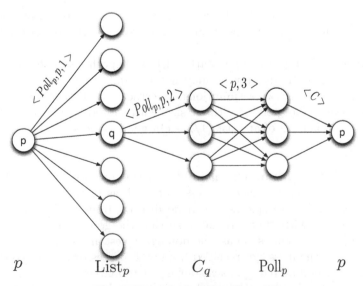

p $List_p$ C_q $Poll_p$ p

Fig. 1. Steps 6-10 of Our Protocol

described in detail in Algorithm 1 listed below. In Figure 1, time increases in the horizontal direction. This figure concerns a fixed processor p that concludes $p \notin C$ in the earlier parts of the algorithm (steps 2-5). For clarity, in this example, only messages that are sent on behalf of p that eventually help p to determine C are shown. Moreover, again for clarity, we show a best case scenario where all nodes in $Poll_p$ are assumed to have received no more than $\sqrt{n} \log^2 n$ type 3 requests. In the first step of this example, p sends the message $< Poll_p, p, 1 >$ to all nodes in $List_p$. The node q is the only node in this set such that $p \in Forward_q$, so q forwards a type 2 message of the form $< Poll_p, p, 2 >$ to all the nodes in C_q. In this example, $C_q = C$. Next all nodes in C_q send the message $< p, 3 >$ to all nodes in $Poll_p$. In this example, all nodes in $Poll_p$ know the set C, so they all send the message $< C >$ to p in the final step.

Algorithm 1. Almost Everywhere to Everywhere

Each processor executes the following steps in any order:

1. Each processor p selects uniformly at random, independently, and with replacement three subsets, $List_p$, $Forward_p$, and $Poll_p$ of processor ID's where: $|List_p| = c\sqrt{n} \log n$; $|Forward_p| = \sqrt{n}$; $|Poll_p| = c \log n$;

Verifying Membership in C:

2. $member_p \leftarrow FALSE$
3. If $p \in C_p$, then p sends a message $< Am\ I\ in\ C? >$ to the members of $Poll_p$;
4. If q receives a message $< Am\ I\ in\ C? >$ from a processor $p \in C_q$, q sends $< Yes >$ back to the p;
5. If p receives a message $< Yes >$ from a majority of members of $Poll_p$ then p sets $member_p \leftarrow TRUE$;

Determing C:

6. p sends a message $< Poll_p, p, 1 >$ (type 1 message) to each processor in $List_p$;
7. For each q: if $< Poll_p, p, 1 >$ is the first type 1 message received from processor p and $p \in Forward_q$, then q sends $< Poll_p, p, 2 >$ (a type 2 message) to every processor in C_q;
8. For each r: if $member_r = TRUE$ then for every processor q, for the first $\sqrt{n}$ type 2 messages of the form $< Poll_p, p, 2 >$ which are received from q, send $< p, 3 >$ (type 3 message) to every processor in $Poll_p$;
9. For each s: for the first $\sqrt{n} \log^2 n$ different type 3 messages of the form $< p, 3 >$ which are each sent by a majority of processors in C_s, send $< C_s, 4 >$ (type 4 message) to p;
10. If s receives the same type 4 message $< C', 4 >$ from a majority of processors in $Poll_s$ then
    (a) s sets $C_s \leftarrow C'$; and
    (b) s answers any remaining type 3 requests that have come from a majority of the current C_s, i.e. for each such request $< p, 3 >$ s sends $< C_s, 4 >$ to p;

---

4   Proof of Correctness

First, we point out that the asynchronicity of the model is not a real problem here because of the following observation:

Observation 1. *In the asynchronous model, if p is waiting to hear from a set of processors such that a majority of processors in the set are good and agree on the same value, and if each sends that value to p, then the adversary cannot prevent p from receiving this value in one timestep.*

In what follows, we show that with high probability, all transmissions which processors need to respond to are sent by a majority of good processors which agree on the same value. We say that a processor is *knowledgeable* if it is good and $C_p = C$.

Lemma 1. *W.h.p., more than a $1/2+\epsilon/2$ fraction of processors of every poll-list are knowledgeable at the start of the protocol and these remain knowledgeable.*

Proof. Let c' be any positive constant and c be the constant in the protocol. Let X be the number of processors which are initially knowledgeable in a fixed poll-list. Then $E[X] = (1/2 + \epsilon)c\log n$. The probability that the number of initially knowledgeable processors on the poll-list is not a majority is less than the probability that $X \leq (1-\delta)E[X]$ for $\delta = (\epsilon/2)/(1/2+\epsilon)$. Using the Chernoff bound, this probability is $\leq e^{(-\delta^2 E[X]/2)} \leq n^{-c'-1}$ for $c = 8(c'+1)(1/2+\epsilon)/\epsilon^2$, i.e., for c a constant, this is $1/n^{c'+1}$.

There are no more than n poll-lists for good processors. Thus, the probability that any poll-list fails to have at least a $1/2 + \epsilon/2$ fraction of initially knowledgeable processors is no greater than the sum of the n individual probabilities of failure or $1/n^{c'}$ for any constant c'.

Next, we prove by contradiction that no knowledgeable processor becomes not knowledgeable. Let p be the first processor which becomes not knowledgeable. This implies that p resets $C_p \neq C$, which implies that $Poll_p$ contains less than a majority of knowledgeable processors. By assumption, the initially knowledgeable processors in $Poll_p$ are still knowledgeable, which implies there must have been less than a majority of initially knowledgeable processors in $Poll_p$. But we have shown this event does not occur w.h.p. for any poll-list.

Lemma 2. *W.h.p., if every type 3 message received by every knowledgeable processor p is responded to by p within $O(\log n/\log\log n)$ steps then Theorem 4 holds. Moreover, a total of $O(n^{3/2}\log^3 n|C|)$ bits are sent.*

Proof. We fix a good processor p and first bound the probability that $Poll_p$ is forwarded to C. The probability that a knowledgeable processor q forwards a type 1 message sent to it by a good processor p is the probability that $p \in Forward_q = 1/\sqrt{n}$. Since each processor p sends out $c\sqrt{n}\log n$ type 1 messages, the probability that all fail to be forwarded is the probability that for every message, the processor q receiving it is either not knowledgeable or q is knowledgeable but $p \notin Forward_q$. Recall that by assumption, initially no more than $1/2 - \epsilon$ fraction of processors are not knowledgeable and by the previous lemma, this number does not grow. The probability that $Poll_p$ is not forwarded to C by a particular processor q which receives it is therefore bounded above by $(1/2 - \epsilon) + (1/2 + \epsilon)(1 - 1/\sqrt{n}) = 1 - \frac{1/2+\epsilon}{\sqrt{n}}$. The probability that all requests to forward fail is $(1 - (1/2 + \epsilon)/\sqrt{n})^{c\sqrt{n}\log n} \leq 1/n^{c/2}$.

If $Poll_p$ is forwarded by a knowledgeable processor then it is sent to every processor in C, by the definition of knowledgeable. From the previous lemma, and a simple Chernoff and union bound, each processor in C verifies it is in C with high probability. Thus, since a good processor never forwards more than $\sqrt{n}$ messages, with high probability all good processors in C will send a message of the form $< p, 3 >$ to each processor in $Poll_p$. In particular, a majority of processors in C will do so. With high probability (from the previous lemma) a majority of processors in $Poll_p$ are knowledgeable and hence upon receiving messages from processors in C will send p the correct message which p receives and decides correctly. Taking the union over all processors p, for any constant c', there is a constant c for the algorithm such that the probability of any processor failing is no greater than $1/n^{c'}$.

The number of bits transmitted by good processors can be calculated as follows. First we consider bits sent by processors that are knowledgeable. For the verification phase, the total number of bits is $\tilde{O}(n \log n)$. For the next phase, each poll-list contains $O(\log n)$ ID's of $O(\log n)$ length for a total of $O(\log^2 n)$ bits. Each good processor forwards no more than $\sqrt{n}$ poll-lists to the members of C for a total of $O(n^{3/2}|C| \log^2 n)$ bits transmitted. With high probability, each member of C transmits $O(n^{3/2} * |poll - list|)$ messages each with at most $O(\log n)$ bits per message to each member of each poll-list in the form of type 3 messages, for $O(n^{3/2}|C| \log^2 n)$ bits in total. The knowledgeable processors which receive type 3 messages respond to them all, for a total of $O(n^{3/2}|C| \log^2 n)$ bits. The total number of bits transmitted by knowledgable processors is thus $O(n^{3/2}|C| \log^2 n)$. In addition, no more than $n(\sqrt{n} \log^2 n)$ type-4 messages are sent by processors while they are not knowledgeable, for a total of $n(\sqrt{n} \log^3 n|C|)$ bits.

It remains to show:

Lemma 3. *W.h.p., every type 3 message received by every knowledgeable processor p is responded to by p within $O(\log n/ \log \log n)$ steps.*

Proof. A knowledgeable processor is *overloaded* if there are more than $\sqrt{n} \log^2 n$ poll-lists received by C which contain it. As there are no more than $n^{3/2}$ type 2 messages processed by C and each poll-list has size $c\log n$, there can be no more than $cn/\log n$ processors which receive more than $\sqrt{n} \log^2 n$ type 3 requests from C.

The adversary can choose its poll lists after seeing the poll lists from all the good processors. We will denote time step i of our algorithm to begin when i units of time have elapsed and end just before $i + 1$ units have elapsed, where a unit of time is defined to be the maximum delay of a message. We will say

$Know_p = FALSE$ at time i if p has not yet received the same type 4 message from a majority of processors in $Poll_p$, i.e. the condition for the if statement in step 10 of our algorithm has not been satisfied, by time i. Otherwise, we will say $Know_p = TRUE$. A processor p is *blocked* at time i if $Know_p = FALSE$ and p is overloaded.

Claim: With high probability, for any time step $j \geq 6$, if there is a processor with $Know_p = FALSE$ at time step $i + j$, then there must be $((\epsilon c \log n)/4)^i (\log \log n)^{i-1}$ distinct blocked processors at time j, for $i = 1, ..., O(\log n / \log \log n)$.

Proof of Claim: Let $L = |poll - list| = c \log n$. We note that since $j \geq 6$, by time step j, w.h.p., all type 1, 2 and 3 messages have been sent out and received. Moreover, the first set of type 4 messages have been sent and received. This proof is by induction on i.

Fix a processor p. Then we can view p as a root of a tree. Each node is a processor; the children of each node q are the processors in $Poll_q$. Note that some processors may appear more than once in the tree. The degree of each node is L.

Base Case: For $i = 1$. Suppose there are fewer than $(\epsilon/4)L$ blocked processors in time step j. Then from Lemma 1, w.h.p., there are $(1/2+\epsilon/2)L$ processors on every poll-list which are knowledgeable. Then there remain $(1/2 + \epsilon/4)L$ knowledgeable processors on $Poll_p$ who are not blocked and will send type 4 messages to p in the next timestep. In time $j + 1$, p will hear from them and decide.

Induction Step: Let $x_i = (\epsilon L/4)^i (\log \log n)^{i-1}$. Assume the induction hypothesis holds for $i - 1$. Then if there is a processor with $Know_p = FALSE$ at time $i + j$, then there must be a set S of size x_{i-1} of blocked processors at time step $j + 1$. Then it must be the case that at time j, reasoning as in the base case, each element of S must have at least x_1 blocked children (i.e., elements of its poll-list). We show that w.h.p. there is no set S' of size less than x_i which satisfies this condition.

Fix a set S, a set of x_1 children for each element of S, and a set S'. Since the children are picked randomly and independently, the probability of having x_1 children for each element of S coming from S' is

$$(x_i/n)^{x_1 x_{i-1}} \leq (x_i/n)^{x_i \log \log n}.$$

The number of ways to choose these sets is no more than

$$\binom{n}{x_{i-1}} L^{x_1 x_{i-1}} \binom{n}{x_i} = (ne/x_{i-1})^{x_{i-1}} L^{x_1 x_{i-1}} (ne/x_i)^{x_i} \leq (ne/x_i)^{c x_i};$$

where the last inequality holds since we can assume that $x_i \leq n/2$. Taking the union bound over all possible such sets, we find that the probability of there existing a set S' is less than

$$(x_i/n)^{(\log \log n - O(1))((\epsilon L/4)/ \log \log n)^i} < 1/n^{c'}$$

for any constant c' and $x_i/n \leq n/\log n$. Taking the union bound over all i yields the claim.

Remaining Proof of Lemma: For $i = O(\log n/\log\log n)$, the required number of blocked processors exceeds $cn/\log n$, the maximum number the adversary is able to block. Hence, every processor decides by time $O(\log n/\log\log n)$.

5   Conclusion and Open Problems

We have shown that classical problems in distributed computing, like Byzantine agreement, universe reduction, and leader election, can be solved with high probability using only $\tilde{O}(n^{3/2})$ bits of communication, even if the adversary has unlimited resources.

Several open problems remain including the following. First, we believe that the protocol from [12] for electing a committee that contains a $2/3 + \epsilon$ fraction of good processors using polylogarithmic bits per processor can be made to work in the asynchronous model. This would imply, together with the results in this paper that universe reduction, Byzantine agreement, and leader election could all be performed with $\tilde{O}(n^{3/2})$ bits in the asynchronous model.

Second, we conjecture that the number of bits required for Byzantine agreement in the full information model with a nonadaptive adversary is $\Omega(n^{3/2})$ in both the synchronous and asynchronous models unless a superpolylogarithmic time is incurred. Third, we ask: Is there is a load-balanced version of the protocol presented here in which each processor needs to send only $\tilde{O}(\sqrt{n})$ bits? Fourth, we ask: Can this bound be beaten if cryptographic assumptions are incorporated into the model? Finally, can other problems like secure mulitparty computation be solved with $o(n^2)$ bits of communication?

Acknowledgements

The authors would like to thank the program committee for a careful, extensive review.

References

1. Attiya, H., Welch, J.: Distributed Computing: Fundamentals, Simulations and Advanced Topics, 2nd edn. John Wiley Interscience, Chichester (2004)
2. Ben-Or, M., Pavlov, E., Vaikuntanathan, V.: Byzantine agreement in the full-information model in o(log n) rounds. In: STOC, pp. 179–186 (2006)
3. Bortnikov, E., Gurevich, M., Keidar, I., Kliot, G., Shraer, A.: Brahms: Byzantine resilient random membership sampling. In: PODC 2008: Proceedings of the twenty-seventh ACM symposium on Principles of distributed computing, Toronto, Canada, pp. 145–154. ACM, New York (2008)

4. Dolev, D., Reischuk, R.: Bounds on information exchange for byzantine agreement. J. ACM 32(1), 191–204 (1985)
5. Feige, U.: Noncryptographic selection protocols. In: FOCS 1999: Proceedings of the 40th Annual Symposium on Foundations of Computer Science, p. 142. IEEE Computer Society, Washington (1999)
6. Garay, J.A., Ostrovsky, R.: Almost-everywhere secure computation. In: Smart, N.P. (ed.) EUROCRYPT 2008. LNCS, vol. 4965, pp. 307–323. Springer, Heidelberg (2008)
7. Georgiou, C., Gilbert, S., Guerraoui, R., Kowalski, D.R.: On the complexity of asynchronous gossip. In: Proceedings of the ACM symposium on Principles of distributed computing (PODC), pp. 135–144 (2008)
8. Goldwasser, S., Pavlov, E., Vaikuntanathan, V.: Fault-tolerant distributed computing in full-information networks. In: FOCS, pp. 15–26 (2006)
9. Gradwohl, R., Vadhan, S.P., Zuckerman, D.: Random selection with an adversarial majority. In: Dwork, C. (ed.) CRYPTO 2006. LNCS, vol. 4117, pp. 409–426. Springer, Heidelberg (2006)
10. Holtby, D., Kapron, B.M., King, V.: Lower bound for scalable byzantine agreement. Distributed Computing 21(4), 239–248 (2008)
11. Kapron, B.M., Kempe, D., King, V., Saia, J., Sanwalani, V.: Fast asynchronous byzantine agreement and leader election with full information. In: SODA, pp. 1038–1047 (2008)
12. King, V., Saia, J., Sanwalani, V., Vee, E.: Scalable leader election. In: SODA 2006: Proceedings of the seventeenth annual ACM-SIAM symposium on Discrete algorithm, pp. 990–999. ACM Press, New York (2006)
13. King, V., Saia, J., Sanwalani, V., Vee, E.: Towards secure and scalable computation in peer-to-peer networks. In: FOCS 2006: Proceedings of the 47th Annual IEEE Symposium on Foundations of Computer Science (FOCS 2006), pp. 87–98. IEEE Computer Society, Washington (2006)
14. Kotla, R., Alvisi, L., Dahlin, M., Clement, A., Wong, E.: Zyzzyva: speculative byzantine fault tolerance. SIGOPS Oper. Syst. Rev. 41(6), 45–58 (2007)

Appendix: Sketch of Almost Everywhere Universe Reduction

Here, we include a sketch of the protocol to compute almost everywhere universe reduction, excerpted from [12]. The processors are assigned to groups of polylogarithmic size; each processor is assigned to multiple groups. In parallel, each group then elects a small number of processors from within their group to move on. We then recursively repeat this step on the set of elected processors until the number of processors left is polylogarithmic.

The method used to run elections is a simple adaptation from the atomic broadcast model to the synchronous distributed model of a subroutine in [5]:

ELECT-SUBCOMMITTEE: *Input is processors $p_1, \ldots, p_k$*
with $k = \Omega(\ln^8 n)$.
1 For $i = 1$ to k,
2   Processor p_i randomly selects one of $k/(c_1 \ln^3 n)$

"bins" and tells the other processors in its
   committee which bin it has selected.
3   The other processors in the committee run
   Byzantine Agreement to come to a consensus on
   which bin p_i has selected.
4   Let B be the bin with the least number of processors
   in it, and let S_B be the set of processors in that bin.
   Arbitrarily add enough processors to S_B to ensure
   $|S_B| = c_1 \ln^3 n$.
5   Return S_B as the elected subcommittee.

Although this approach is intuitively simple, there are several complications
that must be addressed.

(1) The groups must be determined in such a way that the election mechanism
    cannot be sabotaged by the bad processors.
(2) After each step, each elected processor must determine the identities of cer-
    tain other elected processors, in order to hold the next election.
(3) Election results must be communicated to the processors.
(4) To ensure load balancing, a processor which wins too many elections in
    one round cannot be allowed to participate in too many groups in the next
    round.

Item (1): we use a layered network with extractor-like properties. Every processor is assigned to a specific set of nodes on layer 0 of the network. In order to
assign processors to a node A on layer $\ell > 0$, the set of processors assigned to
nodes on layer $\ell - 1$ that are connected to A hold an election. In other words, the
topology of the network determines how the processors are assigned to groups.
By choosing the network to have certain desired properties, we can ensure that
the election mechanism is robust against malicious adversaries.

To accomplish item (2), we use *monitoring sets*. Each node A of the layered
network is assigned a set of nodes from layer 0, which we denote $m(A)$. The job
of the processors from $m(A)$ is simply to know which processors are assigned
to node A. Since the processors of $m(A)$ are fixed in advance and known to all
processors, any processor that needs to know which processors are assigned to A
can simply ask the processors from $m(A)$. (In fact, the querying processor only
needs to randomly select a polylogarithmic subset of processors from $m(A)$ in
order to learn the identities of the processors in A with high probability. This
random sampling will be used to ensure load balancing.)

Since the number of processors that need to know the identities of processors
in node A is polylogarithmic, the processors of $m(A)$ will not need to send too
many messages, but they need to know which processors need to know so they
do not respond to too many bad processors' queries. Hence the monitoring sets
need to inform relevant other monitoring sets of this information.

Item (3): We use a *communication tree* connecting monitoring sets of children in the layered networks with monitoring sets of parents to inform the monitoring sets which processors won each of their respective elections and otherwise pass information to and from the individual processors on layer 0.

Item (4) is addressed by having such processors refrain from further participation.

The protocol results in almost everywhere agreement rather than everywhere agreement, because the adversary can control a small fraction of the monitoring sets by corrupting their nodes. Thus communication paths to some of the nodes are controlled by the adversary.

Brief Announcement: A Leader-free Byzantine Consensus Algorithm

Fatemeh Borran and André Schiper

Ecole Polytechnique Fédérale de Lausanne (EPFL)
1015 Lausanne, Switzerland
{fatemeh.borran,andre.schiper}@epfl.ch

We consider the consensus problem in a partially synchronous system with Byzantine faults. In a distributed system of n processes, where each process has an initial value, Byzantine consensus is the problem of agreeing on a common value, even though some of the processes may fail in arbitrary, even malicious, ways. It is shown in [11] that — in a synchronous system — $3t + 1$ processes are needed to solve the Byzantine consensus problem without signatures, where t is the maximum number of Byzantine processes. In an asynchronous system, Fischer, Lynch and Peterson [7] proved that no deterministic asynchronous consensus protocol can tolerate even a single non-Byzantine (= crash) failure. The problem can however be solved using randomization for benign and Byzantine faults. For Byzantine faults, Ben-Or [2] and Rabin [12] showed that this requires $5t + 1$ processes. Later, Bracha [3] increased the resiliency of the randomized algorithm to $3t + 1$.

In 1988, Dwork, Lynch and Stockmeyer [6], considered an asynchronous system that eventually becomes synchronous (called *partially synchronous system*). The consensus algorithms proposed in [6], ensure safety in all executions, while guaranteeing liveness only if there exists a period of synchrony. Recently, several papers have considered the partially synchronous system model for Byzantine consensus [4,10,8,1,5]. However, [1,5] point out a potential weakness of these Byzantine consensus algorithms, namely that they suffer from "performance failure". According to [1], a performance failure occurs when messages are sent slowly by a Byzantine leader, but without triggering protocol timeouts, and the paper points out that the PBFT leader-based algorithm [4] is vulnerable to such an attack. Interestingly, all deterministic Byzantine consensus algorithms for non-synchronous systems are leader-based. This raises the following fundamental question: is it possible to design a deterministic Byzantine consensus algorithm for a partially synchronous system that is not leader-based? With such an algorithm, performance failure of Byzantine processes might be harmless.

Results. Our results confirm the existence of a deterministic leader-free Byzantine consensus algorithm in a partially synchronous system that is resilient-optimal and signature-free. We started from the observation that leader-free consensus algorithms exist for the synchronous system, both for benign faults (e.g., the *FloodSet* algorithm [9]) and for Byzantine faults (e.g., the algorithm based on interactive consistency [11]). However, these algorithms violate agreement if executed during the asynchronous period of a partially synchronous

I. Keidar (Ed.): DISC 2009, LNCS 5805, pp. 479–480, 2009.
© Springer-Verlag Berlin Heidelberg 2009

system. Therefore we tried to combine one of these algorithms with a second algorithm that ensures agreement in an asynchronous system.

We have applied our methodology by combining the synchronous consensus algorithm of [11] with a new algorithm that employs mechanisms from several consensus algorithms, e.g., Ben-Or [2], and PBFT [4] with strong validity. Let us denote these two algorithms by A_1, respt. A_2. Our combined algorithm is expressed in a round model. In each round, a correct process sends a message to all, receives a subset of messages sent, and computes its new state based on the messages received. Algorithm A_1 ensures that at the end of $t + 1$ rounds, (i) if q is a correct process, any correct process p receives either v_q from q or nothing, where v_q is the value initially sent by process q, and (ii) if q is a faulty process, any correct process p receives either some common value v from q or nothing. Moreover, if all $t + 1$ rounds are executed in synchronous periods, then all correct processes have the same set of messages at the end of $t + 1$ rounds. Algorithm A_2 ensures safety (i.e., agreement and strong validity), while algorithm A_1 provides liveness (i.e., termination) during periods of synchrony. Our leader-free Byzantine consensus algorithm requires $3t + 1$ processes, and $t + 3$ rounds per consensus instance during periods of synchrony.

References

1. Amir, Y., Coan, B., Kirsch, J., Lane, J.: Byzantine Replication Under Attack. In: DSN 2008, pp. 197–206 (2008)
2. Ben-Or, M.: Another advantage of free choice (Extended Abstract): Completely asynchronous agreement protocols. In: PODC 1983, pp. 27–30. ACM, New York (1983)
3. Bracha, G.: An asynchronous [(n - 1)/3]-resilient consensus protocol. In: PODC 1984, pp. 154–162. ACM, New York (1984)
4. Castro, M., Liskov, B.: Practical Byzantine Fault Tolerance and Proactive Recovery. Transactions on Computer Systems (TOCS) 20(4), 398–461 (2002)
5. Clement, A., Wong, E., Alvisi, L., Dahlin, M., Marchetti, M.: Making Byzantine fault tolerant systems tolerate Byzantine faults. In: NSDI 2009, pp. 153–168. USENIX Association (2009)
6. Dwork, C., Lynch, N., Stockmeyer, L.: Consensus in the Presence of Partial Synchrony. JACM 35(2), 288–323 (1988)
7. Fischer, M.J., Lynch, N.A., Paterson, M.S.: Impossibility of Distributed Consensus with one Faulty Process. J. ACM 32(2), 374–382 (1985)
8. Kotla, R., Alvisi, L., Dahlin, M., Clement, A., Wong, E.: Zyzzyva: speculative byzantine fault tolerance. SIGOPS Oper. Syst. Rev. 41(6), 45–58 (2007)
9. Lynch, N.A.: Distributed Algorithms. Morgan Kaufmann, San Francisco (1996)
10. Martin, J.P., Alvisi, A.: Fast Byzantine Consensus. IEEE Transactions on Dependable and Secure Computing 3(3), 202–215 (2006)
11. Pease, M., Shostak, R., Lamport, L.: Reaching Agreement in the Presence of Faults. J. ACM 27(2), 228–234 (1980)
12. Rabin, M.: Randomized Byzantine generals. In: Proc. Symposium on Foundations of Computer Science, pp. 403–409 (1983)

Efficient k-Shot Broadcasting in Radio Networks*

Erez Kantor and David Peleg

Department of Computer Science and Applied Mathematics,
The Weizmann Institute of Science, Rehovot, 76100 Israel
{erez.kantor,david.peleg}@weizmann.ac.il

Abstract. The paper concerns time-efficient k-shot broadcasting in undirected radio networks. In a k-shot broadcasting algorithm, each node in the network is allowed to transmit at most k times. Both known and unknown topology models are considered. For the known topology model, the problem has been studied before by Gąsieniec et al. [14], who established an upper bound of $D + O(kn^{1/(k-2)} \log^2 n)$ and a lower bound of $D + \Omega((n - D)^{1/2k})$ on the length of k-shot broadcasting schedules for n-node graphs of diameter D. We improve both the upper and the lower bound, providing a randomized algorithm for constructing a k-shot broadcasting schedule of length $D + O(kn^{1/2k} \log^{2+1/k} n)$ on undirected graphs, and a lower bound of $D + \Omega(k \cdot (n - D)^{1/2k})$, which almost closes the gap between these bounds. For the unknown topology model, we provide the first k-shot broadcasting algorithm. Assuming that each node knows only the network size n (or a linear upper bound on it), our randomized k-shot broadcasting algorithm completes broadcasting in $O((D + \min\{D \cdot k, \log n\}) \cdot n^{1/(k-1)} \log n)$ rounds with high probability. Moreover, we present an $\Theta(\log n)$-shot broadcasting algorithm that completes broadcasting in at most $O(D \log n + \log^2 n)$ rounds with high probability. This algorithm matches the broadcasting time of the algorithm of Bar-Yehuda et al. [3], which assumes no limitation on the maximum number of transmissions per node.

1 Introduction

In this paper we study the fundamental task of *broadcasting* in synchronous radio networks, in both the known and unknown topology models. A radio network consists of *stations* that can act, at any given time step (round), as either a transmitter or a receiver. The network is modeled as an undirected graph $G(V, E)$, where V represents the set of stations and E represents communication feasibility, i.e., two nodes $u, v \in V$ can communicate directly with each other iff $(u, v) \in E$. In the unknown topology model, we assume that each node knows only a linear upper bound on the number of nodes n, but does not know anything else concerning the topology.

---

* Supported in part by grants from the Minerva Foundation and the Israel Ministry of Science.

I. Keidar (Ed.): DISC 2009, LNCS 5805, pp. 481–495, 2009.
© Springer-Verlag Berlin Heidelberg 2009

We consider a synchronous network, where communication is performed in rounds and is assumed to have the following property: a node $u \in V$ *receives* a message M in a given round if and only if on that round it acts as a receiver and exactly one of its neighbors acts as a transmitter and transmits M. Otherwise, there are two possibilities: if none of u's neighbors transmits, then u hears *silence*, and if at least two of u's neighbors transmit simultaneously, then a *collision* occurs at u. In both cases, u does not receive any message.

We consider *broadcasting*, which is the following communication task. A distinguished node s, called the *source*, has a message M that has to delivered to all other nodes in the network. A broadcasting schedule S in a radio network is a list $(T_1, T_2, \ldots, T_t)$ of subsets of V that describes the order of transmissions: for each round $i = 1, 2, \ldots, t$, the set $T_i \subseteq V$ specifies the nodes that have to act as transmitters on round i. We assume that a node v scheduled to act as a transmitter on round t will transmit the source message M iff its already received it from one of its neighbors in some previous round. The *length* of the schedule S is the number of rounds, t, and S is said to complete broadcasting if by time t, all the network nodes have received M.

Energy efficiency is a central issue in designing the operation of ad-hoc radio networks and sensor networks, as in many cases the only energy sources for the stations are limited lifetime batteries. This paper concerns the use of *k-shot* algorithms, where each node in the network is allowed to transmit at most k times, hence energy is preserved at each of the stations.

Our contribution: We study the k-shot broadcasting in undirected radio networks. Both the known and unknown topology model are considered. For the known topology model, the problem has been studied before by Gąsieniec et al. [14], who established an upper bound of $D + O(kn^{1/(k-2)} \log^2 n)$ and a lower bound of $D + \Omega((n - D)^{1/2k})$ on the length of k-shot broadcasting schedules for n-node graphs of diameter D. We improve both the upper and the lower bound. Specifically, in Section 3 we present a randomized algorithm for constructing a k-shot broadcasting schedule of length $D + O(kn^{1/2k} \log^{2+1/k} n)$ on undirected graphs, which almost matches the lower bound. For the lower bound we show that on binomial bipartite graphs, presented in [14] (see Section 3.5), any broadcasting schedule requires at least $\Omega(k \cdot n^{1/2k})$ rounds in order to complete broadcasting, implying a lower bound of $D + \Omega(k \cdot (n - D)^{1/2k})$ on arbitrary undirected graphs.

For the unknown topology model, we present in Section 2 a first k-shot broadcasting algorithm. Assuming that each node knows only the network size n (or a linear upper bound on it), our randomized k-shot broadcasting algorithm completes broadcasting in $O\left((D + \min\{D \cdot k, \log n\}) \cdot n^{1/(k-1)} \log n\right)$ rounds with high probability. Moreover, we present a $\Theta(\log n)$-shot broadcasting algorithm that completes broadcasting in at most $O(D \log n + \log^2 n)$ rounds with high probability. This algorithm matches the broadcasting time of the algorithm of Bar-Yehuda et al. [3], which assumes no limitation on the maximum number of transmissions per node (and is, in effect, an $O(\log^2 n)$-shot broadcasting algorithm using expected $O(\log n)$ shots per node.) A comparative summary of these results is provided in Table 1.

Table 1. Summary of results on n-node networks of diameter D

Topology	Our result	Previous [14]
Known	$D + O(kn^{1/2k} \log^{2+1/k} n)$ $D + \Omega(k \cdot n^{1/2k})$	$D + O(kn^{1/(k-2)} \log^2 n)$ $D + \Omega(n^{1/2k})$
Unknown	$O\left((D + \min\{D \cdot k, \log n\}) \cdot n^{1/(k-1)} \log n\right)$ $k = \Theta(\log n)$: $\quad O(D \log n + \log^2 n)$	– –

Related work: Deterministic centralized broadcasting in radio networks was first studied by Chlamtac and Kutten [4], who formulated the radio network model. A lower bound of $\Omega(\log^2 n)$ time for broadcasting, even in $O(1)$-diameter networks, was established in [1] by showing the existence of a family of radius-2 n-node networks for which any broadcast schedule requires at least $\Omega(\log^2 n)$ rounds. On the other hand, for the known topology model, a sequence of papers presented increasingly tighter upper bounds. In [5], Chlamtac and Weinstein presented an $O(D \log^2 n)$-time broadcasting algorithm for n-node radio networks of diameter D. In [12], Gaber and Mansour proposed an $O(D + \log^5 n)$-time broadcasting algorithm. Subsequently, Elkin and Kortsarz [11] presented a deterministic algorithm yielding schedules of length $O(D + \log^4 n)$, Gąsieniec et al. [13] presented a deterministic algorithm for constructing schedules of length $D + O(\log^3 n)$ and a randomized algorithm for computing schedules of length $D + O(\log^2 n)$, and finally Kowalski and Pelc [20] gave an optimal deterministic algorithm yielding schedules of $O(D + \log^2 n)$ rounds.

For the unknown topology model, Bar-Yehuda et al. [3] were the first to study distributed broadcasting, and presented a randomized protocol that achieves successful broadcast within $O(D \log n + \log^2 n)$ rounds with high probability. (The paper assumes that every node knows its neighborhood, but the result also holds for a model where each node knows only its own label.) Kushilevitz and Mansour [21] proved a lower bound of $\Omega(D \log(n/D))$ on the problem, and Czumaj and Rytter [9] and Kowalski and Pelc [18] later showed that this bound is tight by presenting a randomized broadcasting algorithm whose time complexity is $O(D \log(n/D) + \log^2 n)$, with high probability.

In the deterministic case, for directed n-node networks of diameter D, Chrobak et al. [6] showed that there exists a deterministic broadcast algorithm with time $O(n \log^2 n)$. Later, Kowalski and Pelc [19] improved this result and established an $O(n \log n \log D)$ bound, and recently, De-Marco [10] established an $O(n \log n \log \log n)$ bound. All proofs are non-constructive. For undirected n-node networks of diameter D, Kowalski and Pelc [18] presented an algorithm working in time $O(n \log n)$ and later Kowalski [17] improved this result and established a broadcast algorithm working in time $O(n \log D)$. On the other hand, a lower bound of $\Omega(n \log D)$ was given in [8] for directed n-node networks of diameter D, and a lower bound of $\Omega(n \log n / \log(n/D))$ was given in [18] for undirected n-node networks of diameter D.

Energy efficient radio broadcasting was studied in the context of geometric networks, where the network nodes are embedded on the Euclidean plane. One of the main problems studied in this context is the *energy efficient broadcast tree* problem, where the goal is to find a transmission schedule that minimizes the total power consumption, based on a directed spanning tree rooted at the source node s. When the stations are spread in d-dimensional Euclidean space ($d > 1$), the minimum spanning tree (MST) based algorithm achieves constant approximation ratio for the problem (see [2,7,16,23]). On the other hand, the problem is known to be NP-hard [7] and if the distance function is arbitrary, then the problem has no logarithmic factor approximation unless $P = NP$ [15].

2   A k-Shot Broadcast Algorithm in Unknown Topology

This section considers k-shot broadcasting in an unknown topology, where the knowledge available to each node is limited to n, the number of nodes in the network (or a linear upper bound on it). The section is organized as follows. Subsection 2.1 presents a k-shot broadcast algorithm that is efficient for $k \leq \frac{\log n}{6}$. In subsection 2.2 we show how to extend this algorithm to a k-shot broadcast algorithm for large k (i.e., $k \approx (\log n)/\delta$ for constant $\delta \geq 1$), which completes broadcasting almost as fast as the best broadcast algorithm without any constraints on the allowed number of transmissions per node.

2.1   A k-Shot Broadcast Algorithm for Small k

Consider a network $G(V, E)$ of diameter D, where $|V| = n$. We present a randomized k-shot broadcast algorithm that completes broadcasting on G in $O((D + \min\{D \cdot k, \log n\}) \cdot n^{1/(k-1)} \log n)$ rounds with high probability. (We say that an event *holds with high probability* if its probability is at least $1 - n^{-1/(k-1)}$.) Let $\Gamma_G(w) \subseteq V$ be the set of neighbors of w in G and let $\deg_G(w) = |\Gamma_G(w)|$ be w's degree in G. (We may omit the subscript G when it is clear from the context.)

The operation of a broadcast algorithm can be viewed from two different angles. One is the viewpoint of a node $v \in V$ that has already received the message M, and whose goal is to deliver the message M to its neighbors $\Gamma(v)$. The other viewpoint is that of a node $w \in V$ that has not received M yet; the goal of the algorithm is to ensure that w does receive M from one of its neighbors in $\Gamma(w)$. Our analysis takes the second viewpoint. In our broadcasting algorithm, time is divided into epochs, with each epoch divided into Ψ phases (for integer $\Psi \geq 1$), and with each phase consisting of $O(\log n)$ rounds (time slots). Consider a node $w \in V$ that has not receive M so far, and let $\Lambda(w) \subseteq \Gamma(w)$ be a subset of w's neighbors that have already received M. Assume that $\Lambda(w) \neq \emptyset$. The algorithm assigns each node to a single transmission round, and its goal (w.r.t. w) is to have a round in which exactly one node of $\Lambda(w)$ will transmit, which will ensure that w receives M on that round. In particular, the broadcasting algorithm invokes Procedure EPOCH k times at each node u, and in each invocation it assigns u to one of Ψ phases. The goal is to assign the set $\Lambda(w)$ to a large number of phases among all considered phases. We say that a phase is *active* with respect to w if a nonempty subset of w's neighbors is assigned to this phase. For a nonempty subset $\Lambda'(w) \subseteq \Lambda(w)$ assigned to the same phase, the algorithm invokes Procedure PHASE, which ensures that there will be a round with exactly one node of $\Lambda'(w)$ transmitting, with probability at least $31/48$ for $|\Lambda(w)| \geq 2$, and with probability 1 for $|\Lambda(w)| = 1$. Thus intuitively, the broadcast algorithm ensures that for small (respectively, large) $\Lambda(w)$ there will be more than $|\Lambda(w)|/2$ (resp., $\Psi/8$) active phases with respect to w with high probability, which implies that w will receive the message with high probability.

We now turn to describing the broadcasting algorithm in detail. We first describe a basic 1-shot transmission procedure named PHASE. Let $\mathcal{T} = \lceil \log n \rceil + 5$. A node that participates in Procedure PHASE randomly selects a number r to be $i \in \{1, ..., \mathcal{T} - 1\}$ with probability 2^{-i} and otherwise selects $r = \mathcal{T}$ (with probability $2^{-\mathcal{T}+1}$). Next, it transmits the message M to all its neighbors on round $Time \equiv r \mod \mathcal{T}$. The formal code is presented in Figure 1.

Procedure PHASE$(M, \mathcal{T})$

1. Random selection:
   (a) Set $r'(v) \leftarrow i$ with probability 2^{-i}, for $i > 0$.
   (b) Set $r(v) \leftarrow \begin{cases} r'(v), & \text{if } r'(v) \leq \mathcal{T}, \\ \mathcal{T}, & \text{otherwise.} \end{cases}$
2. Send the message M to all neighbors on round $Time \equiv r(v) \mod \mathcal{T}$.

Fig. 1. Procedure PHASE

Procedure PHASE is a simple 1-shot procedure, where each node transmits in exactly one round.

Lemma 1. *Consider a node $w \in V$. If a nonempty subset of w's neighbors executes Procedure PHASE during the time interval $[1, \mathcal{T}]$ and they all start at $Time = 1$, then the probability that w receives the message M during this time interval is at least $31/48$.*

(Throughout, proofs are deferred to the full version of the paper.)

Next we describe another 1-shot procedure named EPOCH, which consists of Ψ phases (i.e., $\Psi\mathcal{T}$ rounds). A node executing Procedure EPOCH selects uniformly at random exactly one of Ψ potential phases in which it participates and executes Procedure PHASE. The formal code is presented in Figure 2.

Procedure EPOCH takes at most $\Psi\mathcal{T}$ rounds. We next prove that for any given node w, if a nonempty subset of w's neighbors executes Procedure EPOCH

Procedure EPOCH$(M, \Psi, \mathcal{T})$

1. Select uniformly at random an integer b from the set $\{0, 1, ..., \Psi - 1\}$.
2. On round $Time \equiv b\mathcal{T} + 1 \mod \Psi\mathcal{T}$, invoke Procedure PHASE$(M, \mathcal{T})$.

Fig. 2. Procedure EPOCH

simultaneously, then w will receive the message M with probability at least $1 - 1/\Psi$ during the $\Psi\mathcal{T}$ rounds of the procedure.

We start with a lemma stating three technical observations referring to placing balls in bins. Given x balls and y bins, consider a process in which each ball is placed uniformly and independently (with repetitions) in a random bin. For $x \leq y/8$, we say that the process ended *successfully* when there exists a bin occupied with exactly one ball. In order to give a lower bound for the success probability, we bound from below the probability that more than $x/2$ bins are occupied, which necessarily yields a bin with exactly one ball. For $x > y/8$, we say that the process ended successfully when more than $y/16$ bins are been occupied. Let $\mathcal{P}(x, y)$, (respectively, $\mathcal{P}'(x, y)$) be the probability of success, i.e., of having more than $x/2$, (resp., $y/16$) occupied bins.

Lemma 2. *Let $y \geq 64$. The success probabilities satisfy the following.*

(C1) $\mathcal{P}(x, y) \geq 1 - 1/y$, for $x = 2, 3$,
(C2) $\mathcal{P}(x, y) \geq 1 - (2e/y)^2$, for $3 < x \leq y/8$, and
(C3) $\mathcal{P}'(x, y) > 1 - (2e/y)^2$, for $x > y/8$.

Consider a node $w \in V$. The process of placing balls in bins is used to model a random selection of transmission phases made by w's neighbors. We say that a phase is *active* with respect to w if at least one of its neighbors participates in that phase. Note that success of the first type (where more than $x/2$ bins have been occupied) implies the existence of a phase selected by exactly one neighbor of w among all considered neighbors, which necessarily yields a round where exactly one neighbor of w transmits, and thus implies that w will receive M on that round. Success of the second type (where more than $y/16$ bins have been occupied) implies the existence of more than $y/16$ active phases among all considered subsets of phases, which implies that w will receive M during these phases with high probability.

Using Lemmas 1 and 2, we prove the following.

Lemma 3. *Let $\Psi \geq 64$. Consider a node $w \in V$. If an nonempty subset of w's neighbors executes Procedure EPOCH during the time interval $[1, \Psi\mathcal{T}]$ and they all start at Time $= 1$, then the probability that w receives the message M during this time interval is at least $1 - 1/\Psi$.*

Now we present our k-shot broadcast algorithm, named BROADCAST. In this algorithm, once node receives the source message M, it executes Procedure EPOCH$(M, \Psi, \mathcal{T})$ k times, starting on rounds corresponding to Time $\equiv 1 \mod \Psi\mathcal{T}$. The formal code of Algorithm BROADCAST is presented in Figure 3.

Relying on Lemma 3, we get the following.

Lemma 4. *Let $\Psi \geq 64$ and fix the parameter k. Algorithm BROADCAST(M, k, Ψ) is a k-shot algorithm, and it completes broadcasting on an n-node network of diameter D within $O\left((D + \min\{D \cdot k, \log n\}) \cdot \Psi\mathcal{T}\right)$ rounds with probability at least $(1 - 1/n)(1 - n(1/\Psi)^k)$.*

For a fixed parameter k, let $\Psi = \max\{64, \lceil 2n^{1/(k-1)} \rceil\}$ and $\mathcal{T} = \log n + 5$. Lemma 4 yields:

Algorithm BROADCAST(M, k, Ψ)

1. Wait until receiving the message M.
2. Do k times:
   On round $Time \equiv 1 \mod \Psi T$, execute Procedure EPOCH(M, Ψ, T).

Fig. 3. Algorithm BROADCAST

Theorem 1. *Algorithm* BROADCAST$(M, k, \max\{64, \lceil 2n^{1/(k-1)} \rceil\})$ *is a k-shot algorithm and it completes broadcasting in* $O((D + \min\{D \cdot k, \log n\}) \cdot n^{1/(k-1)} \log n)$ *rounds with probability at least* $1 - n^{-1/(k-1)}$.

2.2   A Fast k-Shot Broadcasting Protocol

We now show that for any constant integer parameter $\delta \geq 1$, setting $k = \lceil (\log n)/\delta \rceil$ and $\Psi = 4^\delta$, Algorithm BROADCAST(M, k, Ψ) is a k-shot algorithm that completes broadcasting in $O(D \log n + \log^2 n) \cdot \Psi = O((D \log n) + \log^2 n)$ rounds with probability at least $1 - 2/n$. For $\delta > 2$, this follows immediately by Lemma 4. That lemma does not apply for $\delta = 1, 2$, since Ψ must be at least 64 for Lemma 3 to apply. Thus, for $\delta = 1, 2$, we analyze the success probability of Procedure EPOCH directly (using Lemma 2).

Observation 2 *Consider a node* $w \in V$. *If a nonempty subset of* w's *neighbors executes Procedure* EPOCH$(M, 4^\delta)$ *during the time interval* $[1, 4^\delta T]$ *and they all start at* $Time = 1$, *then the probability that* w *receives the message* M *during this time interval is at least* $1 - 1/4^\delta$, *for* $\delta = 1, 2$.

Theorem 3. *Consider an* n-*node network. For constant* δ, *let* $k = \lceil (\log n)/\delta \rceil$ *and* $\Psi = 4^\delta$. *Algorithm* BROADCAST(M, k, Ψ) *is a* k-*shot algorithm that completes broadcasting in* $O(D \log n + \log^2 n) \cdot 4^\delta = O((D \log n) + \log^2 n)$ *rounds with probability at least* $1 - 2/n$.

This result should be compared with the BGI algorithm [3], the fundamental broadcast algorithm for wireless networks of unknown topology. The BGI algorithm consists of $2 \log n$ phases. In each phase, each node transmits on average twice, hence the expected number of transmissions per node is $4 \log n$ and each node transmits at most $4 \log^2 n$ times. Note that for $\delta = 1$, Algorithm BROADCAST is fast as the BGI algorithm, and in addition it is energy efficient, as each node transmits at most $\log n$ times.

3   Near-Optimal k-Shot Broadcasting in Known Topology

Consider a radio network modeled as an n-node directed graph $G(V, E)$. In this section we present a (centralized) scheduling algorithm generating k-shot broadcast schedules of length $O(kn^{1/2k} \log^{2+1/k} n)$, which is almost optimal given the aforementioned lower bound of $\Omega(k \cdot n^{1/2k})$. Specifically, we first present a randomized algorithm named RANDSCHEDULE that produces broadcast schedules of length at most $O(kn^{1/2k} \log^{1+1/k} n)$ on bipartite graphs, and then use the technique of [14] to extend the algorithm to one applying to arbitrary graphs (paying an additional logarithmic factor in schedule length).

The randomized algorithm RANDSCHEDULE applies to a bipartite graph $B = (U, L, E)$. Assume that all the nodes of U know the source message M and the goal is to deliver the message to all nodes of L. Assume that $2 \le k < \frac{\log n}{2 \log \log n}$. Note that for $k = 1$ one can use the efficient deterministic 1-shot algorithm described in [14], obtaining schedules of length $O(\sqrt{n})$. Moreover, for $k \ge \frac{\log n}{2 \log \log n}$ one can execute the broadcast algorithm for unknown topology presented in Section 2.

Our randomized scheduling algorithm improves upon the broadcast length of $O(k \cdot n^{1/(k-2)} \log n)$ achieved by Algorithm RANDBROADCAST(k) [14]. The bottleneck of that broadcast algorithm are nodes of degree at most 3. Our algorithm makes use of a technique of partitioning the schedule into sets in base k (see Section 3.1) that overcomes this bottleneck, by ensuring that all the nodes of degree at most 3 will receive the source message with probability 1.

The section is organized as follows. In Section 3.1, we begin with a technical observation referring to partitions of a set into subsets in base k. Next, in Section 3.2, we present a scheduling algorithm that produces a broadcast schedule of length $\tilde{O}(k \cdot \sqrt[k]{\max\{|U|, \sqrt{n}\}})$, only slightly improving on the previous algorithm of [14]. Later, in Section 3.3, we present a composition procedure, and in Section 3.4 we present our final algorithm, which constructs a broadcast schedule of the desired length, $O(kn^{1/2k} \log^{1+1/k} n)$.

3.1   Partitions of a Set to Subsets in Base k

In this subsection we describe a method for partitioning a set into subsets in base k, which will assist us in designing the scheduling algorithm. Let x be a positive integer of the form ψ^k for integer ψ. For simplicity, denote $[y] = \{0, 1, ..., y-1\}$ and $[y]^+ = \{1, ..., y\}$ for any positive integer y, and denote $X = [x] = \{0, 1, ..., x-1\}$. Consider the representation in *base* ψ of an integer $z \in X$. Denote the ℓ'th digit of z in base ψ by $i_\ell(z)$, i.e., $i_\ell(z) = i_\ell = \lfloor \frac{z}{\psi^\ell} \rfloor \mod \psi$. Hence,

$$z = i_{k-1}(z) \cdot \psi^{k-1} + i_{k-2}(z) \cdot \psi^{k-2} + ... + i_1(z) \cdot \psi + i_0(z).$$

For a given function $f : X \to X$, define a sequence of projection functions $f_0, ..., f_{k-1}$, where $f_\ell : X \to [\psi]$ yields the ℓ'th digit of f. i.e., $f_\ell(z) = i_\ell(f(z))$, for any $z \in X$ and $\ell \in [k]$. In addition, define a *partition* of X into a sequence of sets in base k with respect to f as follows:

$$X(f)_\ell^j = \{z \in X \mid f_\ell(z) = j\}.$$

Let $X(f, Z) = \{X(f)_\ell^j \mid X(f)_\ell^j \cap Z \ne \emptyset, \ell \in [k]$ and $j \in [\psi]\}$ and $f(Z) = \{f(z) \mid z \in Z\}$ for any subset $Z \subseteq X$ and let $f_\ell(Z) = \{f_\ell(z) \mid z \in Z\}$ for any subset $Z \subseteq X$ and any $\ell \in [k]$. Note that $X(f, X) = \{X(f)_\ell^j \mid j \in [\psi], \ell \in [k]\}$ is a collection of $k \cdot \psi$ subset of X, and $\{X(f)_\ell^j \mid j \in [\psi]\}$, for any $\ell \in [k]$, is a partition of X into ψ disjoint subsets.

We say that $f : X \to X$ (respectively, $\pi : X \to X$) is a random function (resp., permutation) if it is selected with uniform distribution from the set $\{f : X \to X \mid f \text{ is a function } \}$ (resp., $\{\pi : X \to X \mid \pi \text{ is a permutation}\}$ of functions (resp., permutations) over X. Note that when f is a random function, so is f_ℓ for every $\ell \in [k]$, and conversely, if $f_0, ..., f_{k-1} : X \to [\psi]$ are random functions, then their combined function $f : X \to X$ (such that $f(z) = \sum_{\ell=0}^{k-1} f_\ell(z) \cdot \psi^\ell$) is random as well. Using Lemma 2 again, we have the following.

Lemma 5. *For integers $\psi \geq 64$ and $k \geq 1$, let $x = \psi^k$ and $X = [x]$. For a subset $Z \subseteq X$, we have:*

(C1) If $|Z| \leq 3$, then there exist indices $\ell \in [k]$ and $j \in [\psi]$ such that $|X(\pi)_\ell^j \cap Z| = 1$.

(C2) If $4 \leq |Z| \leq \psi/8$, then the probability that $|X(\pi, Z)| > |Z|/2$ (hence there exists a subset $X(\pi)_\ell^j \in X(\pi, Z)$ such that $|X(\pi)_\ell^j \cap Z| = 1$) is at least $1 - (4e^2)^k \cdot x^{-2}$.

(C3) If $|Z| > \psi/8$, then the probability that $|X(\pi, Z)| > \psi/16$ is at least $1 - (4e^2)^k \cdot x^{-2}$.

3.2 A k-Shot Broadcast Schedule of Length $\tilde{O}(k \cdot \sqrt[k]{\max\{|U|, \sqrt{n}\}})$ on bipartite graphs

Consider a bipartite graph $B(U, L, E)$, where $U = \{u_0, ..., u_{|U|-1}\}$. In this subsection we present an algorithm named RANDSCHEDULE$^-$, for finding a k-shot broadcast schedule whose length depends on $\max\{|U|, \sqrt{n}\}$. The algorithm consists of two stage. The first stage is centralized, and the second stage is local. The algorithm operates as follows. In the first (centralized) stage, initially set $\psi \leftarrow \max\left\{ \left\lceil \sqrt[k]{|U|} \right\rceil, 64 \left\lceil \sqrt[2k]{n} \right\rceil \right\}$, $x \leftarrow \psi^k$, $X \leftarrow [x]$ and $\mathcal{T} \leftarrow 5 + \log n$. Next, select uniformity at random a permutation $\pi : X \to X$. Define a collection of $k\psi$ subsets $X(\pi)_\ell^j$ of X for every $j \in [\psi]$ and $\ell \in [k]$, where $X(\pi)_\ell^0, ..., X(\pi)_\ell^{\psi-1}$, for every $\ell \in [k]$, is a partition of X into ψ disjoint subsets.

In the second (local) stage, each node $u_i \in U$ selects k random numbers $r_0(i), ..., r_{k-1}(i)$ (similarly to the random selection in Procedure PHASE of Subsection 2.1), where $r_\ell(i)$ is selected to be $b \in \{1, ..., \mathcal{T} - 1\}$ with probability 2^{-b} and $r_\ell(i) = \mathcal{T}$ otherwise (with probability $2^{-\mathcal{T}+1}$), for every $\ell \in [k]$. Finally, each subset $X(\pi)_\ell^j$ is partitioned into $\mathcal{T}$ disjoint subsets $X(\pi, r)_{\ell,b}^j$ according to the random number $r_\ell(i)$, i.e., $X(\pi, r)_{\ell,b}^j \leftarrow \{i \mid i \in X(\pi)_j^\ell \text{ and } r_\ell(i) = b\}$.

The schedule is now defined as follows. Order the $k\psi\mathcal{T}$ sets $X(\pi, r)_{\ell,b}^j$ arbitrarily, getting the sequence $X_1, ..., X_{k\psi\mathcal{T}}$. Now, for $s = 1, ..., k\psi\mathcal{T}$, let all the vertices u_i such that $i \in X_s$ transmit simultaneously at round s. Hence the overall time required for this broadcasting schedule is $k\psi\mathcal{T}$ rounds. Note that each vertex belongs to exactly k such subsets.

The formal code of Algorithm RANDSCHEDULE$^-$ is described in Figure 4.

Using Lemma 5, we get:

Lemma 6. *The schedule $\mathcal{S}$ returned by Algorithm RANDSCHEDULE$^-$ maintains the following properties.*

Algorithm RANDSCHEDULE$^-$ $(B(U, L, E))$
/* $U = \{u_0, ..., u_{|U|-1}\}$ and $|U \cup L| = n$ */

    /* Centralized stage */

1. $\psi \leftarrow \max\left\{\left\lceil \sqrt[k]{|U|} \right\rceil, 64 \cdot \lceil \sqrt[2k]{n} \rceil\right\}$, $x \leftarrow \psi^k$, $X \leftarrow [x]$ and $\mathcal{T} \leftarrow 5 + \log n$;
2. Select a random permutation $\pi : X \to X$ over the set X.
3. Construct the sets $X(\pi)_\ell^j$, for every $j \in [\psi]$ and $\ell \in [k]$;
   /* Local stage */
4. For every $u_i \in U$ and $\ell \in [k]$ do:
   (a) Set $\quad r'_\ell(i) \leftarrow b$ with probability 2^{-b}, for $b > 0$.
   (b) Set $\quad r_\ell(i) \leftarrow \begin{cases} r'_\ell(i), & \text{if } r'_\ell(i) \leq \mathcal{T}, \\ \mathcal{T}, & \text{otherwise.} \end{cases}$
5. Construct the transmitting sets $X(\pi, r)_{\ell,b}^j \leftarrow \{i \mid i \in X(\pi)_\ell^j$ and $r_\ell(i) = b\}$, for every $j \in [\psi]$, $\ell \in [k]$ and $b \in [\mathcal{T}]^+$;
6. Return the schedule $\mathcal{S} \leftarrow \langle\{u_i \mid i \in X(\pi, r)_{\ell,b}^j\} : \ell \in [k], j \in [\psi], b \in [\mathcal{T}]^+\rangle$.

Fig. 4. Algorithm RANDSCHEDULE$^-$ $(B(U, L, E))$

(C1) $\mathcal{S}$ is a k-shot schedule.
(C2) For every $w \in L$, there exists a transmitting set $X(\pi, r)_{\ell,b}^j \in \mathcal{S}$ such that $|\Gamma(w) \cap X(\pi, r)_{\ell,b}^j| = 1$ (hence w receives the message), with probability at least $1 - 1/2n$.
(C3) Schedule $\mathcal{S}$ is broadcasting schedule with probability at least $1/2$.

The length of the schedule produced by Algorithm RANDSCHEDULE$^-$ depends on $\max\{|U|, \sqrt{n}\}$, but the size of U may be linear in n. Thus the schedule length is bounded from above by $\tilde{O}(k \cdot n^{1/k})$. In order to reduce the schedule length to $\tilde{O}(k \cdot n^{1/2k})$, we next develop a composition procedure, presented in the next section, that reduces the number of nodes in U by merging some of them into larger "composed nodes", while maintaining some restrictions designed to ensure correctness and efficiency. Later, in Section 3.4, we show how to combine the ideas of Algorithm RANDSCHEDULE$^-$ and the composition procedure to design our final algorithm, named RANDSCHEDULE, that produces a broadcasting schedule of shorter length, $\tilde{O}(k \cdot n^{1/2k})$.

3.3 The Composition Procedure

Consider a bipartite graph $B = (U, L, E)$. This subsection describe a composition procedure named COMP that transforms a bipartite graph $B(U, L, E)$ into another bipartite graph $\mathcal{C} = (\mathcal{U}, L, \mathcal{E})$, where L remains the same and $\mathcal{U}$ is a set of *composed nodes*. Each composed node consists of a subset of U, and together they partition U into disjoint subsets, i.e., $\bigcup_{\mathcal{V} \in \mathcal{U}} \mathcal{V} = U$ and $\mathcal{V}' \cap \mathcal{V}'' = \emptyset$ for every pair of composed nodes $\mathcal{V}', \mathcal{V}'' \in \mathcal{U}$.

Consider a node $w \in L$. We say that there is an *overlap* in $\mathcal{C}$ with respect to w, if there exist two neighbors of w in U that were composed into the same node in $\mathcal{U}$, i.e., there exists a $\mathcal{V} \in \mathcal{U}$ such that $|\mathcal{V} \cap \Gamma_B(w)| \geq 2$.

We use an integral *shrinkage* parameter $\Delta > 1$. The composition procedure maintains the following four properties. First, it ensures that $|\mathcal{U}| \leq \Delta \cdot \sqrt{|L|}$. Second, it ensures that if $\deg_B(w) \leq \Delta$, then ensure that there is no overlap with respect to w in $\mathcal{C}$, i.e., if $\deg_B(w) \leq \Delta$, then $|\mathcal{V} \cap \Gamma_B(w)| \leq 1$ for every $\mathcal{V} \in \mathcal{U}$. Third, if $\deg_B(w) \leq \Delta$, then COMP preserves the degree of w in $\mathcal{C}$, (i.e., $\deg_\mathcal{C}(w) = \deg_B(w)$) and if $\deg_B(w) > \Delta$, then an overlap with respect to w may occur, but the procedure ensures that $\deg_\mathcal{C}(w) \geq \Delta$. Fourth, it ensures that there exists an edge $(\mathcal{V}, w) \in \mathcal{E}$ iff there exists a node $u \in \mathcal{V}$ such that $(u, w) \in E$, i.e., $\mathcal{E} = \{(\mathcal{V}, w) \mid \Gamma_B(w) \cap \mathcal{V} \neq \emptyset\}$.

The composition procedure works as follows. First, initialize the set of composed nodes $\mathcal{U}$ to be a subset with exactly one node for each node in U, i.e., $\mathcal{V}_0 \leftarrow \{u_0\}, \ldots, \mathcal{V}_{|U|-1} \leftarrow \{u_{|U|-1}\}$. Then, update the edge set to satisfy the fourth property, i.e., $\mathcal{E} = \{(\mathcal{V}_i, w) \mid (u_i, w) \in E\}$. Next, in a greedy manner, as long as there exist two composed nodes $\mathcal{V}', \mathcal{V}''$ such that $\mathcal{V}' \cup \mathcal{V}''$ does not create an overlap for any w of degree at most Δ in $\mathcal{C}$ (i.e., $\deg_\mathcal{C}(w) \leq \Delta$), merge these nodes into a single composed node (deleting the other from $\mathcal{U}$), and then update the set of edges, i.e., $\mathcal{V}' \leftarrow \mathcal{V}' \cup \mathcal{V}''$, $\mathcal{U} \leftarrow \mathcal{U} \setminus \{\mathcal{V}''\}$ and $\mathcal{E} \leftarrow \{(\mathcal{V}, w) \mid \Gamma_B(w) \cap \mathcal{V} \neq \emptyset\}$. The formal code is described in Figure 5.

Procedure COMP$(B(U, L, E), \Delta)$

1. For every $u \in U$ do: $\mathcal{V} \leftarrow \{u\}$;
2. $\mathcal{E} \leftarrow \{(\mathcal{V}_i, w) \mid (u_i, w) \in E\}$;
3. While there exist two composed nodes $\mathcal{V}'$ and $\mathcal{V}''$ such that $|(\mathcal{V}' \cup \mathcal{V}'') \cap \Gamma_B(w)| < 1$ for any node $w \in L$ of degree at most Δ in $\mathcal{C}$ (i.e., $\deg_\mathcal{C}(w) \leq \Delta$) do:
   (a) $\mathcal{V}' \leftarrow \mathcal{V}' \cup \mathcal{V}''$;
   (b) $\mathcal{U} \leftarrow \mathcal{U} \setminus \{\mathcal{V}''\}$;
   (c) $\mathcal{E} \leftarrow \{(\mathcal{V}, w) \mid \Gamma_B(w) \cap \mathcal{V} \neq \emptyset\}$;   /* Update edges set */
4. Return $\mathcal{C}(\mathcal{U}, L, \mathcal{E})$;

Fig. 5. Procedure COMP

Lemma 7. *The resulting graph* $\mathcal{C}(\mathcal{U}, L, \mathcal{E})$ *of Procedure* COMP$(B(U, L, E), \Delta)$ *maintains the following properties.*

(P1) $|\mathcal{U}| \leq \Delta \cdot \sqrt{|L|}$.
(P2) There is no overlap in $\mathcal{C}$ with respect to nodes of degree at most $\Delta - 1$, i.e., $|\Gamma_\mathcal{C}(w) \cap \mathcal{V}| \leq 1$ for any $\mathcal{V} \in \mathcal{U}$ and any $w \in L$ such that $\deg_\mathcal{C}(w) < \Delta$.
(P3) $\deg_\mathcal{C}(w) \geq \min\{\deg_B(w), \Delta\}$, with equality when $\deg_B(w) \leq \Delta$.
(P4) There is an edge $(\mathcal{V}, w) \in \mathcal{E}$ if and only if $\Gamma_B(w) \cap \mathcal{V} \neq \emptyset$.

3.4 A k-Shot Broadcasting Schedule on Bipartite Graphs of Length $O(kn^{1/2k} \log^{1+1/k} n)$

Now we are ready to design our final algorithm, named RANDSCHEDULE, that produces a k-shot broadcasting schedule of length $O(kn^{1/2k} \log^{1+1/k} n)$ on bipartite graphs, which is almost optimal. Consider a bipartite graph $B(U, L, E)$, where $U = \{u_0, ..., u_{|U|-1}\}$. Let $y = |U|$ and $Y = [y]$.

Algorithm RANDSCHEDULE operates as follows. First we execute Procedure COMP on $B(U, L, E)$ with parameter $\Delta = 8 \log n$ and get a bipartite graph $C(\mathcal{U}, L, \mathcal{E})$. Subsequently, Algorithm RANDSCHEDULE is similar to Algorithm RANDSCHEDULE$^-$. In particular, we apply the centralized stage of Algorithm RANDSCHEDULE$^-$ on $\mathcal{U}$ by setting $\psi = \max\left\{ \left\lceil \sqrt[k]{|\mathcal{U}|} \right\rceil, 64 \left\lceil \sqrt[2k]{n} \right\rceil \right\}$, $x = \psi^k$ and $X = [x]$. Then we select (uniformly at random) a permutation $\pi : X \to X$ over the set X and define a collection of $k\psi$ subsets $X(\pi)_\ell^j$ of X for every $j \in [\psi]$ and $\ell \in [k]$. Note that y may be linear in n, but x is bounded by $O((64^k + \log n)\sqrt{n})$, since $|\mathcal{U}| = O(\sqrt{n} \log n)$ by property (P1) of Lemma 7. Thus $\psi = O(n^{1/2k} \log^{1/k} n)$.

In the second stage, similarly to the local stage of Algorithm RANDSCHEDULE$^-$, each node $u_i \in U$ selects k random numbers, where $r_\ell(i)$ is randomly set to be $b \in \{1, ..., \mathcal{T} - 1\}$ with probability 2^{-b} and otherwise set to $r_\ell(u) = \mathcal{T}$, for every $\ell \in [k]$. Then, we define a collection of $k\psi$ subsets $Y(\pi, r, B, C)_\ell^j \subseteq Y$, where

$$Y(\pi, r, B, C)_\ell^j = \{i \mid u_i \in \mathcal{V}_l \text{ and } l \in X(\pi)_\ell^j\},$$

for every $j \in [\psi]$ and $\ell \in [k]$. For simplicity, denote $Y_\ell^j = Y(\pi, r, B, C)_\ell^j$. Note that $X(\pi)_\ell^0, ..., X(\pi)_\ell^{\psi-1}$, for any $\ell \in [k]$, is a partition of X into ψ disjoint subsets and $Y_\ell^0, ..., Y_\ell^{\psi-1}$, for any $\ell \in [k]$, is a partition of Y into ψ disjoint subsets. Finally, each subset Y_ℓ^j is partitioned into $\mathcal{T}$ disjoint subsets $Y_{\ell,b}^j = Y(\pi, r, B, C)_{\ell,b}^j$, according to the random numbers $r_\ell(i)$, i.e., $Y_{\ell,b}^j \leftarrow \{i \mid i \in Y_\ell^j \text{ and } r_\ell(i) = b\}$.

The schedule is now defined as follows. Order the $k\psi\mathcal{T}$ sets $Y_{\ell,b}^j$ arbitrarily, getting the sequence $Y_1, ..., Y_{k\psi\mathcal{T}}$. Now for $s = 1, ..., k\psi\mathcal{T}$, let all the vertices u_i such that $i \in Y_s$ transmit simultaneously at round s. Hence the over all time required for this broadcasting schedule is $k\psi\mathcal{T}$ rounds. Note that each vertex belongs to exactly k such subsets.

The formal code of Algorithm RANDSCHEDULE described in Figure 6.

Using Lemmas 5, 6 and 7, we get:

Lemma 8. *Algorithm RANDSCHEDULE returns a k-shot broadcasting schedule of length $O(kn^{1/2k} \log^{1+1/k} n)$ with probability at least $1/2$.*

We can execute Algorithm RANDSCHEDULE repeatedly until getting a schedule that completes broadcast (failing with negligible probability after n attempts). Therefore, we have the following.

Theorem 4. *Algorithm RANDSCHEDULE is a randomized k-shot broadcasting algorithm that constructs (with high probability, in polynomial time) broadcast schedules of length at most $O(k \cdot n^{1/2k} \log^{1+1/k} n)$ on bipartite graphs.*

Moreover, the conclusion of [14] that any $O(f(n))$-time k-shot broadcasting scheme for bipartite graphs admits $D + O(f(n) \log n)$ time broadcast in arbitrary graphs of diameter D (see the relation between Theorem 4.9 and Corollary 4.10 therein) implies the following.

Algorithm RANDSCHEDULE($B(U, L, E)$)

1. $\mathcal{C}(\mathcal{U}, L, \mathcal{E}) \leftarrow$ COMP($B(U, L, E), \Delta = 8 \log n$);
2. $\psi \leftarrow \max \left\{ \left\lceil \sqrt[k]{|\mathcal{U}|} \right\rceil, 64 \left\lceil \sqrt[2k]{n} \right\rceil \right\}$, $x \leftarrow \psi^k$, $X \leftarrow [x]$ and $\mathcal{T} \leftarrow 5 + \log n$;
3. Select a random permutation $\pi : X \rightarrow X$ over the set X.
4. Construct the sets $X(\pi)_\ell^j$, for every $j \in [\psi]$ and $\ell[k]$;
5. Construct the sets $Y_\ell^j = \{i \mid u_i \in \mathcal{V}_l$ and $l \in X(\pi)_\ell^j\}$, for every $j \in [\psi]$ and $\ell[k]$;
6. For every $u_i \in U$ and each $\ell \in [k]$ do:
   (a) Set $r_\ell'(i) \leftarrow b$ with probability 2^{-b}, for $b > 0$.
   (b) Set $r_\ell(i) \leftarrow \begin{cases} r'(i), & \text{if } r'(i) \leq T, \\ T, & \text{otherwise.} \end{cases}$
7. Construct the transmitting sets $Y_{\ell,b}^j \leftarrow \{i \mid i \in Y_\ell^j$ and $r_\ell(i) = b\}$, for every $j \in [\psi]$, $\ell \in [k]$ and $b \in [T]^+$;
8. Return schedule $\mathcal{S} \leftarrow \langle \{u_i \mid i \in Y_{\ell,b}^j\} : \ell \in [k], j \in [\psi], b \in [T]^+\rangle$;

Fig. 6. Algorithm RANDSCHEDULE($B(U, L, E)$)

Corollary 1. *There exist a randomized algorithm for generating (with high probability, in polynomial time) k-shot broadcast schedules of length at most $D + O(k \cdot n^{1/2k} \log^{2+1/k} n)$, in every radio network of size n and diameter D.*

3.5 Lower Bound

We establish a lower bound of $D + \Omega(k \cdot (n - D)^{1/2k})$ for broadcasting in known topologies, improving on the lower bound of $D + \Omega((n - D)^{1/2k})$ presented in [14]. Namely, we show that there exist radio networks in which every k-shot broadcasting schedule requires to be of length at least $D + \Omega(k \cdot (n - D)^{1/2k})$. To prove this, we first show that for any positive integer n there exists an n-node bipartite graph on which any k-shot broadcasting schedule requires to be of length at least $\Omega(k \cdot n^{1/2k})$.

Consider the *binomial graph* $B(x) = (\{s\} \cup U \cup L, E)$ presented in [14]. This graph contains $n = x + \binom{x}{2} + 1$ nodes, where $U = \{u_1, ..., u_x\}$ and $L = \{w_{ij} \mid 1 \leq i < j \leq x\}$. The node s is connected to all the nodes in U, and each node $w_{ij} \in L$ (for $1 \leq i < j \leq x$) is connected to exactly two nodes u_i and u_j in U, i.e., $E = \{(s, u) \mid u \in U\} \bigcup \{(u_i, w_{ij}), (u_j, w_{ij}) \mid 1 \leq i < j \leq x\}$. In the first step, the message is transmitted by s to reach all the nodes in U. Our analysis concerns the process by which the message is disseminated from the nodes of U to the nodes of L.

Lemma 9. *Consider a binomial bipartite graph $B(x)$, where x positive integer. Then any k-shot broadcasting schedule for $B(x)$ requires at least $\frac{k \cdot x^{1/k}}{e} - e$ transmission rounds.*

Recall that the number of nodes in $B(x)$ is $n = \binom{x}{2} + x + 1 \geq x^2/2$, thus t must be greater than $\frac{\sqrt{2}k \cdot n^{1/(2k)}}{e} - e$, yields our lower bounds for bipartite graphs.

Theorem 5. *There exist bipartite graphs of size n in which any k-shot broadcasting schedule requires $\Omega(k \cdot n^{1/2k})$ transmission rounds.*

Using the same argument as in the proof of Theorem 2.1 in [14], we come to the following conclusion.

Corollary 2. *There exist bipartite graphs of size n and diameter D in which any k-shot broadcasting schedule requires $D + \Omega(k \cdot (n - D)^{1/(2k)})$ rounds.*

References

1. Alon, A., Bar-Noy, A., Linial, N., Peleg, D.: A lower bound for radio broadcast. J. Compt. Syst. Science 43, 290–298 (1991)
2. Ambühl, C.: An optimal bound for the MST algorithm to compute energy efficient broadcast trees in wireless networks. In: Caires, L., Italiano, G.F., Monteiro, L., Palamidessi, C., Yung, M. (eds.) ICALP 2005. LNCS, vol. 3580, pp. 1139–1150. Springer, Heidelberg (2005)
3. Bar-Yehuda, R., Goldreich, O., Itai, A.: On the time complexity of broadcast in radio networks: an exponential gap between determinism and randomization. J. Compt. Syst. Science 45, 104–126 (1992)
4. Chlamtac, I., Kutten, S.: On broadcasting in radio networks - problem analysis and protocol design. IEEE Trans. Communications 33, 1240–1246 (1985)
5. Chlamtac, I., Weinstein, O.: The wave expansion approach to broadcasting in multihop radio networks. IEEE Trans. Communications 39, 426–433 (1991)
6. Chrobak, M., Gasieniec, L., Rytter, W.: Fast broadcasting and gossiping in radio networks. In: Proc. 41st Symp. on Foundations of Computer Science (FOCS), pp. 575–581 (2000)
7. Clementi, A.E.F., Crescenzi, P., Penna, P., Rossi, R., Vocca, P.: On the complexity of computing minimum energy consumption broadcast subgraphs. In: Proc. 18th Symp. on Theoretical Aspects of Computer Science (STACS), pp. 12–131 (2001)
8. Clementi, A.E.F., Monti, A., Silvestri, R.: Selective families, superimposed codes, and broadcasting on unknown radio networks. In: Proc. 22nd ACM-SIAM Symp. on Discrete Algorithms (SODA), pp. 709–718 (2001)
9. Czumaj, A., Rytter, W.: Broadcasting algorithms in radio networks with unkown topology. In: Proc. 44rd IEEE Symp. on Foundations of Computer Science (FOCS), pp. 492–501 (2003)
10. De Marco, G.: Distributed broadcast in unknown radio networks. In: Proc. 29th ACM-SIAM Symp. on Discrete Algorithms (SODA), pp. 208–217 (2008)
11. Elkin, M., Kortsarz, G.: Improved schedule for radio broadcast. In: Proc. 26th ACM-SIAM Symp. on Discrete Algorithms (SODA), pp. 222–231 (2005)
12. Gaber, I., Mansour, Y.: Centralized broadcast in multihop radio networks. Journal of Algorithms 46(1), 1–20 (2003)
13. Gasieniec, L., Peleg, D., Xin, Q.: Faster communication in known topology radio networks. In: Proc. 24th ACM symp. on Principles of Distributed Computing (PODC), pp. 129–137 (2005)
14. Gasieniec, L., Kantor, E., Kowalski, D.R., Peleg, D., Su, C.: Time efficient k-shot broadcasting in known topology radio networks. Distributed Computing 21(2), 117–127 (2008)
15. Guha, S., Khuller, S.: Improved methods for approximating node-weighted steiner trees and connected dominating sets. Information and Computation 150, 57–74 (1999)

16. Klasing, R., Navarra, A., Papadopoulos, A., Perennes, S.: Adaptive broadcast consumption (abc), a new heuristic and new bounds for the minimum energy broadcast routing problem. In: Networking, pp. 866–877 (2004)
17. Kowalski, D.R.: On selection problem in radio networks. In: Proc. 24th ACM symp. on Principles of Distributed Computing (PODC), pp. 158–166 (2005)
18. Kowalski, D.R., Pelc, A.: Broadcasting in undirected ad hoc radio networks. In: Proc. 22nd ACM symp. on Principles of Distributed Computing (PODC), pp. 73–82 (2003)
19. Kowalski, D.R., Pelc, A.: Faster deterministic broadcasting in ad hoc radio networks. In: Proc. 20th Symp. on Theoretical Aspects of Computer Science (STACS), pp. 109–120 (2003)
20. Kowalski, D.R., Pelc, A.: Optimal deterministic broadcasting in known topology radio networks. Distributed Computing 19, 185–195 (2007)
21. Kushilevitz, E., Mansour, Y.: An $\omega(d\log(n/d))$ lower bound for broadcast in radio networks. SIAM J. on Computing 27, 702–712 (1998)
22. Mitzenmacher, M., Upfal, E.: Probability and Computing. Cambridge University Press, Cambridge (2005)
23. Wan, P.J., Calinescu, G., Li, X.Y., Frieder, O.: Minimum-energy broadcast routing in static ad hoc wireless networks. In: Proc. 20th Joint Conf. of the IEEE Computer and Communications Societies (INFOCOM), pp. 1162–1171 (2001)

Keeping Mobile Robot Swarms Connected

Alejandro Cornejo[1], Fabian Kuhn[1], Ruy Ley-Wild[2], and Nancy Lynch[1]

[1] MIT, Cambridge MA 02139, USA
{acornejo,fkuhn,lynch}@csail.mit.edu
[2] CMU, Pittsburgh PA 15213, USA
rleywild@cs.cmu.edu

Abstract. Designing robust algorithms for mobile agents with reliable communication is difficult due to the distributed nature of computation, in mobile ad hoc networks (MANETs) the matter is exacerbated by the need to ensure connectivity. Existing distributed algorithms provide coordination but typically assume connectivity is ensured by other means. We present a connectivity service that encapsulates an arbitrary motion planner and can refine any plan to preserve connectivity (the graph of agents remains connected) and ensure progress (the agents advance towards their goal). The service is realized by a distributed algorithm that is *modular* in that it makes no assumptions of the motion-planning mechanism except the ability for an agent to query its position and intended goal position, *local* in that it uses 1-hop broadcast to communicate with nearby agents but doesn't need any network routing infrastructure, and *oblivious* in that it does not depend on previous computations.

We prove the progress of the algorithm in one round is at least $\Omega(\min(d, r))$, where d is the minimum distance between an agent and its target and r is the communication radius. We characterize the worst case configuration and show that when $d \geq r$ this bound is tight and the algorithm is optimal, since no algorithm can guarantee greater progress. Finally we show all agents get ε-close to their targets within $O(D_0/r + n^2/\varepsilon)$ rounds where n is the number of agents and D_0 is the sum of the initial distances to the targets.

1 Introduction

Motivation. Designing robust algorithms for mobile agents with reliable communication is difficult due to the distributed nature of computation. If the agents form a mobile ad hoc network (MANET) there is an additional tension because communication is necessary for motion-planning, but agent movement may destabilize the communication infrastructure. As connectivity is the core property of a communication graph that makes distributed computation possible, algorithms for MANETs must reconcile the interaction between communication and motion planning in order to preserve connectivity.

Existing distributed algorithms for MANETs provide coordination but typically sidestep the issue of connectivity by assuming it is ensured by other means. For example, algorithms on routing [1,2], leader election [3], and mutual exclusion [4] for MANETs assume they run on top of a mobility layer that controls the

I. Keidar (Ed.): DISC 2009, LNCS 5805, pp. 496–511, 2009.
© Springer-Verlag Berlin Heidelberg 2009

trajectories of the agents. Those algorithms deal with connectivity by assuming the mobility layer guarantees that every pair of nodes that need to exchange a message are connected at some instant or transitively through time, otherwise they work on each independent connected cluster. On the other hand, work on flocking [5,6], pattern formation [7], and leader following [8] provides a mobility layer for a MANET that determines how agents will move. Again connectivity is sidestepped by assuming coordination runs atop a network layer that ensures it is always possible to exchange information between every pair of agents. The service we present would thus enable to execute the flocking algorithm of [5] using the routing algorithm of [2], or running the leader follower algorithm of [8] using the leader election service of [3], with the formal guarantee that connectivity is maintained and progress is made. The connectivity service allows an algorithm designer to focus on the problems which are specific to the application (i.e. search and rescue, demining fields, space exploration, etc.) without having to deal with the additional issues that arise when there is no fixed communication infrastructure. We expect algorithms designed on top of this service will be easier to prove correct because the safety and progress properties are maintained orthogonally by the guarantees of the service.

Related work. The problem of preserving connectivity has been addressed before, mainly in the control theory community. However, most proposed solutions are either centralized or preserve connectivity only while performing specific tasks (i.e. converging to a point). For example [9] models connectivity as a constrained optimization problem, but as a result the solution is centralized and does not exploit the locality of distributed computation. Another centralized algorithm for second-order agents is proposed in [10], however it conservatively preserves all edges in the graph. The problem of gathering (rendezvous) all agents to a single point while preserving connectivity is studied in [11,12,13,14]. In [15,16] the authors evaluate through simulations the problem of connected deployment, but do not prove in which configurations the algorithms achieve deployment or preserve connectivity. In contrast in this paper we present a local algorithm that preserves connectivity while performing an arbitrary task, we focus on providing formal safety and progress guarantees. A preliminary version of the algorithm without progress guarantees appeared in [17].

Communication Model. We assume each agent is equipped with a communication device that permits reliable broadcasting to all other agents within some communication radius r. Without loss of generality we suppose $r = 1$ throughout. The service operates in synchronous rounds, it assumes access to a positioning device; relative position between neighboring agents is sufficient, but for ease of exposition we assume absolute position is available. Finally the service assumes the existence of a motion planner which is queried at each round for the desired target position, the service produces a trajectory which preserves connectedness and, when possible, gets closer to the target.

Contributions. We present a distributed connectivity service that modifies an existing motion plan to ensure connectivity using only local information and without making any assumptions of the current and goal configurations. In particular, even if the goal configuration is disconnected, the service guarantees connectivity while trying to get each agent as close as possible to its target. Furthermore, the connectivity service only requires the immediate intended trajectory and the current position, but it is stateless, and hence *oblivious*. The service is also *robust* to the motion of each agent in that the refined plan preserves connectivity irrespective of the agents' speed changes. Therefore agents remain connected throughout their motion even if they only travel a fraction (possibly none) of their trajectory.

Connectivity is a global property, so determining whether an edge can be removed without disconnecting the graph may require traversing the whole graph. However, exploiting the distributed nature of a team of agents requires allowing each agent to perform tasks with a certain degree of independence, so communicating with every agent in the graph before performing each motion is prohibitive. To solve this we parametrize the service with a filtering method that determines which edges must be preserved and which can be removed, we also suggest several local algorithms that can be used to implement this filtering step.

We define *progress* as the quantification of how much closer each agent gets to its target in a single round. Our algorithm guarantees that the total progress is at least $\min(d, r)$ in configurations where every agent wants to move at least some distance d and the communication radius is r. Furthermore, we exhibit a class of configurations where no local algorithm can do better than this bound, hence under these conditions the bound is tight and the algorithm is asymptotically optimal. In the last section we prove all agents get ε-close to their target within $O(D_0/r + n^2/\varepsilon)$ rounds where D_0 is the total initial distance to the targets and n is the number of agents. Since the motion of the agents occurs in a geometric space and the service deals directly with motion planning, most progress arguments rely on geometrical reasoning.

We introduce some notation and definitions in §2. In §3 we present the intersecting disks connectivity service and discuss its parametrization in a filtering function. We prove the algorithm preserves connectivity and produces robust trajectories (§4). In §5 we prove that any lower-bound on progress for chains also applies to general graphs. We start §8 by giving a lower bound on progress of a very restricted class of chains with only two nodes, and in the rest of the section we show how to extend this lower bound to arbitrary chains. We give the termination bound in §9 and conclude in §10.

2   Preliminary Definitions

The *open disk* centered at p with radius r is the set of points at distance less than r from p: $\mathsf{disk}_r(p) := \{q : \|p - q\| < r\}$. The *circle* centered at p with radius r is the set of points at distance r from p: $\mathsf{circle}_r(p) := \{q : \|p - q\| = r\}$. The *closed disk* centered at p with radius r is the set of points at distance at most

r from p: $\overline{\text{disk}}_r(p) := \text{circle}_r(p) \cup \text{disk}_r(p) = \{q : \|p - q\| \leq r\}$. We abbreviate $\text{disk}(p, q) := \text{disk}_{\|p-q\|}(p)$, $\text{circle}(p, q) := \text{circle}_{\|p-q\|}(p)$, $\overline{\text{disk}}(p, q) := \overline{\text{disk}}_{\|p-q\|}(p)$. The *unit disk* of point p is $\text{disk}_1(p)$.

The *lens* of two points p and q is the intersection of their unit disks: $\text{lens}(p, q) := \text{disk}_1(p) \cap \text{disk}_1(q)$. The *cone* of two points p and q is defined as the locus of all the rays with origin in p that pass through $\text{lens}(p, q)$ (the apex is p and the base is $\text{lens}(p, q)$): $\text{cone}(p, q) := \{r : \exists s \in \text{lens}(p, q).r \in \text{ray}(p, s)\}$, where $\text{ray}(p, q) := \{p + \gamma(q - p) : \gamma \geq 0\}$.

A *configuration* $C = \langle I, F \rangle$ is an undirected graph where an agent $i \in I$ has a *source* coordinate $s_i \in \mathbb{R}^2$, a *target* coordinate $t_i \in \mathbb{R}^2$ at distance $d_i = \|s_i - t_i\|$, and every pair of neighboring agents $(i, j) \in F$ are *source-connected* (*i.e.*, $\|s_i - s_j\| \leq r$) where r is the communication radius. We say a configuration C is a *chain* (resp. *cycle*) if the graph is a simple path (resp. cycle).

3   Distributed Connectivity Service

In this section we present a distributed algorithm for refining an arbitrary motion plan into a plan that moves towards the intended goal and preserves global connectivity. No assumptions are made about trajectories generated by the motion planner, the connectivity service only needs to know the current and target positions and produces a straight line trajectory at each round; the composed trajectory observed over a series of rounds need not be linear. The trajectories output by the service are such that connectivity is preserved even if an adversary is allowed to stop or control the speed of each agent independently.

The algorithm is parameterized by a filtering function that determines a sufficient subset of neighbors such that maintaining 1-hop connectivity between those neighbors preserves global connectivity. The algorithm is *oblivious* because it is stateless and only needs access to the current plan, hence it is resilient to changes in the plan over time.

3.1   The Filtering Function

Assuming the communication graph is connected, we are interested in a FILTER subroutine that determines which edges can be removed while preserving connectivity. Let s be the position of an agent with a set N of 1-hop neighbors, we require a function $\text{FILTER}(N, s)$ that returns a subset of neighbors $N' \subseteq N$ such that preserving connectivity with the agents in the subset N' is sufficient to guarantee connectivity.

We will not require for FILTER to be symmetric, hence it may deem necessary for i to preserve j as a neighbor, but not the other way around. However, a FILTER function is *valid* if preserving symmetric edges is sufficient to preserve global connectivity, where an edge (i, j) is symmetric if i should preserve j ($s_j \in N_i'$) and vice versa ($s_i \in N_j'$).

The identity function $\text{FILTER}(N, s) := N$ is trivially valid because connectivity is preserved if no edges are removed. However, ideally we want a FILTER function that in some way "minimizes" the number of edges kept. A natural choice is to compute the minimum spanning tree (MST) of the graph, and return for every agent the set of neighbors which are its one hop neighbors in the MST. Although in some sense this would be the ideal filtering function, it cannot be computed locally and thus it is not suited for the connectivity service.

Nevertheless, there are well known local algorithms that compute sparse connected spanning subgraphs, amongst them is the Gabriel graph (GG) [18], the relative neighbor graph (RNG) [19], and the local minimum spanning tree ($LMST$) [20]. All these structures are connected and can be computed using local algorithms. Since we are looking to remove as many neighbors as possible and $MST \subseteq LMST \subseteq RNG \subseteq GG$, from the above $LMST$ is best suited.

Remark. The connected subgraph represented by symmetric filtered neighbors depends on the positions of the agents, which can vary from one round to the next. Hence, the use of a filtering function enables preserving connectivity without preserving a fixed set of edges (topology) throughout the execution; in fact, it is possible that no edge present in the original graph appears in the final graph.

3.2   The Algorithm

We present a three-phase service (cf. Algorithm 1) that consists of a collection phase, a proposal phase, and an adjustment phase. In the collection phase each agent queries the motion planner and the location service to obtain its current and target positions (s_i and t_i respectively). Each agent broadcasts its position and records the position of neighboring agents discovered within its communication radius.

Algorithm 1. ConnServ run by agent i

                                                              ▷ Collection Phase

$s_i \leftarrow$ *query_positioning_device*()
$t_i \leftarrow$ *query_motion_planner*()
broadcast s_i to all neighbors
$N_i \leftarrow \{s_j \mid$ for each s_j received$\}$
                                                              ▷ Proposal Phase

$N_i' \leftarrow$ FILTER (N_i, s_i)
$R_i \leftarrow \bigcap_{s_j \in N_i'}$ disk$_1(s_j)$
$p_i \leftarrow \text{argmin}_{p \in R_i} \|p - t_i\|$
broadcast p_i to all neighbors
$P_i \leftarrow \{p_j \mid$ for each p_j received$\}$
                                                              ▷ Adjustment Phase

if $\forall s_j \in N_i'.\|p_j - p_i\| \leq r$ **then**
    return trajectory from s_i to p_i
else
    return trajectory from s_i to $s_i + \frac{1}{2}(p_i - s_i)$
end if

In the proposal phase the service queries the FILTER function to determine which neighboring agents are sufficient to preserve connectivity. Using the neighbors returned by FILTER the agent optimistically chooses a target p_i. The target is optimistic in the sense that if none of its neighboring agents move, then moving from source s_i to the target p_i would not disconnect the network. The proposed target p_i is broadcast and the proposals of other agents are collected.

Finally in the adjustment phase, each agent checks whether neighbors kept by the FILTER function will be reachable after each agent moves to their proposed target. If every neighbor will be reachable, then the agent moves from the current position to its proposed target, otherwise it moves halfway to its proposed target, which ensures connectivity is preserved (proved in the next section).

4 Preserving Connectivity

In this section we prove the algorithm preserves network connectivity with any valid FILTER function. Observe that since R_i is the intersection of a set of disks that contain s_i, it follows that R_i is convex and contains s_i. By construction $p_i \in R_i$ and thus by convexity the linear trajectory between s_i and p_i is contained in R_i, so the graph would remain connected if agent i were to move from s_i to p_i and every other agent would remain in place. The following theorems prove a stronger property, namely, the trajectories output guarantee symmetric agents will remain connected, even if they slow down or stop abruptly at any point of their trajectory.

Adjustment Lemma. *The adjusted proposals of symmetric neighbors are connected.*

Proof. The adjusted proposals of symmetric agents i and j are $p'_i = s_i + \frac{1}{2}(p_i - s_i)$ and $p'_j = s_j + \frac{1}{2}(p_j - s_j)$. By construction $\|s_i - p_j\| \leq r$ and $\|s_j - p_i\| \leq r$, so the adjusted proposals are connected:

$$\|p'_i - p'_j\| = \|s_i - s_j + \frac{1}{2}(p_i - p_j + s_j - s_i)\| \leq \frac{1}{2}(\|s_i - p_j\| + \|s_j - p_i\|) \leq r$$

Safety Theorem. *If FILTER is valid, the service preserves connectivity of the graph.*

Proof. Assuming FILTER is valid, it suffices to prove that symmetric neighbors remain connected after one round of the algorithm. Fix symmetric neighbors i and j. If $\|p_i - p_j\| > r$, both adjust their proposals and they remain connected by the Adjustment lemma. If $\|p_i - p_j\| \leq r$ and neither adjust, they trivially remain connected. If $\|p_i - p_j\| \leq r$ but (wlog) i adjusts but j doesn't adjust, then $s_i, p_i \in \mathsf{disk}_1(p_j)$, and by convexity $p'_i \in \mathsf{disk}_1(p_j)$, whence $\|p'_i - p_j\| \leq r$.

Even if two agents are connected and propose connected targets, they might disconnect while following their trajectory to the target. Moreover, agents could stop or slow down unexpectedly (perhaps due to an obstacle) while executing the trajectories. We prove the linear trajectories prescribed by the algorithm for symmetric neighbors are *robust* in that any number of agents can stop or slow down during the execution and connectivity is preserved.

Robustness Theorem. *The linear trajectories followed by symmetric neighbors are robust.*

Proof. Fix symmetric neighbors i and j, we need to prove that all intermediate points on the trajectories are connected. Fix points $q_i := s_i + \gamma_i(p_i - s_i)$ and $q_j := s_j + \gamma_j(p_j - s_j)$ $(\gamma_i, \gamma_j \in [0,1])$ on the trajectory from each source to its proposed target. Since the neighbors are symmetric, $s_i, t_i \in \mathsf{disk}_1(s_j) \cap \mathsf{disk}_1(t_j)$ and by convexity $q_i \in \mathsf{disk}_1(s_j) \cap \mathsf{disk}_1(t_j)$. Similarly $s_j, t_j \in \mathsf{disk}_1(q_i)$ and by convexity $q_j \in \mathsf{disk}_1(q_i)$, whence $\|q_i - q_j\| \leq r$.

5   Ensuring Progress for Graphs

For the algorithm to be useful, besides preserving connectivity (proved in §4) it should also guarantee that agents make progress and eventually reach their intended destination. We start by identifying several subtle conditions without which no local algorithm could both preserve connectivity and guarantee progress.

Cycles. Consider a configuration where nodes are in a cycle, two neighboring nodes want to move apart and break the cycle and every other node wants to remain in place. Clearly no local algorithm can make progress because, without global information, nodes cannot distinguish between being in a cycle or a chain, and in the latter case any movement would violate connectivity. As long as the longest cycle of the graph is bounded by a known constant, say k, using local LMST filtering over $\lfloor k/2 \rfloor$-hops will break all cycles. A way to deal with graphs with arbitrary long cycles without completely sacrificing locality would be to use the algorithm proposed in this paper and switch to a global filtering function to break all cycles when nodes detect no progress has been made for some number of rounds. For proving progress, in the rest of the paper we assume there are no cycles in the filtered graph.

Target-connectedness. If the proposed targets are disconnected, clearly progress cannot be achieved without violating connectivity, hence its necessary to assume the target graph is connected. For simplicity, in the rest of the paper we assume that the current graph is a subgraph of the target graph, this avoids reasoning about filtering when proving progress and one can check that as a side effect the adjustment phase is never required.

5.1   Dependency Graphs

Fix some node in an execution of the ConnServ algorithm, on how many other nodes does its trajectory depend on? Let $\mathsf{region}(S) := \bigcap_{s \in S} \mathsf{disk}_1(s)$ and let proposal$(S, t) := \text{argmin}_{p \in \text{region}(S)} \|p - t\|$, then a node with filtered neighbor set N' and target t depends on k neighbors (has dependency k) if there exists a subset $S \subseteq N'$ of size $|S| = k$ such that proposal$(S, t) = $ proposal(N', t) but proposal$(S', t) \neq$ proposal(N', t) for any subset $S' \subseteq N'$ of smaller size $|S'| < k$.

The dependency of a node can be bounded by the size of its filtered neighborhood. If the filtering function is LMST then the number of neighbors is at most 6 or 5 depending on whether the distances to neighbors are unique (*i.e.* breaking ties using unique ID's). The following lemma gives a tighter upper bound on the dependency of a neighbor which is independent of the filtering function.

Lemma 6. *Every agent depends on at most two neighbors.*

Proof. Fix agent i with filtered neighbors N' and target t, let $R = \text{region}(N')$. If $t \in R$ then proposal$(N', t) = $ proposal$(\varnothing, t) = t$ and agent i depends on no neighbors. If $t \notin R$ then proposal(N', t) returns a point p in the boundary of region R. Since R is the intersection of a finite set of disks it follows that p is either in the boundary of a single disk so i depends on a single neighbor, or the intersection of two disks so i depends on at most two neighbors.

Given the above, for any configuration $C = \langle I, F \rangle$ we can consider its dependency graph $D = \langle I, E \rangle$ where there exists a directed edge $(u, v) \in E$ iff node u depends on node v. Hence, D is a directed subgraph of C with maximum out-degree 2. Moreover since graphs with cycles cannot be handled by any local connectivity service, then for the purpose of proving progress we assume C has no undirected cycles. This implies that the only directed cycles in D are simple cycles of length 2, we refer to such dependency graphs as *nice* graphs.

A *prechain* H is a sequence of vertices $\langle v_i \rangle_{i \in 1..n}$ such that there is a simple cycle between v_i, v_{i+1} $(i \in 1..n-1)$. Observe that a vertex v is a singleton prechain. Below we prove that any nice dependency graph D contains a nonempty prechain H with no out-edges.

Theorem 7. *Every finite nice graph $G = \langle V, E \rangle$ contains a nonempty prechain $H \subseteq V$ with no out edges.*

Proof. Fix a graph $G = \langle V, E \rangle$ and consider the graph G' that results from iteratively contracting the vertices $u, v \in V$ if $(u, v) \in E$ and $(v, u) \in E$. Clearly G' is also a finite nice graph and any vertex v' in G' is a prechain of G, however G' does not contain any directed cycles.

We follow a directed path in G' starting at an arbitrary vertex u', since the graph is finite and contains no cycles, we must eventually reach some vertex v' with no outgoing edges, such a vertex is a prechain and has no outgoing edges, which implies the theorem.

Therefore by theorem 7 any lower bound on progress for chains also holds for general configurations. In particular the lower bound of $\Omega(\min(d, r))$ for chains proved in the next section applies for general graphs as well.

8   Ensuring Progress for Chains

In this section we restrict our attention to chain configurations and show that, if agents execute the connectivity service's refined plan, the total progress of the configuration is at least $\min(d, r)$, where d is the minimum distance between any agent and its target and r is the communication radius. We introduce some terminology to classify chains according to their geometric attributes, then we prove the progress bound for a very restricted class of chains. Finally, we establish the result for all chains by showing that the progress of an arbitrary chain is bounded below by the progress of a restricted chain.

Terminology. Each agent has a local coordinate system where the source is the origin $(s_i = \langle 0, 0 \rangle)$ and the target is directly above it $(t_i = \langle 0, d_i \rangle)$. The left side of agent i is defined as $L_i := \{\langle x, y \rangle : x \leq 0\}$ and the right side as $R_i := \{\langle x, y \rangle : x > 0\}$ where points are relative to the local coordinate system. An agent in a chain is *balanced* if it has one neighbor on its left side, and the other on its right side; a configuration is balanced if every agent is balanced.

A configuration is *d-uniform* if every agent is at distance d from its target $(d_i = d$ for every agent $i)$. Given a pair of agents i and j, they are *source-separated* if $\|s_i - s_j\| = 1$; they are *target-separated* if $\|s_i - s_j\| = 1$; and they are *target-parallel* if the rays $\mathsf{ray}(s_i, t_i)$ and $\mathsf{ray}(s_j, t_j)$ are parallel. An agent i with neighbors j and k is *straight* if s_i, s_j and s_k are collinear; a chain configuration is straight if all agents are straight.

Given an agent with source s, target t and a (possibly empty) subset of neighbors $S \subseteq N$, its proposed target w.r.t. S is defined as $t^* = \mathsf{proposal}(S, t)$. The *progress* of the agent would be $\delta(s, t; S) := \|s - t\| - \|t^* - t\|$, which we abbreviate as δ_i for agent i when the s_i, t_i and S_i are clear from context. Observe that since $\mathsf{region}(S \cup S') \subseteq \mathsf{region}(S)$, $\delta(s, t; S \cup S') \leq \delta(s, t; S)$. The *progress* of a configuration C is the sum every agent's progress: $\mathsf{prog}(C) := \sum_i \delta_i$.

Proof Overview. We first characterize the progress of agents in a balanced and source-separated chain and show the progress bound specifically for chains that are d-uniform, source- and target-separated, balanced, and straight (§8.2). Then we show how to remove each of the requirements of a chain being straight, balanced, source- and target-separated, and d-uniform (§8.3). Ultimately, this means that an *arbitrary* target-connected chain configuration $C = \langle I, F \rangle$ can be transformed into a d-uniform, source- and target-separated, balanced, straight chain configuration C' such that $\mathsf{prog}(C) \geq \mathsf{prog}(C') \geq \min(d, r)$, where d is the minimum distance between each source and its target in the original configuration C $(d := \min_{i \in I} \|s_i - t_i\|)$ and the communication radius is r. At each removal step we show that imposing a particular constraint on a more relaxed configuration does not increase progress, so that the lower bound for the final (most constrained) configuration is also a lower bound for the original (unconstrained) configuration. The bound shows that straight chains (the most constrained configurations) are the worst-case configurations since their progress is a lower bound for all chains. We show the lower bound is tight for d-uniform configurations by exhibiting a chain with progress exactly $\min(d, r)$ (§8.3).

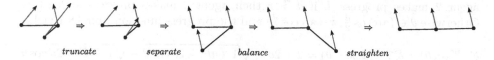

Fig. 1. Transformation overview from arbitrary to restricted chains

8.1 Progress Function for Balanced and Separated Chains

We explicitly characterize the progress of an agent in a balanced, source-separated chain. In such a configuration, if an agent has source s with target t, the source-target distance is $d := \|s-t\|$ and the position of its neighbors s_{-1}, s_{+1} (if any) can be uniquely determined by the angles of the left ($\lambda := \angle t, s, s_{-1}$) and right neighbor ($\rho := \angle t, s, s_{+1}$). Since an agent's progress is determined by it's neighbors, its progress can be defined as a function $\delta^{\angle}(d, \lambda, \rho)$.

If the agent doesn't depend on either neighbor, it can immediately move to its target and its progress is d. If it (partially) depends on a single (left or right) neighbor at angle θ, then progress is $\delta^{single}(d, \theta) := d + 1 - \sqrt{1 + d^2 - 2d\cos\theta}$. If it (partially) depends on both neighbors at angles ρ and λ, then progress is $\delta^{both}(d, \lambda, \rho) := d - \sqrt{2 + d^2 - 2d\cos\rho + 2\cos(\rho + \lambda) - 2d\cos\lambda}$. If completely immobilized by one or both of its neighbors, its progress is 0. Therefore the progress of an agent is described by the following piecewise function, parametrized by the source-target distance d and the angle to its neighbors ρ and λ. Observe that the agent i's progress function is monotonically decreasing in ρ and λ.

$$\delta^{\angle}(d, \lambda, \rho) = \begin{cases} d & \rho \le \cos^{-1}\frac{d}{2} \text{ and } \lambda \le \cos^{-1}\frac{d}{2} \\ \delta^{single}(d, \rho) & \rho > \cos^{-1}\frac{d}{2} \text{ and } \sin(\rho + \lambda) \ge d\sin\lambda \\ \delta^{single}(d, \lambda) & \lambda > \cos^{-1}\frac{d}{2} \text{ and } \sin(\rho + \lambda) \ge d\sin\rho \\ \delta^{both}(d, \lambda, \rho) & \rho + \lambda < \pi \text{ and } \sin(\rho + \lambda) < d\sin\rho, d\sin\lambda \\ 0 & \rho + \lambda \ge \pi \end{cases}$$

8.2 Progress for Restricted Chains

We prove a lower bound on progress of $\min(d, r)$ for d-uniform, source- and target-separated, balanced, straight chains with communication radius r. Let $C_k(d, \theta)$ represent a d-uniform, source- and target-separated, straight chain of k nodes, where $\angle t_i, s_i, s_{i+1} = \theta$ for $i \in 1..n - 1$. We first establish the progress bound for chains of two nodes and then extend it to more than two nodes.

Progress Theorem for Restricted 2-Chains. *For any $\theta \in [0, \pi]$, the chain $C_2(d, \theta)$ makes progress at least $\min(d, r)$ ($\mathsf{prog}(C_2(d, \theta)) \ge \min(d, r)$).*

Proof. Suppose $\theta \le \arccos\frac{d}{2}$, then if $d \le r$ agent 1 makes progress d, if $d > r$ then agent 1 makes progress at least r. Similarly if $\theta \ge \pi - \arccos\frac{d}{2}$ and $d \le r$

agent 2 makes progress d, if $d > r$ then agent 2 makes progress at least r. Otherwise $\theta \in (\arccos \frac{d}{2}, \pi - \arccos \frac{d}{2})$ and the progress function from §8.1 yields

$$\delta^{\text{single}}(d, \theta) + \delta^{\text{single}}(d, \pi - \theta) = 2 + 2d - \sqrt{1 + d^2 - 2d \cos \theta} - \sqrt{1 + d^2 + 2d \cos \theta}$$

The partial derivative is $d \sin \theta (1/\sqrt{1 + d^2 + 2d \cos \theta} - 1/\sqrt{1 + d^2 - 2d \cos \theta})$, whose only root in $(0, \pi)$ is $\theta = \frac{\pi}{2}$, which is a local minimum. We use the first order Taylor approximation as an upper bound of $\sqrt{1 + d^2}$ and since $d^2 < d$:

$$\text{prog}(C_2(d, \theta)) \geq \text{prog}(C_2(d, \frac{\pi}{2})) \geq 2\delta^{\text{single}}(d, \frac{\pi}{2})$$

$$\geq 2 + 2d - 2\sqrt{1 + d^2}) \geq 2 + 2d - 2 - d^2 \geq d$$

Progress Theorem for Restricted n-Chains. *Configurations $C_n(d, \theta)$ ($n > 2$) and $C_2(d, \theta)$ have the same progress ($\text{prog}(C_n(d, \theta)) = \text{prog}(C_2(d, \theta))$).*

Proof. Since C_n is straight and separated, internal nodes make no progress ($\delta_i = 0$ for $i \in 2..n - 1$). The first node in C_n (and C_2) has a single neighbor at angle θ, so $\delta_1^n = \delta_1^2$. Similarly the last node in C_n (and C_2) has a single neighbor at angle $\pi - \theta$, so $\delta_n^n = \delta_2^2$. Therefore $\text{prog}(C_n(d, \theta)) = \text{prog}(C_2(d, \theta))$.

8.3   Progress for Arbitrary Chains

We prove that the progress of an *arbitrary* chain is bounded by below by the progress of a restricted chain, hence the progress bound proved in the previous section for restricted chains extends to all chains. Furthermore, we show the bound is tight for d-uniform configurations by exhibiting a class of chains for which progress is exactly $\min(d, r)$.

To extend the progress result from restricted to arbitrary chains, we exhibit a sequence of transformations (cf. Fig 1) that show how to transform an arbitrary chain to be d-uniform, source-separated, target-separated, balanced and straight. Each transformation doesn't increase progress and preserves the configuration's properties. The proofs rely heavily on geometric reasoning and are the most technical part of the progress bound. Due to space restrictions we list the lemmas without proof, see [21] for the detailed proofs.

Truncation Lemma. *Suppose a source s with target t and neighbors S. Let $t^T = s + \gamma(t - s)$ with $\gamma \in [0, 1]$ be its truncated target, then $\delta(s, t; S) \geq \delta(s, t^T; S)$.*

Separation Lemma. *A d-uniform configuration C can be transformed into a d-uniform, source- and target-separated configuration C' with $\text{prog}(C) \geq \text{prog}(C')$.*

Balancing Lemma. *Fix a configuration C where agent i has neighbors $i - 1$ and $i + 1$ on the same side. Let C' be the configuration obtained by reflecting every s_j and t_j for $j > i$ (or $j < i$) around agent i's y-axis. Then $\text{prog}(C) \geq \text{prog}(C')$.*

Straightening Lemma. *Fix a configuration C described by $\{\theta_i\}_{i \in 1..n-1}$ and a straight configuration C' described by $\{\theta_i'\}_{i \in 1..n-1}$ where every angle is θ_{n-1} ($\theta_i' := \theta_{n-1}$ for $i \in 1..n$). Then $\mathsf{prog}(C) \geq \mathsf{prog}(C')$.*

With these transformations in place we are ready to prove a bound on the progress of an arbitrary chain.

Progress Theorem for Chains. *The progress of a chain $C = \langle I, F \rangle$ is $\mathsf{prog}(C) \geq \min(\min_{i \in I} d_i, r)$.*

Proof. By the Truncation lemma we can set all the source-target distances to $d = \min(\min_{i \in I} d_i, r)$ to obtain a d-uniform chain. Using the Separation, Balancing, and Straightening lemmas there exists an angle $\theta \in [0, \pi]$ such that the straight chain $C_n(d, \theta)$ has less progress than C ($\mathsf{prog}(C) \geq \mathsf{prog}(C_n(d, \theta))$).

Finally by the Progress theorem for straight n-chains we have $\mathsf{prog}(C_n(d, \theta)) = \mathsf{prog}(C_2(d, \theta))$, and by the progress lemma progress for 2-chains we have $\mathsf{prog}(C_2(d, \theta)) \geq d$ for any θ. Hence, $\mathsf{prog}(C) \geq \mathsf{prog}(C_n(d, \theta)) = \mathsf{prog}(C_2(d, \theta)) \geq d$.

Optimality Theorem. *The lower bound on progress is tight for d-uniform configurations: there are chains that cannot make more than $\min(d, r)$ progress under any local service, and ConnServ achieves exactly that much progress.*

Proof. For any n, we exhibit a chain of n agents with progress exactly $\min(d, r)$. Fix n and consider the straight chain $C_n(d, 0)$, the first agent has progress $\min(d, r)$ ($\delta_1^n = \min(d, r)$) while every other agent has no progress ($\delta_i^n = 0$ for $i > 1$), therefore $\mathsf{prog}(C_n(0, d)) = \min(d, r)$. This class of of chains cannot make more than $\min(d, r)$ progress under any local service and ConnServ achieves exactly that much progress.

9   Termination

Consider an arbitrary chain of agents running the connectivity service. How many rounds does it take the agents to get (arbitrarily close) to their target? Let $d_i[k]$ be the source-target distance of agent i after round k, we say an agent is ε-close to its target at round k iff $d_i[k] \leq \varepsilon$. Given the initial source-target distance $d_i[0]$ of each agent, we will give an upper bound on k to guarantee every agent is ε-close.

So far we proved that while the target of every agent is outside its communication radius r, the collective distance traveled is r; moreover this is tight up to a constant factor. However, once an agent has its target within its communication radius, we can only argue that collective progress is proportional to the smallest source-target distance (since we truncate to the smallest distance). Unfortunately this is not enough to give an upper bound on k.

Let $D_k = \sum_i d_i[k]$ and $d_{\min}[k] = \min_i d_i[k]$, then $D_{k+1} \leq D_k - \min(d_{\min}[k], r)$. However, if $d_{\min}[k] = 0$ this yields $D_{k+1} \leq D_k$ and we cannot prove termination. The following lemma allows us to sidestep this limitation. We call a chain *almost*

d-uniform if all the inner nodes are d-uniform and the outermost nodes have source-target distance 0.

Progress Theorem for Almost-Uniform Chains. *An* almost d-uniform *chain C_n of size $n \geq 3$ has progress* $\mathsf{prog}(C_n) \geq \delta^{\angle}(d, \frac{\pi}{2}, \arccos \frac{d}{2}) \geq \gamma_0 d$ *where* $\gamma_0 := 1 - \sqrt{2 - \sqrt{3}}$.

Proof. Observe that the Balancing and Separation theorems still apply. Moreover, by the independence lemma and the monotonicity of the progress function we can assume the endpoints are at an angle of $\arccos \frac{d}{2}$ to their neighboring source-target vector.

Hence, for $n = 3$ we need to consider one configuration, and by the target-connectedness assumption it's clear that the inner node makes full progress and hence $\mathsf{prog}(C_3) \geq d$. For $n > 3$ there is a family of possible chains determined by the angles between the inner nodes, we proceed by a complete induction on n. Observe that we can assume the progress of the internal nodes depends on both of its neighbors, since otherwise we could argue about a smaller subchain.

Case 1. Base case. Let $n = 4$, clearly only the two internal nodes make progress, therefore we have $\mathsf{prog}(C_4) = \delta^{\mathsf{both}}(d, \arccos \frac{d}{2}, \alpha) + \delta^{\mathsf{both}}(d, \pi - \alpha, \arccos \frac{d}{2})$ where α is the angle between the two internal nodes. If $\alpha \leq \arccos \frac{d}{2}$ or $\pi - \alpha \leq \arccos \frac{d}{2}$, then $\mathsf{prog}(C_4) \geq d$. For $\arccos \frac{d}{2} \leq \alpha \leq \pi - \arccos \frac{d}{2}$ we define the restricted minimization problem $\alpha^* = \mathrm{argmin}_\alpha \, \mathsf{prog}(C_4)$. There is a unique minimum at $\alpha^* = \frac{\pi}{2}$ and hence $\mathsf{prog}(C_4) \geq 2\delta^{\angle}(d, \frac{\pi}{2}, \arccos \frac{d}{2}) \geq \gamma_0 d$.

Case 2. Inductive step. Consider a chain of length $n > 4$ with $n - 2$ interior nodes. Let S be the set of angles between the first $n-3$ interior nodes and let α be the angle between the last interior nodes. The progress of the chain is $\mathsf{prog}(C_n) = p(S, \alpha) + \delta^{\angle}(d, \alpha, \arccos \frac{d}{2})$, where $p(S, \alpha)$ represents the progress of the first $n-3$ interior nodes. Similarly for a chain of length $n+1$ there are $n-1$ interior nodes, and its progress is $\mathsf{prog}(C_{n+1}) = p(S, \alpha) + \delta^{\angle}(d, \alpha, \beta) + \delta^{\angle}(d, \pi - \beta, \arccos \frac{d}{2})$.

We prove the bound by cases on α. If $\alpha \leq \frac{\pi}{2}$, we can minimize the last two terms of $\mathsf{prog}(C_{n+1})$ by solving $\min_{\alpha, \beta} \delta^{\angle}(d, \alpha, \beta) + \delta^{\angle}(d, \pi - \beta, \arccos \frac{d}{2})$, which has a single minimum at $\alpha = \beta = \frac{\pi}{2}$, and thus $\mathsf{prog}(C_{n+1}) = p(S, \alpha) + \delta^{\angle}(d, \alpha, \beta) + \delta^{\angle}(d, \pi - \beta, \arccos \frac{d}{2}) \geq \delta^{\angle}(d, \frac{\pi}{2}, \frac{\pi}{2}) + \delta^{\angle}(d, \frac{\pi}{2}, \arccos \frac{d}{2}) \geq \gamma_0 d$.

If $\alpha > \frac{\pi}{2}$, by the inductive hypothesis we have $\mathsf{prog}(C_n) \geq \gamma_0 d$ and it suffices to show $\mathsf{prog}(C_{n+1}) \geq \mathsf{prog}(C_n)$. This is equivalent to proving $\delta^{\angle}(d, \alpha, \beta) + \delta^{\angle}(d, \pi - \beta, \arccos \frac{d}{2}) - \delta^{\angle}(a, \alpha, \arccos \frac{d}{2}) \geq 0$ for $\alpha > \frac{\pi}{2}$ and any β, which also holds.

Intuitively, the progress theorem for almost-uniform chains proves that once subset of the agents reach their target, the rest of the agents make almost the same progress as before. Intuitively, it seems reasonable to expect that if a subset of the agents get ε-close to their target (for small enough ε) a similar result should hold. This is at the core of the termination theorem which proves an upper bound on the number of rounds needed for nodes to be ε-close to their targets.

We say the targets of two nodes are ℓ-connected if they are at distance ℓ of each other. So far we have assumed neighboring nodes have connected targets, that is, they are r-connected. To prove the next theorem we require a stronger assumption, namely, that targets are $(r - 2\varepsilon)$-connected.

Termination Theorem. *Under the $(r - 2\varepsilon)$-connected assumption, nodes get ε-close within $O(D_0/r + n^2/\varepsilon)$ rounds.*

Proof. Since targets are $(r - 2\varepsilon)$-close, we can assume each node stops at the first round when they are ε-close to their target and the resulting configuration is connected. Therefore we can consider the source-target distance of a node to be either greater than ε when it is not ε-close, or zero once it is ε-close.

If initially every node i is at distance $d_i \geq r$ from its target, it takes at most D_0/r rounds before there exists some node i with $d_i < r$. If there is a node i with source-target distance $d_i < r$ it follows that $D_k < r\frac{n^2}{2}$, we argue that from this point on we can assume a progress of at least $\gamma_0\varepsilon$ per round until every node reaches its target, therefore the total number of rounds is $O(D_0/r + n^2/\varepsilon)$.

Consider a chain $C = \langle I, F \rangle$ and let the subset $S_k \subseteq I$ represent the set of agents which are already at their target at round k ($i \in S_k$ iff $d_i[k] = 0$). If $S_k = I$ then we are done, otherwise there exists a subchain $C' \subseteq C$ where all agents except possibly the endpoints have $d_i[k] > \varepsilon$. Hence, by the progress theorem for almost-uniform chains the progress is at least $\gamma_0\varepsilon$.

10   Conclusion

In this paper we present a local, oblivious connectivity service (§3) that encapsulates an arbitrary motion planner and can refine any plan to preserve connectivity (the graph of agents remains connected) and ensure progress (the agents advance towards their goal). We prove the algorithm not only preserves connectivity, but also produces robust trajectories so if an arbitrary number of agents stop or slow down along their trajectories the graph will remain connected (§4).

We also prove a tight lower bound of $\min(d, r)$ on progress for d-uniform configurations (§8). The truncation lemma allows this lower bound to apply to general configurations using the minimum distance between any agent and its goal. Thus, when each agent's target is within a constant multiple of the communication radius, the lower bound implies the configuration will move at a constant speed towards the desired configuration.

As the agents get closer to their goal, this bound no longer implies constant speed convergence. We prove a bound of $O(D_0/r + n^2/\varepsilon)$ on the number of rounds until nodes are ε-close. This bound requires assuming targets are $(r - 2\varepsilon)$-connected, though we conjecture that it is possible to remove this assumption. The D_0/r term in the bound is necessary because when the initial source-target distance is large enough, clearly no service can guarantee robust, connected trajectories if agents advance faster than one communication radius per round.

It would be tempting to prove agents advance at a rate proportional to the mean (instead of the minimum) source-target distance, which would imply a termination bound of $O(D_0/r + n \log \frac{n}{\varepsilon})$. However, it is possible to construct an example which shows that the progress is less than $\gamma \cdot mean$, for any constant $\gamma > 0$. An alternative approach we intend to pursue in future work is to directly argue about the number of rounds it takes the agents to reach their target. This may give a tighter bound on the rate of convergence over quantifying the distance traveled by the agents in a single round, which necessarily assumes a worst case configuration at every step.

References

1. Johnson, D., Maltz, D.: Dynamic Source Routing in Ad Hoc Wireless Networks. Computer Communications Review - SIGCOMM (1996)
2. Perkins, C., Royer, E.: Ad-hoc On-Demand Distance Vector Routing. In: Workshop on Mobile Computing Systems and Applications (1999)
3. Malpani, N., Welch, J., Vaidya, N.: Leader Election Algorithms for Mobile Ad-hoc Networks. In: DIAL-M: Workshop in Discrete Algorithms and Methods for Mobile Computing and Communications (2000)
4. Walter, J., Welch, J., Vaidya, N.: A Mutual Exclusion Algorithm for Ad Hoc Mobile Networks. Wireless Networks (2001)
5. Regmi, A., Sandoval, R., Byrne, R., Tanner, H., Abdallah, C.: Experimental Implementation of Flocking Algorithms in Wheeled Mobile Robots. In: Proceedings of the American Control Conference 2005, pp. 4917–4922 (2005)
6. Hayes, A., Dormiani-Tabatabaei, P.: Self-organized flocking with agent failure: Offline optimization and demonstration with real robots. In: ICRA (2002)
7. Fierro, R., Das, A.: A modular architecture for formation control. Robot Motion and Control (2002)
8. Carpin, S., Parker, L.E.: Cooperative Leader Following in a Distributed Multi-Robot System. In: ICRA (2002)
9. Zavlanos, M.M., Pappas, G.J.: Controlling Connectivity of Dynamic Graphs. In: CDC-ECC, pp. 6388–6393 (2005)
10. Savla, K., Notarstefano, G., Bullo, F.: Maintaining limited-range connectivity among second-order agents. SIAM Journal on Control and Optimization (2007)
11. Ando, H., Oasa, Y., Suzuki, I., Yamashita, M.: Distributed memoryless point convergence algorithm for mobilerobots with limited visibility. ICRA 15(5), 818–828 (1999)
12. Flocchini, P., Prencipe, G., Santoro, N., Widmayer, P.: Gathering of asynchronous robots with limited visibility. Theor. Comput. Sci. 337(1-3), 147–168 (2005)
13. Ganguli, A., Cortés, J., Bullo, F.: Multirobot rendezvous with visibility sensors in nonconvex environments. CoRR abs/cs/0611022 (2006)
14. Souissi, S., Défago, X., Yamashita, M.: Using eventually consistent compasses to gather oblivious mobile robots with limited visibility. In: SSS, pp. 484–500 (2006)
15. Lee, G., Chong, N.Y., Defago, X.: Robust Self-Deployment for a Swarm of Autonomous Mobile Robots with Limited Visibility Range. In: Robot and Human interactive Communication (2007)
16. Maja, A.H., Howard, A., Matari, M.J., Sukhatme, G.S.: An Incremental Self-Deployment Algorithm for Mobile Sensor Networks. Autonomous Robots, Special Issue on Intelligent Embedded Systems 13, 113–126 (2001)

17. Cornejo, A., Lynch, N.: Connectivity Service for Mobile Ad-Hoc Networks. In: Spatial Computing Workshop (2008)
18. Gabriel, K., Sokal, R.: A new statistical approach to geographic variation analysis. Systematic Zoology 18(3), 259–278 (1969)
19. Toussaint, G.T.: The relative neighbourhood graph of a finite planar set. Pattern Recognition 12(4), 261–268 (1980)
20. Li, N., Hou, J.C., Sha, L.: Design and analysis of an MST-based topology control algorithm. INFOCOM 3, 1702–1712 (2003)
21. Cornejo, A., Kuhn, F., Lynch, N., Ley-Wild, R.: Keeping mobile robot swarms connected. MIT-CSAIL-TR-2009-027 (2009), http://hdl.handle.net/1721.1/45568

Consensus and Mutual Exclusion
in a Multiple Access Channel

Jurek Czyzowicz[1,*], Leszek Gąsieniec[2,**], Dariusz R. Kowalski[2,***],
and Andrzej Pelc[1,†]

[1] Département d'informatique, Université du Québec en Outaouais,
Gatineau, Québec J8X 3X7, Canada
[2] Department of Computer Science, University of Liverpool, Liverpool L69 3BX, UK

Abstract. We consider deterministic feasibility and time complexity of two fundamental tasks in distributed computing: consensus and mutual exclusion. Processes have different labels and communicate through a multiple access channel. The adversary wakes up some processes in possibly different rounds. In any round every awake process either listens or transmits. The message of a process i is heard by all other awake processes, if i is the only process to transmit in a given round. If more than one process transmits simultaneously, there is a collision and no message is heard. We consider three characteristics that may or may not exist in the channel: collision detection (listening processes can distinguish collision from silence), the availablity of a global clock showing the round number, and the knowledge of the number n of all processes.

If none of the above three characteristics is available in the channel, we prove that consensus and mutual exclusion are infeasible; if at least one of them is available, both tasks are feasible and we study their time complexity. Collision detection is shown to cause an exponential gap in complexity: if it is available, both tasks can be performed in time logarithmic in n, which is optimal, and without collision detection both tasks require linear time. We then investigate both consensus and mutual exclusion in the absence of collision detection, but under alternative presence of the two other features. With global clock, we give an algorithm whose time complexity linearly depends on n and on the wake-up time, and an algorithm whose complexity does not depend on the wake-up time and differs from the linear lower bound only by a factor $O(\log^2 n)$. If n is known, we also show an algorithm whose complexity differs from the linear lower bound only by a factor $O(\log^2 n)$.

Keywords: consensus, mutual exclusion, multiple access channel, collision detection.

* Partially supported by NSERC discovery grant.
** Partially funded by the Royal Society International Joint Project, IJP - 2007/R1.
*** This work was supported by the Engineering and Physical Sciences Research Council [grant number EP/G023018/1].
† Partially supported by NSERC discovery grant and by the Research Chair in Distributed Computing at the Université du Québec en Outaouais.

I. Keidar (Ed.): DISC 2009, LNCS 5805, pp. 512–526, 2009.
© Springer-Verlag Berlin Heidelberg 2009

1   Introduction

The background and the problem. We consider deterministic feasibility and time complexity of two fundamental tasks in distributed computing: consensus and mutual exclusion. Processes have different integer labels from 1 to n, and each of them knows its own label. In the sequel we identify processes with their labels. They communicate through a multiple access channel (MAC) which is a well known and thoroughly studied communication medium. In order to capture the notion of collisions, that are the main difficulty of communicating over a MAC, time is considered as slotted into *rounds*, similarly as in the literature on radio communication, cf., e.g., [1,3,7,12,14,16].

The adversary wakes up some processes in possibly different rounds. In each round every awake process either listens or transmits. Transmitting processes do not hear anything. The message of process i is heard by all other awake listening processes, if i is the only process to transmit in a given round. If more than one process transmits simultaneously, there is a *collision* and no message is heard. We consider three features that may or may not exist in the MAC: collision detection (CD), the availablity of a global clock showing the round number (GC), and the knowledge of the number n of all processes (KN). Collision detection is the capacity of listening processes to distiguish collision (when more than one process transmits in a given round) from "silence" (when no process transmits). "Silence" is in fact the background noise occurring in the MAC when no process transmits, and a collision slightly increases the level of this noise. Hence detecting this difference requires a more sensitive receiving device. Global clock permits awake processes to see the same round number. In the absence of it, individual clocks of awake processes tick at the same rate indicating rounds, but each clock starts at 0 when the process is woken up by the adversary. Finally, knowledge of the number n of all processes may or may not be available, but we never assume the knowledge of the number of processes ever woken up or the knowledge of their waking rounds. We focus on the problem of whether consensus and mutual exclusion are deterministically feasible, and if so, what is their deterministic time complexity, depending on which of the features CD, GC, KN are available in the MAC over which processes communicate. It should be stressed that the fact that the adversary wakes up an arbitrary unknown subset of processes and that these processes are woken up in arbitrary rounds, significantly increases the difficulty of the problem.

The tasks and the power of the adversary. Since communication between processes is done over a MAC, we define a *transmission schedule* that is an infinite binary sequence π determining the communication actions of a process. For any non-negative integer i, $\pi(i) = 1$ means that the process transmits in round i after its wakeup, and $\pi(i) = 0$ means that the process listens in round i after its wakeup. Round 0 is the round in which the process is woken up.

We now describe the two tasks under consideration, in the context of the communication over a MAC, and define the power of the adversary for each task. The adversary wakes up some of the processes in some, possibly different rounds. Every process starts executing its protocol in its wake-up round. Actions of an awake process in a given round depend on its label, on its input value, on the previously heard messages (or noise, if collision detection is available), on the number of rounds since its wake-up, on the global round number, if there is a global clock, and on the number n of processes, if this number is known.

Consensus

Let $\{1, ..., \alpha\}$, for $\alpha \geq 2$, be the range of possible input values of processes. The adversary chooses a function $v : \{1, ..., n\} \longrightarrow \{1, ..., \alpha\}$ which assigns an input value to every process. A consensus algorithm is distributedly run by all awake processes. Each action of a process can be either listening or transmitting some message and/or deciding a value from $\{1, ..., \alpha\}$. The following three conditions must be satisfied:

Termination: each awake process eventually decides

Validity: a decision is on one of the input values of awake processes

Agreement: all awake processes decide the same value

The time complexity of a consensus algorithm is the maximum number of rounds, over all awake processes, between the wake-up time and the decision time.

Mutual Exclusion

A mutual exclusion algorithm is distributedly run by all awake processes. Each process executes a protocol partitioned into the following sections:

Entry (trying): the part of the protocol executed in preparation for entering the critical section

Critical: the part of the protocol to be protected from concurrent execution

Exit: the part of the protocol executed on leaving the critical section

Remainder: the rest of the protocol

Each process executes these sections cyclically in the order: *remainder, entry, critical, and exit.* In the traditional mutual exclusion problem, as defined in [2,31] in the context of the shared-memory model, the adversary controls the sections *remainder* and *critical* (in particular it controls their duration in each cycle, only subject to the obvious assumption that this duration in each cycle is finite), while an algorithm provides a protocol for the *entry* and *exit* sections of each process. In the model of communication over a MAC, each action of a process can be either listening or transmitting some message, as well as changing sections of the protocol: entering the *critical* section, if the process is currently in the *entry* section, and entering the *remainder* section, if the process is currently in the *exit* section. We assume that changing sections occurs momentarily between consecutive rounds, i.e., in each round a process is exactly in one section of the protocol.

The following assumption is specific for mutual exclusion with communication over a MAC, replacing the traditional communication by shared variables: the MAC is not used by the adversary in the sections *remainder* and *critical* (otherwise the adversary would have an unlimited power of creating collisions in the MAC, thus preventing communication if collision detection is not available). Instead, the protocol can use the MAC while a process is in the *critical* section by sending the message "occupied".

Any mutual exclusion algorithm has to satisfy the following two properties:

Exclusion: in every round of any execution, at most one process is in the *critical* section.

No deadlock: in every round r of any execution, if there is a process in the entry section at round r then some process will enter the *critical* section eventually after round r.

Note that we do not require the *no lockout* property, stronger than *no deadlock*: in every round r of any execution, if there is a process in the entry section at round r, then *this* process will enter the critical section eventually after round r.

The time complexity of a mutual exclusion algorithm, called the *makespan*, is the maximum number of rounds in any interval when there is some process in the *entry* section and there is no process in the *critical* section.

Our results. If none of the three characteristics (collision detection, global clock, knowledge of the number n of all processes) is available in the channel, we prove that consensus and mutual exclusion are infeasible. If at least one of them is available, both tasks are feasible and we study their time complexity. Collision detection is shown to cause an exponential gap in complexity. If it is available, both tasks can be performed in logarithmic time, which is optimal. More precisely, consensus with values in the range $\{1, ..., \alpha\}$ can be performed in time $O(\min(\log n, \log \alpha))$ and mutual exclusion in time $O(\log n)$, and both these orders of magnitude are tight. If collision detection is not available, we show that both consensus and mutual exclusion require time $\Omega(n)$. We then investigate both consensus and mutual exclusion in the absence of collision detection, but under alternative presence of the two other characteristics. With global clock, we give an algorithm for consensus and mutual exclusion whose time complexity linearly depends on n and on the wake-up time, and an algorithm whose complexity does not depend on the wake-up time and differs from the linear lower bound only by a factor $O(\log^2 n)$. If n is known, we also show an algorithm whose complexity differs from the linear lower bound only by a factor $O(\log^2 n)$.

The paper is organized as follows. In Section 2 we show infeasibility of the considered tasks in the weakest model. In Section 3 we present a consensus algorithm with collision detection, show that it is optimal and prove a linear lower bound on the complexity of our tasks without collision detection. In Sections 4 and 5 we present consensus algorithms assuming the availability only of a global clock, resp. only of the knowledge of the number of processes, in the absence of the two other characteristics. Section 6 is devoted to presenting a scheme that transforms a consensus algorithm to a mutual exclusion algorithm. Thus we obtain corollaries for the complexity of mutual exclusion from the previous results. Section 7 contains conclusions and open problems. Due to lack of space, proofs of the results are omitted. They will appear in the full version of the paper.

Related work. The multiple access channel (MAC) is a well-studied communication medium. Research concerning the MAC can be divided into two parts: one assuming that some communicating processes are woken up by the adversary in possibly different rounds (this is the model used in this paper), and the other assuming that all processes are awake from the beginning. In the first model two tasks were mainly studied in the literature: the wake-up problem in which one process has to transmit alone in some round, thus waking up all other processes [9,17,24,26] and the continuous broadcast, in which processes start to broadcast possibly multiple messages in different rounds, the broadcast being successful when the process transmits alone in some round. The latter problem is subject to dynamic packet arrival, either modeled by an adversarial queuing framework (see, e.g., [4,11]), or by queue-free framework (see, e.g., [28]), or by stochastic distributions (see, e.g., [21]).

One of the fundamental problems investigated assuming that all processes communicating over a MAC are awake from the beginning is the leader election problem. For deterministic leader election without collision detection and with a known number n of processes, matching bounds on time $\Omega(n \log n)$ and $O(n \log n)$ follow from [14], with the upper bound being non-constructive. A constructive upper bound $O(n \operatorname{polylog}(n))$ follows from [24]. For the time of deterministic algorithms with collision detection, matching bounds are also known: $\Omega(\log n)$ follows from [22], and $O(\log n)$ follows from [5,23,35]. For the expected time of randomized algorithms without collision detection, the same matching bounds are known: $\Omega(\log n)$ follows from [30] and $O(\log n)$ from [3]. Randomized leader election with collision detection can be done faster: matching bounds $\Omega(\log \log n)$ (for fair protocols) and $O(\log \log n)$ were proved in [36]. Further references can be found in [25,32]. Communication with possible failures (e.g., crash or Byzantine) has been investigated in the above model, e.g., in [15,18,20].

It should be noted that the MAC is equivalent to a special case of the popular radio network model, namely when the underlying graph is complete. General radio networks were intensely studied in the context of the broadcasting problem, starting with the seminal paper [10]. Most researchers worked in the model without collision detection: deterministic broadcasting in this model was studied, e.g., in [8,14,16] and randomized broadcasting in [1,16,29,30]. Fewer papers were devoted to broadcasting with collision detection, cf. [8,19]. Communication with possible failures (such as crash, Byzantine, probabilistic) has also been studied in multi-hop radio network models, see, e.g., [15,27,34]

Consensus and mutual exclusion are two classic problems in distributed computing, mostly studied assuming that processes communicate by shared variables or through message passing networks [2,31]. In [6], feasibility and complexity of consensus in a multiple access channel with *synchronized* starting points and crash failures were studied in the context of different collision detectors— the tools introduced in that work by the analogy to classic failure detectors. To the best of our knowledge, consensus and mutual exclusion were never studied in the context of a multiple access channel with non-synchronized wake-up times.

2   Infeasibility in the Weakest Model

We start with a negative result that neither consensus nor mutual exclusion are feasible in the weakest of all models considered in this paper, the model in which none of the assumptions CD, GC, KN holds.

Theorem 1. *Consensus and mutual exclusion are infeasible without collision detection, without a global clock and with an unknown number n of processes.*

The above impossibility result should be contrasted with the positive solution of the wake-up problem in the same model. Indeed, it was shown in [17] that wake-up in a MAC can be achieved in polynomial time without a global clock, collision detection or the knowledge of the number of processes. Hence wake-up in the weakest of our models is strictly easier than consensus. This difference can be also viewed as follows. Consider the special case of the consensus problem in which the input value of each process is equal to its label. This is called *label consensus* and it is clearly equivalent to leader election. While wake-up in the weakest model is feasible and all other awake processes can elect as the leader the first process to speak alone, this process itself cannot become aware that it is the leader.

3   Impact of Collision Detection

Collision detection permits a listening process to distinguish between silence and collision noise, which occurs when at least two messages are sent. Hence any listening process hears either the silence, or collision noise, or the content of the message transmitted. We say that a listening process hears *signal* μ, if one or more processes transmit in the given round. A round is called *silent* for a listening process i, if i hears silence in this round, and it is *noisy* for i, if i hears signal μ.

3.1   Availability of Collision Detection

We first prove a lower bound on the time of consensus and on the makespan of mutual exclusion even in the strongest of our models.

Theorem 2. *Any consensus algorithm, even with collision detection, global clock and known number n of processes, requires time $\Omega(min(\log n, \log \alpha))$. Any mutual exclusion algorithm, even with collision detection, global clock and known number n of processes, has makespan $\Omega(\log n)$.*

We now present a consensus algorithm matching the above lower bound $\Omega(min(\log n, \log \alpha))$, if collision detection is available, even without the global clock or the knowledge of n.

We first design a consensus algorithm working in time $O(\log \alpha)$. Let $B_{v(i)} = b_1 b_2 \ldots b_l$ denote the string of bits in the binary representation of the input value $v(i)$ of process i, written in reverse order, i.e. starting from the least significant bit. Only meaningful bits of this representation are considered. Hence the last bit b_l of $B_{v(i)}$ always equals 1 and $|B_{v(i)}| = \lceil \log v(i) \rceil$. Consider the first round r when some process is woken up. In the case when there is only one process woken up in round r the consensus value is the input value of this process. Otherwise, the consensus value $v(i^*)$ is the input value of process i^* woken up in round r, such that for any process i woken up in round r, $B_{v(i)} \preceq B_{v(i^*)}$, where $\preceq$ denotes the natural lexicographic order of bit-strings (we also write $B_{v(i)} \prec B_{v(j)}$, if $B_{v(i)} \preceq B_{v(j)}$ and $B_{v(i)} \neq B_{v(j)}$).

The transmission schedule $\pi_{i,v(i)}$ begins with 0001 followed by the infinite sequence of repetitions of bit-string $b_1 b_2 1 \ldots b_{l-1} 1 b_l 001$, that we will call the *value transmission pattern*. The only message ever transmitted by a process is the *contact* message consisting of bit 1. During the algorithm execution each process i may be either *active*, when it follows its transmission schedule $\pi_{i,v(i)}$, or *passive*, when it listens forever. At least one process remains active forever. This process will follow its value transmission pattern periodically and its input value becomes the consensus value. Passive processes decode this value from a sequence of silent and noisy rounds.

Algorithm ConsensusCD1 (integer v)

1 *active:* Listen for three rounds;
            if silence is always heard **then** transmit in round 4 **else goto** *passive*;
2   Follow value transmission pattern for v;
            if μ is heard at some listening round **then goto** *passive*;
3   Decide on v;
4   **forever** follow value transmission pattern for v periodically.

5 *passive:* Wait until silence is heard for two consecutive rounds $\rho, \rho+1$;
6   Start counting rounds $r_1, r_2, \ldots$, with $r_1 = \rho + 2$;
           Listen until silence is heard in the first odd-numbered round r_{2k+1};
           For each even-numbered round r_{2j}, for $0 < 2j < 2k+1$,
               store bit 0 if silence was heard and bit 1 otherwise;
           Interpret the reverse of the stored bit-string as a binary
               representation of value x;
           Decide on x.

Each process i runs Algorithm ConsensusCD1 with its input value $v(i)$ as the parameter v.

Lemma 1. *Algorithm* ConsensusCD1 *reaches consensus with collision detection in time* $O(\log \alpha)$.

We now present our main consensus algorithm with collision detection, working in time $O(\min(\log n, \log \alpha))$. It essentially consists in running in parallel ConsensusCD1$(v(i))$ and ConsensusCD1(i). This may be done by reserving odd-numbered rounds for one algorithm and even-numbered rounds for the other one.

Since global clock is not available, some synchronization is necessary in order for each process to recognize at some point the round parity. Similarly as before we consider the string $B'_i=b'_1b'_2 \ldots b'_m$ - which is the inverse of the binary representation of label i. We call the *label transmission pattern* of process i the sequence of bits $b'_1 1 b'_2 1 \ldots b'_{m-1} 1 b'_m 001$. Unless specified otherwise, the message transmitted in each transmission round is the contact message.

Algorithm `ConsensusCD2` (integer i, integer v)

1 *active:* Listen for six rounds;
         if silence is always heard **then** transmit in round 7 **else goto** *passive*;
2   Starting from the 7th round after wake-up consider the numbering of
         rounds $r_1, r_2, \ldots$
         Follow $b_1 1 b_2 1 \ldots b_{l-1} 1 b_l 001$ - the value transmission pattern of v in
         the odd-numbered rounds
         Follow $b'_1 1 b'_2 1 \ldots b'_{m-1} 1 b'_m 001$ - the label transmission pattern for i in
         the even-numbered rounds
         if μ is heard at some listening round in the above patterns
         then goto *passive*;
3   **if** the end of the value transmission pattern is achieved **then**
         Decide on v
         forever follow the pattern $0000011 b_1 1 b_2 1 \ldots b_{l-1} 1 b_l$ periodically;
4   **if** the end of the label transmission pattern is achieved **then**
         Decide on v
         forever follow the pattern 000001 periodically, where v is
         transmitted in each transmission round.

5 *passive:* Listen until silence is heard for five consecutive rounds;
         Listen until silence is heard again for five consecutive rounds $\rho + 1$,
         $\ldots, \rho + 5$ and signal μ is heard in round $\rho + 6$;
6   **if** silence is heard in round $\rho + 7$ **then**
         Decide on x (in this case a message was heard in round $\rho + 6$);
7   **else** Start counting rounds $r_1, r_2, \ldots$, with $r_1 = \rho + 7$
         Listen until silence is heard in the first odd-numbered round r_{2k+1}
         For each even-numbered round r_{2j}, for $2j < 2k + 1$,
            store bit 0 if silence was heard and bit 1 otherwise
         Interpret the reverse of the stored bit-string as a binary
            representation of integer x
         Decide on x.

Each process i runs Algorithm `ConsensusCD2` with its label i and its input value $v(i)$ as the parameters of the algorithm.

Theorem 3. *Algorithm* `ConsensusCD2` *reaches consensus with collision detection in time* $O(\min(\log n, \log \alpha))$.

3.2   Absence of Collision Detection

The following lower bound on the complexity of consensus and mutual exclusion in the absence of collision detection shows an exponential gap caused by the lack of this characteristic of the MAC.

Theorem 4. *Any consensus (resp. mutual exclusion) algorithm in the model without collision detection, even with global clock and known number n of processes, requires time (resp. makespan) at least $n/2$.*

4   Global Clock

In this section we assume that a global clock is available to all awake processes, but we do not assume collision detection or the knowledge of the number n of processes. We present algorithms for consensus based on the following scheme.

Algorithmic scheme GlobalClock
The set of natural numbers (corresponding to the round numbers given by the global clock) is partitioned into an infinite family $A_1, A_2, \ldots$ of pairwise disjoint infinite sets. The set A_i is the set of rounds reserved for process i, i.e., no other process transmits in these rounds. Process i that was woken up in (global) round t listens in rounds $t, t + 1, \ldots, t'$, where $t' + 1$ is the first integer larger than t belonging to A_i. If silence was heard in all these rounds, then process i decides on its value $v(i)$ and in all rounds larger than t' transmits value $v(i)$. If some value w was heard in one of the rounds $t, t + 1, \ldots, t'$, then process i decides on value w and remains silent forever.

Lemma 2. *The algorithmic scheme GlobalClock reaches consensus with global clock, for any family $A_1, A_2, \ldots$ of pairwise disjoint infinite sets of natural numbers.*

Depending on the particular family of sets $A_1, A_2, \ldots$, the algorithmic scheme GlobalClock can produce various consensus algorithms. We show two such algorithms with incomparable complexities. The first one, Algorithm GlobalClock1, has complexity $O(n + t)$, where t is the largest wake-up round of any process. It matches the lower bound $\Omega(n)$ from Theorem 4, for small values of t.

Algorithm GlobalClock1
It is enough to define the family of sets $A_1, A_2, \ldots$. First partition the set N of natural numbers into consecutive segments $C_0, C_1, \ldots$ called *blocks*. Block C_i has length 2^i. For a fixed i, let $r_1, \ldots, r_{2^i}$ be elements of C_i. We define the function $f_i : C_i \longrightarrow N$ by $f_i(r_j) = j$. This gives the function $f : N \longrightarrow N$ defined as f_i on block C_i. The function f corresponds to the sequence $(1, 1, 2, 1, 2, 3, 4, 1, 2, 3, 4, 5, 6, 7, 8, \ldots)$. Now the set A_i is defined as $f^{-1}(\{i\})$.

Lemma 3. *Algorithm* GlobalClock1 *reaches consensus with global clock in time* $O(n + t)$*, where t is the largest wake-up round of any process.*

While the complexity of Algorithm GlobalClock1 matches the lower bound $\Omega(n)$ for small values of t, it may be arbitrarily large (as compared to the number of processes), if processes are woken up late in global history. Hence it is natural to seek a consensus algorithm whose complexity does not depend on the times of wake-up of processes by the adversary. Our next algorithm, also based on the algorithmic scheme GlobalClock, satisfies this requirement.

Algorithm GlobalClock2

Again it suffices to define the family of sets $A_1, A_2, \dots$. First partition the set N of natural numbers into consecutive blocks $B_0, B_1, \dots$. Block B_i has length $8 \cdot 2^i \cdot i^2$ and it is formed of positions enumerated from 1 to $8 \cdot 2^i \cdot i^2$. We subdivide B_i into $i + 1$ pairwise disjoint lists $S_i(1), \dots, S_i(i)$ and R_i. Consider a list $S_i(l)$, where $2^{k-1} \leq l \leq 2^k - 1$ for some $1 \leq k \leq \lceil \log i \rceil$. The consecutive elements of such $S_i(l)$ are positions $2^k \cdot x + 2^{k-1}$ in B_i for all integers x satisfying $x \equiv l \pmod{2^{k-1}}$. Note that consecutive elements in such $S_i(l)$ are at distance $2^k \cdot 2^{k-1} = 2^{2k-1}$ in B_i.

We now show that for any $1 \leq l_1 < l_2 \leq i$ the lists $S_i(l_1)$ and $S_i(l_2)$ do not intersect. First, if $2^{k-1} \leq l_1 < l_2 \leq 2^k - 1$ for some $1 \leq k \leq \lceil \log i \rceil$, then values $x_1 \equiv l_1 \pmod{2^{k-1}}$ and $x_2 \equiv l_2 \pmod{2^{k-1}}$ can only be equal when $|l_1 - l_2| > 2^{k-1}$, which is impossible. Assume now that $2^{k_1-1} \leq l_1 \leq 2^{k_1} - 1$ and $2^{k_2-1} \leq l_2 \leq 2^{k_2} - 1$, for some $1 \leq k_1 < k_2 \leq \lceil \log i \rceil$. Note that in this case integers in $S_i(l_1)$ are certain multiples of 2^{k_1-1} but not multiples of 2^{k_1}. Since integers in $S_i(l_2)$ are certain multiples of 2^{k_2-1} which are multiples of 2^{k_1} when $k_2 > k_1$, the intersection of $S_i(l_1)$ and $S_i(l_2)$ is also empty. Finally, the list R_i contains all remaining positions in B_i, i.e., $R_i = B_i \setminus (S_i(1) \cup \cdots \cup S_i(l))$.

For each i and for $l = 1, \dots, i$, we now define functions $g_l : S_i(l) \longrightarrow \{2^{l-1}, \dots, 2^l - 1\}$ as follows. The function g_l assigns elements from the set $\{2^{l-1}, \dots, 2^l - 1\}$ to consecutive elements from the list $S_i(l)$ in a round-robin fashion, i.e., forming the sequence of values $(2^{l-1}, \dots, 2^l - 1, 2^{l-1}, \dots, 2^l - 1, 2^{l-1}, \dots, 2^l - 1, \dots)$. We additionally define the function h_i as the function constantly equal 1 on the domain R_i.

Since the lists $S_i(1), \dots, S_i(i), R_i$ form a disjoint partition of the block B_i, the above functions define, for each i, a function $\phi_i : B_i \longrightarrow \{1, \dots, 2^i - 1\}$. This in turn gives the function $\phi : N \longrightarrow N$ defined as ϕ_i on block B_i. Now the set A_i is defined as $\phi^{-1}(\{i\})$.

Lemma 4. *Algorithm* GlobalClock2 *reaches consensus with global clock in time* $O(n \log^2 n)$.

By interleaving algorithms GlobalClock1 and GlobalClock2 on even and odd rounds, respectively, listening in the first two rounds after wake-up and keeping silence on both threads as soon as a process hears some value in one of the threads, we get the following result.

Theorem 5. *There exists an algorithm reaching consensus with global clock in time $O(\min(n+t, n\log^2 n))$, where t is the largest wake-up round of any process.*

5   Known Number of Processes

In this section, we assume that the number n of all processes is known to every process, but we do not assume global clock or collision detection.

Our consensus algorithm uses the notion of a *fixed transmission schedule*, introduced in [17]. A fixed transmission schedule of process i is a finite binary sequence π_i depending only on the label i of the process and on the parameter n. The interpretation of π_i is the following. If process i is woken up in round t, then i transmits in round $t + u - 1$ if $\pi_i(u) = 1$ and i listens in round $t + u - 1$ if $\pi_i(u) = 0$. It was proved in [17] that, for every n, there exists a set of fixed transmission schedules $\{\pi_i : i = 1, ..., n\}$ of length $s \in O(n\log^2 n)$, such that regardless of the (non-empty) set of processes woken up by the adversary and regardless of the wake-up rounds of these processes, there exists a process and a round $t^* + s'$, where t^* is the earliest wake-up round of any process and $s' \leq s$, in which this process transmits alone. Thus the easier problem of wake-up can be solved in time $O(n\log^2 n)$. Our aim is to give a consensus algorithm with the same time complexity.

Algorithm KnownNumber
Starting in its wake-up round t, process i listens for s rounds. If it hears some input value in one of these rounds, it decides on this value and remains silent forever. If it hears silence in all these s rounds, it starts transmitting its input value according to the schedule π_i. If it hears some input value in one of the following s rounds, it decides on this value and remains silent forever. If it does not hear any message in all the $2s$ rounds, it decides on its own input value and transmits it according to the schedule π_i repeated periodically forever.

Theorem 6. *Algorithm KnownNumber reaches consensus in time $O(n\log^2 n)$, for any known number n of processes.*

6   From Consensus to Mutual Exclusion

In this section we propose a generic mutual exclusion algorithm, called MACMEX, which uses a consensus algorithm as a subroutine and solves the problem of mutual exclusion, preserving the complexity of the consensus solution. Using the consensus algorithms developped in the previous sections, we obtain mutual exclusion algorithms in the respective models.

Consider our consensus algorithms in the case when the input value of every process is equal to the label of the process (label consensus). All our algorithms have the following two properties.

P1. Every process listens in the round in which it is woken up.

P2. If the decision is on value i, no process other than i transmits in the round when i makes its decision.

Hence all our consensus algorithms, considered in the case of label consensus, can be transformed by having the winning process i transmit a special message "my label i won" in the round r when process i decides on its value and in all subsequent rounds. Indeed, all processes awake in round r will hear this message in round r, decide on i and remain silent forever, and all processes woken up in some round $r' > r$ will hear this message in round r', decide on i and remain silent forever. The complexities of the transformed algorithms remain the same. Hence we may assume that the label consensus subroutine used by Algorithm MACMEX has the following two properties.

P'1. Every process listens in the round in which it is woken up.

P'2. Starting from the round in which process i decides on its own value, process i transmits the message "my label i won" forever, and all other processes listen forever.

Algorithm MACMEX

Entry section. Process i executes a consensus subroutine satifying properties P'1 and P'2, with its label as the input value, until one of the following events occurs:

- process i decides on its own label;
  in this case process i enters the *critical* section
- process i hears either the message "occupied" or the message "my label j won";
  in this case process i stops the execution of the consensus subroutine and listens on the MAC in the next round
- process i hears the message "released";
  in this case process i starts a new execution of the consensus subroutine with its label as the input value.

Critical section. Process i transmits the message "occupied" on the MAC in each round when it is in the *critical* section. The rest of the behavior of the process in this section is controlled by the adversary.

Exit section. Process i transmits the message "released" on the MAC and leaves the section.

The proof of correctness of Algorithm MACMEX is based on the following invariant.

Lemma 5. *Exactly one of the following properties holds in any round r:*

Q1 the message "occupied" is heard in round r and its sender is the only process in the critical *section in this round; additionally, no process is in the* exit *section and no process executes the consensus subroutine in round r; or*

*Q2 the message "released" is heard in round r and its sender is the only process
     in the* exit *section in this round; additionally, no process is in the critical
     section and no process executes the consensus subroutine in round r; or*

*Q3 there is at least one process executing the consensus subroutine in round r;
     additionally, all such processes are exactly those in the* entry *section and no
     process is in the* critical *or* exit *sections in round r; or*

Q4 all processes are in the remainder *section in round r.*

Using Lemma 5 we can prove the following theorem.

Theorem 7. *Algorithm* MACMEX *with a consensus subroutine satisfying properties P'1 and P'2, is a mutual exclusion algorithm with no deadlock. Moreover, the makespan of the* MACMEX *algorithm is the same as the time complexity of the consensus subroutine.*

Combining Theorem 7 with Theorems 3, 5 and 6 for the label-consensus version of the problem, we derive the following conclusions for mutual exclusion.

Theorem 8. *Algorithm* MACMEX *is a mutual exclusion algorithm with no deadlock in a multiple access channel having at least one of the following characteristics: collision detection, global clock, or the knowledge of the number n of processes. The makespan of algorithm* MACMEX *is:*

(i) $O(\log n)$, if collision detection is assumed;

*(ii) $O(\min(n + t, n \log^2 n))$, if global clock is assumed and t is the largest round
      of the wake-up of any process;*

(iii) $O(n \log^2 n)$, if knowledge of n is assumed.

*Moreover, the first bound is tight, while the two others differ from the lower
bound $\Omega(n)$ without collision detection at most by a factor of $O(\log^2 n)$.*

7   Conclusion and Open Problems

We provided almost optimal algorithms for consensus and mutual exclusion with processes communicating over a MAC. It would be interesting to close the $O(\log^2 n)$ factor gaps in the models without collision detection but with global clock or with a known number of processes. (In the model with collision detection our algorithms have optimal complexity.) It also remains open how randomization influences the complexity of these problems with MAC communication. Another set of open problems concerns energy consumption. We may assume that processes can not only transmit or listen, but can switch off. Then a natural measure of efficiency is the maximum or average number of rounds in which a process is active (listens or transmits). Finally, in the case of mutual exclusion, we guaranteed no deadlock, but not the stronger *no lockout* property. It remains open if mutual exclusion with no lockout is feasible in all models except the weakest one, and if so, what is its complexity.

References

1. Alon, N., Bar-Noy, A., Linial, N., Peleg, D.: A lower bound for radio broadcast. J. of Computer and System Sciences 43, 290–298 (1991)
2. Attiya, H., Welch, J.: Distributed Computing. John Wiley and Sons, Inc., Chichester (2004)
3. Bar-Yehuda, R., Goldreich, O., Itai, A.: On the time complexity of broadcast in radio networks: an exponential gap between determinism and randomization. Journal of Computer and System Sciences 45, 104–126 (1992)
4. Bender, M.A., Farach-Colton, M., He, S., Kuszmaul, B.C., Leiserson, C.E.: Adversarial contention resolution for simple channels. In: Proceedings, 17th Annual ACM Symposium on Parallel Algorithms (SPAA), pp. 325–332 (2005)
5. Capetanakis, J.: Tree algorithms for packet broadcast channels. IEEE Transactions on Information Theory 25, 505–515 (1979)
6. Chockler, G., Demirbas, M., Gilbert, S., Lynch, N.A., Newport, C.C., Nolte, T.: Consensus and collision detectors in radio networks. Distributed Computing 21, 55–84 (2008)
7. Chlamtac, I., Kutten, S.: On broadcasting in radio networks - problem analysis and protocol design. IEEE Transactions on Communications 33, 1240–1246 (1985)
8. Chlebus, B.S., Gąsieniec, L., Gibbons, A., Pelc, A., Rytter, W.: Deterministic broadcasting in unknown radio networks. Distributed Computing 15, 27–38 (2002)
9. Chlebus, B.S., Gąsieniec, L., Kowalski, D.R., Radzik, T.: On the wake-up problem in radio networks. In: Caires, L., Italiano, G.F., Monteiro, L., Palamidessi, C., Yung, M. (eds.) ICALP 2005. LNCS, vol. 3580, pp. 347–359. Springer, Heidelberg (2005)
10. Chlebus, B.S., Kowalski, D.R.: A better wake-up in radio networks. In: Proceedings, 23rd ACM Symposium on Principles of Distributed Computing (PODC), pp. 266–274 (2004)
11. Chlebus, B.S., Kowalski, D.R., Rokicki, M.A.: Adversarial queuing on the multiple-access channel. In: Proceedings, 25th ACM Symposium on Principles of Distributed Computing (PODC), pp. 92–101 (2006)
12. Chrobak, M., Gąsieniec, L., Kowalski, D.R.: The wake-up problem in multi-hop radio networks. SIAM J. Comput. 36, 1453–1471 (2007)
13. Chrobak, M., Gasieniec, L., Rytter, W.: Fast broadcasting and gossiping in radio networks. J. Algorithms 43, 177–189 (2002)
14. Clementi, A.E.F., Monti, A., Silvestri, R.: Selective families, superimposed codes, and broadcasting on unknown radio networks. In: Proceedings, 12th Ann. ACM-SIAM Symp. on Discrete Algorithms (SODA), pp. 709–718 (2001)
15. Clementi, A.E.F., Monti, A., Silvestri, R.: Round robin is optimal for fault-tolerant broadcasting on wireless networks. In: Meyer auf der Heide, F. (ed.) ESA 2001. LNCS, vol. 2161, pp. 452–463. Springer, Heidelberg (2001)
16. Czumaj, A., Rytter, W.: Broadcasting algorithms in radio networks with unknown topology. In: Proceedings, 44th IEEE Symposium on Foundations of Computer Science (FOCS), pp. 492–501 (2003)
17. Gąsieniec, L., Pelc, A., Peleg, D.: The wakeup problem in synchronous broadcast systems. SIAM Journal on Discrete Mathematics 14, 207–222 (2001)
18. Dolev, S., Gilbert, S., Guerraoui, R., Newport, C.C.: Gossiping in a multi-channel radio network. In: Pelc, A. (ed.) DISC 2007. LNCS, vol. 4731, pp. 208–222. Springer, Heidelberg (2007)

19. Fusco, E.G., Pelc, A.: Acknowledged broadcasting in ad hoc radio networks. Information Processing Letters 109, 136–141 (2008)
20. Gilbert, S., Guerraoui, R., Newport, C.C.: Of malicious motes and suspicious sensors: On the efficiency of malicious interference in wireless networks. Theor. Comput. Sci. 410, 546–569 (2009)
21. Goldberg, L.A., Jerrum, M., Kannan, S., Paterson, M.: A bound on the capacity of backoff and acknowledgment-based protocols. SIAM J. Comput. 33, 313–331 (2004)
22. Greenberg, A.G., Winograd, S.: A lower bound on the time needed in the worst case to resolve conflicts deterministically in multiple access channels. J. ACM 32, 589–596 (1985)
23. Hayes, J.F.: An adaptive technique for local distribution. IEEE Transactions on Communications 26, 1178–1186 (1978)
24. Indyk, P.: Explicit constructions of selectors and related combinatorial structures, with applications. In: Proceedings, 13th ACM-SIAM Symposium on Discrete Algorithms (SODA), pp. 697–704 (2002)
25. Jurdzinski, T., Kutylowski, M., Zatopianski, J.: Efficient algorithms for leader election in radio networks. In: Proceedings, 21st Annual ACM Symposium on Principles of Distributed Computing (PODC), pp. 51–57 (2002)
26. Jurdziński, T., Stachowiak, G.: Probabilistic algorithms for the wakeup problem in single-hop radio networks. In: Bose, P., Morin, P. (eds.) ISAAC 2002. LNCS, vol. 2518, pp. 535–549. Springer, Heidelberg (2002)
27. Koo, C.-Y., Bhandari, V., Katz, J., Vaidya, N.H.: Reliable broadcast in radio networks: the bounded collision case. In: Proceedings, 25th Annual ACM Symposium on Principles of Distributed Computing (PODC), pp. 258–264 (2006)
28. Kowalski, D.R.: On selection problem in radio networks. In: Proceedings, 24th ACM Symposium on Principles of Distributed Computing (PODC), pp. 158–166 (2005)
29. Kowalski, D.R., Pelc, A.: Deterministic broadcasting time in radio networks of unknown topology. In: Proceedings, 22nd ACM Symposium on Principles of Distributed Computing (PODC), pp. 73–82 (2003)
30. Kushilevitz, Y., Mansour, Y.: An $\Omega(D \log(N/D))$ lower bound for broadcast in radio networks. SIAM J. on Computing 27, 702–712 (1998)
31. Lynch, N.A.: Distributed Algorithms. Morgan Kaufmann Publ., Inc., San Francisco (1996)
32. Nakano, K., Olariu, S.: Uniform leader election protocols for radio networks. IEEE Transactions on Parallel Distributed Systems 13, 516–526 (2002)
33. Pelc, A.: Activating anonymous ad hoc radio networks. Distributed Computing 19, 361–371 (2007)
34. Pelc, A., Peleg, D.: Feasibility and complexity of broadcasting with random transmission failures. In: Proceedings, 24th Annual ACM Symposium on Principles of Distributed Computing (PODC), pp. 334–341 (2005)
35. Tsybakov, B.S., Mikhailov, V.A.: Free synchronous packet access in a broadcast channel with feedback. Prob. Inf. Transmission 14, 259–280 (1978); Translated from Russian original. Prob. Peredach. Inf. (1977)
36. Willard, D.E.: Log-logarithmic selection resolution protocols in a multiple access channel. SIAM J. on Computing 15, 468–477 (1986)

Brief Announcement:
Efficient Utilization of Multiple Interfaces in Wireless Ad Hoc Networks

Roy Friedman and Alex Kogan

Department of Computer Science, Technion, Israel
{roy,sakogan}@cs.technion.ac.il

A wireless ad hoc network is composed of devices that are capable of communicating directly with their neighbors (roughly speaking, nodes that are nearby). Many such devices are battery-operated, e.g., laptops, smart-phones and PDAs. Thus, their operational life-time before the battery should be recharged or replaced is limited. Among all subsystems operating inside these devices, wireless communication is accounted for the major consumption of power [1, 2]. Additionally, platforms enabled with multiple wireless communication interfaces are becoming quite common. This turns the problem of efficient power usage by the wireless communication subsystem even more acute.

Known proximity wireless communication technologies include established standards, such as Blue-Tooth (BT) and WiFi, along with emerging standards, such as ZigBee and WiMax. These technologies differ dramatically from one another in their maximum transmission range, energy requirements and available bandwidth [2,3]. Since the power consumed by radios in *idle* state is on the same order of magnitude as in active state (i.e., *sending* and *receiving* states) [1,2,3], a systematic approach for creating power-efficient networks is required. Using such an approach, one should be able to shut down as many power-consuming radios as possible, while still maintain a connected topology. In addition, in order to keep latency and network capacity under some predetermined boundaries, a desired property of such a topology is to ensure that the number of low-bandwidth hops traversed by each transmission is limited by some threshold.

Most previous research on power utilization in wireless networks considers devices equipped with a single radio. The proposed solutions maintain energy-efficient topology by selecting overlays of active nodes or by adjusting transmission ranges of the nodes. The drawbacks in both approaches include lost connectivity and non-trivial assumptions, such as the availability of accurate location information or the use of radios with variable transmission ranges. In addition, applying these solutions separately on each of the available interfaces will not benefit from the potential of an integrated approach.

Our contributions: Our first contribution is the introduction of a formal approach for reducing the energy consumption of wireless networks consisting of nodes owning two interfaces, one of which has a smaller transmission range and a lower power consumption than the other. Specifically, we formulate a

I. Keidar (Ed.): DISC 2009, LNCS 5805, pp. 527–528, 2009.

new optimization problem, which we call *k-Weighted Connected Dominating Set* (*kWCDS*). It is a generalization of the well-known graph theoretic problem of finding minimal *Connecting Dominating Set* (*CDS*). In the definition of *kWCDS*, we distinguish between *short* and *long* communication edges, corresponding to the interface with shorter and longer transmission ranges, respectively. A solution to the *kWCDS* problem is a set of nodes, so that every node in the system is close enough (up to k short communication edges) to some node in the set, while all nodes in the set form a sub-network connected by long edges. An arbitrary parameter k controls the latency that applications running on devices may experience (e.g., instead of passing through one long edge, a message may pass through up to k short edges). Each node in the system is assigned a weight, which is set to the reciprocal of the remaining battery power of the node, and we seek a solution having minimal total weight of nodes in the selected set. Consequently, an optimal solution to the *kWCDS* problem provides a power-efficient topology where nodes in the selected set stay with both interfaces turned on, while all other nodes turn off their power-hungry long range interface.

Second, we provide a centralized *kWCDS* algorithm with a proven approximation factor. This protocol includes two phases: building a k-Weighted Dominating Set (*kWDS*) and then extending it to a *kWCDS*. We also prove that whenever nodes are uniformly distributed, every *kWDS* is w.h.p. also *kWCDS*. This is regardless of how the *kWDS* was obtained. (Notice that this is in contrast to the *CDS* problem, where most dominating sets are not connected.) The significance of this third contribution of our work is that in many practical settings, the second phase of the protocol can be skipped, and a *kWCDS* is obtained very efficiently.

Our fourth contribution includes presenting two distributed asynchronous protocols for the *kWCDS* problem. The first of these is a distributed version of the centralized algorithm with a proven approximation factor, which is directly derived from the centralized algorithm. The second protocol is heuristic. It does not have a proven approximation factor, but in practice behaves similarly in most settings, yet is much more message efficient. A formal time and message communication complexity analysis is provided for both.

Finally, we simulate the performance of our algorithms with typical parameters of WiFi and BT technologies and show that as the number of nodes in the system increases, more than 95% of the nodes may turn off their WiFi radios while remaining connected to the rest of the network at the BT level.

References

1. Feeney, L.M., Nilsson, M.: Investigating the energy consumption of a wireless network interface in an ad hoc networking environment. In: Proc. IEEE INFOCOM, pp. 1548–1557 (2001)
2. Pering, T., Agarwal, Y., Gupta, R., Power, C.: Coolspots: Reducing the power consumption of wireless mobile devices with multiple radio interfaces. In: Proc. ACM MOBISYS, pp. 220–232 (2006)
3. Bahl, P., Adya, A., Padhye, J., Walman, A.: Reconsidering wireless systems with multiple radios. ACM SIGCOMM Comput. Commun. Rev. 34(5), 39–46 (2004)

Brief Announcement: The Speed of Broadcasting in Random Networks – Density Does Not Matter

Nikolaos Fountoulakis, Anna Huber, and Konstantinos Panagiotou

Max-Planck-Institute for Informatics
Stuhlsatzenhausweg 85, Campus E1.4
Saarbrücken, D-66123 Germany
{fountoul,ahuber,kpanagio}@mpi-inf.mpg.de

1 Introduction

We consider the problem of spreading information in large random networks with small average degree. Randomized broadcasting is among the most fundamental and well-studied communication primitives in distributed computing, and has also applications in several other disciplines, like e.g. in mathematical theories of epidemics. A particularly popular example [1] is the maintenance of consistency in a distributed database, which is replicated at many hundreds or thousands of sites in a large, heterogeneous network. Obviously, efficient broadcasting algorithms are crucial in order to ensure that all copies of the database converge quickly and effectively to the same content.

A classical protocol in the context of randomized broadcasting, which is also the main topic of our study, is the *push model* [2,1]. There, initially some information is placed on one of the nodes. In each succeeding stage, every informed node passes the information to another node, that it chooses uniformly at random and independently among its neighbors. The crucial question now is: how long does it take until all nodes have received the information? There are several advantages of considering a broadcast algorithm like this: it is simple, local, and scalable, and thus independent of the network topology. Moreover, it is highly robust against network and link failures, which makes it highly reliable.

In the case where the underlying network is the complete graph on n vertices, Frieze and Grimmett [2] proved that *with high probability*[1] *(w.h.p.)* the push protocol completes the broadcasting of the message within $(1 \pm \varepsilon)(\log_2 n + \ln n)$ stages. In other words, if a node can "talk" to *any other* node in the network, then the broadcast time will be almost surely very close to $\log_2 n + \ln n$. This bound was later improved by Pittel [3] to $\log_2 n + \ln n \pm \alpha(n)$, where $\alpha(n)$ is any function that tends to ∞ when $n \to \infty$. Feige et al. considered in [4] networks that are different from the complete graph. Among other results, they showed that if the underlying network is a random graph $G_{n,p}$, where $p \geq \frac{(1+\varepsilon)\ln n}{n}$, then the message will arrive at all nodes with high probability within $\Theta(\ln n)$ stages. Moreover, they also showed that the protocol is efficient on hypercubes,

---

[1] With probability tending to 1 when $n \to \infty$.

I. Keidar (Ed.): DISC 2009, LNCS 5805, pp. 529–530, 2009.
© Springer-Verlag Berlin Heidelberg 2009

and derived bounds that hold for arbitrary graphs. Elsässer and Sauerwald determined in [5] similar bounds for several classes of Cayley graphs, thus generalizing upon [4].

Our Contribution

Let $G = (V, E)$ be a graph on n vertices, where we will assume that $V = \{1, \ldots, n\}$. We define $T(G)$ as the number of stages needed by the push protocol until all vertices have been informed, if the information is initially placed on node 1. Note that *regardless* of the underlying network topology $T(G) \geq \log_2 n$, as the number of informed vertices can at most double in each round. Consequently, all the results mentioned above state that the push model is, up to multiplicative constants, an asymptotically optimal protocol for disseminating information.

However, it is not at all well-understood *how much* the structure of the underlying network affects the performance of the push model. Although, for example, we know from the results in [4] that on a random graph $G_{n,p}$ the protocol requires with high probability at most $C \ln n$ rounds, for some $C > 0$, we have *a priori* no bounds that quantify how slower (or faster?) the protocol is compared to the case where the network is the complete graph. In particular, it is not clear in which way the average degree of the underlying graph influences the speed of the protocol. Our main result states that the number of stages is essentially *unaffected* by the density of the underlying graph:

Theorem 1. *Let* $0 < \alpha(n) \leq \ln^{1/9} n$ *be any function with the property* $\lim_{n \to \infty} \alpha(n) = \infty$. *Let* $p \geq \frac{\alpha(n) \ln n}{n}$. *Then w.h.p.*

$$|T(G_{n,p}) - (\log_2 n + \ln n)| < \alpha(n)^{-1/7} \ln n.$$

In other words, if the average degree of $G_{n,p}$ is slightly larger than $\ln n$, then the broadcast time of the push model essentially *coincides* with the broadcast time on the complete graph, which was shown in [2] to be very close to $\log_2 n + \ln n$. This confirms the robustness and the efficiency of the push model.

References

1. Demers, A., Greene, D., Hauser, C., Irish, W., Larson, J., Shenker, S., Sturgis, H., Swinehart, D., Terry, D.: Epidemic algorithms for replicated database maintenance. In: PODC 1987: Proceedings of the 6th annual ACM Symposium on Principles of distributed computing, New York, NY, USA, pp. 1–12 (1987)
2. Frieze, A., Grimmett, G.: The shortest-path problem for graphs with random arc-lengths. Discrete Applied Mathematics 10, 57–77 (1985)
3. Pittel, B.: On spreading a rumor. SIAM Journal on Applied Mathematics 47(1), 213–223 (1987)
4. Feige, U., Peleg, D., Raghavan, P., Upfal, E.: Randomized broadcast in networks. Random Structures and Algorithms 1(4), 447–460 (1990)
5. Elsässer, R., Sauerwald, T.: Broadcasting vs. Mixing and information dissemination on cayley graphs. In: Thomas, W., Weil, P. (eds.) STACS 2007. LNCS, vol. 4393, pp. 163–174. Springer, Heidelberg (2007)

Author Index